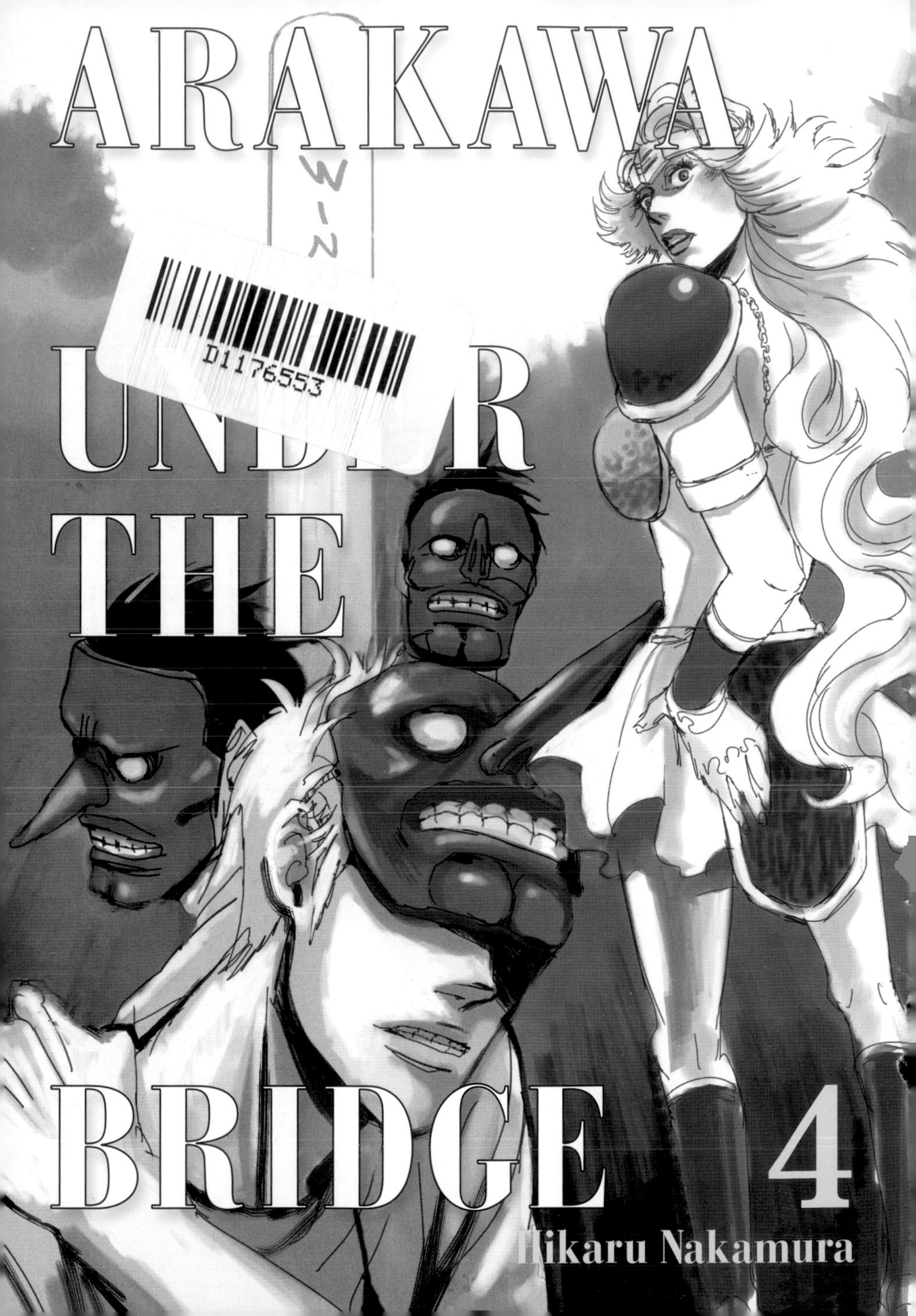
ARAKAWA
UNDER
THE
BRIDGE
4
Hikaru Nakamura

CONTENTS

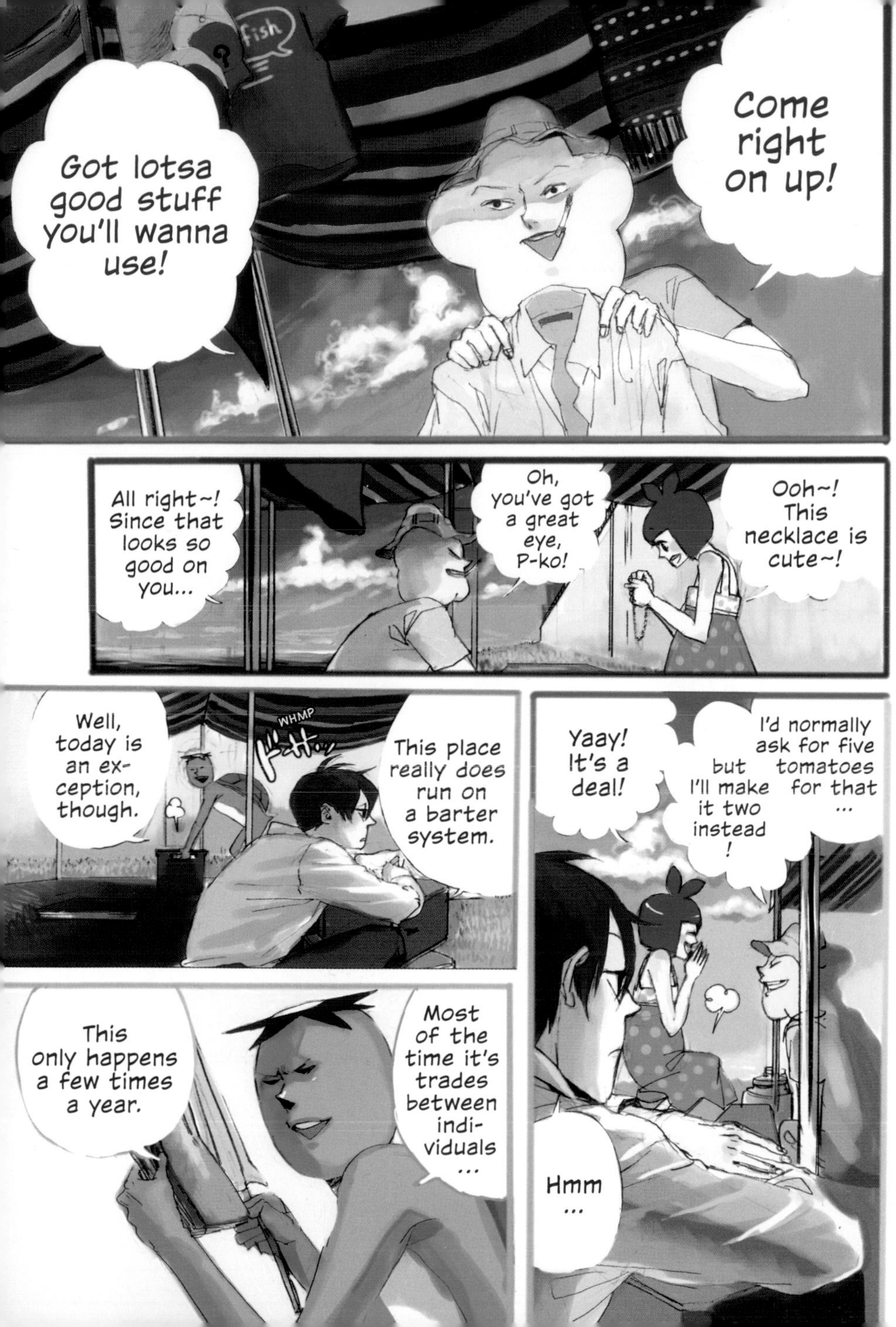
fish
Come right on up!
Got lotsa good stuff you'll wanna use!
Ooh~! This necklace is cute~!
Oh, you've got a great eye, P-ko!
All right~! Since that looks so good on you...
I'd normally ask for five tomatoes for that...
but I'll make it two instead!
Yaay! It's a deal!
Hmm...
This place really does run on a barter system.
WHMP
Well, today is an exception, though.
Most of the time it's trades between individuals...
This only happens a few times a year.

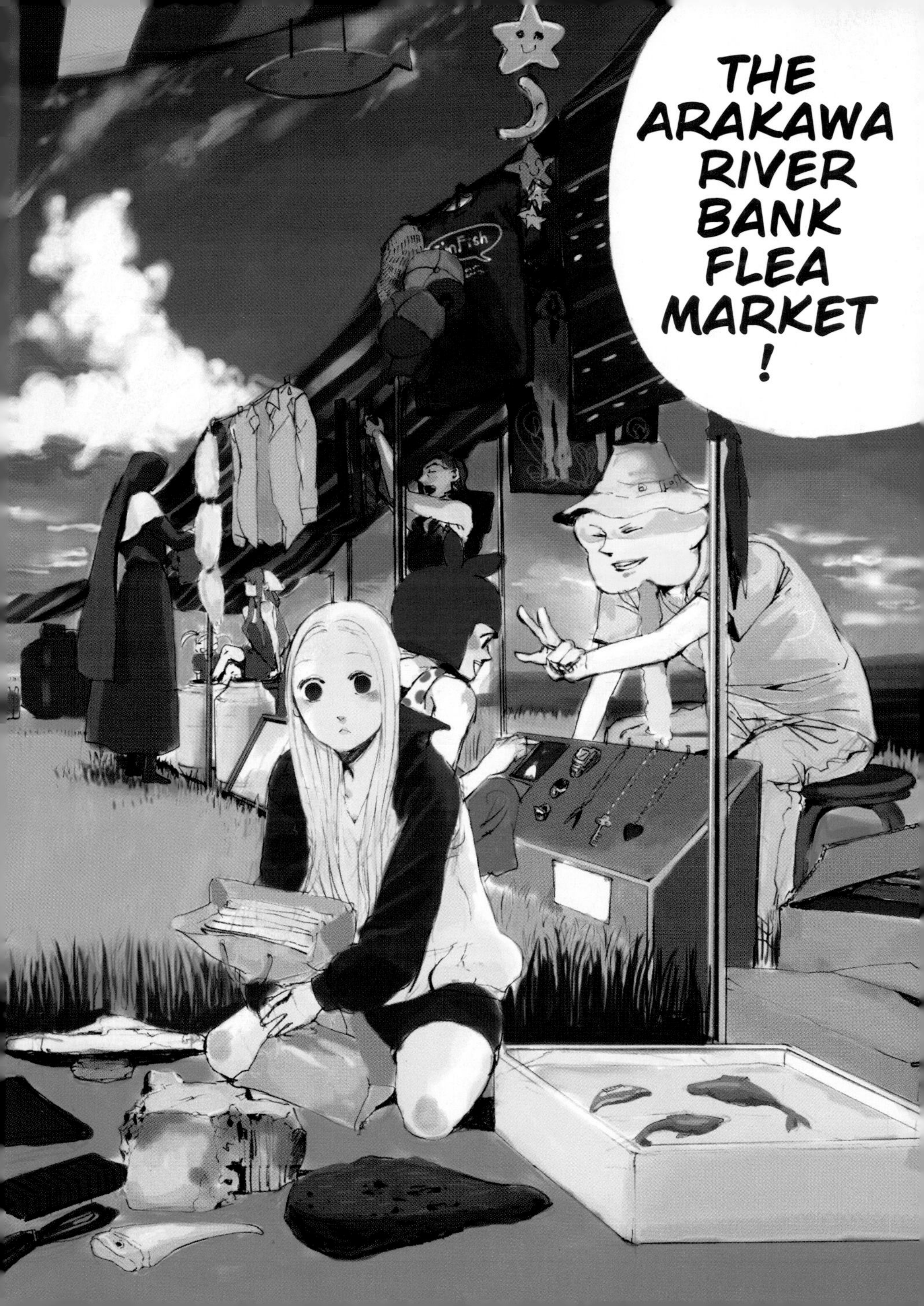
THE ARAKAWA RIVER BANK FLEA MARKET!

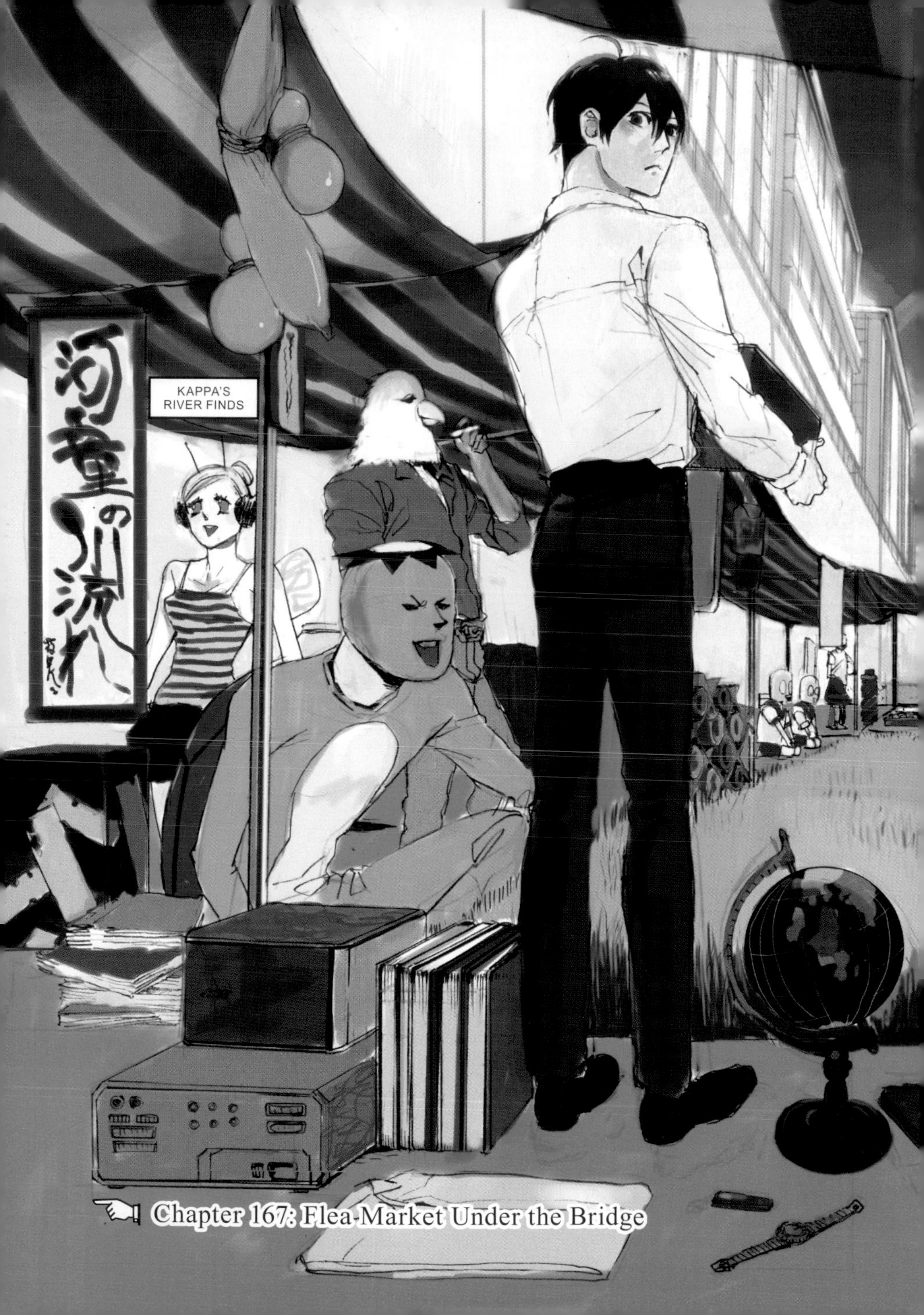
河童の川流れ
KAPPA'S RIVER FINDS

Chapter 167: Flea Market Under the Bridge

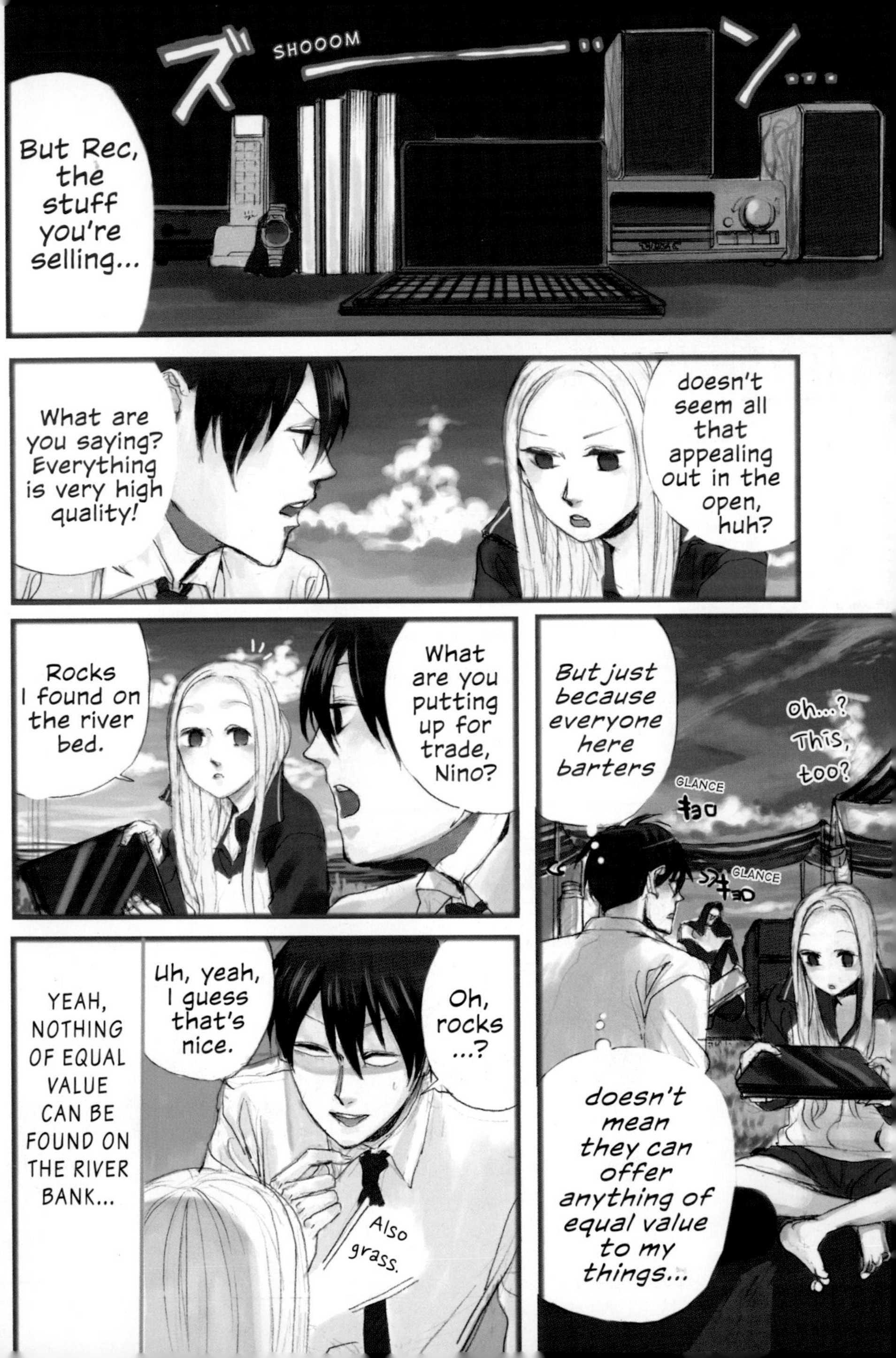
ズーーン...
SHOOOM
But Rec, the stuff you're selling...
doesn't seem all that appealing out in the open, huh?
What are you saying? Everything is very high quality!
But just because everyone here barters
Oh...? This, too?
GLANCE
キョロ
GLANCE
キョロ
doesn't mean they can offer anything of equal value to my things...
What are you putting up for trade, Nino?
Rocks I found on the river bed.
Oh, rocks ...?
Uh, yeah, I guess that's nice.
Also grass.
YEAH, NOTHING OF EQUAL VALUE CAN BE FOUND ON THE RIVER BANK...

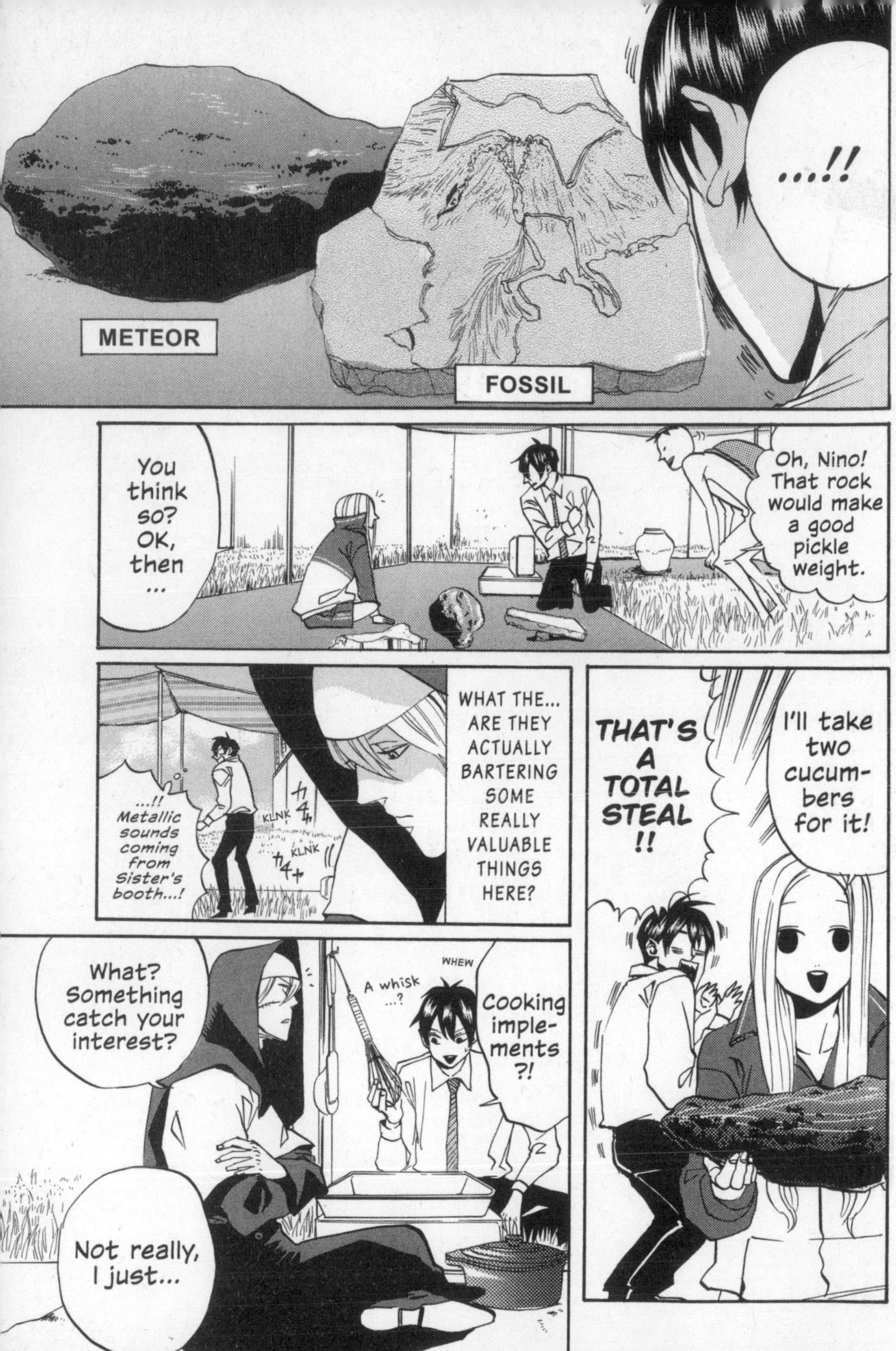
...!!
FOSSIL
METEOR
Oh, Nino! That rock would make a good pickle weight.
You think so? OK, then ...
I'll take two cucum-bers for it!
THAT'S A TOTAL STEAL !!
WHAT THE... ARE THEY ACTUALLY BARTERING SOME REALLY VALUABLE THINGS HERE?
KLNK
KLNK
...!! Metallic sounds coming from Sister's booth...!
Cooking imple-ments ?!
WHEW
A whisk ...?
What? Something catch your interest?
Not really, I just...

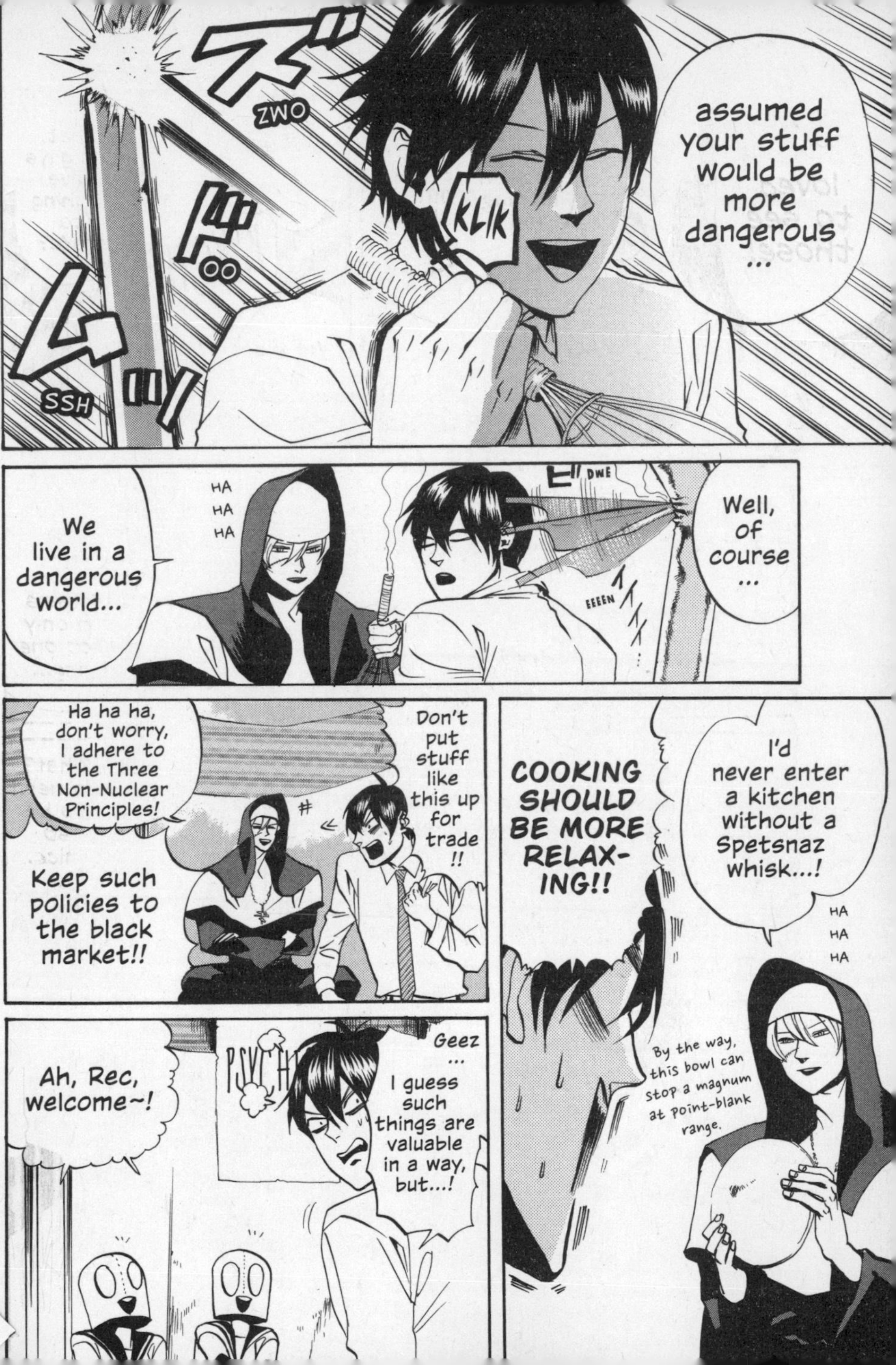
assumed your stuff would be more dangerous ...
KLIK
ZWO
SSH
Well, of course ...
DWE
EEEEN
HA HA HA
We live in a dangerous world...
I'd never enter a kitchen without a Spetsnaz whisk...!
COOKING SHOULD BE MORE RELAX-ING!!
HA HA HA
By the way, this bowl can stop a magnum at point-blank range.
Don't put stuff like this up for trade !!
Ha ha ha, don't worry, I adhere to the Three Non-Nuclear Principles!
Keep such policies to the black market!!
Geez ... I guess such things are valuable in a way, but...!
Ah, Rec, welcome~!

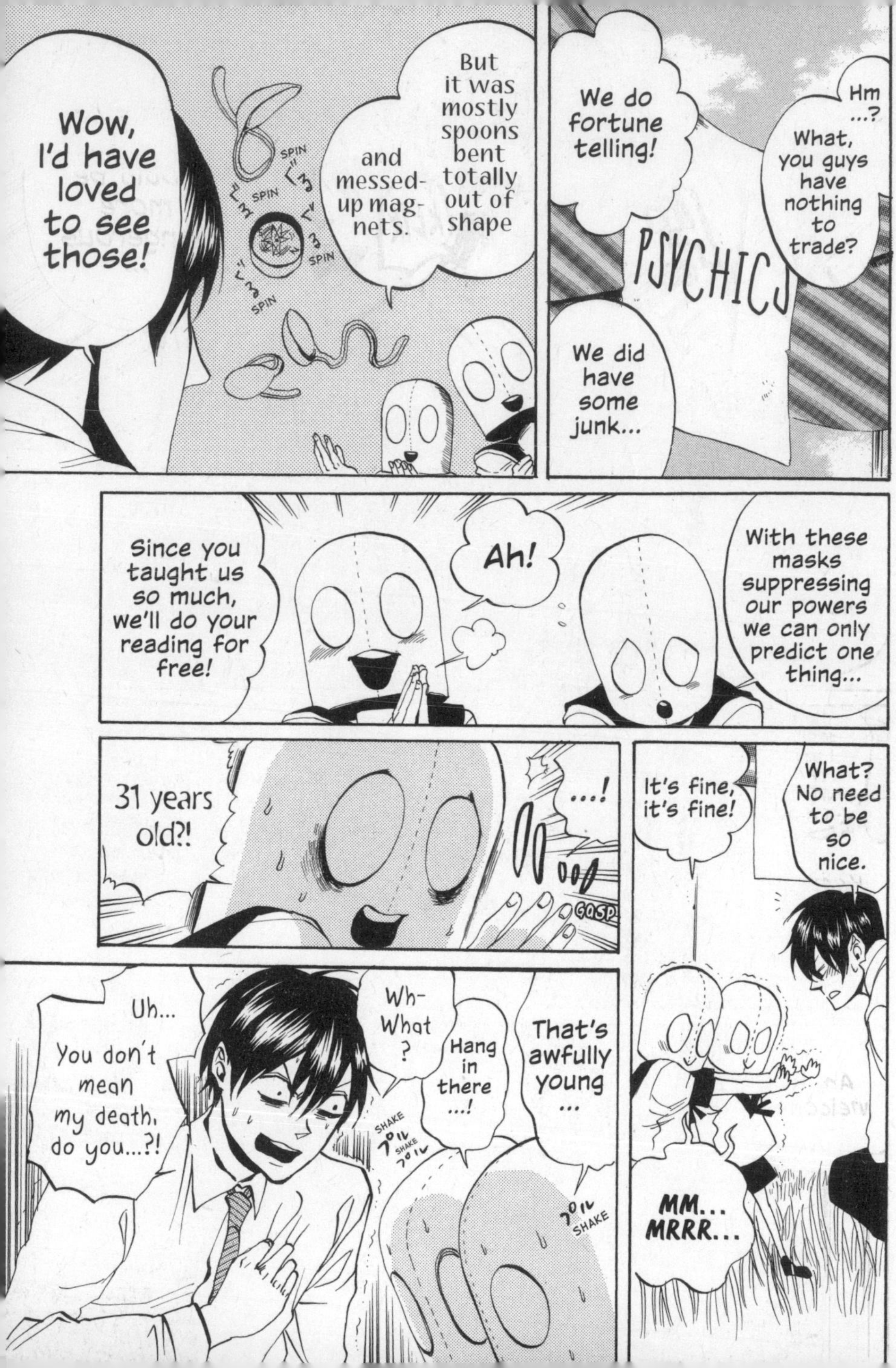

Hm ...? What, you guys have nothing to trade?
We do fortune telling!
PSYCHICS
We did have some junk...
But it was mostly spoons bent totally out of shape
and messed-up mag-nets.
SPIN
SPIN
SPIN
SPIN
Wow, I'd have loved to see those!
With these masks suppressing our powers we can only predict one thing...
Ah!
Since you taught us so much, we'll do your reading for free!
What? No need to be so nice.
It's fine, it's fine!
...!
GASP!
31 years old?!
MM... MRRR...
SHAKE
That's awfully young ...
Hang in there ...!
Wh- What ?
SHAKE
SHAKE
Uh...
You don't mean my death, do you...?!

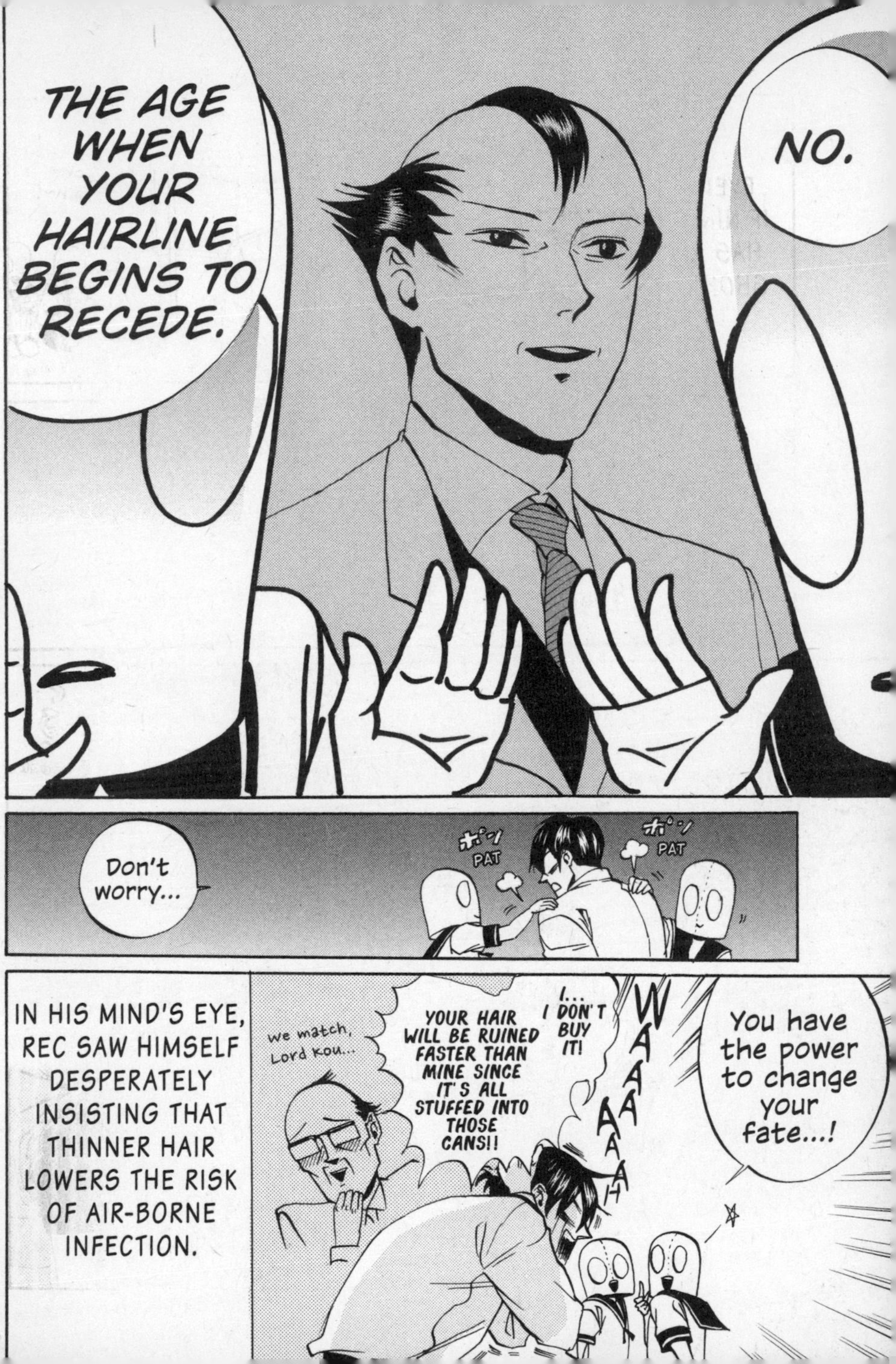
NO.
THE AGE WHEN YOUR HAIRLINE BEGINS TO RECEDE.
ポン PAT
ポン PAT
Don't worry...
You have the power to change your fate...!
WAAAAAAH
I... I DON'T BUY IT!
YOUR HAIR WILL BE RUINED FASTER THAN MINE SINCE IT'S ALL STUFFED INTO THOSE CANS!!
we match, Lord Kou...
IN HIS MIND'S EYE, REC SAW HIMSELF DESPERATELY INSISTING THAT THINNER HAIR LOWERS THE RISK OF AIR-BORNE INFECTION.

Chapter 168: Love Present Struggle

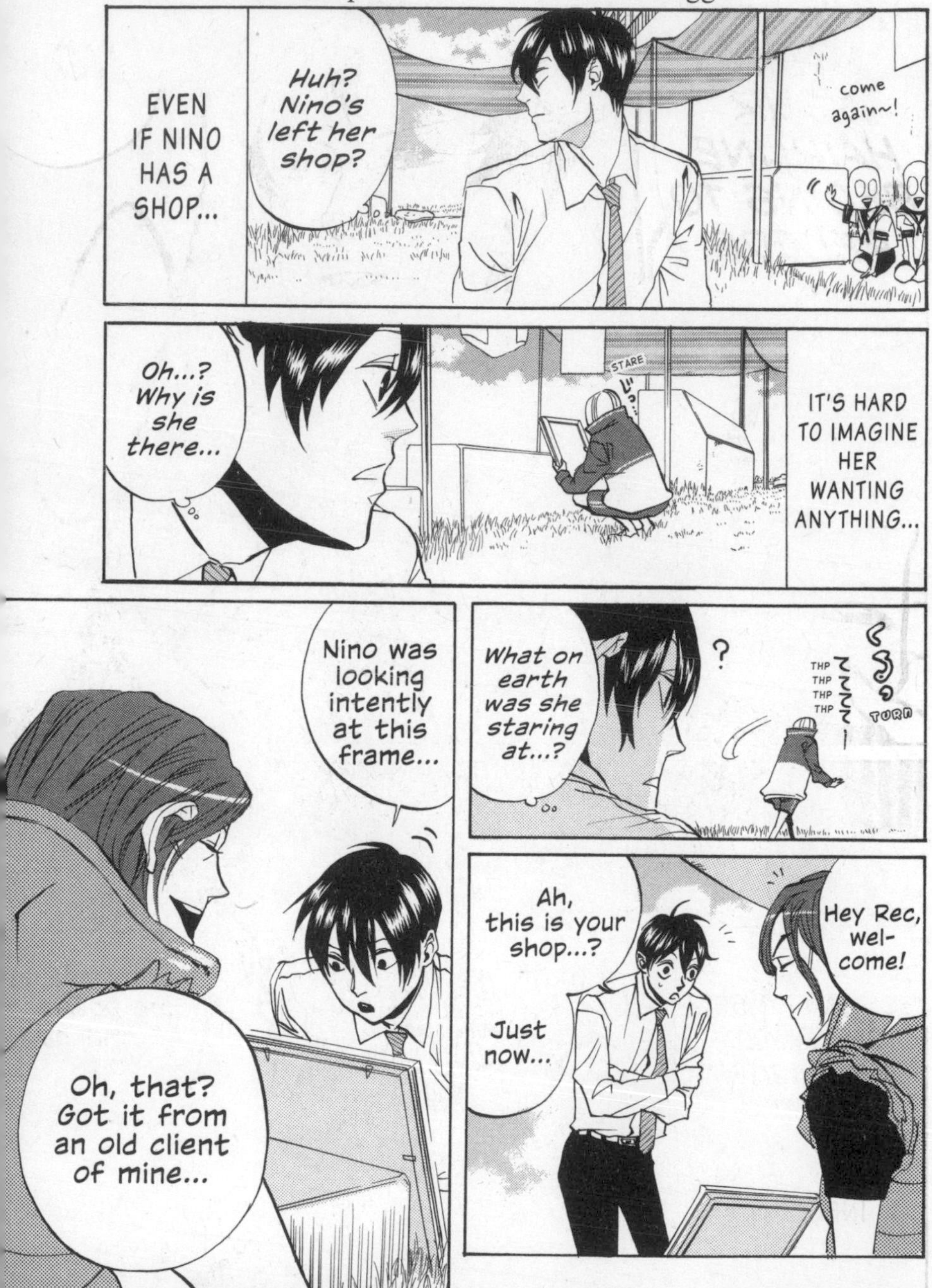
come again~!
Huh? Nino's left her shop?
EVEN IF NINO HAS A SHOP...
IT'S HARD TO IMAGINE HER WANTING ANYTHING...
STARE
Oh...? Why is she there...
TURN
THP THP THP THP
?
What on earth was she staring at...?
Hey Rec, wel-come!
Ah, this is your shop...?
Just now...
Nino was looking intently at this frame...
Oh, that? Got it from an old client of mine...

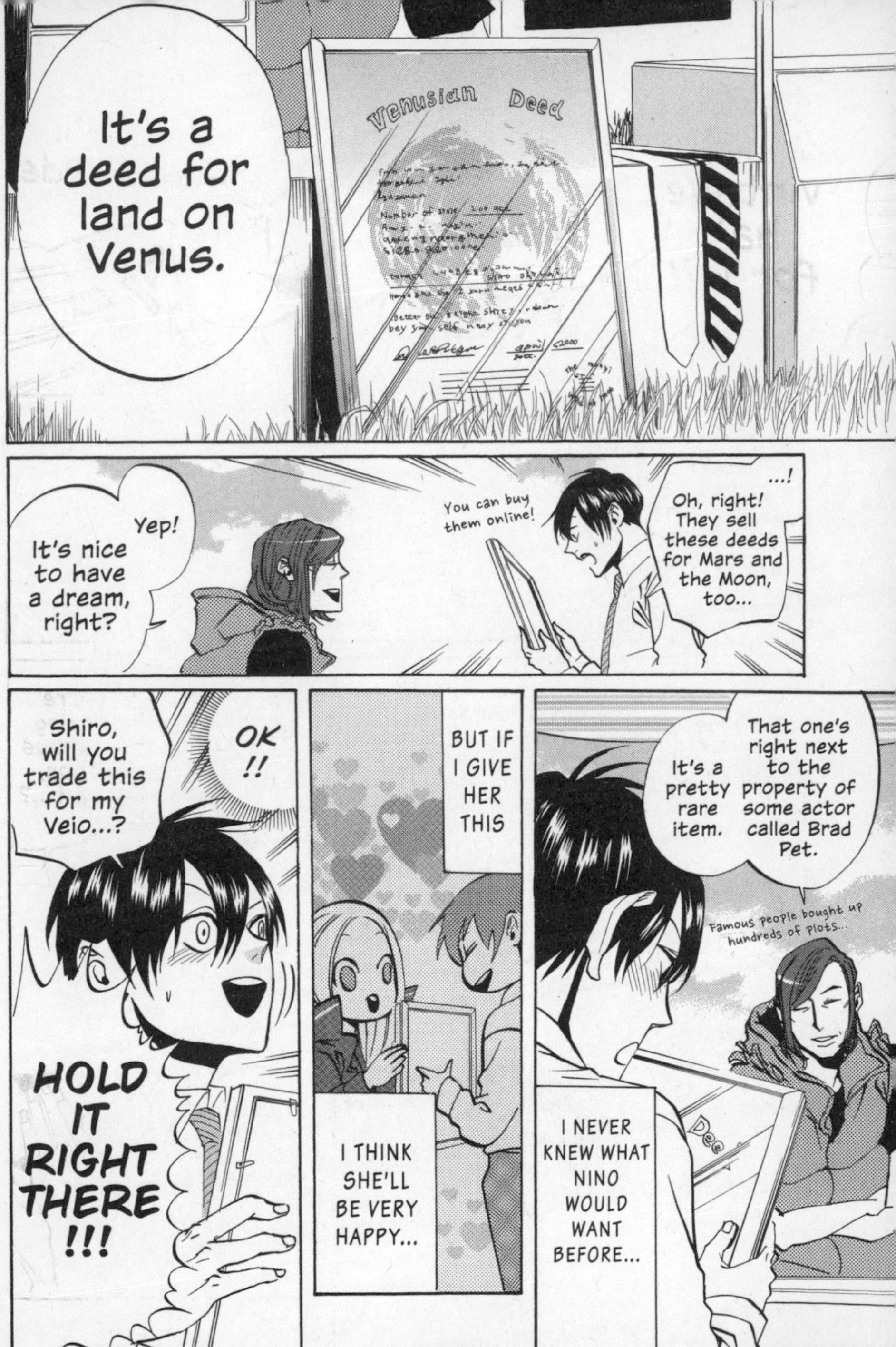
It's a deed for land on Venus.
Venusian Deed
...!
Oh, right! They sell these deeds for Mars and the Moon, too...
You can buy them online!
Yep! It's nice to have a dream, right?
That one's right next to the property of some actor called Brad Pet.
It's a pretty rare item.
Famous people bought up hundreds of plots...
I NEVER KNEW WHAT NINO WOULD WANT BEFORE...
BUT IF I GIVE HER THIS
I THINK SHE'LL BE VERY HAPPY...
Shiro, will you trade this for my Veio...?
OK !!
HOLD IT RIGHT THERE !!!

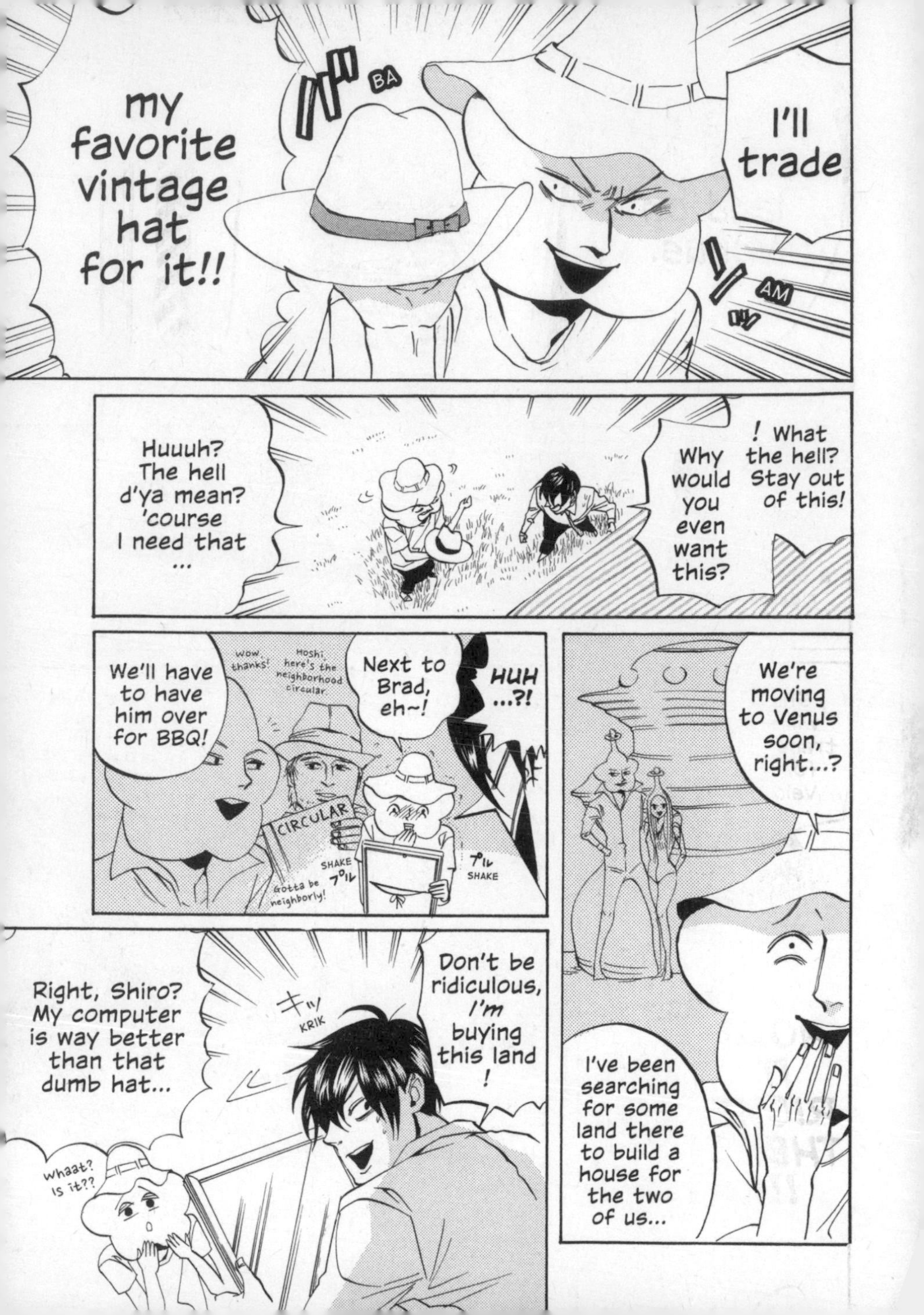
I'll trade
BA
AM
my favorite vintage hat for it!!
! What the hell? Stay out of this!
Why would you even want this?
Huuuh? The hell d'ya mean? 'course I need that ...
We're moving to Venus soon, right...?
I've been searching for some land there to build a house for the two of us...
HUH ...?!
Next to Brad, eh~!
Hoshi, here's the neighborhood circular.
wow, thanks!
We'll have to have him over for BBQ!
CIRCULAR
SHAKE
SHAKE
Gotta be neighborly!
Don't be ridiculous, *I'm* buying this land!
KRIK
Right, Shiro? My computer is way better than that dumb hat...
Whaat? Is it??

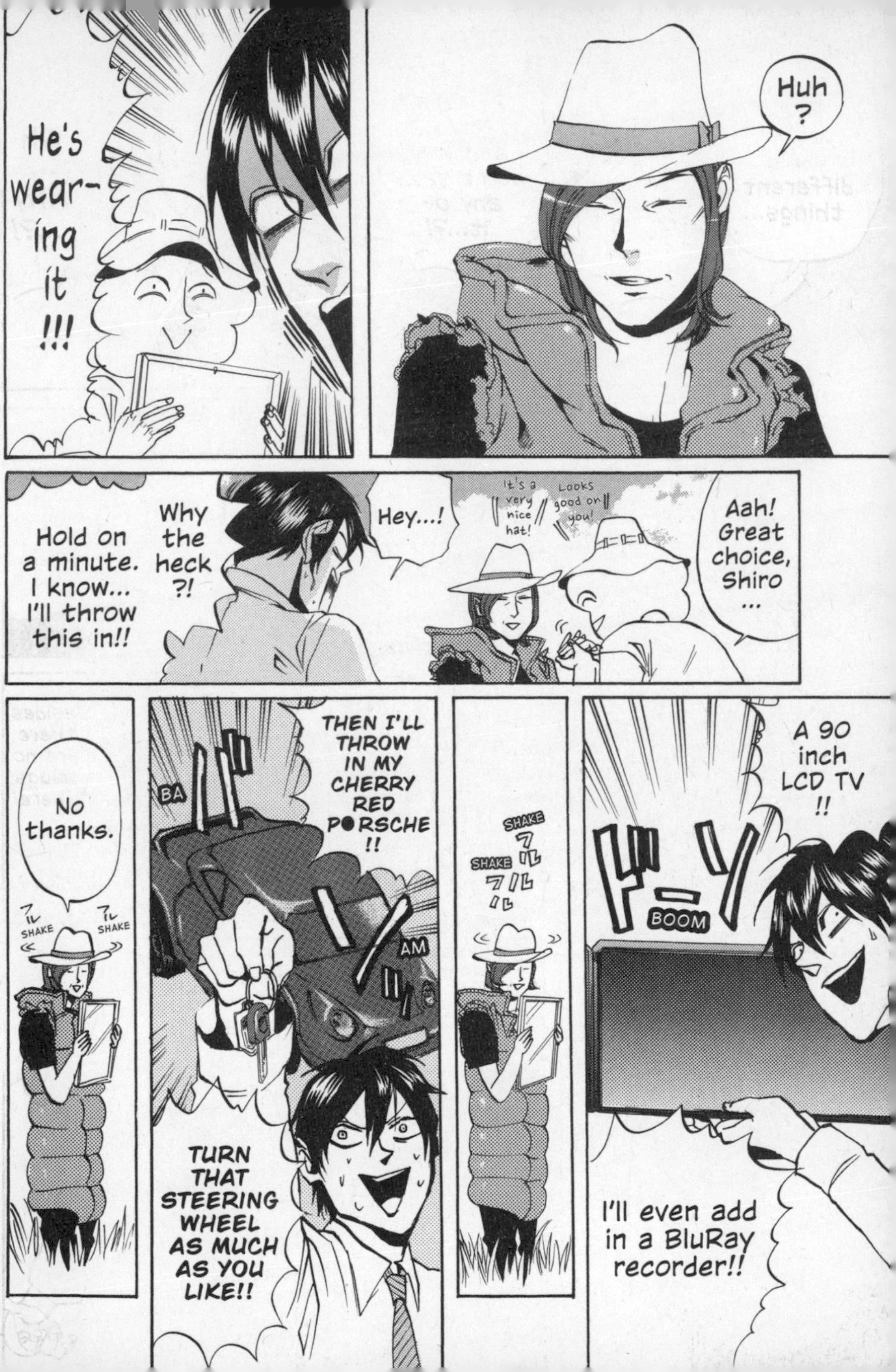
Huh?
He's wear-ing it!!!
Aah! Great choice, Shiro...
Looks good on you!
It's a very nice hat!
Hey...!
Why the heck?!
Hold on a minute. I know... I'll throw this in!!
A 90 inch LCD TV!!
BOOM
I'll even add in a BluRay recorder!!
SHAKE
SHAKE
THEN I'LL THROW IN MY CHERRY RED PORSCHE!!
BA
AM
TURN THAT STEERING WHEEL AS MUCH AS YOU LIKE!!
No thanks.
SHAKE
SHAKE

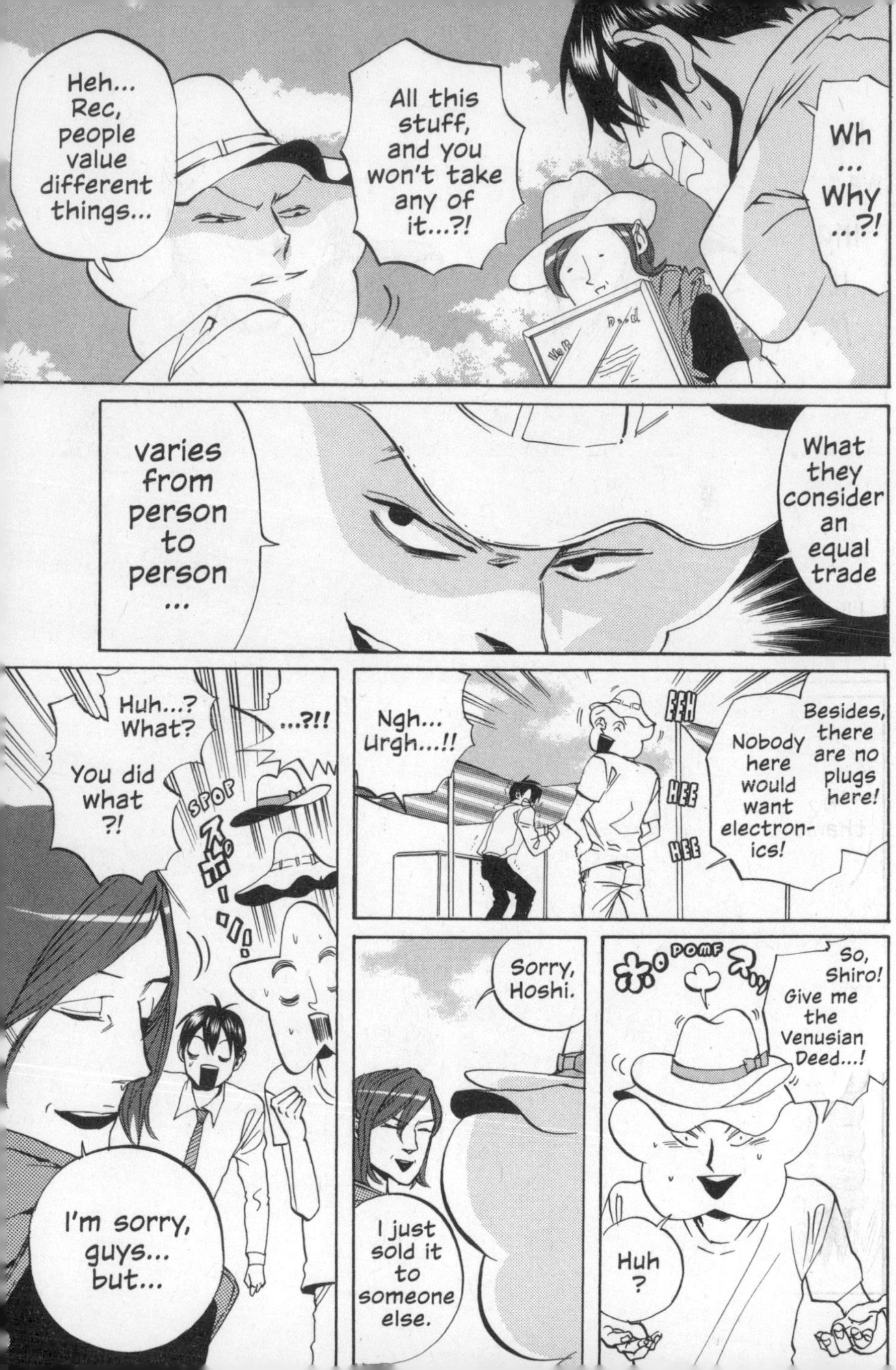
Wh... Why...?!
All this stuff, and you won't take any of it...?!
Heh... Rec, people value different things...
What they consider an equal trade
varies from person to person...
Besides, there are no plugs here!
Nobody here would want electron-ics!
EEH
HEE
HEE
Ngh... Urgh...!!
So, Shiro! Give me the Venusian Deed...!
DOMF
Huh?
Sorry, Hoshi.
I just sold it to someone else.
Huh...? What?
...?!!
You did what?!
SPOP
I'm sorry, guys... but...

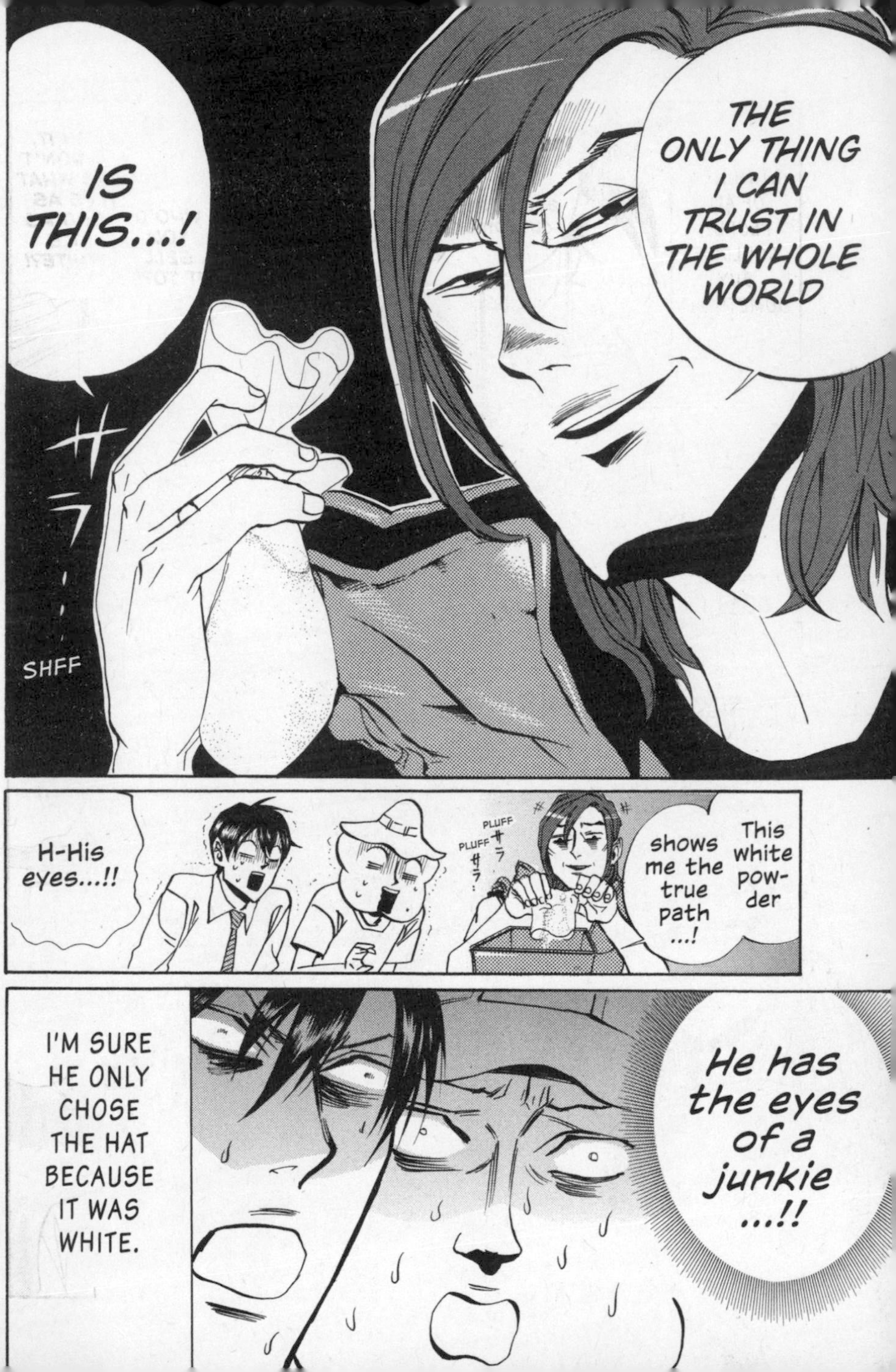
THE ONLY THING I CAN TRUST IN THE WHOLE WORLD
IS THIS...!
サラ…
SHFF
This white powder
shows me the true path ...!
PLUFF サラ
PLUFF サラ
H-His eyes...!!
He has the eyes of a junkie ...!!
I'M SURE HE ONLY CHOSE THE HAT BECAUSE IT WAS WHITE.

Chapter 169: I Want to See You Smile

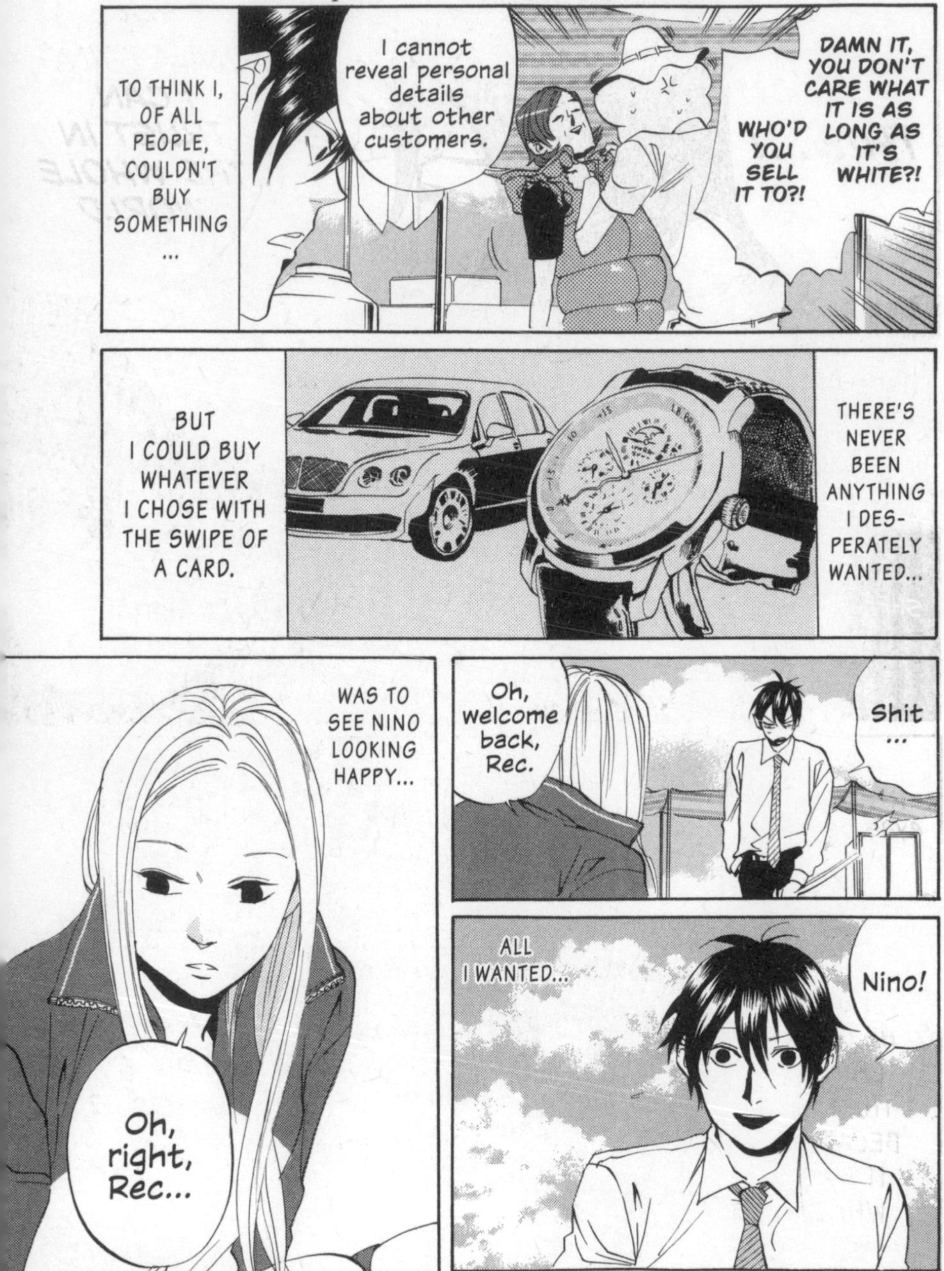
DAMN IT, YOU DON'T CARE WHAT IT IS AS LONG AS IT'S WHITE?!
WHO'D YOU SELL IT TO?!
I cannot reveal personal details about other customers.
TO THINK I, OF ALL PEOPLE, COULDN'T BUY SOMETHING ...
THERE'S NEVER BEEN ANYTHING I DES-PERATELY WANTED...
BUT I COULD BUY WHATEVER I CHOSE WITH THE SWIPE OF A CARD.
Shit ...
Oh, welcome back, Rec.
Nino!
ALL I WANTED...
WAS TO SEE NINO LOOKING HAPPY...
Oh, right, Rec...

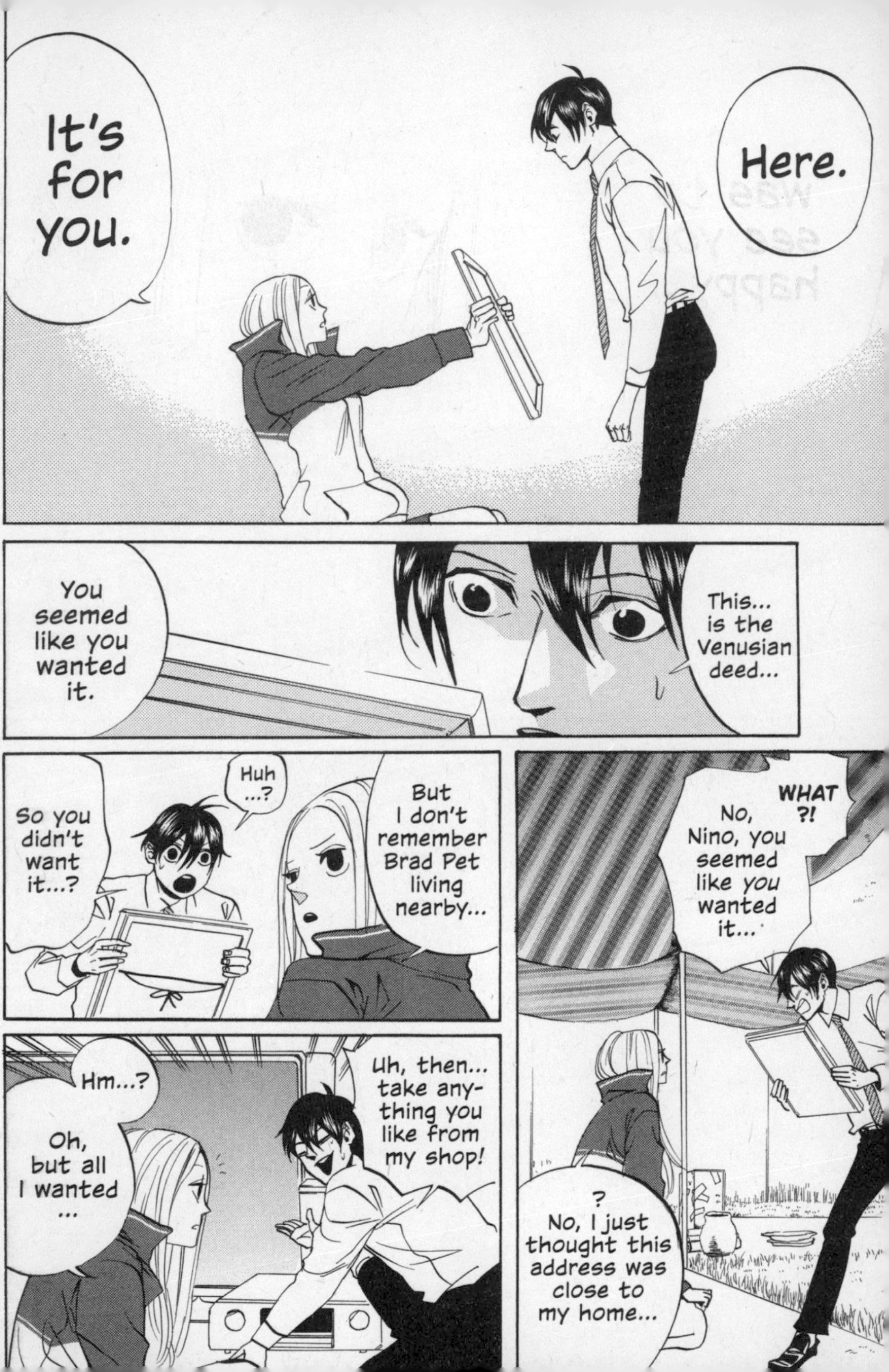
Here.
It's for you.
This... is the Venusian deed...
You seemed like you wanted it.
WHAT ?!
No, Nino, you seemed like *you* wanted it...
?
No, I just thought this address was close to my home...
But I don't remember Brad Pet living nearby...
Huh ...?
So you didn't want it...?
Uh, then... take anything you like from my shop!
Hm...?
Oh, but all I wanted ...

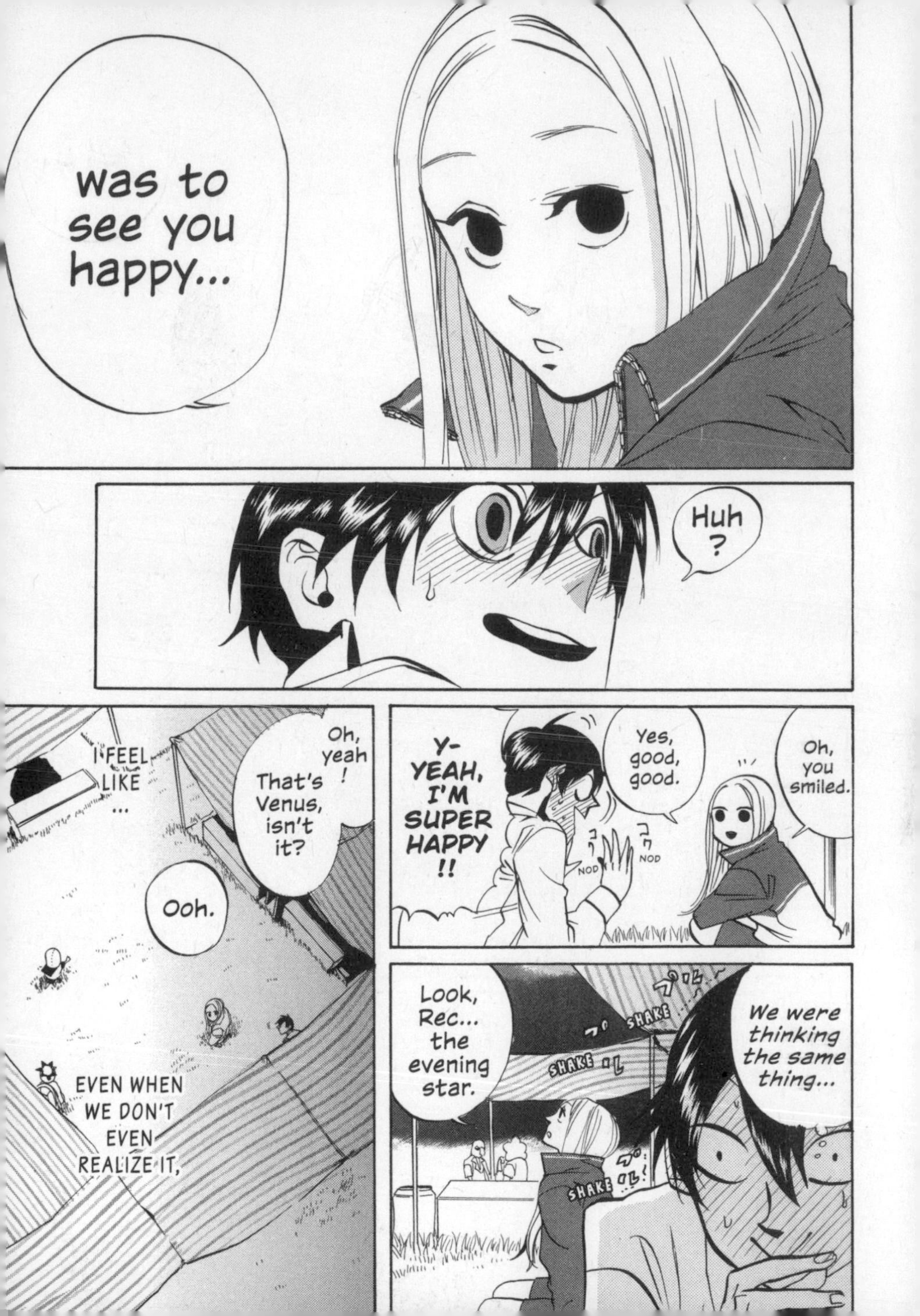
was to see you happy...
Huh?
Oh, you smiled.
Yes, good, good.
NOD
NOD
Y-YEAH, I'M SUPER HAPPY!!
We were thinking the same thing...
SHAKE
SHAKE
SHAKE
Look, Rec... the evening star.
Oh, yeah! That's Venus, isn't it?
I FEEL LIKE ...
Ooh.
EVEN WHEN WE DON'T EVEN REALIZE IT,

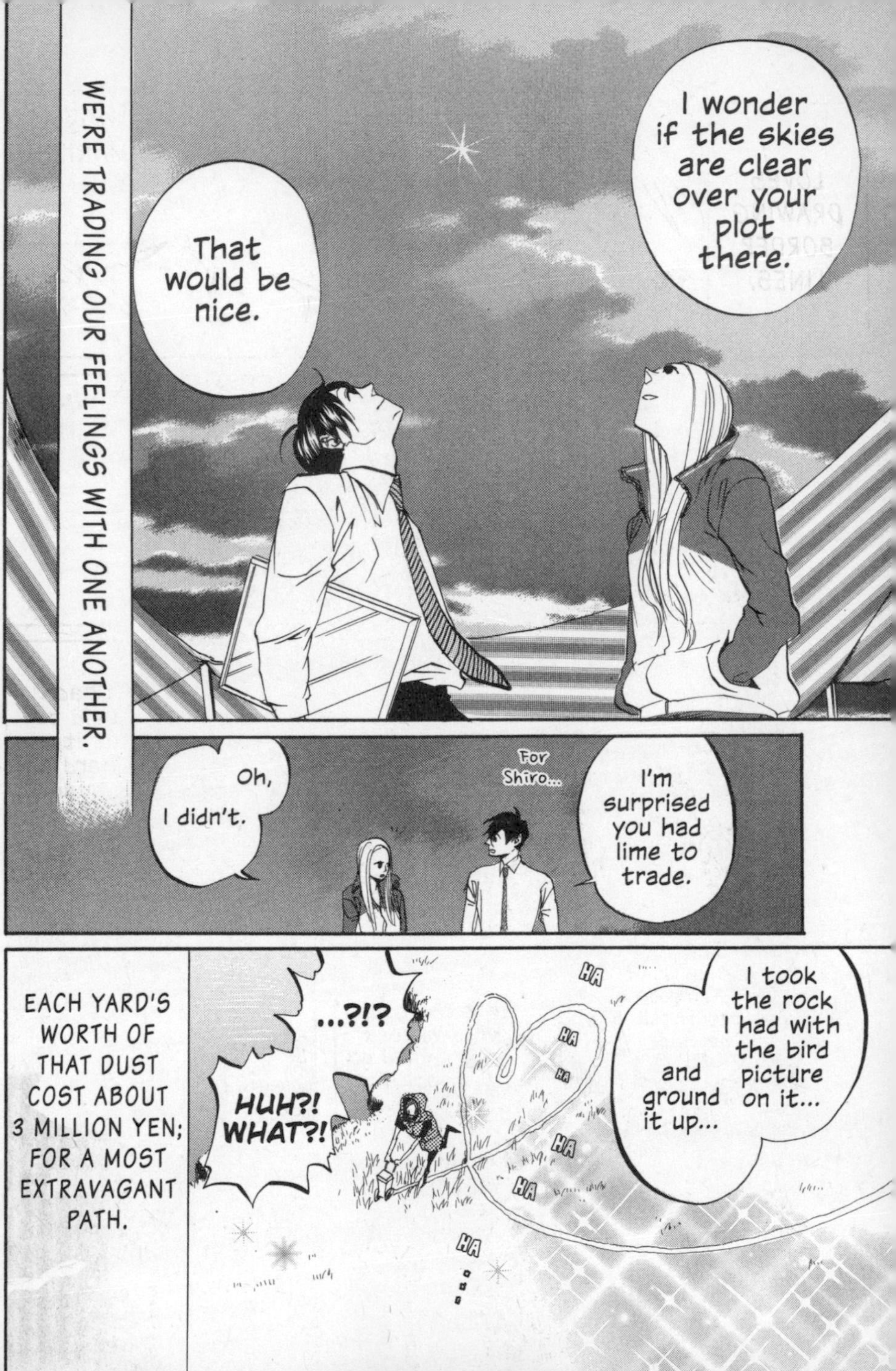
I wonder if the skies are clear over your plot there.
That would be nice.
WE'RE TRADING OUR FEELINGS WITH ONE ANOTHER.
For Shiro...
I'm surprised you had lime to trade.
Oh, I didn't.
I took the rock I had with the bird picture on it...
and ground it up...
HA
HA
HA
HA
HA
HA
HUH?! WHAT?!
...?!?
EACH YARD'S WORTH OF THAT DUST COST ABOUT 3 MILLION YEN; FOR A MOST EXTRAVAGANT PATH.

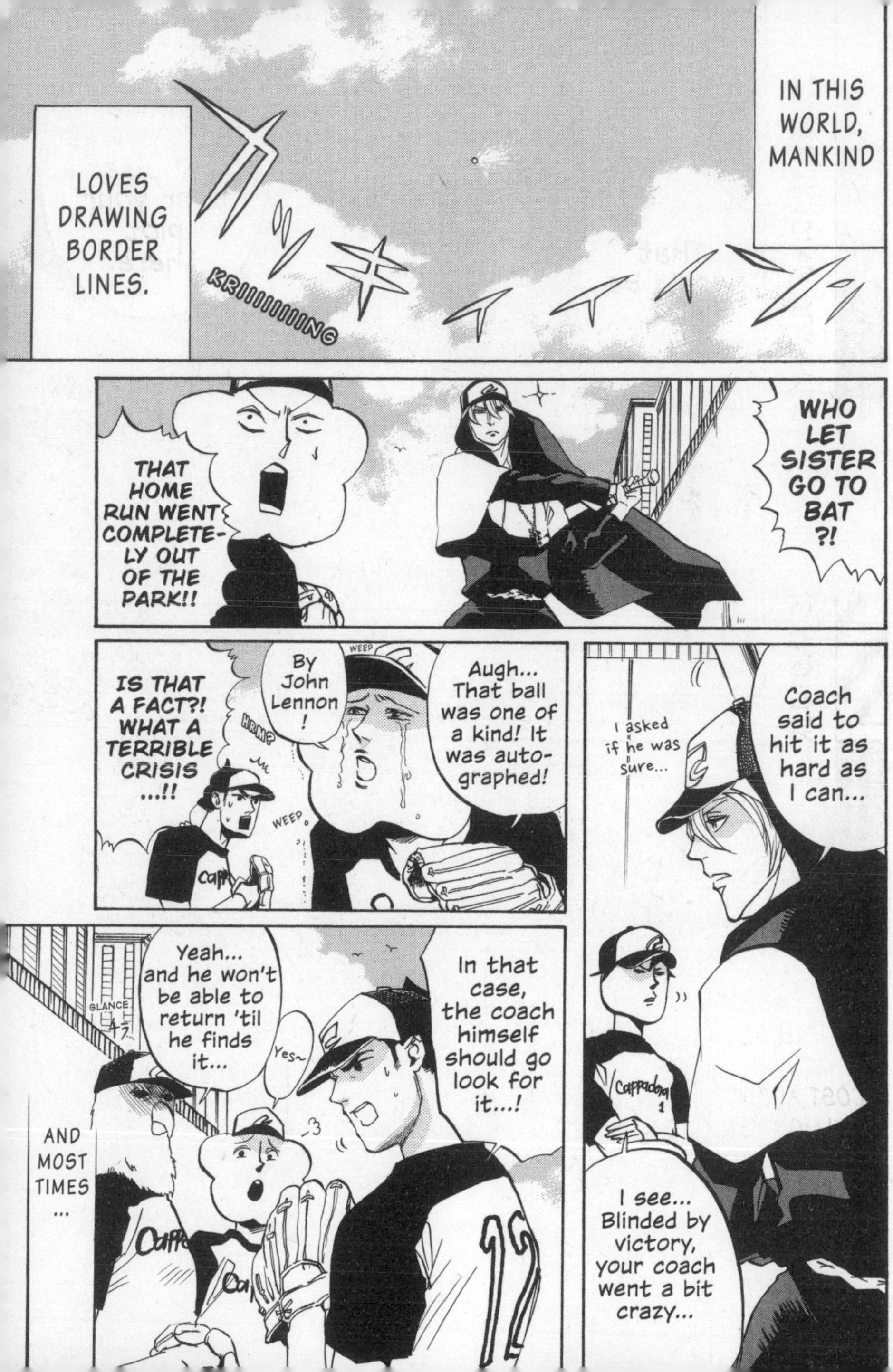
IN THIS WORLD, MANKIND
KRIIIIIIIIIING
LOVES DRAWING BORDER LINES.
WHO LET SISTER GO TO BAT?!
THAT HOME RUN WENT COMPLETELY OUT OF THE PARK!!
Coach said to hit it as hard as I can...
I asked if he was sure...
I see... Blinded by victory, your coach went a bit crazy...
Augh... That ball was one of a kind! It was autographed!
WEEP
By John Lennon!
HRM?
IS THAT A FACT?! WHAT A TERRIBLE CRISIS...!!
WEEP
In that case, the coach himself should go look for it...!
Yeah... and he won't be able to return 'til he finds it...
Yes~
GLANCE
AND MOST TIMES...

ADVENTURE WAITS BEYOND THOSE BORDER LINES.

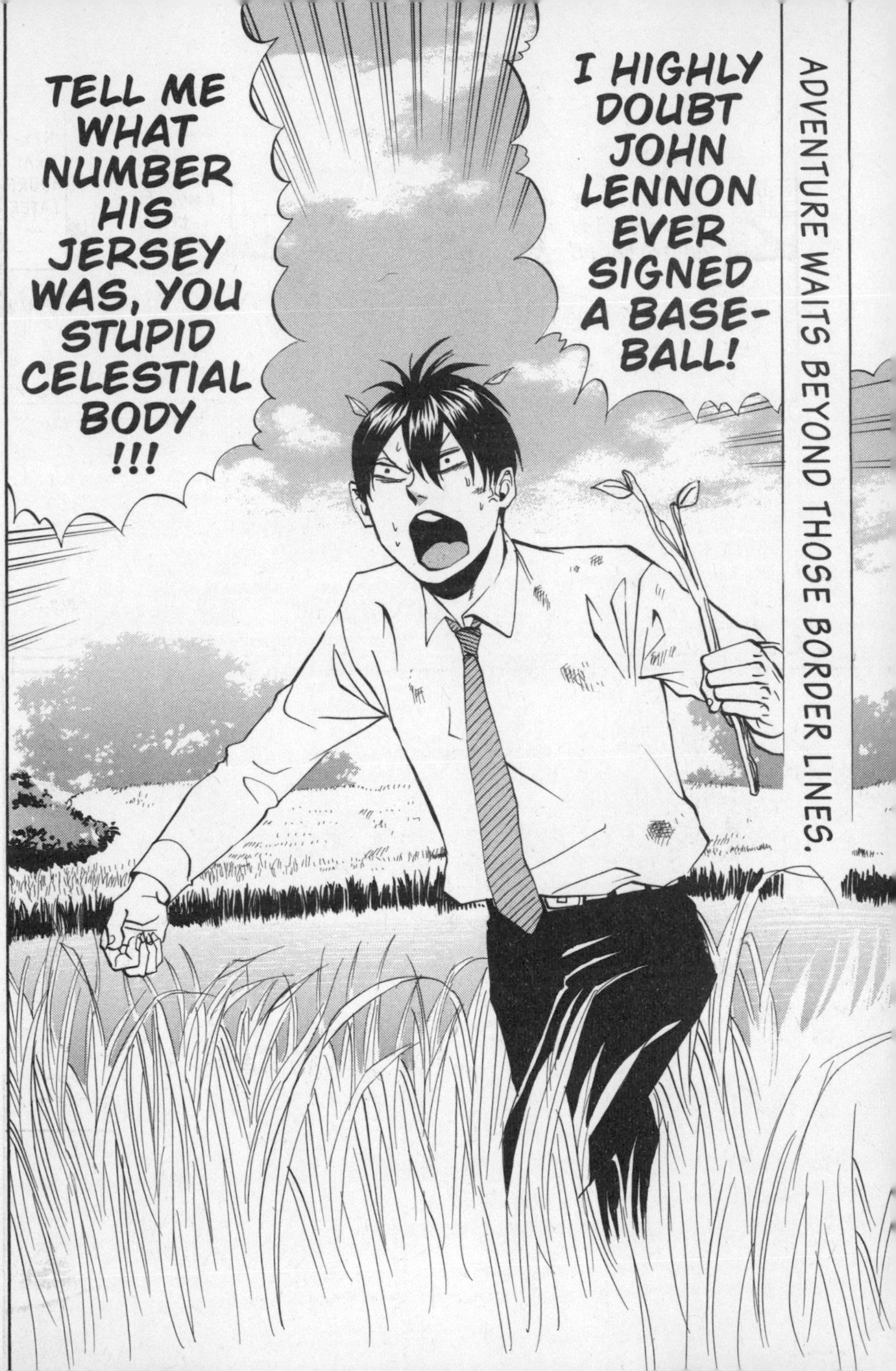
I HIGHLY DOUBT JOHN LENNON EVER SIGNED A BASE-BALL!
TELL ME WHAT NUMBER HIS JERSEY WAS, YOU STUPID CELESTIAL BODY !!!

Chapter 170: Across the Border

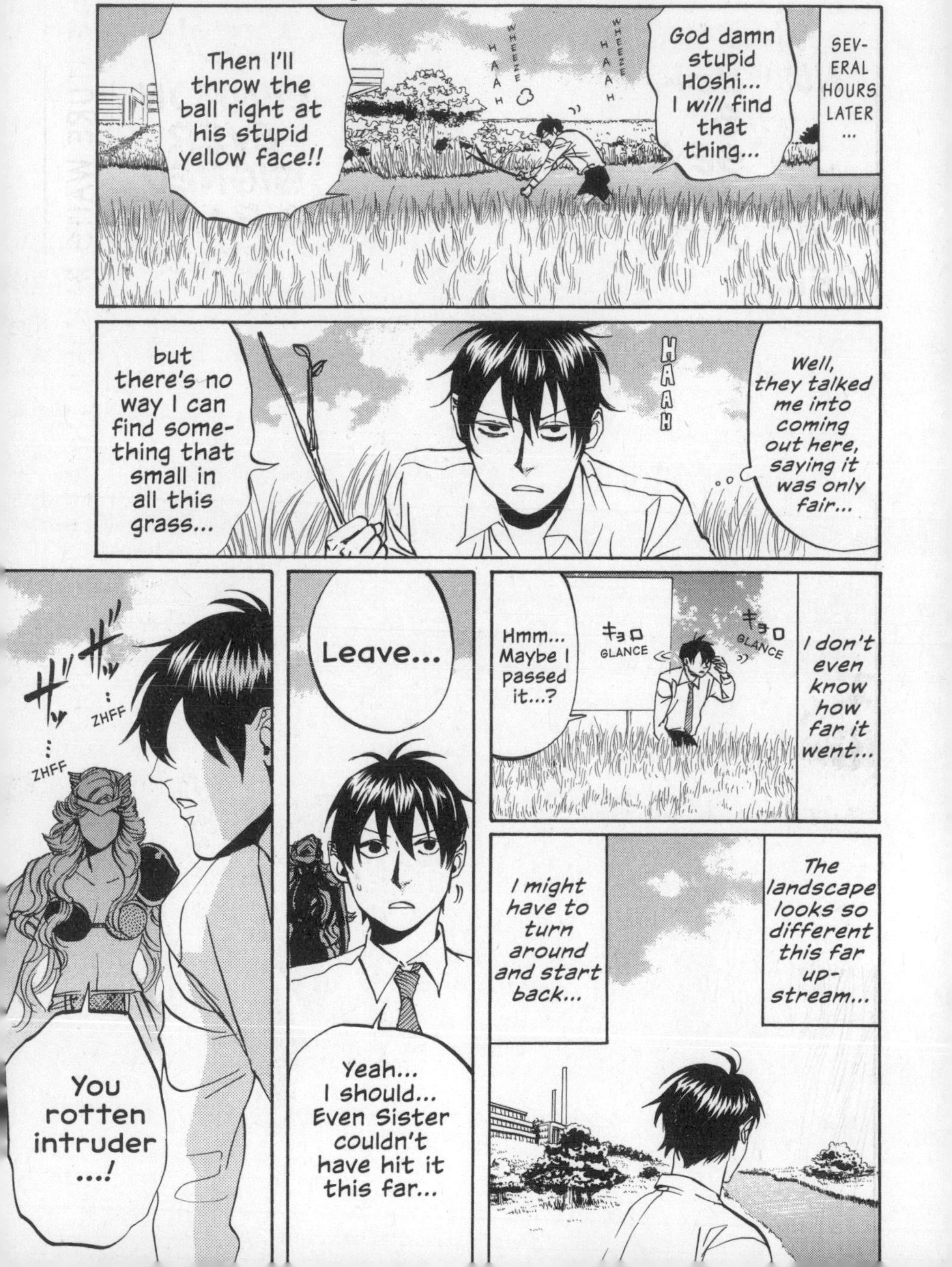
SEV-ERAL HOURS LATER...
God damn stupid Hoshi... I will find that thing...
HAAH WHEEZE
HAAH WHEEZE
Then I'll throw the ball right at his stupid yellow face!!
Well, they talked me into coming out here, saying it was only fair...
HAAAH
but there's no way I can find some-thing that small in all this grass...
I don't even know how far it went...
GLANCE
GLANCE
Hmm... Maybe I passed it...?
The landscape looks so different this far up-stream...
I might have to turn around and start back...
Leave...
Yeah... I should... Even Sister couldn't have hit it this far...
ZHFF
ZHFF
You rotten intruder...!

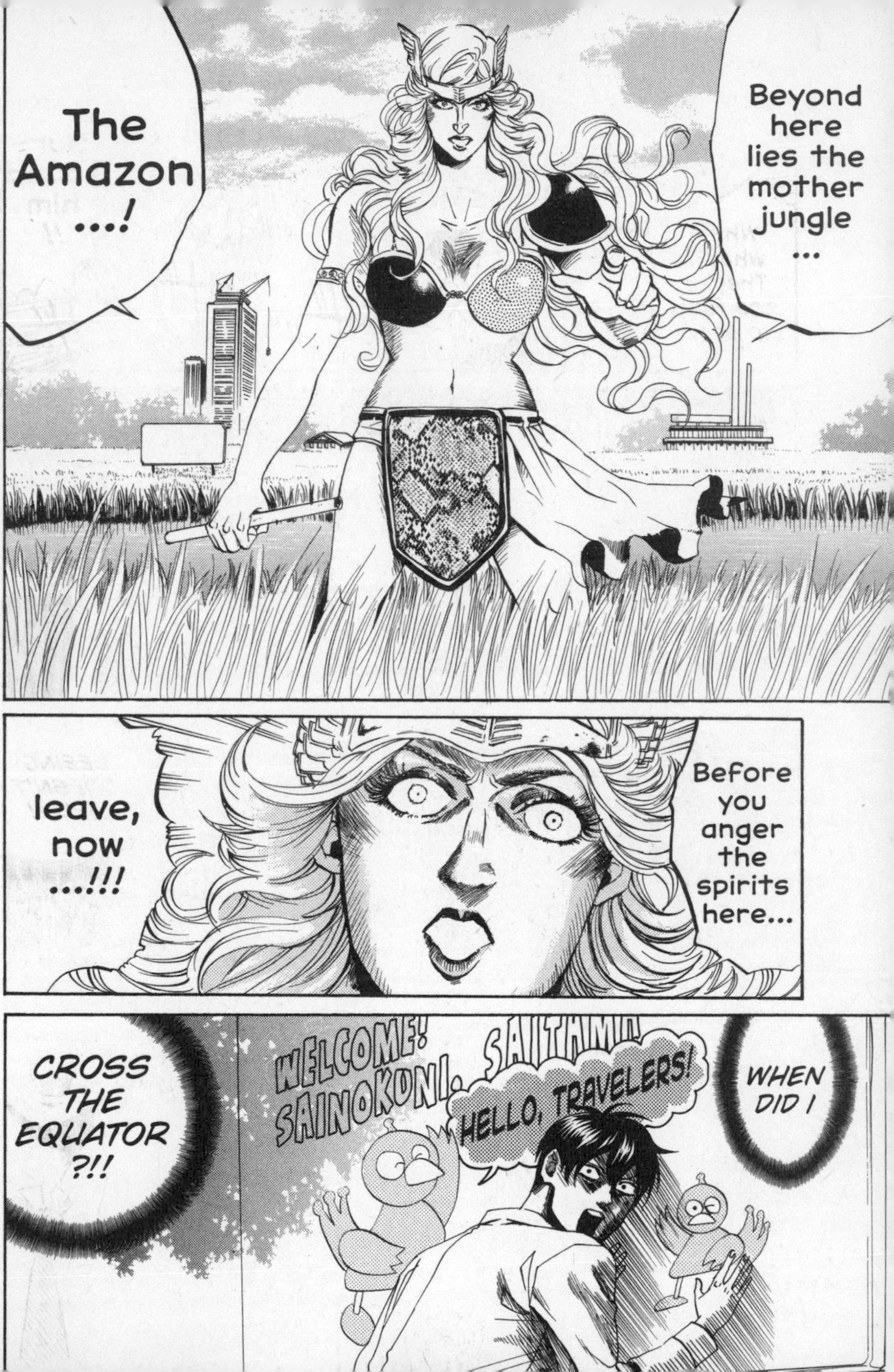
Beyond here lies the mother jungle ...
The Amazon ...!
Before you anger the spirits here...
leave, now ...!!!
WHEN DID I
WELCOME! SAINOKUNI, SAITAMA
HELLO, TRAVELERS!
CROSS THE EQUATOR ?!!

Chapter 171: Sainokuni's Amazoness (and Tengu)

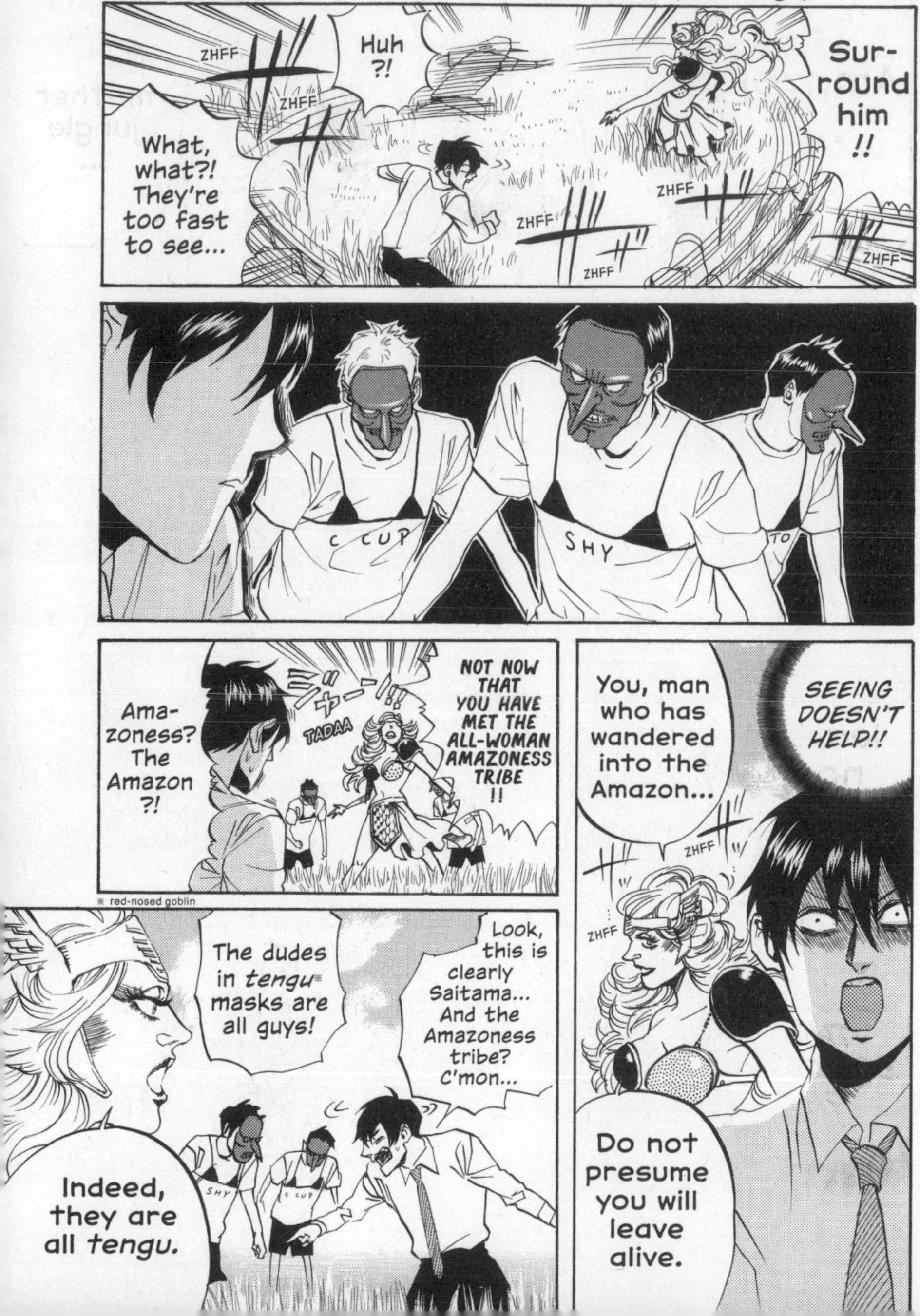

Sur-round him!!
Huh?!
ZHFF
ZHFF
What, what?! They're too fast to see...
ZHFF
ZHFF
ZHFF
ZHFF
TO
SHY
C CUP
SEEING DOESN'T HELP!!
You, man who has wandered into the Amazon...
ZHFF
ZHFF
Do not presume you will leave alive.
NOT NOW THAT YOU HAVE MET THE ALL-WOMAN AMAZONESS TRIBE!!
TADAA
Ama-zoness? The Amazon?!
Look, this is clearly Saitama... And the Amazoness tribe? C'mon...
The dudes in *tengu*※ masks are all guys!
Indeed, they are all *tengu*.
SHY
C CUP

※ red-nosed goblin

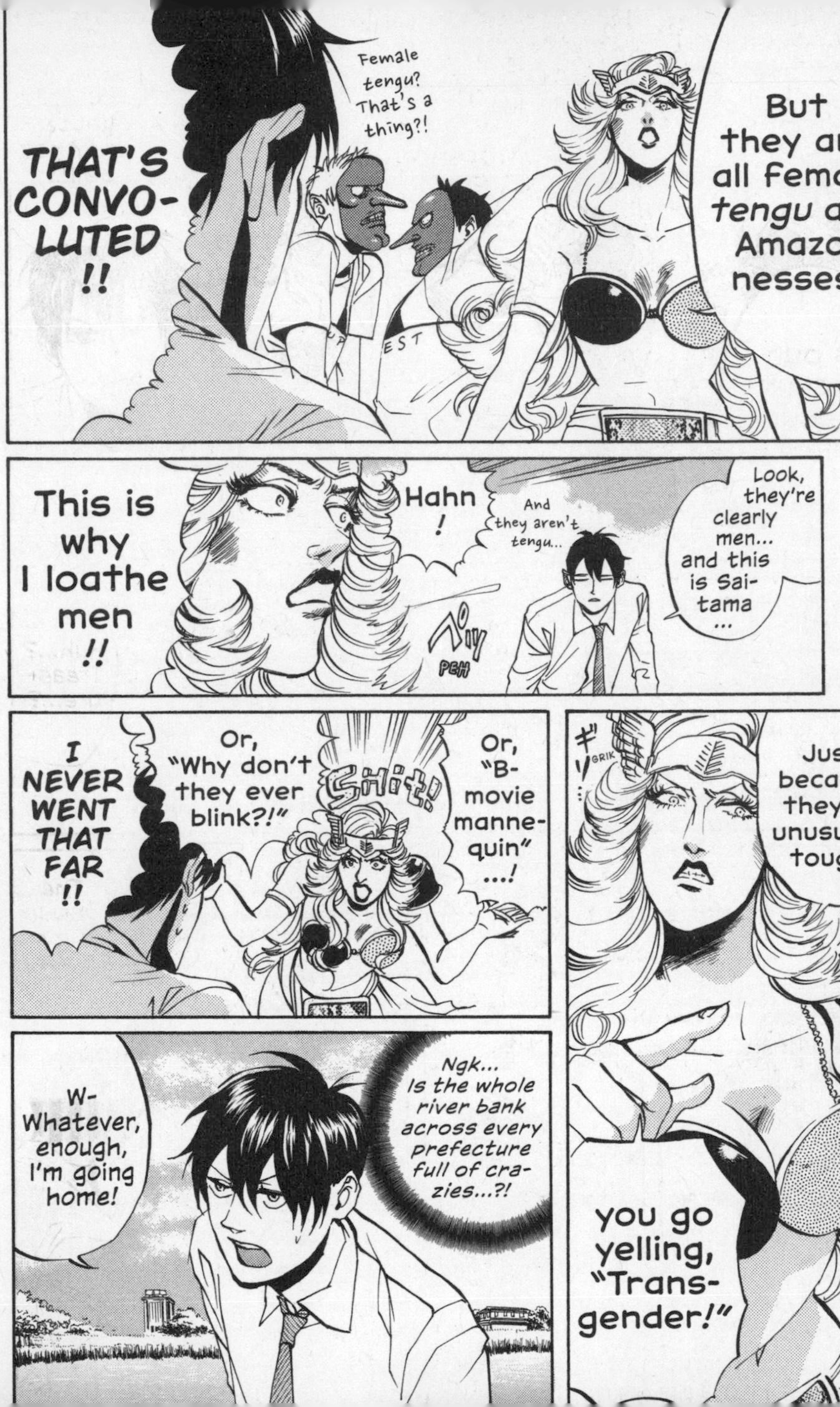

But they are all female *tengu* and Amazonesses.
Female tengu? That's a thing?!
THAT'S CONVOLUTED!!
Look, they're clearly men... and this is Saitama...
And they aren't tengu...
Hahn!
ペッ
PEH
This is why I loathe men!!
ギリ
GRIK
Just because they're unusually tough,
you go yelling, "Transgender!"
Or, "B-movie mannequin"...!
Shit!
Or, "Why don't they ever blink?!"
I NEVER WENT THAT FAR!!
Ngk... Is the whole river bank across every prefecture full of crazies...?!
W-Whatever, enough, I'm going home!

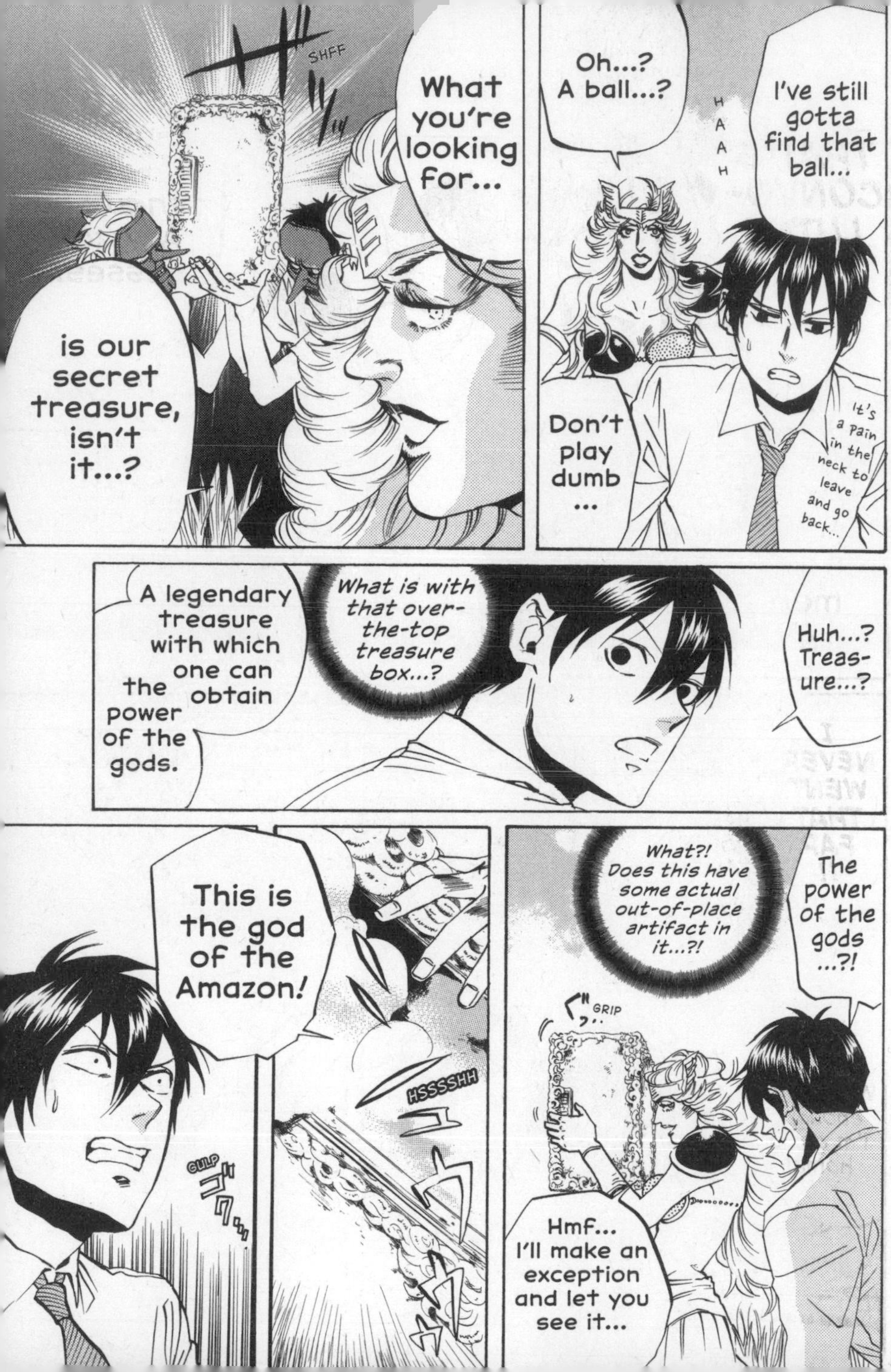
I've still gotta find that ball...
HAAH
Oh...? A ball...?
It's a pain in the neck to leave and go back...
Don't play dumb ...
What you're looking for...
SHFF
is our secret treasure, isn't it...?
Huh...? Treasure...?
What is with that over-the-top treasure box...?
A legendary treasure with which one can obtain the power of the gods.
The power of the gods ...?!
What?! Does this have some actual out-of-place artifact in it...?!
GRIP
Hmf... I'll make an exception and let you see it...
HSSSSHH
This is the god of the Amazon!
GULP

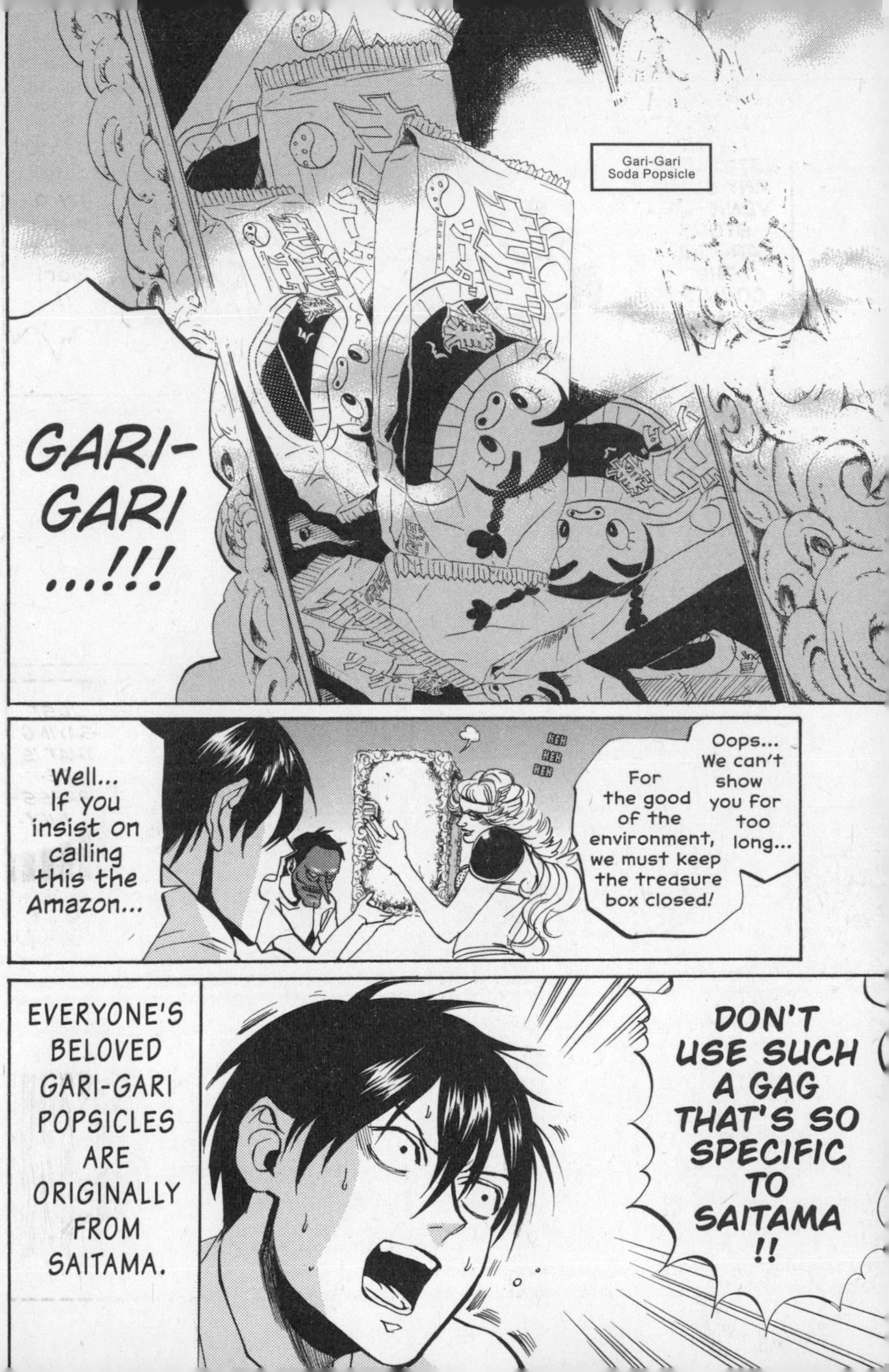
Gari-Gari Soda Popsicle
GARI-GARI ...!!!
Oops... We can't show you for too long...
For the good of the environment, we must keep the treasure box closed!
HEH HEH HEH
Well... If you insist on calling this the Amazon...
DON'T USE SUCH A GAG THAT'S SO SPECIFIC TO SAITAMA !!
EVERYONE'S BELOVED GARI-GARI POPSICLES ARE ORIGINALLY FROM SAITAMA.

Chapter 172: Arakawa, Where Mystery Begets Mystery

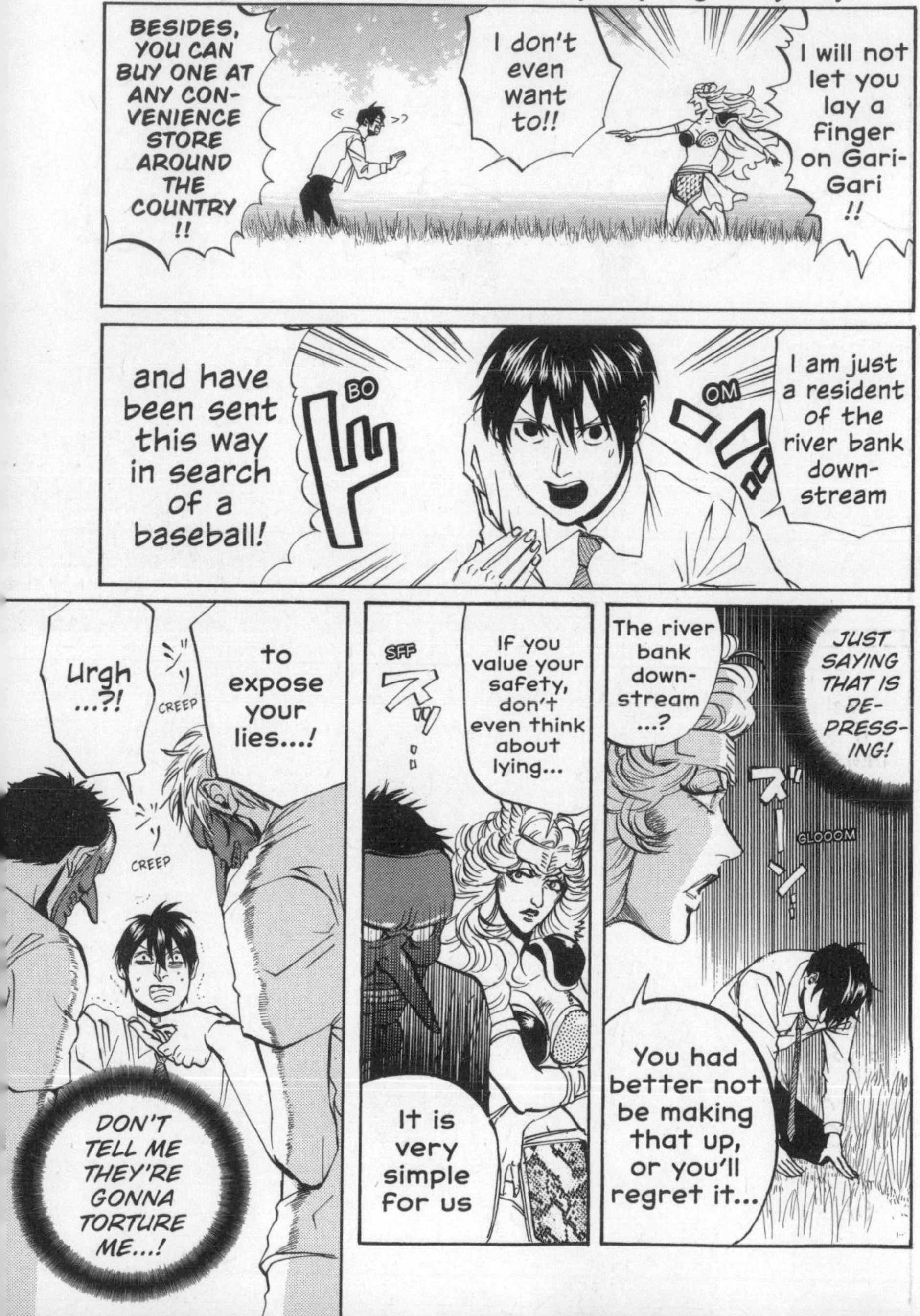
I will not let you lay a finger on Gari-Gari !!
I don't even want to!!
BESIDES, YOU CAN BUY ONE AT ANY CON-VENIENCE STORE AROUND THE COUNTRY !!
I am just a resident of the river bank down-stream
OM
BO
and have been sent this way in search of a baseball!
JUST SAYING THAT IS DE-PRESS-ING!
The river bank down-stream ...?
GLOOOM
You had better not be making that up, or you'll regret it...
If you value your safety, don't even think about lying...
SFF
It is very simple for us
to expose your lies...!
CREEP
Urgh ...?!
CREEP
DON'T TELL ME THEY'RE GONNA TORTURE ME...!

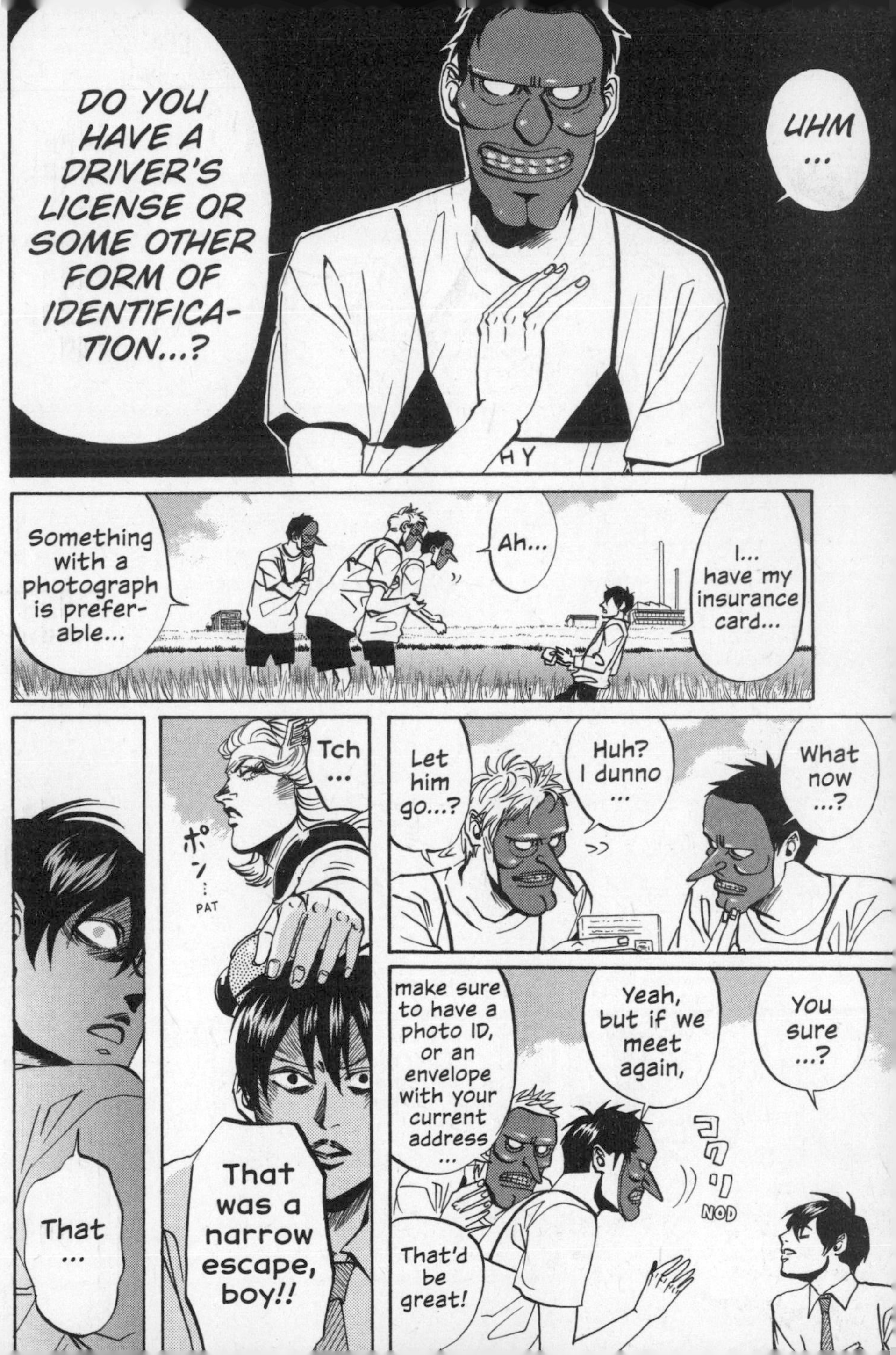
UHM ...
DO YOU HAVE A DRIVER'S LICENSE OR SOME OTHER FORM OF IDENTIFICA-TION...?
HY
I... have my insurance card...
Ah...
Something with a photograph is prefer-able...
What now ...?
Huh? I dunno ...
Let him go...?
You sure ...?
Yeah, but if we meet again,
make sure to have a photo ID, or an envelope with your current address ...
コクリ
NOD
That'd be great!
Tch ...
ポン
PAT
That was a narrow escape, boy!!
That ...

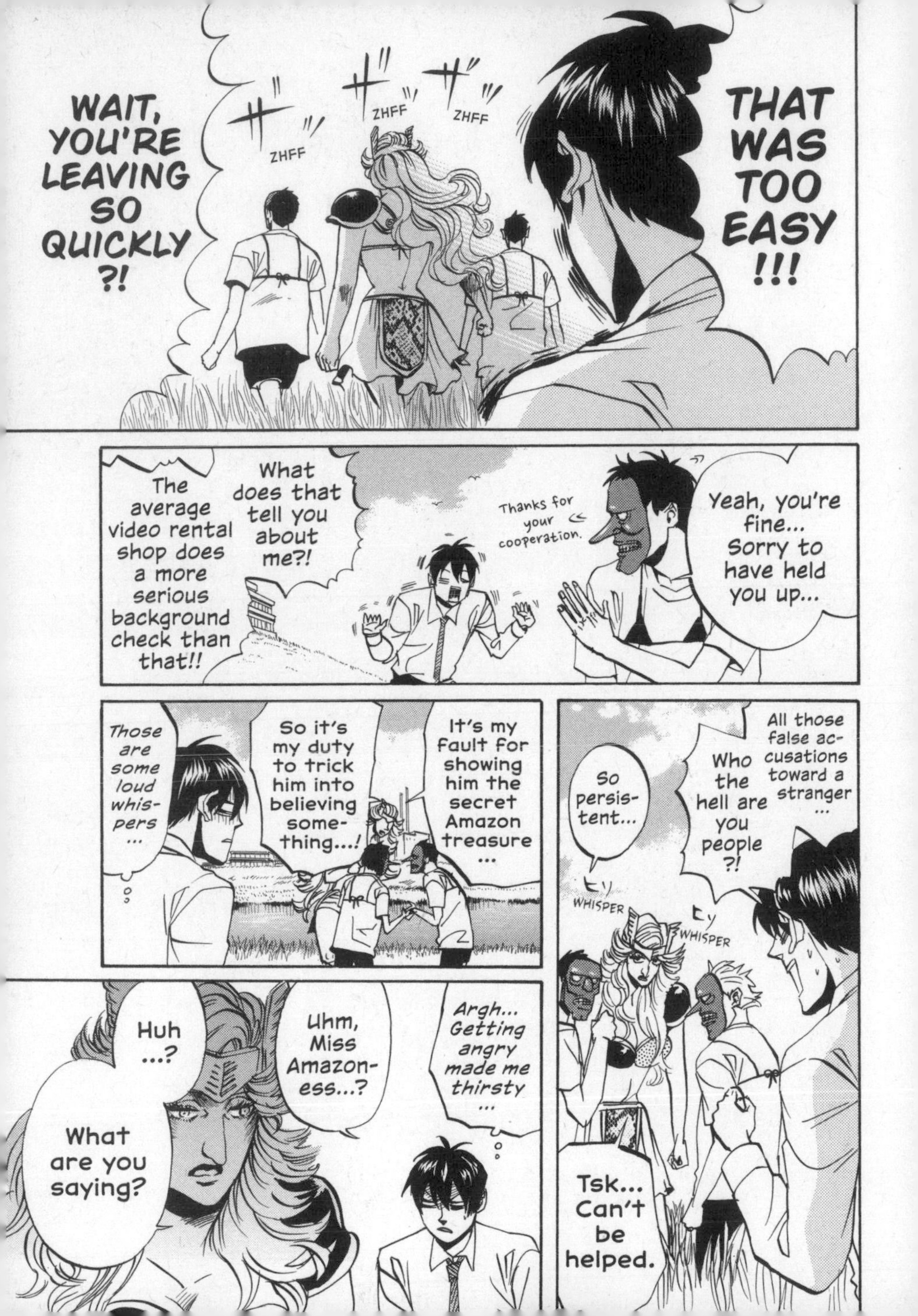
THAT WAS TOO EASY!!!
ZHFF
ZHFF
ZHFF
WAIT, YOU'RE LEAVING SO QUICKLY?!
Yeah, you're fine... Sorry to have held you up...
Thanks for your cooperation.
What does that tell you about me?!
The average video rental shop does a more serious background check than that!!
All those false accusations toward a stranger...
Who the hell are you people?!
So persistent...
WHISPER
WHISPER
Tsk... Can't be helped.
It's my fault for showing him the secret Amazon treasure...
So it's my duty to trick him into believing something...!
Those are some loud whispers...
Argh... Getting angry made me thirsty...
Uhm, Miss Amazoness...?
Huh...?
What are you saying?

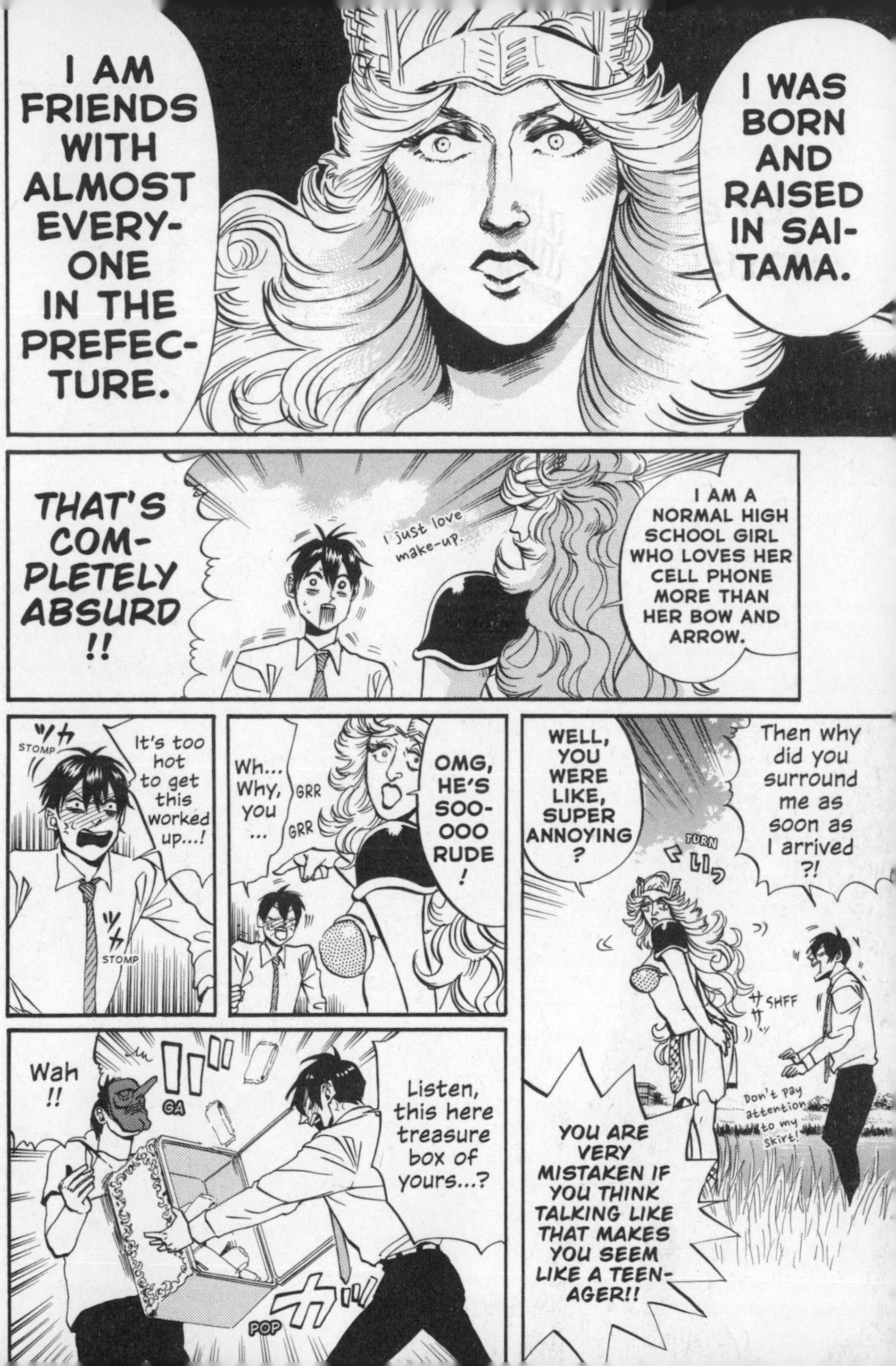
I WAS BORN AND RAISED IN SAI-TAMA.
I AM FRIENDS WITH ALMOST EVERY-ONE IN THE PREFEC-TURE.
I AM A NORMAL HIGH SCHOOL GIRL WHO LOVES HER CELL PHONE MORE THAN HER BOW AND ARROW.
I just love make-up.
THAT'S COM-PLETELY ABSURD !!
Then why did you surround me as soon as I arrived ?!
WELL, YOU WERE LIKE, SUPER ANNOYING ?
TURN
SHFF
Don't pay attention to my skirt!
YOU ARE VERY MISTAKEN IF YOU THINK TALKING LIKE THAT MAKES YOU SEEM LIKE A TEEN-AGER!!
OMG, HE'S SOO-OOO RUDE !
Wh... Why, you ...
GRR
GRR
STOMP
It's too hot to get this worked up...!
STOMP
Listen, this here treasure box of yours...?
GA
Wah !!
POP

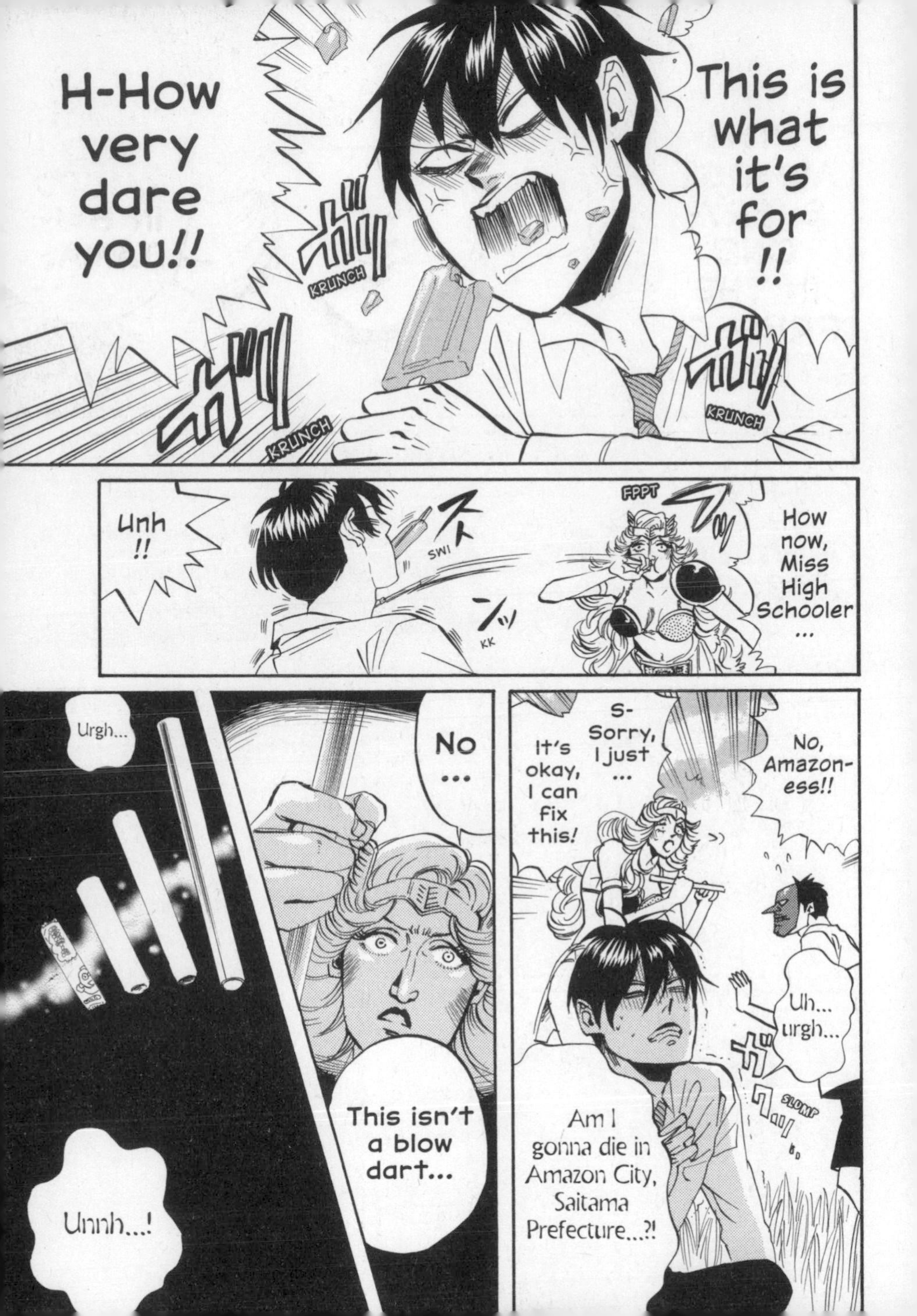
This is what it's for!!
KRUNCH
H-How very dare you!!
KRUNCH
KRUNCH
How now, Miss High Schooler...
FPPT
KK
SWI
Unh!!
No, Amazon-ess!!
S-Sorry, I just...
It's okay, I can fix this!
Uh... urgh...
SLUMP
Am I gonna die in Amazon City, Saitama Prefecture...?!
No...
This isn't a blow dart...
Urgh...
Unnh...!

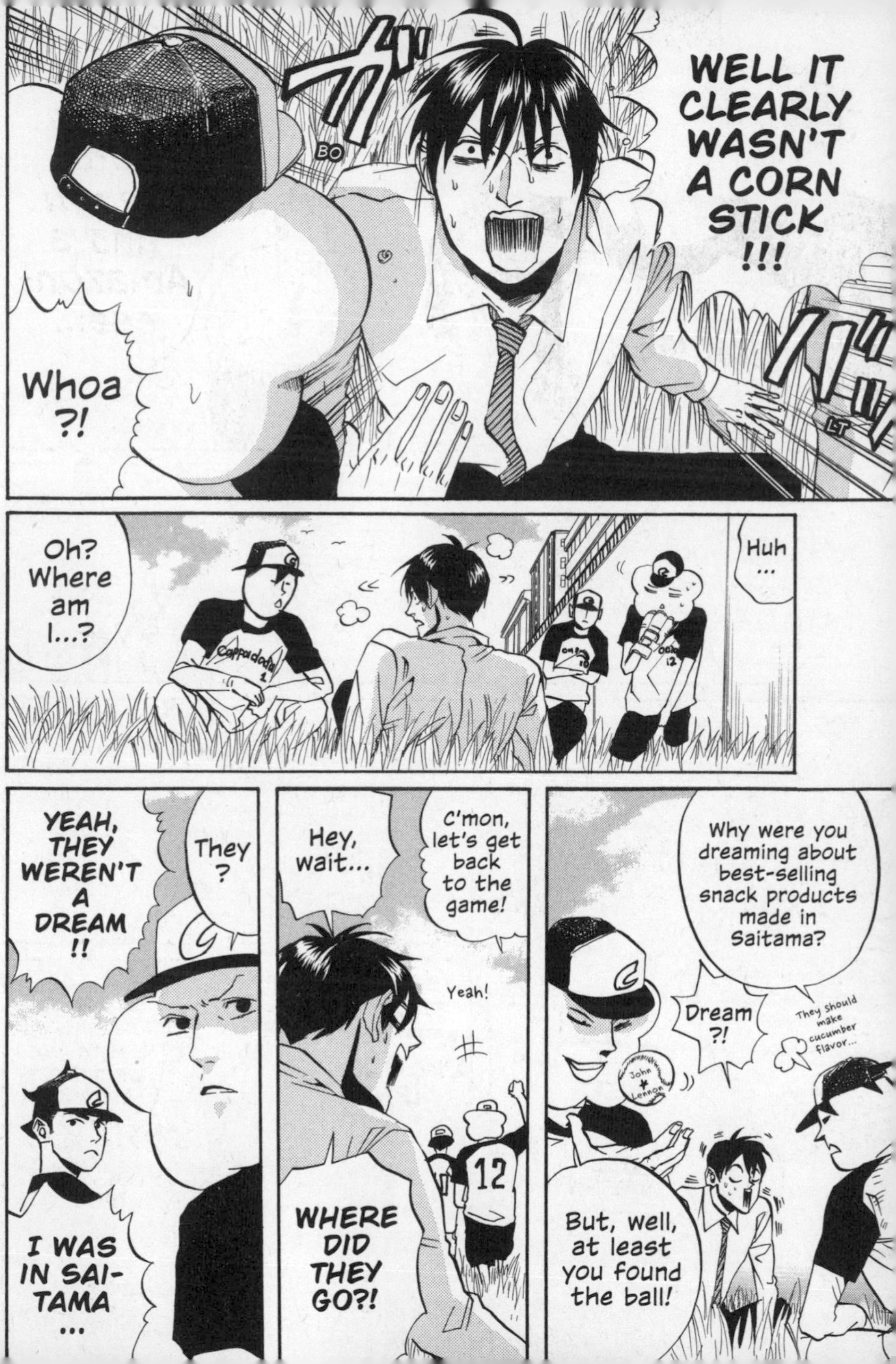
WELL IT CLEARLY WASN'T A CORN STICK !!!
BO
LT
Whoa ?!
Huh ...
Oh? Where am I...?
Why were you dreaming about best-selling snack products made in Saitama?
Dream ?!
They should make cucumber flavor...
John Lennon
But, well, at least you found the ball!
C'mon, let's get back to the game!
Hey, wait...
Yeah!
12
WHERE DID THEY GO?!
They ?
YEAH, THEY WEREN'T A DREAM !!
I WAS IN SAI-TAMA ...

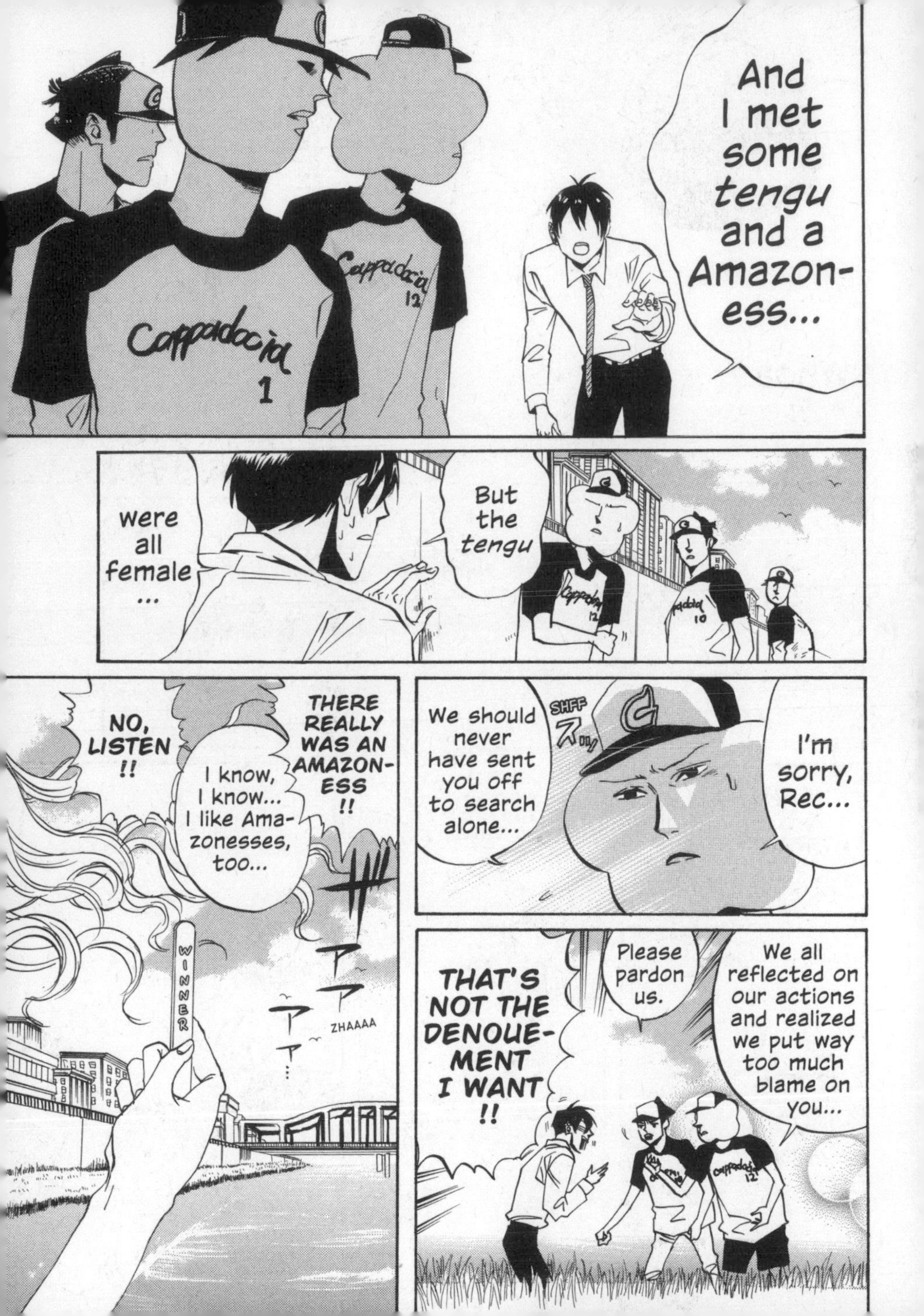
And I met some *tengu* and a Amazon-ess...
Cappadocia 12
Cappadocia 1
But the *tengu*
were all female...
I'm sorry, Rec...
SHFF
We should never have sent you off to search alone...
We all reflected on our actions and realized we put way too much blame on you...
Please pardon us.
THAT'S NOT THE DENOUEMENT I WANT!!
THERE REALLY WAS AN AMAZON-ESS!!
NO, LISTEN!!
I know, I know... I like Amazonesses, too...
WINNER
ZHAAAA

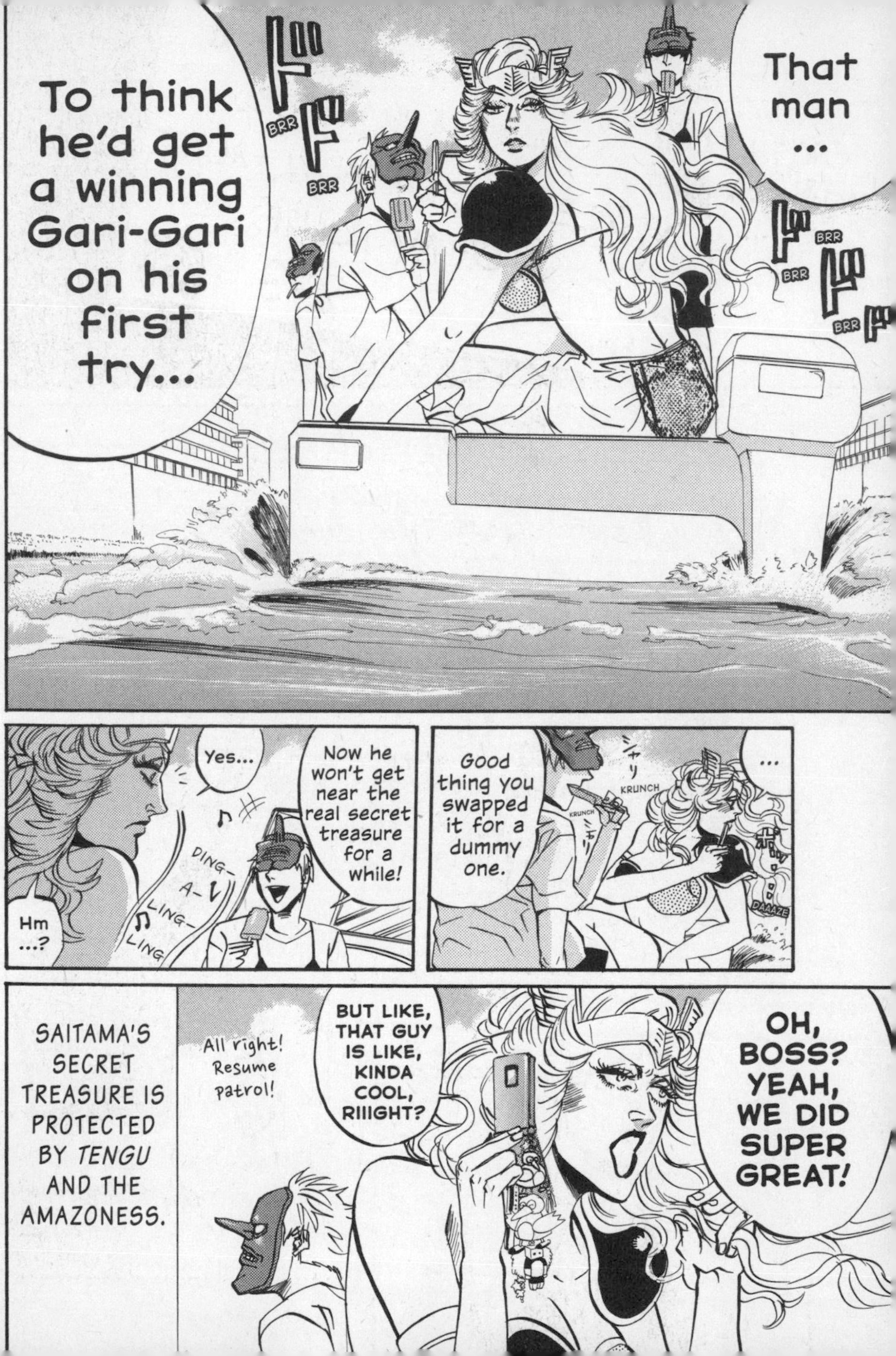
That man ...
BRR
BRR
BRR
BRR
BRR
To think he'd get a winning Gari-Gari on his first try...
...
KRUNCH
KRUNCH
DAAAZE
Good thing you swapped it for a dummy one.
Now he won't get near the real secret treasure for a while!
Yes...
DING-A-LING-LING
Hm ...?
OH, BOSS? YEAH, WE DID SUPER GREAT!
BUT LIKE, THAT GUY IS LIKE, KINDA COOL, RIIIGHT?
All right! Resume patrol!
SAITAMA'S SECRET TREASURE IS PROTECTED BY *TENGU* AND THE AMAZONESS.

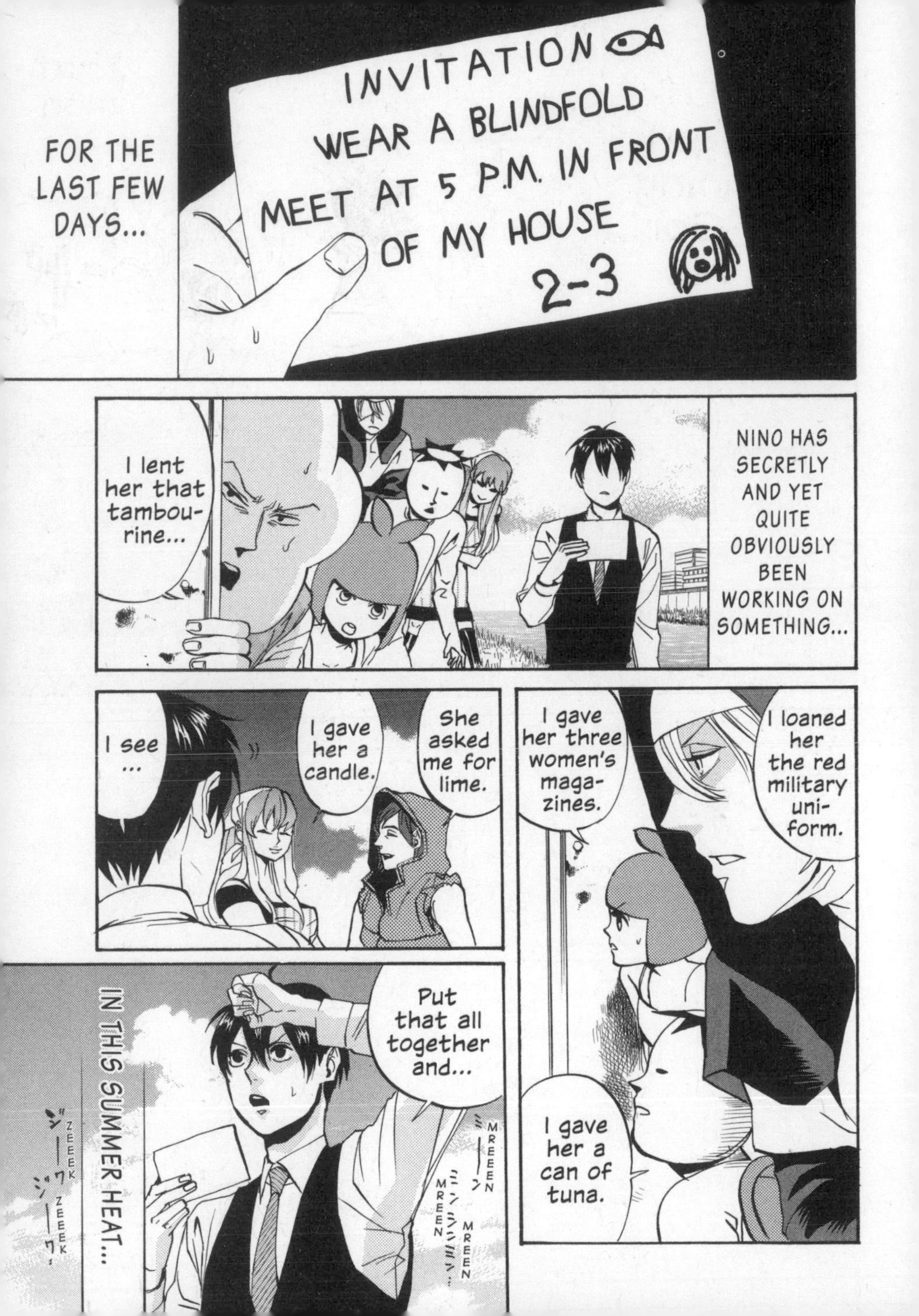
INVITATION
WEAR A BLINDFOLD
MEET AT 5 P.M. IN FRONT OF MY HOUSE
2-3
FOR THE LAST FEW DAYS...
NINO HAS SECRETLY AND YET QUITE OBVIOUSLY BEEN WORKING ON SOMETHING...
I lent her that tambourine...
I loaned her the red military uniform.
I gave her three women's magazines.
I gave her a can of tuna.
She asked me for lime.
I gave her a candle.
I see ...
Put that all together and...
MREEEN
MREEEN
MREEEN
ZEEEK
ZEEEK
IN THIS SUMMER HEAT...

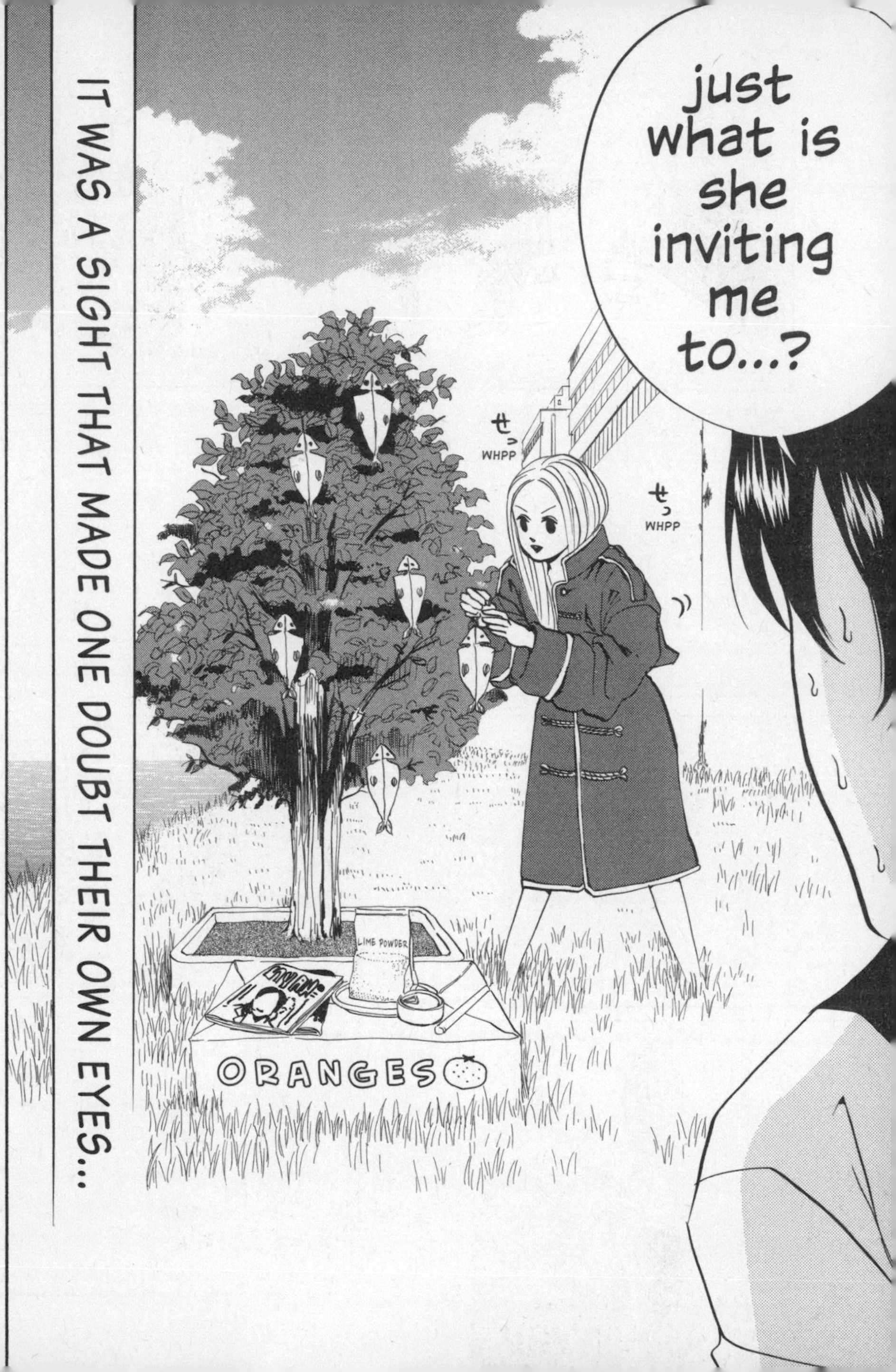
just what is she inviting me to...?
せっ WHPP
せっ WHPP
LIME POWDER
ORANGES
IT WAS A SIGHT THAT MADE ONE DOUBT THEIR OWN EYES...

Chapter 173: What Day Is Today?

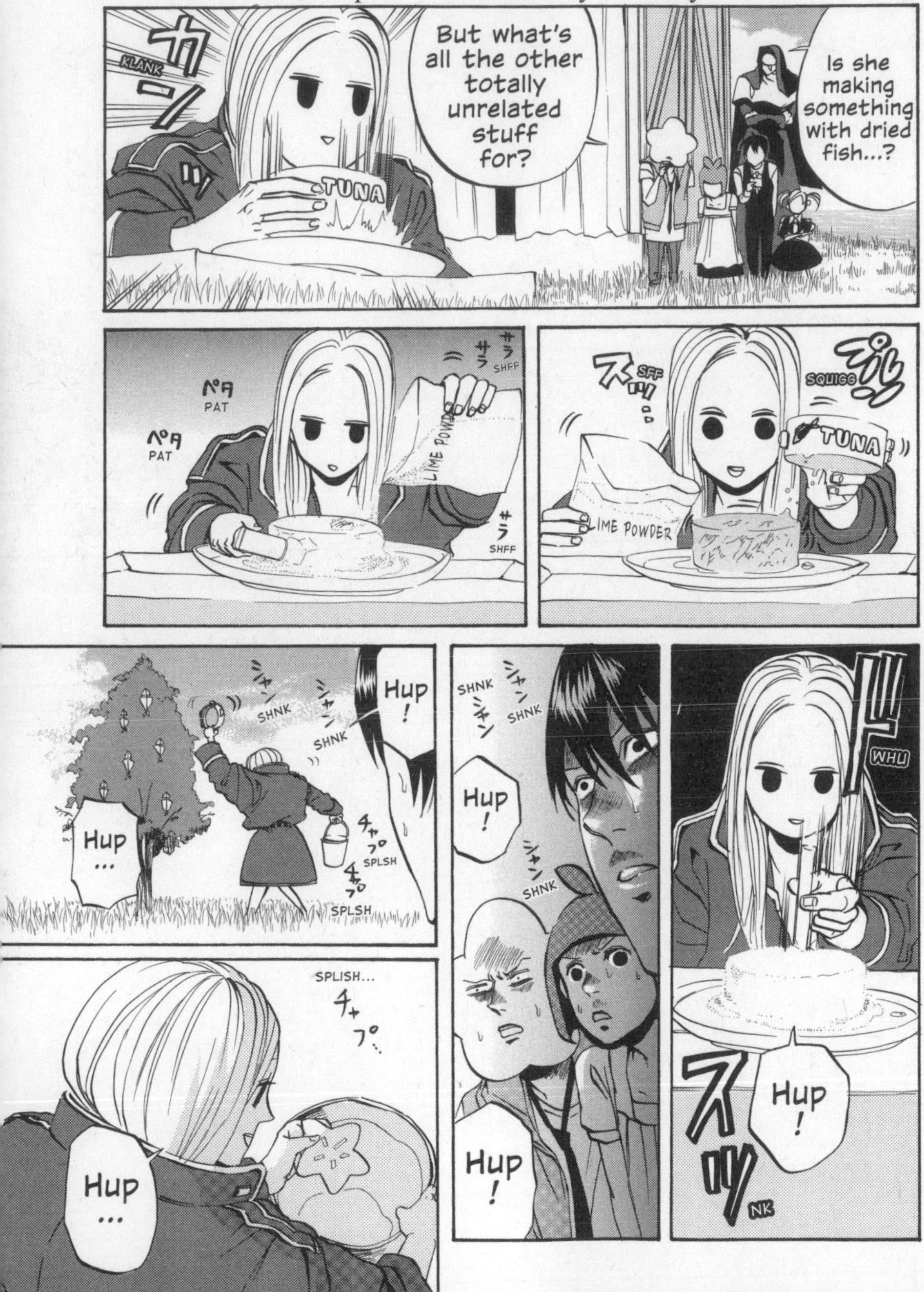
Is she making something with dried fish...?
But what's all the other totally unrelated stuff for?
KLANK
TUNA
SQUIGG
SFF
TUNA
LIME POWDER
SHFF
PAT
PAT
LIME POWDER
SHFF
WHU
Hup!
NK
SHNK
SHNK
Hup!
SHNK
Hup!
Hup!
SHNK
SHNK
SPLSH
SPLSH
Hup...
SPLISH...
Hup...

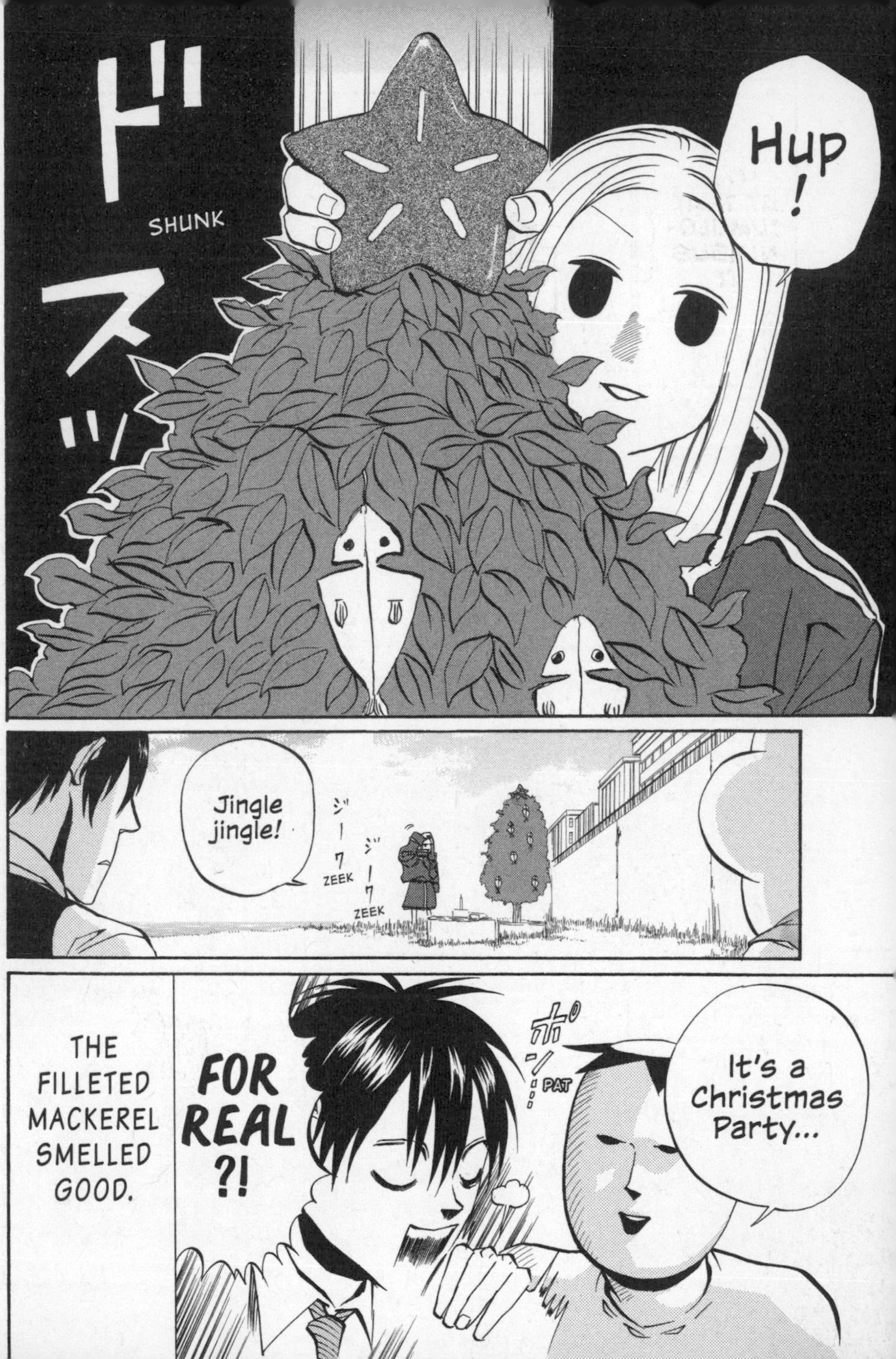
Hup!
ドリ
SHUNK
スッ
Jingle jingle!
ジーク
ZEEK
ジーク
ZEEK
It's a Christmas Party...
ポン
PAT
FOR REAL?!
THE FILLETED MACKEREL SMELLED GOOD.

Chapter 174: Couple's Christmas

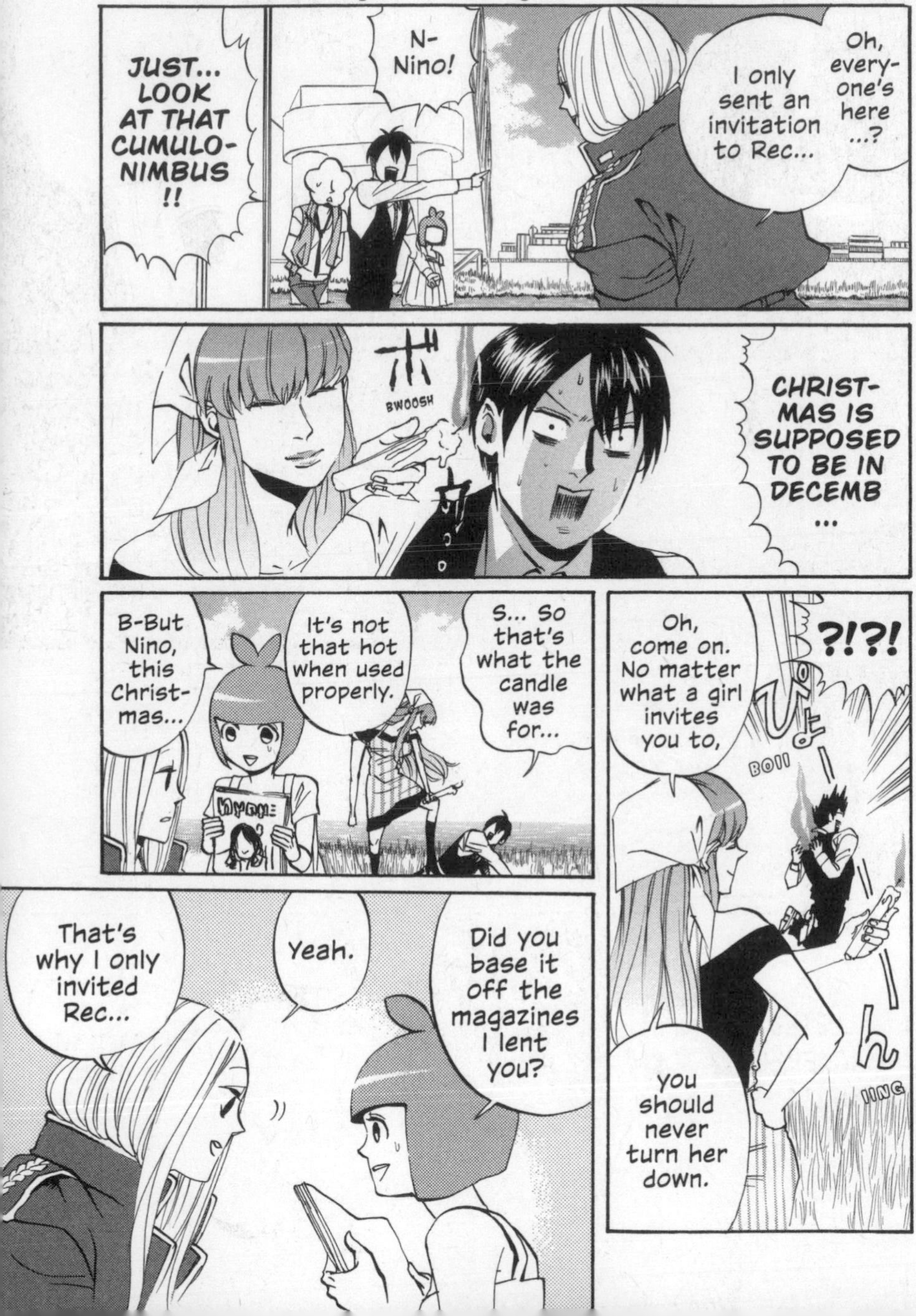
Oh, every-one's here ...?
I only sent an invitation to Rec...
N-Nino!
JUST... LOOK AT THAT CUMULO-NIMBUS !!
CHRIST-MAS IS SUPPOSED TO BE IN DECEMB ...
BWOOSH
?!?!
Oh, come on. No matter what a girl invites you to,
BOII
IING
you should never turn her down.
S... So that's what the candle was for...
It's not that hot when used properly.
B-But Nino, this Christ-mas...
Did you base it off the magazines I lent you?
Yeah.
That's why I only invited Rec...

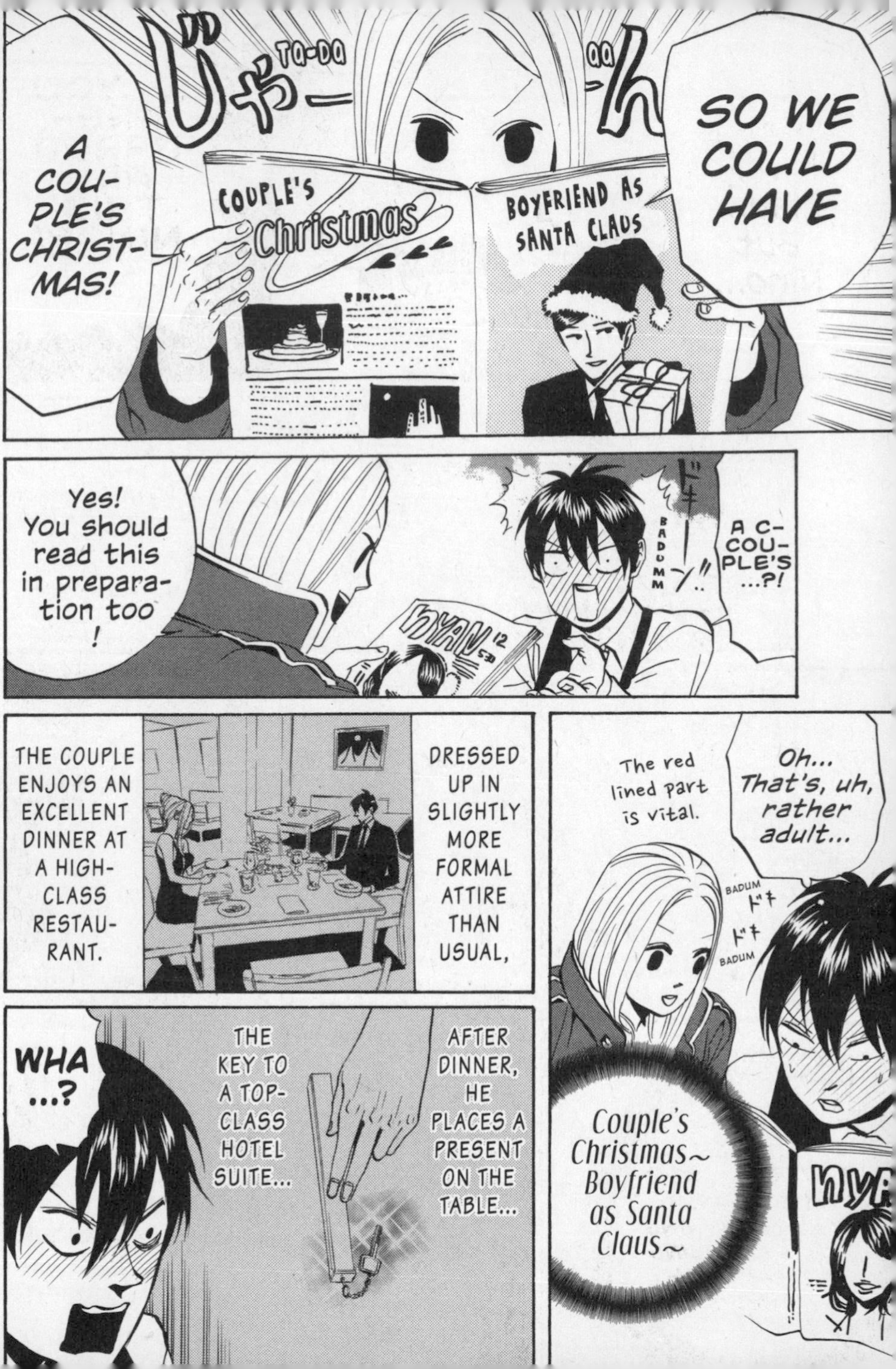
じゃーん
TA-DA
aa
SO WE COULD HAVE
A COUPLE'S CHRISTMAS!
COUPLE'S Christmas
BOYFRIEND AS SANTA CLAUS
A C-COUPLE'S ...?!
ドキーン
BADUMM
Yes! You should read this in preparation too!
NYAN
12
Oh... That's, uh, rather adult...
The red lined part is vital.
BADUM
ドキ
ドキ
BADUM
Couple's Christmas~ Boyfriend as Santa Claus~
NYA
DRESSED UP IN SLIGHTLY MORE FORMAL ATTIRE THAN USUAL,
THE COUPLE ENJOYS AN EXCELLENT DINNER AT A HIGH-CLASS RESTAURANT.
AFTER DINNER, HE PLACES A PRESENT ON THE TABLE...
THE KEY TO A TOP-CLASS HOTEL SUITE...
WHA...?

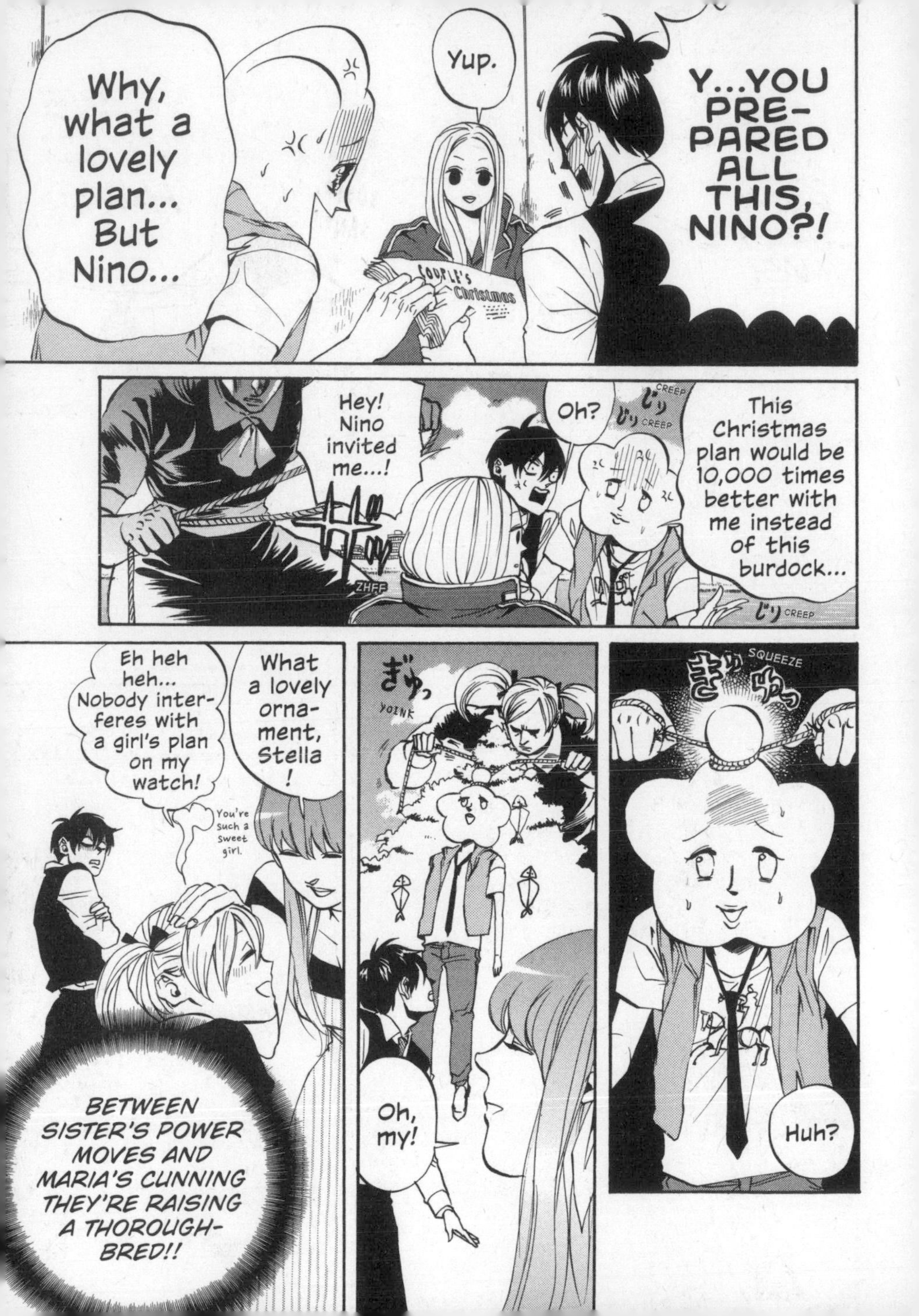
Y...YOU PRE-PARED ALL THIS, NINO?!
Yup.
COUPLE'S Christmas
Why, what a lovely plan... But Nino...
CREEP
This Christmas plan would be 10,000 times better with me instead of this burdock...
CREEP
Oh?
CREEP
Hey! Nino invited me...!
ZHFF
SQUEEZE
Huh?
YOINK
Oh, my!
What a lovely ornament, Stella!
Eh heh heh... Nobody interferes with a girl's plan on my watch!
You're such a sweet girl.
BETWEEN SISTER'S POWER MOVES AND MARIA'S CUNNING THEY'RE RAISING A THOROUGH-BRED!!

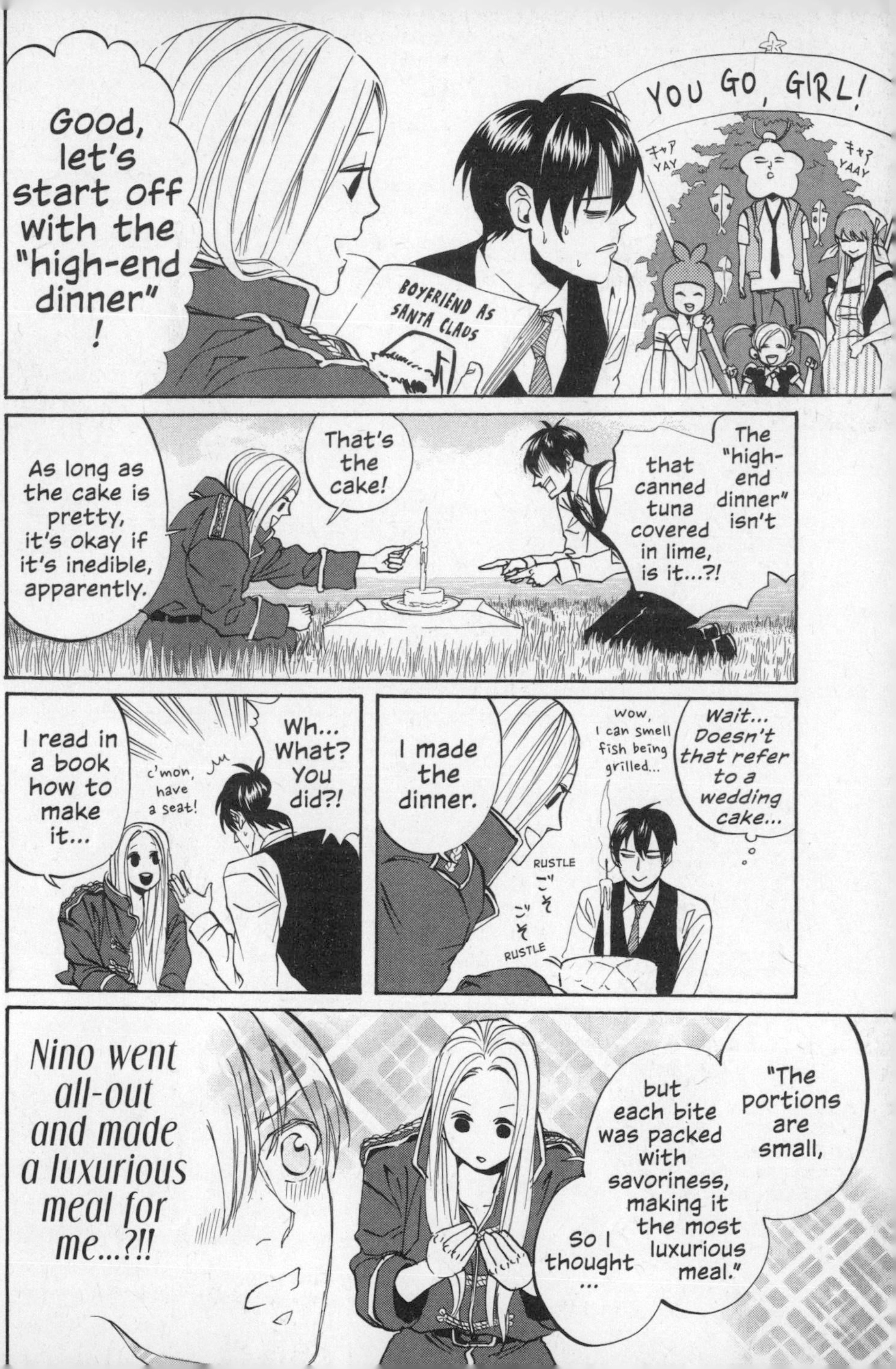
YOU GO, GIRL!
キャア YAAY
キャア YAY
Good, let's start off with the "high-end dinner"!
BOYFRIEND AS SANTA CLAUS
The "high-end dinner" isn't that canned tuna covered in lime, is it...?!
That's the cake!
As long as the cake is pretty, it's okay if it's inedible, apparently.
Wait... Doesn't that refer to a wedding cake...
Wow, I can smell fish being grilled...
I made the dinner.
ごそごそ RUSTLE RUSTLE
Wh... What? You did?!
c'mon, have a seat!
I read in a book how to make it...
"The portions are small,
but each bite was packed with savoriness, making it the most luxurious meal."
So I thought...
Nino went all-out and made a luxurious meal for me...?!!

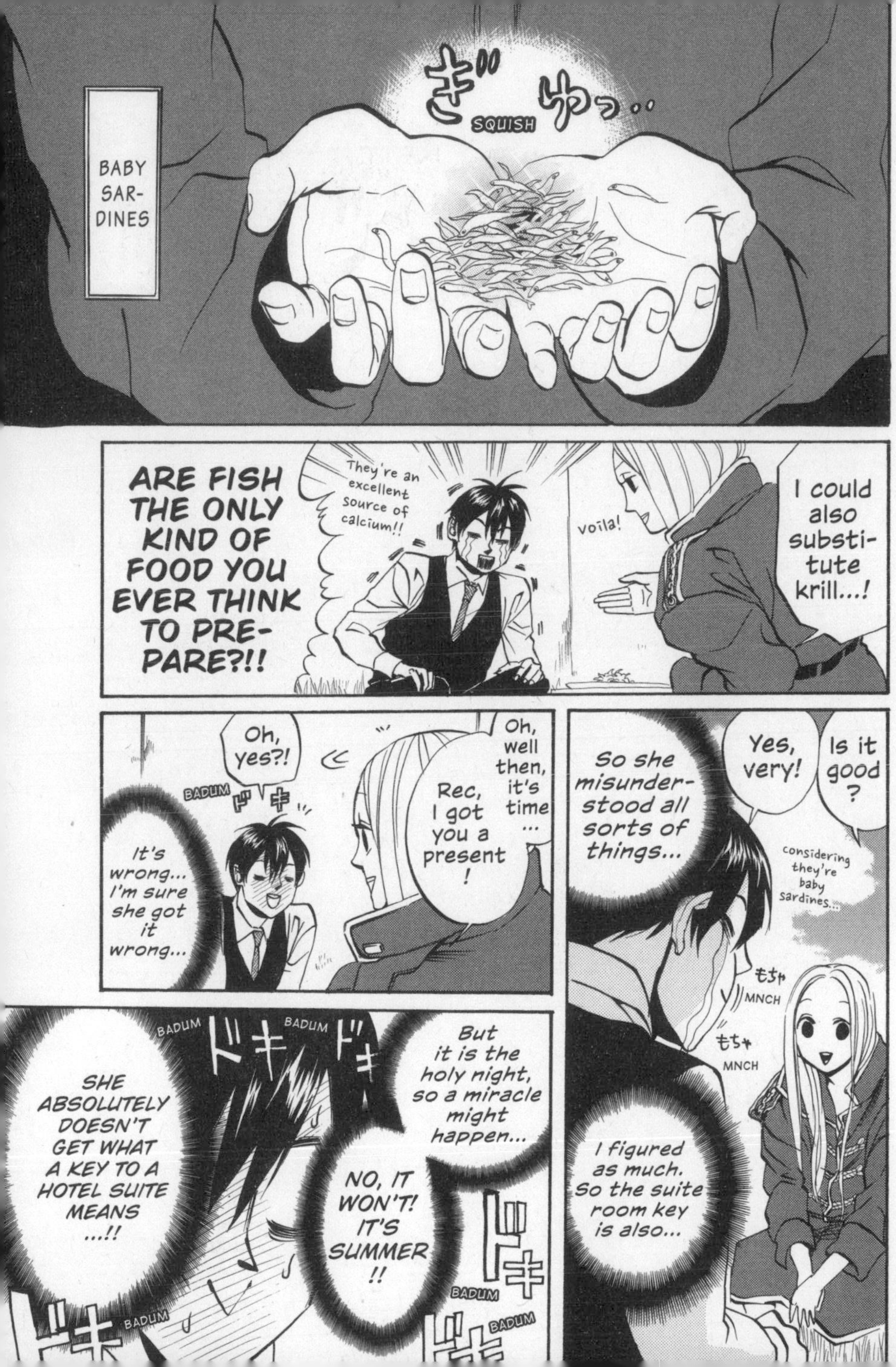
ぎゅっ..
SQUISH
BABY SARDINES
I could also substitute krill...!
voila!
They're an excellent source of calcium!!
ARE FISH THE ONLY KIND OF FOOD YOU EVER THINK TO PREPARE?!!
Is it good?
Yes, very!
So she misunderstood all sorts of things...
considering they're baby sardines...
もちゃ
MNCH
もちゃ
MNCH
I figured as much. So the suite room key is also...
Oh, well then, it's time...
Rec, I got you a present!
Oh, yes?!
ドキ
BADUM
It's wrong... I'm sure she got it wrong...
But it is the holy night, so a miracle might happen...
ドキ
BADUM
ドキ
BADUM
SHE ABSOLUTELY DOESN'T GET WHAT A KEY TO A HOTEL SUITE MEANS ...!!
NO, IT WON'T! IT'S SUMMER!!
ドキ
BADUM
ドキ
BADUM
ドキ
BADUM

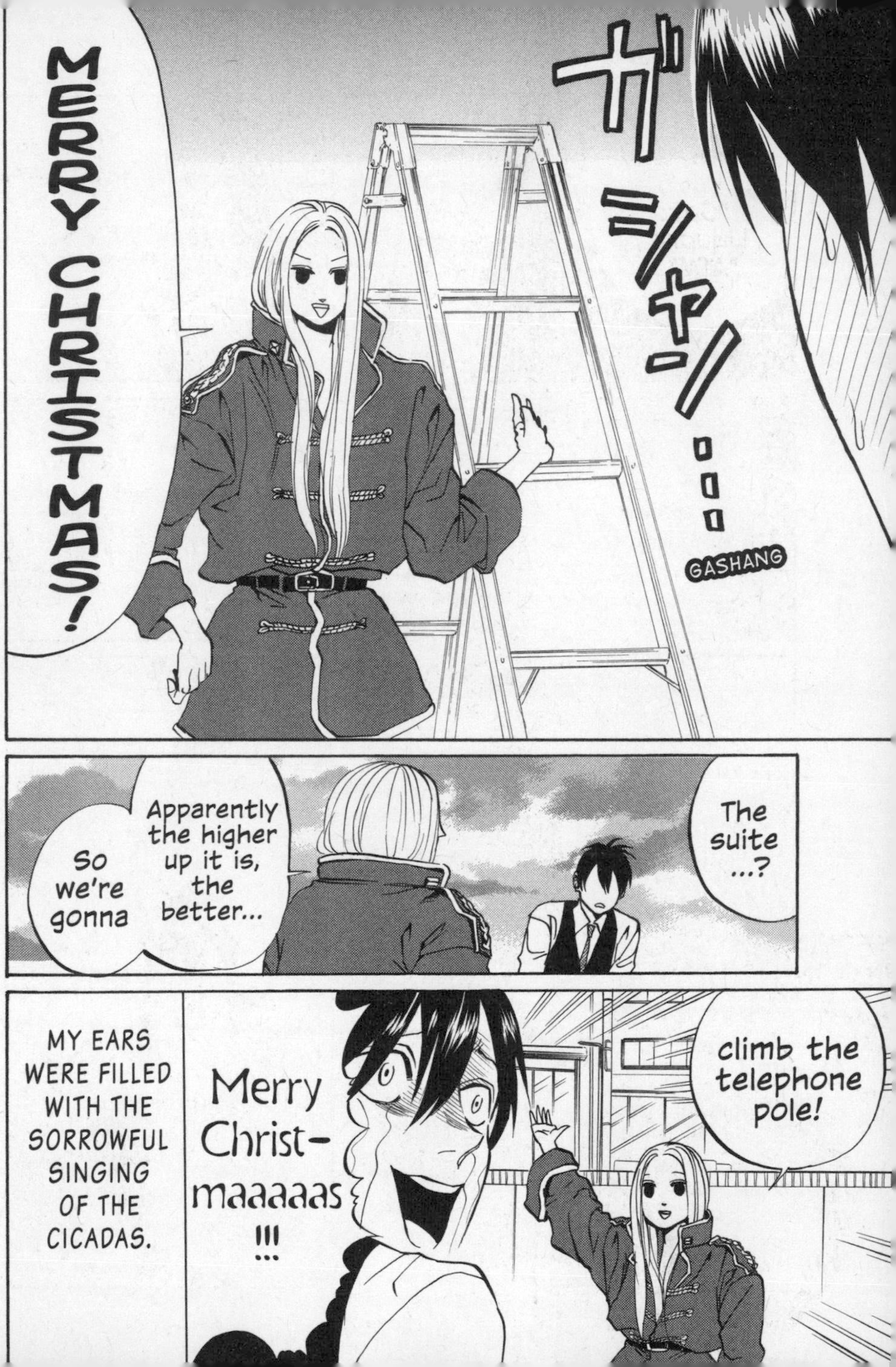
ガシャン…
GASHANG
MERRY CHRISTMAS!
The suite ...?
Apparently the higher up it is, the better...
So we're gonna
climb the telephone pole!
Merry Christ-maaaaas!!!...
MY EARS WERE FILLED WITH THE SORROWFUL SINGING OF THE CICADAS.

Chapter 175: The Arakawa Suite

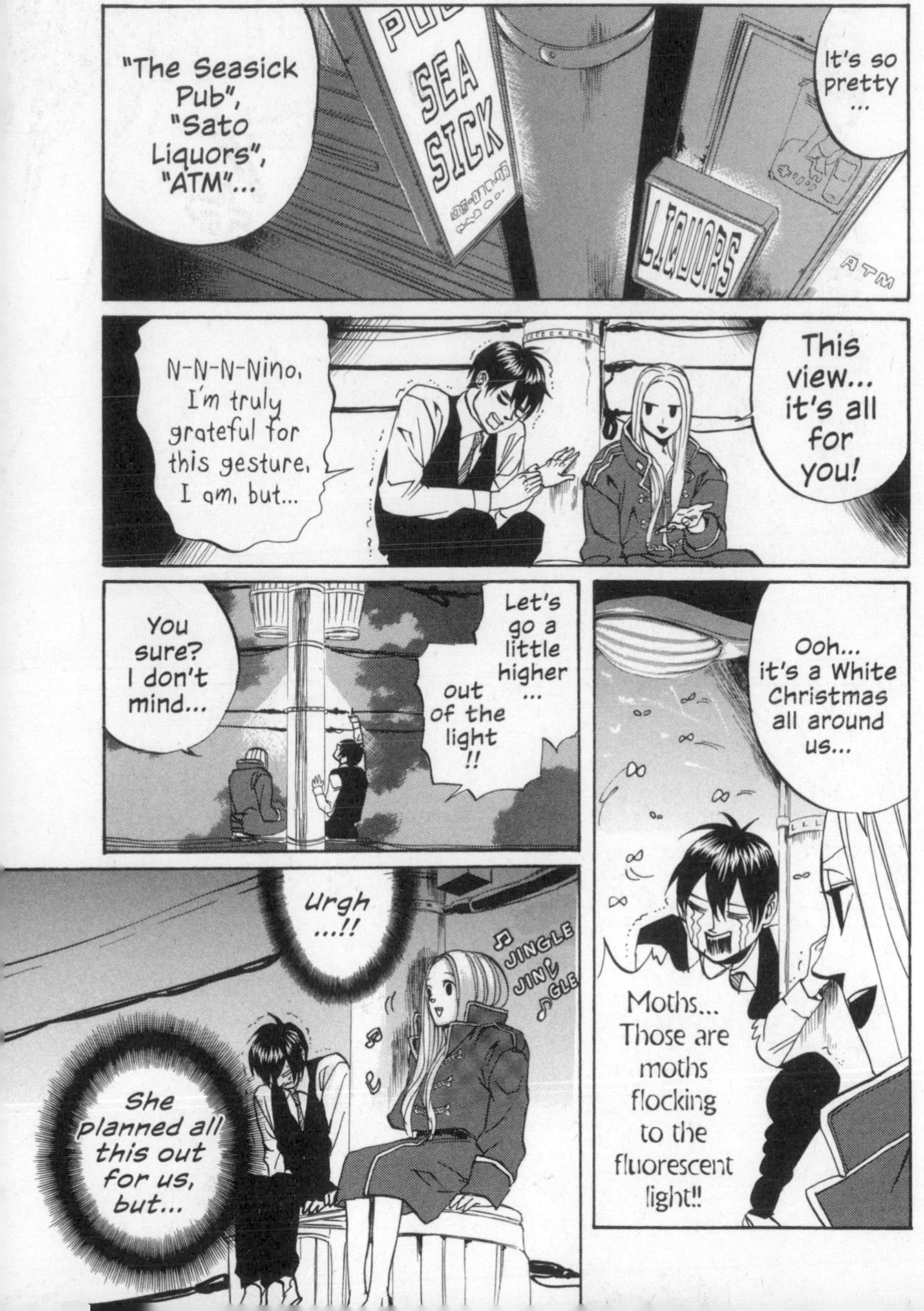
It's so pretty ...
"The Seasick Pub", "Sato Liquors", "ATM"...
PUB
SEA SICK
LIQUORS
ATM
This view... it's all for you!
N-N-N-Nino, I'm truly grateful for this gesture, I am, but...
Ooh... it's a White Christmas all around us...
Moths... Those are moths flocking to the fluorescent light!!
Let's go a little higher ... out of the light !!
You sure? I don't mind...
Urgh ...!!
JINGLE JINGLE
She planned all this out for us, but...

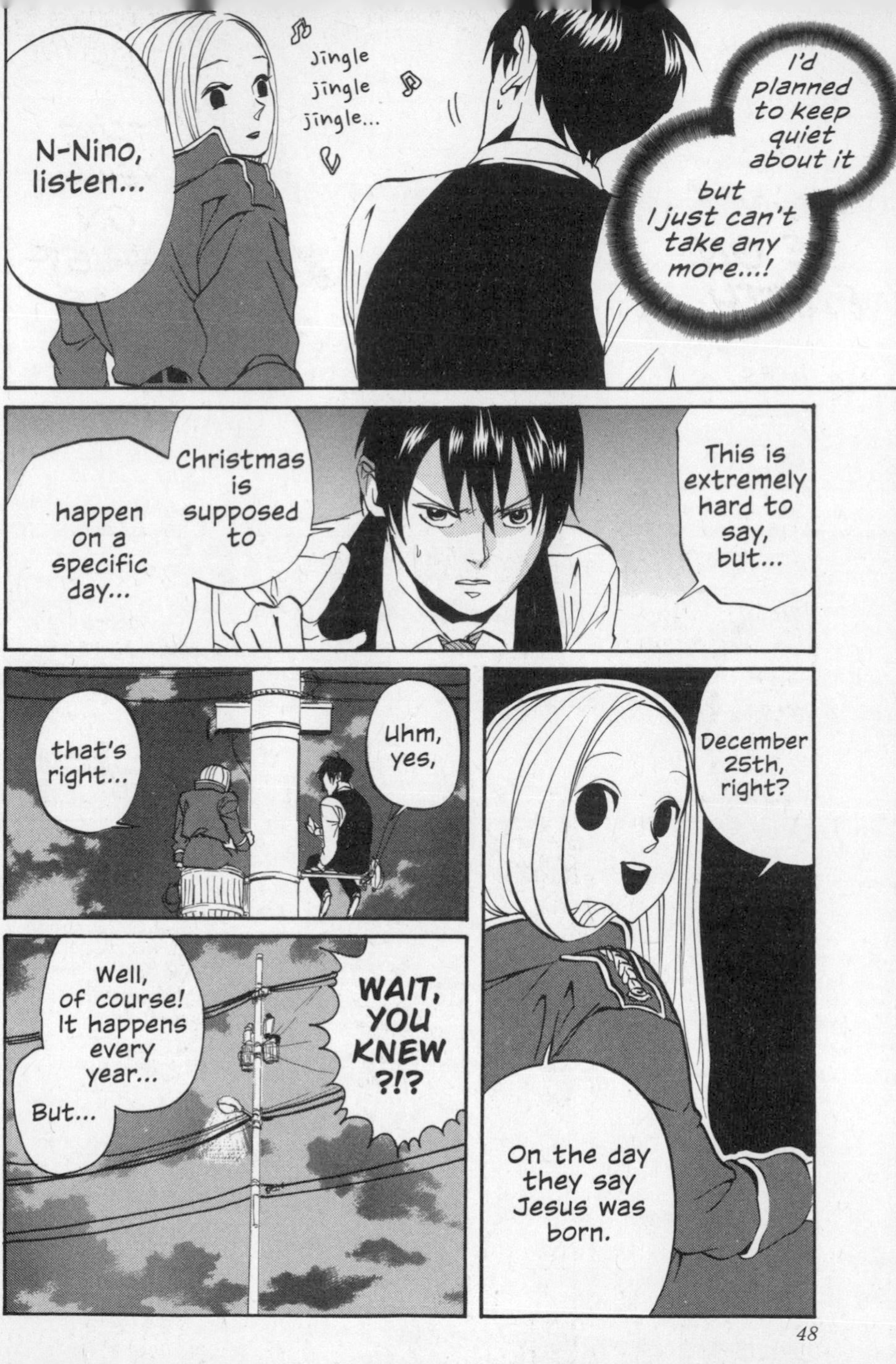
I'd planned to keep quiet about it but I just can't take any more...!
Jingle jingle jingle...
N-Nino, listen...
This is extremely hard to say, but...
Christmas is supposed to happen on a specific day...
December 25th, right?
On the day they say Jesus was born.
Uhm, yes,
that's right...
WAIT, YOU KNEW ?!?
Well, of course! It happens every year...
But...

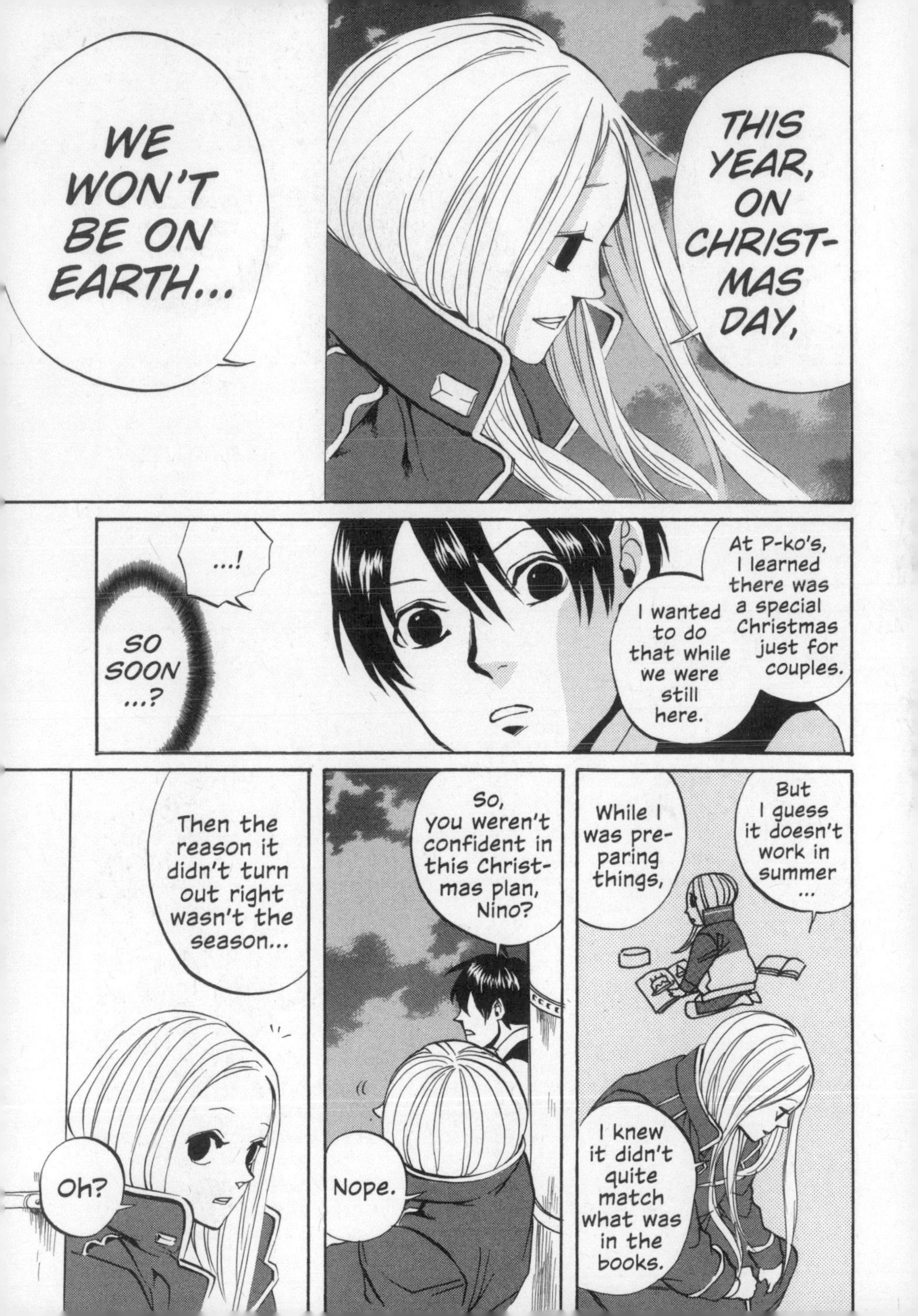
THIS YEAR, ON CHRIST-MAS DAY,
WE WON'T BE ON EARTH...
At P-ko's, I learned there was a special Christmas just for couples.
I wanted to do that while we were still here.
...!
SO SOON ...?
But I guess it doesn't work in summer ...
While I was pre-paring things,
I knew it didn't quite match what was in the books.
So, you weren't confident in this Christ-mas plan, Nino?
Nope.
Then the reason it didn't turn out right wasn't the season...
Oh?

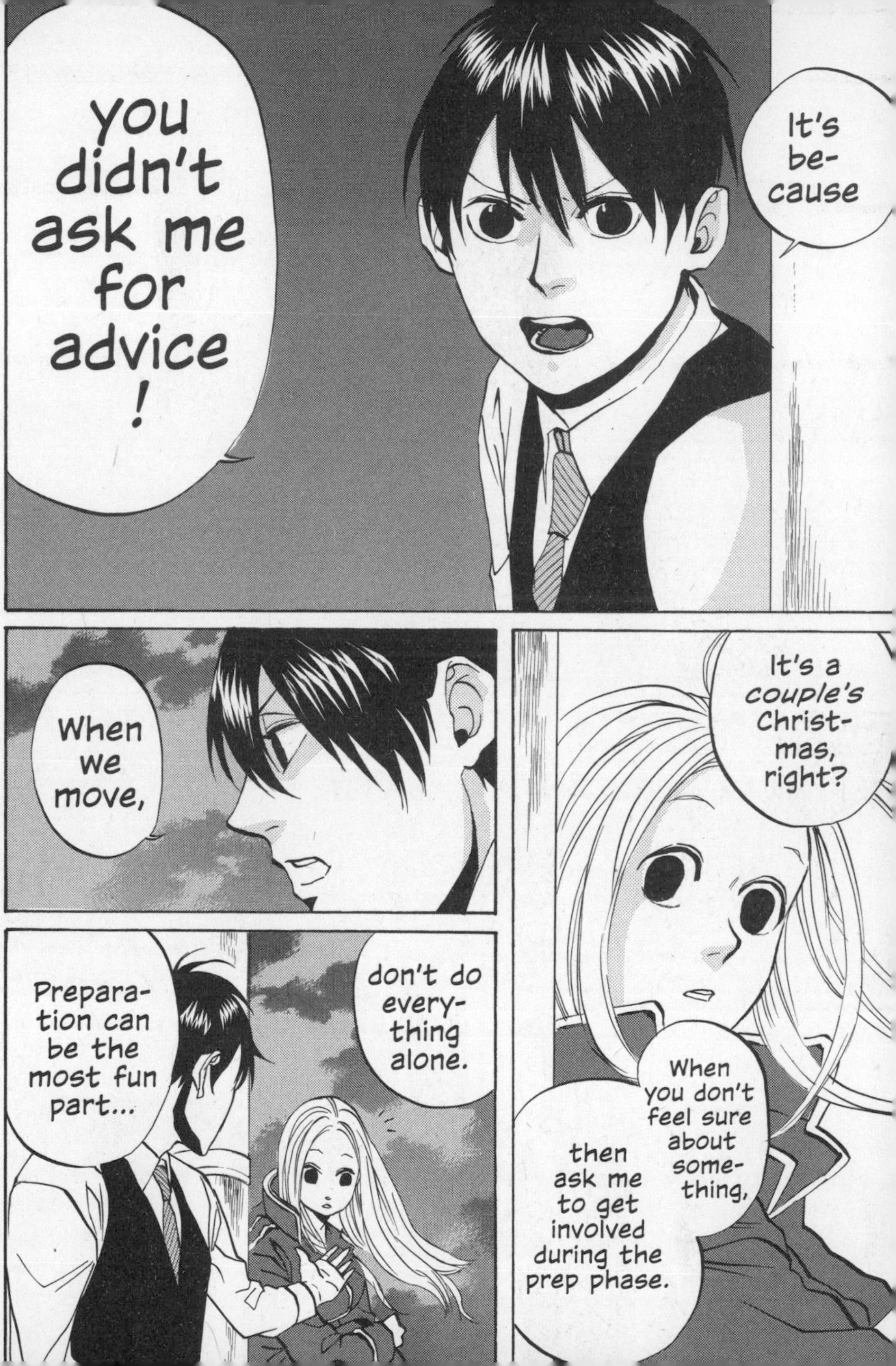
It's be-cause
you didn't ask me for advice!
It's a couple's Christmas, right?
When you don't feel sure about some-thing,
then ask me to get involved during the prep phase.
When we move,
don't do every-thing alone.
Prepara-tion can be the most fun part...

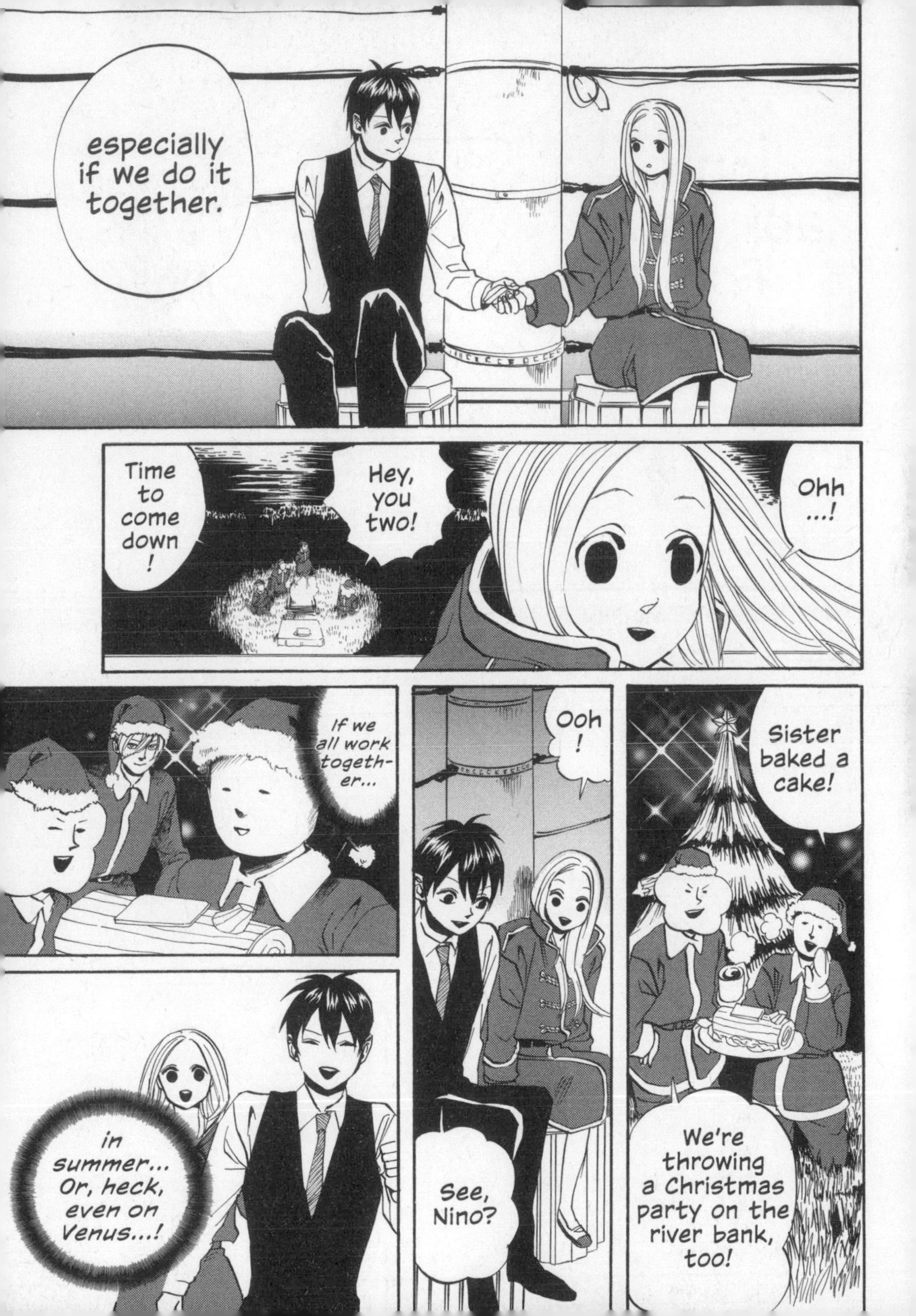
especially if we do it together.
Ohh ...!
Hey, you two!
Time to come down!
Sister baked a cake!
We're throwing a Christmas party on the river bank, too!
Ooh!
See, Nino?
If we all work togeth-er...
in summer... Or, heck, even on Venus...!

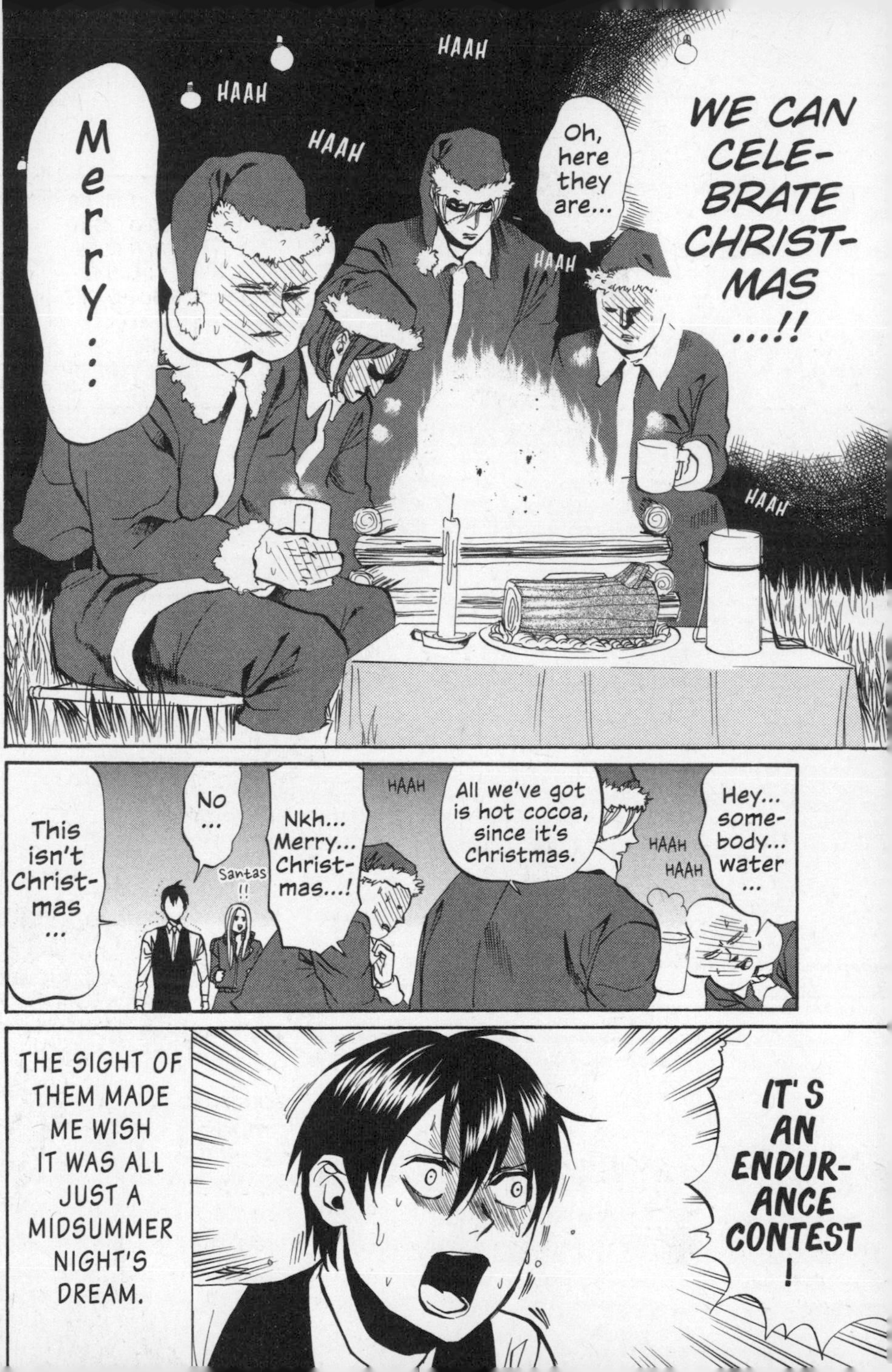
WE CAN CELEBRATE CHRISTMAS ...!!
HAAH
HAAH
Oh, here they are...
HAAH
HAAH
HAAH
Merry...
HAAH
Hey... somebody... water...
HAAH
HAAH
All we've got is hot cocoa, since it's Christmas.
HAAH
Nkh... Merry... Christmas...!
Santas !!
No ...
This isn't Christmas ...
IT'S AN ENDURANCE CONTEST !
THE SIGHT OF THEM MADE ME WISH IT WAS ALL JUST A MIDSUMMER NIGHT'S DREAM.

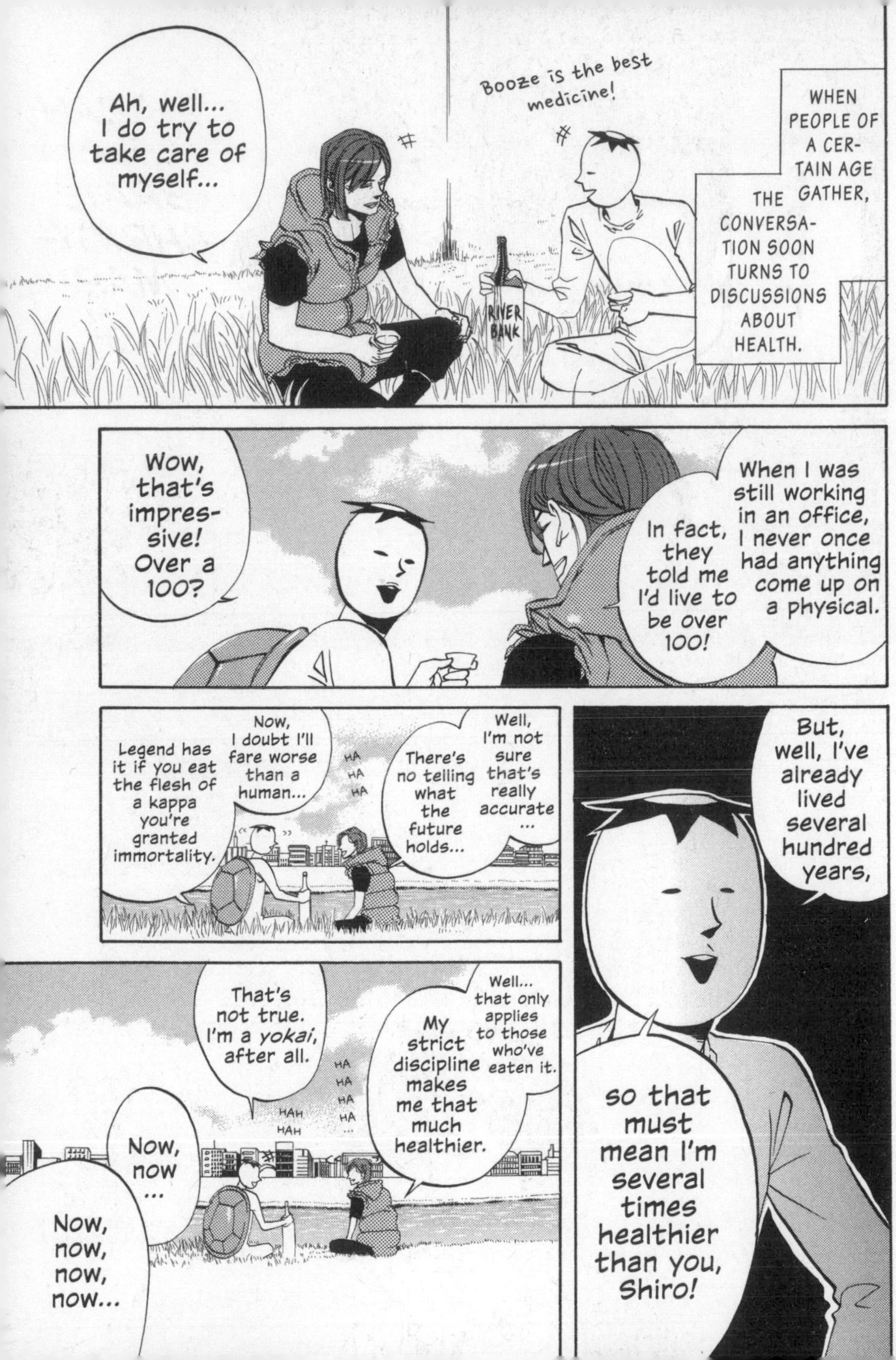
WHEN PEOPLE OF A CERTAIN AGE GATHER, THE CONVERSATION SOON TURNS TO DISCUSSIONS ABOUT HEALTH.
Booze is the best medicine!
RIVER BANK
Ah, well... I do try to take care of myself...
When I was still working in an office, I never once had anything come up on a physical.
In fact, they told me I'd live to be over 100!
Wow, that's impressive! Over a 100?
But, well, I've already lived several hundred years,
so that must mean I'm several times healthier than you, Shiro!
Well, I'm not sure that's really accurate ...
There's no telling what the future holds...
HA HA HA
Now, I doubt I'll fare worse than a human...
Legend has it if you eat the flesh of a kappa you're granted immortality.
Well... that only applies to those who've eaten it.
My strict discipline makes me that much healthier.
HA HA HA HA ...
That's not true. I'm a *yokai*, after all.
HAH HAH
Now, now ...
Now, now, now, now...

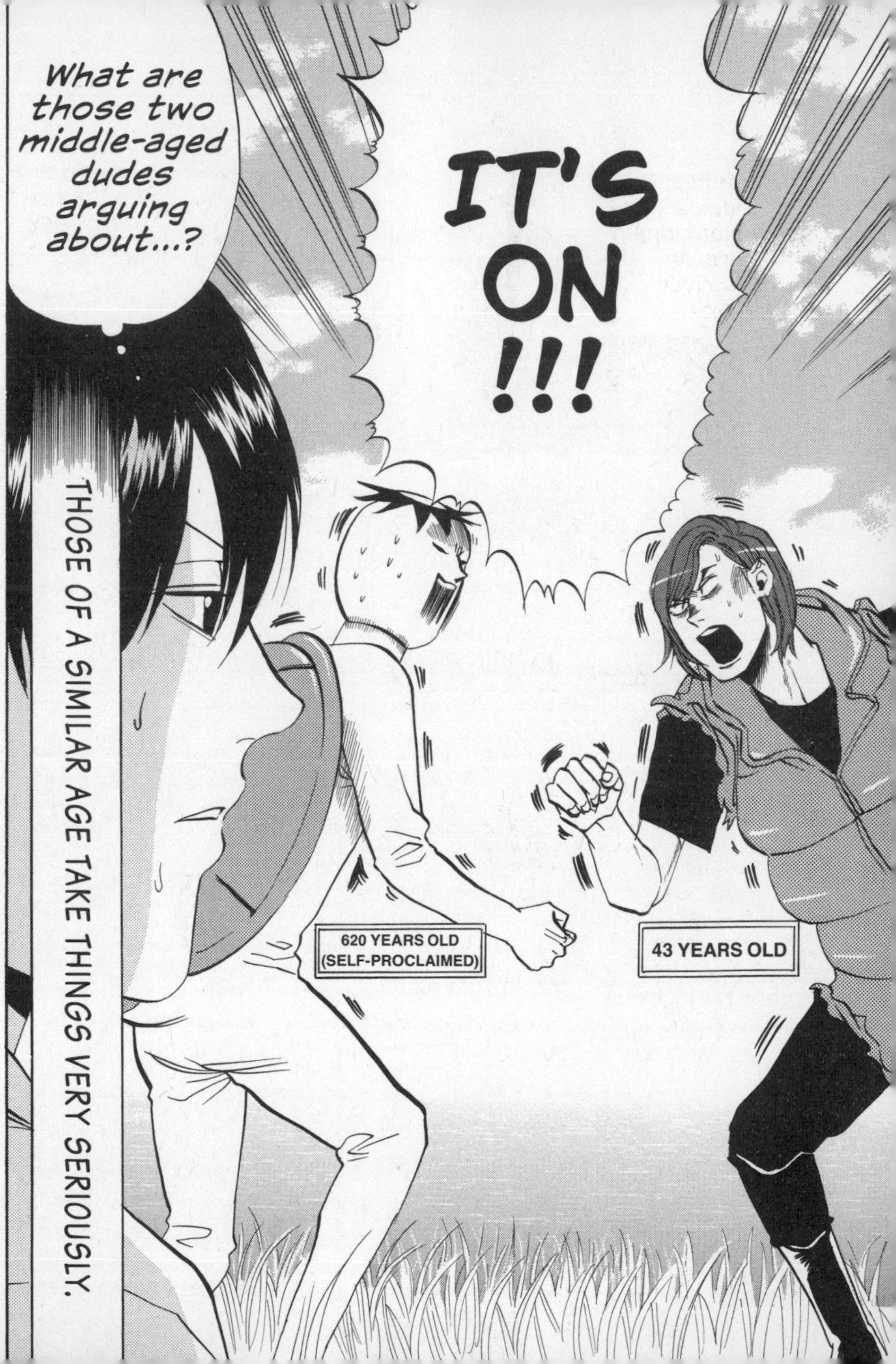
IT'S ON!!!
43 YEARS OLD
620 YEARS OLD (SELF-PROCLAIMED)
What are those two middle-aged dudes arguing about...?
THOSE OF A SIMILAR AGE TAKE THINGS VERY SERIOUSLY.

Chapter 176: Check-Up Under the Bridge

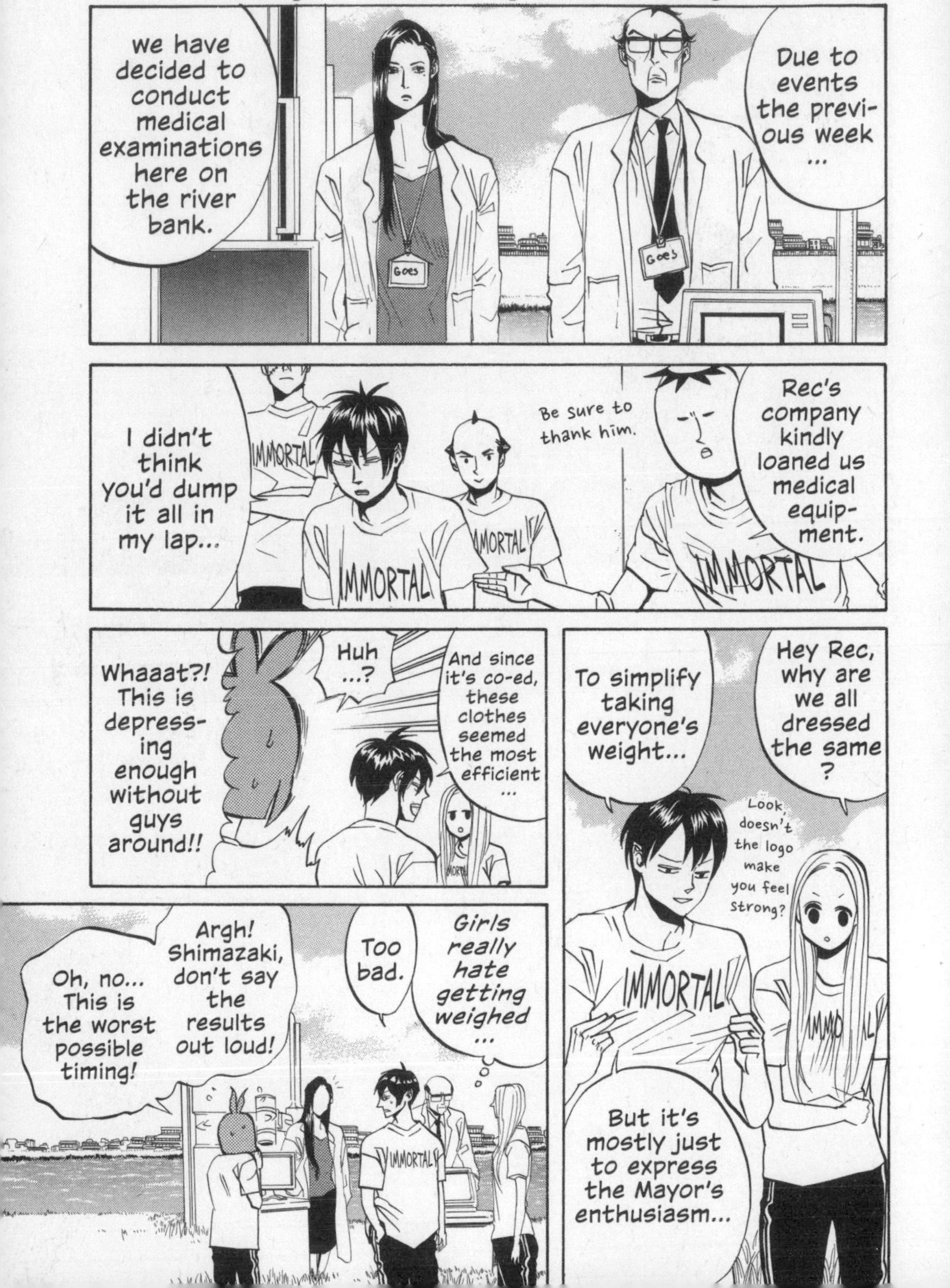

Due to events the previous week...
we have decided to conduct medical examinations here on the river bank.
Rec's company kindly loaned us medical equipment.
Be sure to thank him.
I didn't think you'd dump it all in my lap...
Hey Rec, why are we all dressed the same?
To simplify taking everyone's weight...
Look, doesn't the logo make you feel strong?
But it's mostly just to express the Mayor's enthusiasm...
And since it's co-ed, these clothes seemed the most efficient...
Huh...?
Whaaat?! This is depressing enough without guys around!!
Girls really hate getting weighed...
Too bad.
Argh! Shimazaki, don't say the results out loud!
Oh, no... This is the worst possible timing!

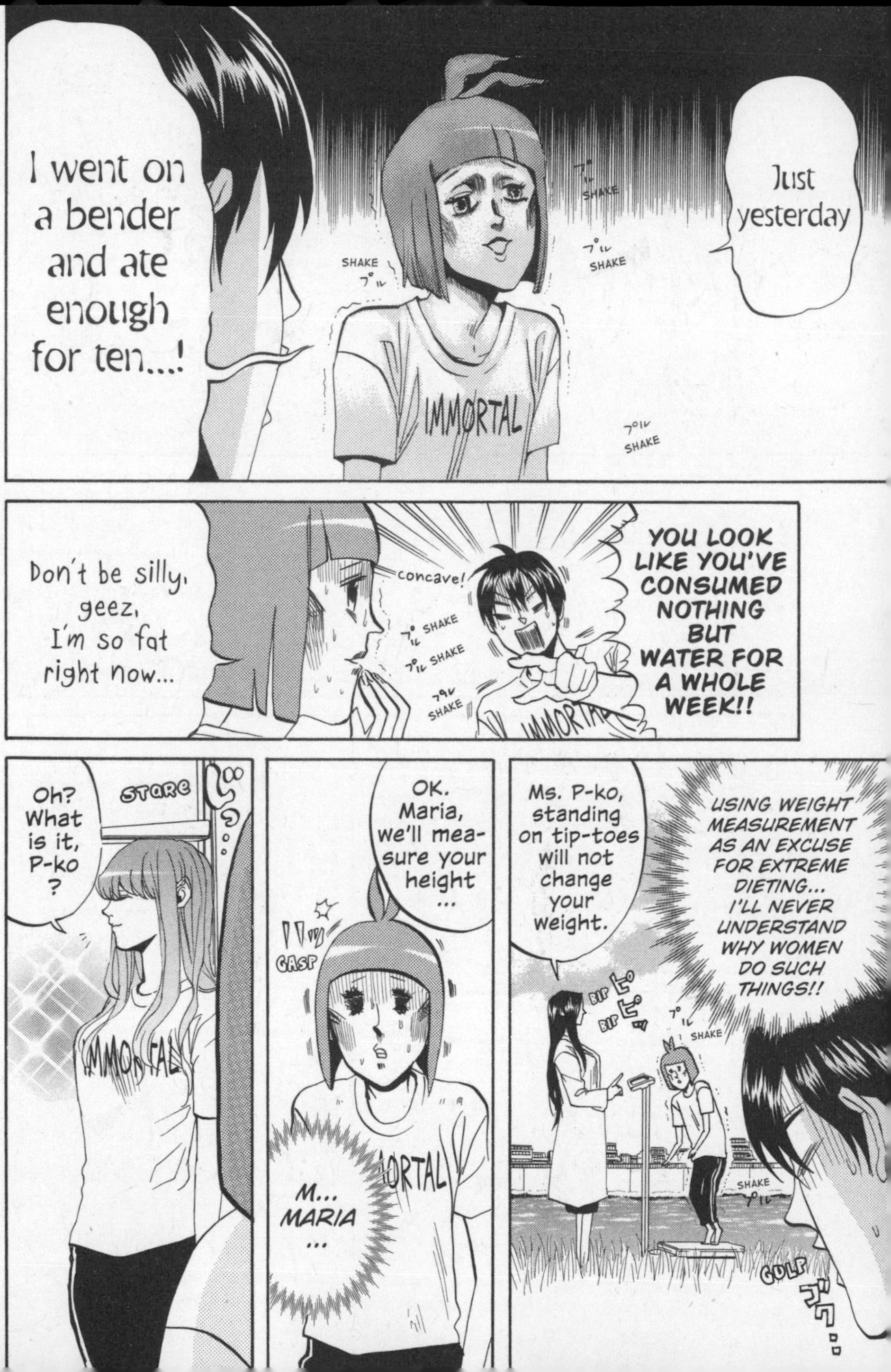
Just yesterday
SHAKE
SHAKE
SHAKE
SHAKE
I went on a bender and ate enough for ten...!
YOU LOOK LIKE YOU'VE CONSUMED NOTHING BUT WATER FOR A WHOLE WEEK!!
concave!
SHAKE
SHAKE
SHAKE
Don't be silly, geez, I'm so fat right now...
USING WEIGHT MEASUREMENT AS AN EXCUSE FOR EXTREME DIETING... I'LL NEVER UNDERSTAND WHY WOMEN DO SUCH THINGS!!
Ms. P-ko, standing on tip-toes will not change your weight.
BIP BIP
SHAKE
SHAKE
GULP
OK. Maria, we'll mea-sure your height ...
GASP
M... MARIA ...
STARE
Oh? What is it, P-ko?

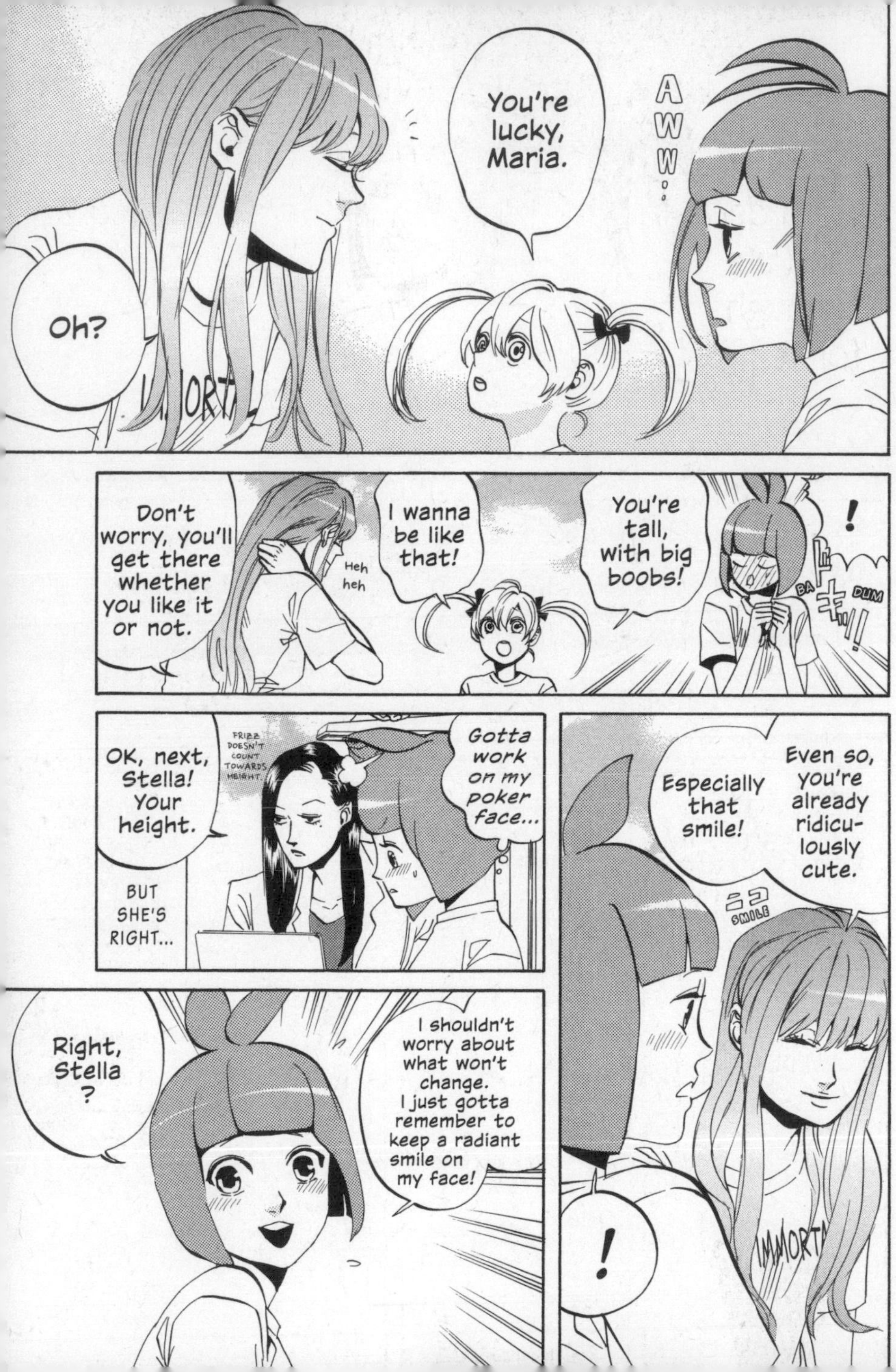

AWWW...
You're lucky, Maria.
Oh?
!
BA DUM
You're tall, with big boobs!
I wanna be like that!
Heh heh
Don't worry, you'll get there whether you like it or not.
Even so, you're already ridiculously cute.
Especially that smile!
ニコ SMILE
!
Gotta work on my poker face...
FRIZZ DOESN'T COUNT TOWARDS HEIGHT.
OK, next, Stella! Your height.
BUT SHE'S RIGHT...
I shouldn't worry about what won't change. I just gotta remember to keep a radiant smile on my face!
Right, Stella?

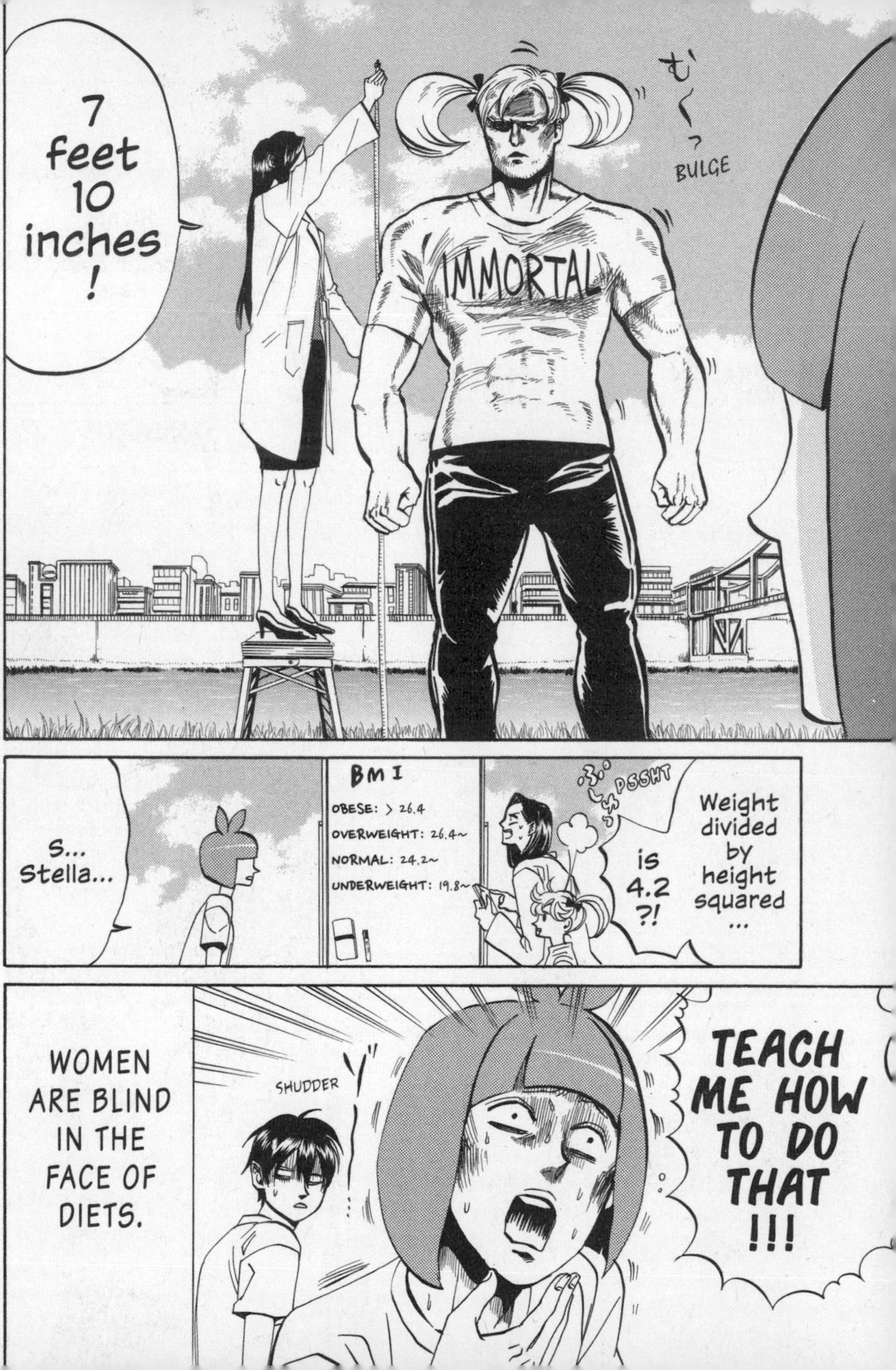
7 feet 10 inches !
むくっ
BULGE
IMMORTAL
Weight divided by height squared ...
is 4.2 ?!
PSSHT
BMI
OBESE: > 26.4
OVERWEIGHT: 26.4~
NORMAL: 24.2~
UNDERWEIGHT: 19.8~
S... Stella...
TEACH ME HOW TO DO THAT !!!
SHUDDER
WOMEN ARE BLIND IN THE FACE OF DIETS.

Chapter 177: Shimazaki Gone Wild

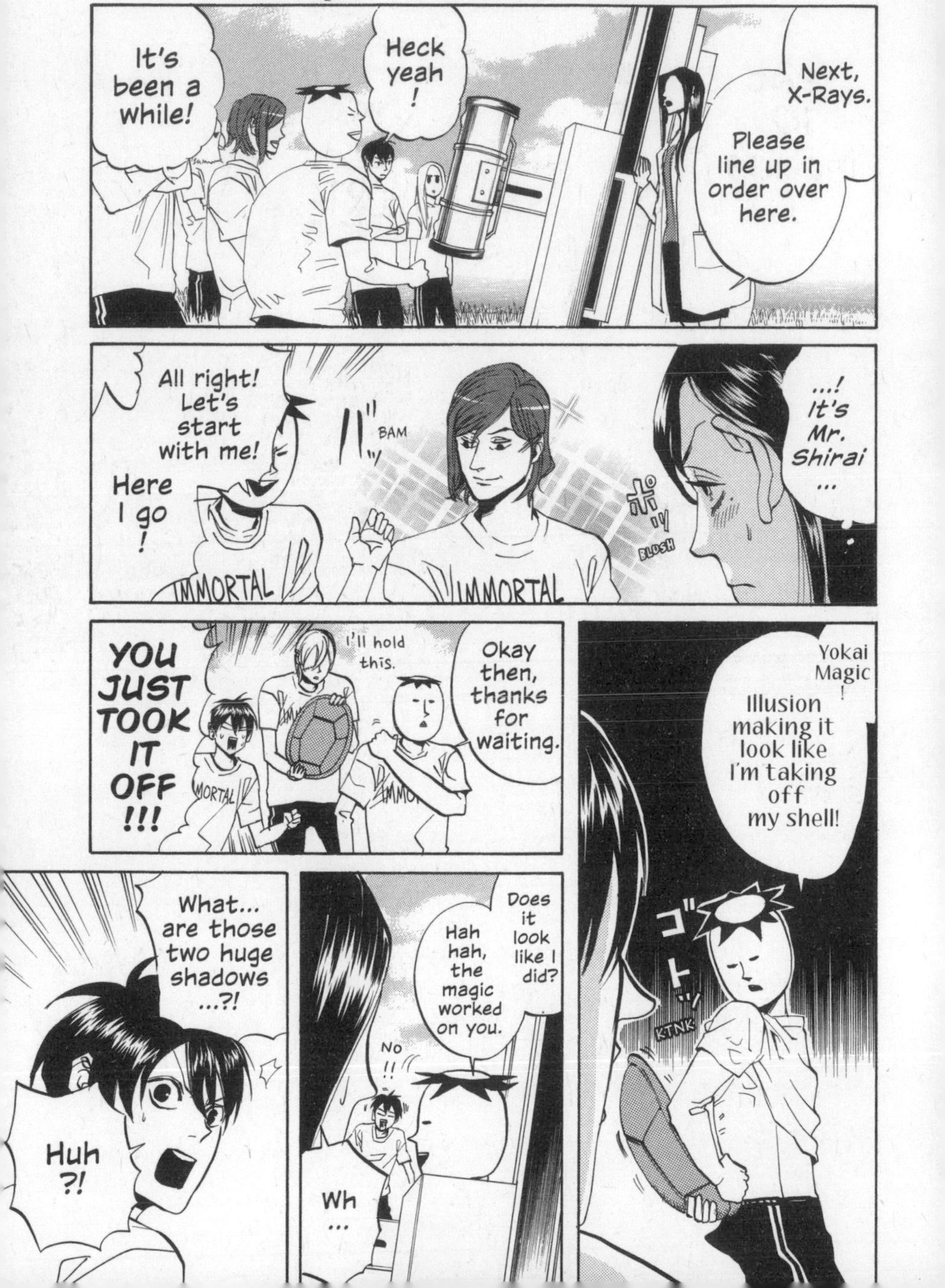

Next, X-Rays.
Please line up in order over here.
Heck yeah!
It's been a while!
...! It's Mr. Shirai ...
BLUSH
BAM
All right! Let's start with me!
Here I go!
Yokai Magic!
Illusion making it look like I'm taking off my shell!
KTNK
Okay then, thanks for waiting.
I'll hold this.
YOU JUST TOOK IT OFF!!!
Does it look like I did?
Hah hah, the magic worked on you.
NO!!
Wh ...
What... are those two huge shadows ...?!
Huh?!

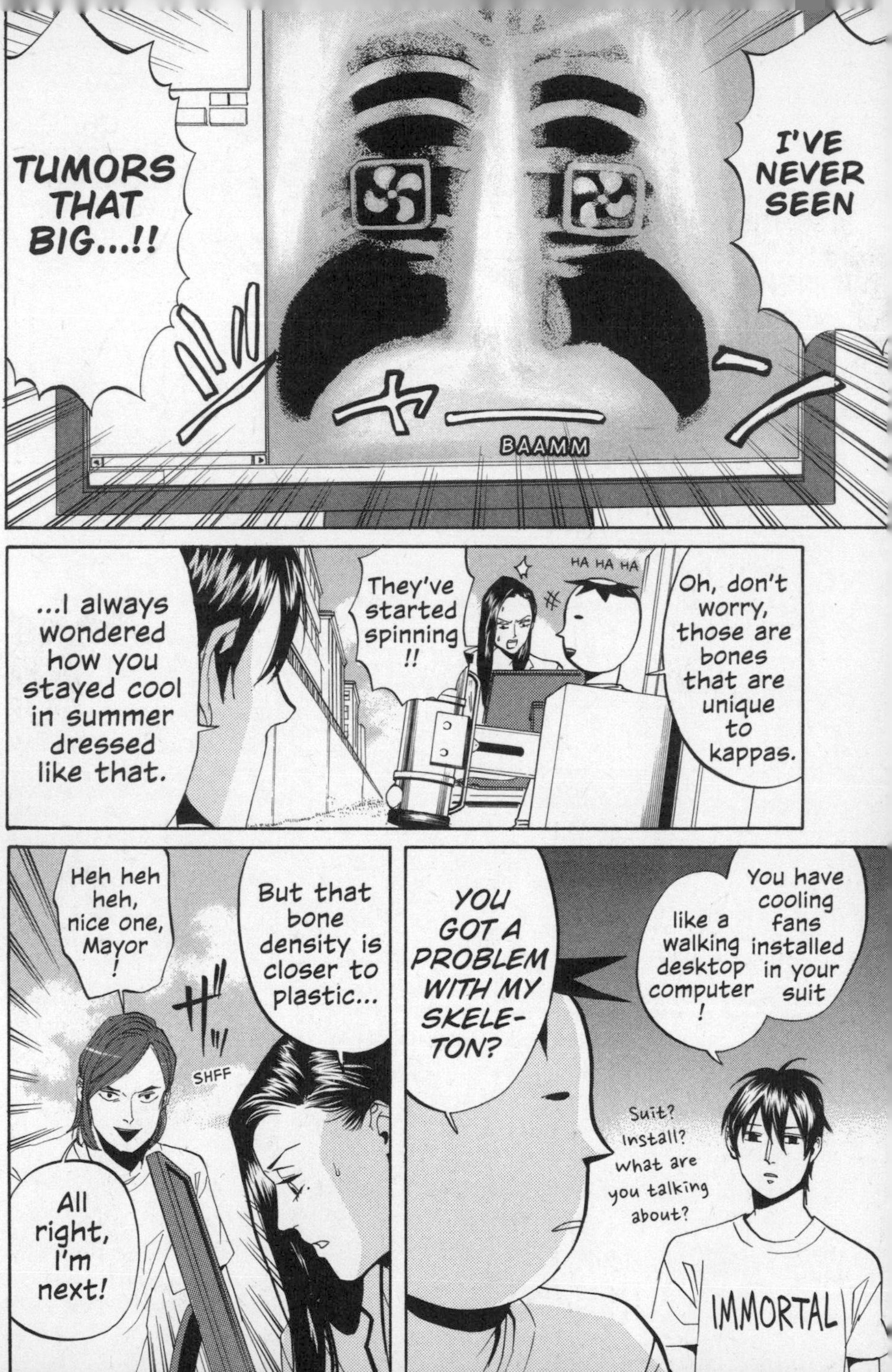
I'VE NEVER SEEN
TUMORS THAT BIG...!!
BAAMM
Oh, don't worry, those are bones that are unique to kappas.
HA HA HA
They've started spinning !!
...I always wondered how you stayed cool in summer dressed like that.
You have cooling fans installed in your suit
like a walking desktop computer !
Suit? Install? what are you talking about?
IMMORTAL
YOU GOT A PROBLEM WITH MY SKELE-TON?
But that bone density is closer to plastic...
Heh heh heh, nice one, Mayor !
SHFF
All right, I'm next!

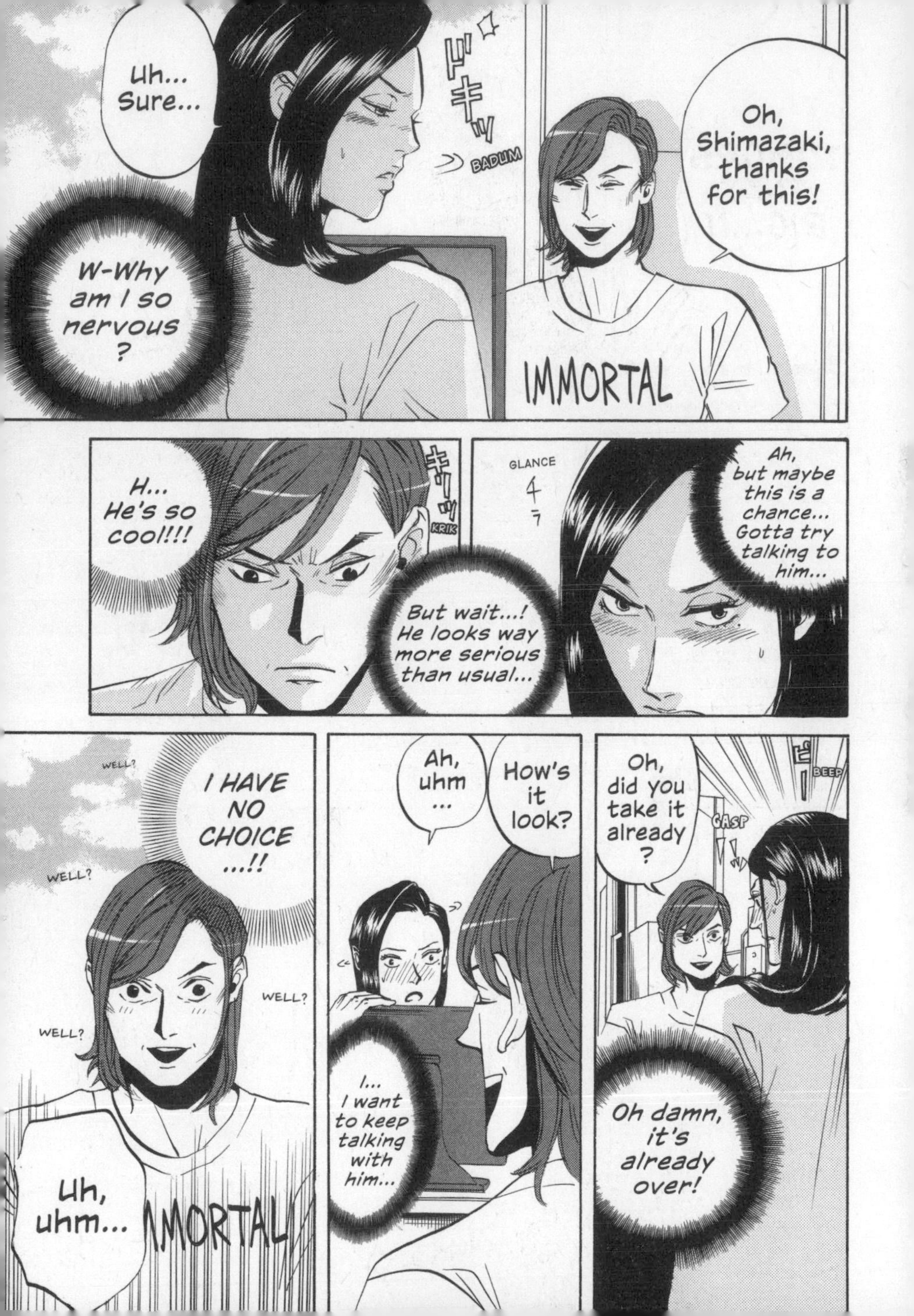
Oh, Shimazaki, thanks for this!
IMMORTAL
BADUM
Uh... Sure...
W-Why am I so nervous?
Ah, but maybe this is a chance... Gotta try talking to him...
GLANCE
But wait...! He looks way more serious than usual...
KRIK
H... He's so cool!!!
Oh, did you take it already?
BEEP
GASP
Oh damn, it's already over!
How's it look?
Ah, uhm ...
I... I want to keep talking with him...
I HAVE NO CHOICE ...!!
WELL?
WELL?
WELL?
WELL?
Uh, uhm...
IMMORTAL

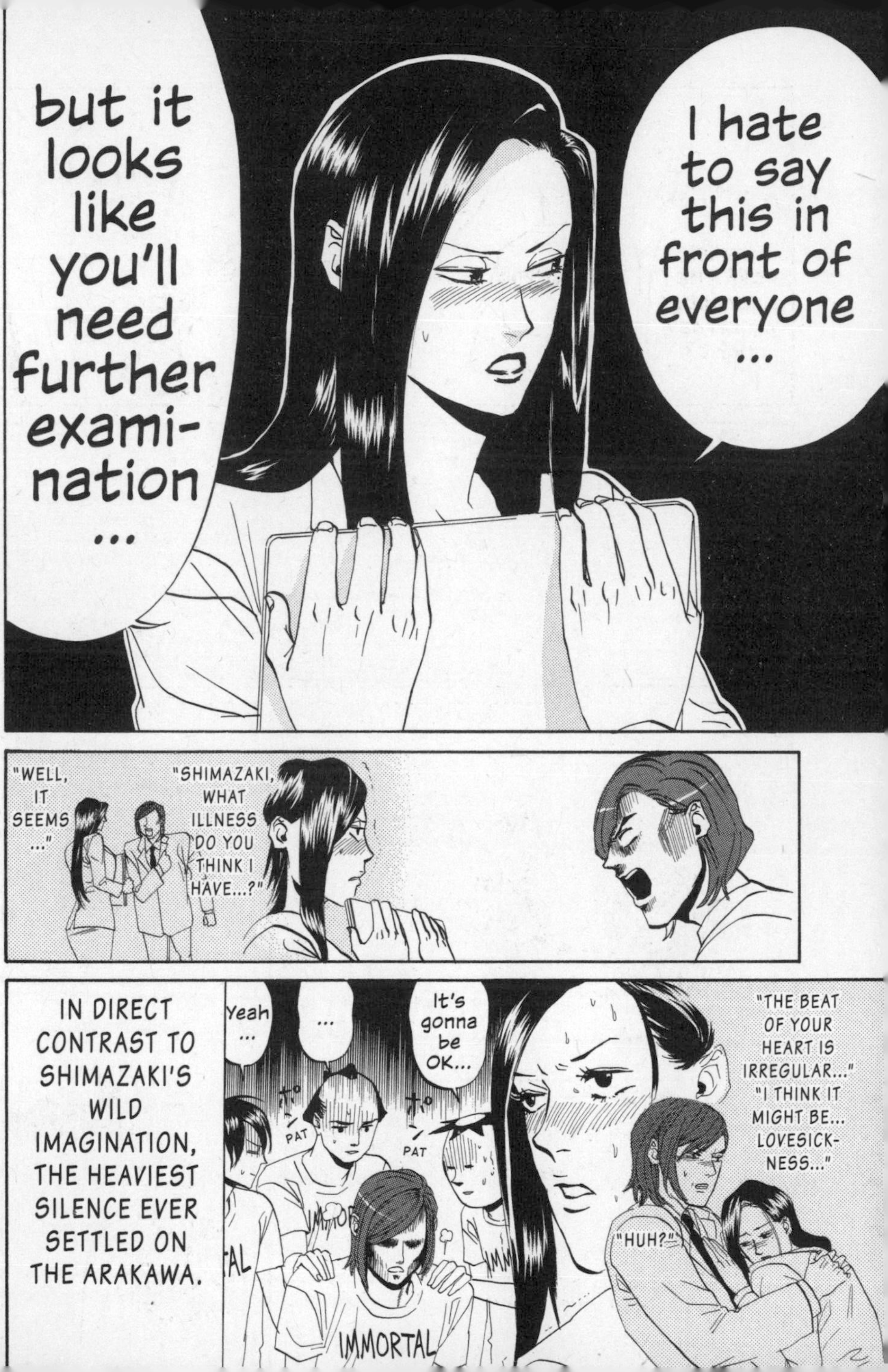
I hate to say this in front of everyone...
but it looks like you'll need further examination...
"SHIMAZAKI, WHAT ILLNESS DO YOU THINK I HAVE...?"
"WELL, IT SEEMS..."
"THE BEAT OF YOUR HEART IS IRREGULAR..."
"I THINK IT MIGHT BE... LOVESICKNESS..."
"HUH?"
It's gonna be OK...
PAT
...
PAT
Yeah...
IMMORTAL
IMMORTAL
IN DIRECT CONTRAST TO SHIMAZAKI'S WILD IMAGINATION, THE HEAVIEST SILENCE EVER SETTLED ON THE ARAKAWA.

Chapter 178: Unfettered Frailty

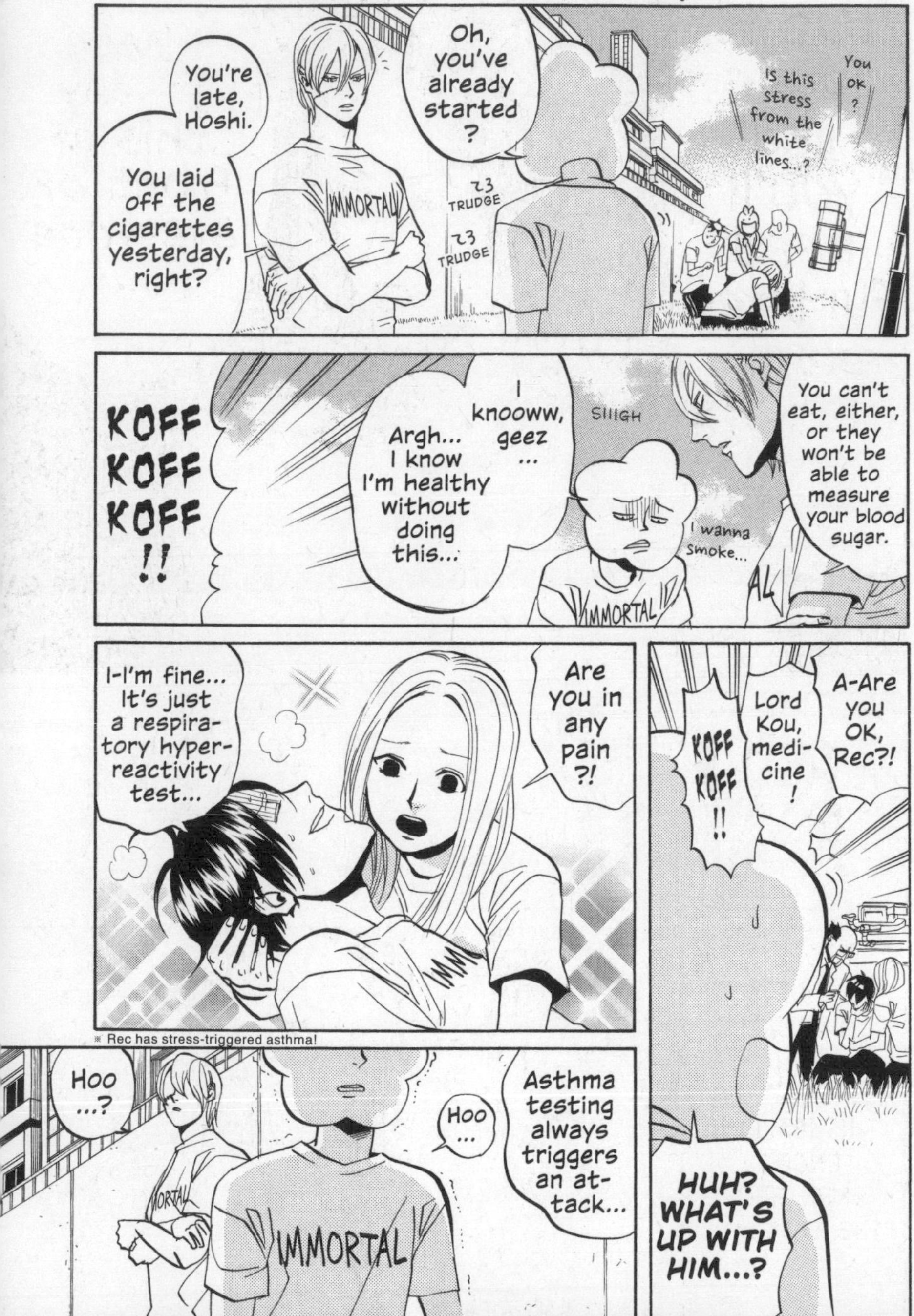

You OK?
Is this stress from the white lines...?
Oh, you've already started?
TRUDGE
TRUDGE
You're late, Hoshi.
You laid off the cigarettes yesterday, right?
You can't eat, either, or they won't be able to measure your blood sugar.
SIIIGH
I wanna smoke...
I knooww, geez...
Argh... I know I'm healthy without doing this...
KOFF KOFF KOFF!!
A-Are you OK, Rec?!
Lord Kou, medicine!
KOFF KOFF!!
HUH? WHAT'S UP WITH HIM...?
Are you in any pain?!
I-I'm fine... It's just a respiratory hyper-reactivity test...
Asthma testing always triggers an attack...
Hoo...
Hoo...?

※ Rec has stress-triggered asthma!

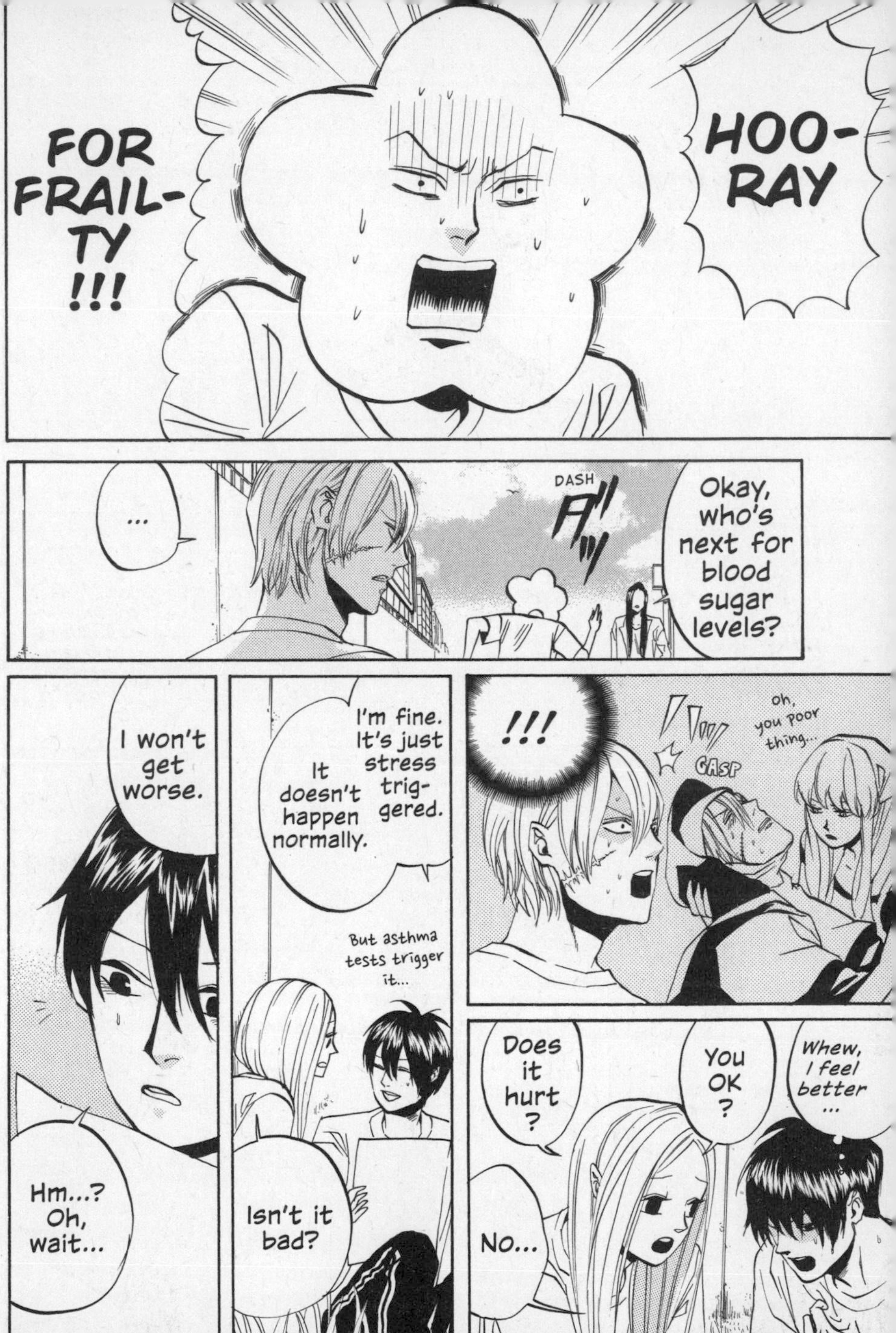
HOO-RAY
FOR FRAIL-TY!!!
Okay, who's next for blood sugar levels?
DASH
...
Oh, you poor thing...
GASP
!!!
Whew, I feel better...
You OK?
Does it hurt?
No...
I'm fine. It's just stress trig-gered.
It doesn't happen normally.
But asthma tests trigger it...
Isn't it bad?
I won't get worse.
Hm...? Oh, wait...

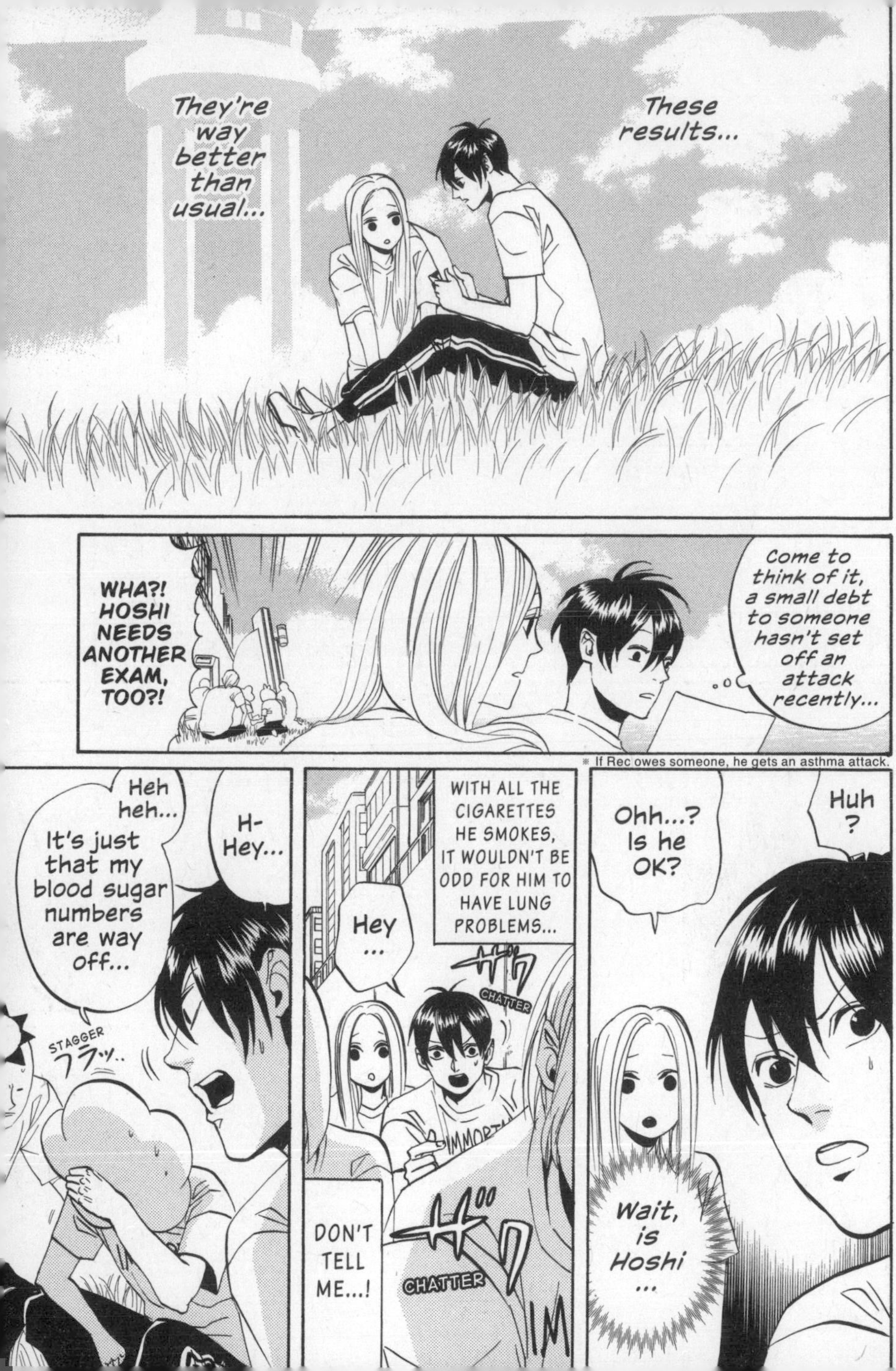
These results...
They're way better than usual...
Come to think of it, a small debt to someone hasn't set off an attack recently...
WHA?! HOSHI NEEDS ANOTHER EXAM, TOO?!
※ If Rec owes someone, he gets an asthma attack.
Huh?
Ohh...? Is he OK?
Wait, is Hoshi ...
WITH ALL THE CIGARETTES HE SMOKES, IT WOULDN'T BE ODD FOR HIM TO HAVE LUNG PROBLEMS...
Hey ...
CHATTER
CHATTER
DON'T TELL ME...!
H- Hey...
Heh heh... It's just that my blood sugar numbers are way off...
STAGGER

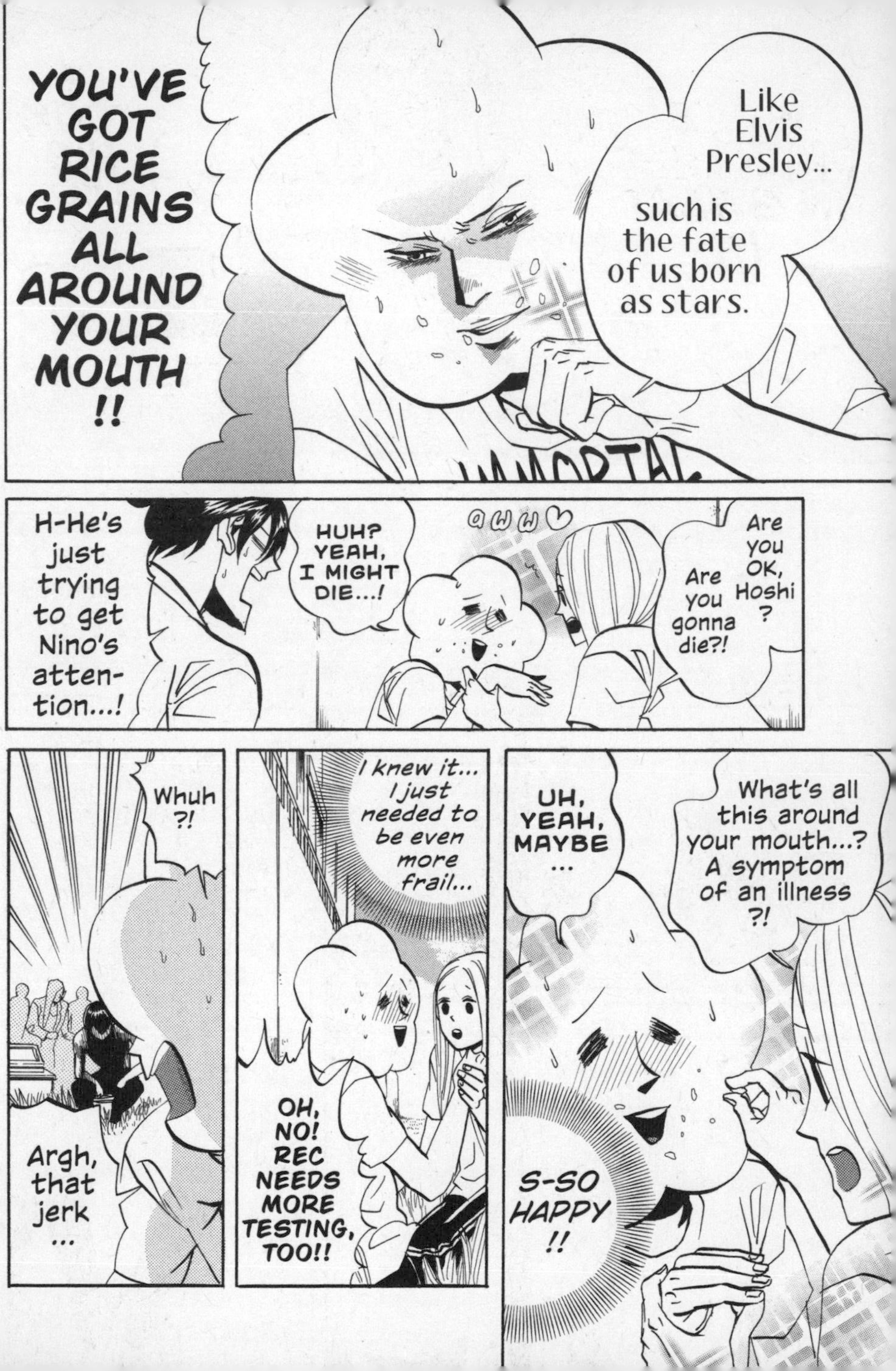
Like Elvis Presley... such is the fate of us born as stars.
YOU'VE GOT RICE GRAINS ALL AROUND YOUR MOUTH!!
Are you OK, Hoshi?
Are you gonna die?!
HUH? YEAH, I MIGHT DIE...!
H-He's just trying to get Nino's atten-tion...!
What's all this around your mouth...? A symptom of an illness?!
UH, YEAH, MAYBE...
S-SO HAPPY!!
I knew it... I just needed to be even more frail...
OH, NO! REC NEEDS MORE TESTING, TOO!!
Whuh?!
Argh, that jerk...

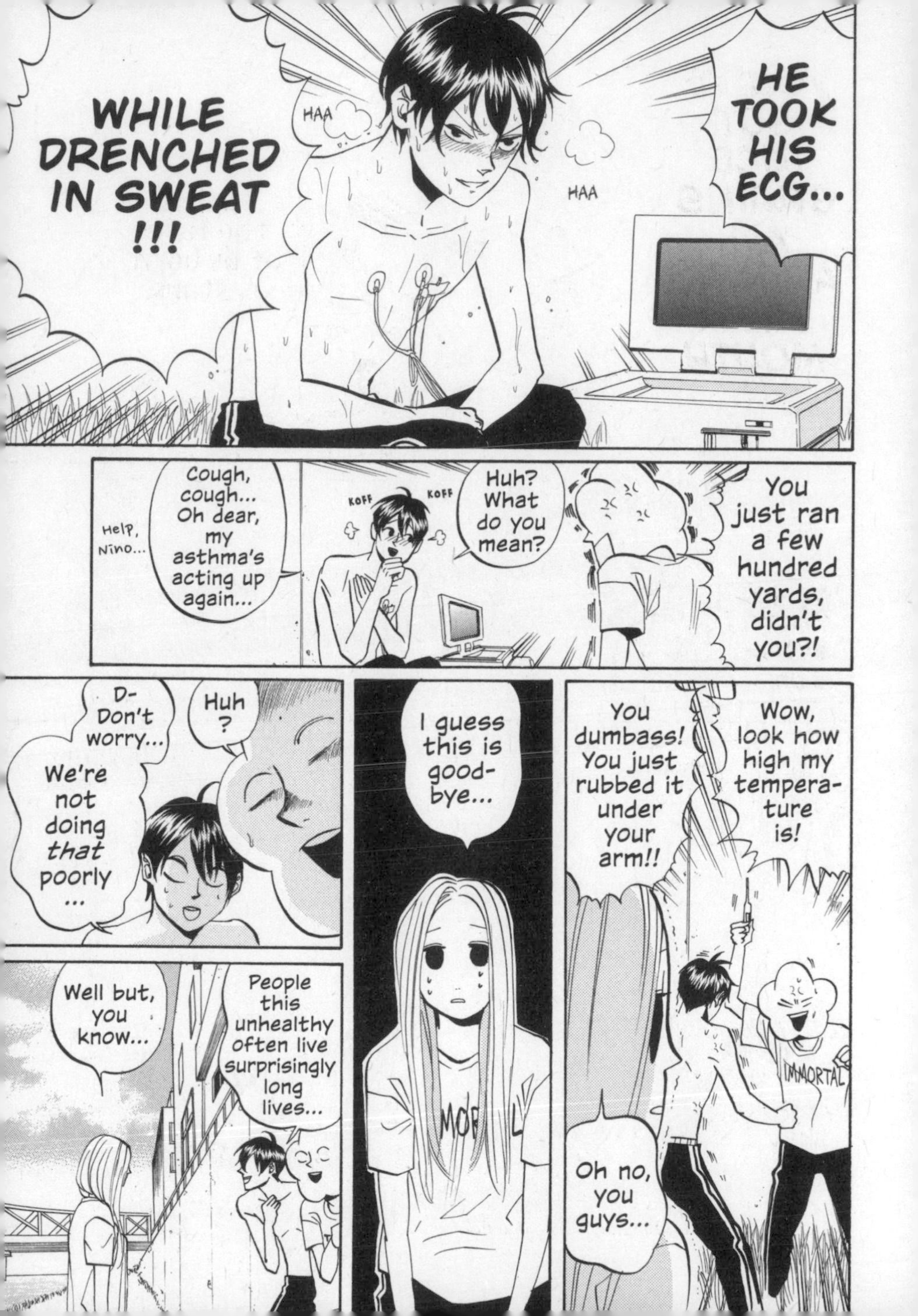
HE TOOK HIS ECG...
HAA
HAA
WHILE DRENCHED IN SWEAT !!!
You just ran a few hundred yards, didn't you?!
Huh? What do you mean?
KOFF
KOFF
Cough, cough... Oh dear, my asthma's acting up again...
Help, Nino...
Wow, look how high my temperature is!
You dumbass! You just rubbed it under your arm!!
IMMORTAL
Oh no, you guys...
I guess this is good-bye...
MORTAL
Huh?
D- Don't worry...
We're not doing *that* poorly ...
People this unhealthy often live surprisingly long lives...
Well but, you know...

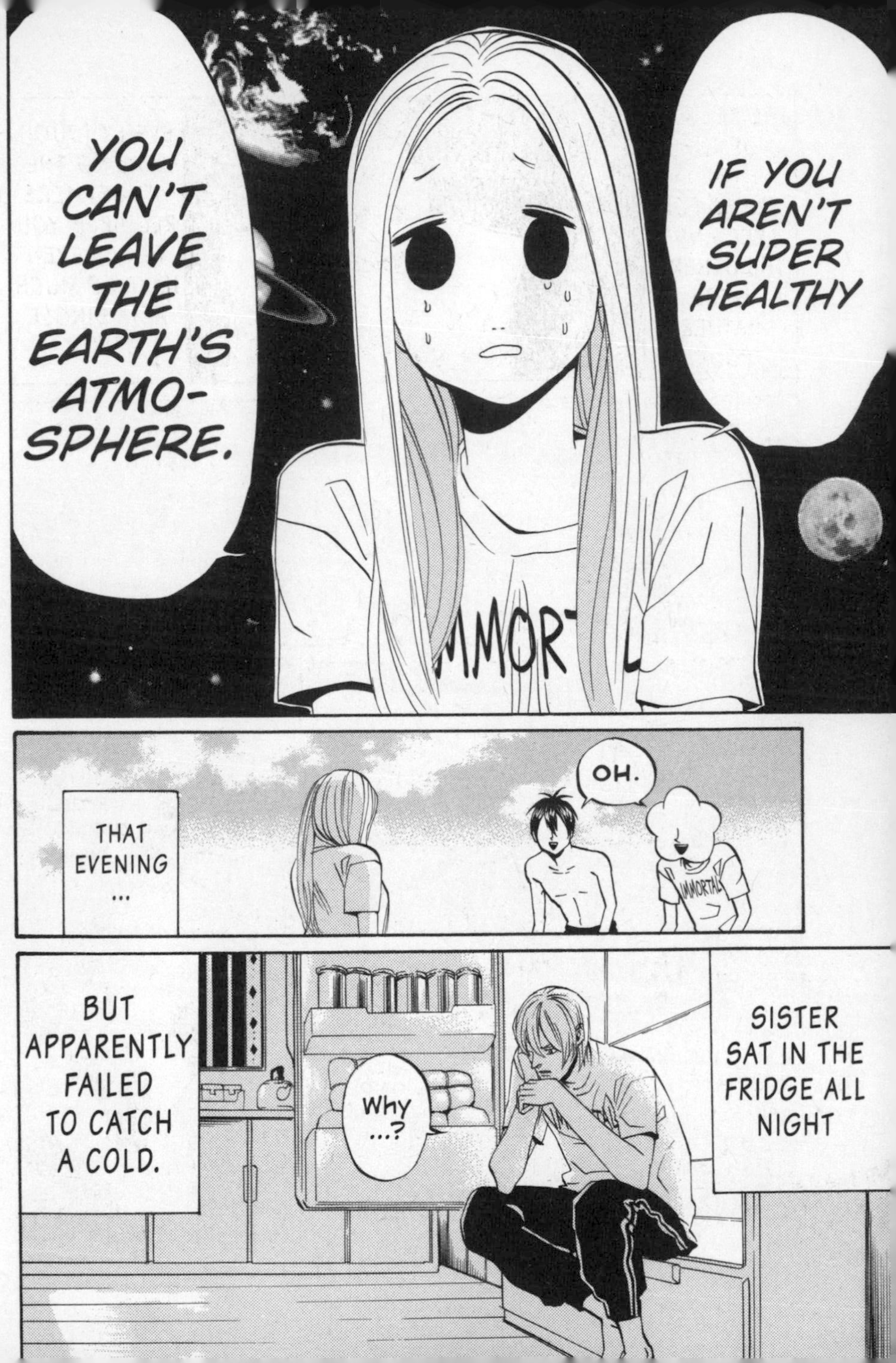
IF YOU AREN'T SUPER HEALTHY
YOU CAN'T LEAVE THE EARTH'S ATMOSPHERE.
OH.
IMMORTAL
THAT EVENING ...
SISTER SAT IN THE FRIDGE ALL NIGHT
Why ...?
BUT APPARENTLY FAILED TO CATCH A COLD.

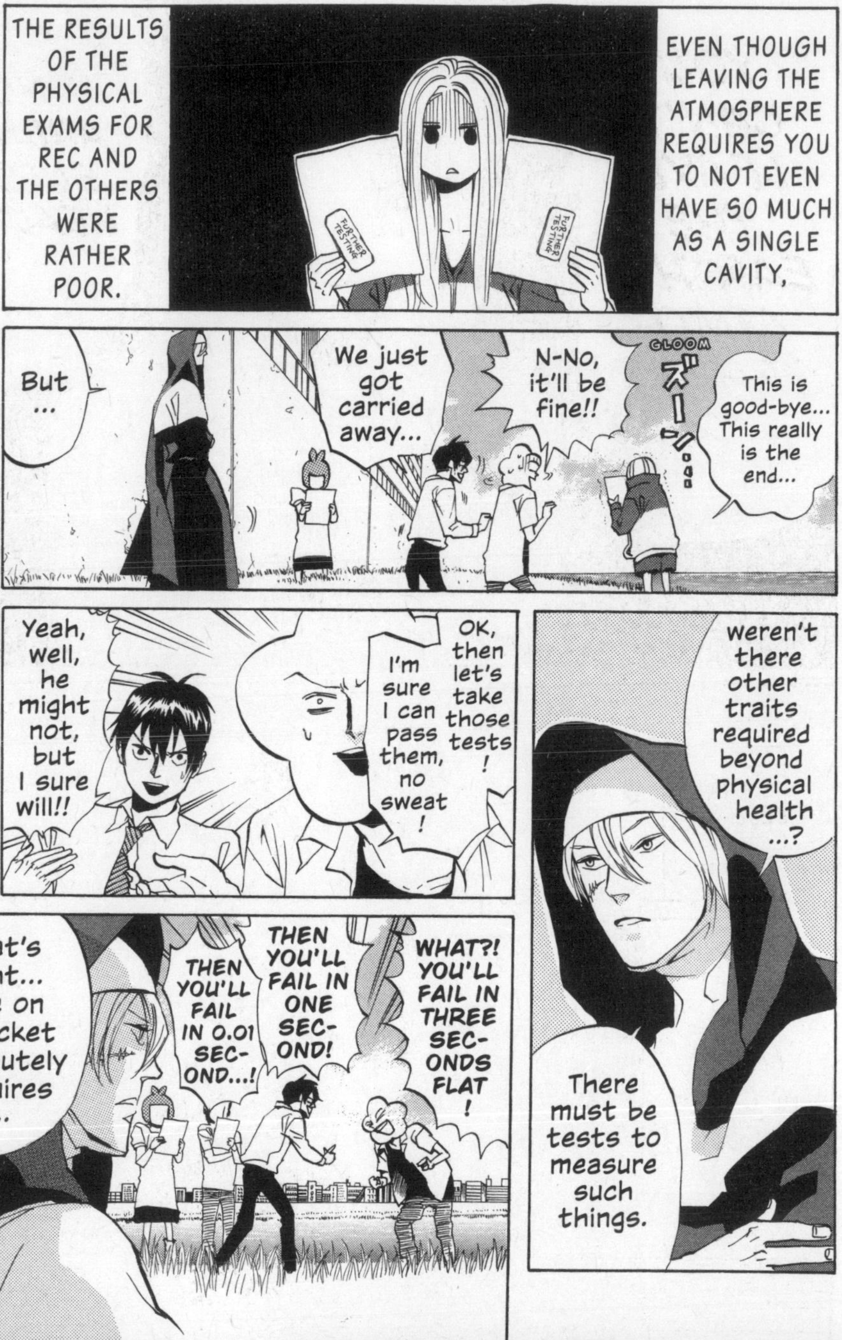
EVEN THOUGH LEAVING THE ATMOSPHERE REQUIRES YOU TO NOT EVEN HAVE SO MUCH AS A SINGLE CAVITY,
FURTHER TESTING
FURTHER TESTING
THE RESULTS OF THE PHYSICAL EXAMS FOR REC AND THE OTHERS WERE RATHER POOR.
This is good-bye... This really is the end...
GLOOM
ズーー
N-No, it'll be fine!!
We just got carried away...
But ...
weren't there other traits required beyond physical health ...?
There must be tests to measure such things.
OK, then let's take those tests!
I'm sure I can pass them, no sweat!
Yeah, well, he might not, but I sure will!!
WHAT?! YOU'LL FAIL IN THREE SECONDS FLAT!
THEN YOU'LL FAIL IN ONE SECOND!
THEN YOU'LL FAIL IN 0.01 SECOND...!
That's right... Life on a rocket absolutely requires ...

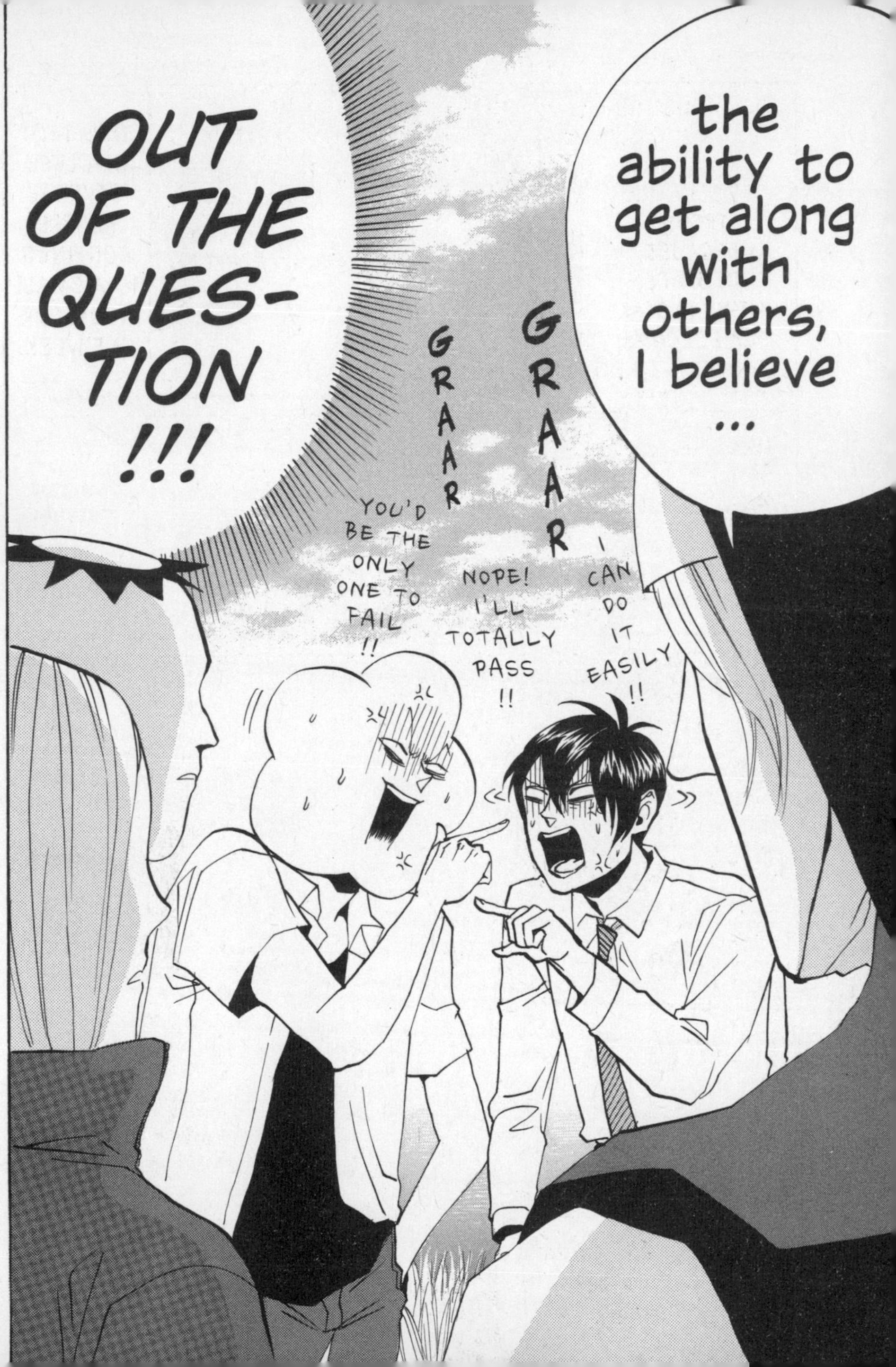
the ability to get along with others, I believe ...
OUT OF THE QUES-TION !!!
GRAAR
GRAAR
I CAN DO IT EASILY !!
NOPE! I'LL TOTALLY PASS !!
YOU'D BE THE ONLY ONE TO FAIL !!

Chapter 179: Astronaut Qualification Test Under the Bridge

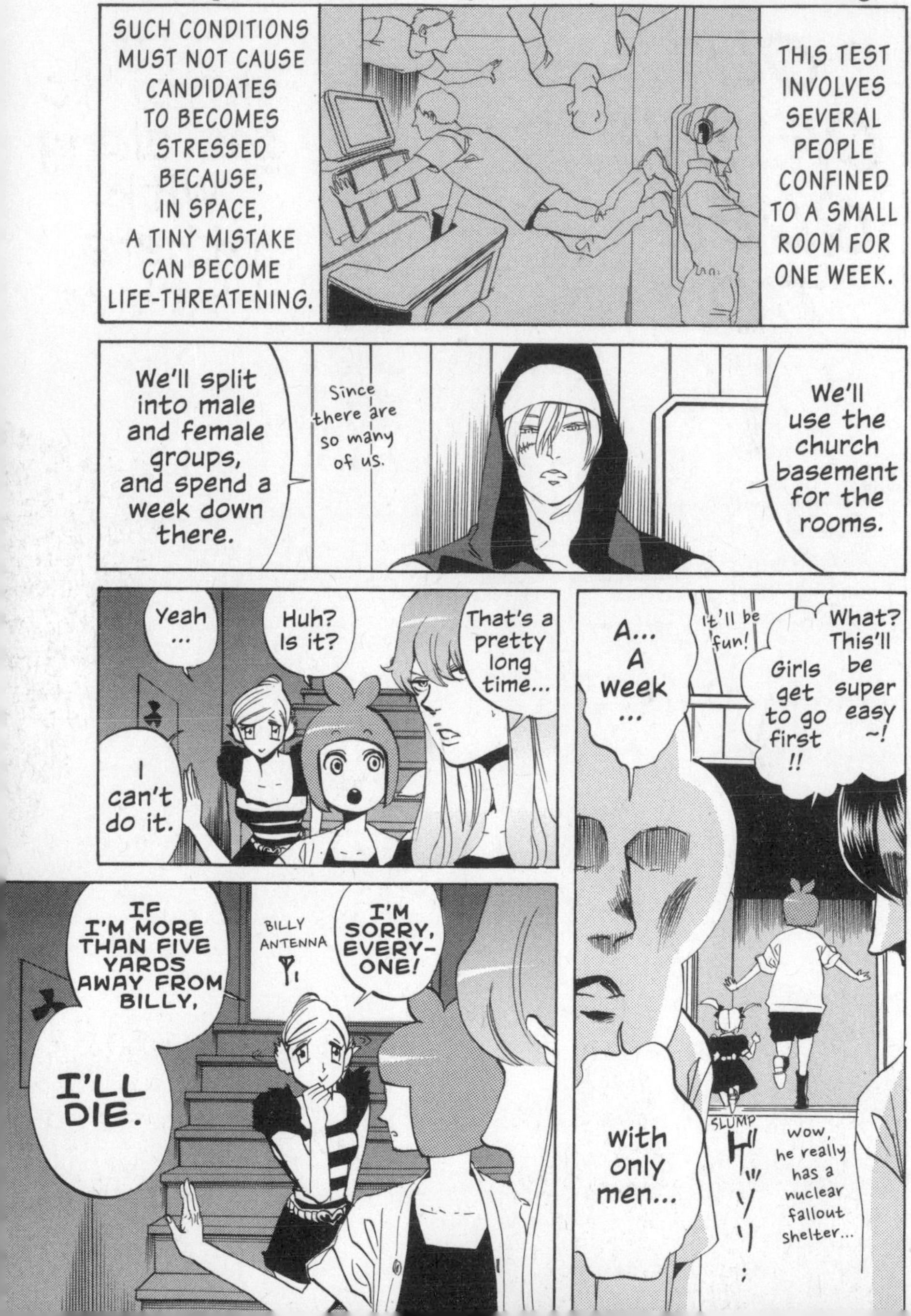
THIS TEST INVOLVES SEVERAL PEOPLE CONFINED TO A SMALL ROOM FOR ONE WEEK.
SUCH CONDITIONS MUST NOT CAUSE CANDIDATES TO BECOMES STRESSED BECAUSE, IN SPACE, A TINY MISTAKE CAN BECOME LIFE-THREATENING.
We'll use the church basement for the rooms.
Since there are so many of us.
We'll split into male and female groups, and spend a week down there.
What? This'll be super easy ~!
It'll be fun!
Girls get to go first !!
A... A week ...
with only men...
SLUMP
wow, he really has a nuclear fallout shelter...
That's a pretty long time...
Huh? Is it?
Yeah ...
I can't do it.
I'M SORRY, EVERY-ONE!
BILLY ANTENNA
IF I'M MORE THAN FIVE YARDS AWAY FROM BILLY,
I'LL DIE.

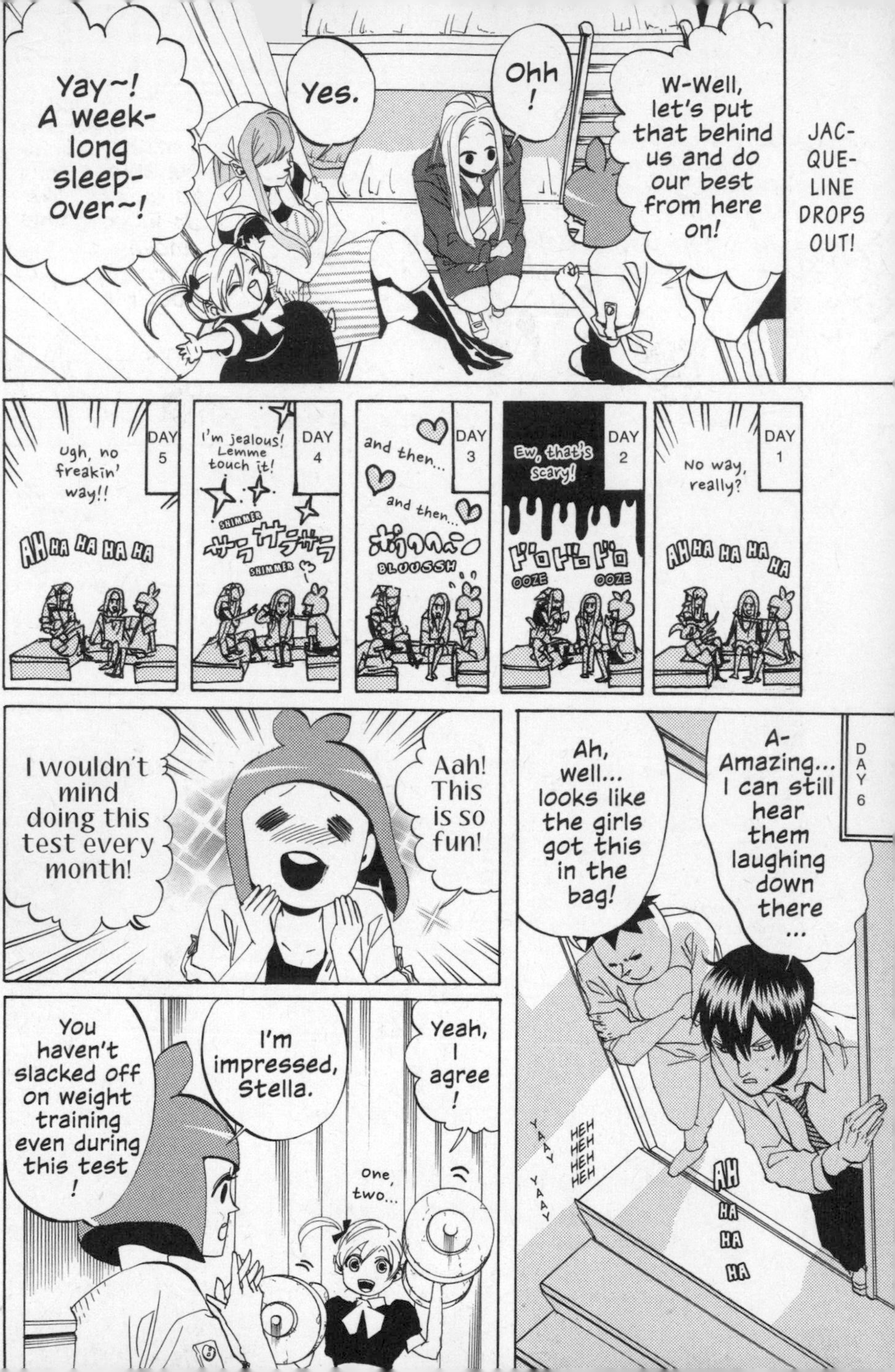
JACQUELINE DROPS OUT!
W-Well, let's put that behind us and do our best from here on!
Ohh!
Yes.
Yay~! A week-long sleepover~!
DAY 1
No way, really?
AHHA HA HA HA HA
DAY 2
Ew, that's scary!
ドロドロドロ
OOZE OOZE
DAY 3
and then...
and then...
BLUUSSH
DAY 4
I'm jealous! Lemme touch it!
サラサラサラ
SHIMMER SHIMMER
DAY 5
Ugh, no freakin' way!!
AHHA HA HA HA
DAY 6
A-Amazing... I can still hear them laughing down there...
Ah, well... looks like the girls got this in the bag!
YAAY YAAY
HEH HEH HEH HEH
AH HA HA HA
Aah! This is so fun!
I wouldn't mind doing this test every month!
Yeah, I agree!
I'm impressed, Stella.
You haven't slacked off on weight training even during this test!
One, two...

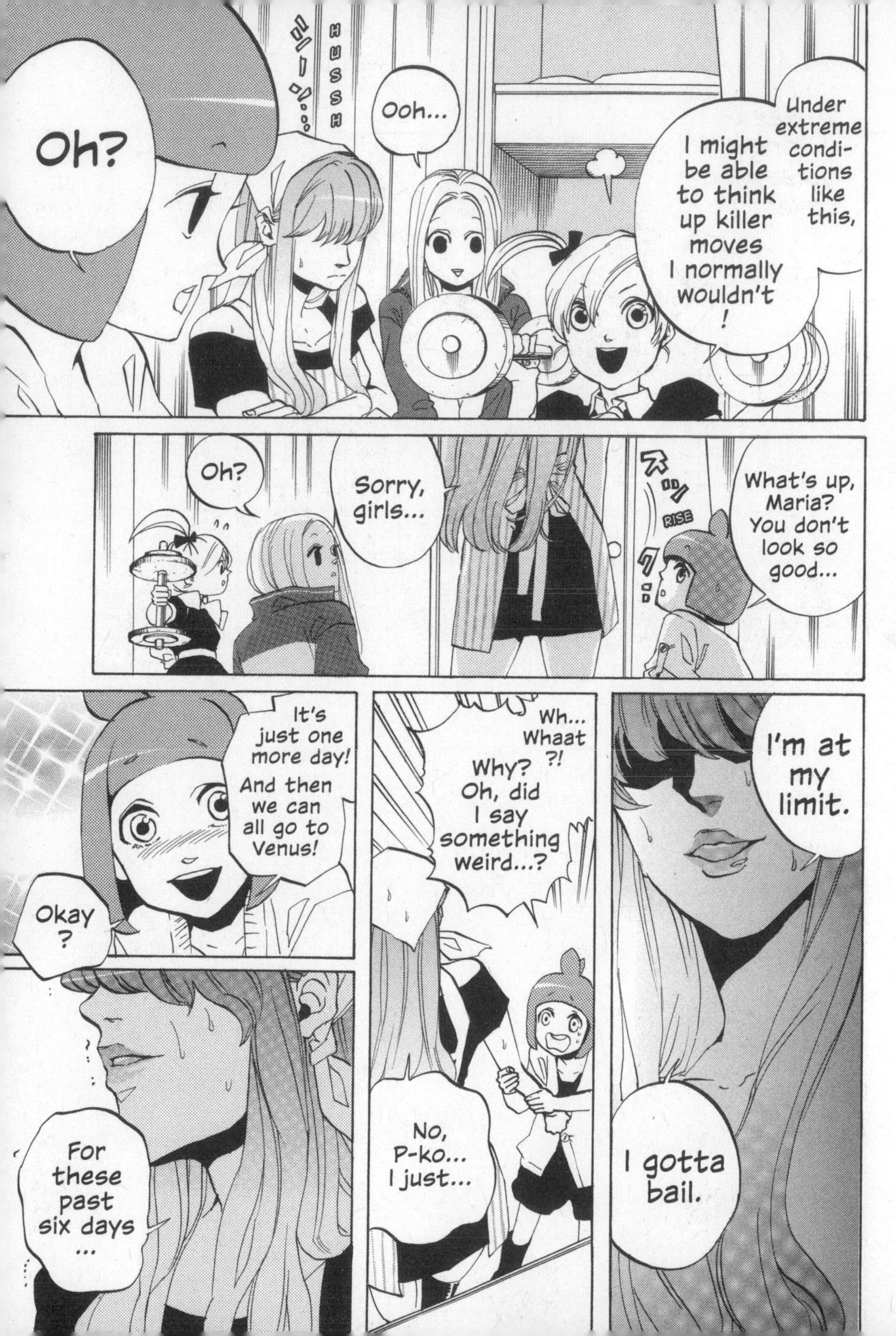
Under extreme condi- tions like this,
I might be able to think up killer moves I normally wouldn't !
Ooh...
HUSSH
Oh?
What's up, Maria? You don't look so good...
RISE
Sorry, girls...
Oh?
I'm at my limit.
Wh... Whaat ?!
Why? Oh, did I say something weird...?
It's just one more day!
And then we can all go to Venus!
Okay ?
I gotta bail.
No, P-ko... I just...
For these past six days ...

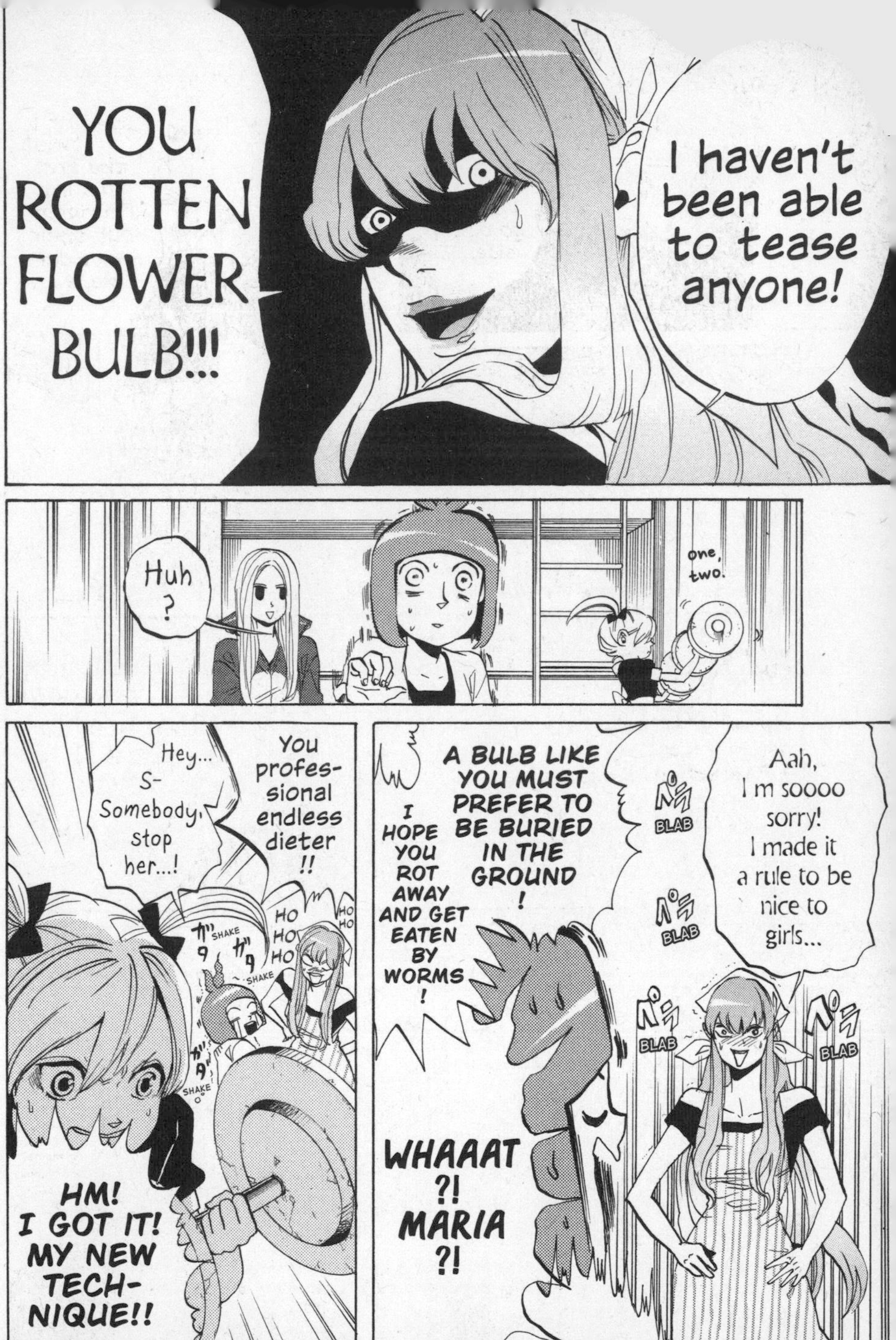
I haven't been able to tease anyone!
YOU ROTTEN FLOWER BULB!!!
one, two.
Huh?
Aah, I m soooo sorry! I made it a rule to be nice to girls...
BLAB
BLAB
BLAB
BLAB
A BULB LIKE YOU MUST PREFER TO BE BURIED IN THE GROUND!
I HOPE YOU ROT AWAY AND GET EATEN BY WORMS!
WHAAAT?! MARIA?!
You profes-sional endless dieter!!
Hey... S-Somebody, stop her...!
HO HO HO
HO HO
SHAKE
SHAKE
SHAKE
HM! I GOT IT! MY NEW TECH-NIQUE!!

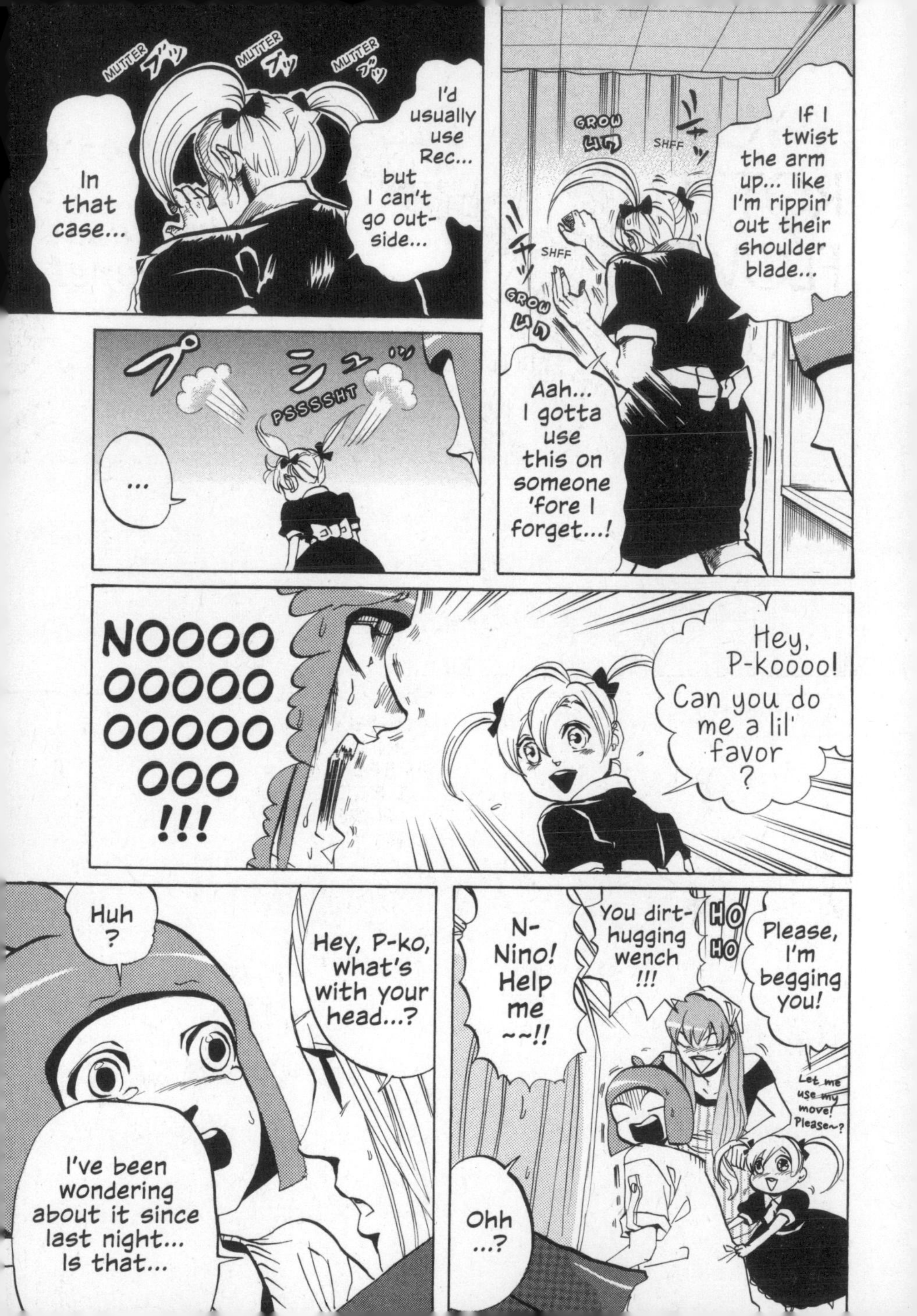

If I twist the arm up... like I'm rippin' out their shoulder blade...
SHFF
GROW
SHFF
GROW
Aah... I gotta use this on someone 'fore I forget...!
MUTTER
MUTTER
MUTTER
I'd usually use Rec... but I can't go outside...
In that case...
PSSSSHT
...
Hey, P-koooo! Can you do me a lil' favor?
NOOOOOOOOOOOOOOOOOOO!!!
Please, I'm begging you!
HO HO
You dirt-hugging wench!!!
N-Nino! Help me ~~!!
Let me use my move! Please~?
Ohh ...?
Hey, P-ko, what's with your head...?
Huh?
I've been wondering about it since last night... Is that...

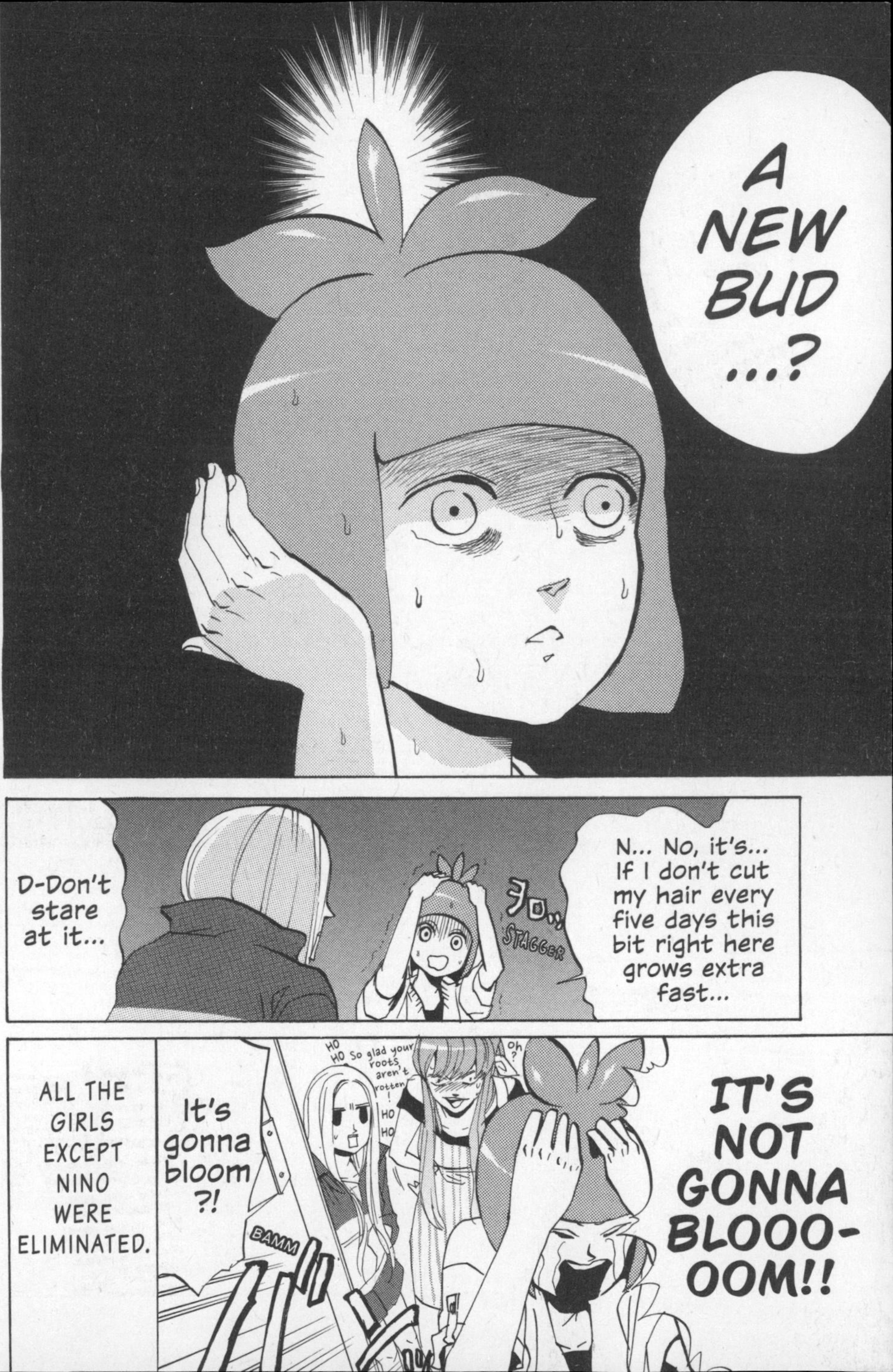
A NEW BUD ...?
N... No, it's... If I don't cut my hair every five days this bit right here grows extra fast...
ヨロ
STAGGER
D-Don't stare at it...
IT'S NOT GONNA BLOOO-OOM!!
oh?
HO HO So glad your roots aren't rotten! HO HO
It's gonna bloom?!
BAMM
ALL THE GIRLS EXCEPT NINO WERE ELIMINATED.

Chapter 180: The Ultimate Endurance Contest

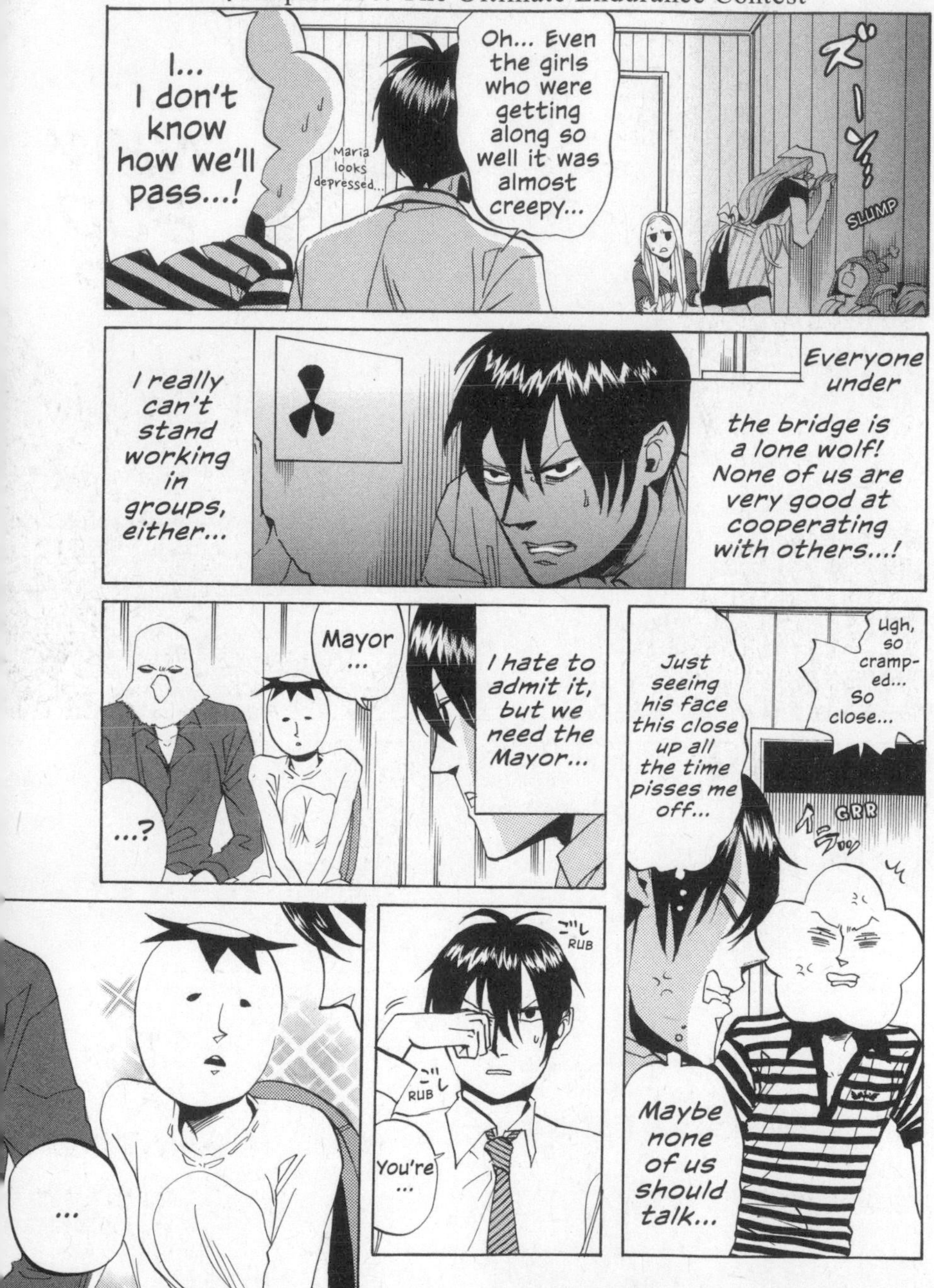
SLUMP
Oh... Even the girls who were getting along so well it was almost creepy...
Maria looks depressed...
I... I don't know how we'll pass...!
Everyone under the bridge is a lone wolf! None of us are very good at cooperating with others...!
I really can't stand working in groups, either...
Ugh, so cramped... So close...
Just seeing his face this close up all the time pisses me off...
GRR
Maybe none of us should talk...
I hate to admit it, but we need the Mayor...
Mayor...
...?
RUB
RUB
You're...
...

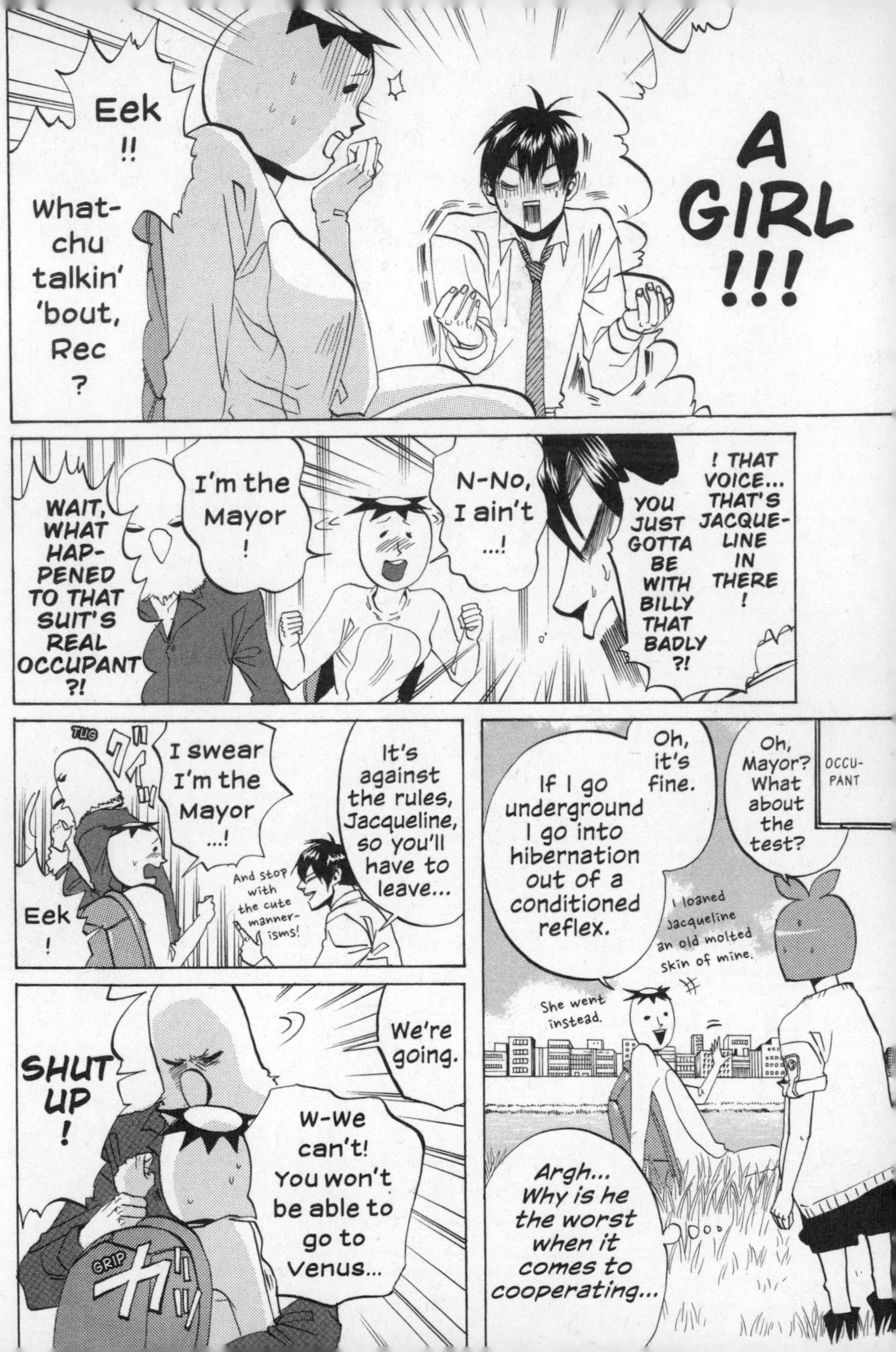
A GIRL !!!
Eek !!
What-chu talkin' 'bout, Rec ?
! THAT VOICE... THAT'S JACQUE-LINE IN THERE !
YOU JUST GOTTA BE WITH BILLY THAT BADLY ?!
N-No, I ain't ...!
I'm the Mayor !
WAIT, WHAT HAP-PENED TO THAT SUIT'S REAL OCCUPANT ?!
OCCU-PANT
Oh, Mayor? What about the test?
Oh, it's fine.
If I go underground I go into hibernation out of a conditioned reflex.
I loaned Jacqueline an old molted skin of mine.
She went instead.
Argh... Why is he the worst when it comes to cooperating...
TUG
It's against the rules, Jacqueline, so you'll have to leave...
And stop with the cute manner-isms!
I swear I'm the Mayor ...!
Eek !
We're going.
W-We can't! You won't be able to go to Venus...
SHUT UP !
GRIP

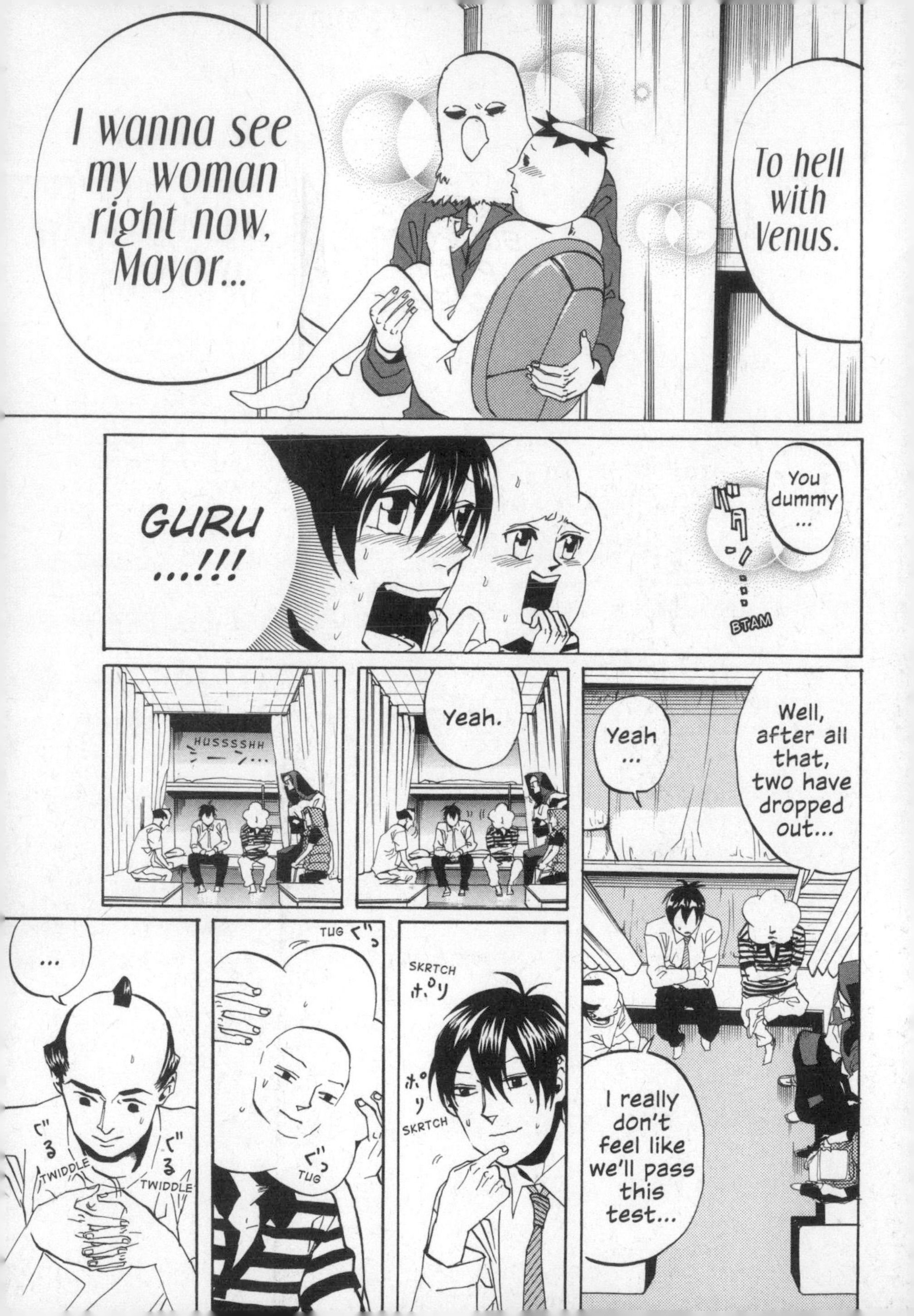
To hell with Venus.
I wanna see my woman right now, Mayor...
You dummy ...
BTAM
GURU ...!!!
Well, after all that, two have dropped out...
Yeah ...
I really don't feel like we'll pass this test...
Yeah.
HUSSSSHH
SKRTCH
SKRTCH
TUG
TUG
...
TWIDDLE
TWIDDLE

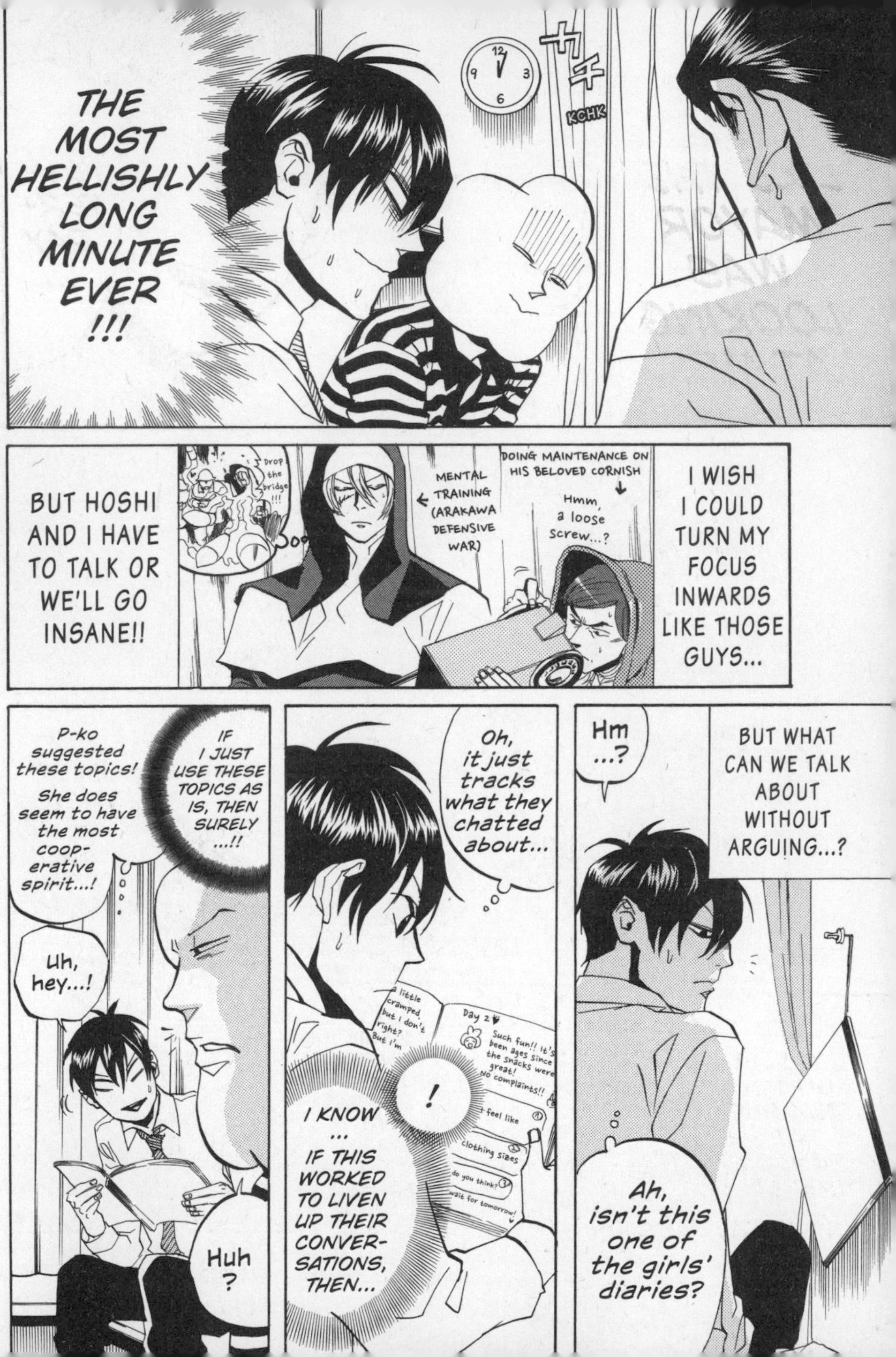
KCHK
THE MOST HELLISHLY LONG MINUTE EVER !!!
I WISH I COULD TURN MY FOCUS INWARDS LIKE THOSE GUYS...
DOING MAINTENANCE ON HIS BELOVED CORNISH
Hmm, a loose screw...?
MENTAL TRAINING (ARAKAWA DEFENSIVE WAR)
Drop the bridge!!!
BUT HOSHI AND I HAVE TO TALK OR WE'LL GO INSANE!!
BUT WHAT CAN WE TALK ABOUT WITHOUT ARGUING...?
Hm ...?
Ah, isn't this one of the girls' diaries?
Oh, it just tracks what they chatted about...
Day 2
Such fun!! It's been ages since the snacks were great! No complaints!!
feel like
clothing sizes
do you think?
wait for tomorrow!
a little cramped but I don't right? But I'm
!
I KNOW ... IF THIS WORKED TO LIVEN UP THEIR CONVERSATIONS, THEN...
IF I JUST USE THESE TOPICS AS IS, THEN SURELY ...!!
P-ko suggested these topics! She does seem to have the most cooperative spirit...!
Uh, hey...!
Huh ?

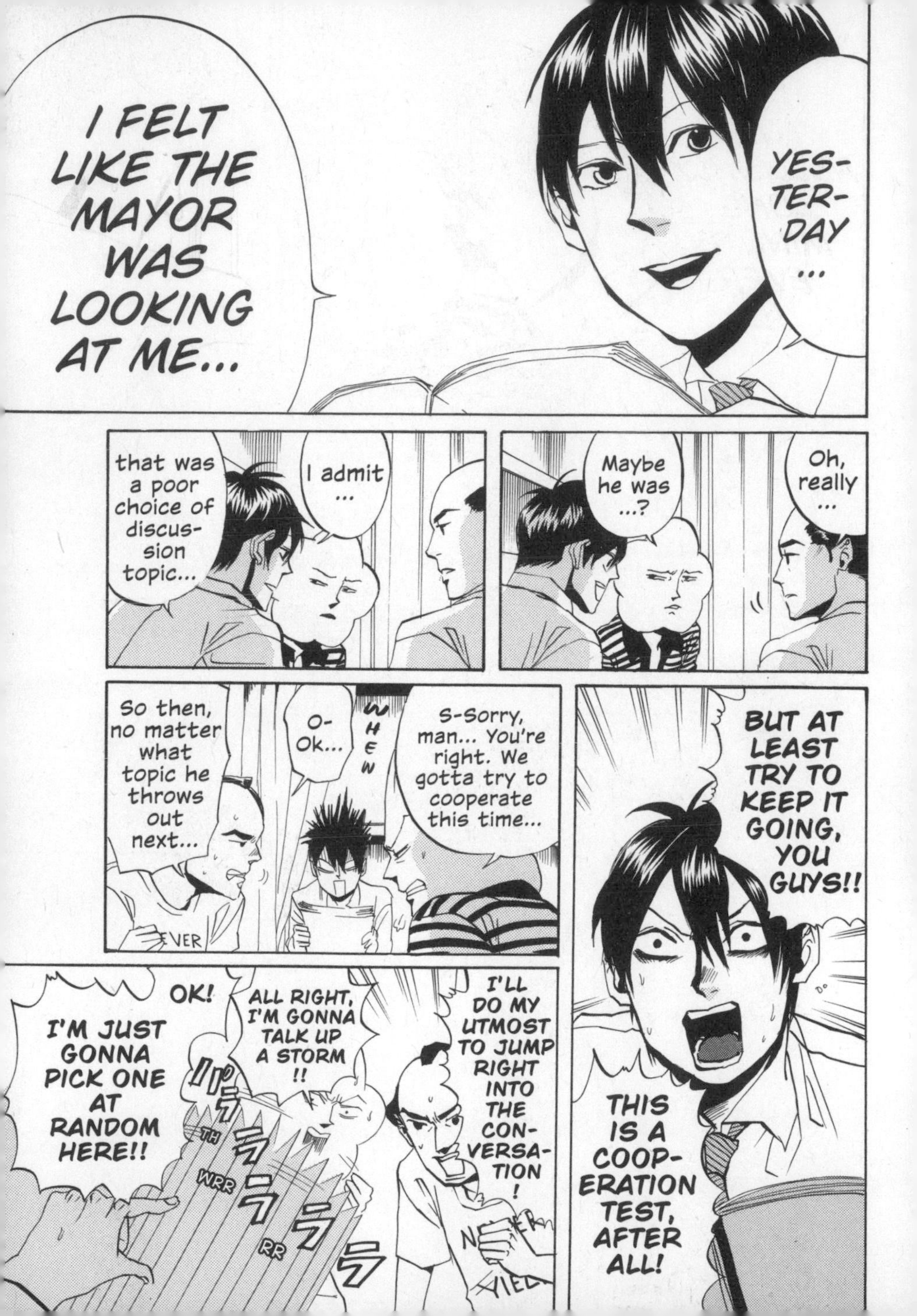
YES-TER-DAY...
I FELT LIKE THE MAYOR WAS LOOKING AT ME...
Oh, really...
Maybe he was...?
I admit...
that was a poor choice of discus-sion topic...
BUT AT LEAST TRY TO KEEP IT GOING, YOU GUYS!!
DO
THIS IS A COOP-ERATION TEST, AFTER ALL!
S-Sorry, man... You're right. We gotta try to cooperate this time...
WHEW
O-Ok...
So then, no matter what topic he throws out next...
EVER
I'LL DO MY UTMOST TO JUMP RIGHT INTO THE CON-VERSA-TION!
ALL RIGHT, I'M GONNA TALK UP A STORM!!
OK!
I'M JUST GONNA PICK ONE AT RANDOM HERE!!
TH
WRR
RR

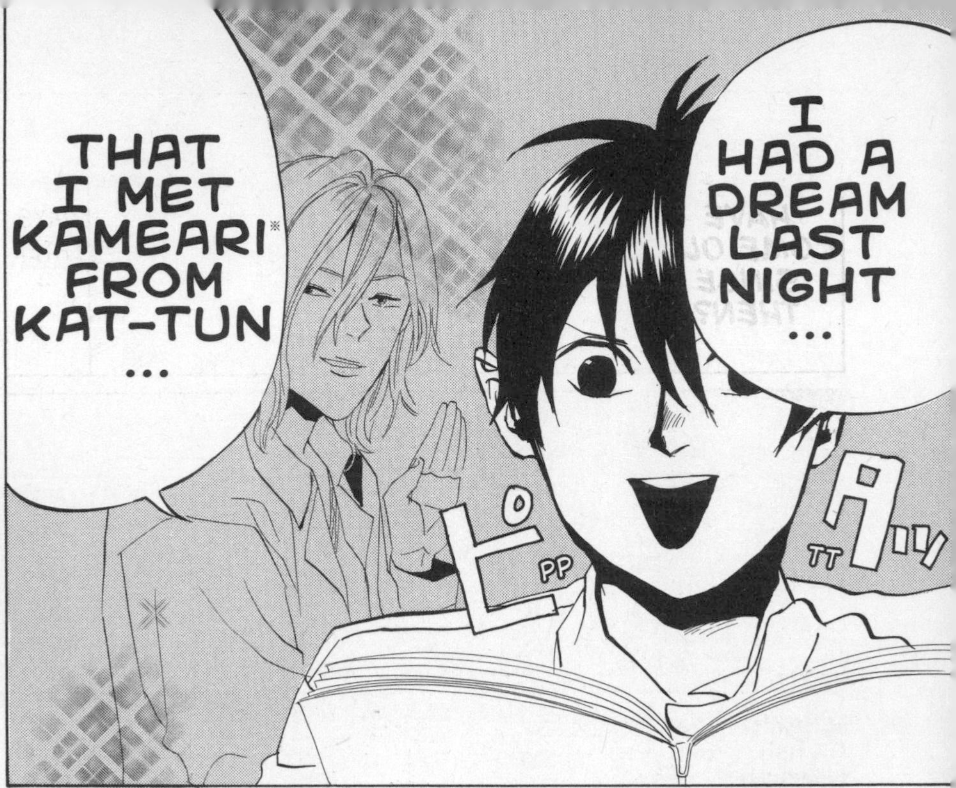
I HAD A DREAM LAST NIGHT ...
TT
PP
THAT I MET KAMEARI※ FROM KAT-TUN ...

※ Pun on name of band member "Kamenashi".

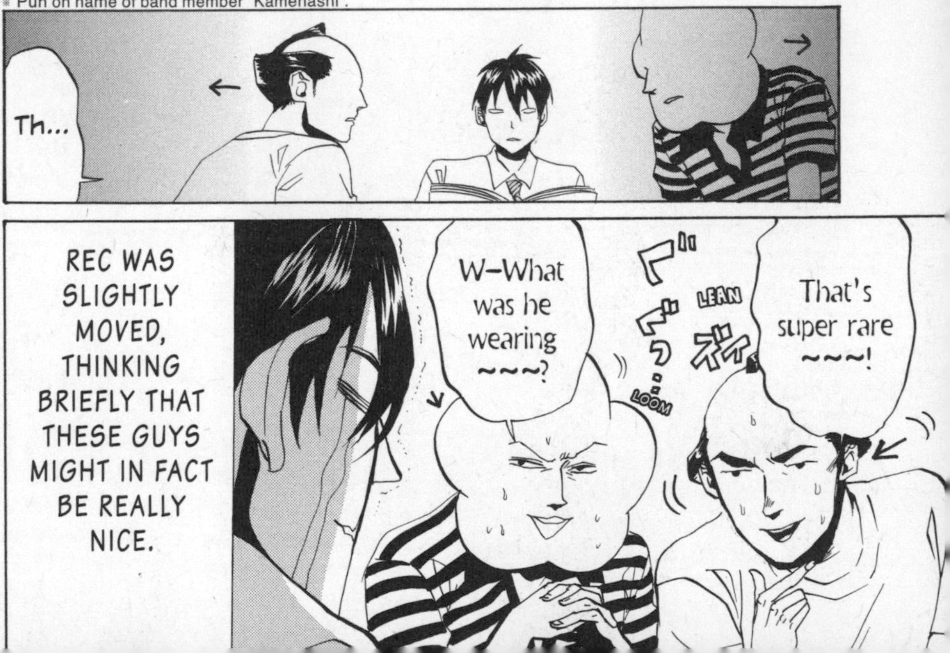
Th...
That's super rare ~~~!
LEAN
LOOM
W-What was he wearing ~~~?
REC WAS SLIGHTLY MOVED, THINKING BRIEFLY THAT THESE GUYS MIGHT IN FACT BE REALLY NICE.

Chapter 181: Elegy for the Men

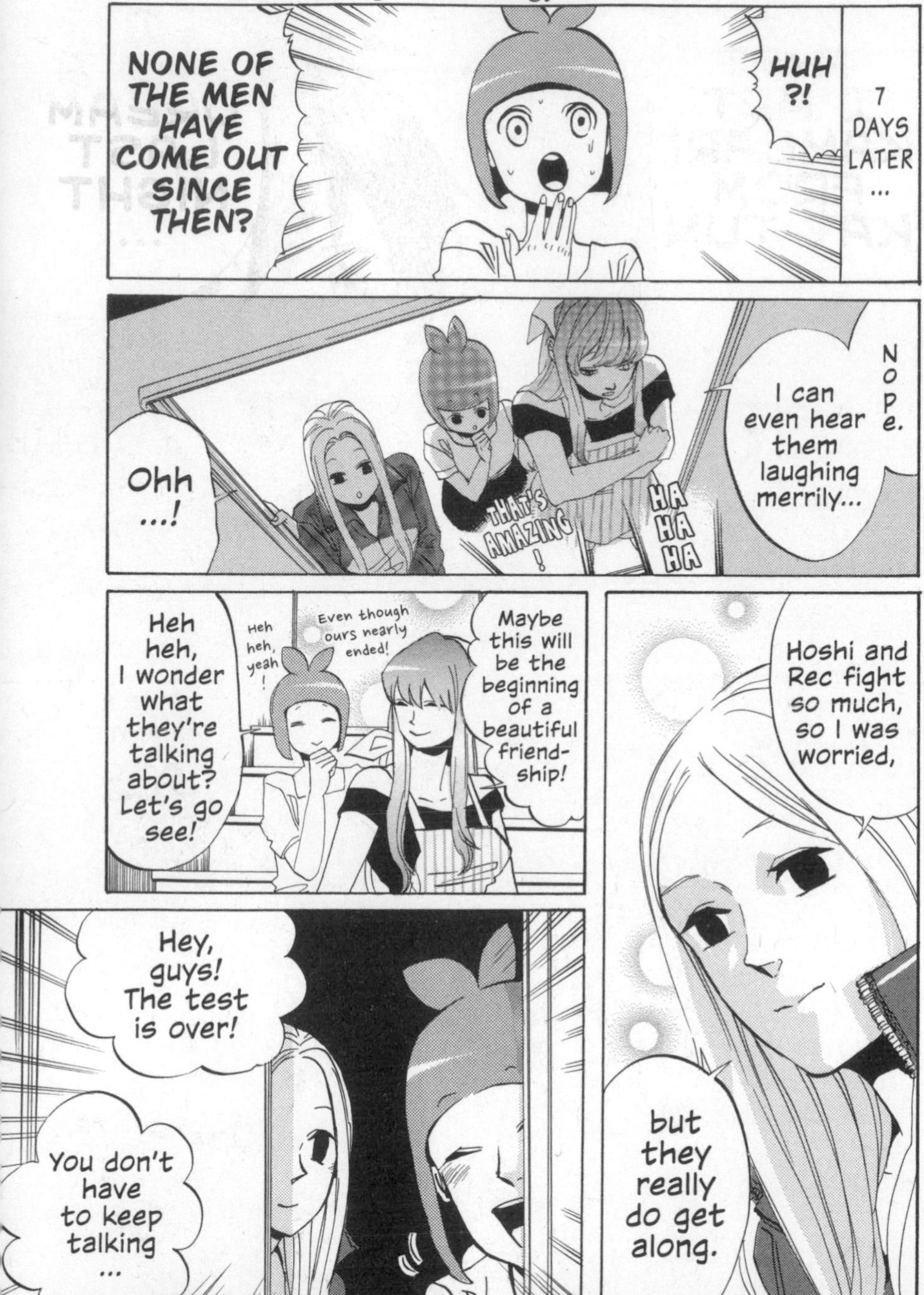
7 DAYS LATER ...
HUH ?!
NONE OF THE MEN HAVE COME OUT SINCE THEN?
Nope.
I can even hear them laughing merrily...
HA HA HA
THAT'S AMAZING !
Ohh ...!
Hoshi and Rec fight so much, so I was worried,
but they really do get along.
Maybe this will be the beginning of a beautiful friend-ship!
Even though ours nearly ended!
Heh heh, yeah !
Heh heh, I wonder what they're talking about? Let's go see!
Hey, guys! The test is over!
You don't have to keep talking ...

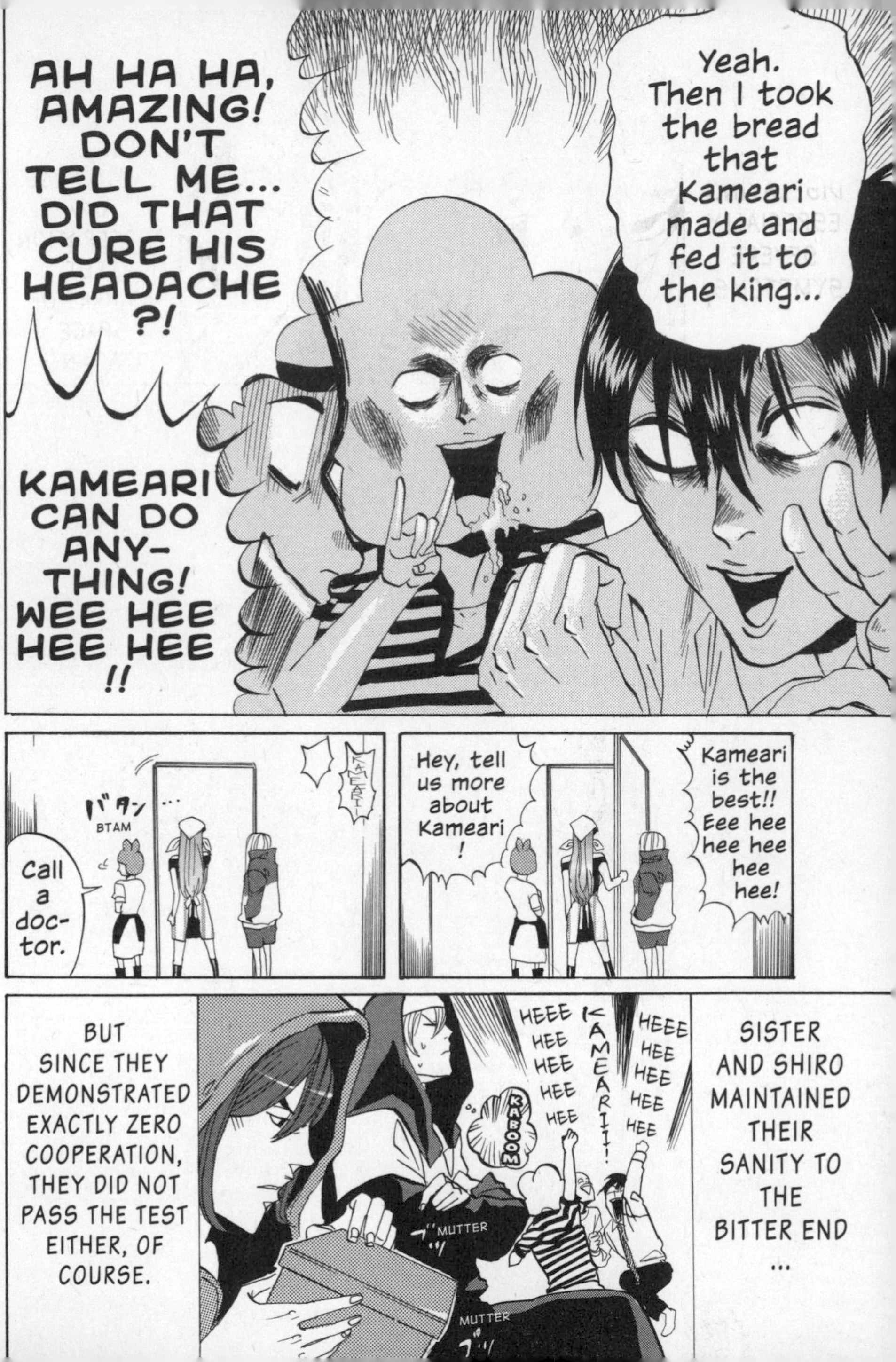
Yeah. Then I took the bread that Kameari made and fed it to the king...
AH HA HA, AMAZING! DON'T TELL ME... DID THAT CURE HIS HEADACHE?!
KAMEARI CAN DO ANY-THING! WEE HEE HEE HEE!!
Kameari is the best!! Eee hee hee hee hee hee!
Hey, tell us more about Kameari!
KAMEARI
...
バタン
BTAM
Call a doc-tor.
SISTER AND SHIRO MAINTAINED THEIR SANITY TO THE BITTER END...
HEEE HEE HEE HEE HEE
KAMEARI!!
HEEE HEE HEE HEE HEE
KABOOM
MUTTER
MUTTER
BUT SINCE THEY DEMONSTRATED EXACTLY ZERO COOPERATION, THEY DID NOT PASS THE TEST EITHER, OF COURSE.

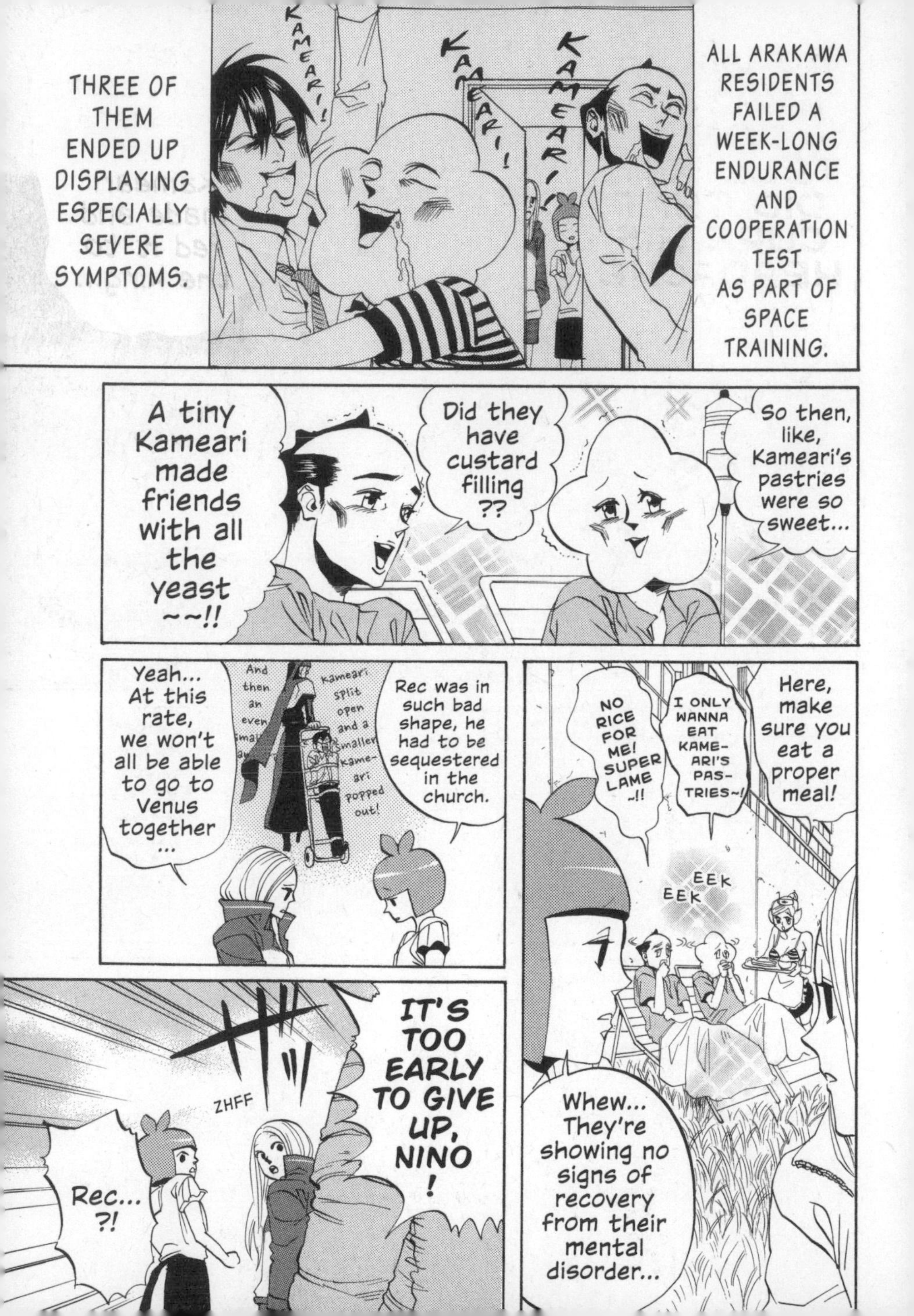
ALL ARAKAWA RESIDENTS FAILED A WEEK-LONG ENDURANCE AND COOPERATION TEST AS PART OF SPACE TRAINING.
KAMEARI!
KAMEARI!
KAMEARI!
KAMEARI!
THREE OF THEM ENDED UP DISPLAYING ESPECIALLY SEVERE SYMPTOMS.
So then, like, Kameari's pastries were so sweet...
Did they have custard filling??
A tiny Kameari made friends with all the yeast ~~!!
Here, make sure you eat a proper meal!
I ONLY WANNA EAT KAME-ARI'S PAS-TRIES~!
NO RICE FOR ME! SUPER LAME ~!!
EEK EEK
Whew... They're showing no signs of recovery from their mental disorder...
Rec was in such bad shape, he had to be sequestered in the church.
Kameari split open and a smaller Kame-ari popped out!
Yeah... At this rate, we won't all be able to go to Venus together ...
IT'S TOO EARLY TO GIVE UP, NINO!
ZHFF
Rec... ?!

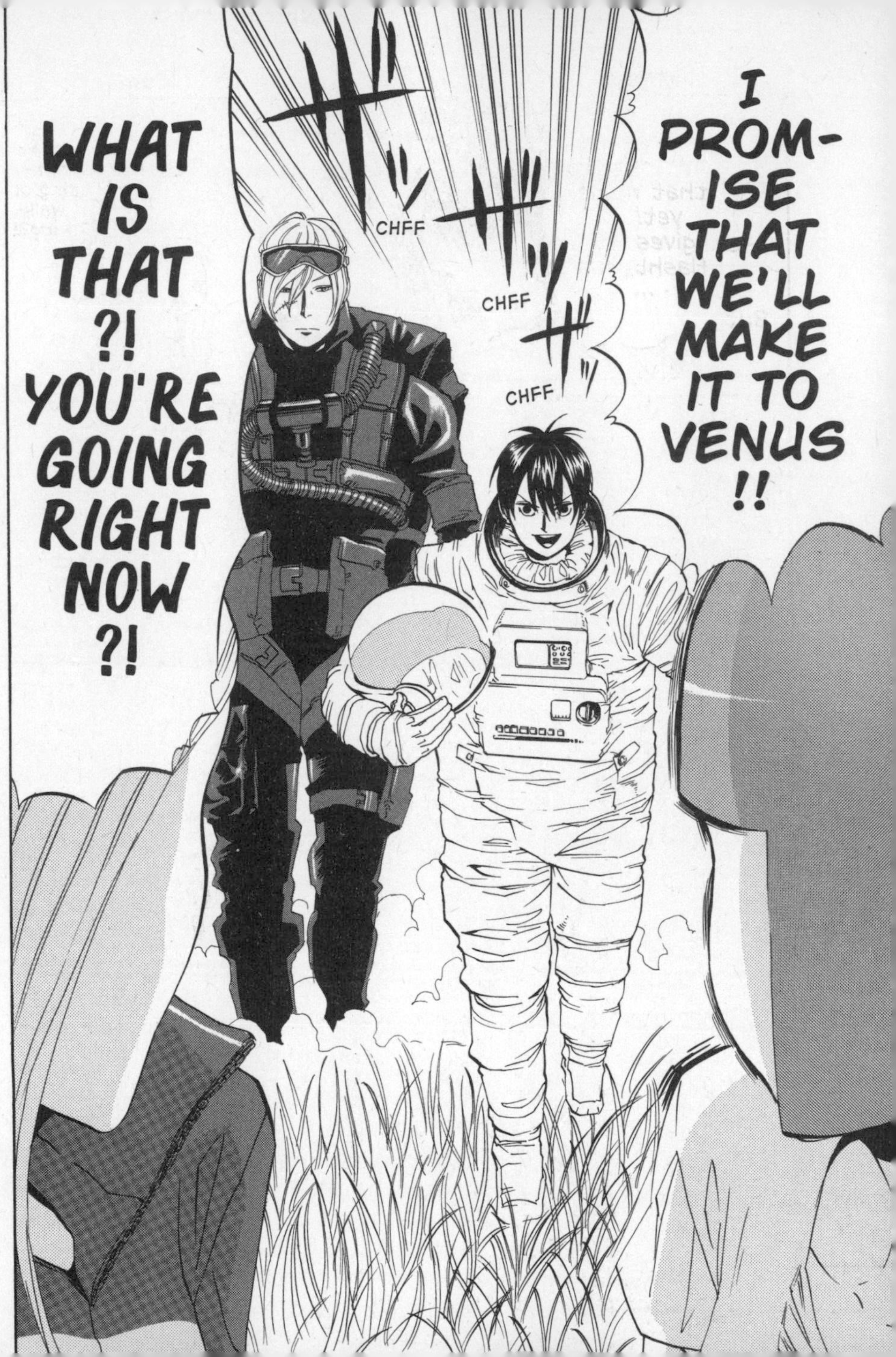
I PROMISE THAT WE'LL MAKE IT TO VENUS!!
CHFF
CHFF
CHFF
WHAT IS THAT?! YOU'RE GOING RIGHT NOW?!

Chapter 182: The Arakawa Space Station Plan

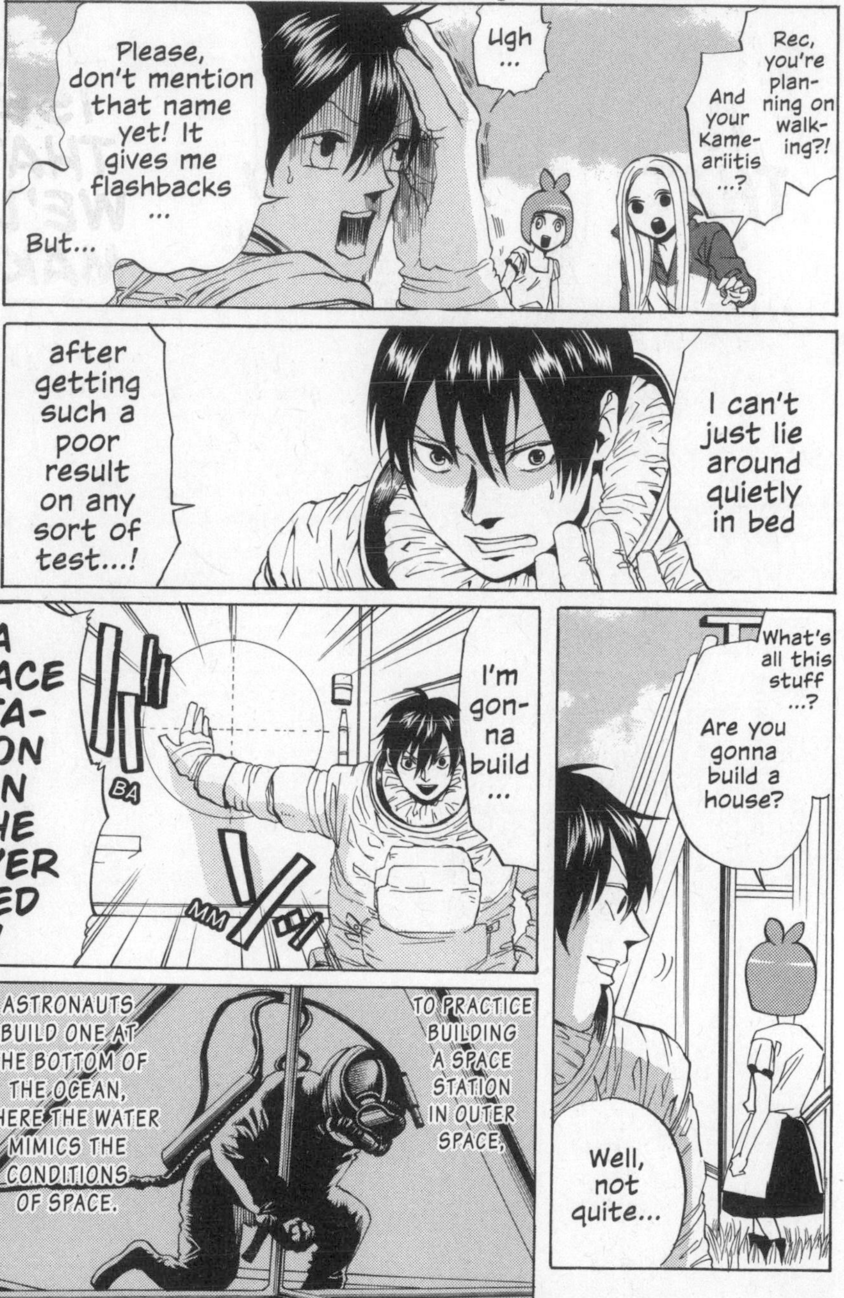
Rec, you're plan-ning on walk-ing?!
And your Kame-ariitis ...?
Ugh ...
Please, don't mention that name yet! It gives me flashbacks ...
But...
I can't just lie around quietly in bed
after getting such a poor result on any sort of test...!
What's all this stuff ...?
Are you gonna build a house?
Well, not quite...
I'm gon-na build ...
A SPACE STA-TION ON THE RIVER BED !
BA
MM
TO PRACTICE BUILDING A SPACE STATION IN OUTER SPACE,
ASTRONAUTS BUILD ONE AT THE BOTTOM OF THE OCEAN, WHERE THE WATER MIMICS THE CONDITIONS OF SPACE.

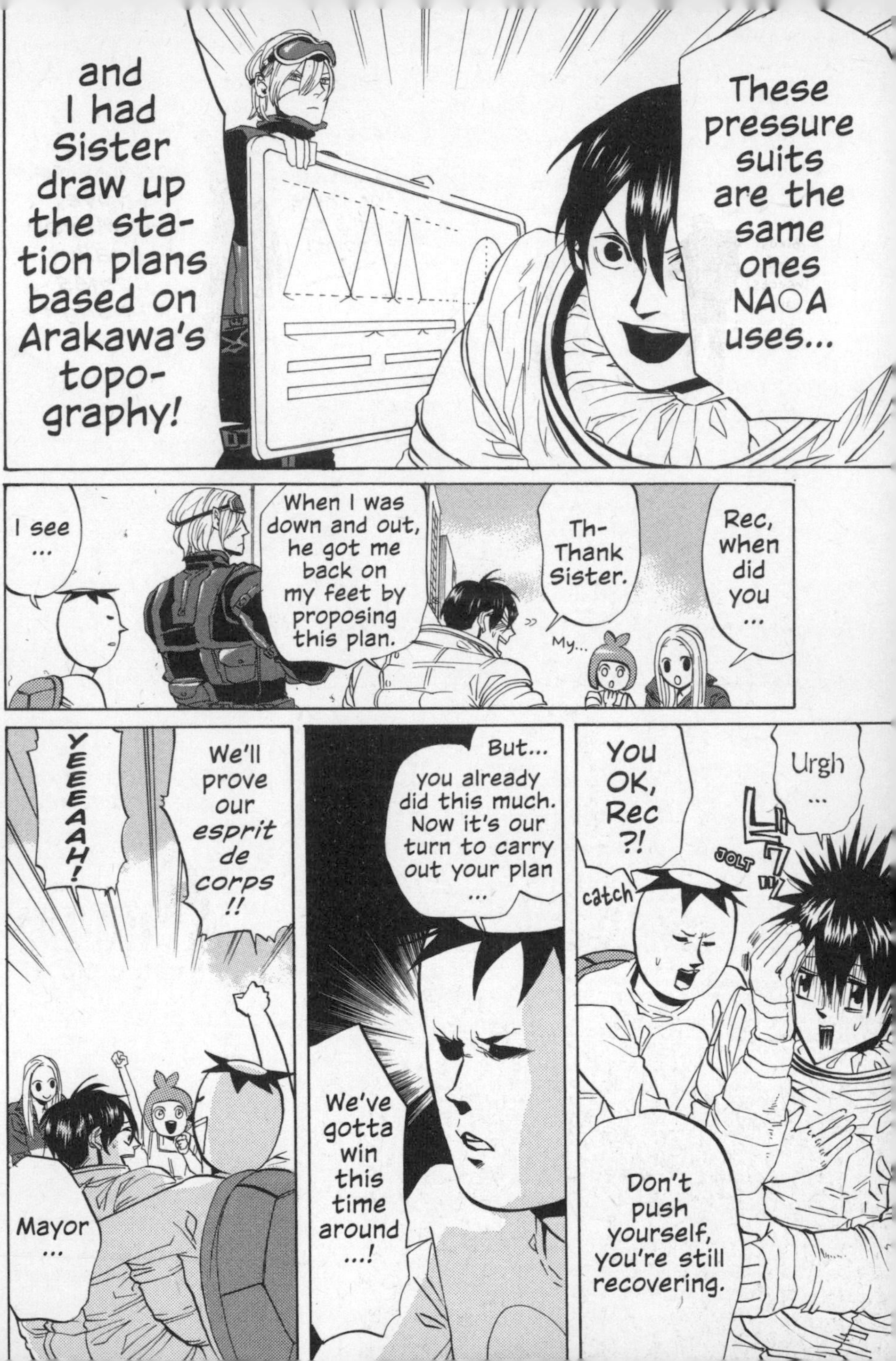
These pressure suits are the same ones NA○A uses...
and I had Sister draw up the station plans based on Arakawa's topography!
Rec, when did you ...
My...
Th- Thank Sister.
When I was down and out, he got me back on my feet by proposing this plan.
I see ...
Urgh ...
JOLT
You OK, Rec ?!
catch
Don't push yourself, you're still recovering.
But... you already did this much. Now it's our turn to carry out your plan ...
We've gotta win this time around ...!
We'll prove our *esprit de corps* !!
YEEEAAAH!
Mayor ...

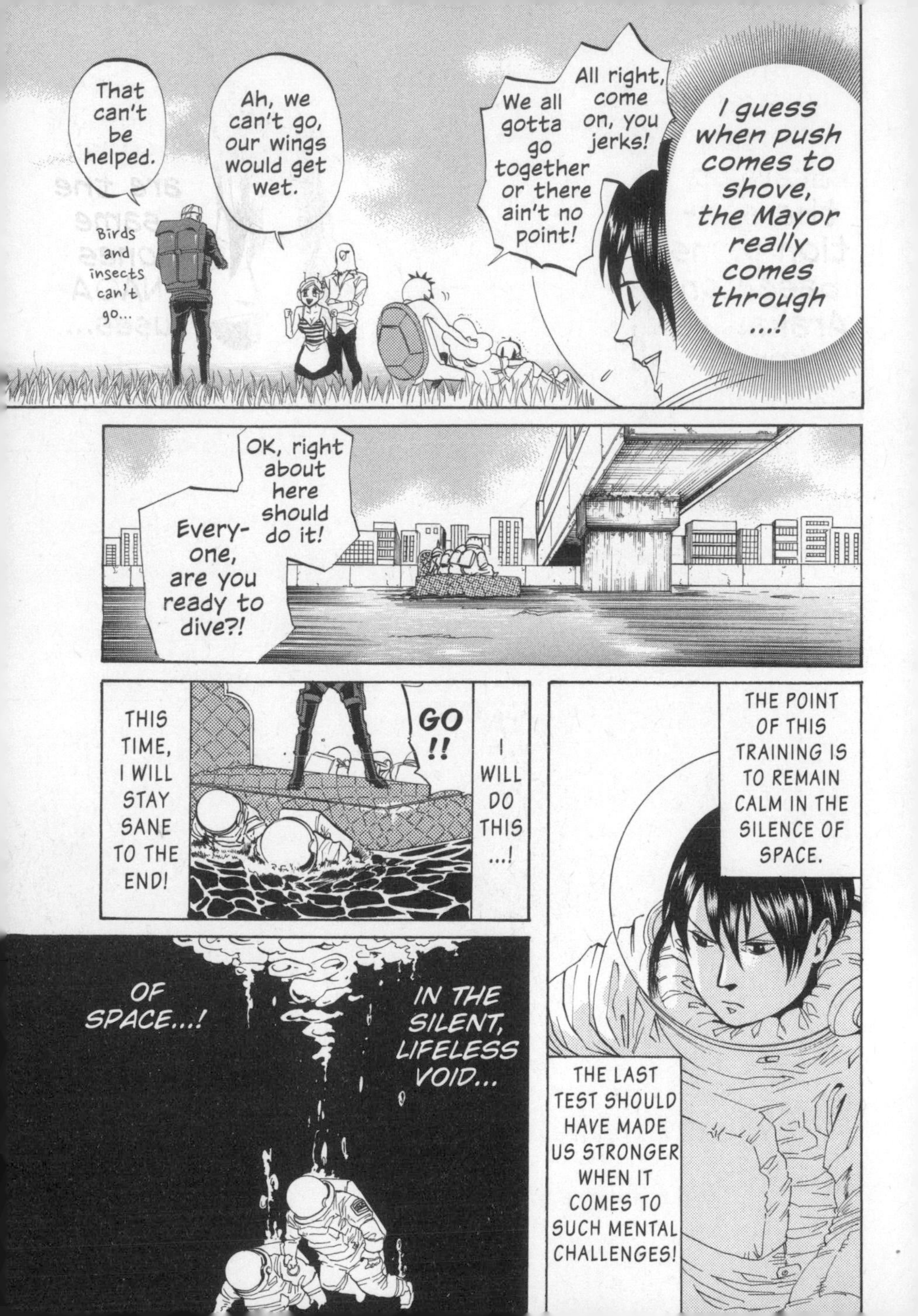
I guess when push comes to shove, the Mayor really comes through...!
All right, come on, you jerks!
We all gotta go together or there ain't no point!
Ah, we can't go, our wings would get wet.
That can't be helped.
Birds and insects can't go...
OK, right about here should do it!
Every-one, are you ready to dive?!
THE POINT OF THIS TRAINING IS TO REMAIN CALM IN THE SILENCE OF SPACE.
THE LAST TEST SHOULD HAVE MADE US STRONGER WHEN IT COMES TO SUCH MENTAL CHALLENGES!
I WILL DO THIS...!
GO!!
THIS TIME, I WILL STAY SANE TO THE END!
IN THE SILENT, LIFELESS VOID...
OF SPACE...!

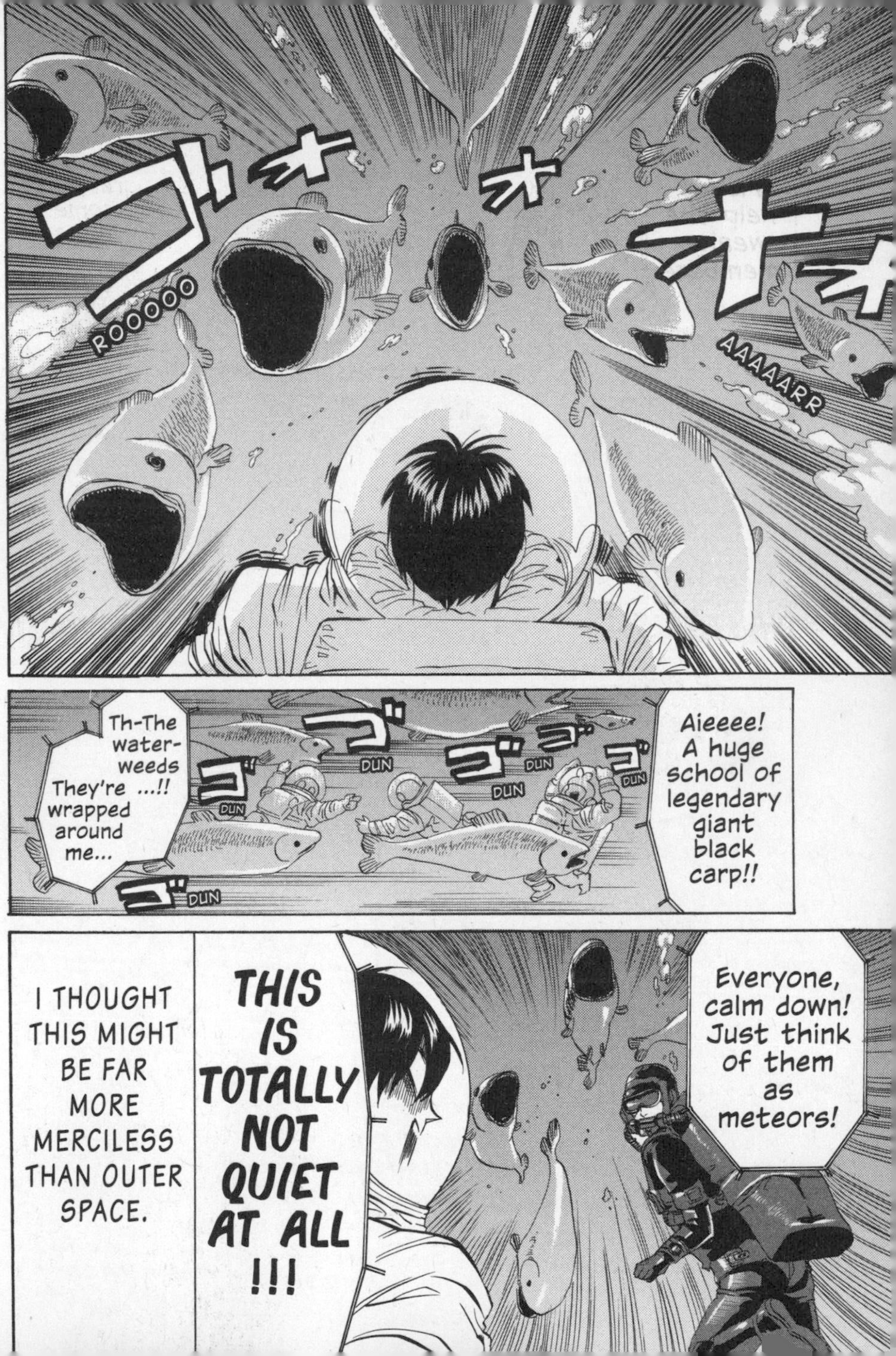
ROOOOO
AAAAAARR
Aieeee! A huge school of legendary giant black carp!!
DUN
DUN
DUN
DUN
DUN
Th-The water-weeds ...!!
They're wrapped around me...
DUN
Everyone, calm down! Just think of them as meteors!
THIS IS TOTALLY NOT QUIET AT ALL!!!
I THOUGHT THIS MIGHT BE FAR MORE MERCILESS THAN OUTER SPACE.

Chapter 183: Deep Blue

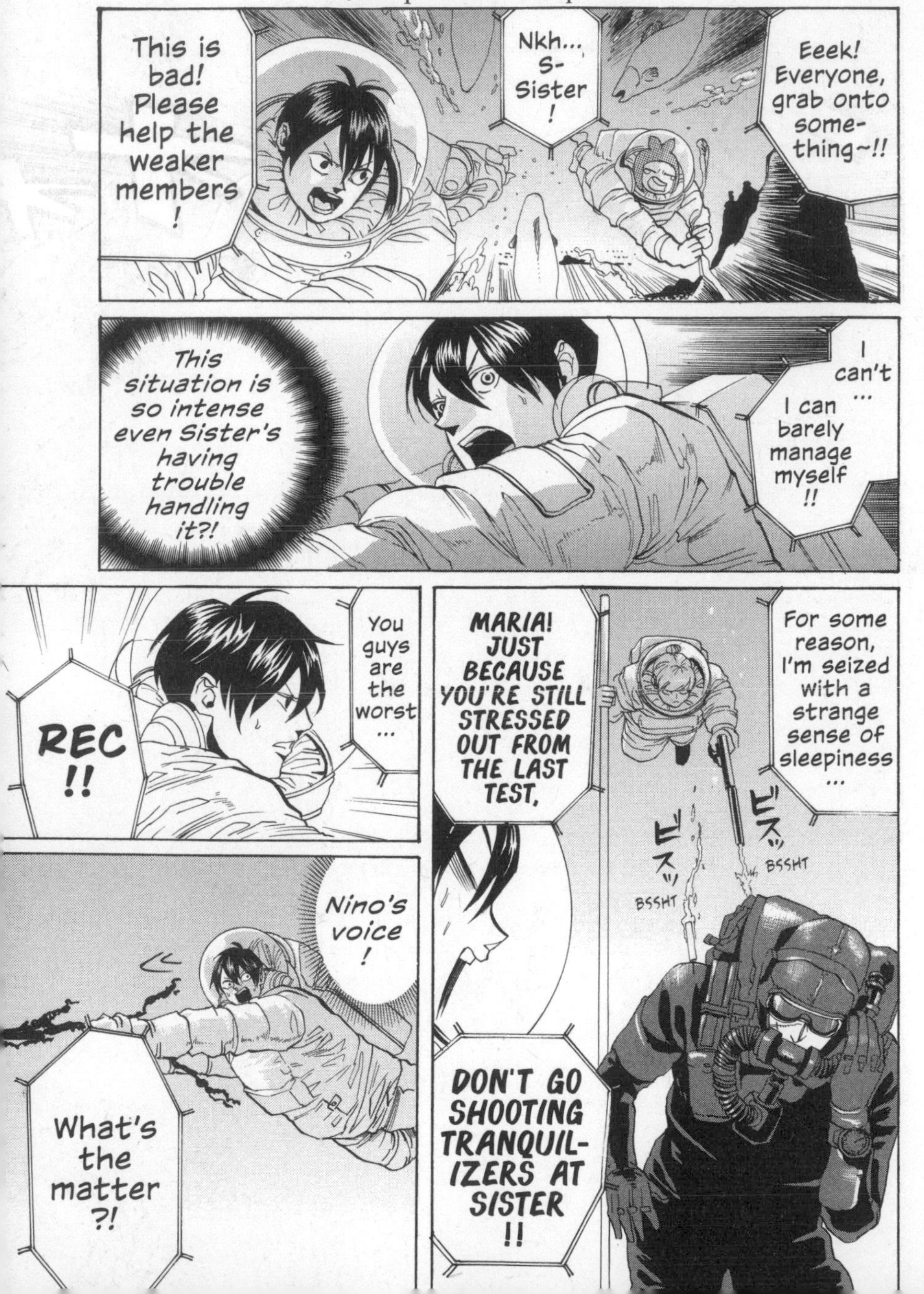
Eeek! Everyone, grab onto some-thing~!!
Nkh..., S-Sister!
This is bad! Please help the weaker members!
I can't ... I can barely manage myself!!
This situation is so intense even Sister's having trouble handling it?!
For some reason, I'm seized with a strange sense of sleepiness...
ビスッ
BSSHT
ビスッ
BSSHT
MARIA! JUST BECAUSE YOU'RE STILL STRESSED OUT FROM THE LAST TEST,
DON'T GO SHOOTING TRANQUIL-IZERS AT SISTER!!
You guys are the worst...
REC!!
Nino's voice!
What's the matter?!

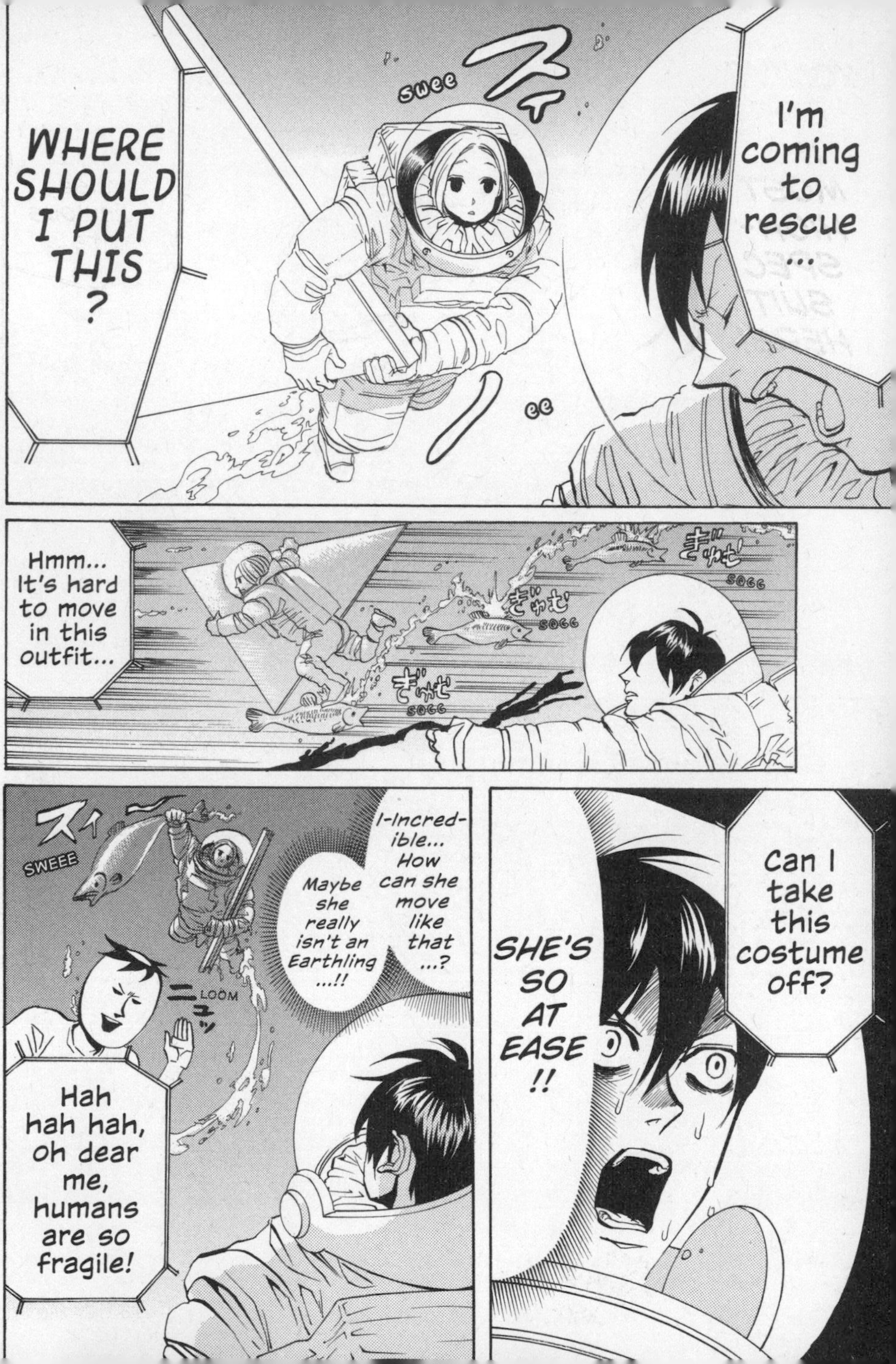
I'm coming to rescue ...
swee
ee
WHERE SHOULD I PUT THIS ?
SOGG
SOGG
SOGG
Hmm... It's hard to move in this outfit...
Can I take this costume off?
SHE'S SO AT EASE !!
I-Incred-ible... How can she move like that ...?
Maybe she really isn't an Earthling ...!!
SWEEE
LOOM
Hah hah hah, oh dear me, humans are so fragile!

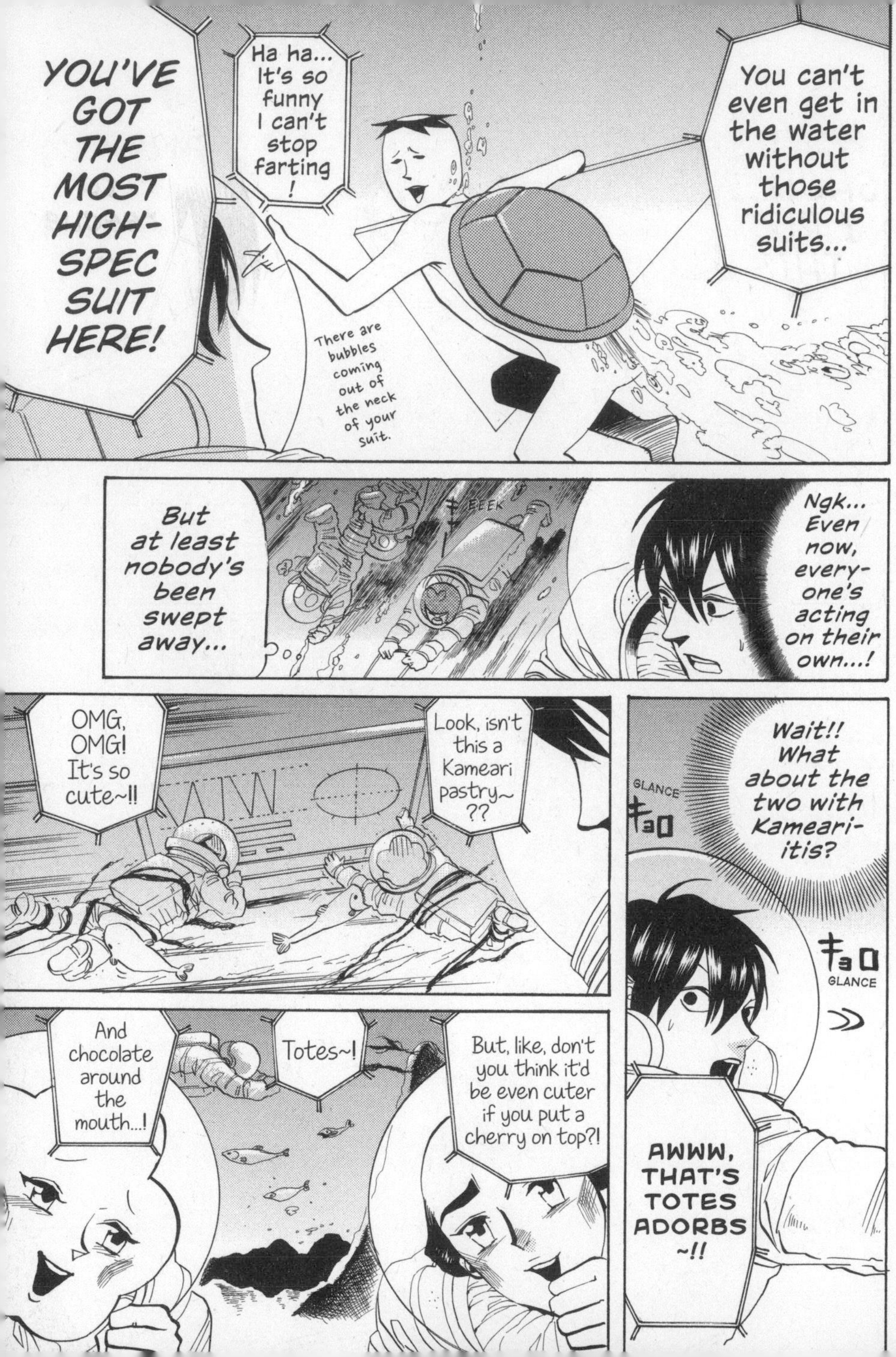
You can't even get in the water without those ridiculous suits...
Ha ha... It's so funny I can't stop farting!
YOU'VE GOT THE MOST HIGH-SPEC SUIT HERE!
There are bubbles coming out of the neck of your suit.
Ngk... Even now, everyone's acting on their own...!
EEEK
But at least nobody's been swept away...
Wait!! What about the two with Kameari-itis?
GLANCE
GLANCE
Look, isn't this a Kameari pastry~??
OMG, OMG! It's so cute~!!
AWWW, THAT'S TOTES ADORBS~!!
But, like, don't you think it'd be even cuter if you put a cherry on top?!
Totes~!
And chocolate around the mouth...!

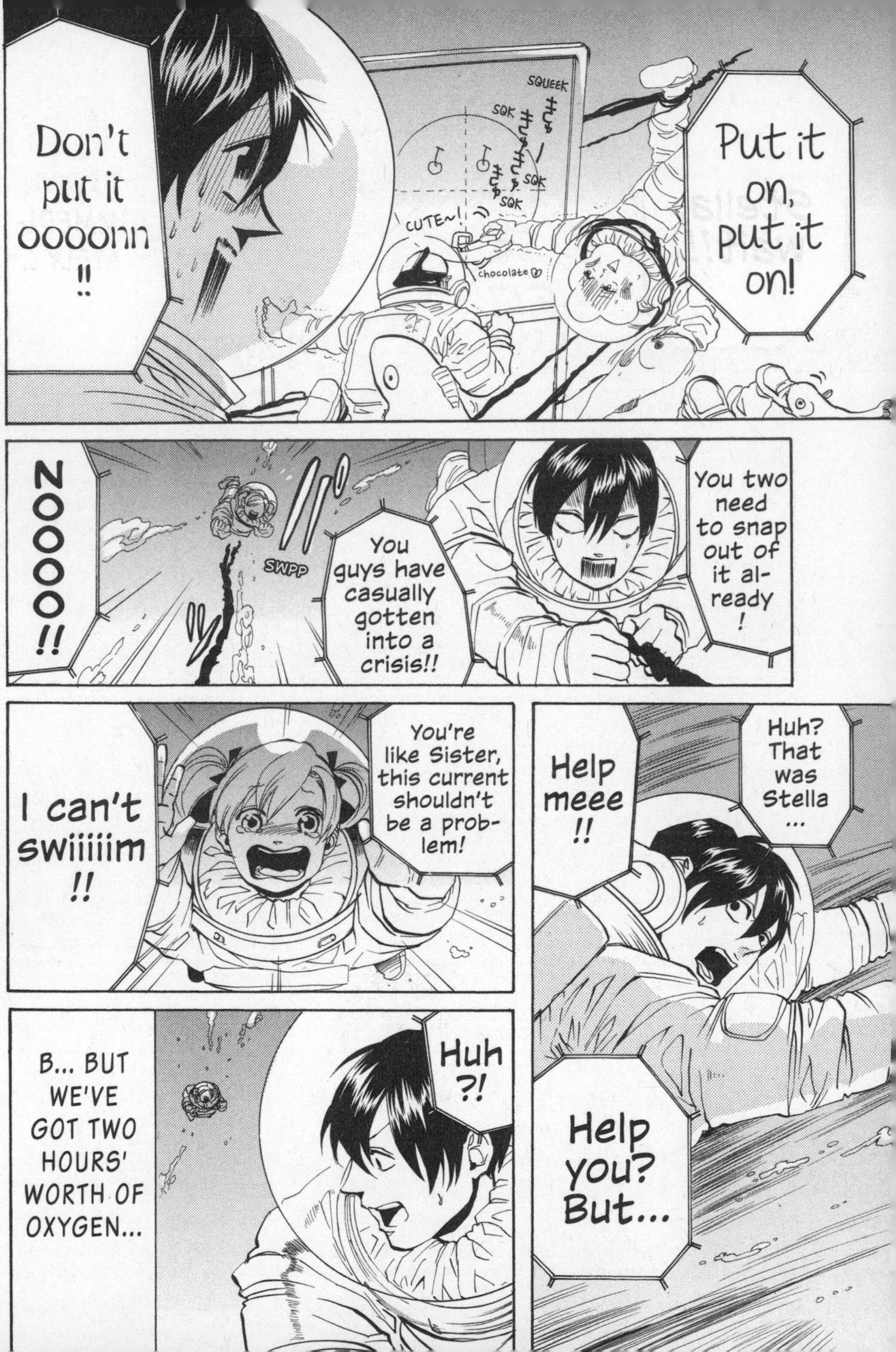
Put it on, put it on!
SQUEEK
SQK
SQK
SQK
CUTE~!
chocolate
Don't put it oooonn!!
You two need to snap out of it al-ready!
You guys have casually gotten into a crisis!!
SWPP
NOOOO!!
Huh? That was Stella...
Help meee!!
Help you? But...
You're like Sister, this current shouldn't be a prob-lem!
I can't swiiiiim!!
Huh?!
B... BUT WE'VE GOT TWO HOURS' WORTH OF OXYGEN...

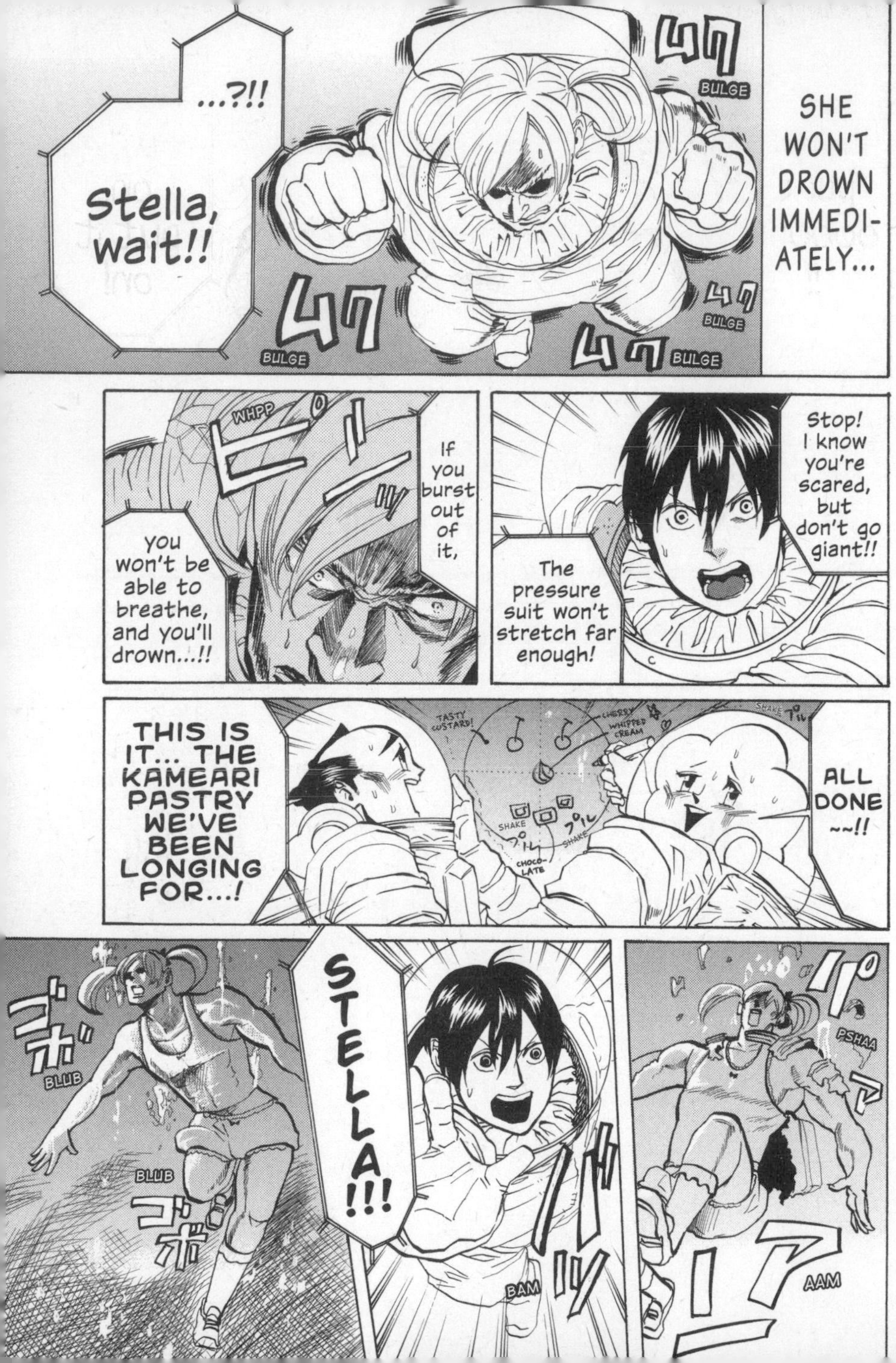
SHE WON'T DROWN IMMEDI-ATELY...
BULGE
...?!!
Stella, wait!!
BULGE
BULGE
BULGE
Stop! I know you're scared, but don't go giant!!
The pressure suit won't stretch far enough!
WHPP
If you burst out of it,
you won't be able to breathe, and you'll drown...!!
SHAKE
ALL DONE ~~!!
TASTY CUSTARD!
CHERRY
WHIPPED CREAM
SHAKE
SHAKE
CHOCO-LATE
THIS IS IT... THE KAMEARI PASTRY WE'VE BEEN LONGING FOR...!
PSHAA
AAM
STELLA!!!
BAM
BLUB
BLUB

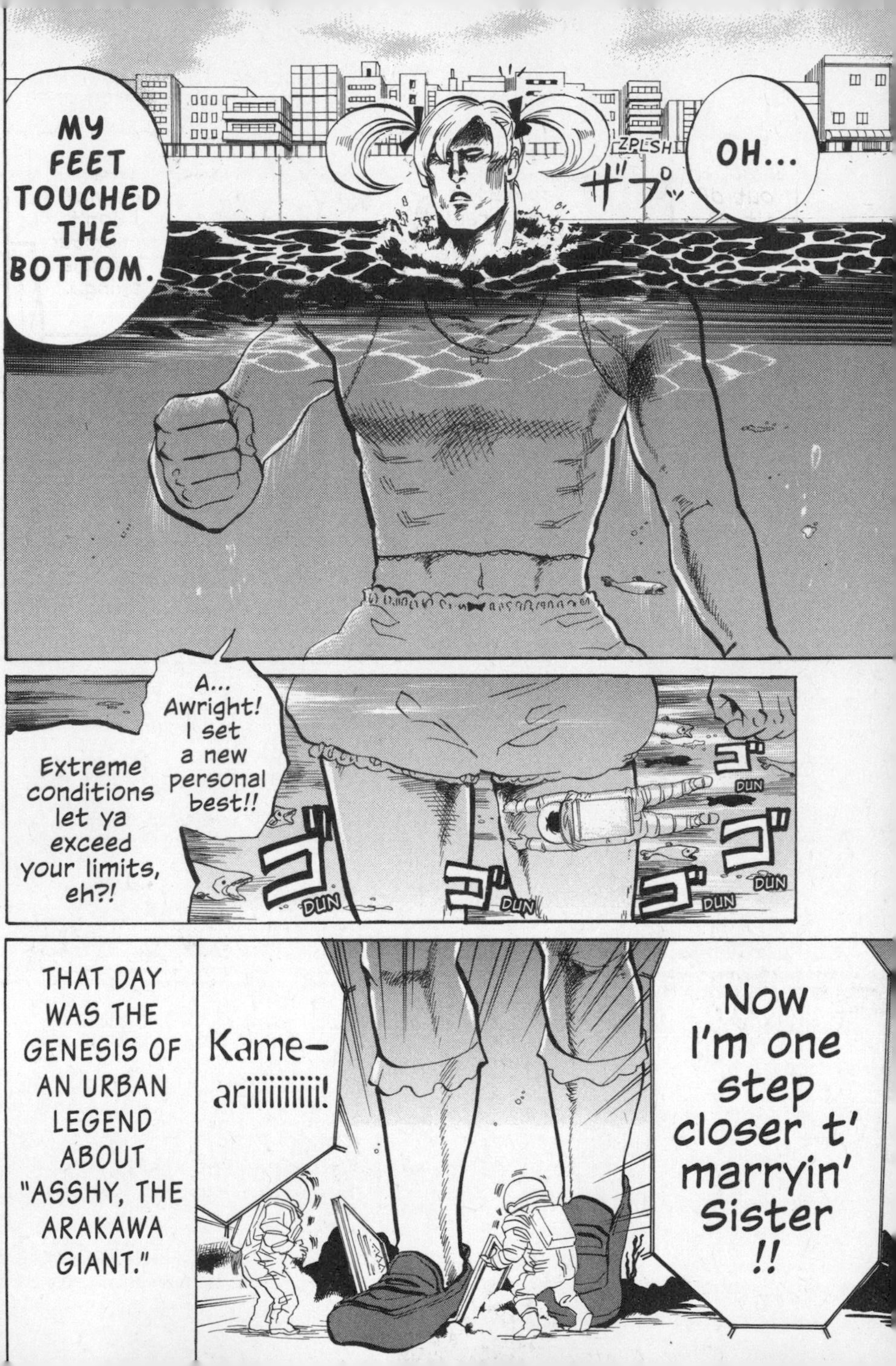
OH...
ZPLSH
ザプッ
MY FEET TOUCHED THE BOTTOM.
A... Awright! I set a new personal best!!
Extreme conditions let ya exceed your limits, eh?!
ゴ DUN
ゴ DUN
ゴ DUN
ゴ DUN
ゴ DUN
Now I'm one step closer t' marryin' Sister !!
Kame-ariiiiiiiiiii!
THAT DAY WAS THE GENESIS OF AN URBAN LEGEND ABOUT "ASSHY, THE ARAKAWA GIANT."

Chapter 184: Dreams of Seeing Space with Friends

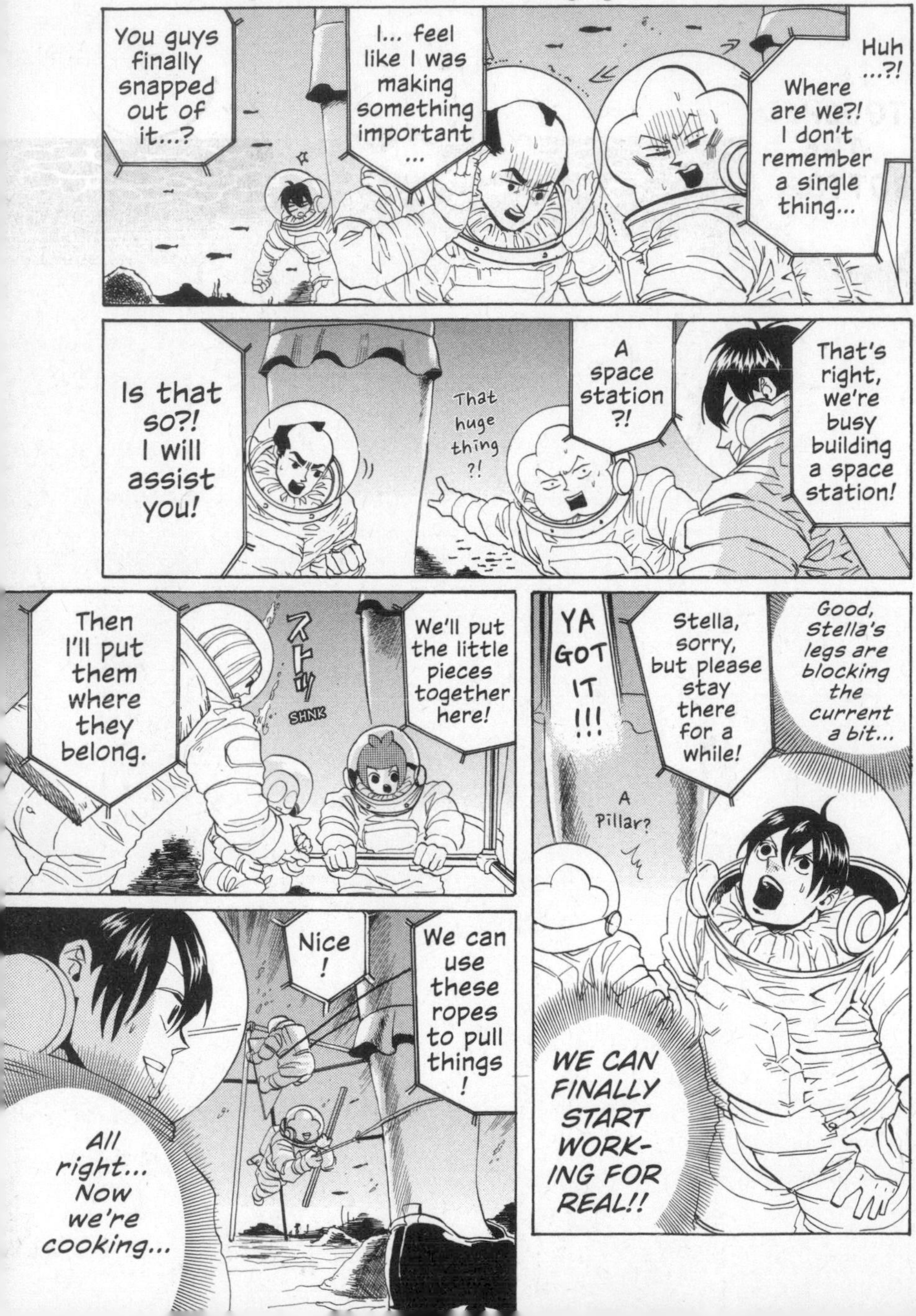
Huh ...?! Where are we?! I don't remember a single thing...
I... feel like I was making something important ...
You guys finally snapped out of it...?
That's right, we're busy building a space station!
A space station ?!
That huge thing ?!
Is that so?! I will assist you!
Good, Stella's legs are blocking the current a bit...
Stella, sorry, but please stay there for a while!
YA GOT IT !!!
A Pillar?
WE CAN FINALLY START WORK-ING FOR REAL!!
We'll put the little pieces together here!
ストッ
SHNK
Then I'll put them where they belong.
We can use these ropes to pull things !
Nice !
All right... Now we're cooking...

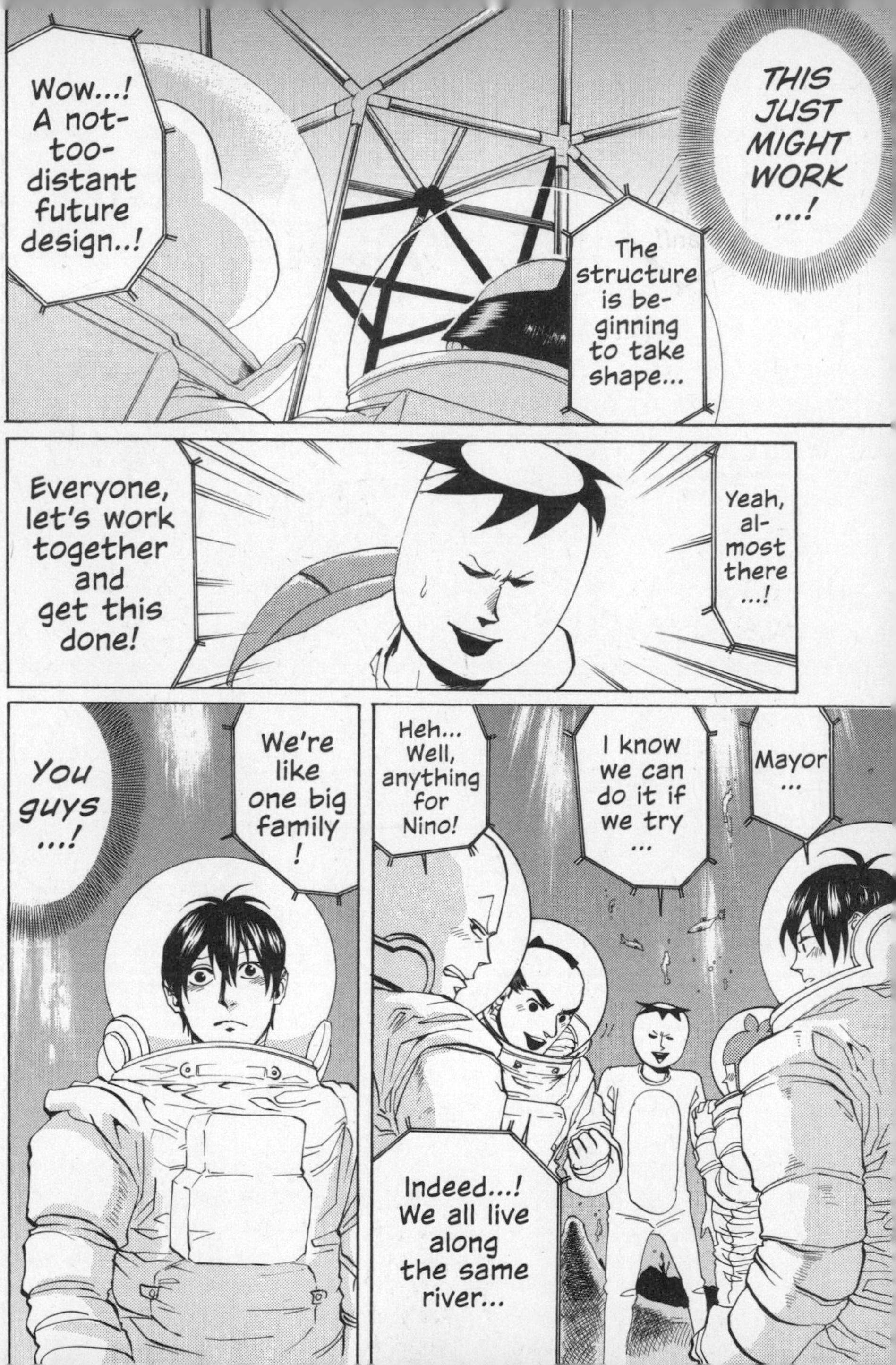
THIS JUST MIGHT WORK ...!
The structure is be-ginning to take shape...
Wow...! A not-too-distant future design..!
Yeah, al-most there ...!
Everyone, let's work together and get this done!
Mayor ...
I know we can do it if we try ...
Heh... Well, anything for Nino!
Indeed...! We all live along the same river...
We're like one big family !
You guys ...!

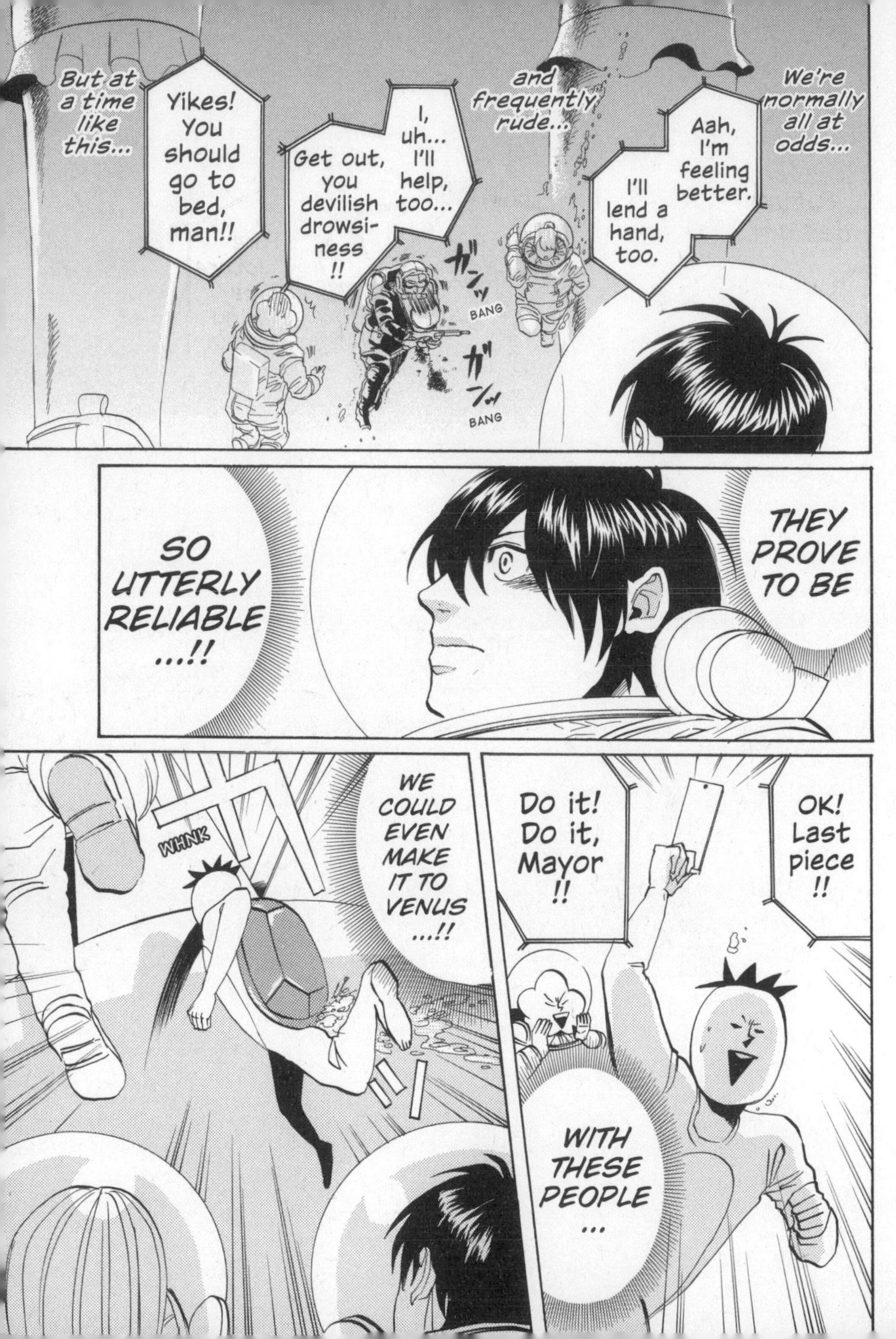
We're normally all at odds...
Aah, I'm feeling better.
I'll lend a hand, too.
and frequently rude...
I, uh... I'll help, too...
Get out, you devilish drowsiness !!
BANG
BANG
Yikes! You should go to bed, man!!
But at a time like this...
THEY PROVE TO BE
SO UTTERLY RELIABLE ...!!
OK! Last piece !!
Do it! Do it, Mayor !!
WITH THESE PEOPLE ...
WE COULD EVEN MAKE IT TO VENUS ...!!
WHNK

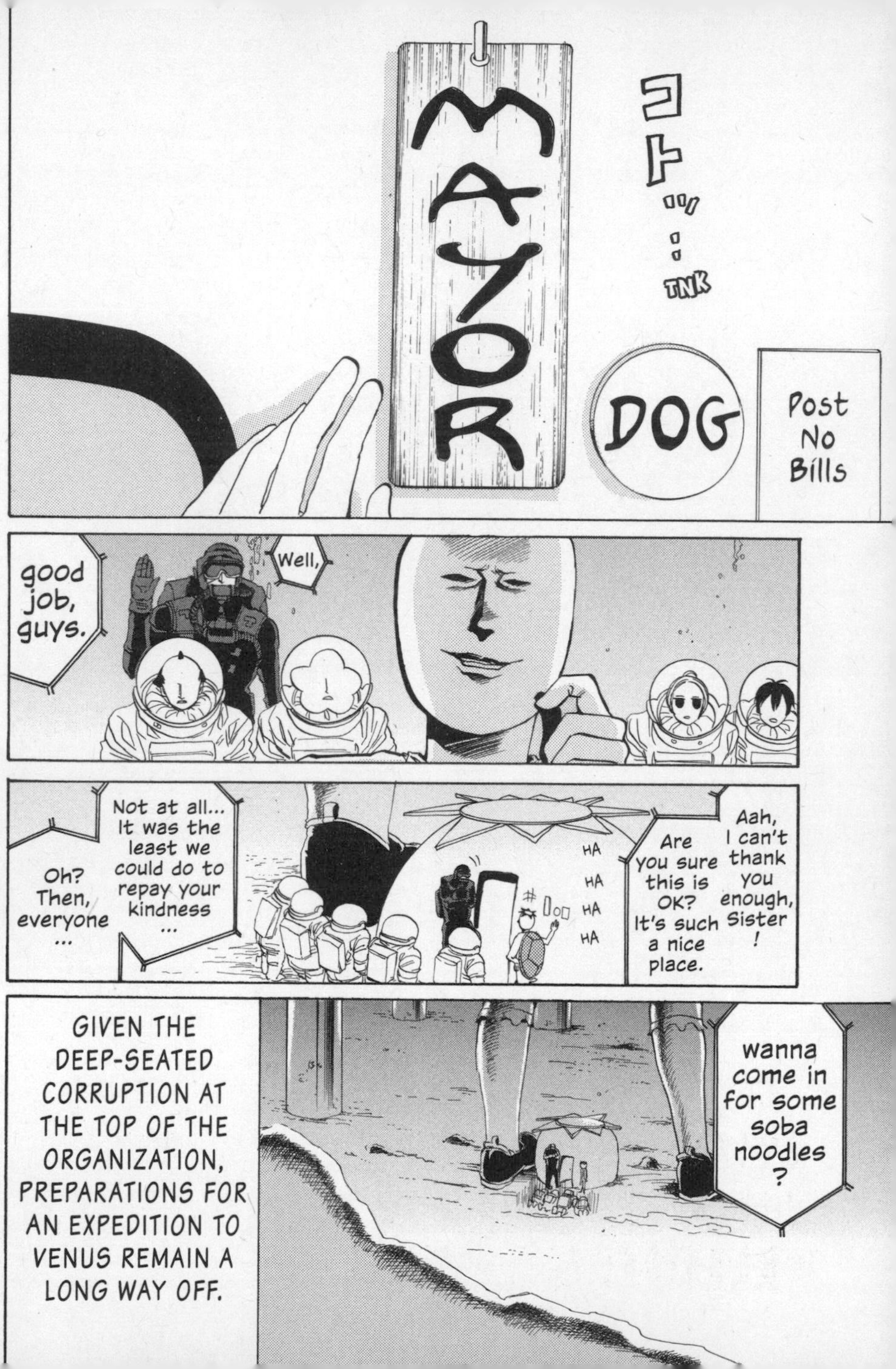
Post No Bills
DOG
コトッ
TNK
MAYOR
Well,
good job, guys.
Aah, I can't thank you enough, Sister!
Are you sure this is OK? It's such a nice place.
HA HA HA HA
Not at all... It was the least we could do to repay your kindness...
Oh? Then, everyone...
wanna come in for some soba noodles?
GIVEN THE DEEP-SEATED CORRUPTION AT THE TOP OF THE ORGANIZATION, PREPARATIONS FOR AN EXPEDITION TO VENUS REMAIN A LONG WAY OFF.

ARAKAWA
UNDER
THE BRIDGE

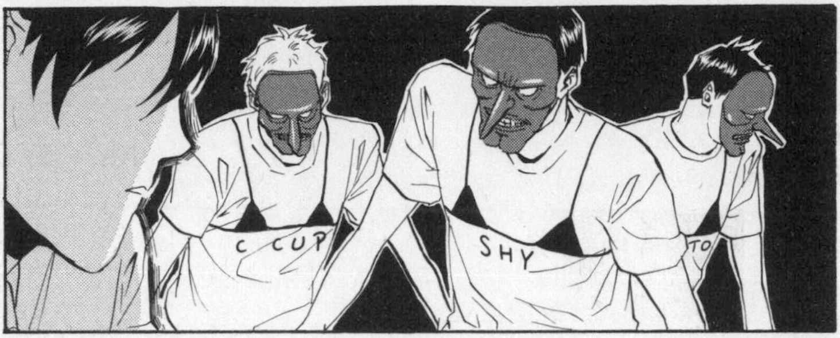
C CUP
SHY

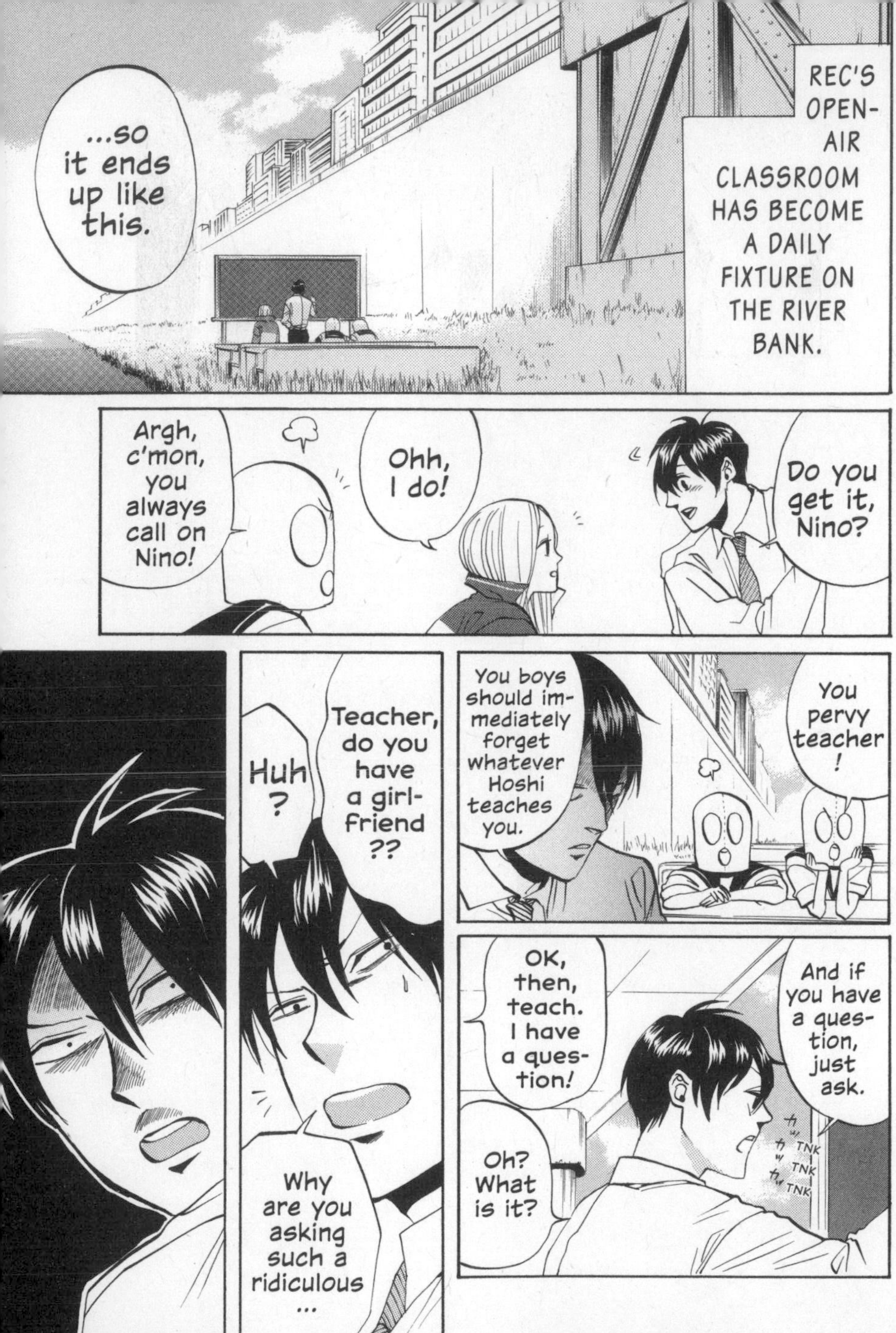
REC'S OPEN-AIR CLASSROOM HAS BECOME A DAILY FIXTURE ON THE RIVER BANK.
...so it ends up like this.
Do you get it, Nino?
Ohh, I do!
Argh, c'mon, you always call on Nino!
You pervy teacher!
You boys should immediately forget whatever Hoshi teaches you.
And if you have a question, just ask.
OK, then, teach. I have a question!
Oh? What is it?
TNK TNK TNK
Teacher, do you have a girlfriend??
Huh?
Why are you asking such a ridiculous ...

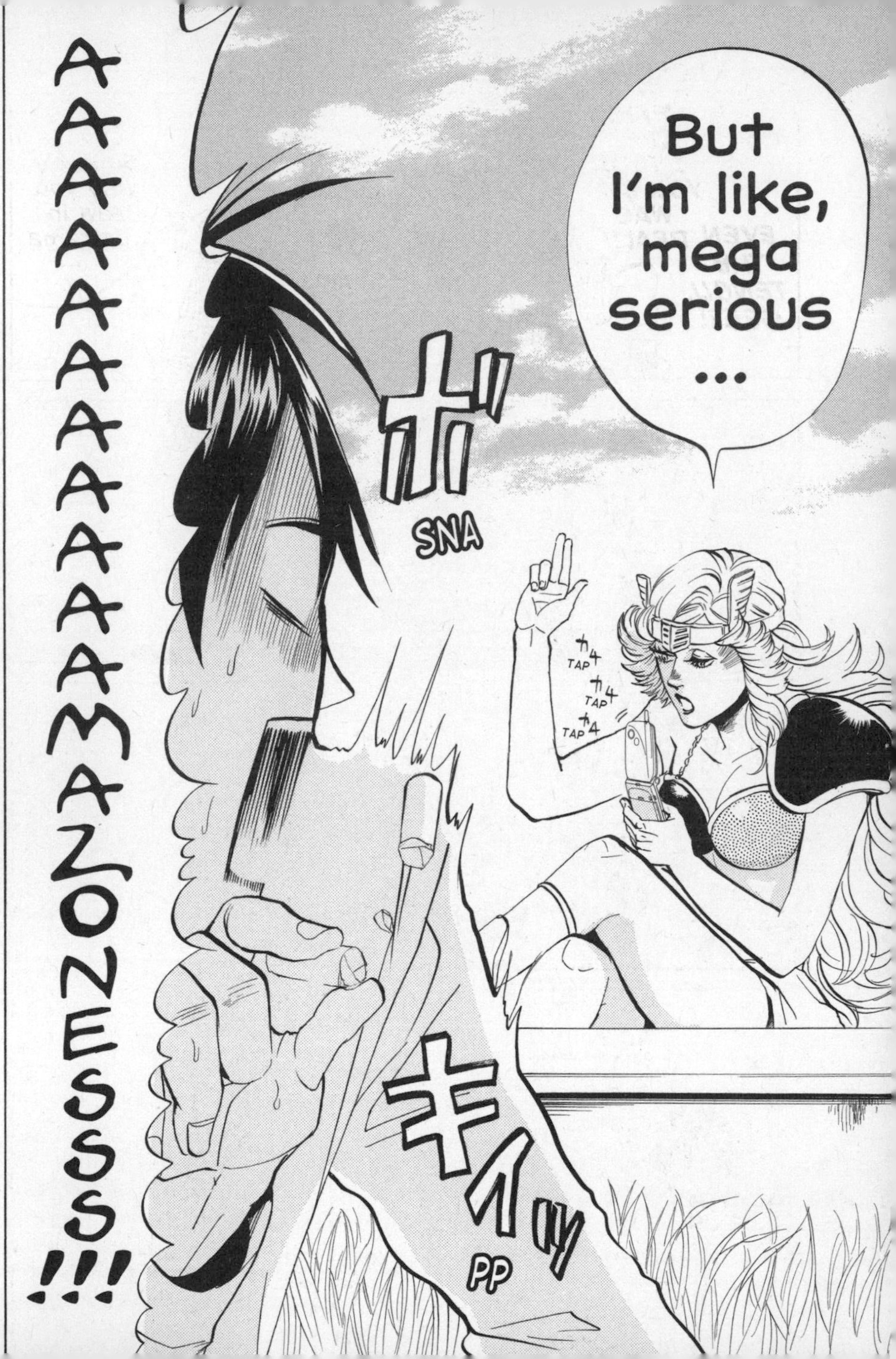

But I'm like, mega serious ...
TAP
TAP
TAP
SNA
PP
AAAAAAAAAAAMAZONESSS!!!

Chapter 185: The New Student is an Amazoness

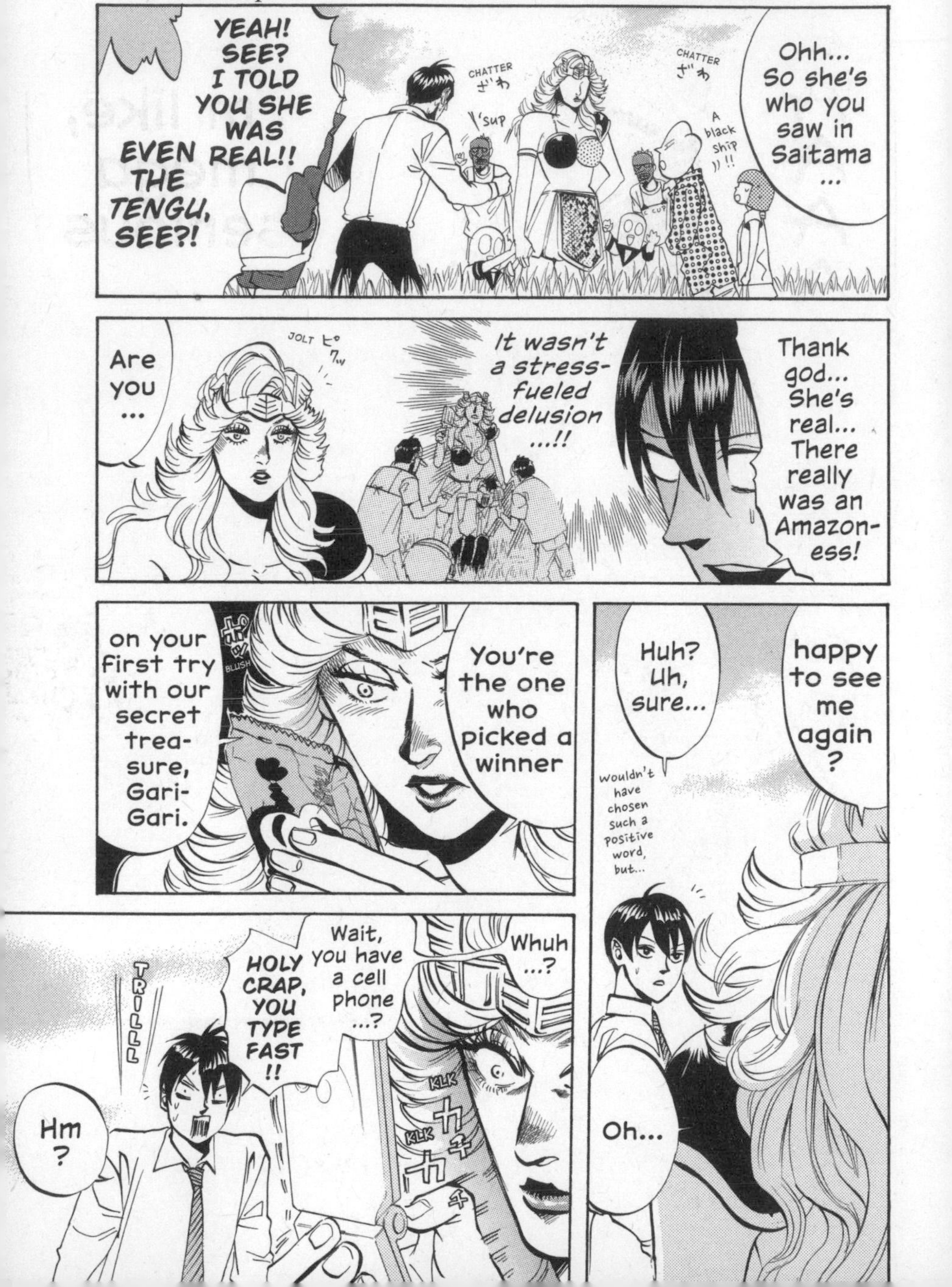
Ohh... So she's who you saw in Saitama ...
CHATTER ざわ
A black ship!!
CHATTER ざわ
'sup
YEAH! SEE? I TOLD YOU SHE WAS REAL!!
EVEN THE TENGU, SEE?!
Thank god... She's real... There really was an Amazoness!
It wasn't a stress-fueled delusion ...!!
JOLT ピクッ
Are you ...
happy to see me again?
Huh? Uh, sure...
wouldn't have chosen such a positive word, but...
Oh...
You're the one who picked a winner
BLUSH ポッ
on your first try with our secret treasure, Gari-Gari.
Whuh ...?
Wait, you have a cell phone ...?
KLK カチ
KLK カチ
HOLY CRAP, YOU TYPE FAST!!
TRILLL
Hm ?

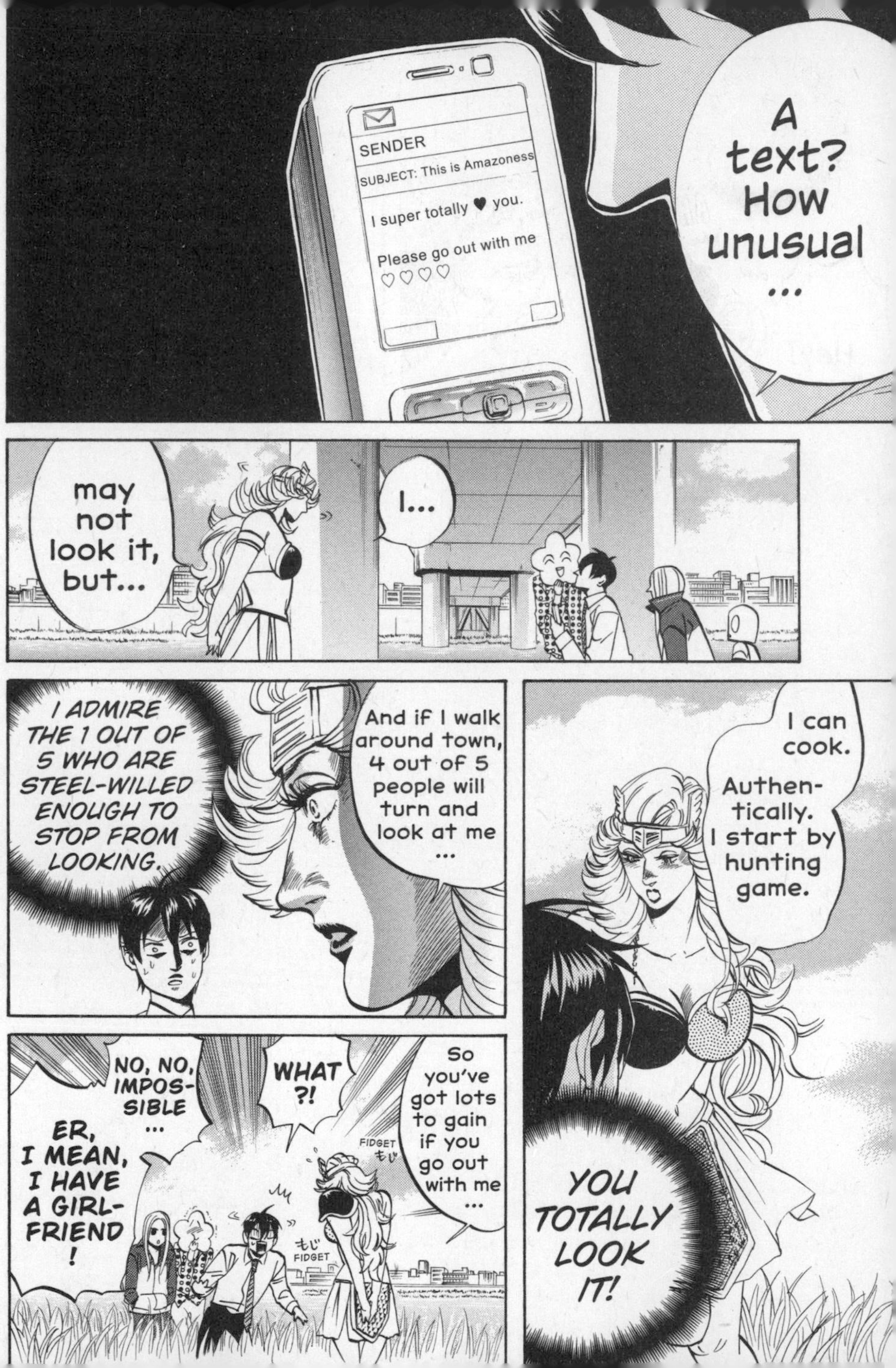
A text? How unusual ...
SENDER
SUBJECT: This is Amazoness
I super totally ♥ you.
Please go out with me
♡♡♡♡
I...
may not look it, but...
I can cook.
Authen-tically. I start by hunting game.
YOU TOTALLY LOOK IT!
And if I walk around town, 4 out of 5 people will turn and look at me ...
I ADMIRE THE 1 OUT OF 5 WHO ARE STEEL-WILLED ENOUGH TO STOP FROM LOOKING.
So you've got lots to gain if you go out with me ...
FIDGET もじ
もじ FIDGET
WHAT ?!
NO, NO, IMPOS-SIBLE ...
ER, I MEAN, I HAVE A GIRL-FRIEND !

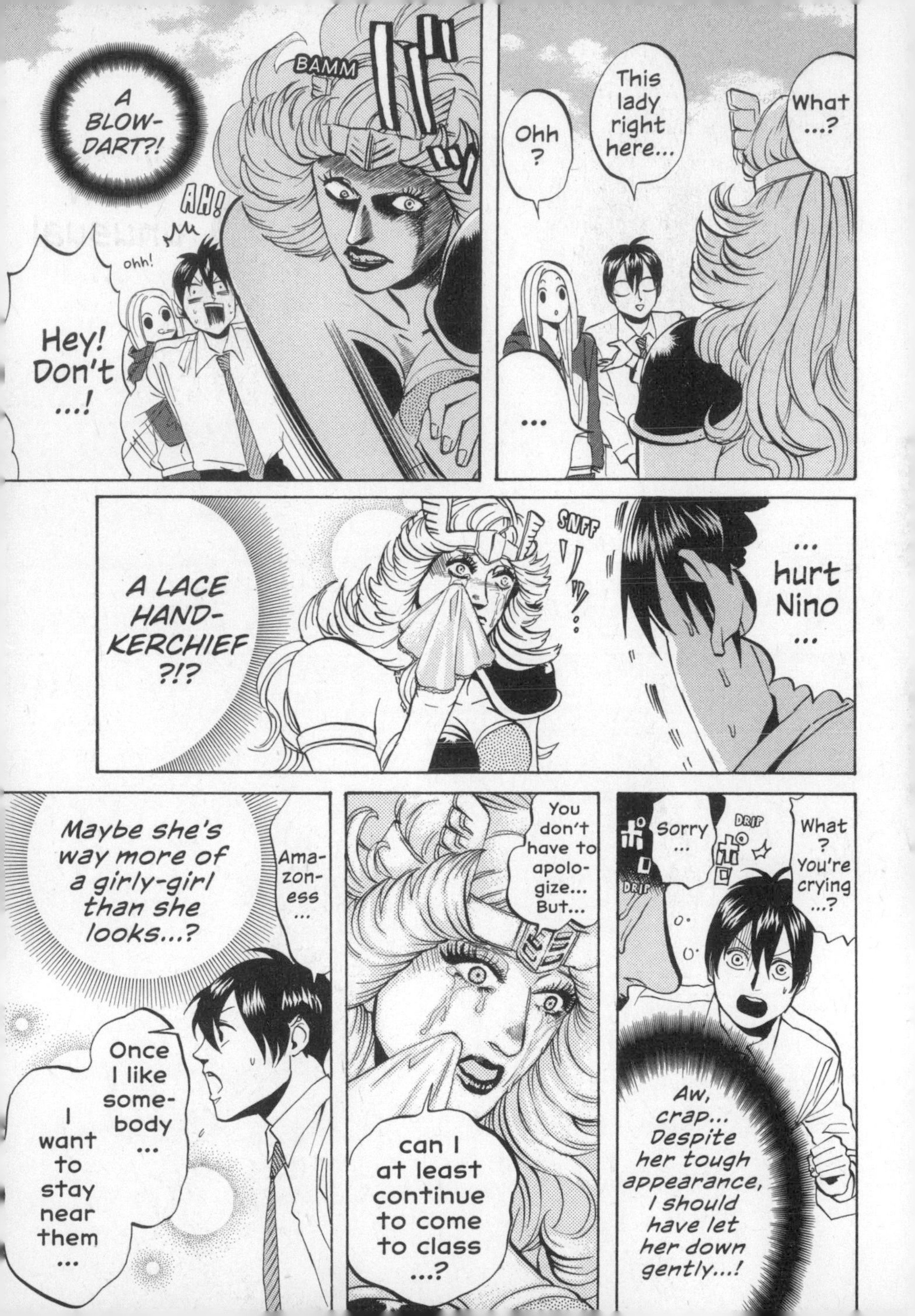
What ...?
This lady right here...
Ohh ?
...
BAMM
A BLOW-DART?!
AH!
ohh!
Hey! Don't ...!
... hurt Nino ...
SNFF
A LACE HAND-KERCHIEF ?!?
What ? You're crying ...?
DRIP
Sorry ...
DRIP
Aw, crap... Despite her tough appearance, I should have let her down gently...!
You don't have to apolo-gize... But...
can I at least continue to come to class ...?
Ama-zon-ess ...
Maybe she's way more of a girly-girl than she looks...?
Once I like some-body ...
I want to stay near them ...

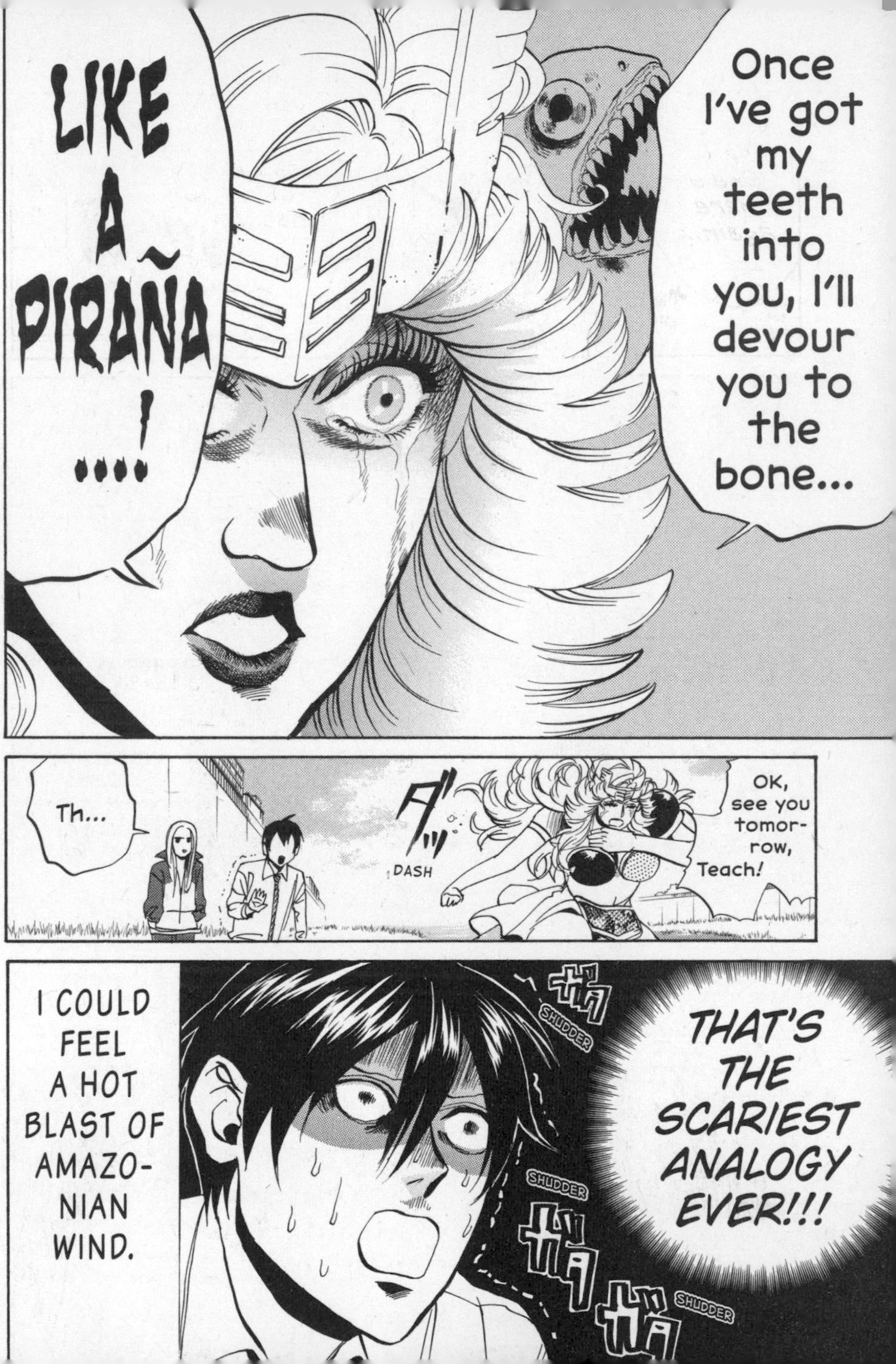
Once I've got my teeth into you, I'll devour you to the bone...
LIKE A PIRAÑA....!
OK, see you tomorrow, Teach!
DASH
Th...
THAT'S THE SCARIEST ANALOGY EVER!!!
SHUDDER
SHUDDER
SHUDDER
I COULD FEEL A HOT BLAST OF AMAZONIAN WIND.

Chapter 186: Love in a Song

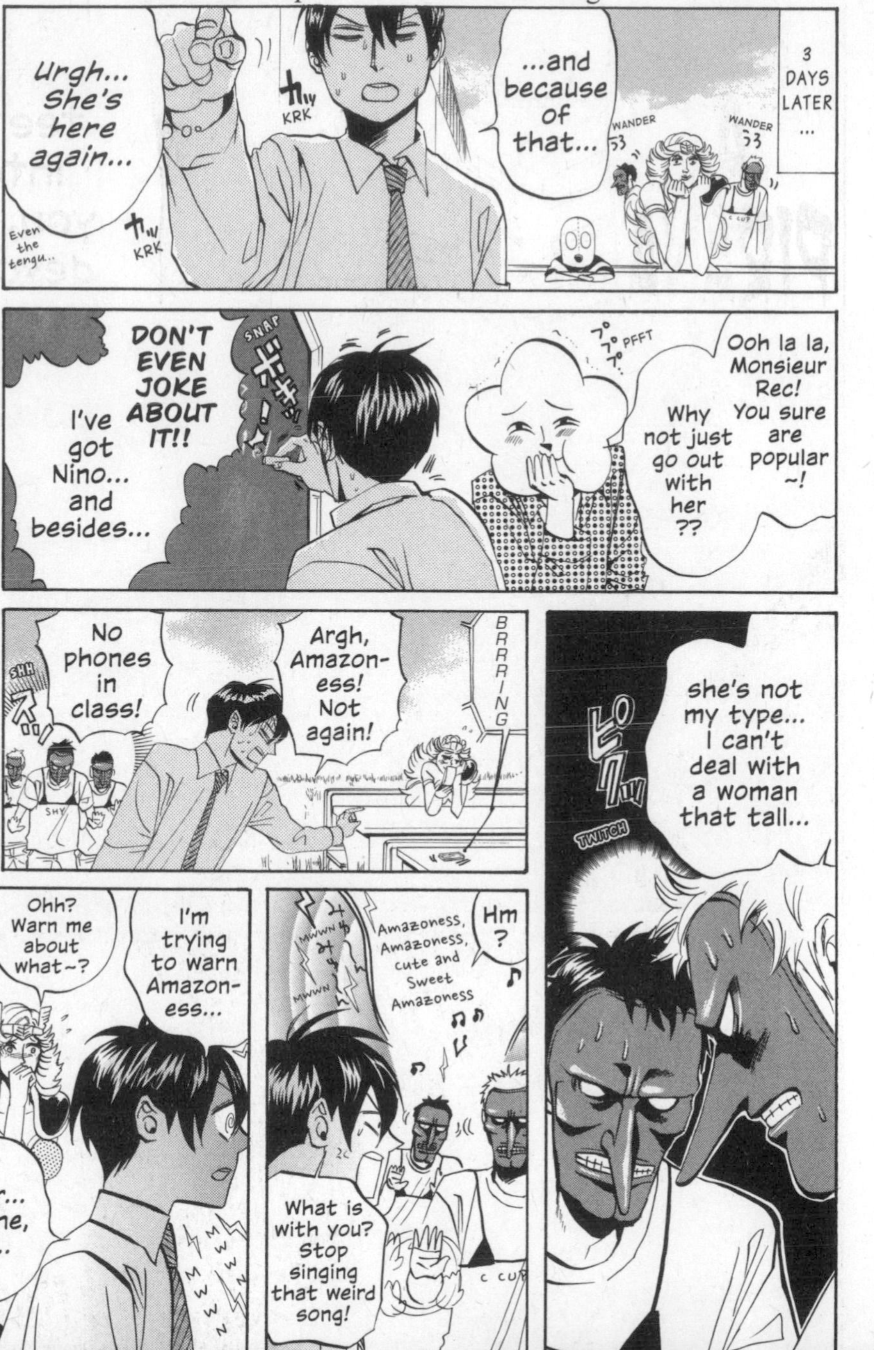
3 DAYS LATER...
WANDER
WANDER
...and because of that...
Urgh... She's here again...
KRK
KRK
Even the tengu...
C CUP
Ooh la la, Monsieur Rec! You sure are popular~!
Why not just go out with her??
PFFT
SNAP
DON'T EVEN JOKE ABOUT IT!!
I've got Nino... and besides...
she's not my type... I can't deal with a woman that tall...
TWITCH
BRRRING
Argh, Amazoness! Not again!
No phones in class!
SHH
SHY
Hm?
Amazoness, Amazoness, cute and Sweet Amazoness
MWWN
MWWN
What is with you? Stop singing that weird song!
C CUP
I'm trying to warn Amazoness...
Ohh? Warn me about what~?
Your... phone, it...
MWWN
MWWN

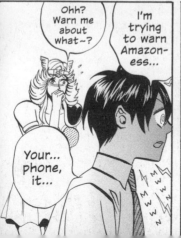

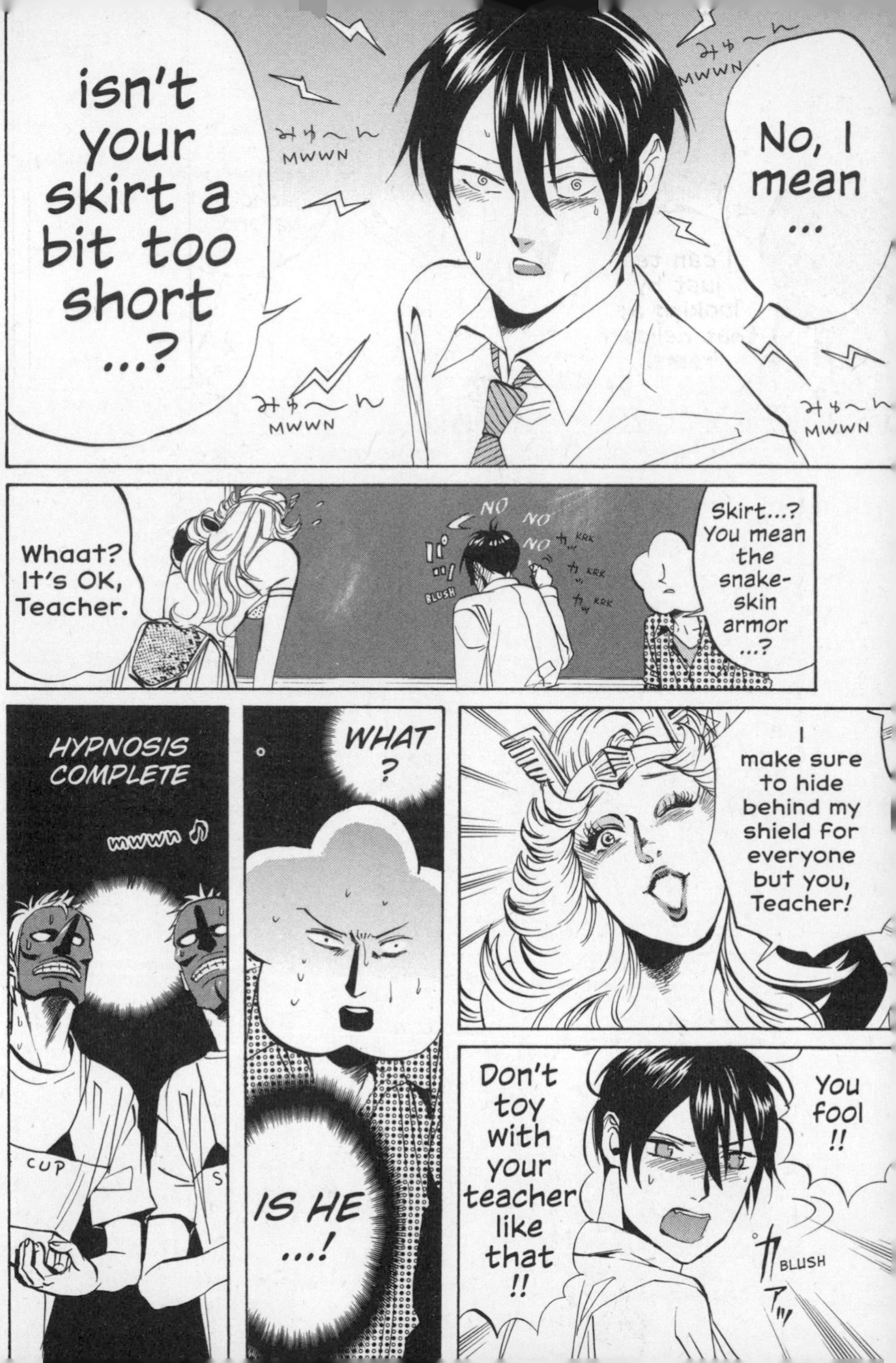
みゅ〜ん MWWN
No, I mean ...
みゅ〜ん MWWN
isn't your skirt a bit too short ...?
みゅ〜ん MWWN
みゅ〜ん MWWN
Skirt...? You mean the snake-skin armor ...?
NO NO NO
KRK KRK KRK
BLUSH
Whaat? It's OK, Teacher.
I make sure to hide behind my shield for everyone but you, Teacher!
You fool !!
Don't toy with your teacher like that !!
BLUSH
WHAT ?
IS HE ...!
HYPNOSIS COMPLETE
mwwn ♪
CUP

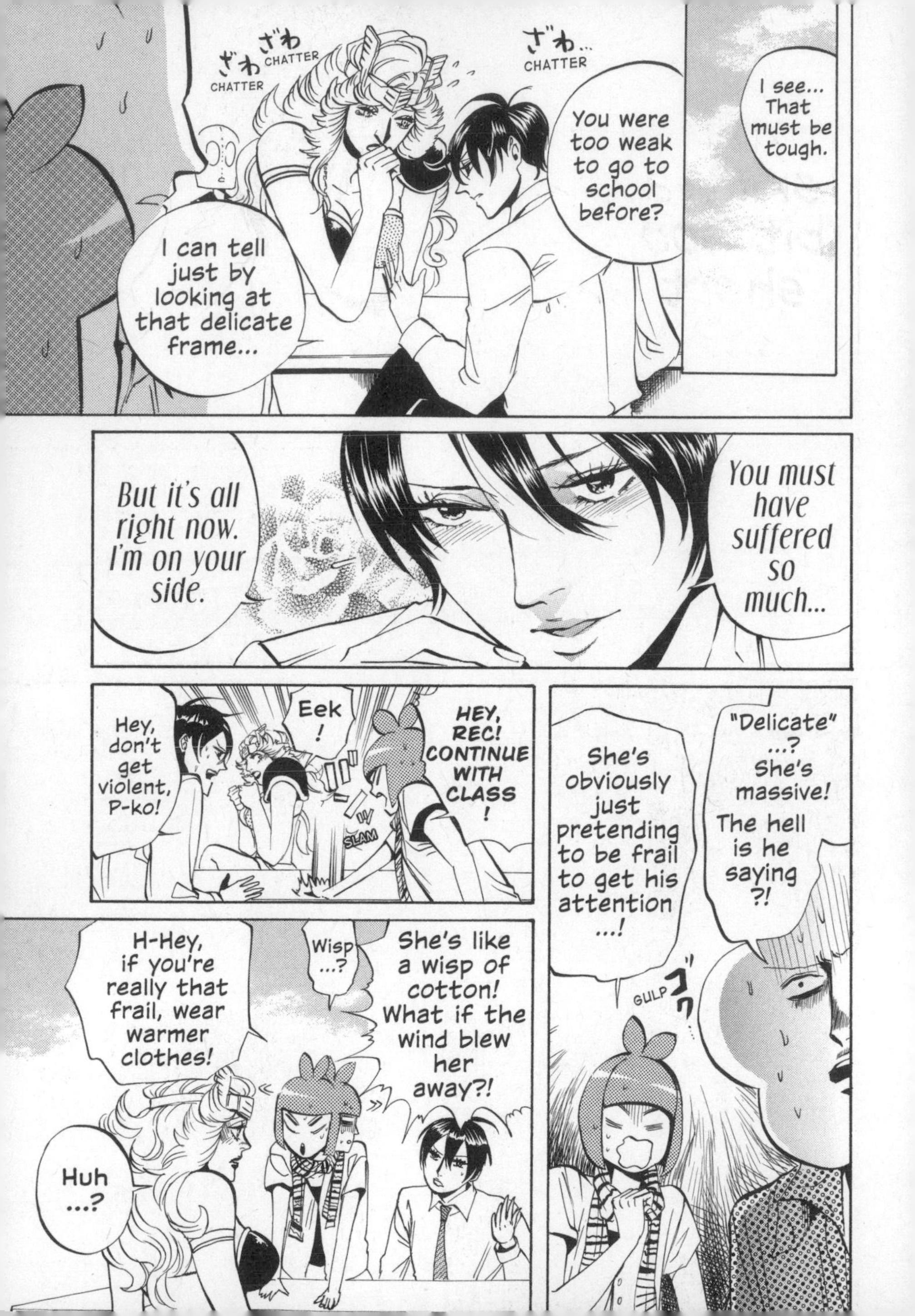
I see... That must be tough.
You were too weak to go to school before?
ざわ... CHATTER
ざわ CHATTER
ざわ CHATTER
I can tell just by looking at that delicate frame...
You must have suffered so much...
But it's all right now. I'm on your side.
"Delicate" ...? She's massive!
The hell is he saying?!
She's obviously just pretending to be frail to get his attention ...!
GULP
HEY, REC! CONTINUE WITH CLASS!
Eek!
SLAM
Hey, don't get violent, P-ko!
She's like a wisp of cotton! What if the wind blew her away?!
Wisp ...?
H-Hey, if you're really that frail, wear warmer clothes!
Huh ...?

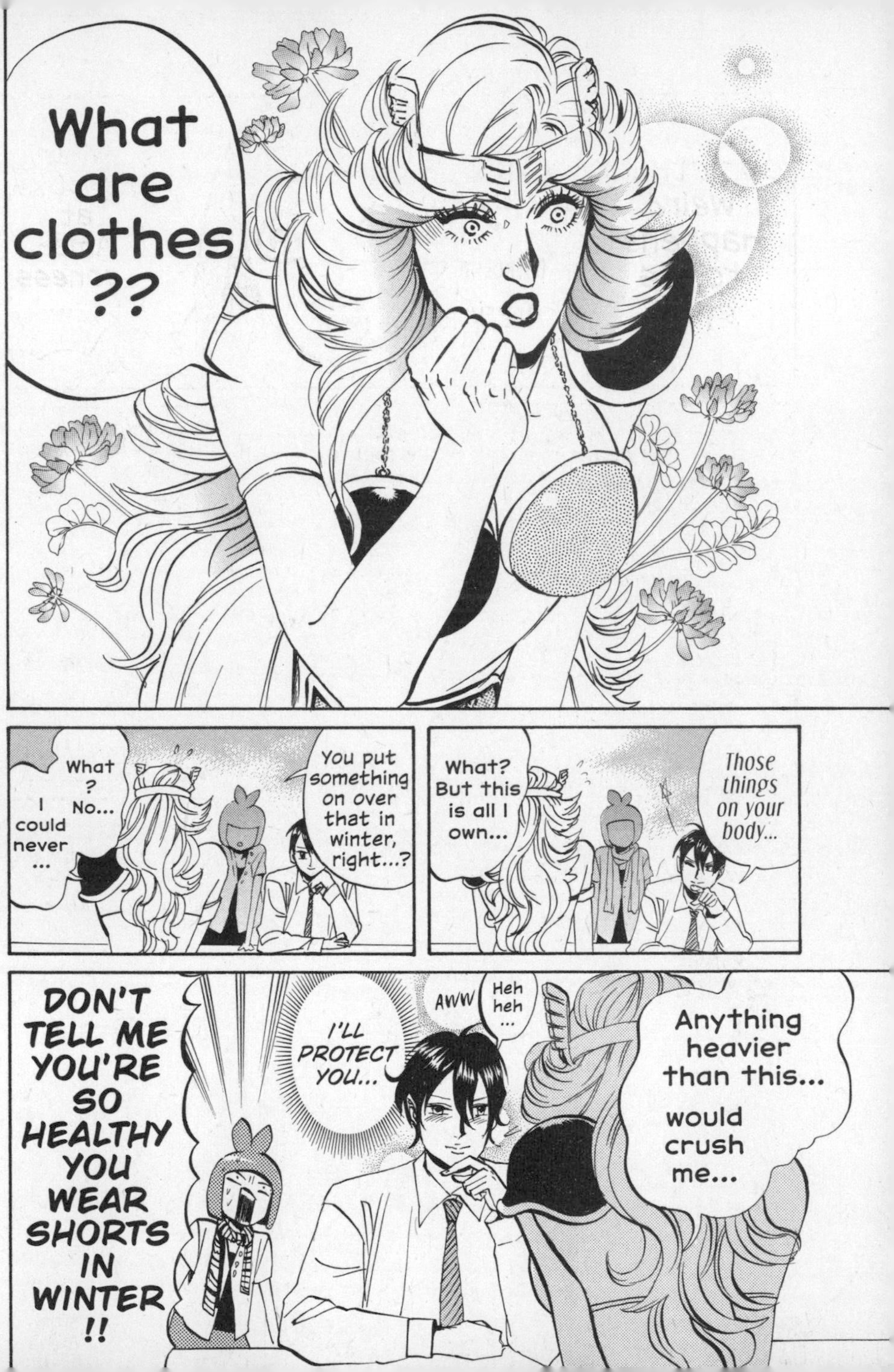
What are clothes ??
Those things on your body...
What? But this is all I own...
You put something on over that in winter, right...?
What? No...
I could never ...
Anything heavier than this... would crush me...
Heh heh ...
AWW
I'LL PROTECT YOU...
DON'T TELL ME YOU'RE SO HEALTHY YOU WEAR SHORTS IN WINTER !!

Chapter 187: Raging Love

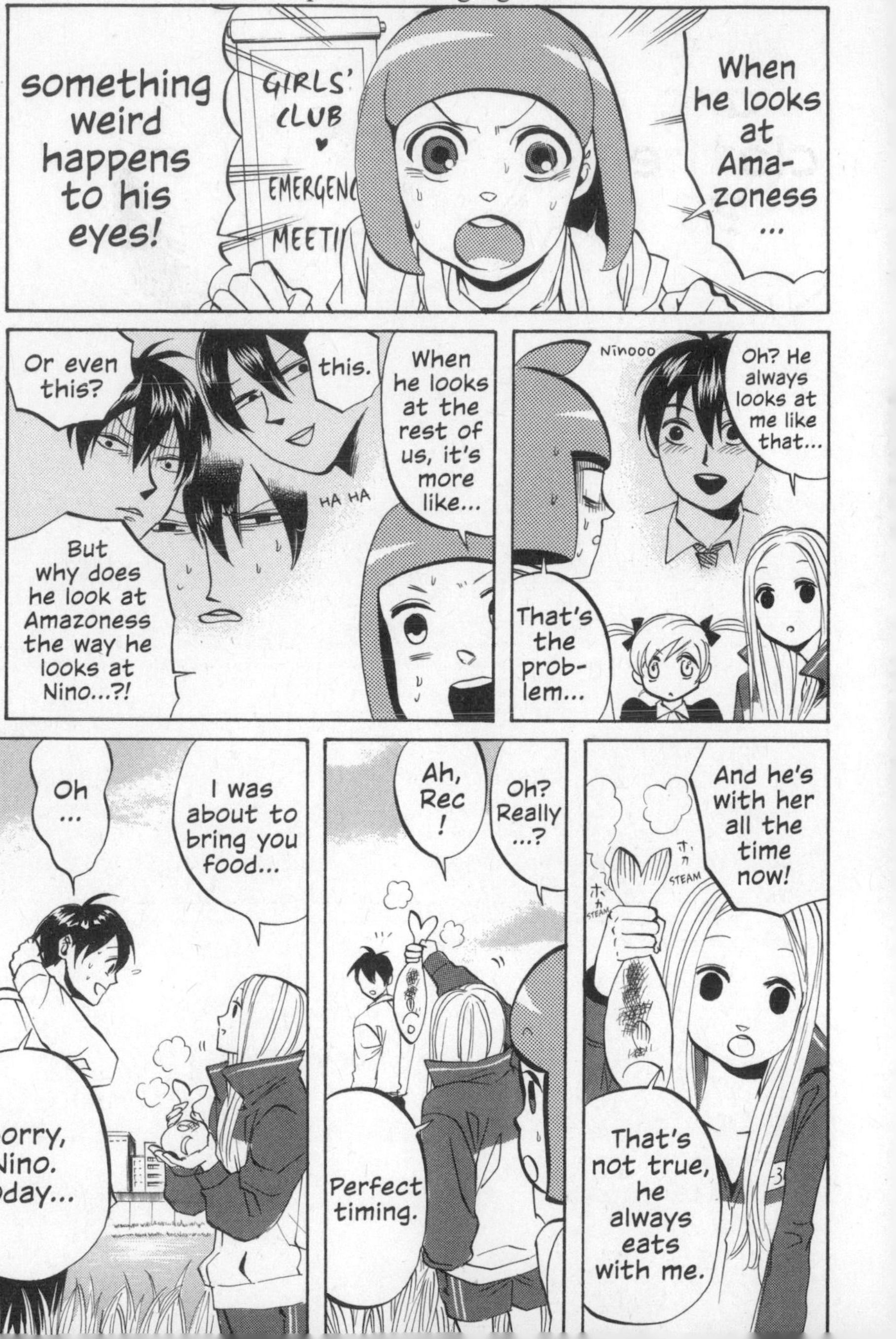
When he looks at Amazoness...
GIRLS' CLUB ♥ EMERGENC MEETI
something weird happens to his eyes!
Oh? He always looks at me like that...
Ninooo
That's the prob-lem...
When he looks at the rest of us, it's more like...
this.
Or even this?
HA HA
But why does he look at Amazoness the way he looks at Nino...?!
And he's with her all the time now!
STEAM
STEAM
That's not true, he always eats with me.
Oh? Really...?
Ah, Rec!
Perfect timing.
I was about to bring you food...
Oh...
Sorry, Nino. Today...

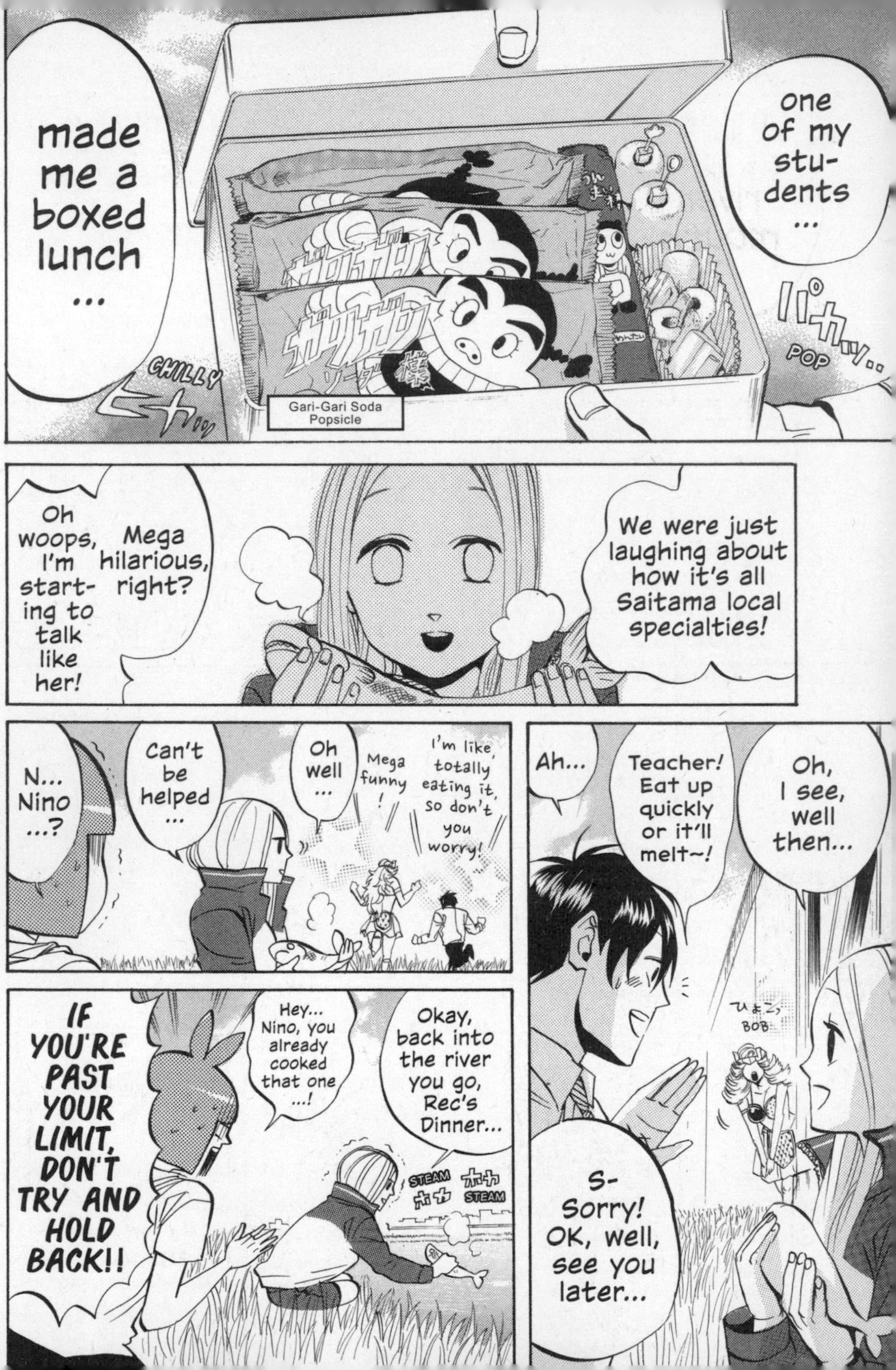
one of my stu-dents ...
パカッ
POP
made me a boxed lunch ...
CHILLY
ヒヤッ
Gari-Gari Soda Popsicle
We were just laughing about how it's all Saitama local specialties!
Mega hilarious, right?
Oh woops, I'm start-ing to talk like her!
Oh, I see, well then...
Teacher! Eat up quickly or it'll melt~!
Ah...
ひょこっ
BOB
S-Sorry! OK, well, see you later...
I'm like, totally eating it, so don't you worry!
Mega funny!
Oh well ...
Can't be helped ...
N... Nino ...?
Okay, back into the river you go, Rec's Dinner...
STEAM
ホカ
Hey... Nino, you already cooked that one ...!
IF YOU'RE PAST YOUR LIMIT, DON'T TRY AND HOLD BACK!!

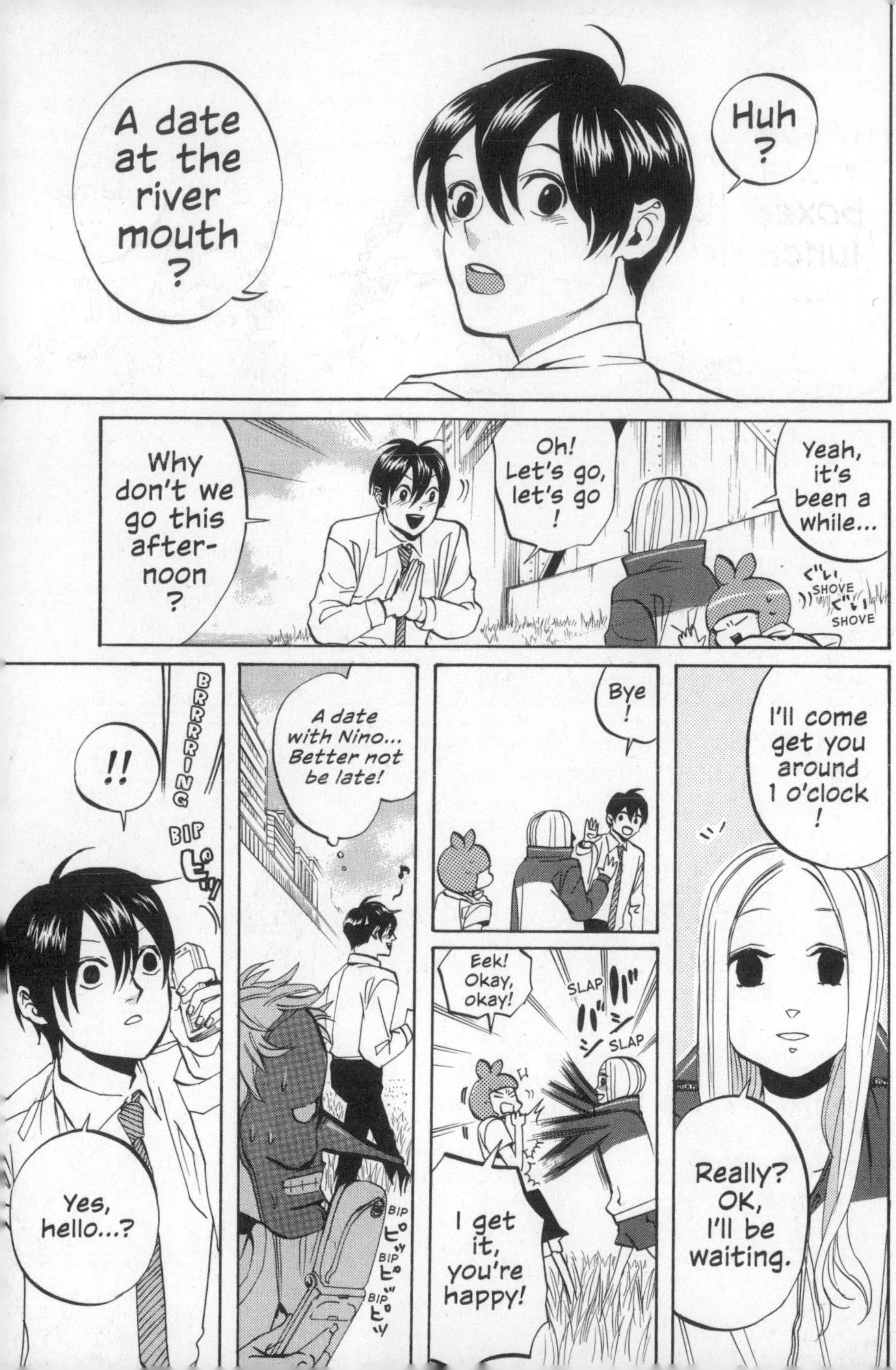
Huh?
A date at the river mouth?
Yeah, it's been a while...
SHOVE
SHOVE
Oh! Let's go, let's go!
Why don't we go this afternoon?
I'll come get you around 1 o'clock!
Really? OK, I'll be waiting.
Bye!
Eek! Okay, okay!
SLAP
SLAP
I get it, you're happy!
A date with Nino... Better not be late!
BIP
BIP
BIP
BRRRRING
BIP
!!
Yes, hello...?

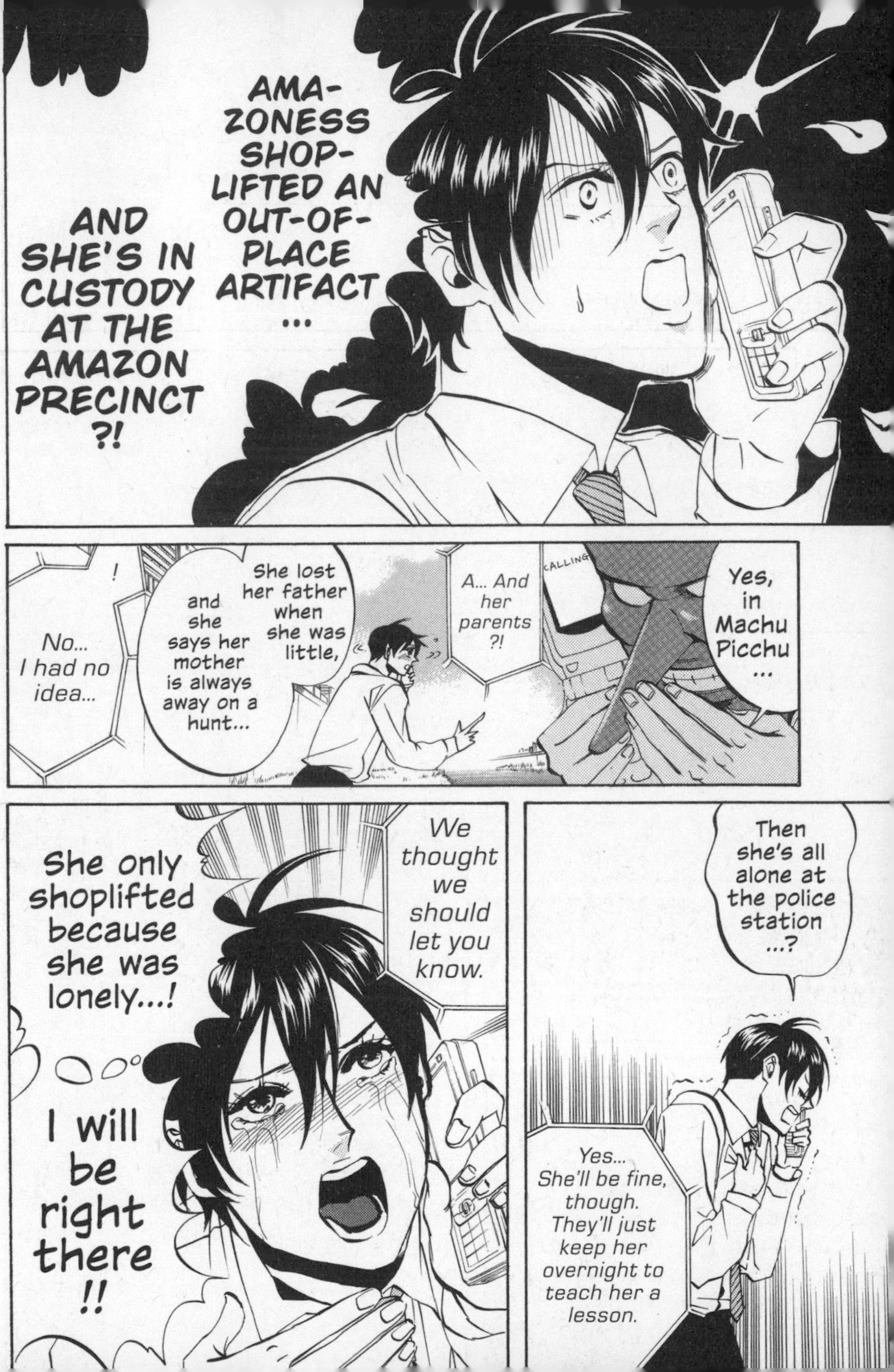
AMA-ZONESS SHOP-LIFTED AN OUT-OF-PLACE ARTIFACT ...
AND SHE'S IN CUSTODY AT THE AMAZON PRECINCT ?!
CALLING
Yes, in Machu Picchu ...
A... And her parents ?!
She lost her father when she was little,
and she says her mother is always away on a hunt...
!
No... I had no idea...
Then she's all alone at the police station ...?
Yes... She'll be fine, though. They'll just keep her overnight to teach her a lesson.
We thought we should let you know.
She only shoplifted because she was lonely...!
I will be right there !!

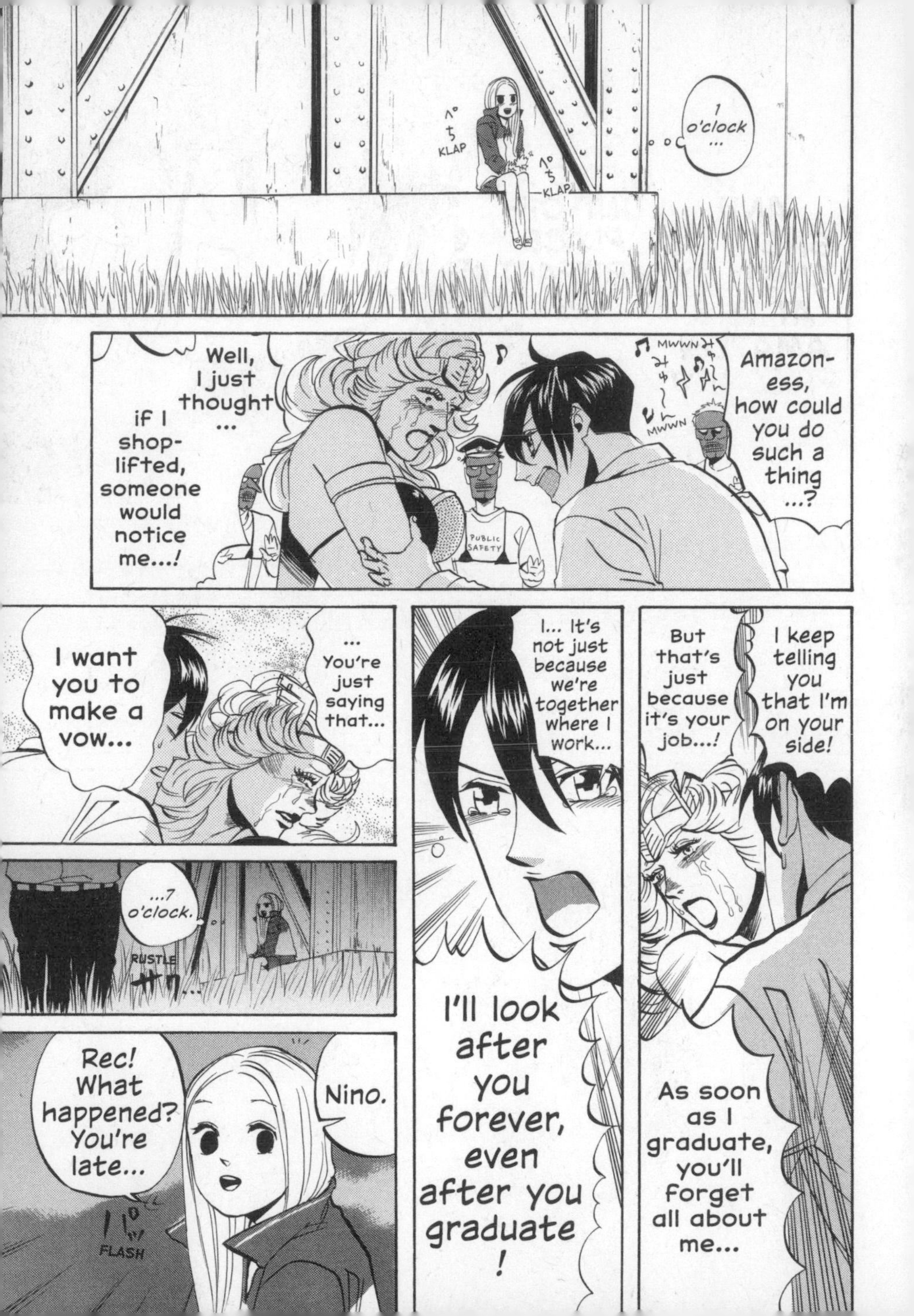
1 o'clock ...
KLAP
KLAP
Amazon-ess, how could you do such a thing ...?
MWWN
MWWN
Well, I just thought ... if I shop-lifted, someone would notice me...!
PUBLIC SAFETY
I keep telling you that I'm on your side!
But that's just because it's your job...!
As soon as I graduate, you'll forget all about me...
I... It's not just because we're together where I work...
I'll look after you forever, even after you graduate!
... You're just saying that...
I want you to make a vow...
...7 o'clock.
RUSTLE
Nino.
Rec! What happened? You're late...
FLASH

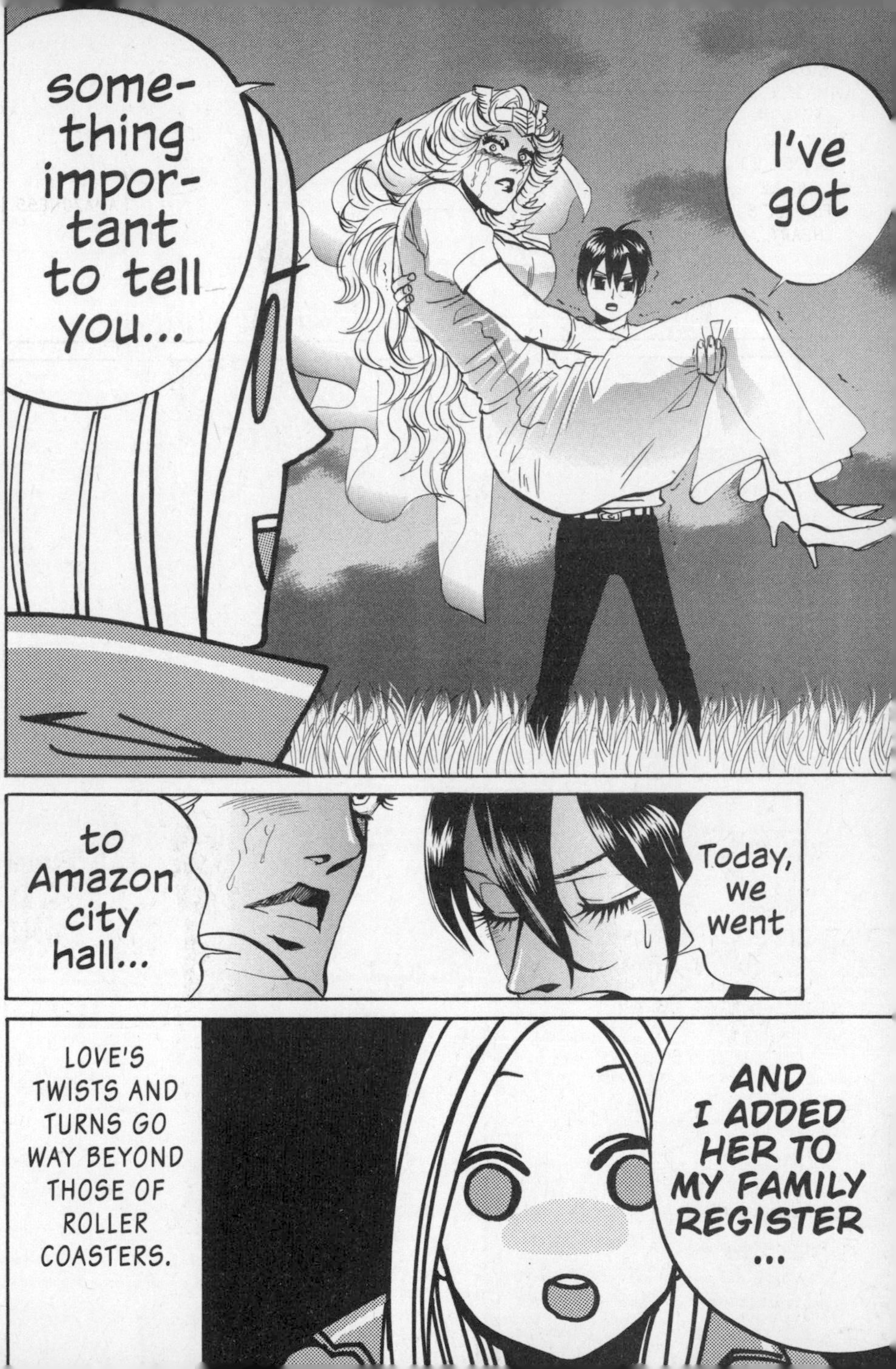
I've got
something important to tell you...
Today, we went
to Amazon city hall...
AND I ADDED HER TO MY FAMILY REGISTER...
LOVE'S TWISTS AND TURNS GO WAY BEYOND THOSE OF ROLLER COASTERS.

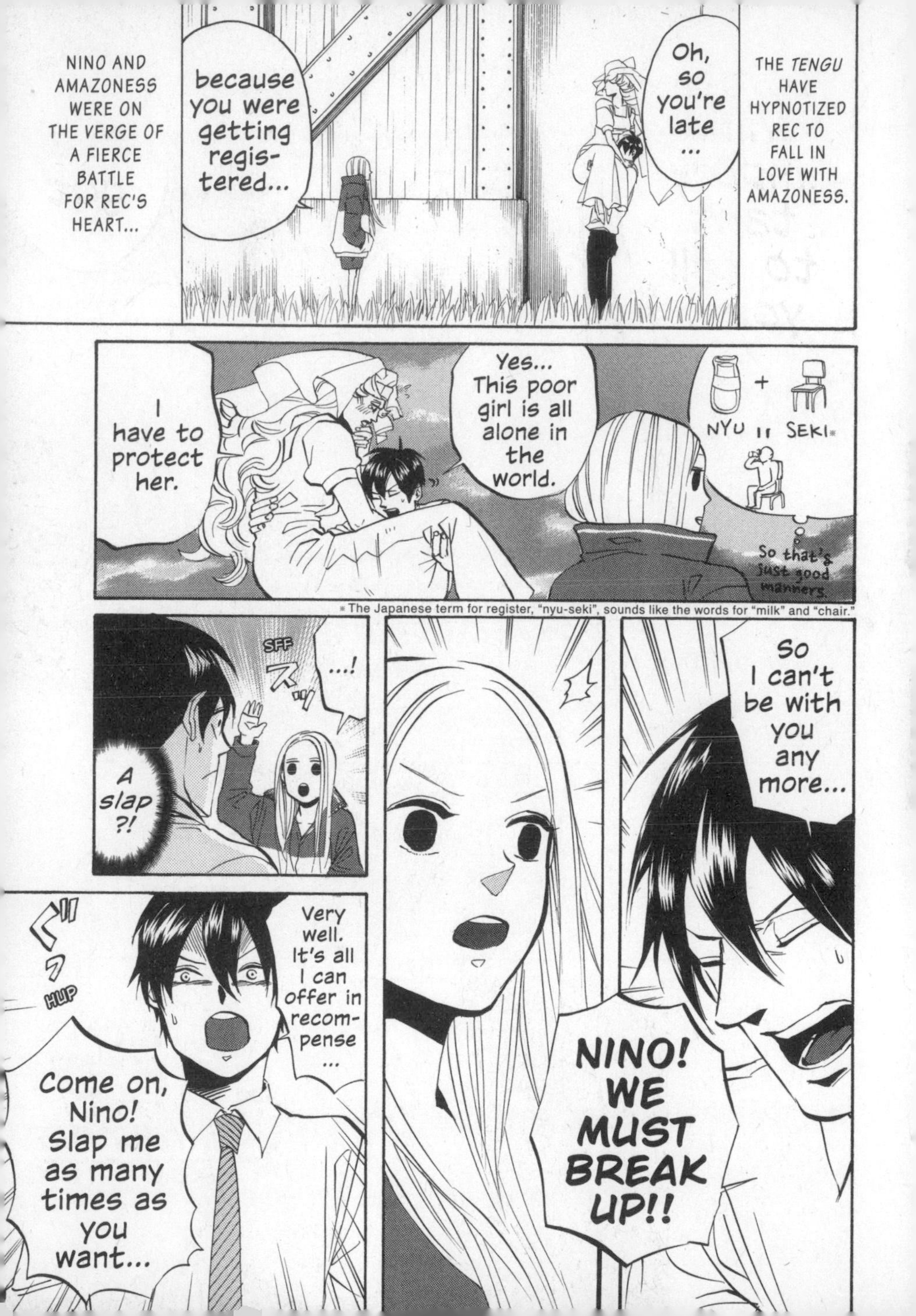
THE TENGU HAVE HYPNOTIZED REC TO FALL IN LOVE WITH AMAZONESS.
Oh, so you're late...
because you were getting regis-tered...
NINO AND AMAZONESS WERE ON THE VERGE OF A FIERCE BATTLE FOR REC'S HEART...
NYU + SEKI*
So that's just good manners.
Yes... This poor girl is all alone in the world.
I have to protect her.
So I can't be with you any more...
NINO! WE MUST BREAK UP!!
...!
SFF
A slap?!
Very well. It's all I can offer in recom-pense...
HUP
Come on, Nino! Slap me as many times as you want...

* The Japanese term for register, "nyu-seki", sounds like the words for "milk" and "chair."

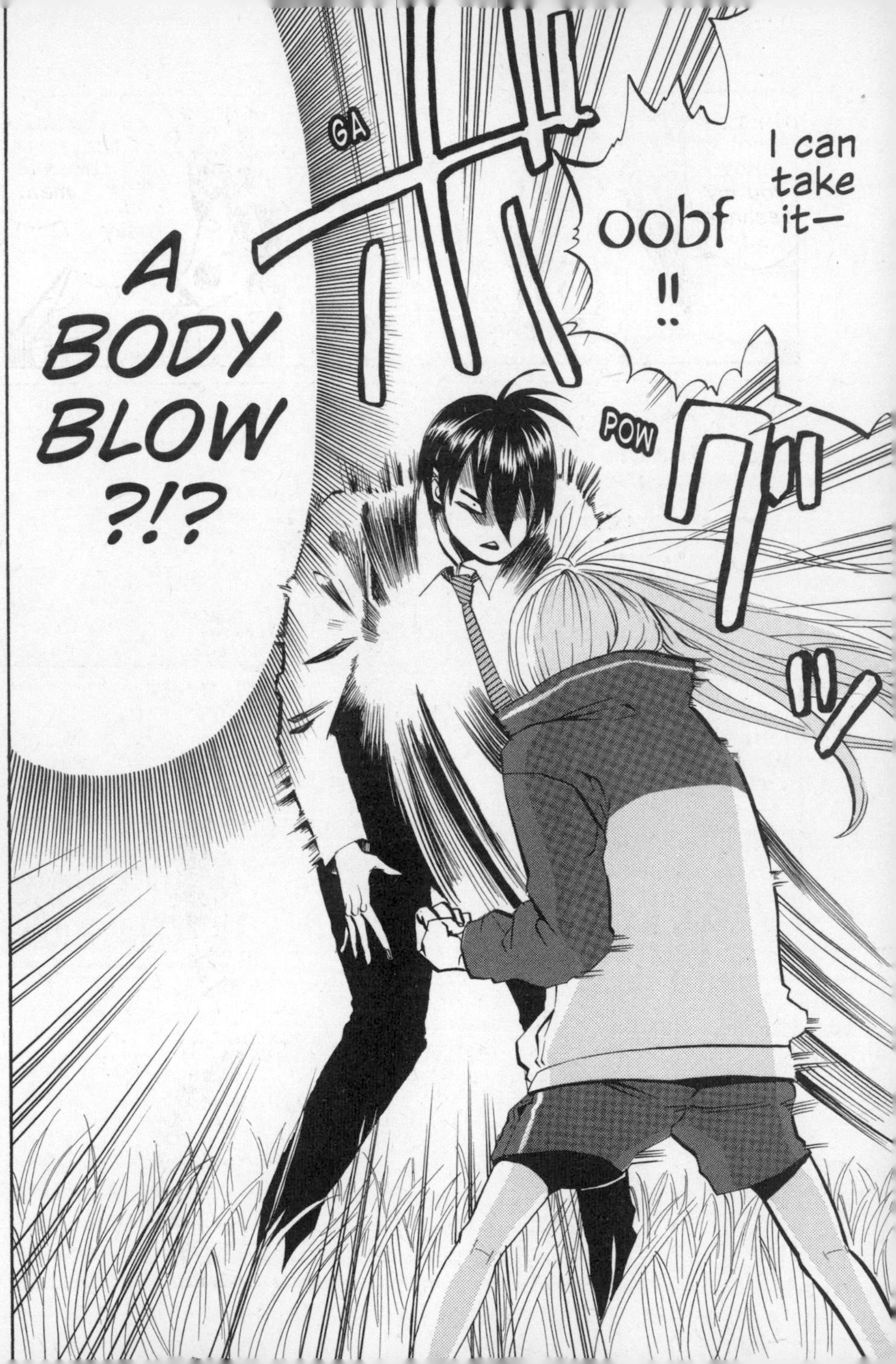
I can take it—
oobf !!
GA
POW
A BODY BLOW ?!?

Chapter 188: Expressions of Love

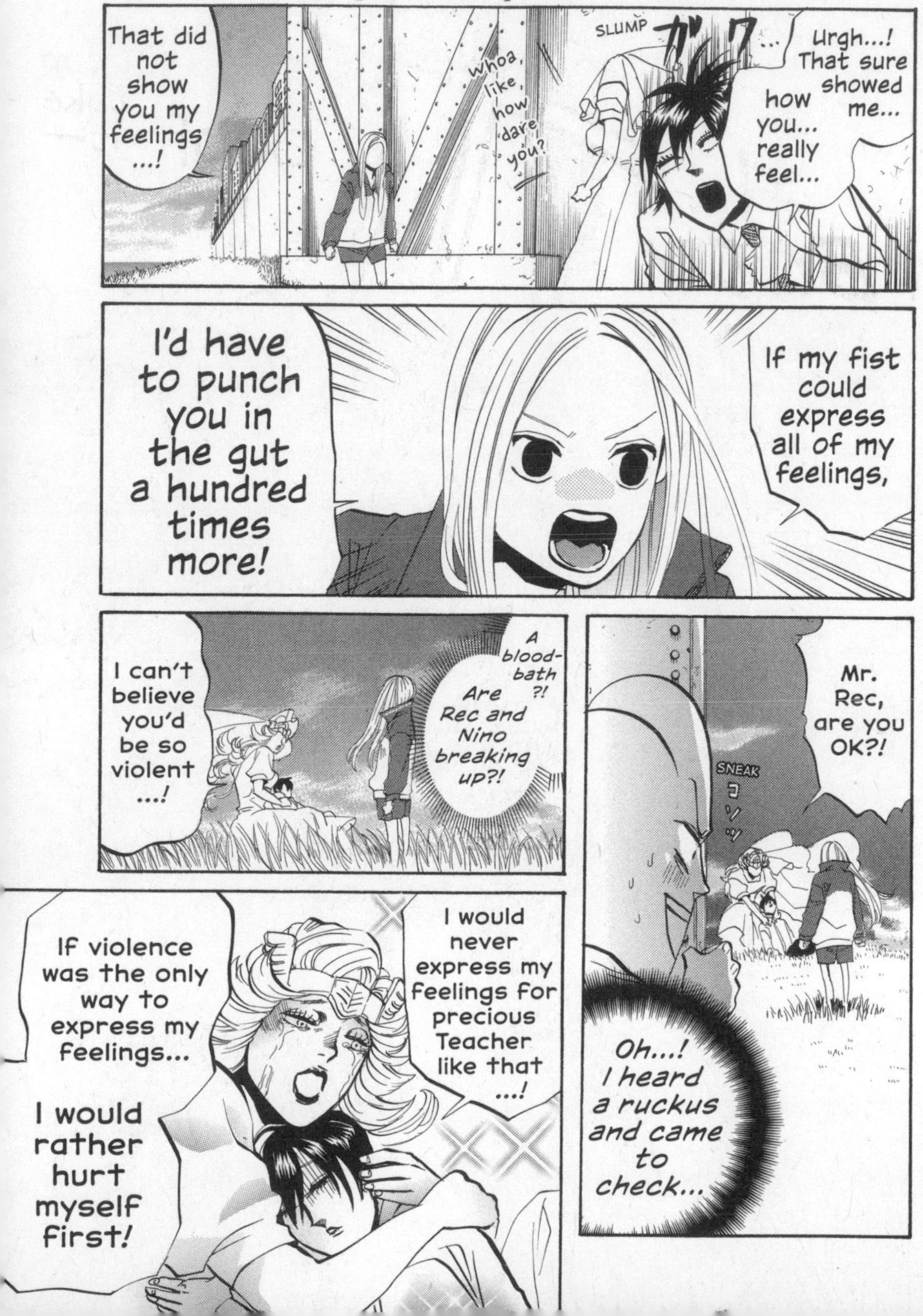
SLUMP
ガク
Urgh...! That sure showed me... how you... really feel...
whoa, like, how dare you?
That did not show you my feelings...!
If my fist could express all of my feelings,
I'd have to punch you in the gut a hundred times more!
Mr. Rec, are you OK?!
SNEAK
Oh...! I heard a ruckus and came to check...
A blood-bath?!
Are Rec and Nino breaking up?!
I can't believe you'd be so violent...!
I would never express my feelings for precious Teacher like that...!
If violence was the only way to express my feelings...
I would rather hurt myself first!

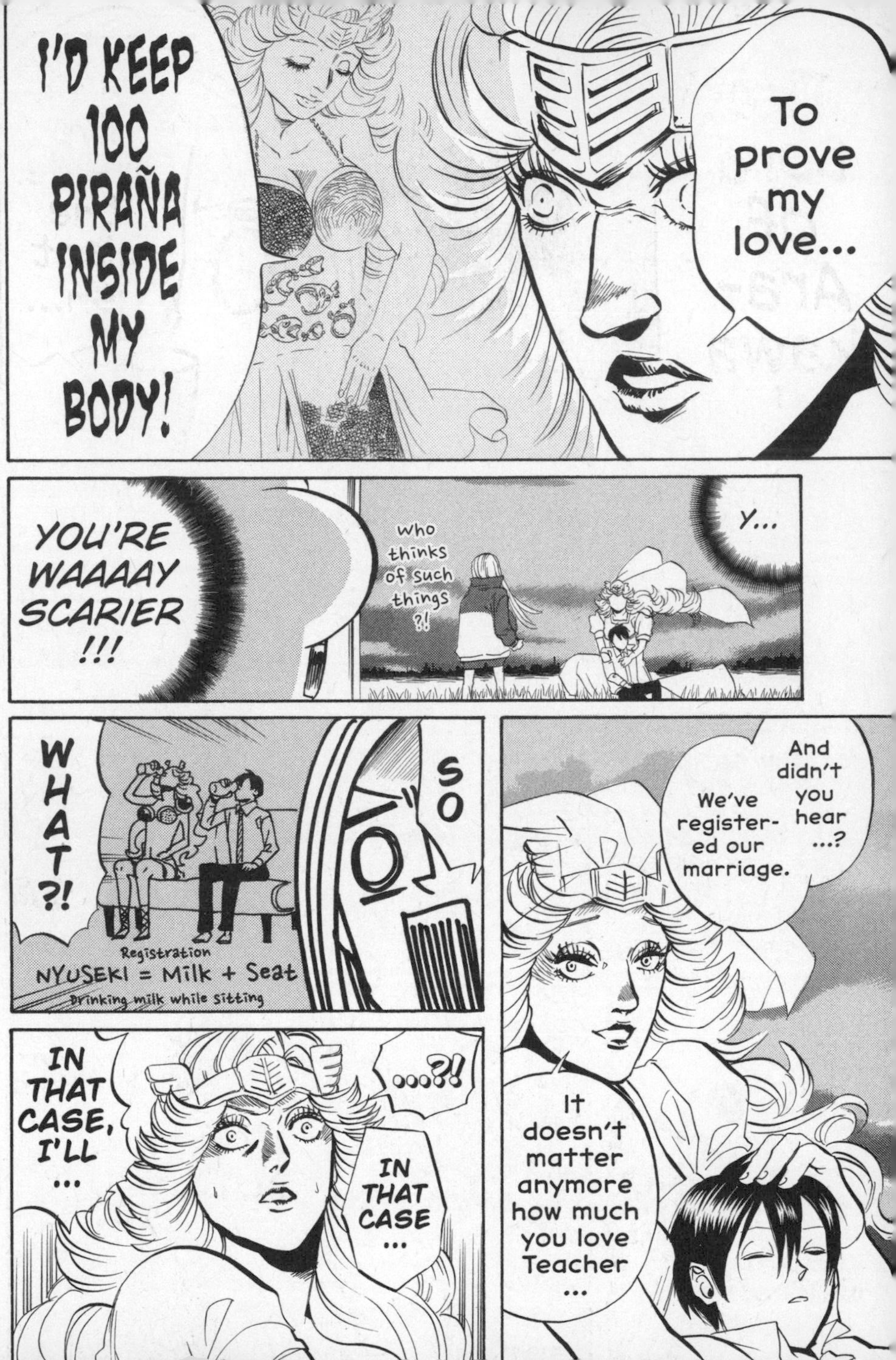
To prove my love...
I'D KEEP 100 PIRAÑA INSIDE MY BODY!
Y...
who thinks of such things ?!
YOU'RE WAAAAY SCARIER !!!
And didn't you hear ...?
We've register-ed our marriage.
It doesn't matter anymore how much you love Teacher ...
SO
WHAT ?!
Registration
NYUSEKI = Milk + Seat
Drinking milk while sitting
...?!
IN THAT CASE ...
IN THAT CASE, I'LL ...

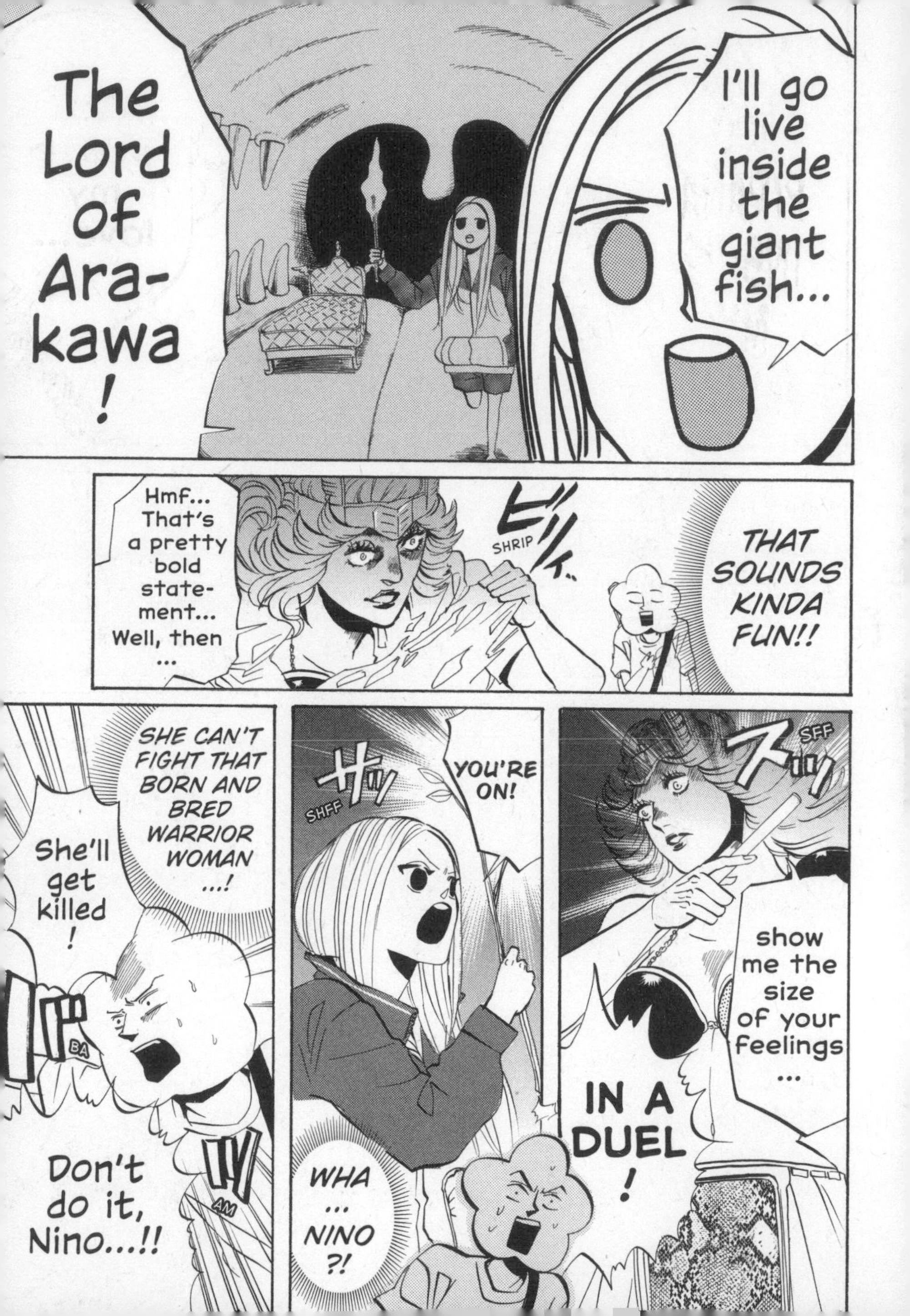
I'll go live inside the giant fish...
The Lord of Arakawa!
THAT SOUNDS KINDA FUN!!
SHRIP
Hmf... That's a pretty bold statement... Well, then ...
SFF
show me the size of your feelings ...
IN A DUEL!
SHFF
YOU'RE ON!
WHA ... NINO?!
SHE CAN'T FIGHT THAT BORN AND BRED WARRIOR WOMAN ...!
She'll get killed!
BA
AM
Don't do it, Nino...!!

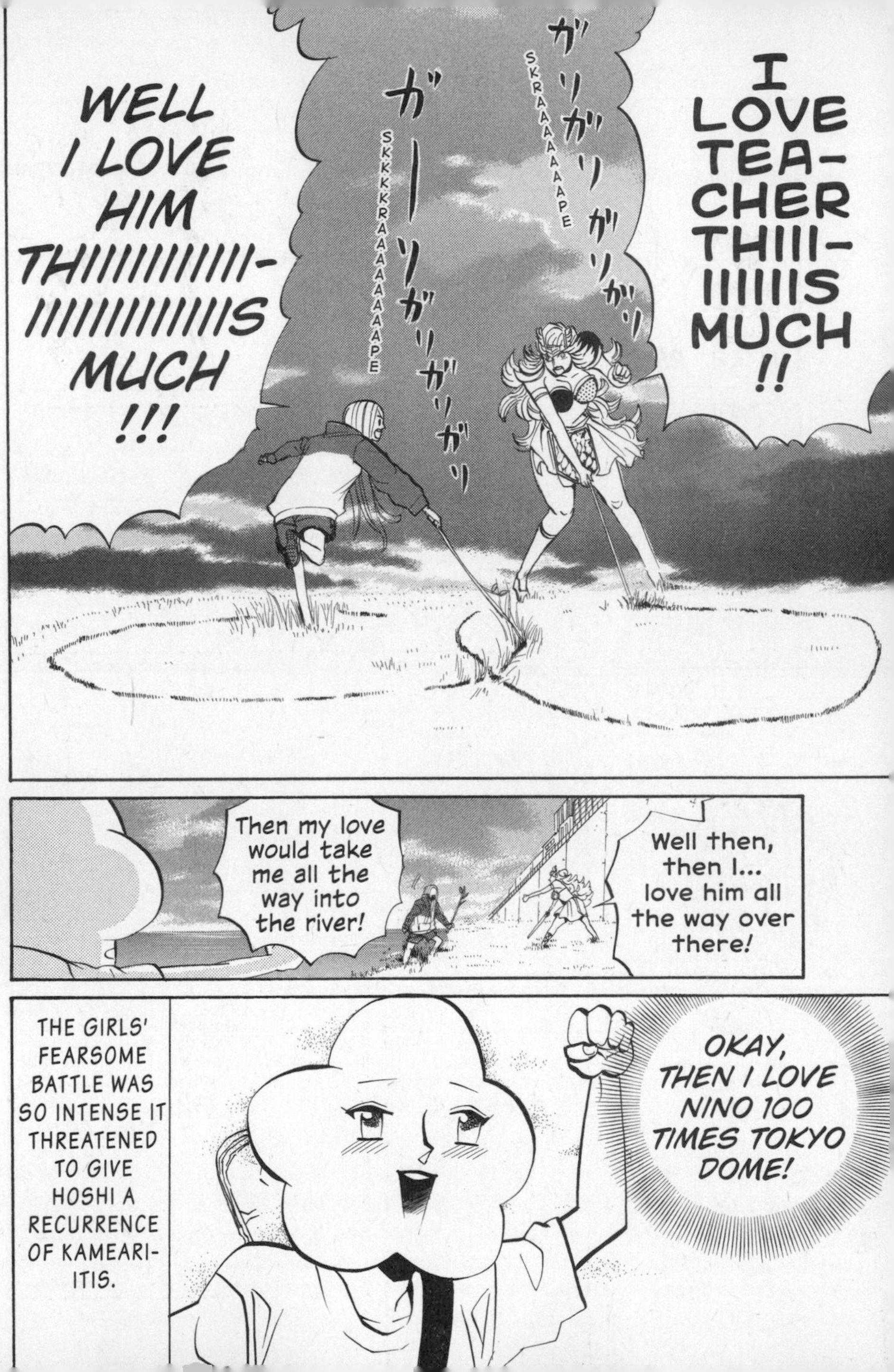
I LOVE TEACHER THIIII-IIIIIIS MUCH!!
ガリガリガリガリ
SKRAAAAAAAAPE
ガーリガリガリガリ
SKKKKRAAAAAAAAAAAPE
WELL I LOVE HIM THIIIIIIIIIIII-IIIIIIIIIIIIIS MUCH!!!
Well then, then I... love him all the way over there!
Then my love would take me all the way into the river!
OKAY, THEN I LOVE NINO 100 TIMES TOKYO DOME!
THE GIRLS' FEARSOME BATTLE WAS SO INTENSE IT THREATENED TO GIVE HOSHI A RECURRENCE OF KAMEARI-ITIS.

Chapter 189: Unyielding Emotions

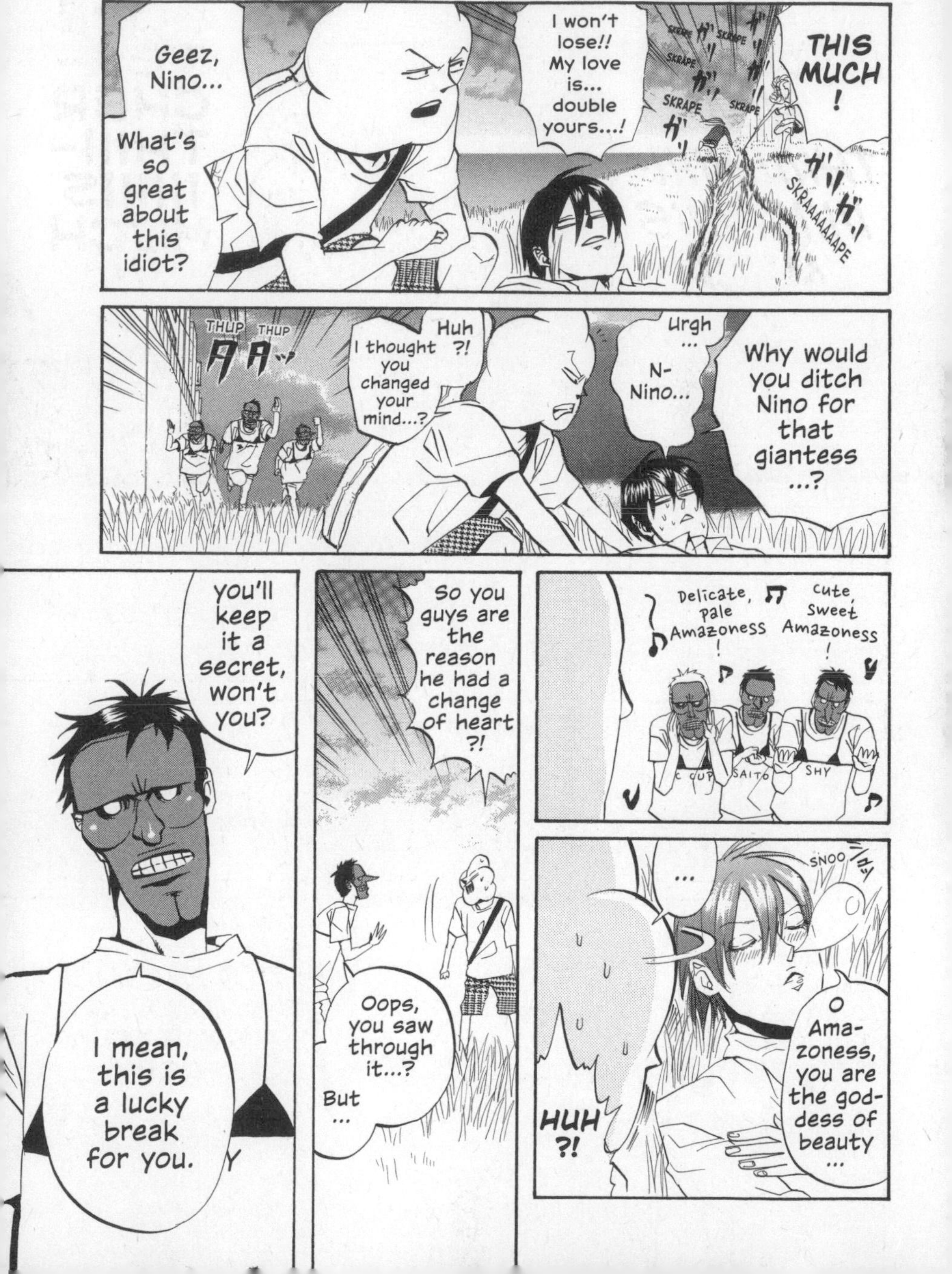
SKRAPE
SKRAPE
SKRAPE
SKRAPE
SKRAPE
THIS MUCH!
I won't lose!! My love is... double yours...!
Geez, Nino...
What's so great about this idiot?
SKRAAAAAAAPE
Why would you ditch Nino for that giantess...?
Urgh... N-Nino...
Huh?!
I thought you changed your mind...?
THUP THUP
Cute, Sweet Amazoness!
Delicate, Pale Amazoness!
SHY
SAITO
C CUP
SNOO
O Amazoness, you are the goddess of beauty...
...
HUH?!
So you guys are the reason he had a change of heart?!
Oops, you saw through it...?
But...
you'll keep it a secret, won't you?
I mean, this is a lucky break for you.

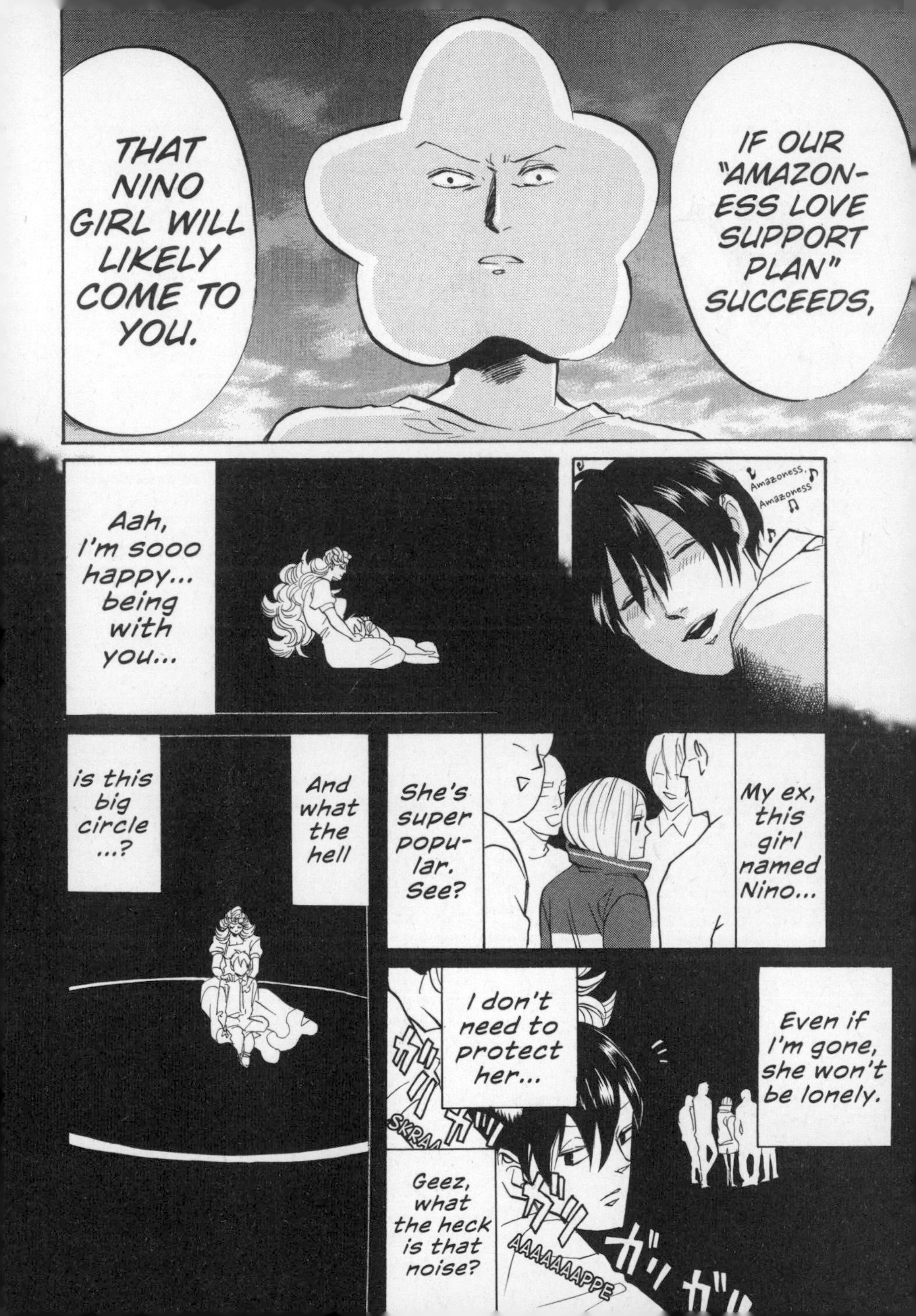
IF OUR "AMAZONESS LOVE SUPPORT PLAN" SUCCEEDS,
THAT NINO GIRL WILL LIKELY COME TO YOU.
Amazoness, Amazoness
Aah, I'm sooo happy... being with you...
My ex, this girl named Nino...
She's super popular. See?
And what the hell
is this big circle ...?
Even if I'm gone, she won't be lonely.
I don't need to protect her...
SKRAA
Geez, what the heck is that noise?
AAAAAAAPPE

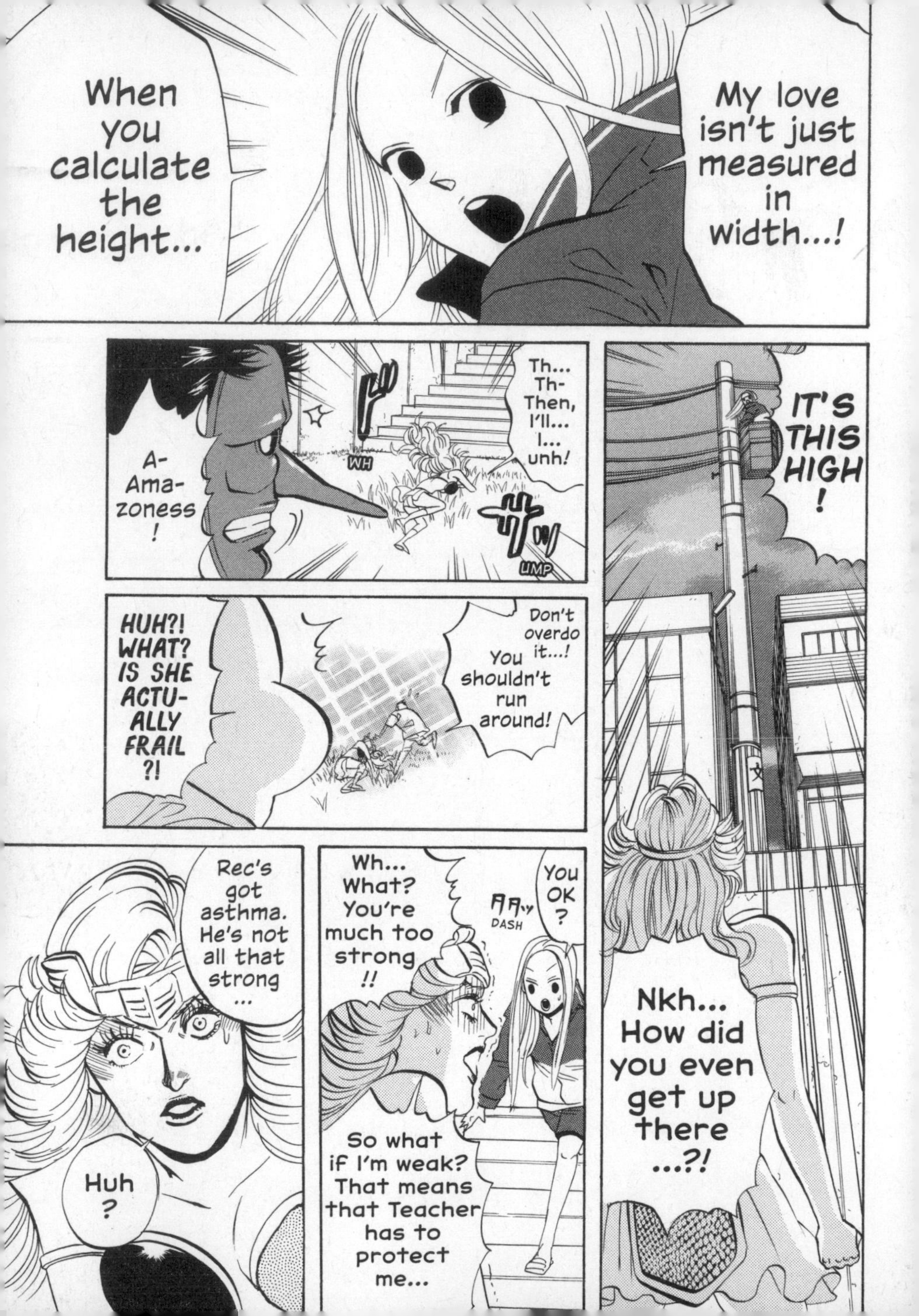

My love isn't just measured in width...!
When you calculate the height...
IT'S THIS HIGH!
Nkh... How did you even get up there ...?!
Th... Th-Then, I'll... I... unh!
WH
UMP
A-Amazoness!
Don't overdo it...! You shouldn't run around!
HUH?! WHAT? IS SHE ACTUALLY FRAIL?!
You OK?
DASH
Wh... What? You're much too strong!!
So what if I'm weak? That means that Teacher has to protect me...
Rec's got asthma. He's not all that strong...
Huh?

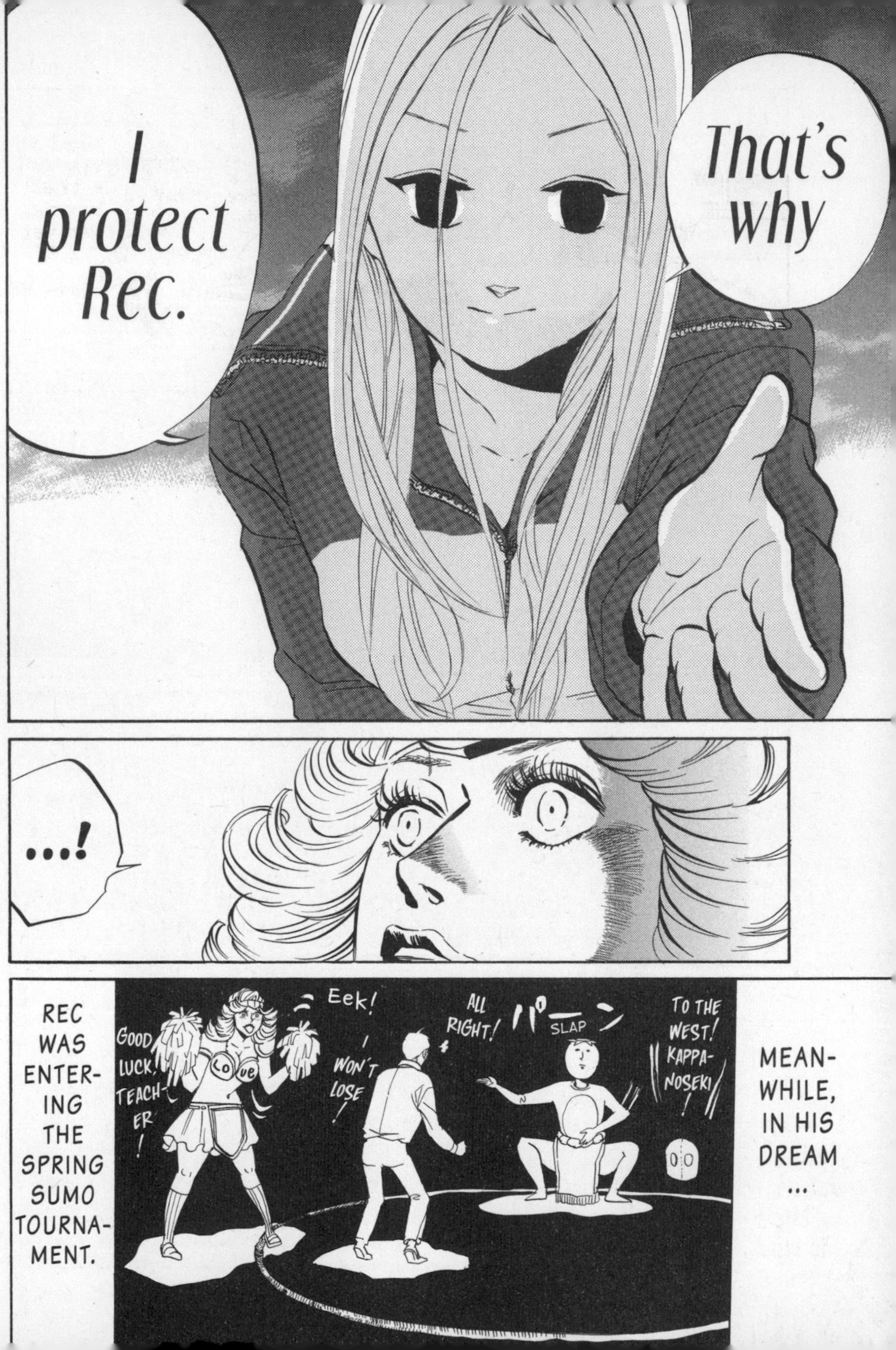
That's why
I protect Rec.
...!
MEAN-WHILE, IN HIS DREAM ...
TO THE WEST! KAPPA-NOSEKI!
SLAP
ALL RIGHT!
Eek!
I WON'T LOSE!
GOOD LUCK, TEACH-ER!
REC WAS ENTER-ING THE SPRING SUMO TOURNA-MENT.

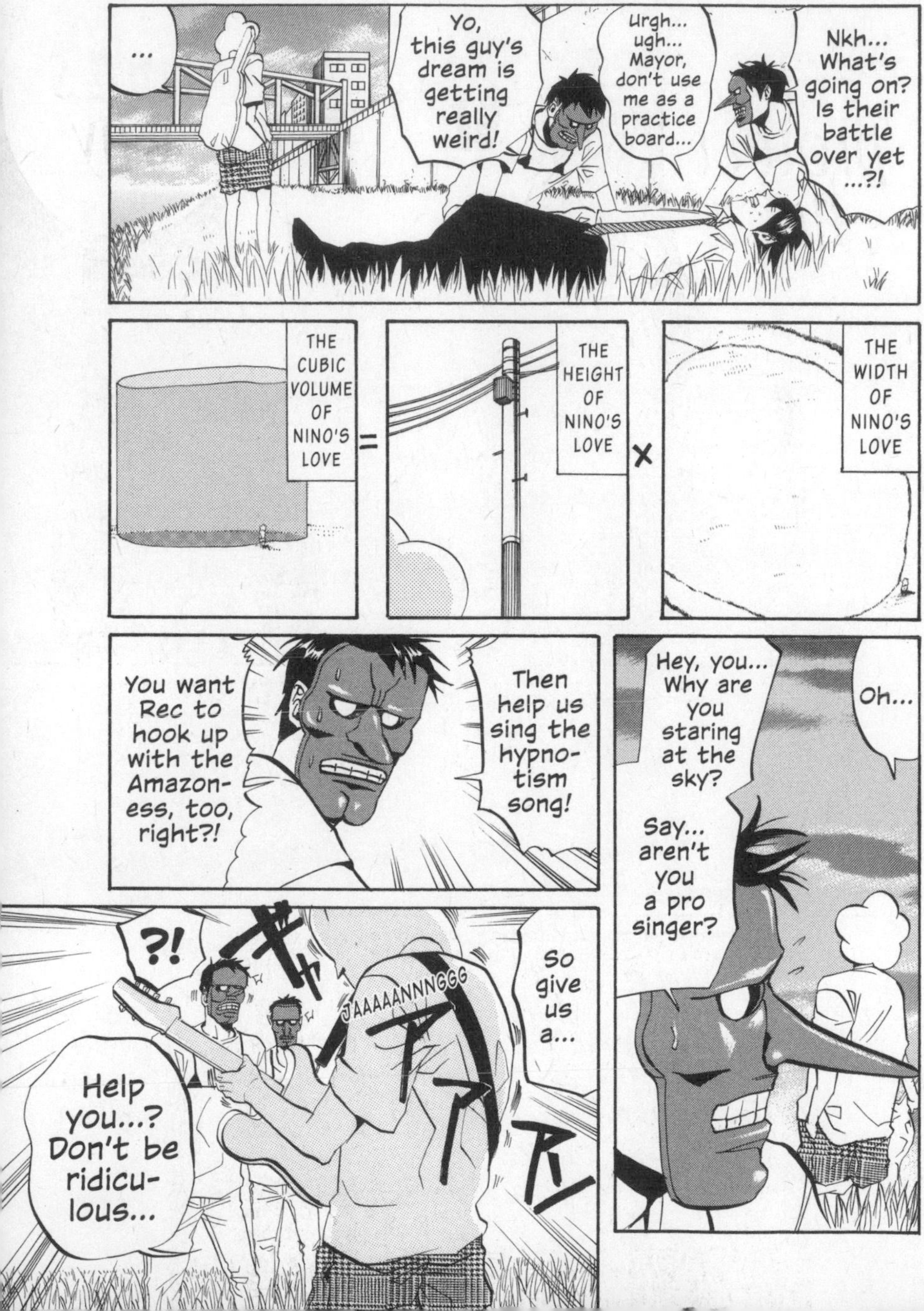
Nkh... What's going on? Is their battle over yet ...?!
Urgh... ugh... Mayor, don't use me as a practice board...
Yo, this guy's dream is getting really weird!
...
THE WIDTH OF NINO'S LOVE
×
THE HEIGHT OF NINO'S LOVE
=
THE CUBIC VOLUME OF NINO'S LOVE
Oh...
Hey, you... Why are you staring at the sky?
Say... aren't you a pro singer?
Then help us sing the hypno-tism song!
You want Rec to hook up with the Amazon-ess, too, right?!
So give us a...
JAAAAANNNGGG
?!
Help you...? Don't be ridicu-lous...

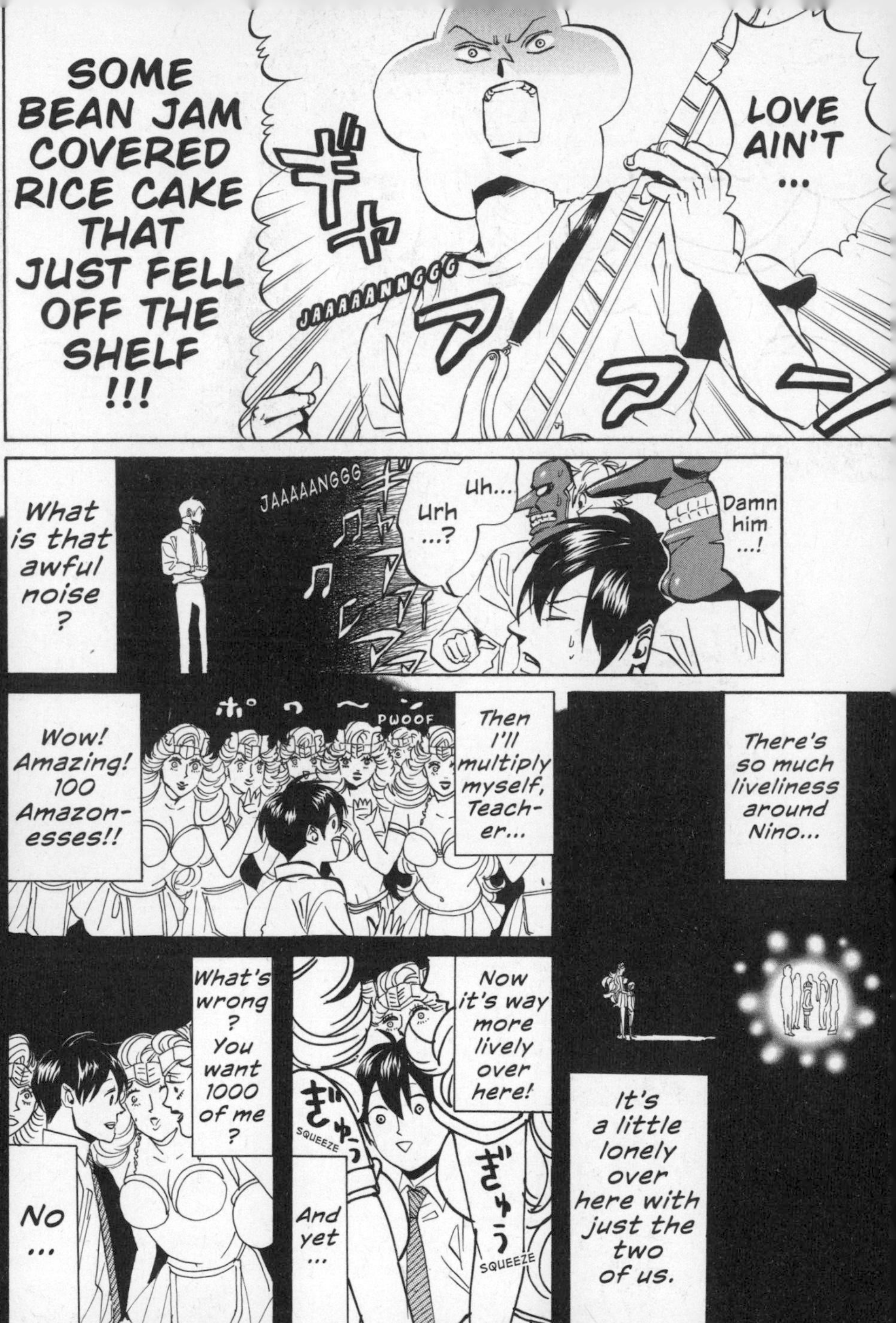

LOVE AIN'T ...
JAAAAANNGGG
SOME BEAN JAM COVERED RICE CAKE THAT JUST FELL OFF THE SHELF !!!
Damn him ...!
Uh...
Urh ...?
JAAAAANGGG
What is that awful noise ?
There's so much liveliness around Nino...
Then I'll multiply myself, Teacher...
PWOOF
Wow! Amazing! 100 Amazonesses!!
It's a little lonely over here with just the two of us.
Now it's way more lively over here!
SQUEEZE
SQUEEZE
And yet ...
What's wrong ? You want 1000 of me ?
No ...

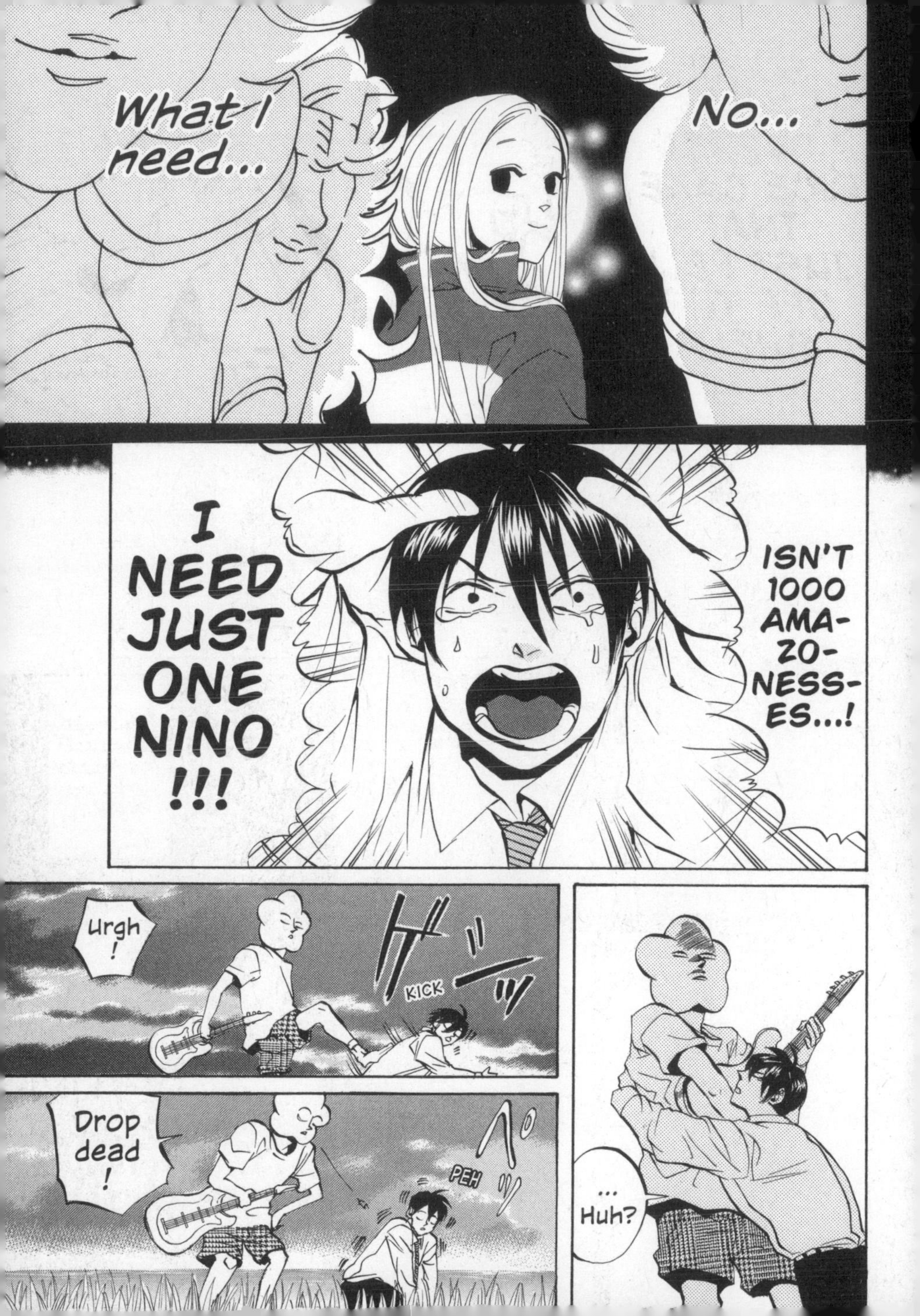

No...
What I need...
ISN'T 1000 AMAZONESSES...!
I NEED JUST ONE NINO!!!
... Huh?
Urgh!
KICK
Drop dead!
PEH

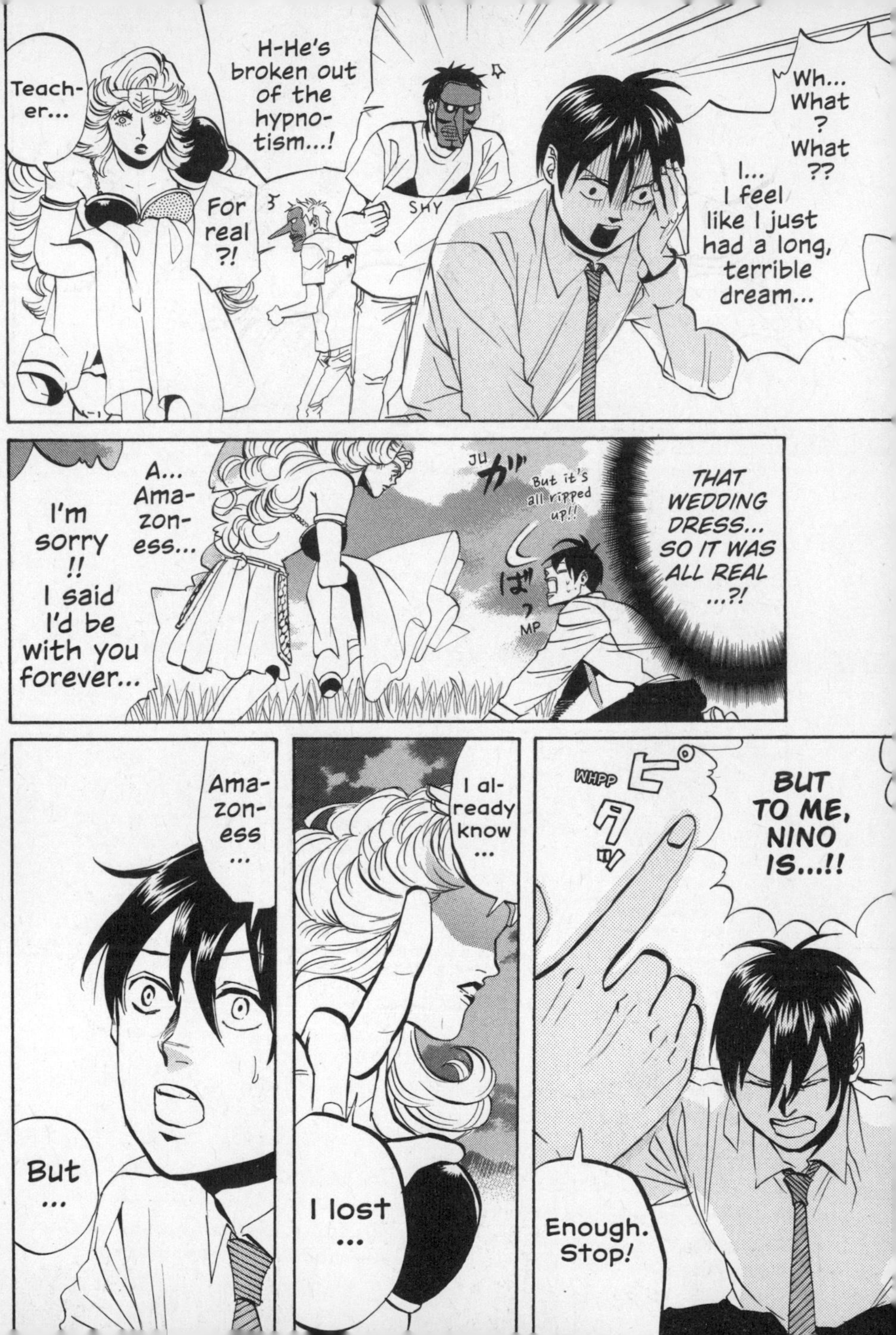
Wh... What? What??
I... I feel like I just had a long, terrible dream...
H-He's broken out of the hypnotism...!
Teacher...
For real?!
SHY
THAT WEDDING DRESS... SO IT WAS ALL REAL...?!
JU ガ
But it's all ripped up!!
ば MP
A... Amazoness...
I'm sorry!! I said I'd be with you forever...
BUT TO ME, NINO IS...!!
WHPP ピタッ
Enough. Stop!
I already know...
I lost...
Amazoness...
But...

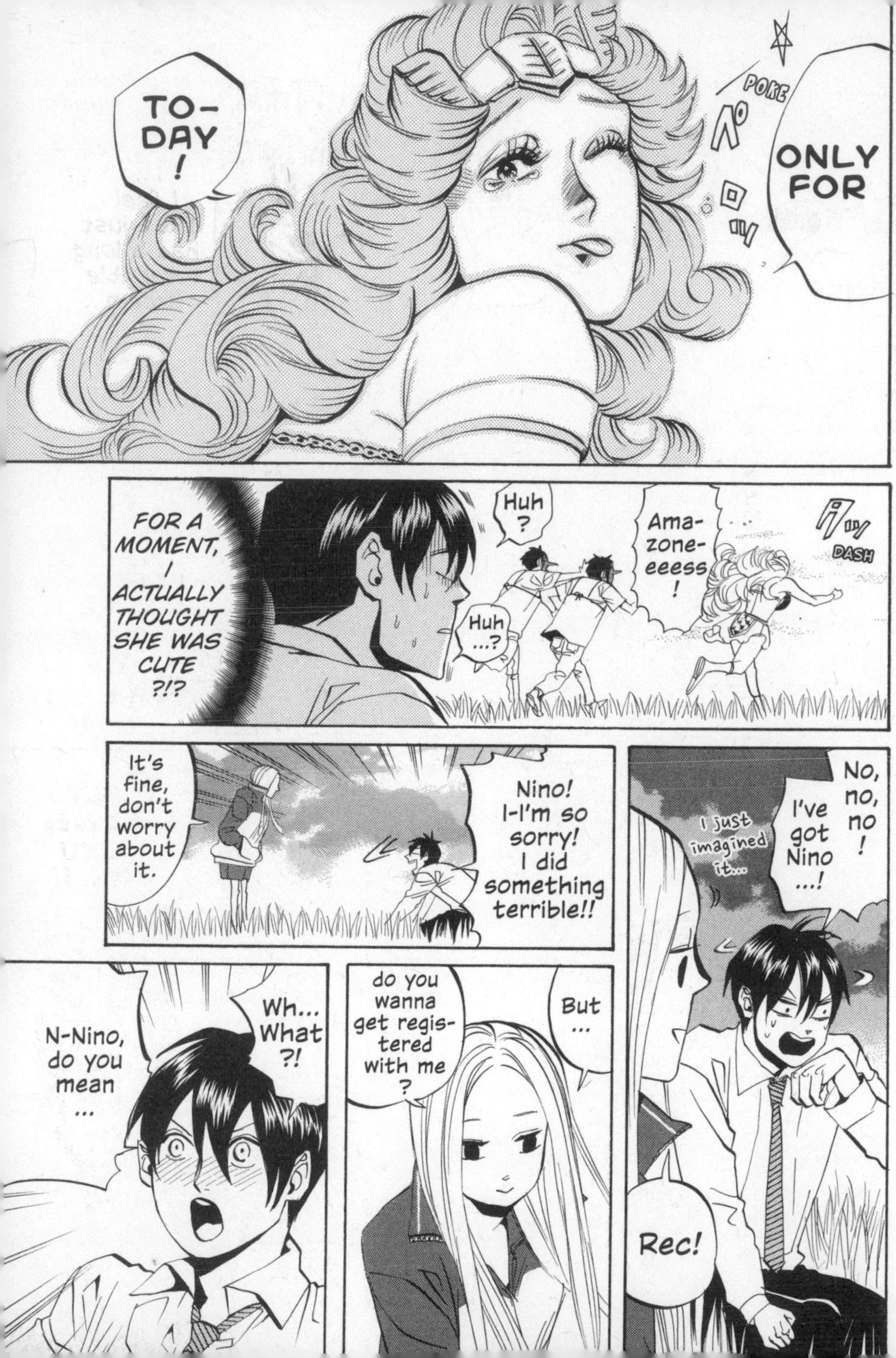
ONLY FOR
POKE
TO-DAY!
DASH
Ama-zone-eeess!
Huh?
Huh...?
FOR A MOMENT, I ACTUALLY THOUGHT SHE WAS CUTE?!?
No, no, no!
I've got Nino...!
I just imagined it...
Rec!
Nino! I-I'm so sorry! I did something terrible!!
It's fine, don't worry about it.
But...
do you wanna get regis-tered with me?
Wh... What?!
N-Nino, do you mean...

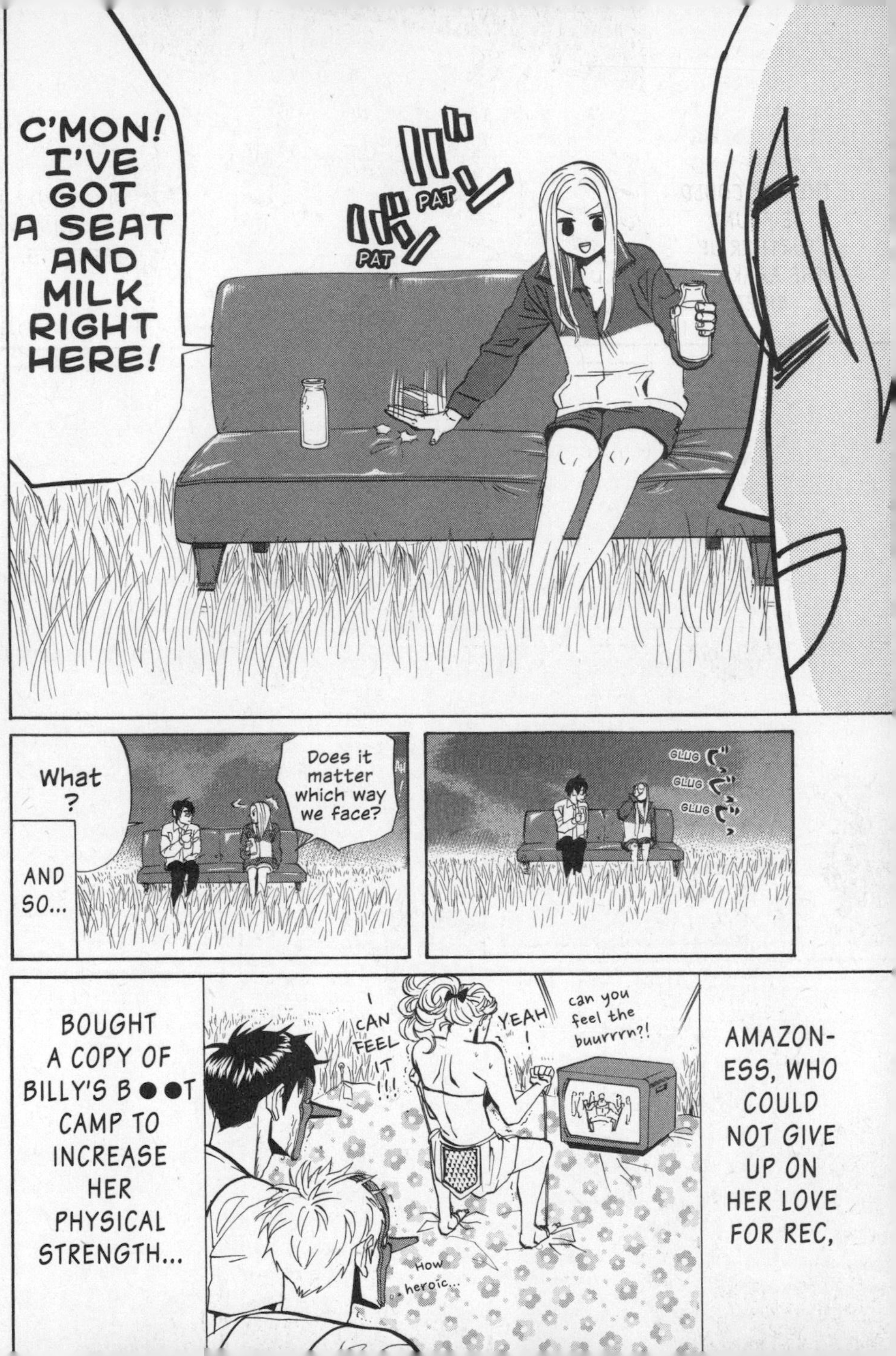
C'MON! I'VE GOT A SEAT AND MILK RIGHT HERE!
PAT
PAT
GLUG
GLUG
GLUG
Does it matter which way we face?
What?
AND SO...
AMAZON-ESS, WHO COULD NOT GIVE UP ON HER LOVE FOR REC,
can you feel the buurrrn?!
YEAH!
I CAN FEEL IT!!!
How heroic...
BOUGHT A COPY OF BILLY'S B●●T CAMP TO INCREASE HER PHYSICAL STRENGTH...

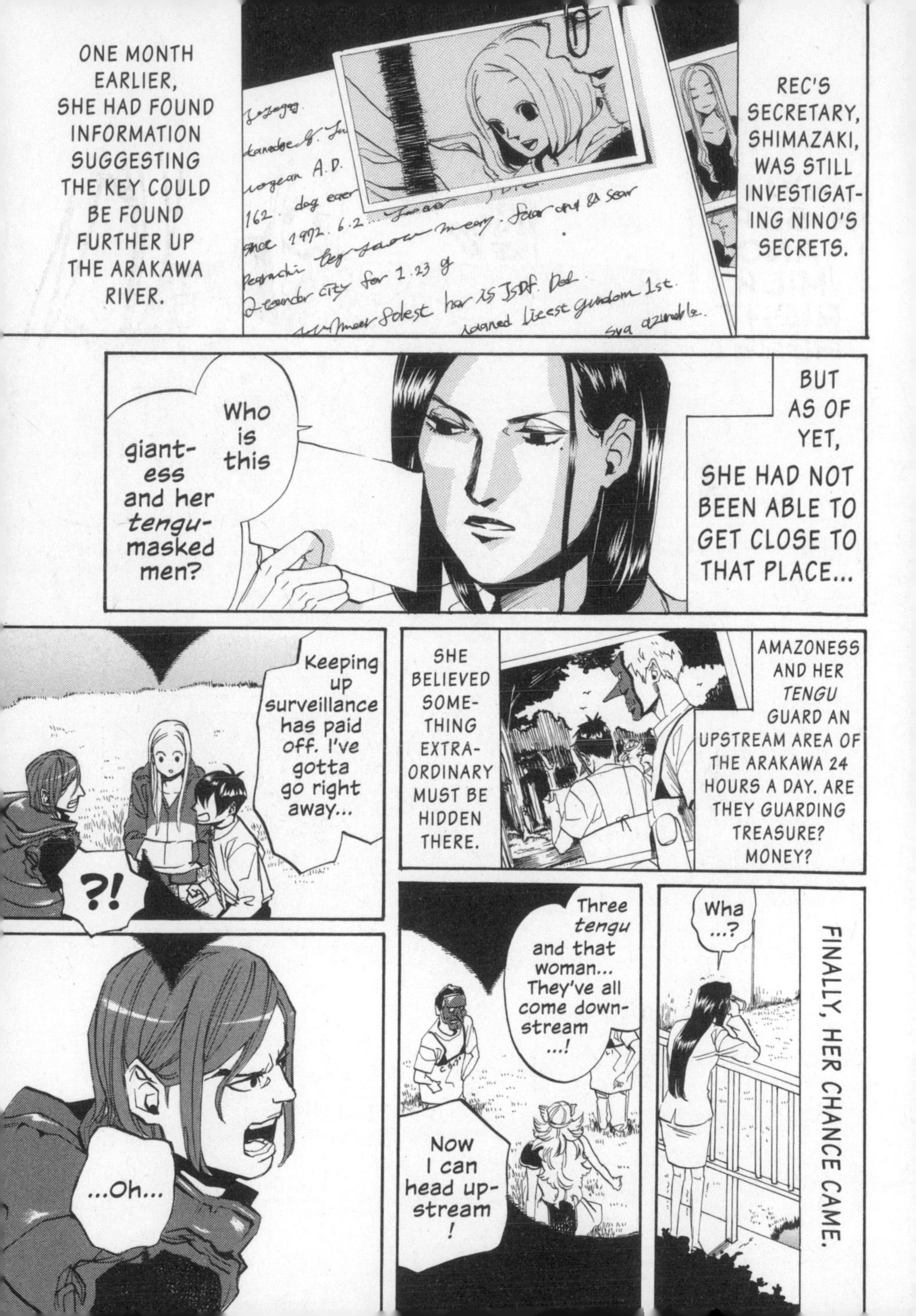
REC'S SECRETARY, SHIMAZAKI, WAS STILL INVESTIGATING NINO'S SECRETS.
ONE MONTH EARLIER, SHE HAD FOUND INFORMATION SUGGESTING THE KEY COULD BE FOUND FURTHER UP THE ARAKAWA RIVER.
BUT AS OF YET, SHE HAD NOT BEEN ABLE TO GET CLOSE TO THAT PLACE...
Who is this giantess and her *tengu*-masked men?
AMAZONESS AND HER *TENGU* GUARD AN UPSTREAM AREA OF THE ARAKAWA 24 HOURS A DAY. ARE THEY GUARDING TREASURE? MONEY?
SHE BELIEVED SOMETHING EXTRAORDINARY MUST BE HIDDEN THERE.
Keeping up surveillance has paid off. I've gotta go right away...
?!
FINALLY, HER CHANCE CAME.
Wha...?
Three *tengu* and that woman... They've all come downstream...!
Now I can head upstream!
...Oh...

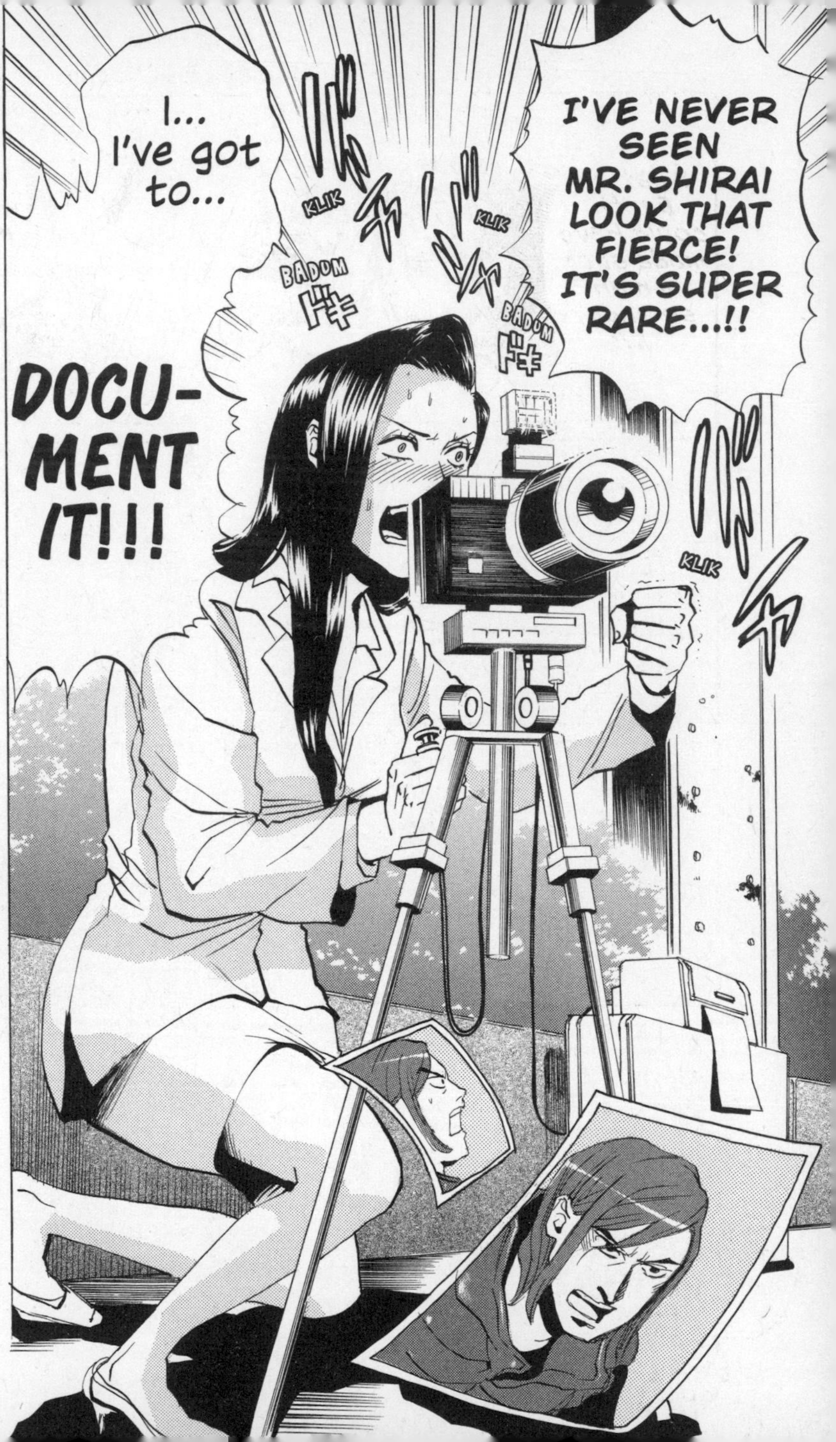

SHIMAZAKI HAS NOT YET ESCAPED SHIRO'S LOVE TRAP...

Chapter 191: The Boundaries of Pride

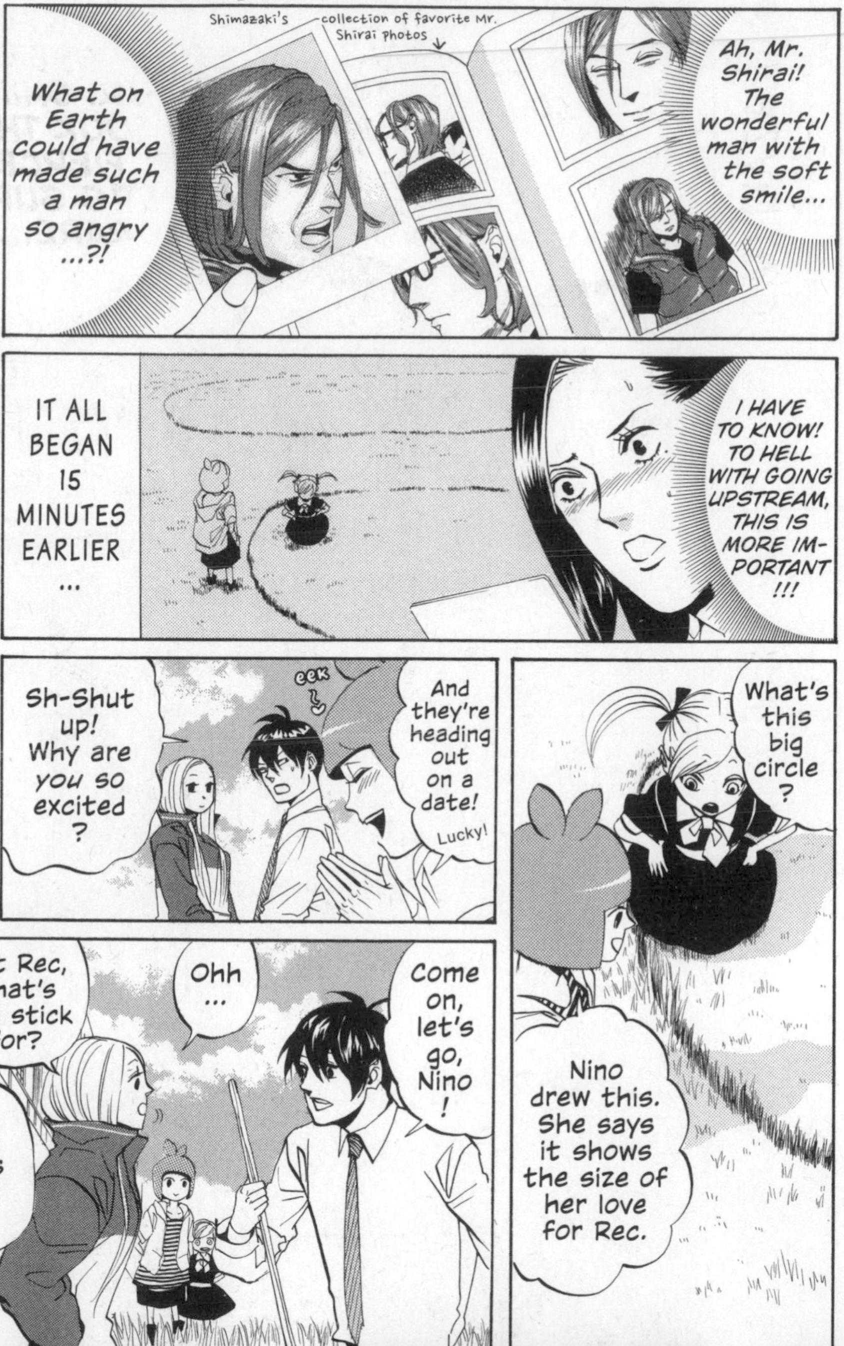
Ah, Mr. Shirai! The wonderful man with the soft smile...
Shimazaki's collection of favorite Mr. Shirai photos
What on Earth could have made such a man so angry ...?!
I HAVE TO KNOW! TO HELL WITH GOING UPSTREAM, THIS IS MORE IMPORTANT !!!
IT ALL BEGAN 15 MINUTES EARLIER ...
What's this big circle ?
Nino drew this. She says it shows the size of her love for Rec.
And they're heading out on a date!
eek
Lucky!
Sh-Shut up! Why are you so excited ?
Come on, let's go, Nino !
Ohh ...
But Rec, what's the stick for?
Oh, this ...?

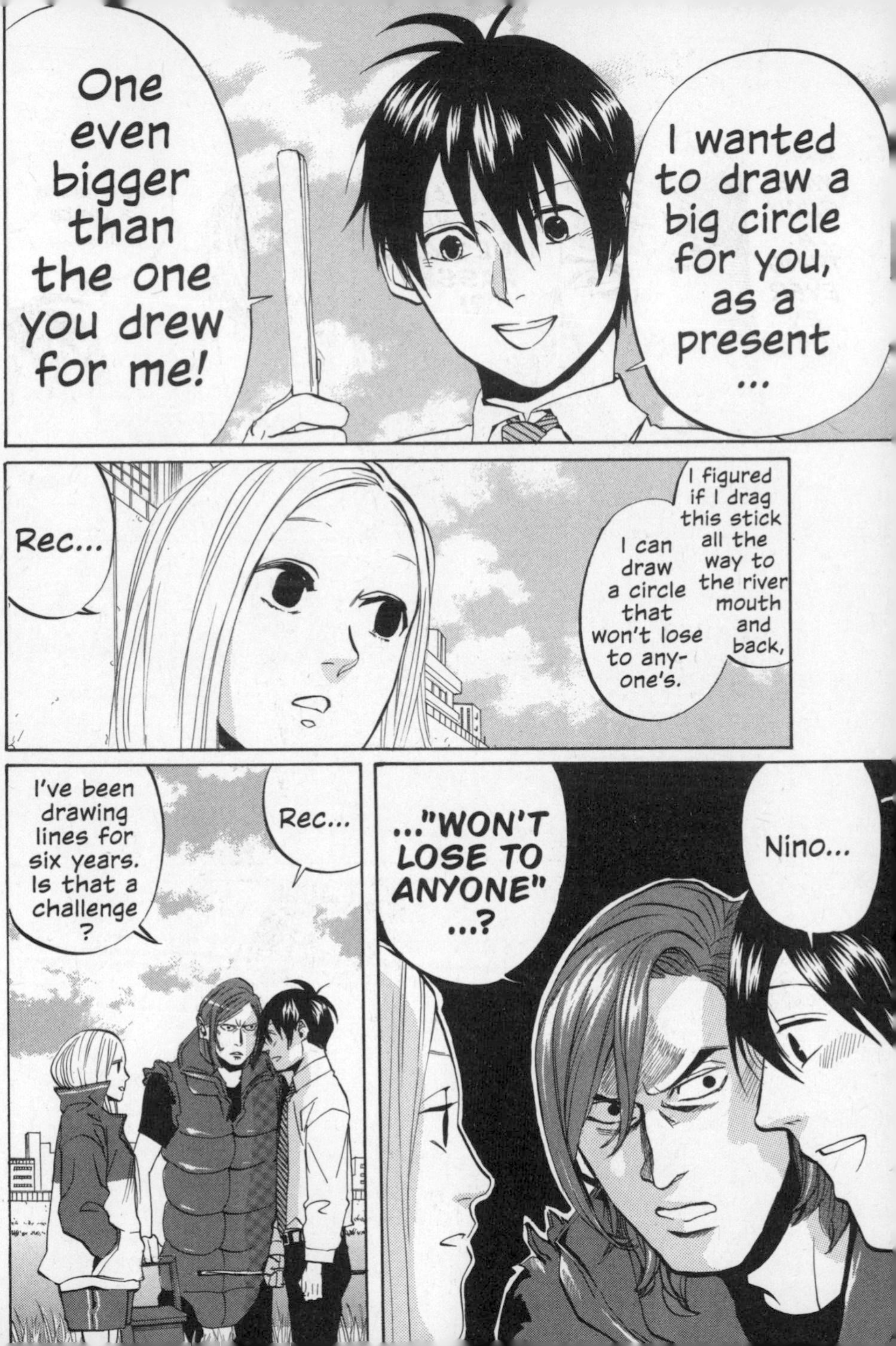
I wanted to draw a big circle for you, as a present ...
One even bigger than the one you drew for me!
I figured if I drag this stick all the way to the river mouth and back,
I can draw a circle that won't lose to anyone's.
Rec...
Nino...
..."WON'T LOSE TO ANYONE" ...?
Rec...
I've been drawing lines for six years. Is that a challenge ?

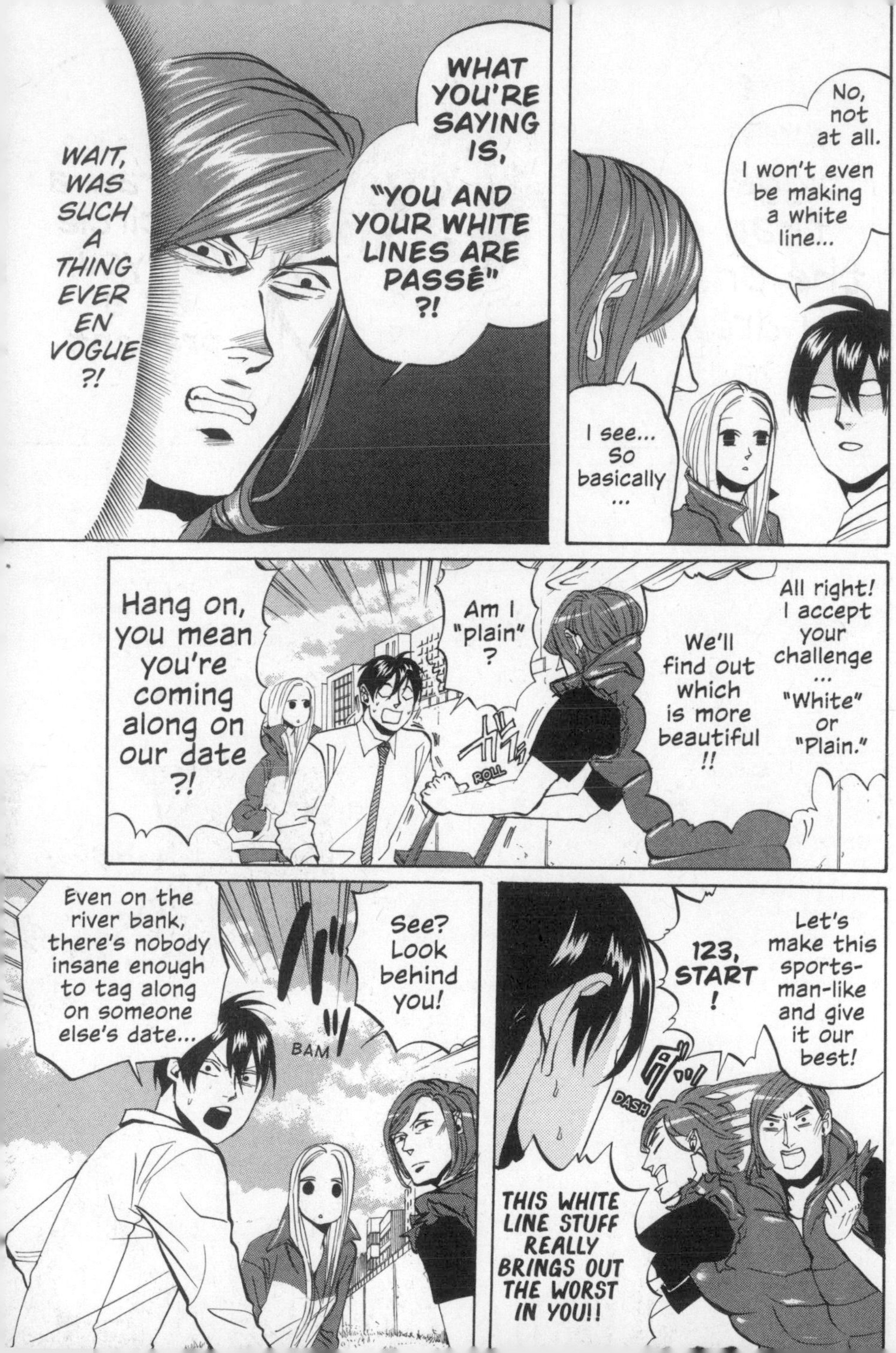
No, not at all. I won't even be making a white line...
I see... So basically...
WHAT YOU'RE SAYING IS, "YOU AND YOUR WHITE LINES ARE PASSÉ" ?!
WAIT, WAS SUCH A THING EVER EN VOGUE ?!
All right! I accept your challenge... "White" or "Plain."
We'll find out which is more beautiful !!
Am I "plain" ?
Hang on, you mean you're coming along on our date ?!
ROLL
Let's make this sports-man-like and give it our best!
123, START !
DASH
THIS WHITE LINE STUFF REALLY BRINGS OUT THE WORST IN YOU!!
See? Look behind you!
BAM
Even on the river bank, there's nobody insane enough to tag along on someone else's date...

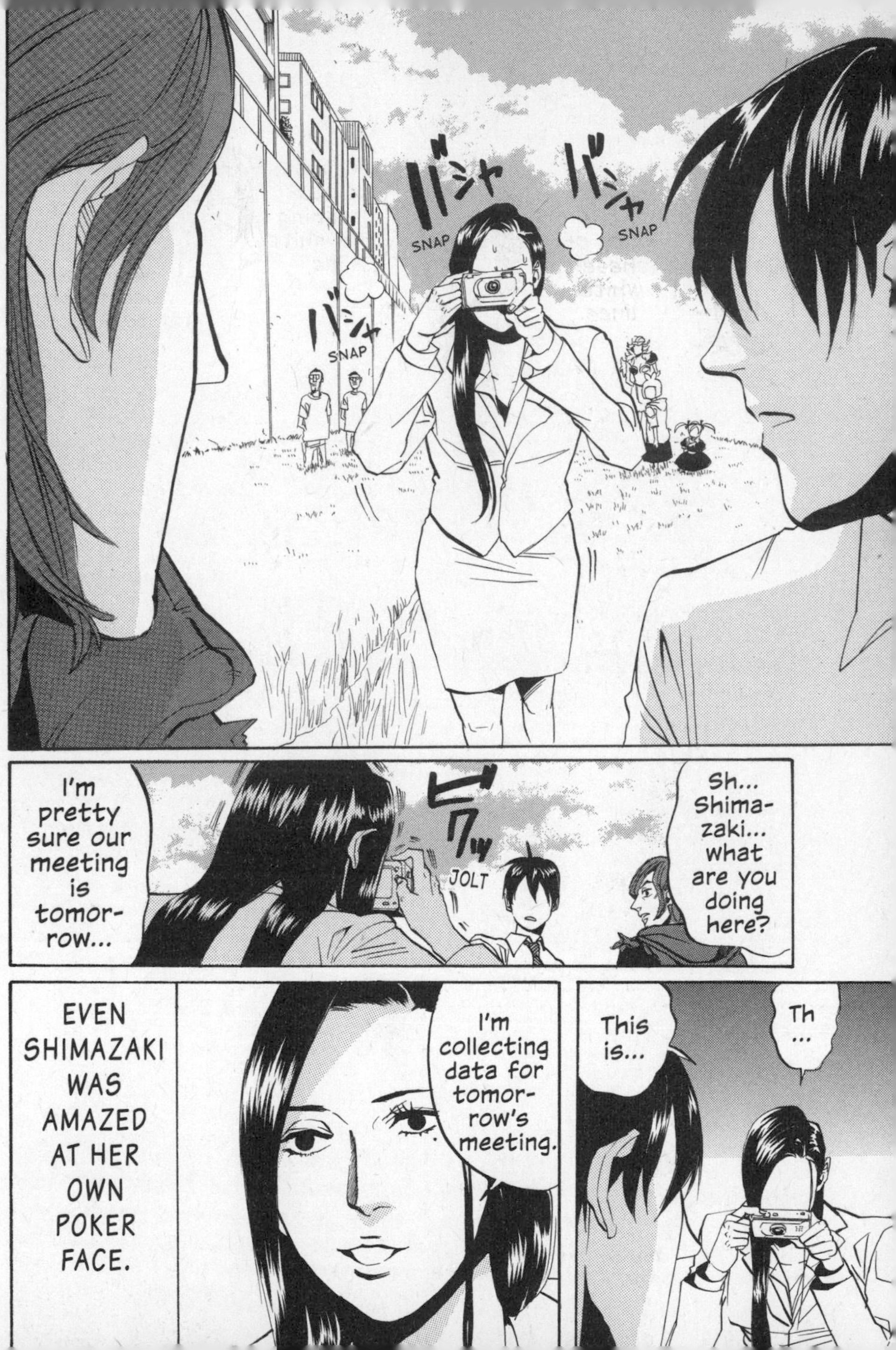
バシャ
SNAP
バシャ
SNAP
バシャ
SNAP
Sh... Shimazaki... what are you doing here?
ビクッ
JOLT
I'm pretty sure our meeting is tomorrow...
Th...
This is...
I'm collecting data for tomorrow's meeting.
EVEN SHIMAZAKI WAS AMAZED AT HER OWN POKER FACE.

Chapter 192: Love Signposts

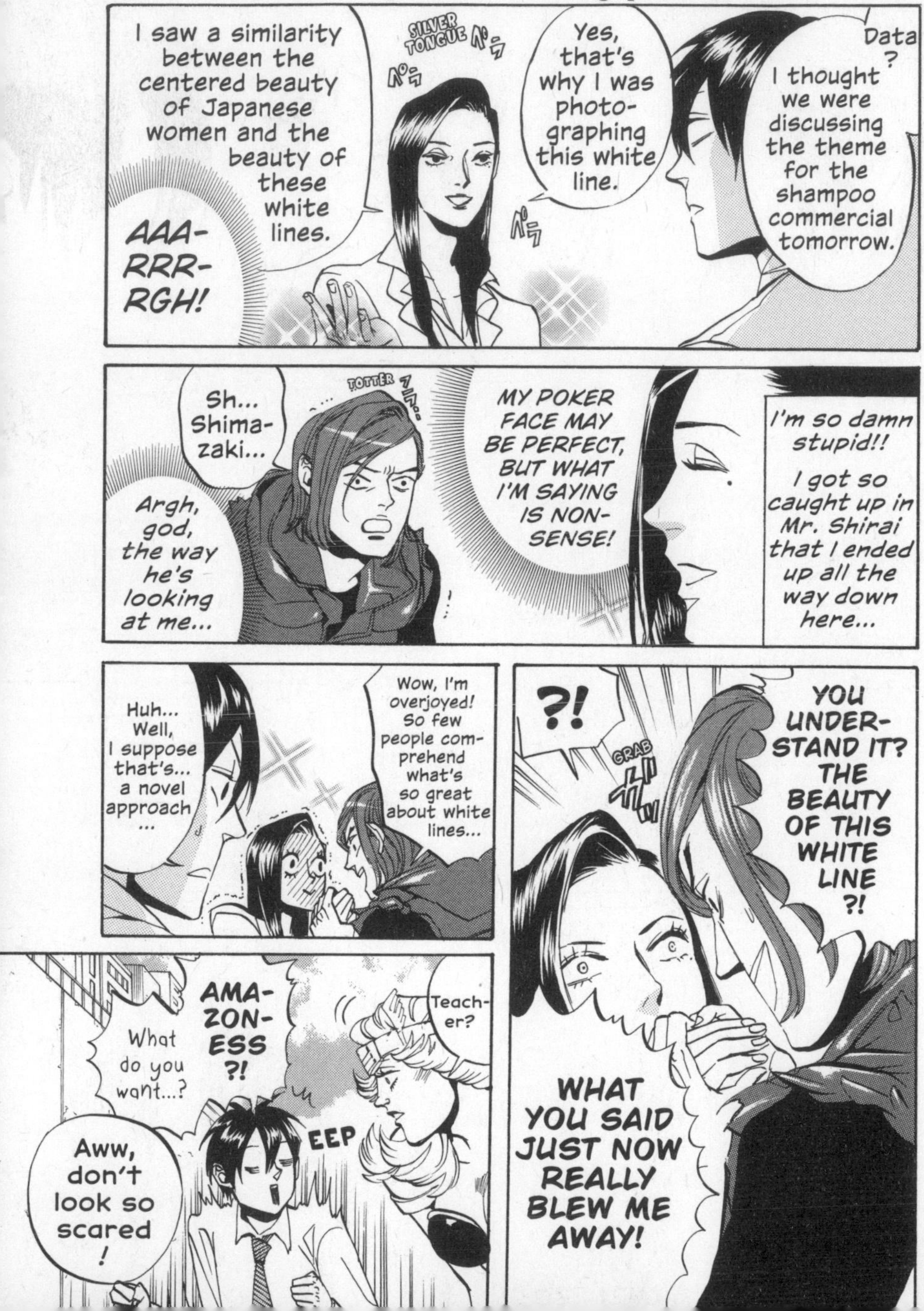

Data? I thought we were discussing the theme for the shampoo commercial tomorrow.
Yes, that's why I was photographing this white line.
SILVER TONGUE
I saw a similarity between the centered beauty of Japanese women and the beauty of these white lines.
AAARRRRGH!
I'm so damn stupid!! I got so caught up in Mr. Shirai that I ended up all the way down here...
MY POKER FACE MAY BE PERFECT, BUT WHAT I'M SAYING IS NONSENSE!
TOTTER
Sh... Shimazaki...
Argh, god, the way he's looking at me...
?!
GRAB
YOU UNDERSTAND IT? THE BEAUTY OF THIS WHITE LINE?!
WHAT YOU SAID JUST NOW REALLY BLEW ME AWAY!
Wow, I'm overjoyed! So few people comprehend what's so great about white lines...
Huh... Well, I suppose that's... a novel approach...
Teacher?
AMAZONESS?!
What do you want...?
EEP
Aww, don't look so scared!

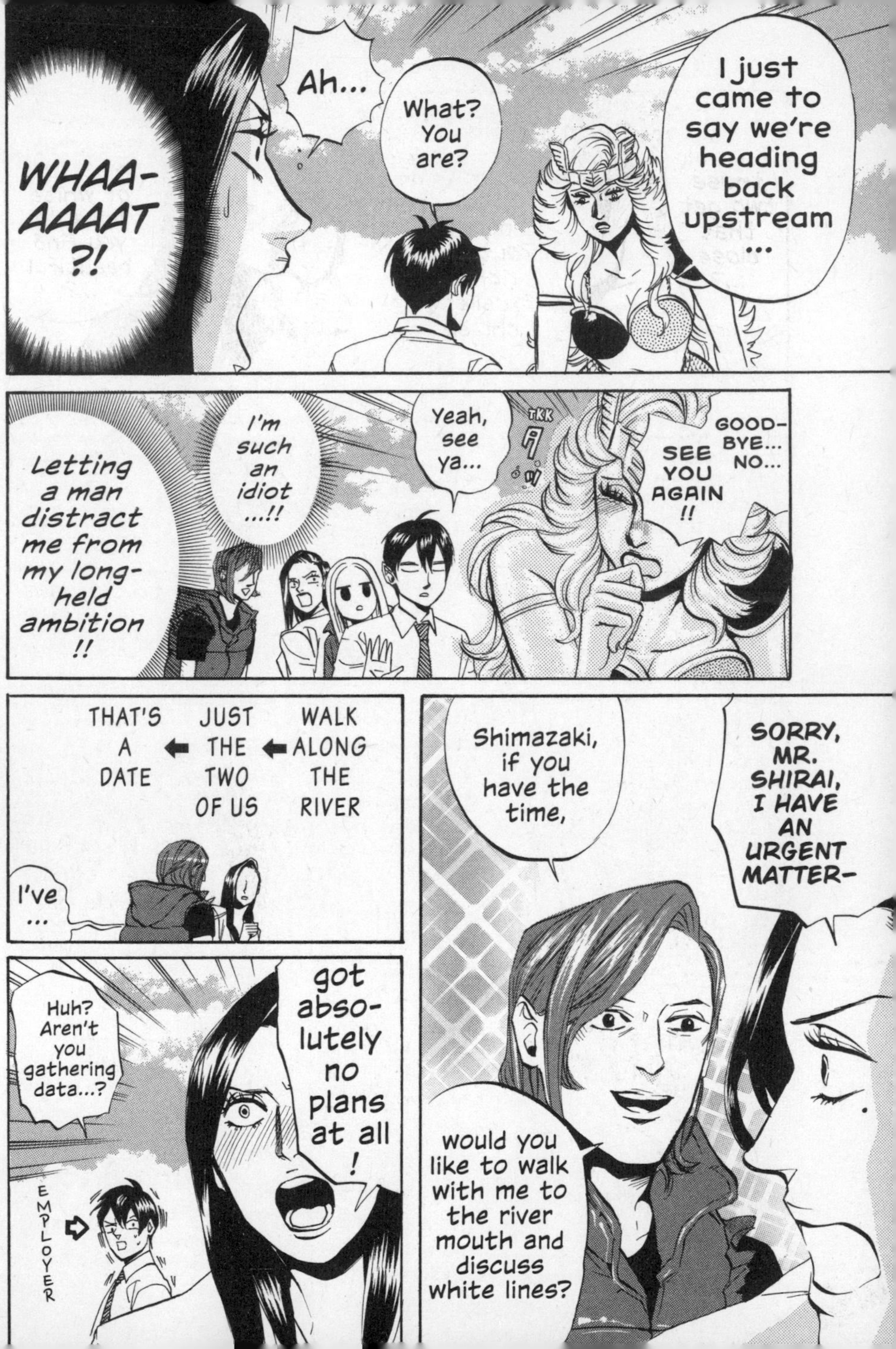

I just came to say we're heading back upstream ...
What? You are?
Ah...
WHAA-AAAAT ?!
GOOD-BYE... NO... SEE YOU AGAIN !!
TKK
Yeah, see ya...
I'm such an idiot ...!!
Letting a man distract me from my long-held ambition !!
SORRY, MR. SHIRAI, I HAVE AN URGENT MATTER-
Shimazaki, if you have the time,
would you like to walk with me to the river mouth and discuss white lines?
WALK ALONG THE RIVER
JUST THE TWO OF US
THAT'S A DATE
I've ...
got absolutely no plans at all !
Huh? Aren't you gathering data...?
EMPLOYER

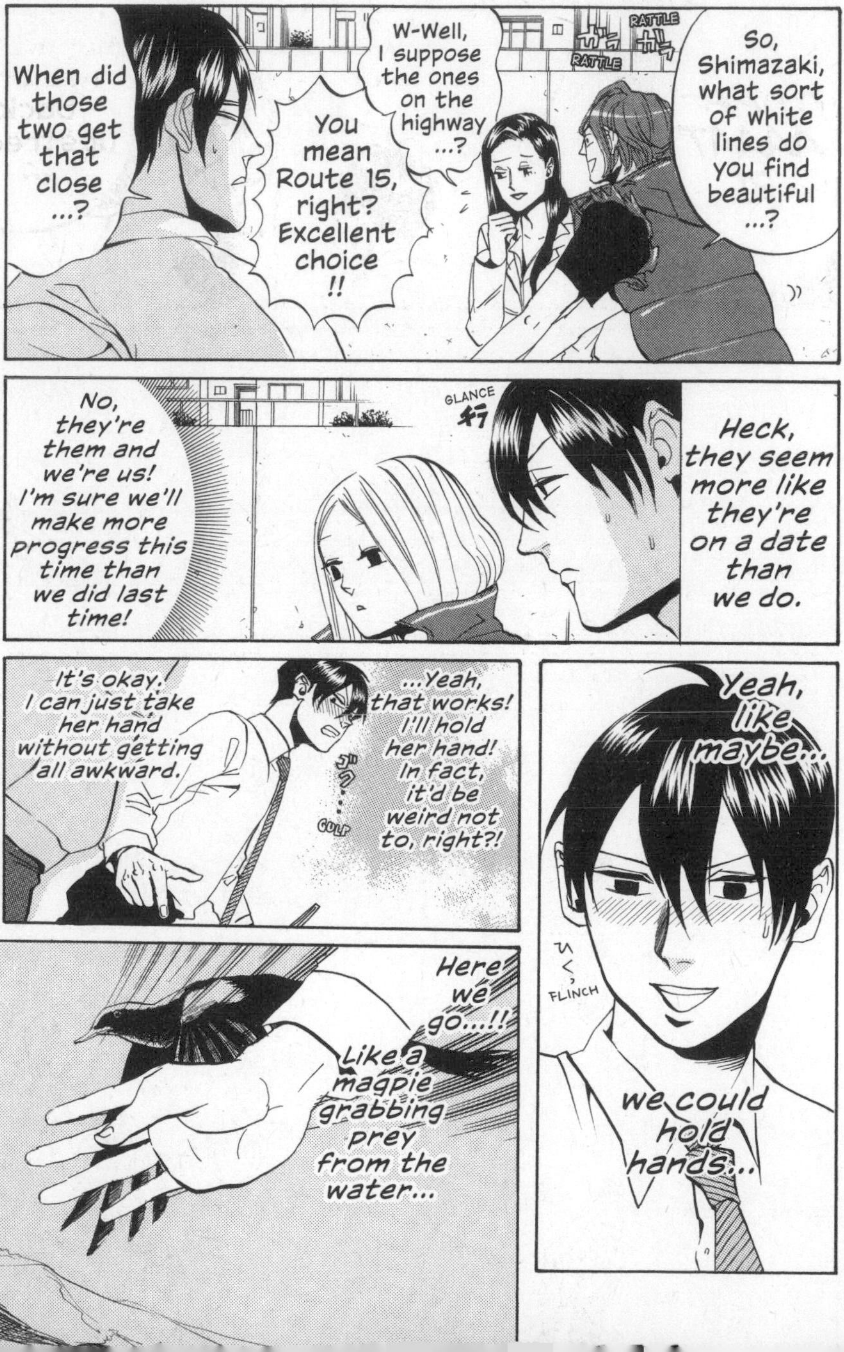
So, Shimazaki, what sort of white lines do you find beautiful ...?
RATTLE
RATTLE
W-Well, I suppose the ones on the highway ...?
You mean Route 15, right? Excellent choice !!
When did those two get that close ...?
Heck, they seem more like they're on a date than we do.
GLANCE
No, they're them and we're us! I'm sure we'll make more progress this time than we did last time!
Yeah, like maybe...
FLINCH
we could hold hands...
...Yeah, that works! I'll hold her hand! In fact, it'd be weird not to, right?!
It's okay. I can just take her hand without getting all awkward.
GULP
Here we go...!!
Like a magpie grabbing prey from the water...

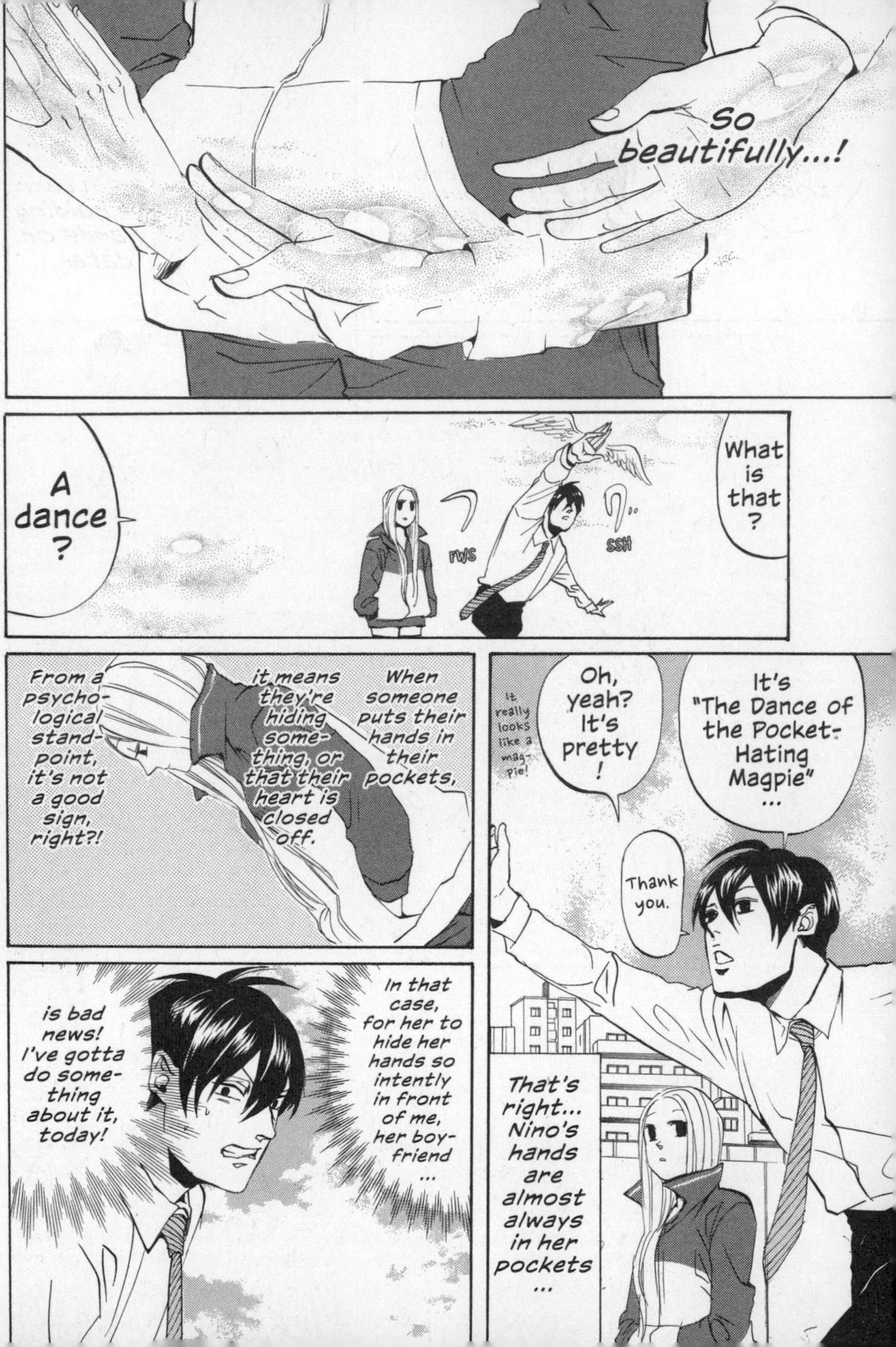
So beautifully...!
What is that?
SSH
FWS
A dance?
It's "The Dance of the Pocket-Hating Magpie"...
Oh, yeah? It's pretty!
It really looks like a magpie!
Thank you.
That's right... Nino's hands are almost always in her pockets...
When someone puts their hands in their pockets,
it means they're hiding something, or that their heart is closed off.
From a psychological standpoint, it's not a good sign, right?!
In that case, for her to hide her hands so intently in front of me, her boyfriend...
is bad news! I've gotta do something about it, today!

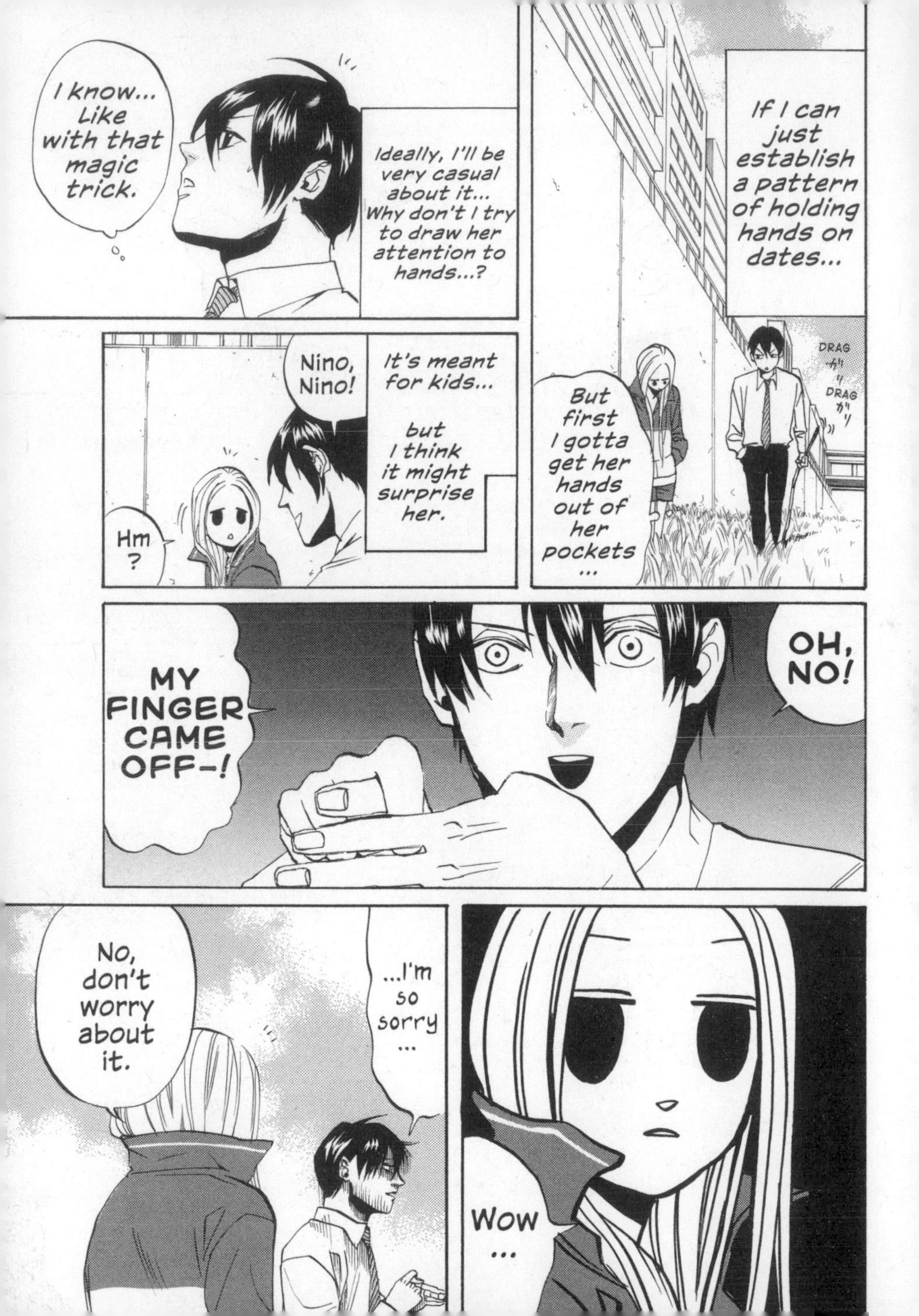
If I can just establish a pattern of holding hands on dates...
But first I gotta get her hands out of her pockets...
DRAG ガリ
DRAG ガリ
Ideally, I'll be very casual about it... Why don't I try to draw her attention to hands...?
I know... Like with that magic trick.
It's meant for kids... but I think it might surprise her.
Nino, Nino!
Hm?
OH, NO!
MY FINGER CAME OFF-!
Wow...
...I'm so sorry...
No, don't worry about it.

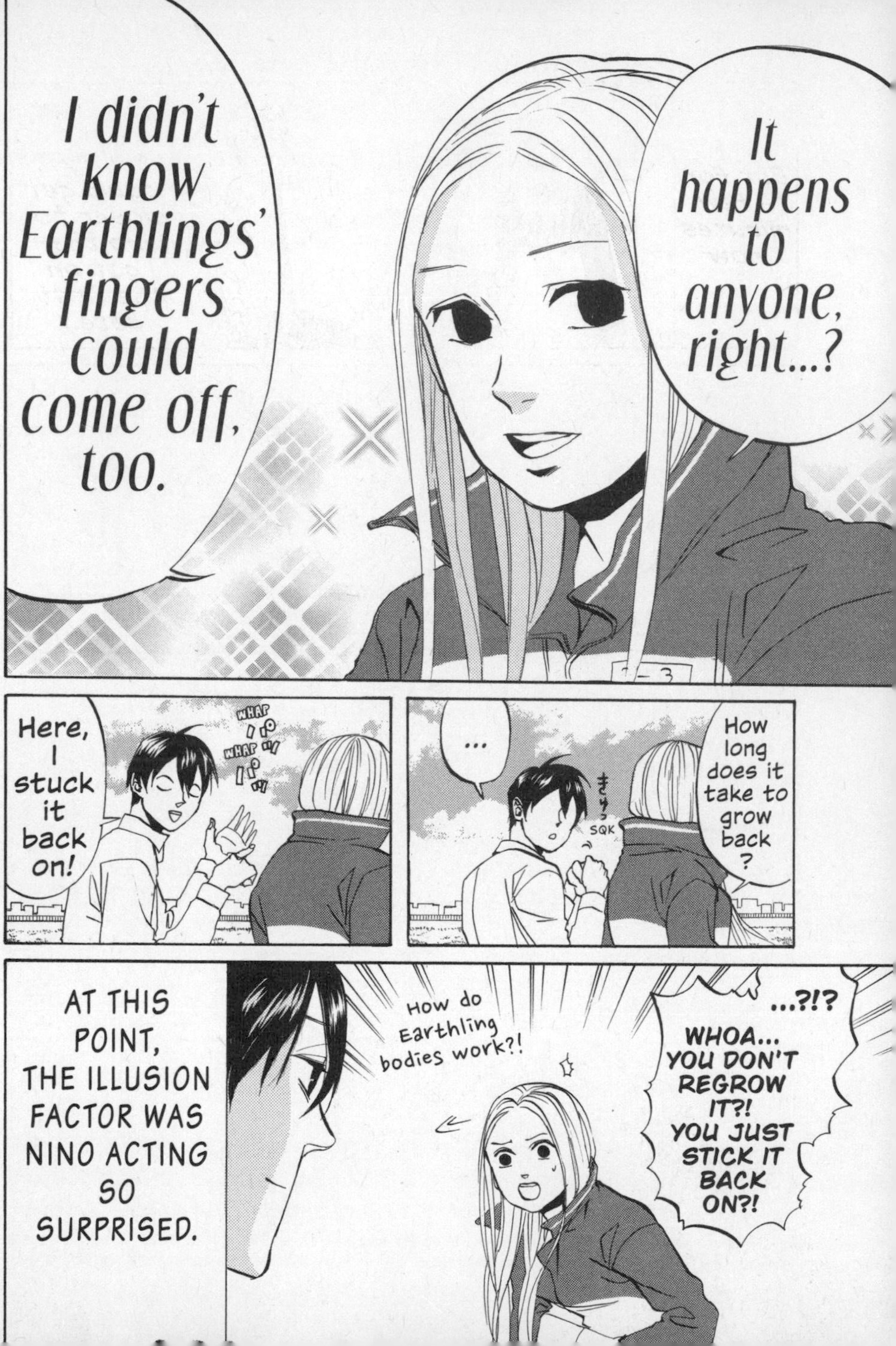

It happens to anyone, right...?
I didn't know Earthlings' fingers could come off, too.
How long does it take to grow back?
...
SQK
WHAP WHAP
Here, I stuck it back on!
...?!?
WHOA... YOU DON'T REGROW IT?! YOU JUST STICK IT BACK ON?!
How do Earthling bodies work?!
AT THIS POINT, THE ILLUSION FACTOR WAS NINO ACTING SO SURPRISED.

Chapter 193: Love Circle, Love Line

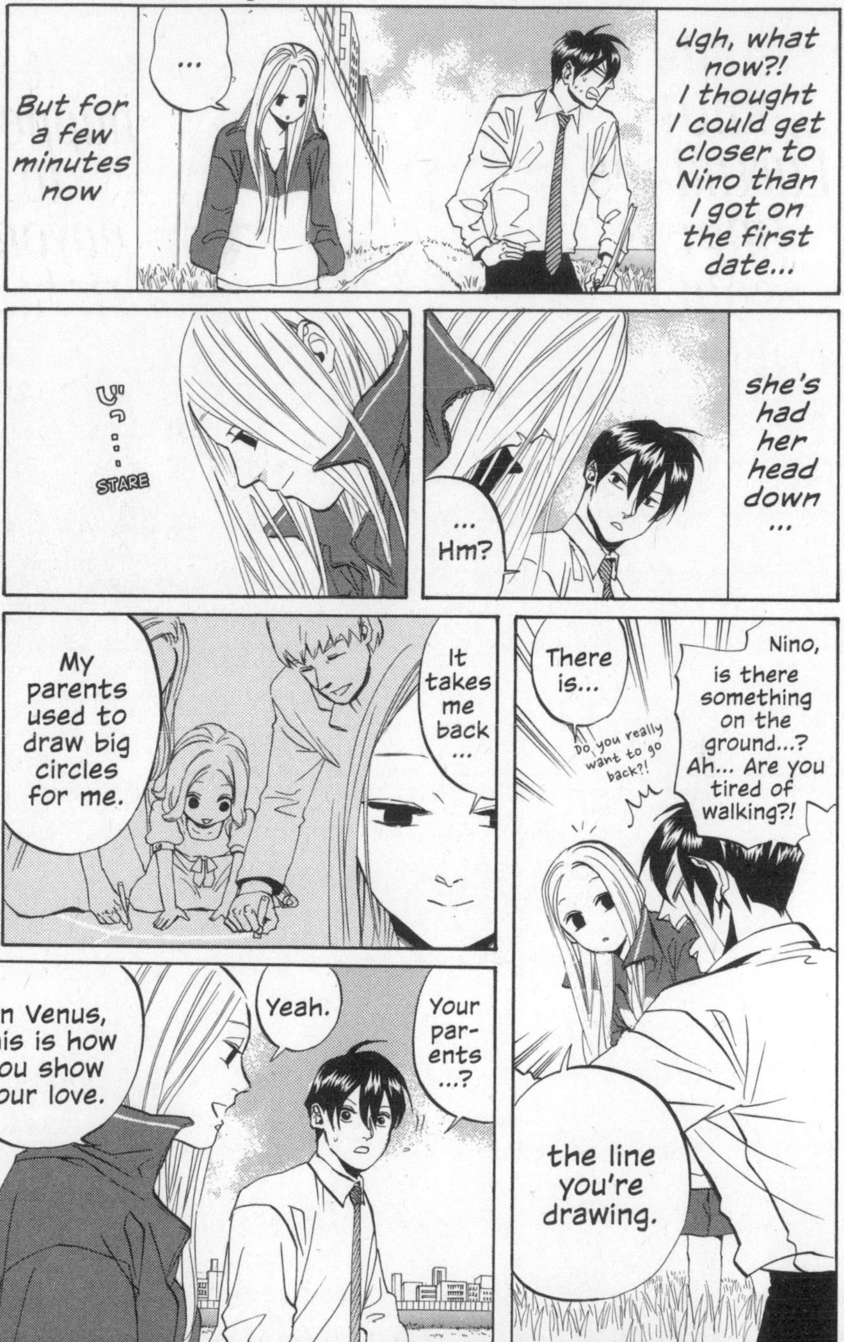
Ugh, what now?! I thought I could get closer to Nino than I got on the first date...
...
But for a few minutes now
she's had her head down...
... Hm?
じっ...
STARE
Nino, is there something on the ground...? Ah... Are you tired of walking?!
Do you really want to go back?!
There is...
the line you're drawing.
It takes me back...
My parents used to draw big circles for me.
Your parents...?
Yeah.
On Venus, this is how you show your love.

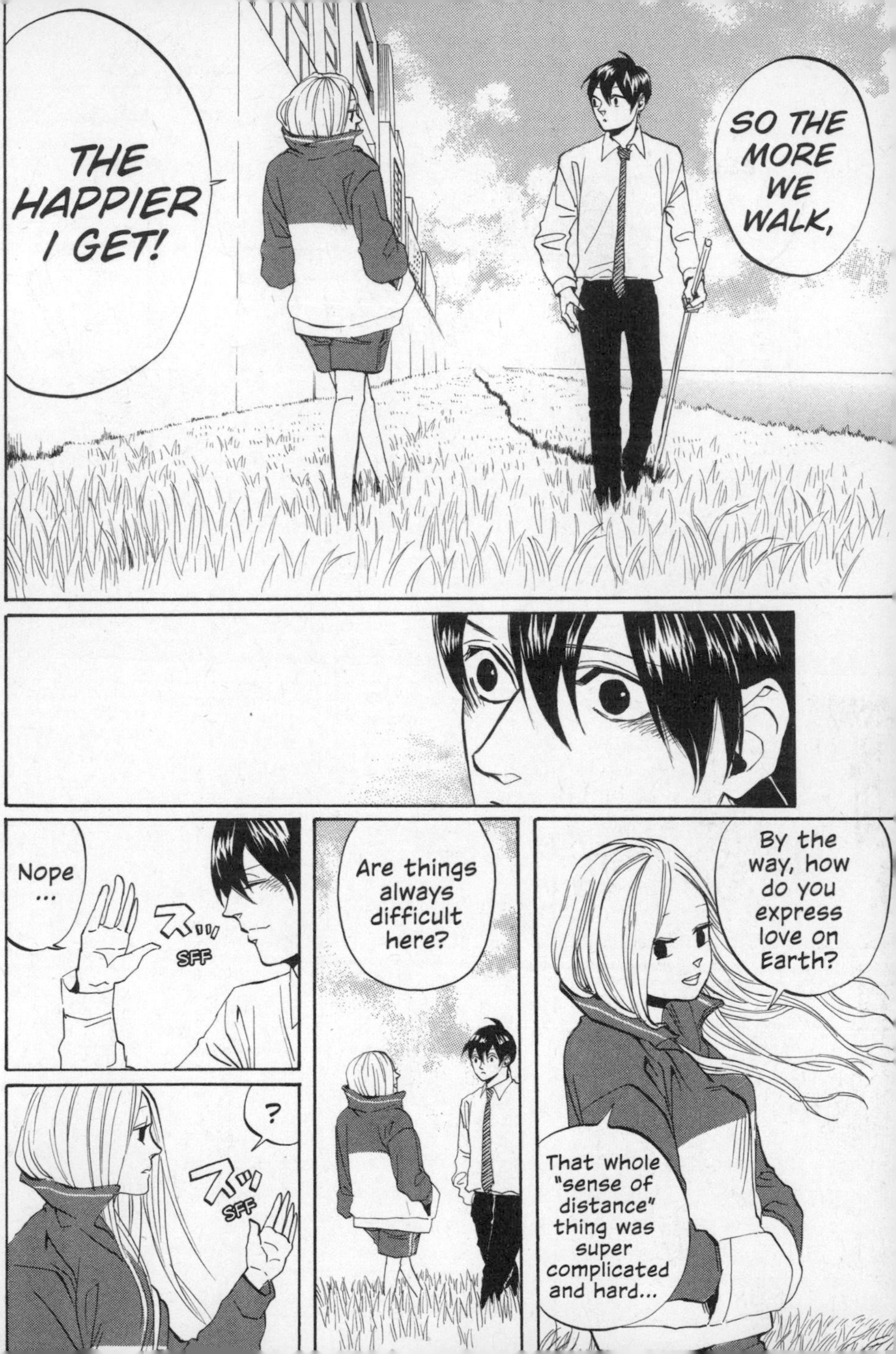
SO THE MORE WE WALK,
THE HAPPIER I GET!
By the way, how do you express love on Earth?
That whole "sense of distance" thing was super complicated and hard...
Are things always difficult here?
Nope ...
SFF
?
SFF

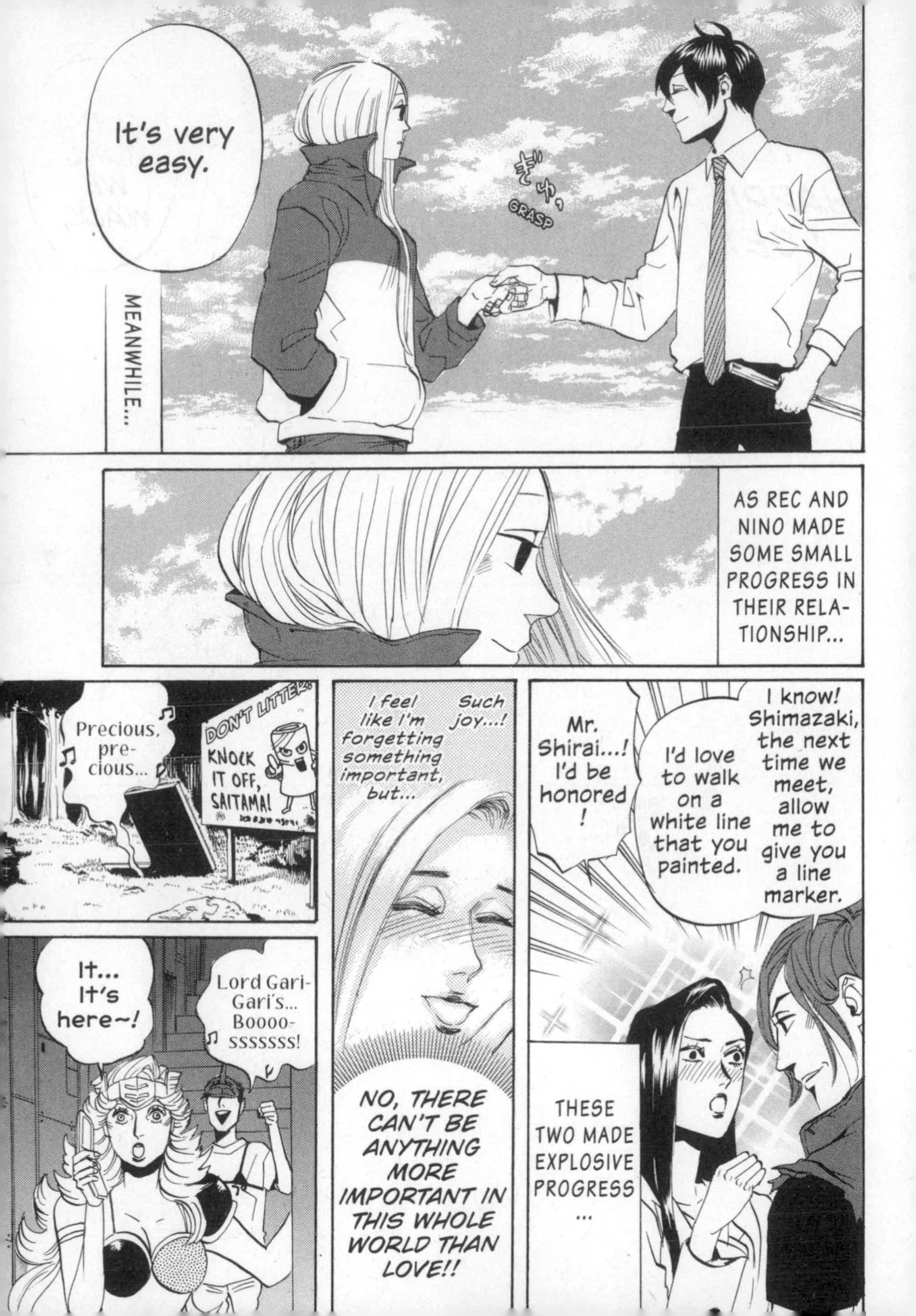
It's very easy.
ぎゅ
GRASP
MEANWHILE...
AS REC AND NINO MADE SOME SMALL PROGRESS IN THEIR RELATIONSHIP...
I know! Shimazaki, the next time we meet, allow me to give you a line marker.
I'd love to walk on a white line that you painted.
Mr. Shirai...! I'd be honored!
THESE TWO MADE EXPLOSIVE PROGRESS...
Such joy...!
I feel like I'm forgetting something important, but...
NO, THERE CAN'T BE ANYTHING MORE IMPORTANT IN THIS WHOLE WORLD THAN LOVE!!
DON'T LITTER!
KNOCK IT OFF, SAITAMA!
Precious, pre-cious...
Lord Gari-Gari's... Boooo-sssssss!
It... It's here~!

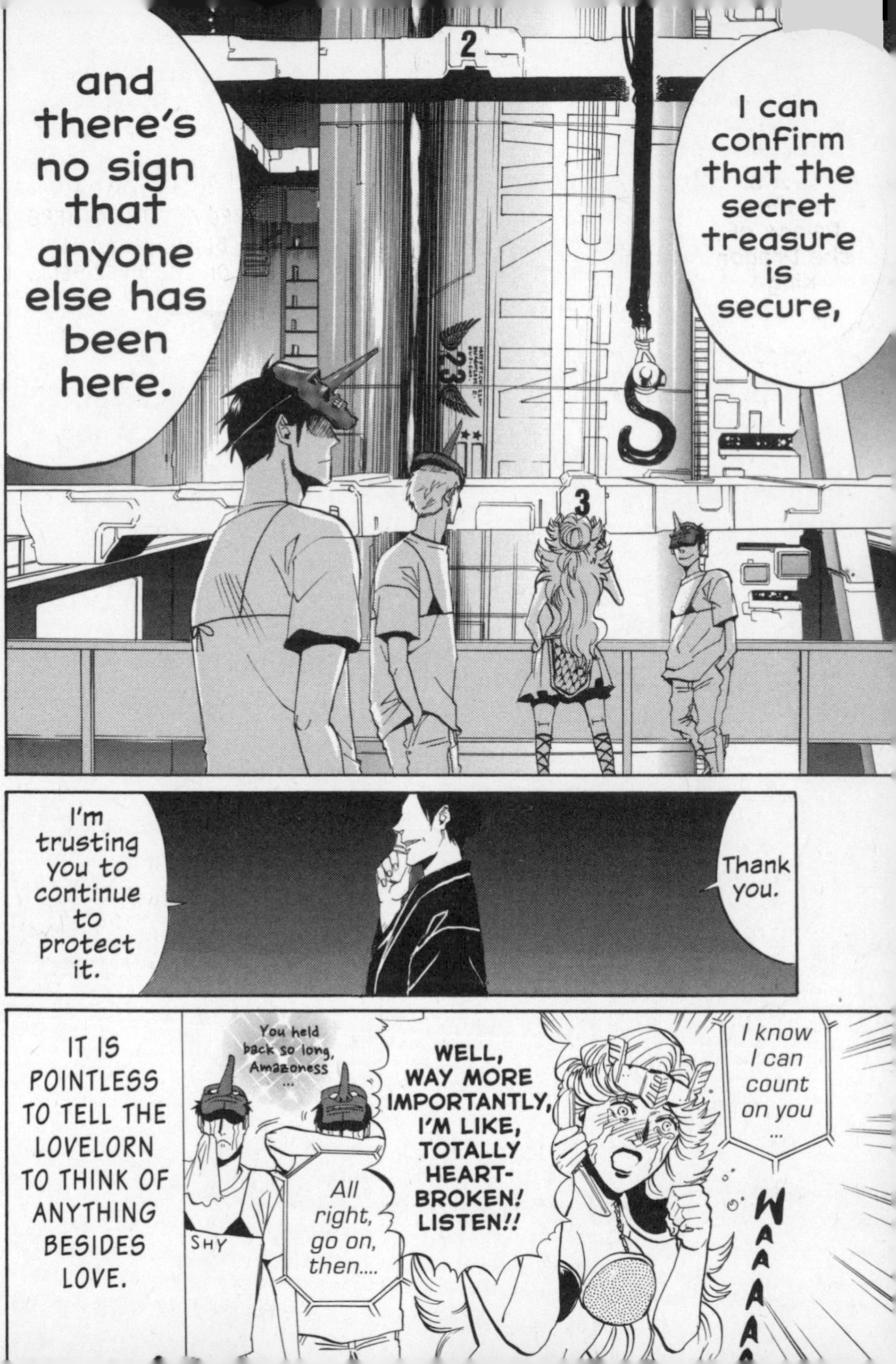
I can confirm that the secret treasure is secure,
and there's no sign that anyone else has been here.
Thank you.
I'm trusting you to continue to protect it.
I know I can count on you ...
WAAAAA
WELL, WAY MORE IMPORTANTLY, I'M LIKE, TOTALLY HEART-BROKEN! LISTEN!!
You held back so long, Amazoness ...
All right, go on, then....
SHY
IT IS POINTLESS TO TELL THE LOVELORN TO THINK OF ANYTHING BESIDES LOVE.

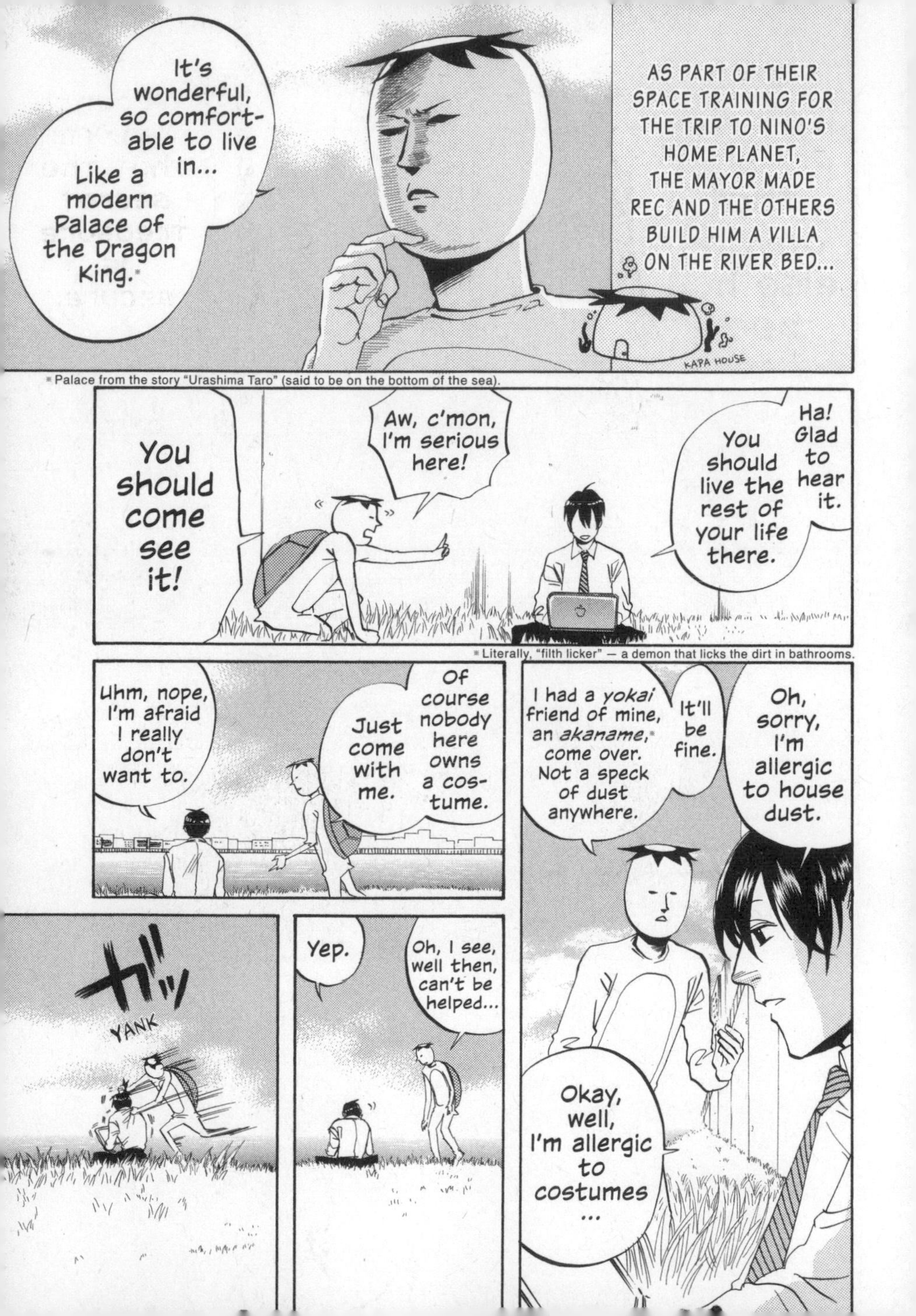
AS PART OF THEIR SPACE TRAINING FOR THE TRIP TO NINO'S HOME PLANET, THE MAYOR MADE REC AND THE OTHERS BUILD HIM A VILLA ON THE RIVER BED...
KAPA HOUSE
It's wonderful, so comfortable to live in...
Like a modern Palace of the Dragon King.*
Ha! Glad to hear it.
You should live the rest of your life there.
Aw, c'mon, I'm serious here!
You should come see it!
Oh, sorry, I'm allergic to house dust.
It'll be fine.
I had a *yokai* friend of mine, an *akaname*,* come over. Not a speck of dust anywhere.
Okay, well, I'm allergic to costumes...
Of course nobody here owns a costume.
Just come with me.
Uhm, nope, I'm afraid I really don't want to.
Oh, I see, well then, can't be helped...
Yep.
ガッ
YANK

* Palace from the story "Urashima Taro" (said to be on the bottom of the sea).

* Literally, "filth licker" — a demon that licks the dirt in bathrooms.

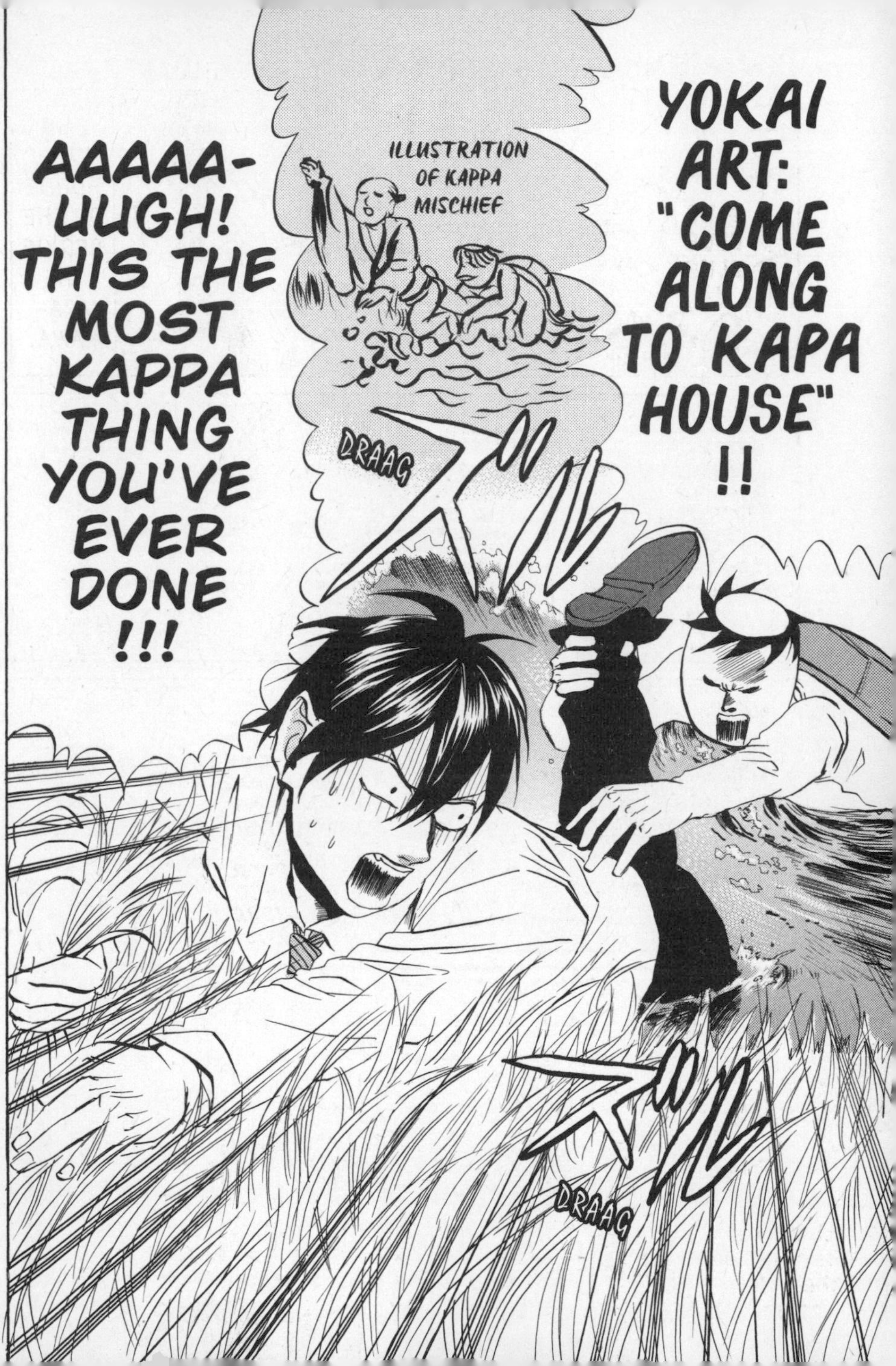
YOKAI ART: "COME ALONG TO KAPA HOUSE" !!
ILLUSTRATION OF KAPPA MISCHIEF
DRAAG
AAAAA-UUGH! THIS THE MOST KAPPA THING YOU'VE EVER DONE !!!
DRAAG

Chapter 194: Welcome to the River Bed

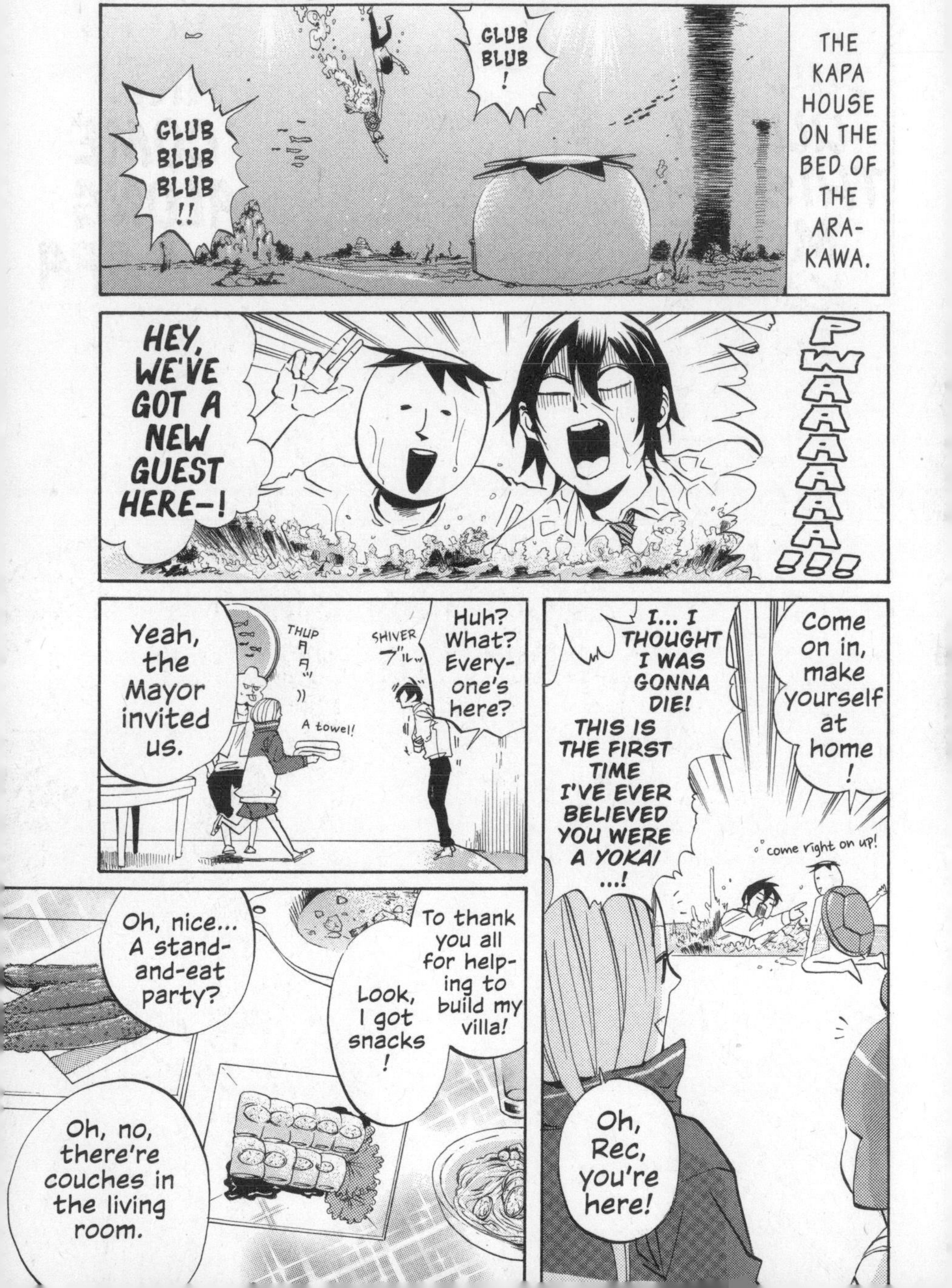
THE KAPA HOUSE ON THE BED OF THE ARA-KAWA.
GLUB BLUB !
GLUB BLUB BLUB !!
PWAAAAAA!!!
HEY, WE'VE GOT A NEW GUEST HERE-!
Come on in, make yourself at home !
I... I THOUGHT I WAS GONNA DIE! THIS IS THE FIRST TIME I'VE EVER BELIEVED YOU WERE A YOKAI ...!
come right on up!
Oh, Rec, you're here!
Huh? What? Every-one's here?
SHIVER
THUP
A towel!
Yeah, the Mayor invited us.
To thank you all for help-ing to build my villa!
Oh, nice... A stand-and-eat party?
Look, I got snacks !
Oh, no, there're couches in the living room.

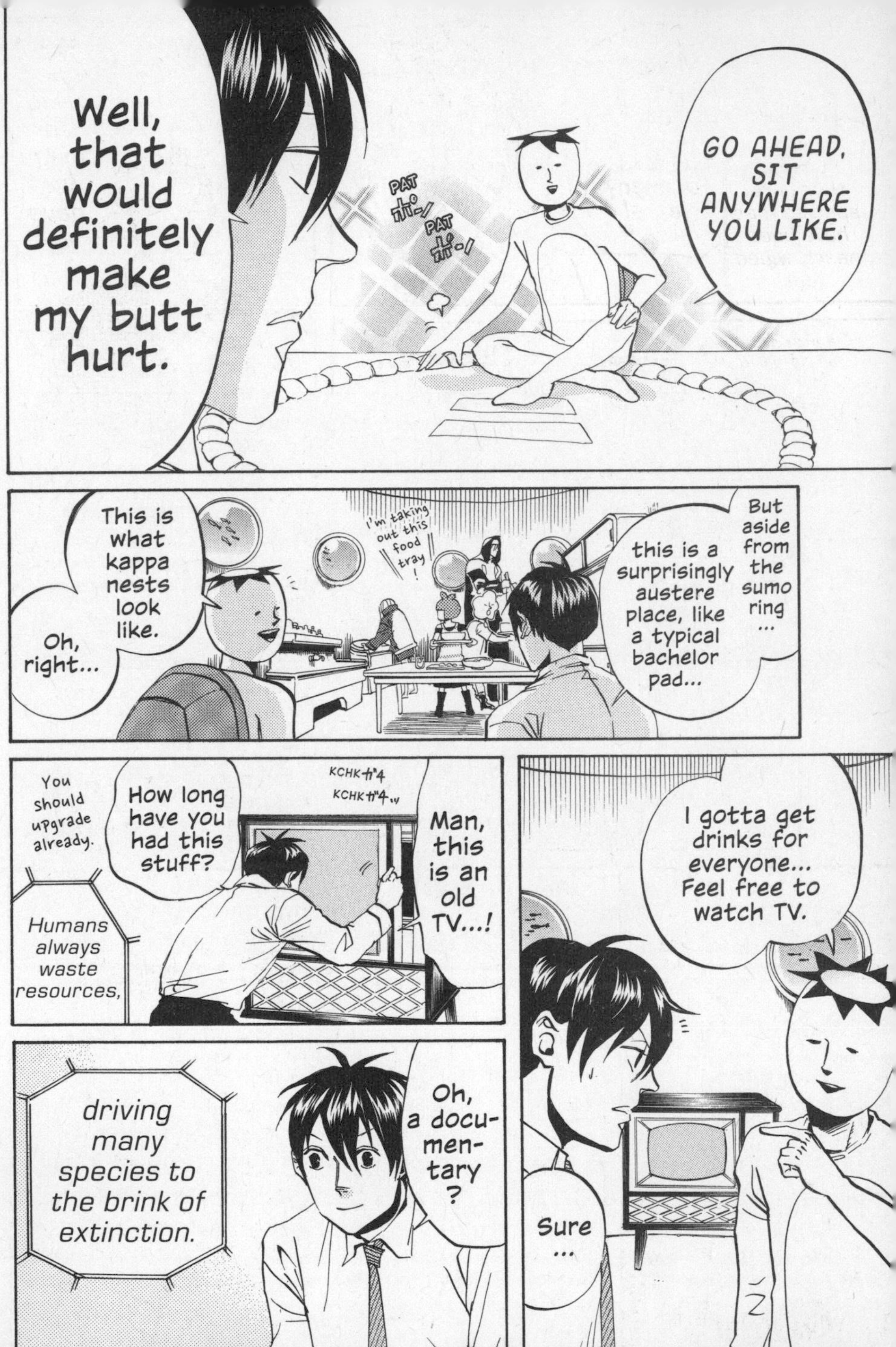
GO AHEAD. SIT ANYWHERE YOU LIKE.
PAT
PAT
Well, that would definitely make my butt hurt.
But aside from the sumo ring...
this is a surprisingly austere place, like a typical bachelor pad...
I'm taking out this food tray!
This is what kappa nests look like.
Oh, right...
I gotta get drinks for everyone... Feel free to watch TV.
Sure...
Man, this is an old TV...!
KCHK
KCHK
How long have you had this stuff?
You should upgrade already.
Humans always waste resources,
Oh, a documentary?
driving many species to the brink of extinction.

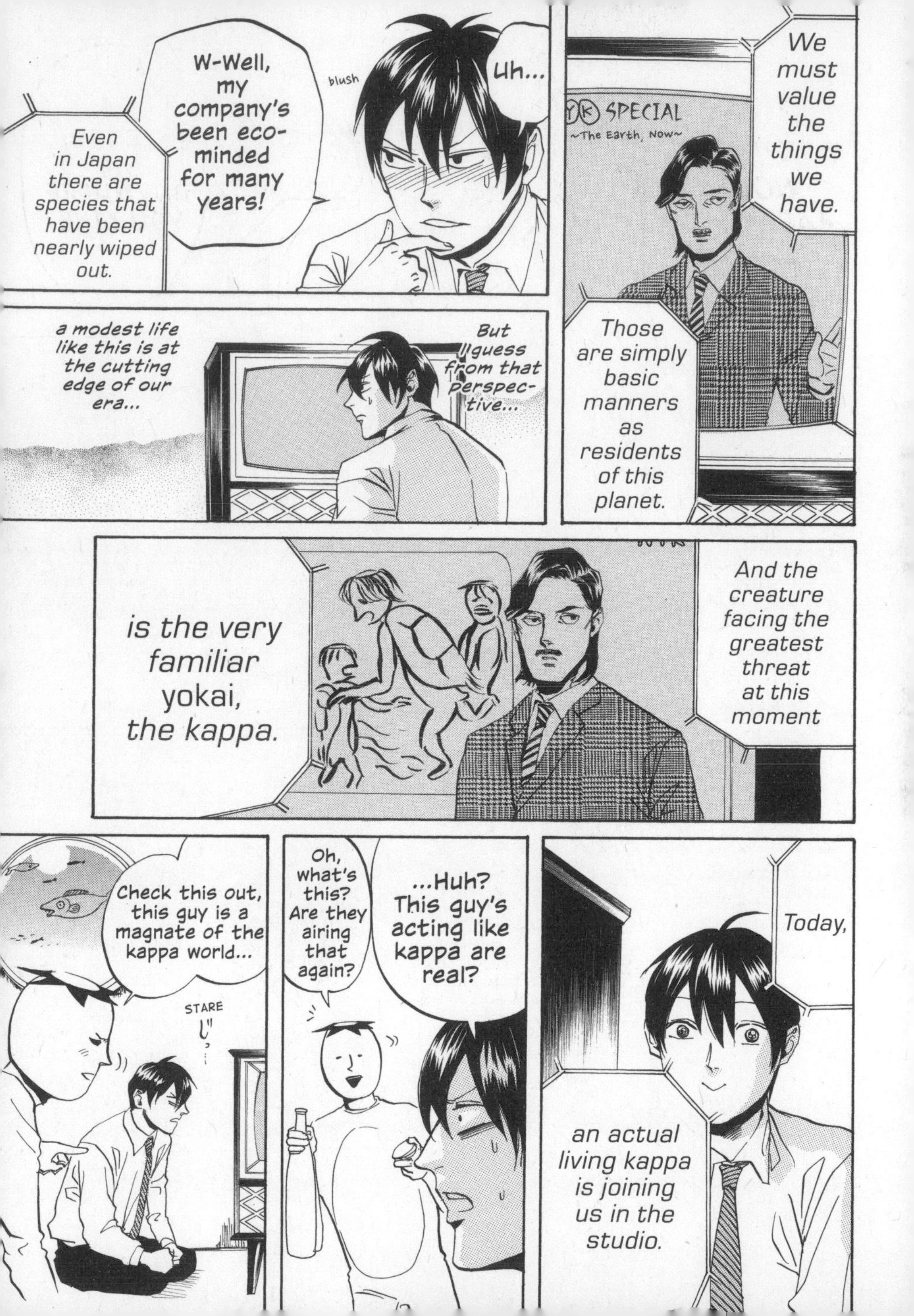

Y K SPECIAL
~The Earth, Now~
We must value the things we have.
Those are simply basic manners as residents of this planet.
Uh...
blush
W-Well, my company's been eco-minded for many years!
Even in Japan there are species that have been nearly wiped out.
But I guess from that perspective...
a modest life like this is at the cutting edge of our era...
And the creature facing the greatest threat at this moment
is the very familiar yokai, the kappa.
Today,
an actual living kappa is joining us in the studio.
...Huh? This guy's acting like kappa are real?
Oh, what's this? Are they airing that again?
Check this out, this guy is a magnate of the kappa world...
STARE

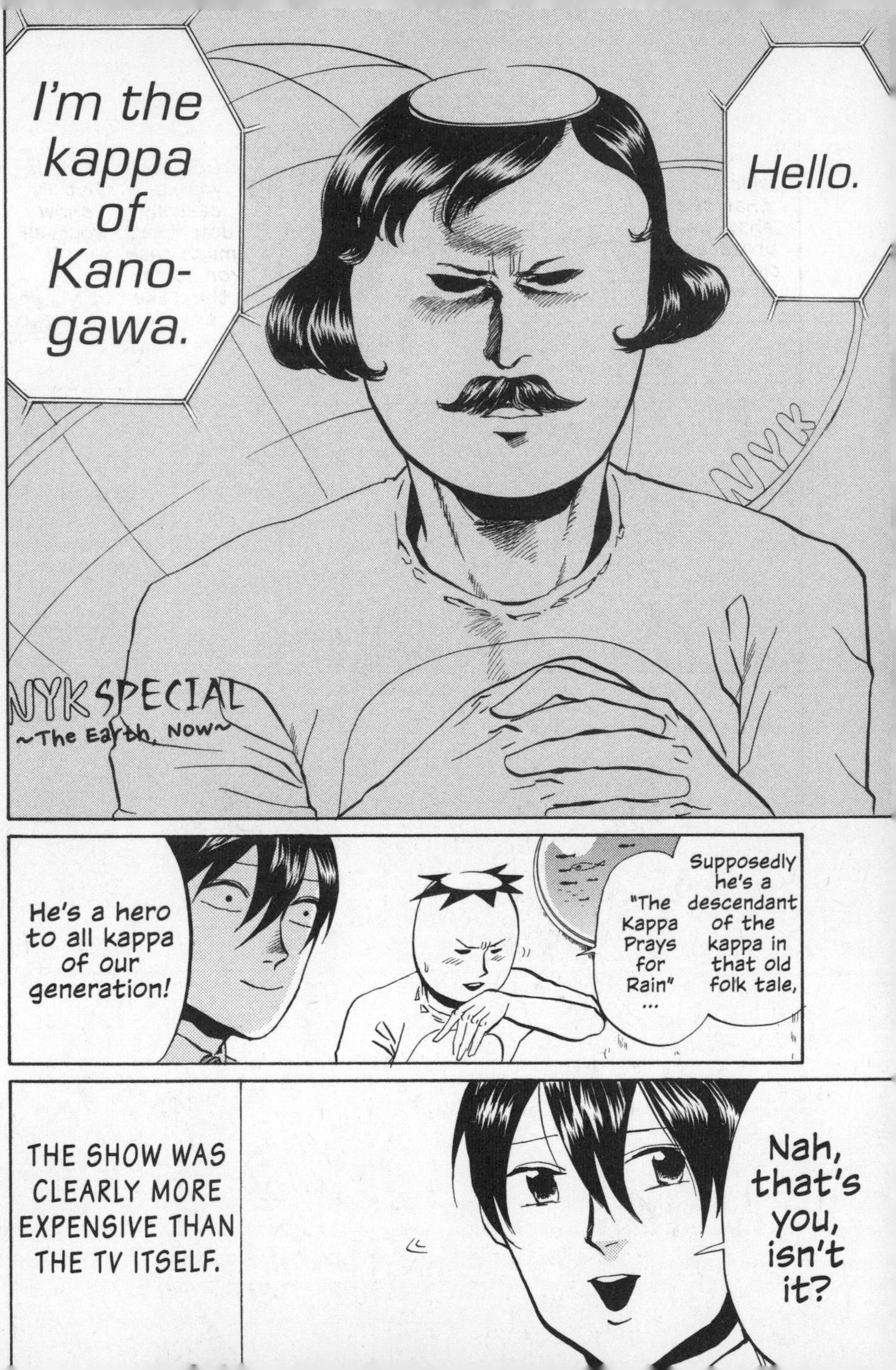
Hello.
I'm the kappa of Kano-gawa.
NYK SPECIAL
~The Earth, Now~
Supposedly he's a descendant of the kappa in that old folk tale, "The Kappa Prays for Rain"...
He's a hero to all kappa of our generation!
Nah, that's you, isn't it?
THE SHOW WAS CLEARLY MORE EXPENSIVE THAN THE TV ITSELF.

Chapter 195: The Mayor's Secret

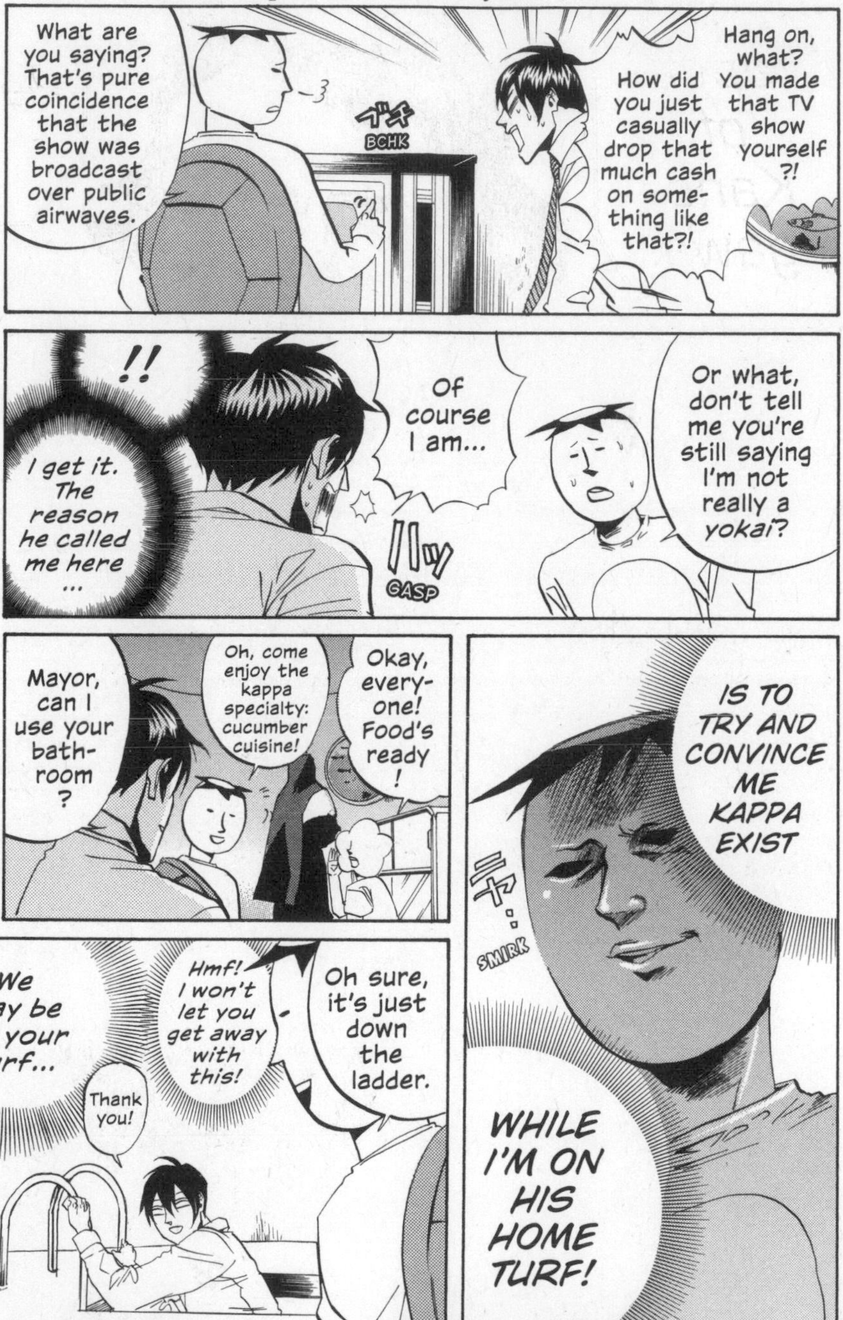

Hang on, what? You made that TV show yourself?!
How did you just casually drop that much cash on some-thing like that?!
BCHK
What are you saying? That's pure coincidence that the show was broadcast over public airwaves.
Or what, don't tell me you're still saying I'm not really a yokai?
Of course I am...
GASP
!!
I get it. The reason he called me here ...
IS TO TRY AND CONVINCE ME KAPPA EXIST
SMIRK
WHILE I'M ON HIS HOME TURF!
Okay, every-one! Food's ready!
Oh, come enjoy the kappa specialty: cucumber cuisine!
Mayor, can I use your bath-room?
Oh sure, it's just down the ladder.
Hmf! I won't let you get away with this!
We may be on your turf...
Thank you!

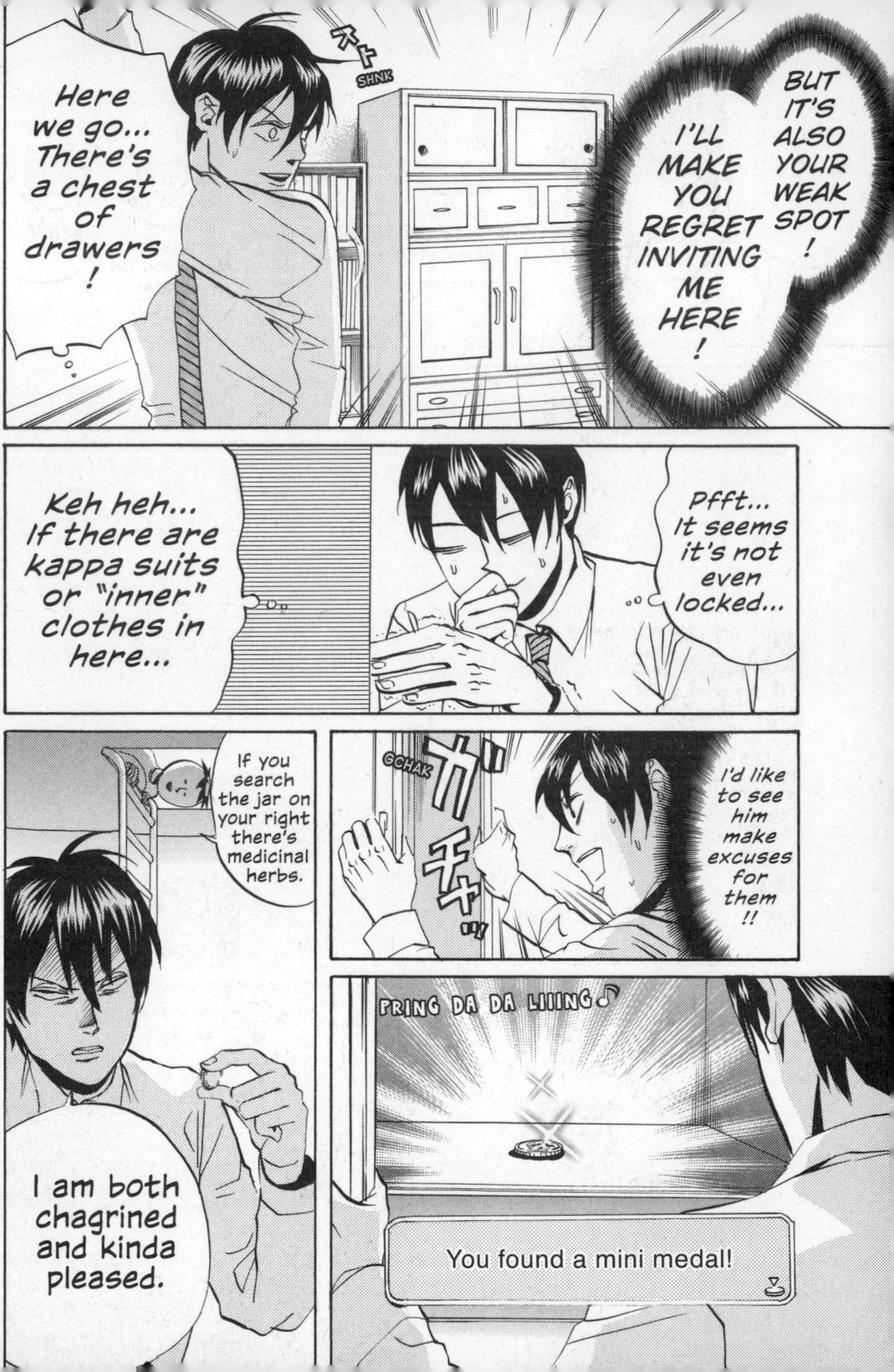
BUT IT'S ALSO YOUR WEAK SPOT!
I'LL MAKE YOU REGRET INVITING ME HERE!
SHNK
Here we go... There's a chest of drawers!
Pfft... It seems it's not even locked...
Keh heh... If there are kappa suits or "inner" clothes in here...
I'd like to see him make excuses for them!!
GCHAK
PRING DA DA LIIING♪
You found a mini medal!
If you search the jar on your right there's medicinal herbs.
I am both chagrined and kinda pleased.

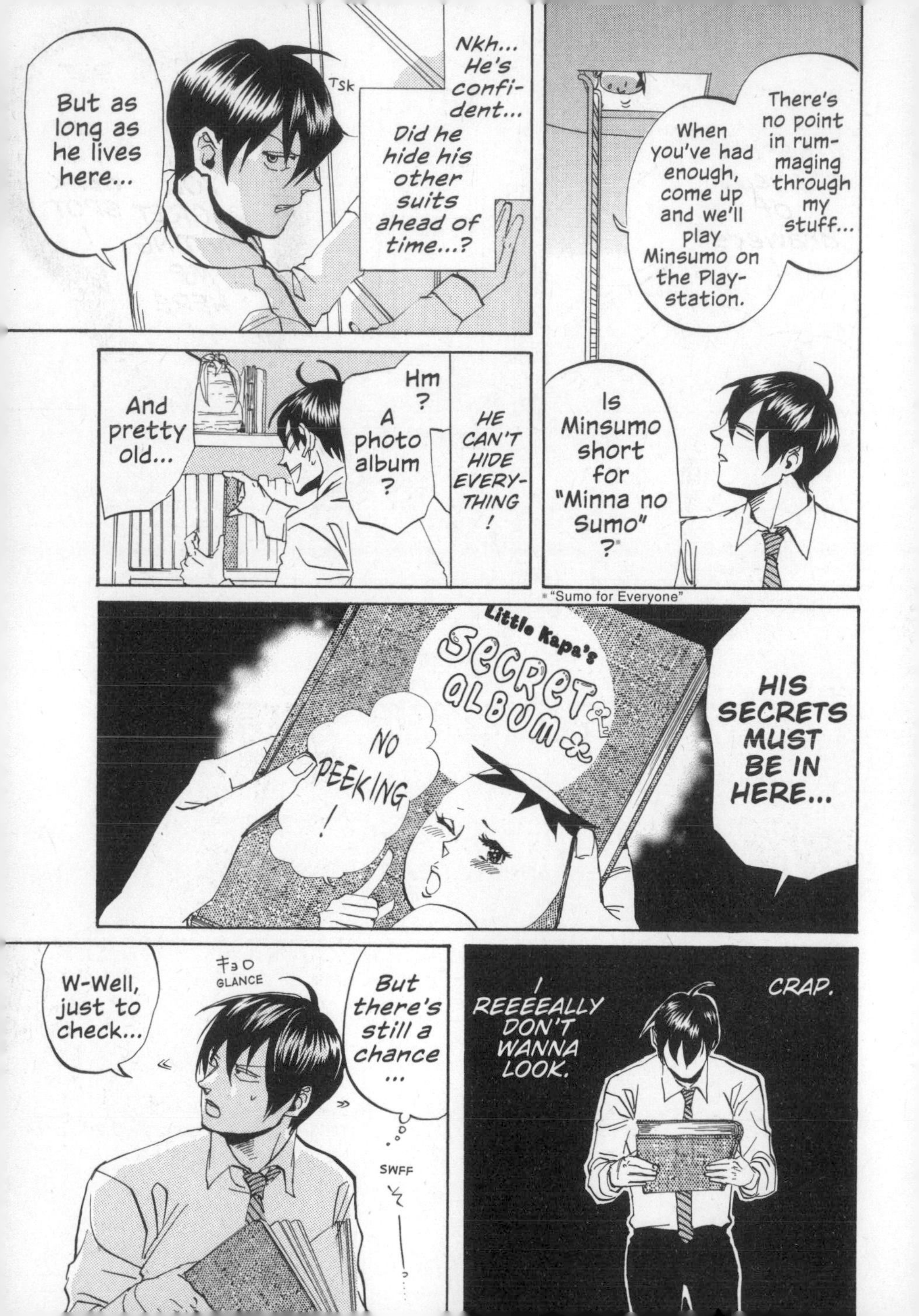
There's no point in rummaging through my stuff...
When you've had enough, come up and we'll play Minsumo on the Playstation.
Is Minsumo short for "Minna no Sumo"?*
Nkh... He's confident...
Did he hide his other suits ahead of time...?
Tsk
But as long as he lives here...
HE CAN'T HIDE EVERYTHING!
Hm? A photo album?
And pretty old...
* "Sumo for Everyone"
HIS SECRETS MUST BE IN HERE...
Little Kapa's Secret Album
NO PEEKING!
CRAP.
I REEEEALLY DON'T WANNA LOOK.
But there's still a chance...
キョロ
GLANCE
W-Well, just to check...
SWFF

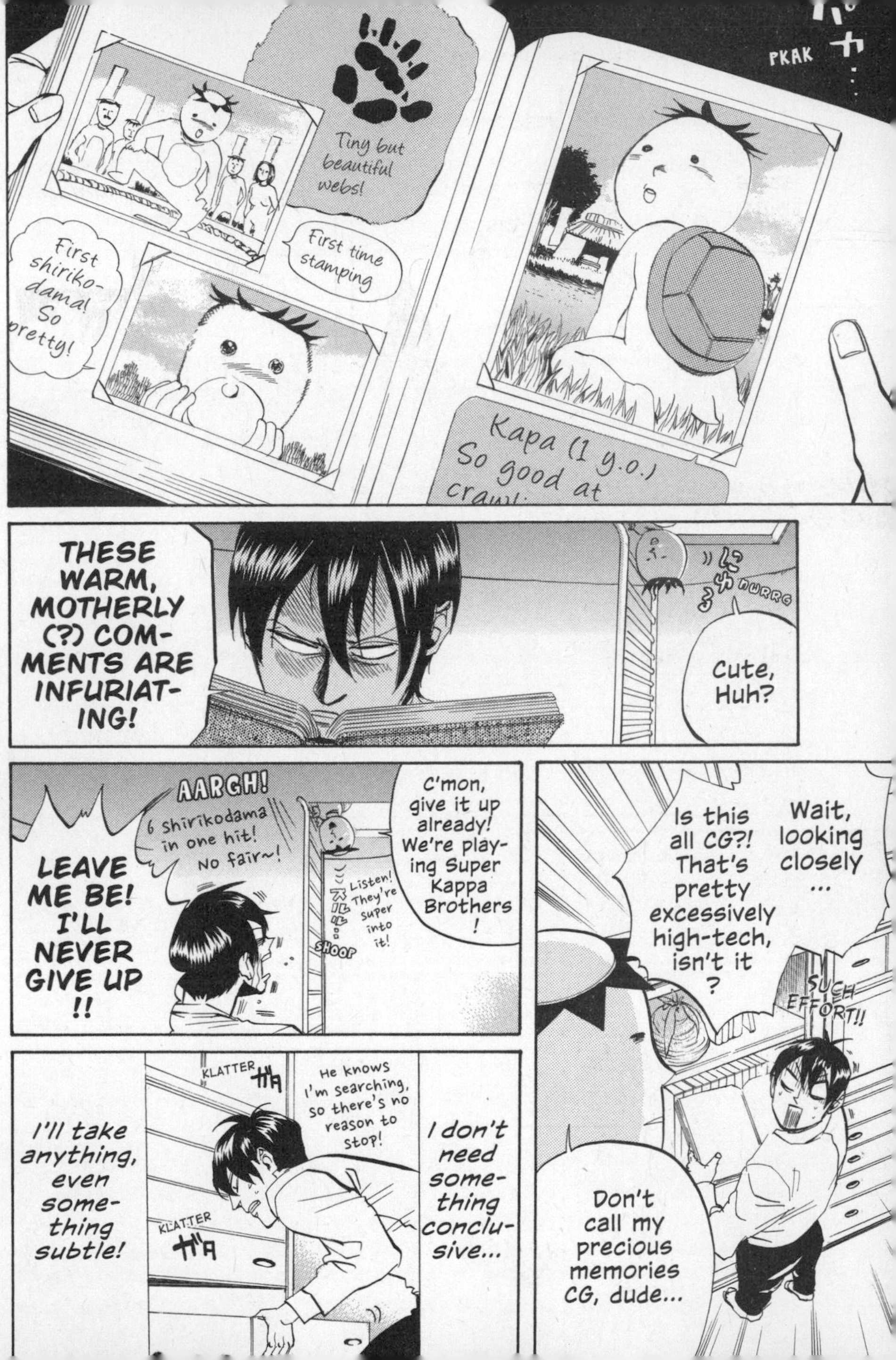
PKAK
Kapa (1 y.o.) So good at crawl
Tiny but beautiful webs!
First time stamping
First shirikodama! So pretty!
NURRG
Cute, Huh?
THESE WARM, MOTHERLY (?) COMMENTS ARE INFURIATING!
Wait, looking closely...
Is this all CG?! That's pretty excessively high-tech, isn't it?
SUCH EFFORT!!
Don't call my precious memories CG, dude...
C'mon, give it up already! We're playing Super Kappa Brothers!
Listen! They're super into it!
SHOOP
AARGH!
6 shirikodama in one hit! No fair~!
LEAVE ME BE! I'LL NEVER GIVE UP!!
I don't need something conclusive...
He knows I'm searching, so there's no reason to stop!
KLATTER
KLATTER
I'll take anything, even something subtle!

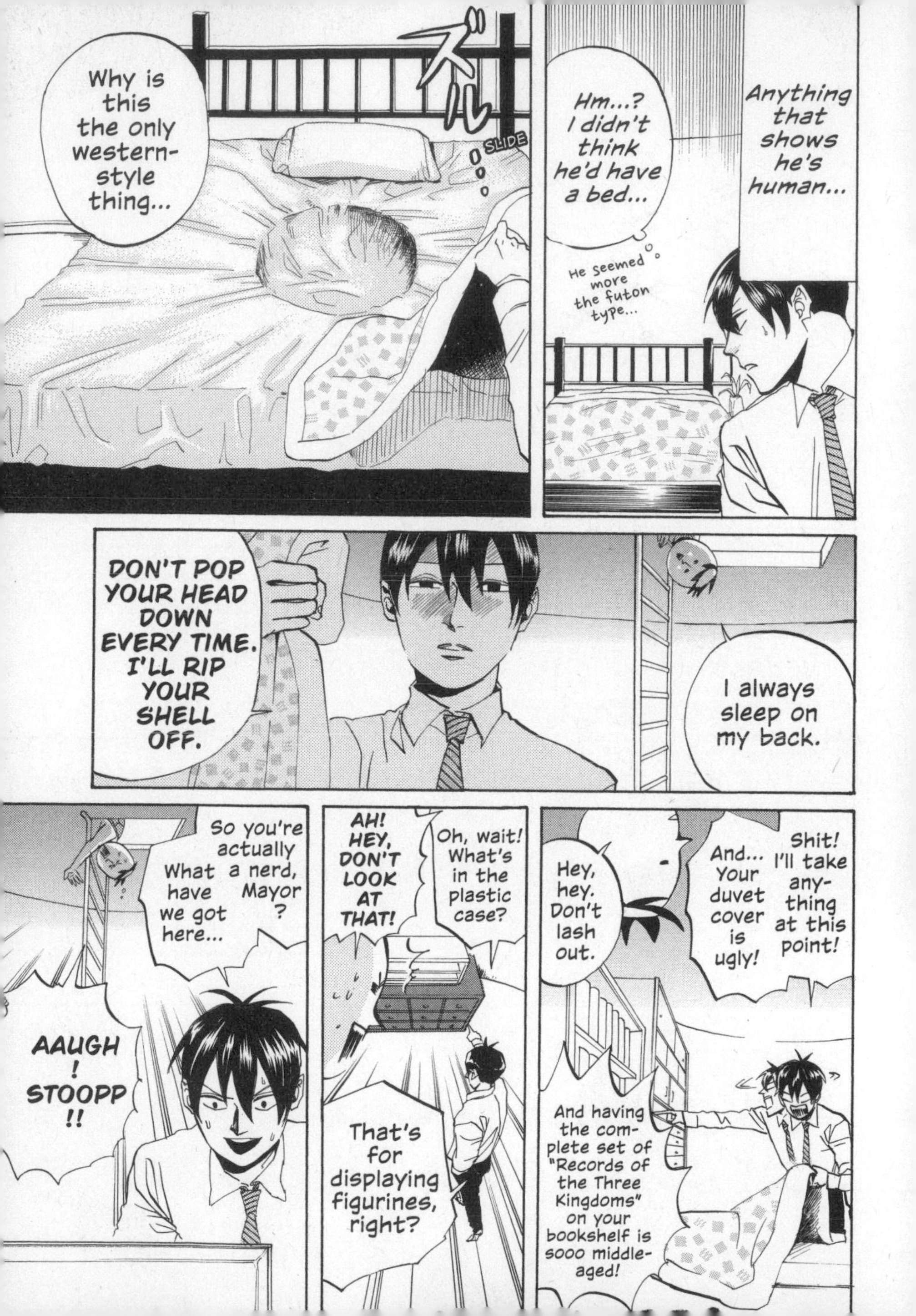
Anything that shows he's human...
Hm...? I didn't think he'd have a bed...
He seemed more the futon type...
ズル
SLIDE
Why is this the only western-style thing...
I always sleep on my back.
DON'T POP YOUR HEAD DOWN EVERY TIME. I'LL RIP YOUR SHELL OFF.
Shit! I'll take anything at this point!
And... Your duvet cover is ugly!
Hey, hey. Don't lash out.
And having the complete set of "Records of the Three Kingdoms" on your bookshelf is sooo middle-aged!
Oh, wait! What's in the plastic case?
AH! HEY, DON'T LOOK AT THAT!
That's for displaying figurines, right?
So you're actually a nerd, Mayor?
What have we got here...
AAUGH! STOOPP!!

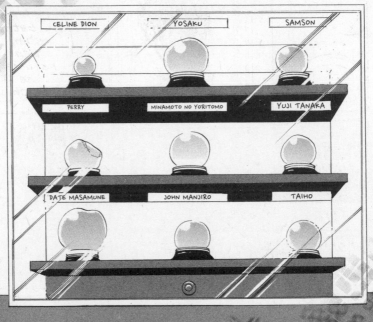

CELINE DION	YOSAKU	SAMSON
PERRY	MINAMOTO NO YORITOMO	YUJI TANAKA
DATE MASAMUNE	JOHN MANJIRO	TAIHO

Which one do you like best, Rec?

The one in the middle's the rarest...

MINA-MOTO NO YORITOMO'S SHIRIKO-DAMA.

THEY JUST LOOK LIKE SUPER BALLS TO ME.

I'M NEVER GONNA LOSE TO YOU!!

I won't give up my shirikodama!!

I could add your *shirikodama* to my collection, if you'd like...

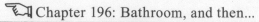

Chapter 196: Bathroom, and then...

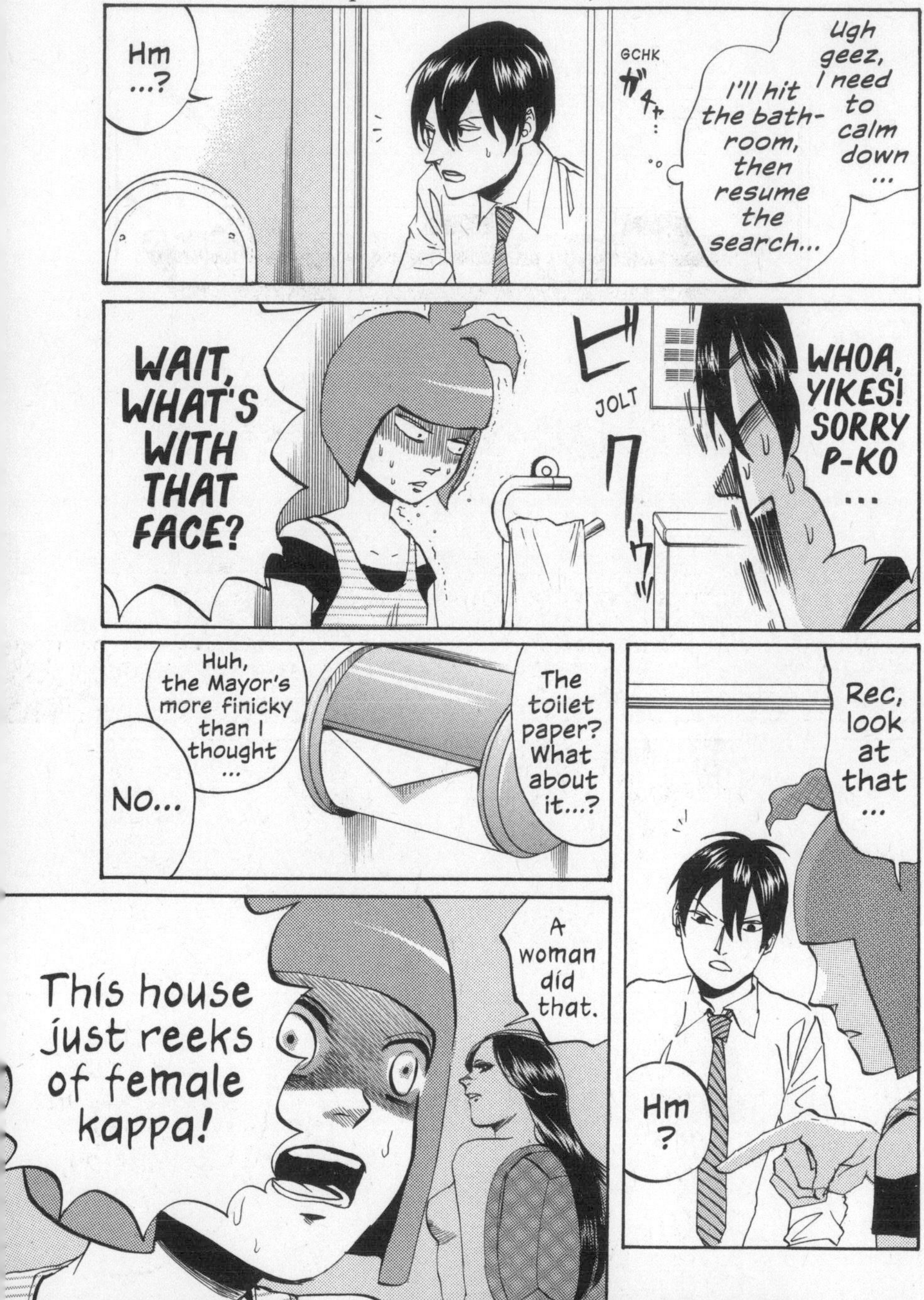
Ugh geez, I need to calm down...
I'll hit the bathroom, then resume the search...
GCHK
Hm...?
WHOA, YIKES! SORRY P-KO...
JOLT
WAIT, WHAT'S WITH THAT FACE?
Rec, look at that...
Hm?
The toilet paper? What about it...?
Huh, the Mayor's more finicky than I thought...
No...
A woman did that.
This house just reeks of female kappa!

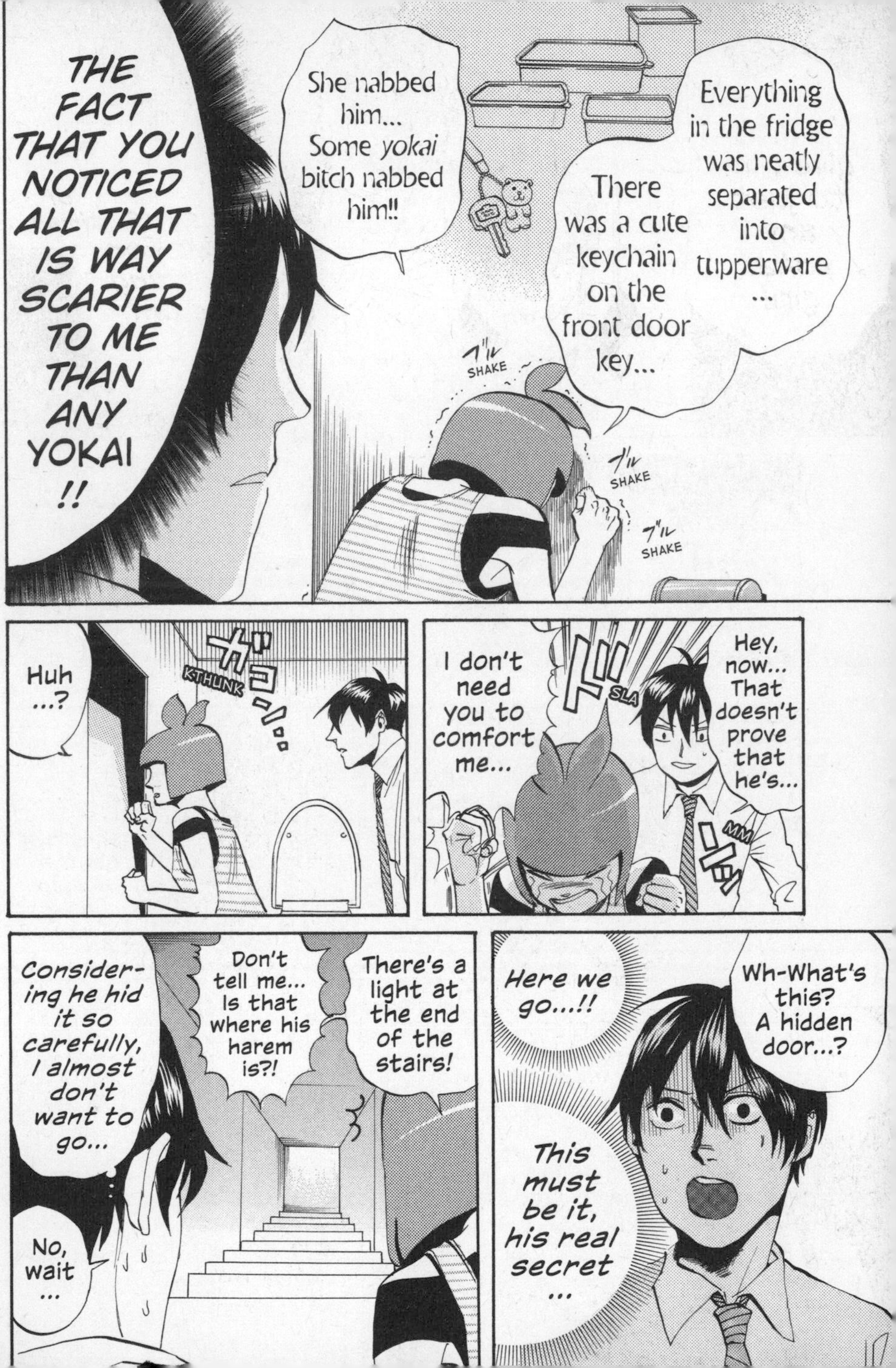

Everything in the fridge was neatly separated into tupperware ...
There was a cute keychain on the front door key...
She nabbed him... Some *yokai* bitch nabbed him!!
SHAKE
SHAKE
SHAKE
THE FACT THAT YOU NOTICED ALL THAT IS WAY SCARIER TO ME THAN ANY YOKAI !!
Hey, now... That doesn't prove that he's...
SLA
I don't need you to comfort me...
MM
KTHUNK
Huh ...?
Wh-What's this? A hidden door...?
Here we go...!!
This must be it, his real secret ...
There's a light at the end of the stairs!
Don't tell me... Is that where his harem is?!
Consider-ing he hid it so carefully, I almost don't want to go...
No, wait ...

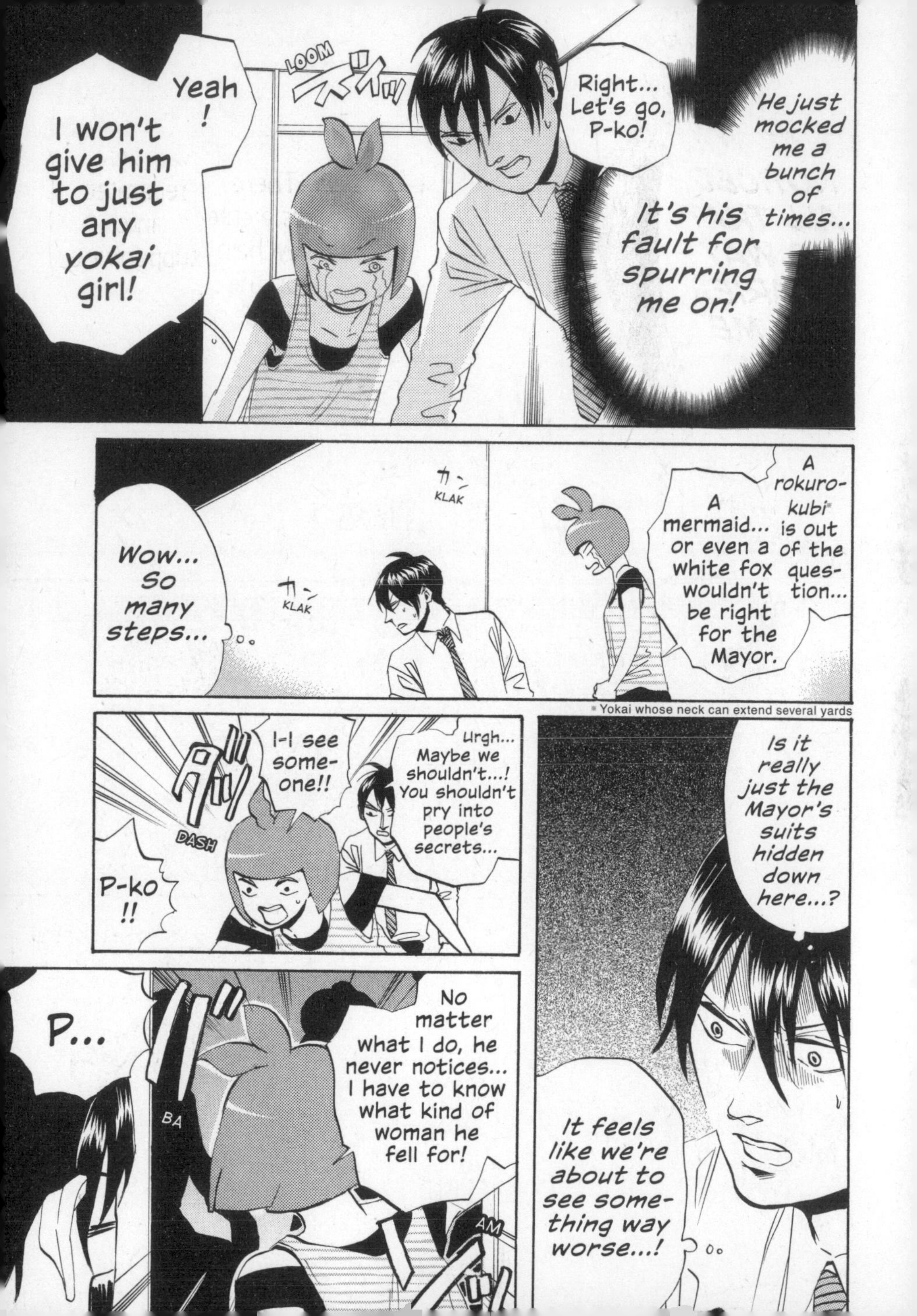
He just mocked me a bunch of times...
It's his fault for spurring me on!
Right... Let's go, P-ko!
LOOM
Yeah!
I won't give him to just any yokai girl!
A rokuro-kubi* is out of the question...
A mermaid... or even a white fox wouldn't be right for the Mayor.
KLAK
KLAK
Wow... So many steps...
Is it really just the Mayor's suits hidden down here...?
It feels like we're about to see something way worse...!
Urgh... Maybe we shouldn't...! You shouldn't pry into people's secrets...
I-I see someone!!
DASH
P-ko!!
No matter what I do, he never notices... I have to know what kind of woman he fell for!
BA
AM
P...

* Yokai whose neck can extend several yards

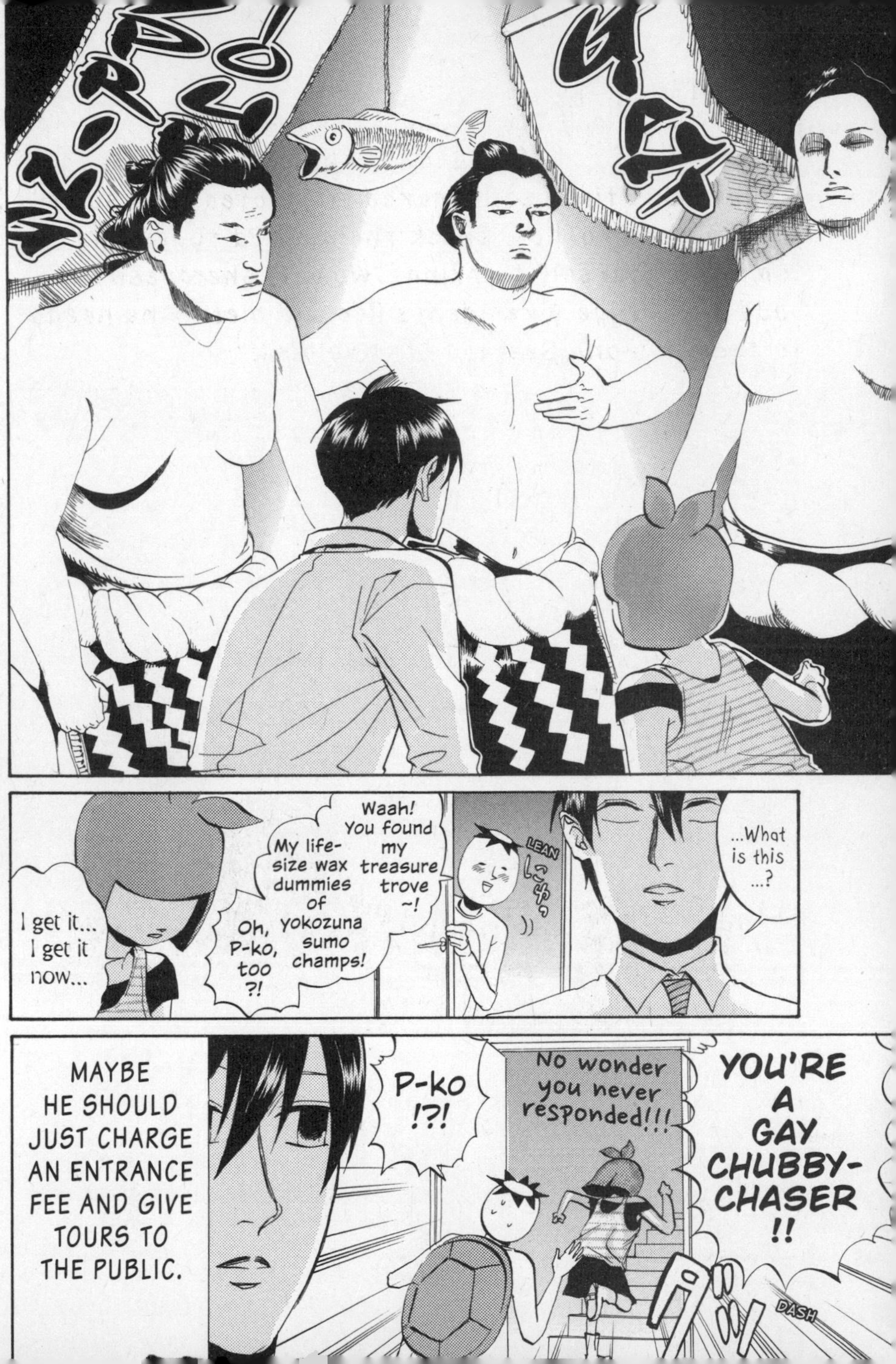
...What is this ...?
LEAN
Waah! You found my treasure trove ~!
My life-size wax dummies of yokozuna sumo champs!
Oh, P-ko, too ?!
I get it... I get it now...
YOU'RE A GAY CHUBBY-CHASER !!
DASH
No wonder you never responded!!!
P-ko !?!
MAYBE HE SHOULD JUST CHARGE AN ENTRANCE FEE AND GIVE TOURS TO THE PUBLIC.

AFTERWORD

Thank you for reading this volume of Arakawa! I had nine extra pages (a lot) this time, so I figured I'd belatedly do some character profiles. Check their blood types and smile to yourself thinking, "Wow, if she doesn't add more type A residents Rec will die! (if he needs a transfusion). See you next volume!

2/27/2008 Hikaru Nakamura

By the way, I'm type O, Taurus

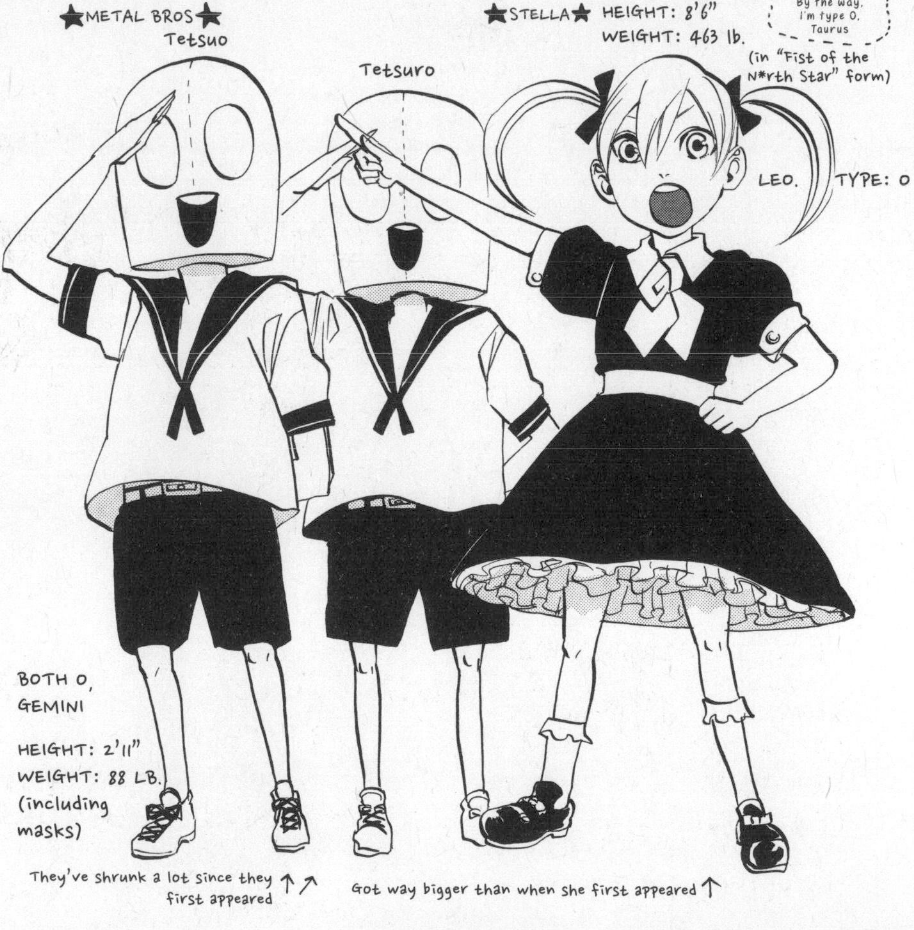
★METAL BROS★
Tetsuo
Tetsuro
★STELLA★ HEIGHT: 8'6"
WEIGHT: 463 lb.
(in "Fist of the N*rth Star" form)
LEO. TYPE: O
BOTH O, GEMINI
HEIGHT: 2'11"
WEIGHT: 88 LB. (including masks)
They've shrunk a lot since they first appeared ↑↗
Got way bigger than when she first appeared ↑

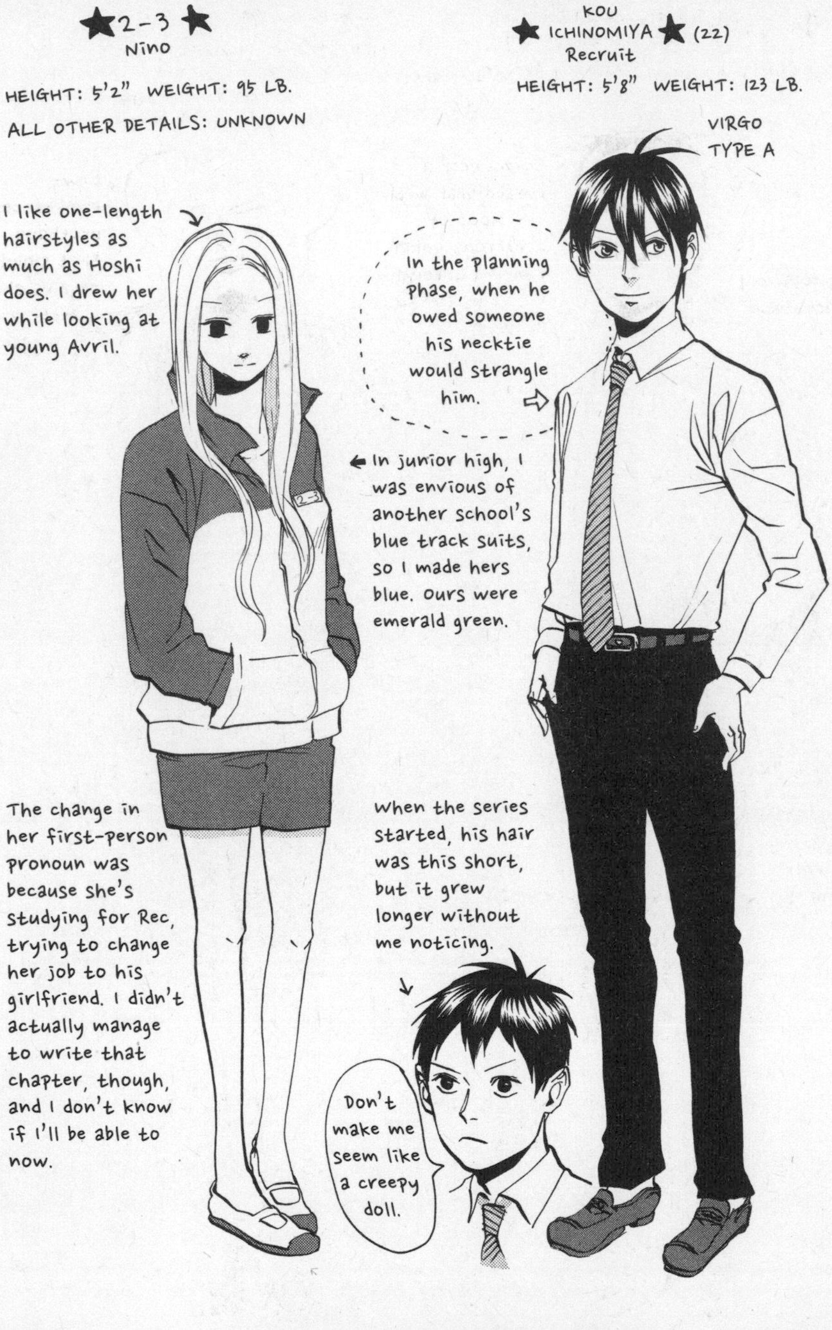

KOU ICHINOMIYA (22)
Recruit
HEIGHT: 5'8" WEIGHT: 123 LB.
VIRGO
TYPE A
In the planning phase, when he owed someone his necktie would strangle him.
When the series started, his hair was this short, but it grew longer without me noticing.
Don't make me seem like a creepy doll.
2-3
Nino
HEIGHT: 5'2" WEIGHT: 95 LB.
ALL OTHER DETAILS: UNKNOWN
I like one-length hairstyles as much as Hoshi does. I drew her while looking at young Avril.
In junior high, I was envious of another school's blue track suits, so I made hers blue. Ours were emerald green.
The change in her first-person pronoun was because she's studying for Rec, trying to change her job to his girlfriend. I didn't actually manage to write that chapter, though, and I don't know if I'll be able to now.

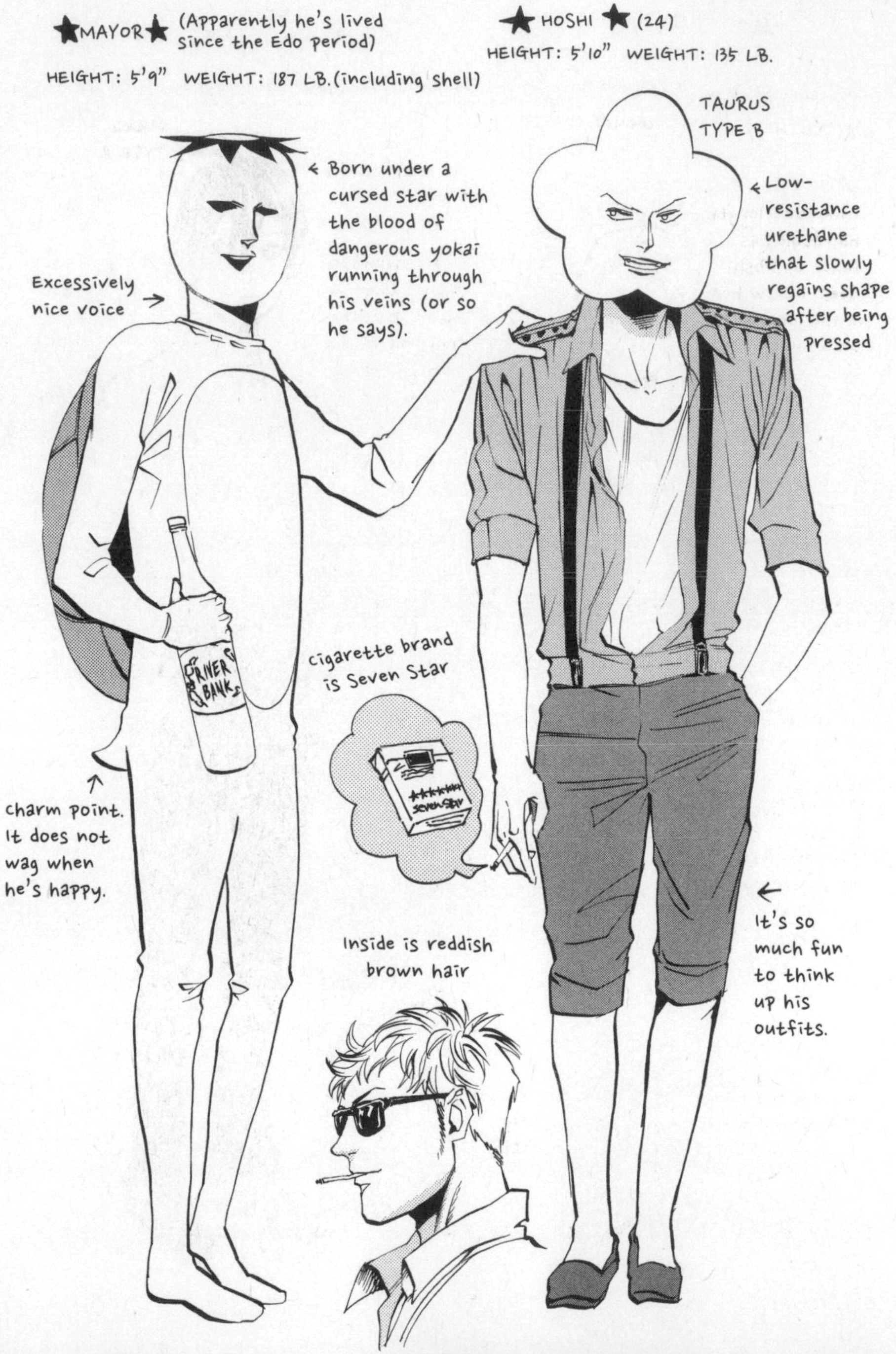
★MAYOR★ (Apparently he's lived since the Edo period)
HEIGHT: 5'9" WEIGHT: 187 LB. (including shell)
★HOSHI★ (24)
HEIGHT: 5'10" WEIGHT: 135 LB.
TAURUS TYPE B
← Born under a cursed star with the blood of dangerous yokai running through his veins (or so he says).
← Low-resistance urethane that slowly regains shape after being pressed
Excessively nice voice →
RIVER BANK
cigarette brand is Seven Star
SEVEN STAR
↑ charm point. It does not wag when he's happy.
← It's so much fun to think up his outfits.
Inside is reddish brown hair

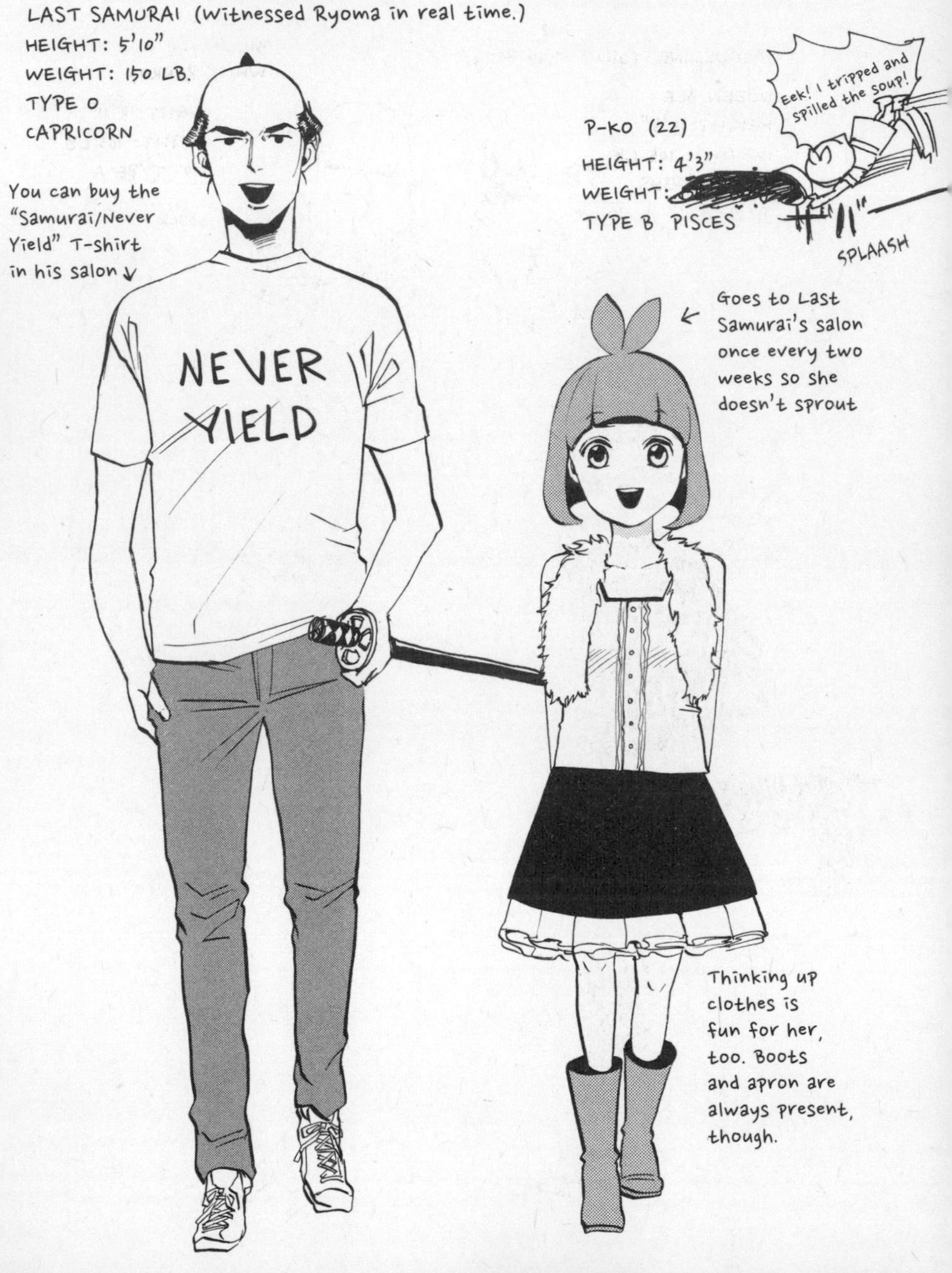
Eek! I tripped and spilled the soup!
SPLAASH
P-KO (22)
HEIGHT: 4'3"
WEIGHT: [redacted]
TYPE B PISCES
Goes to Last Samurai's salon once every two weeks so she doesn't sprout
Thinking up clothes is fun for her, too. Boots and apron are always present, though.
LAST SAMURAI (Witnessed Ryoma in real time.)
HEIGHT: 5'10"
WEIGHT: 150 LB.
TYPE O
CAPRICORN
You can buy the "Samurai/Never Yield" T-shirt in his salon
NEVER YIELD

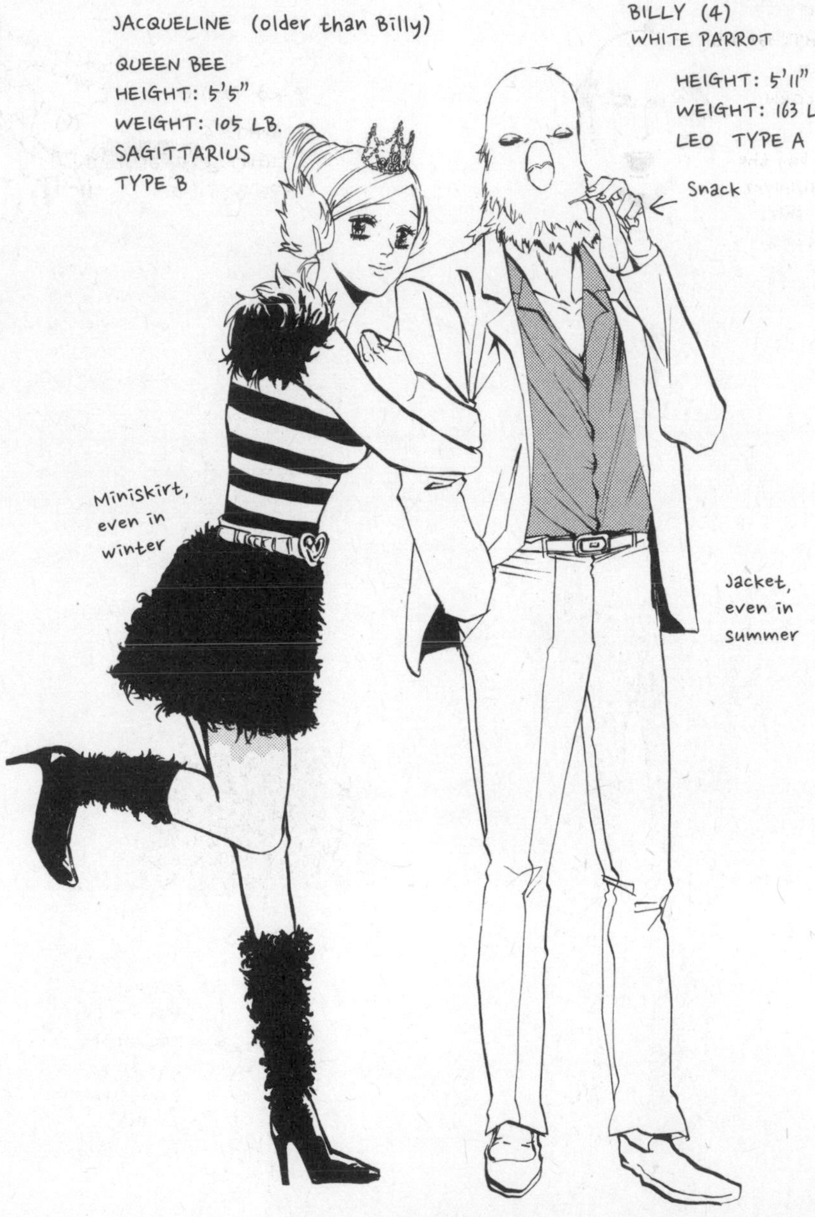
BILLY (4)
WHITE PARROT
HEIGHT: 5'11"
WEIGHT: 163 LB.
LEO TYPE A
Snack
JACQUELINE (older than Billy)
QUEEN BEE
HEIGHT: 5'5"
WEIGHT: 105 LB.
SAGITTARIUS
TYPE B
Jacket, even in summer
Miniskirt, even in winter

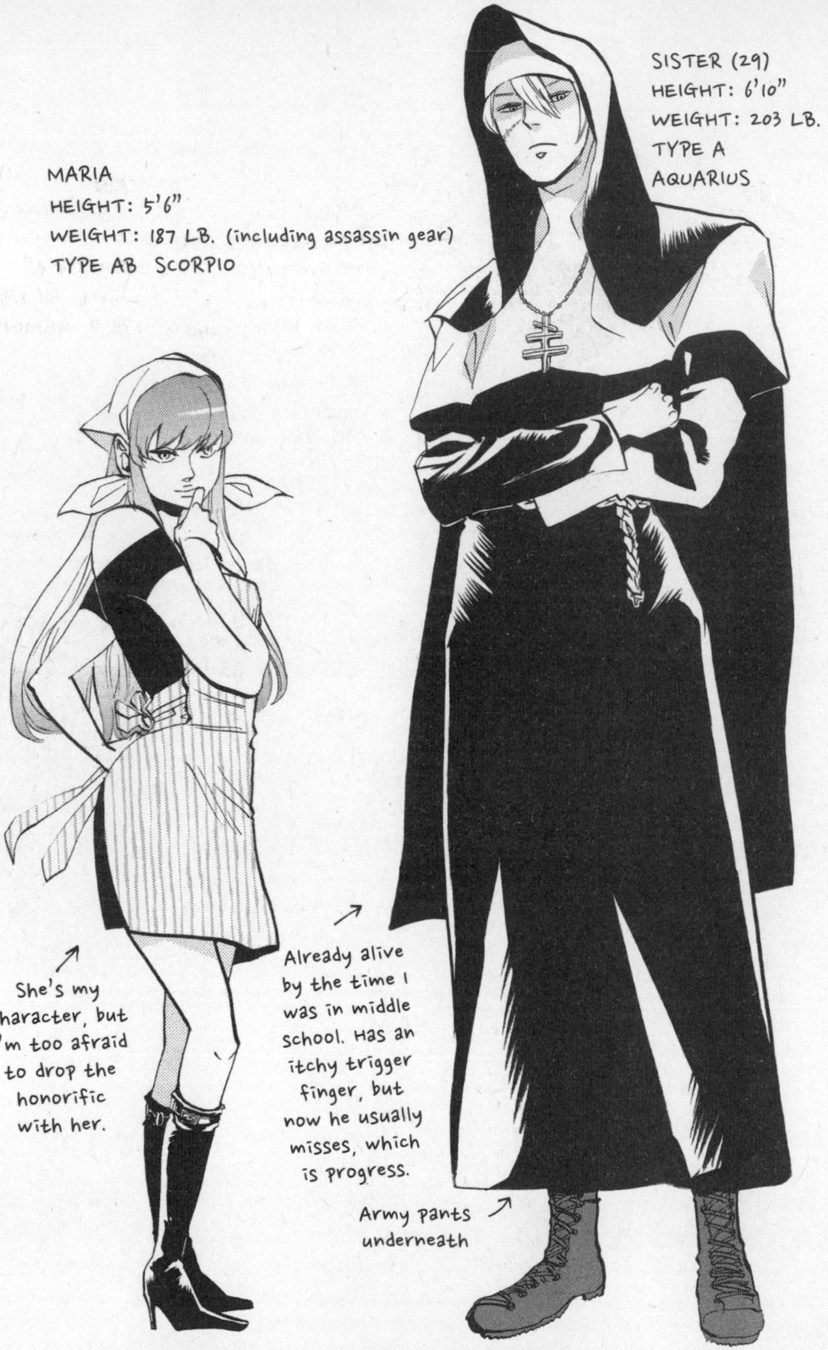
SISTER (29)
HEIGHT: 6'10"
WEIGHT: 203 LB.
TYPE A
AQUARIUS
MARIA
HEIGHT: 5'6"
WEIGHT: 187 LB. (including assassin gear)
TYPE AB SCORPIO
Army pants underneath
Already alive by the time I was in middle school. Has an itchy trigger finger, but now he usually misses, which is progress.
She's my character, but I'm too afraid to drop the honorific with her.

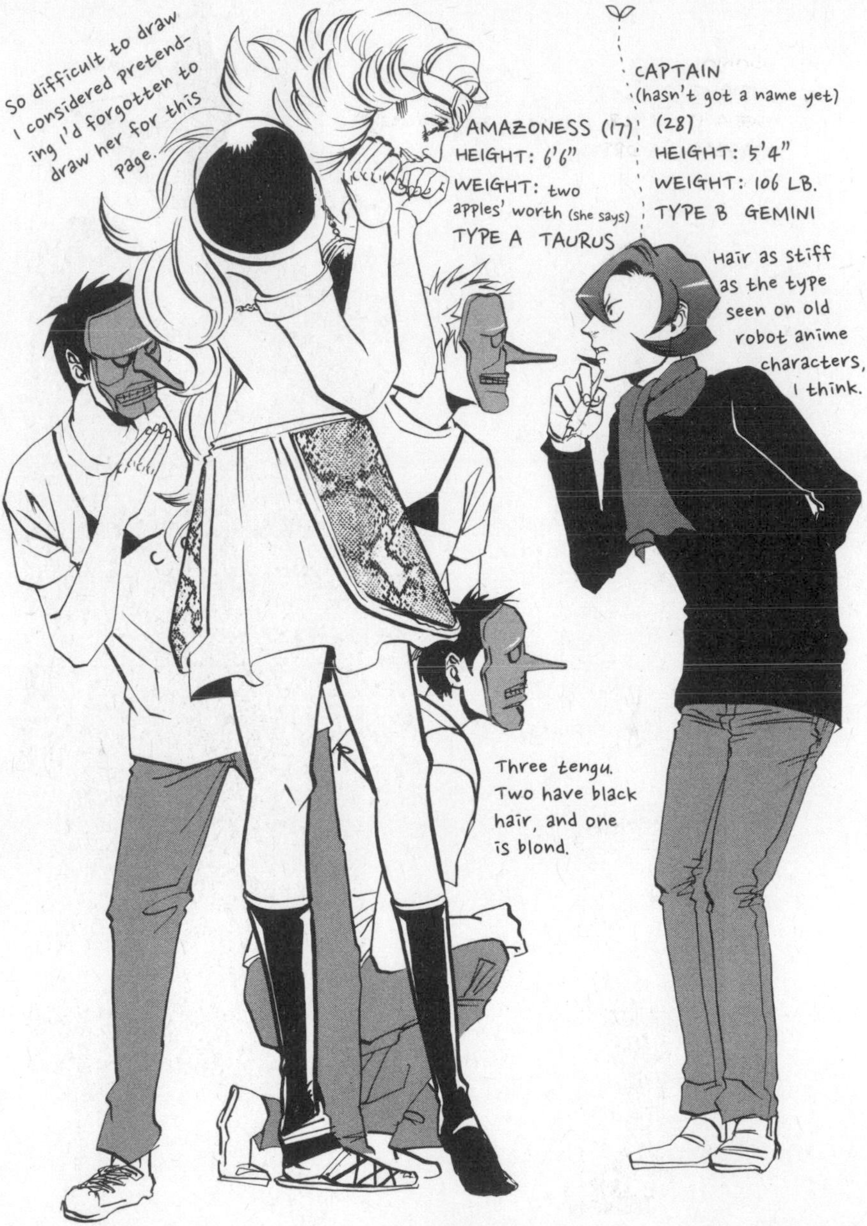
So difficult to draw I considered pretending I'd forgotten to draw her for this page.
AMAZONESS (17)
HEIGHT: 6'6"
WEIGHT: two apples' worth (she says)
TYPE A TAURUS
CAPTAIN
(hasn't got a name yet)
(28)
HEIGHT: 5'4"
WEIGHT: 106 LB.
TYPE B GEMINI
Hair as stiff as the type seen on old robot anime characters, I think.
Three tengu. Two have black hair, and one is blond.

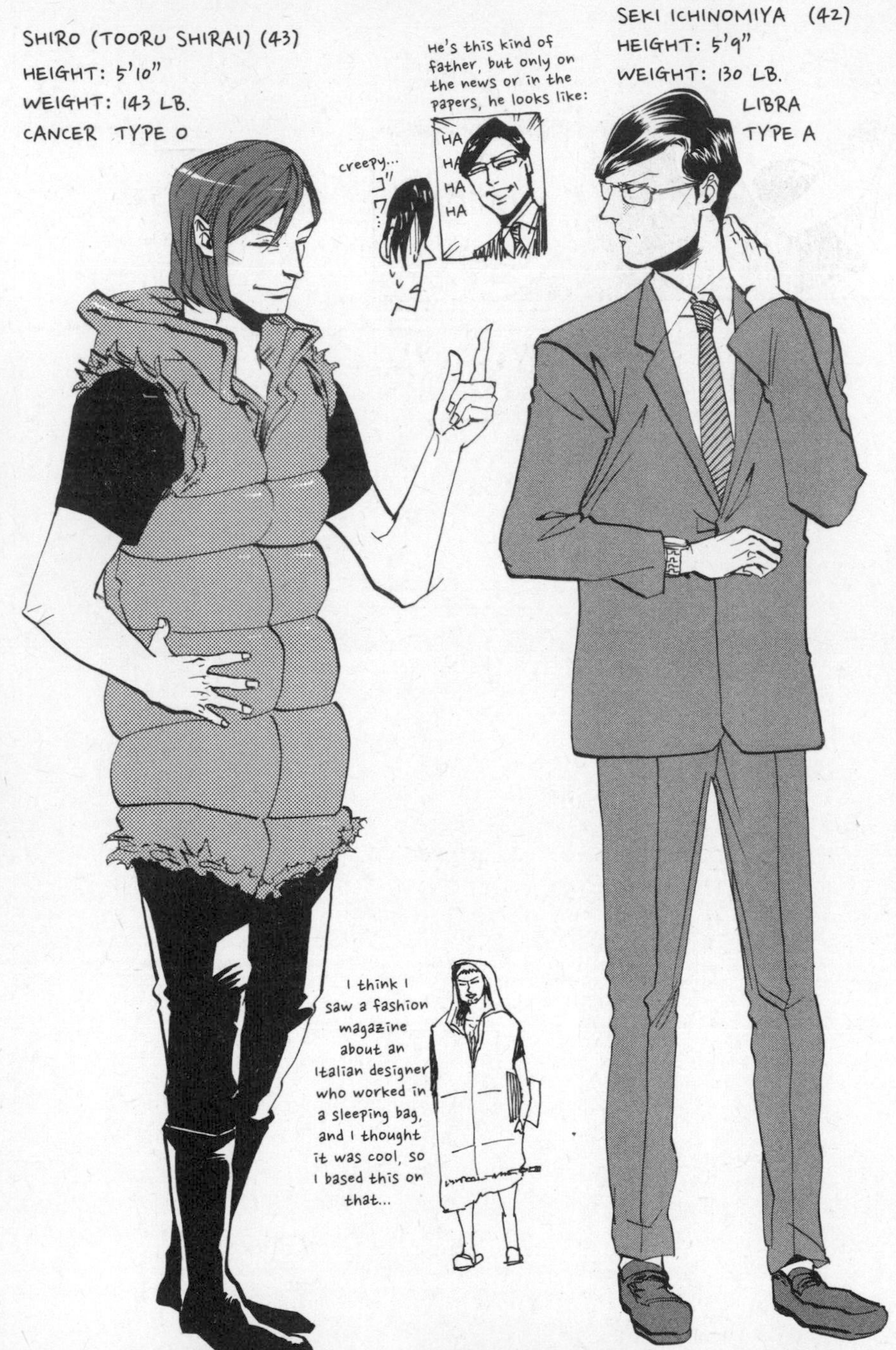
SEKI ICHINOMIYA (42)
HEIGHT: 5'9"
WEIGHT: 130 LB.
LIBRA
TYPE A
He's this kind of father, but only on the news or in the papers, he looks like:
HA
HA
HA
HA
creepy...
SHIRO (TOORU SHIRAI) (43)
HEIGHT: 5'10"
WEIGHT: 143 LB.
CANCER TYPE O
I think I saw a fashion magazine about an Italian designer who worked in a sleeping bag, and I thought it was cool, so I based this on that...

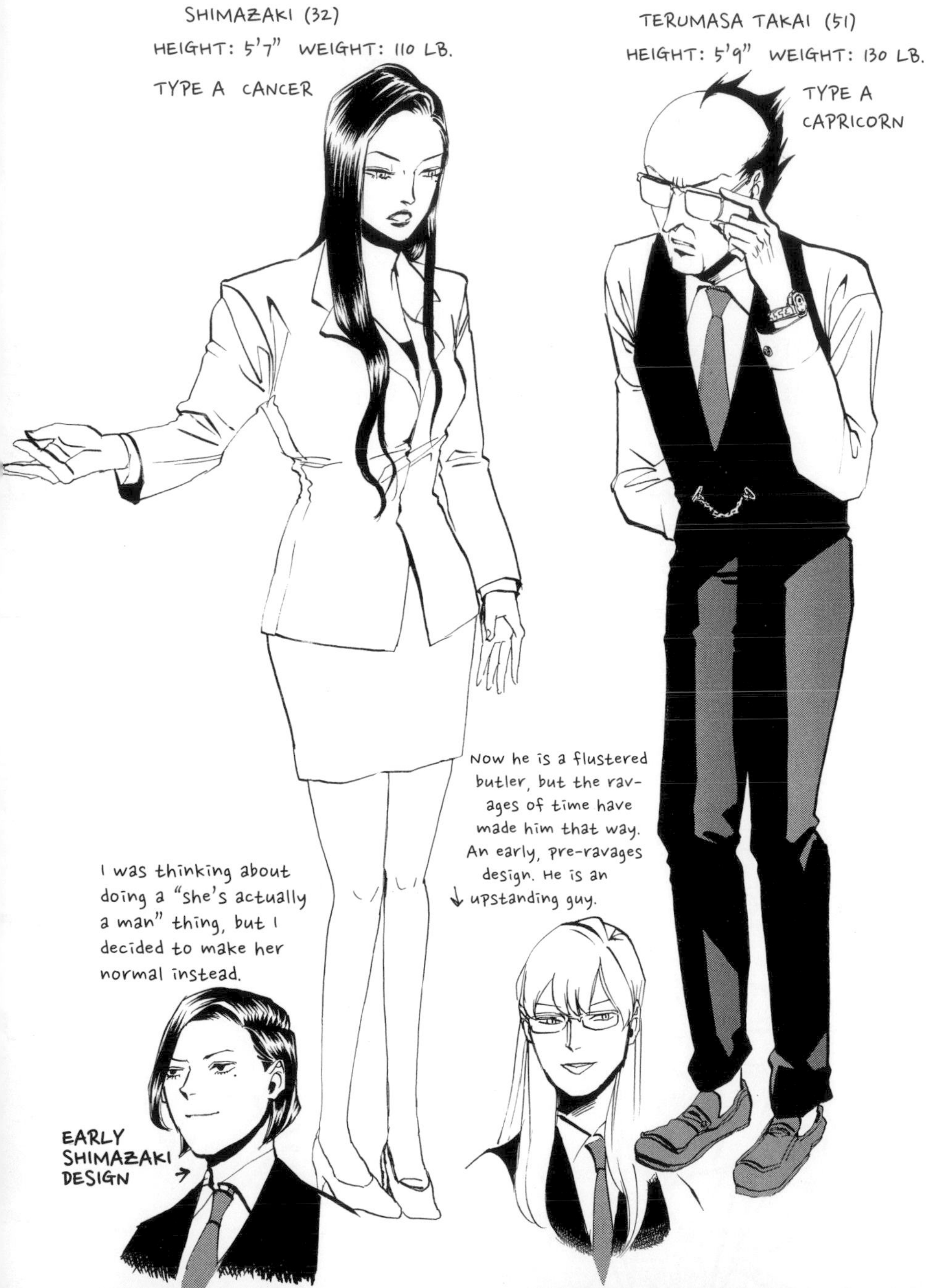
TERUMASA TAKAI (51)
HEIGHT: 5'9" WEIGHT: 130 LB.
TYPE A CAPRICORN
SHIMAZAKI (32)
HEIGHT: 5'7" WEIGHT: 110 LB.
TYPE A CANCER
Now he is a flustered butler, but the rav-ages of time have made him that way. An early, pre-ravages design. He is an upstanding guy.
I was thinking about doing a "she's actually a man" thing, but I decided to make her normal instead.
EARLY SHIMAZAKI DESIGN

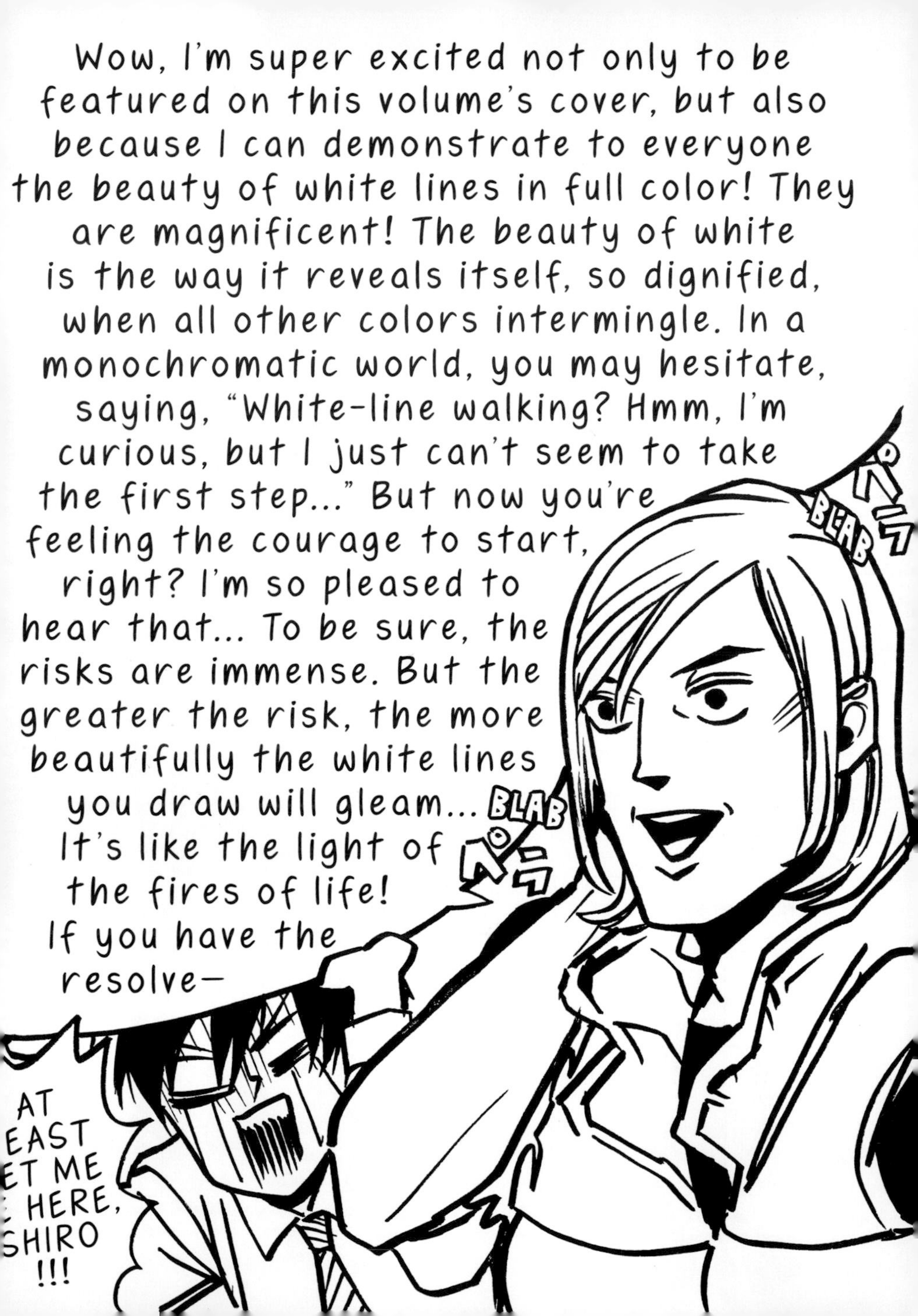

Wow, I'm super excited not only to be featured on this volume's cover, but also because I can demonstrate to everyone the beauty of white lines in full color! They are magnificent! The beauty of white is the way it reveals itself, so dignified, when all other colors intermingle. In a monochromatic world, you may hesitate, saying, "White-line walking? Hmm, I'm curious, but I just can't seem to take the first step..." But now you're feeling the courage to start, right? I'm so pleased to hear that... To be sure, the risks are immense. But the greater the risk, the more beautifully the white lines you draw will gleam... It's like the light of the fires of life! If you have the resolve—
BLAB
BLAB
AT EAST ET ME HERE, SHIRO !!!

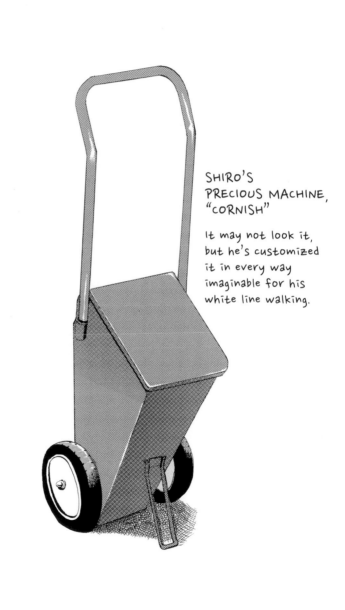

SHIRO'S
PRECIOUS MACHINE,
"CORNISH"

It may not look it,
but he's customized
it in every way
imaginable for his
white line walking.

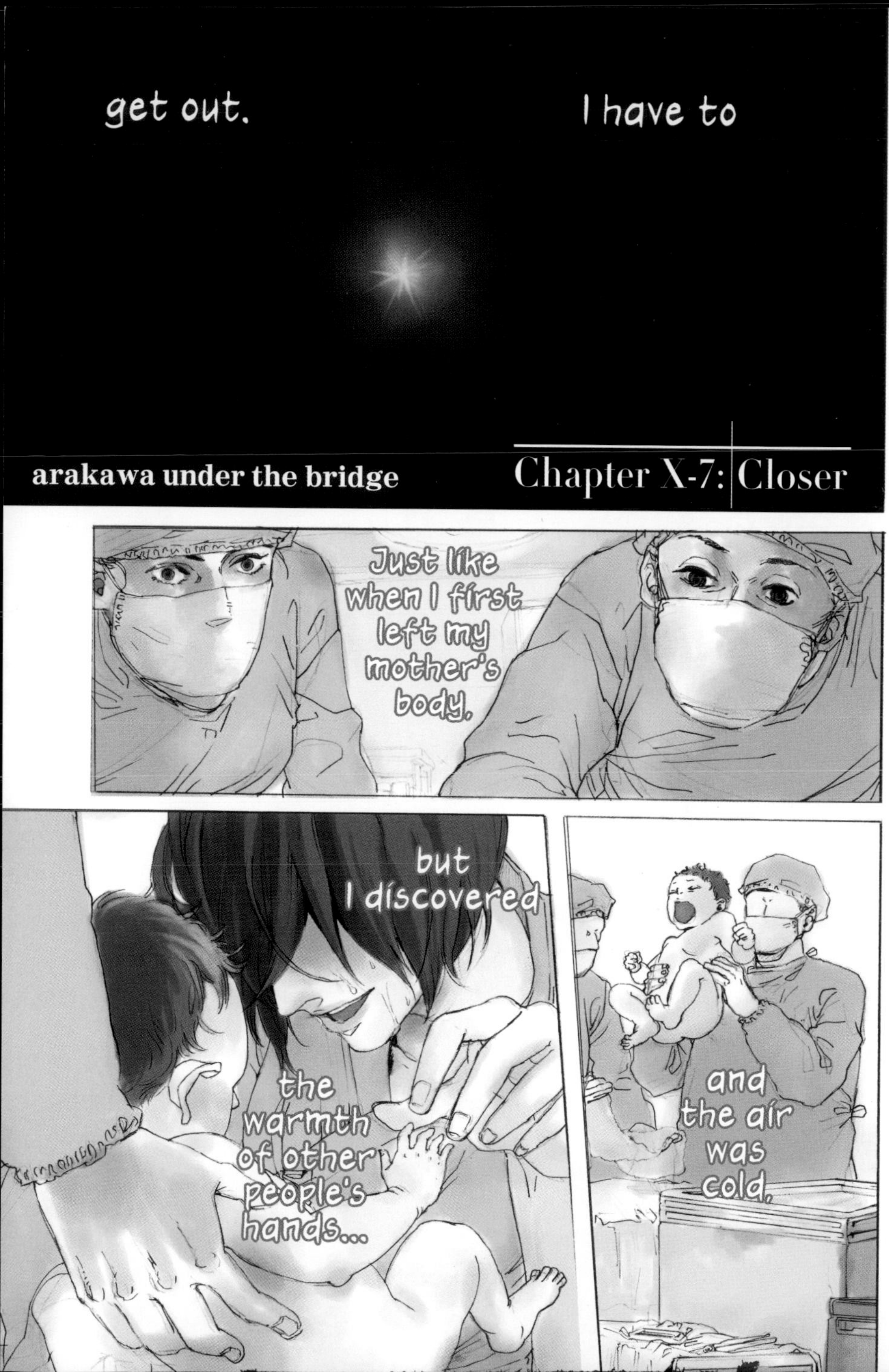
I have to
get out.
arakawa under the bridge
Chapter X-7: Closer
Just like when I first left my mother's body,
and the air was cold,
but I discovered
the warmth of other people's hands...

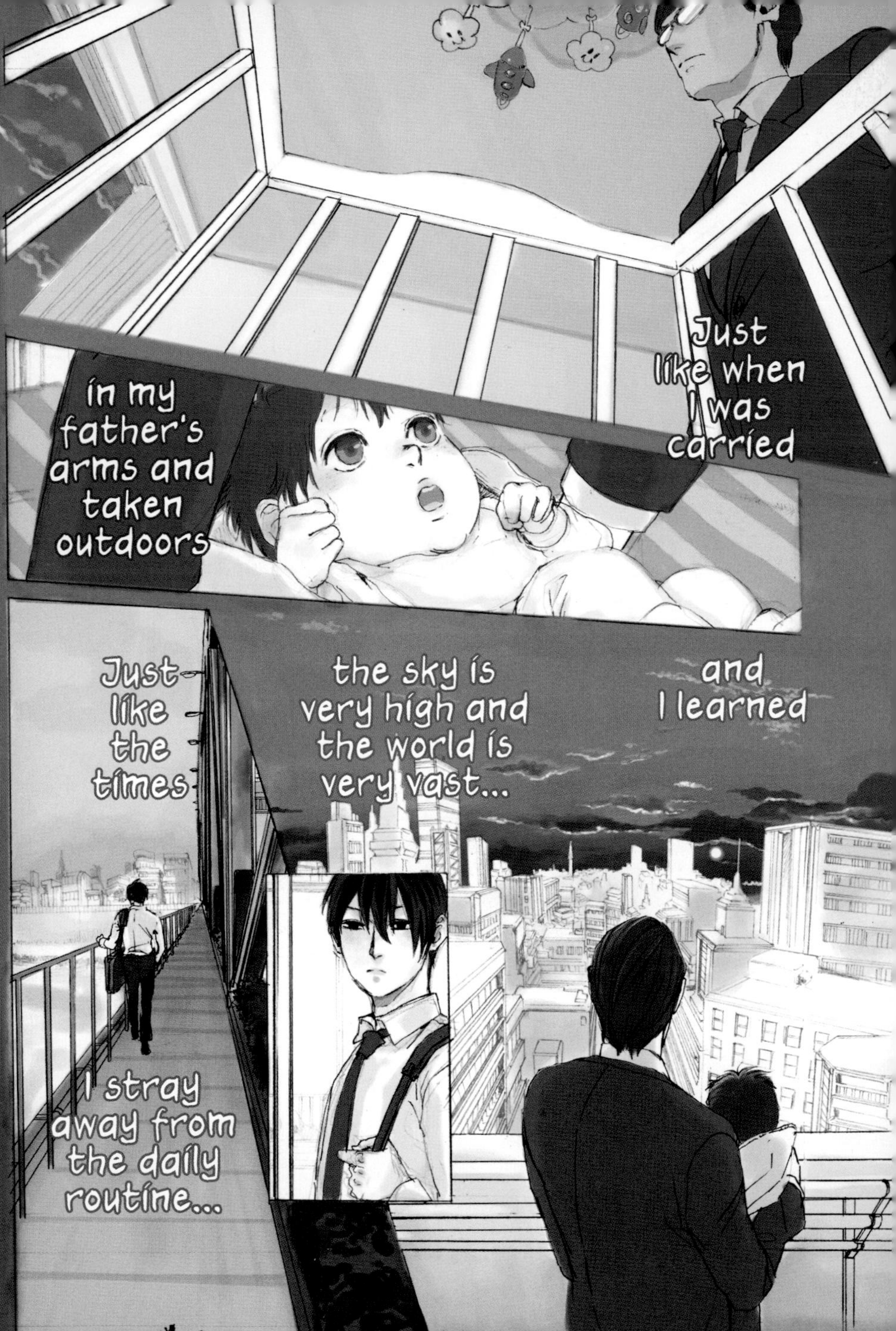
Just like when I was carried
in my father's arms and taken outdoors
and I learned
the sky is very high and the world is very vast...
Just like the times
I stray away from the daily routine...

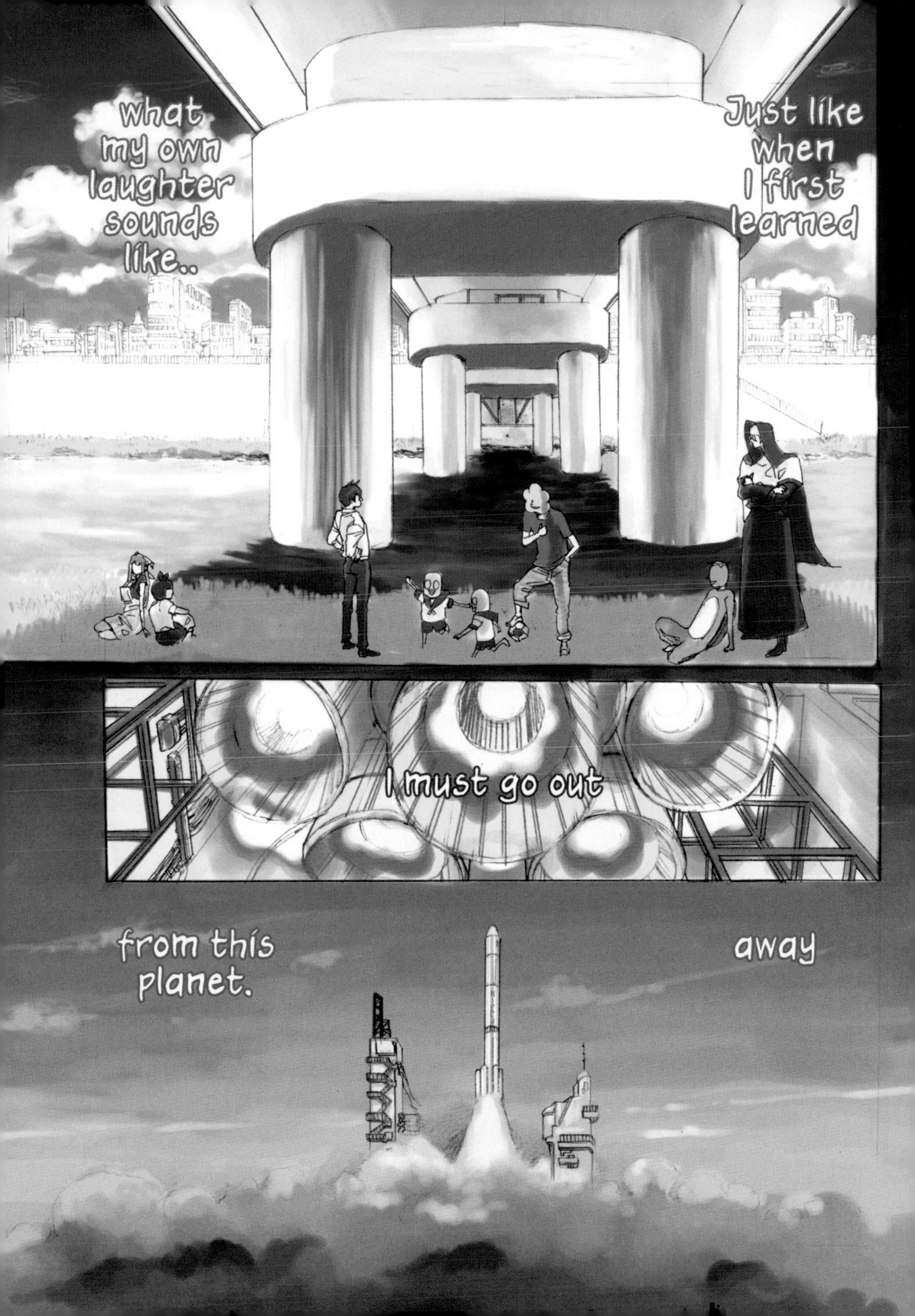
Just like when I first learned
what my own laughter sounds like..
I must go out
away
from this planet.

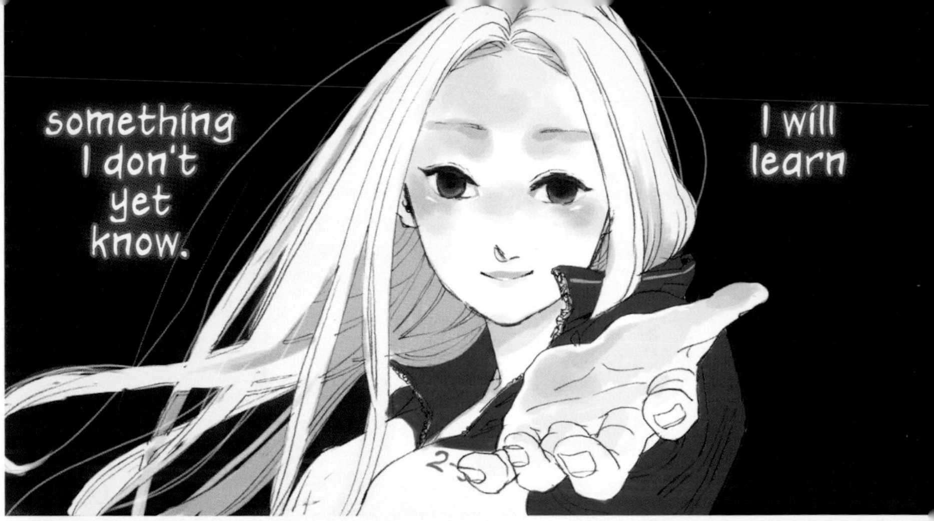
I will learn
something I don't yet know.

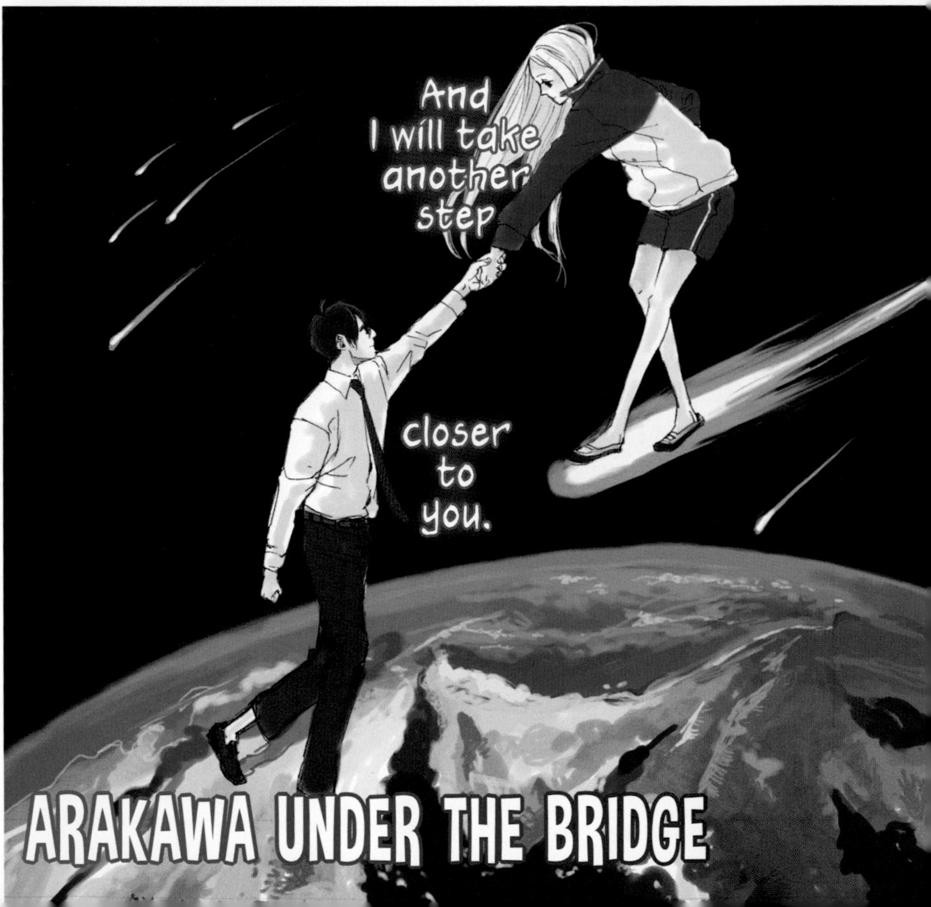
And I will take another step
closer to you.
ARAKAWA UNDER THE BRIDGE

The other day I said good-bye to the desk I had bought with the prize money from the first prize I ever won. It was like something you'd find in a teacher's office. I bought it second-hand. Thanks for those seven years! It was metal, so my arms would half-freeze in winter, but it was a good desk that never budged.

—Hikaru Nakamura

I moved from a place with lots of tall buildings to somewhere with lots of green. All that green suddenly around me made me feel like I'd moved back home.

—Hikaru Nakamura

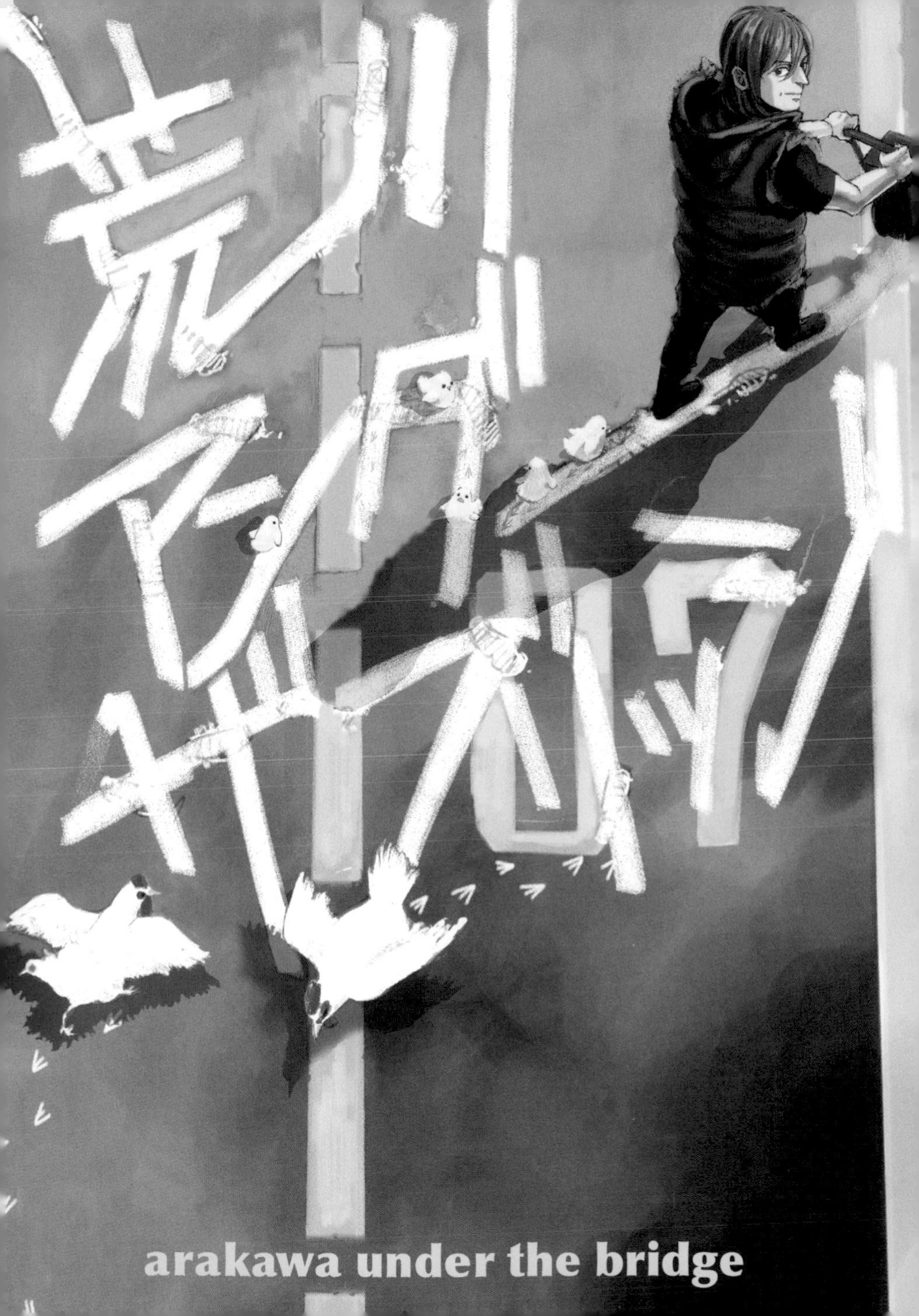
荒川アンダーザブリッジ
arakawa under the bridge

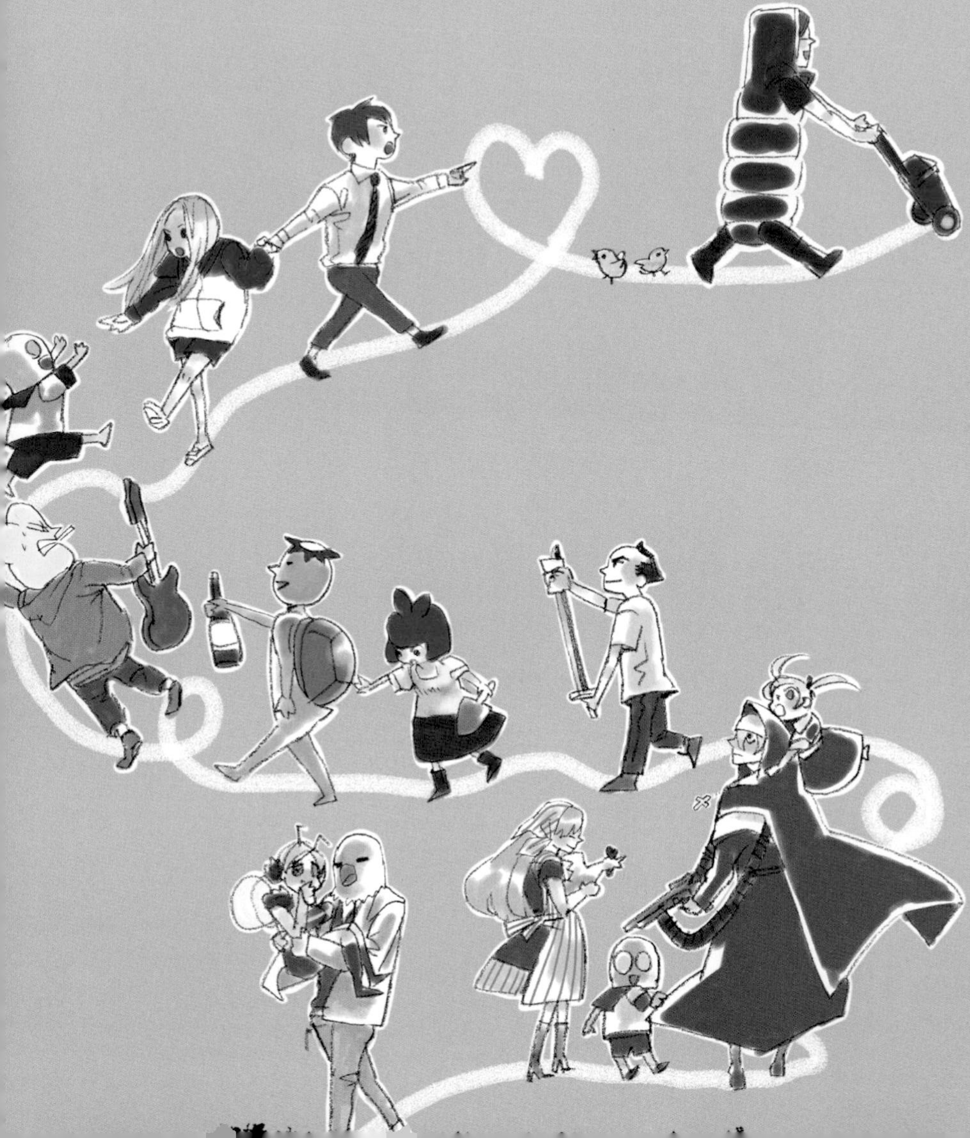

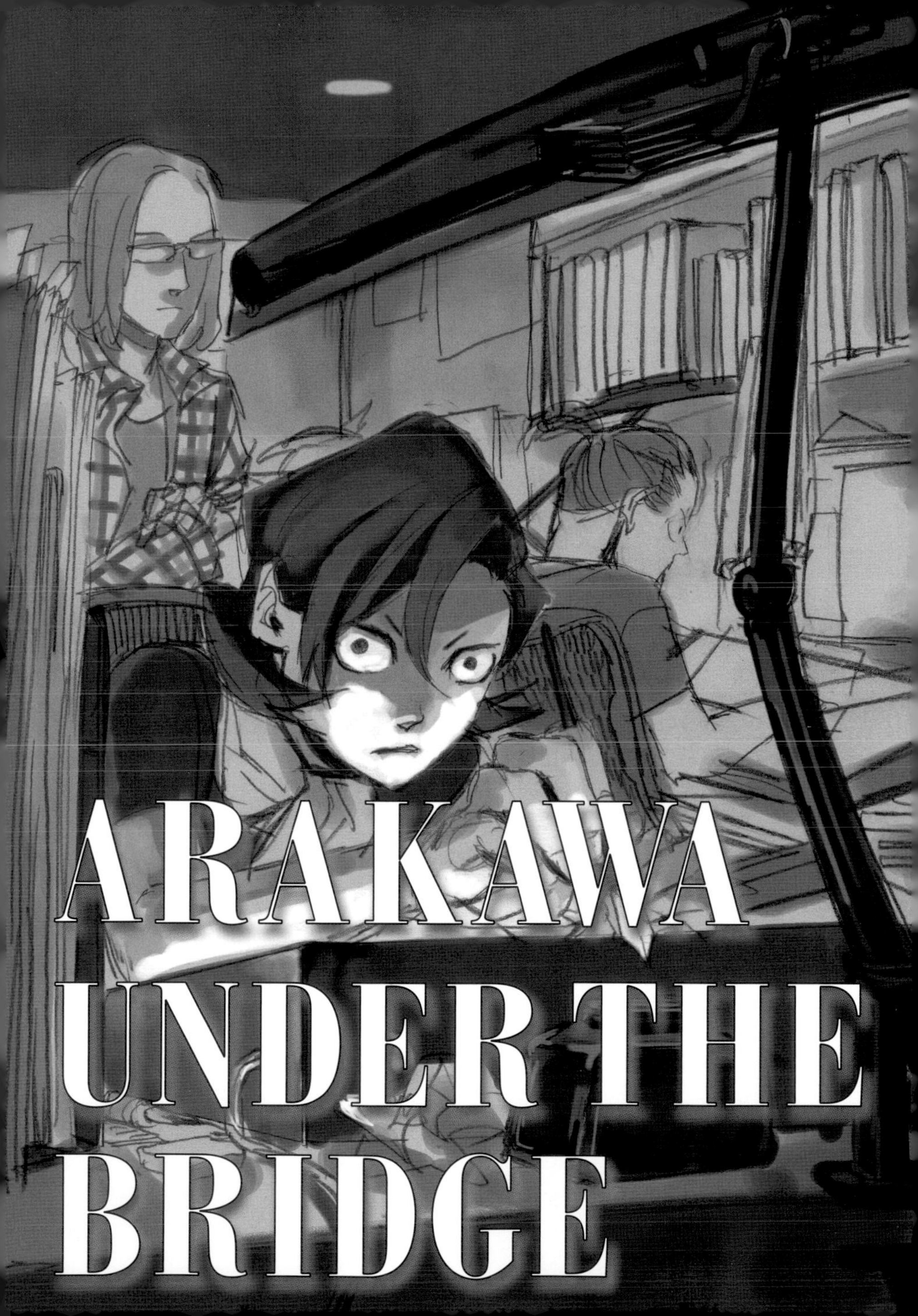
ARAKAWA
UNDER THE
BRIDGE

CONTENTS

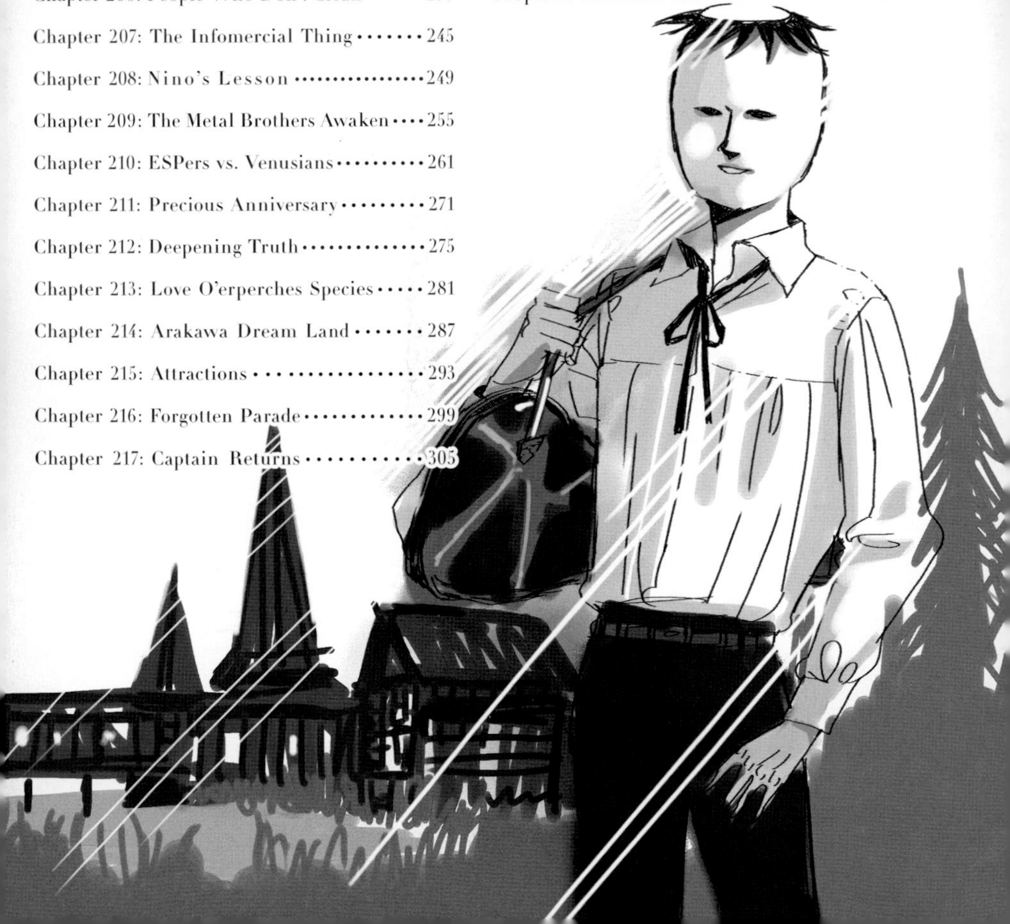

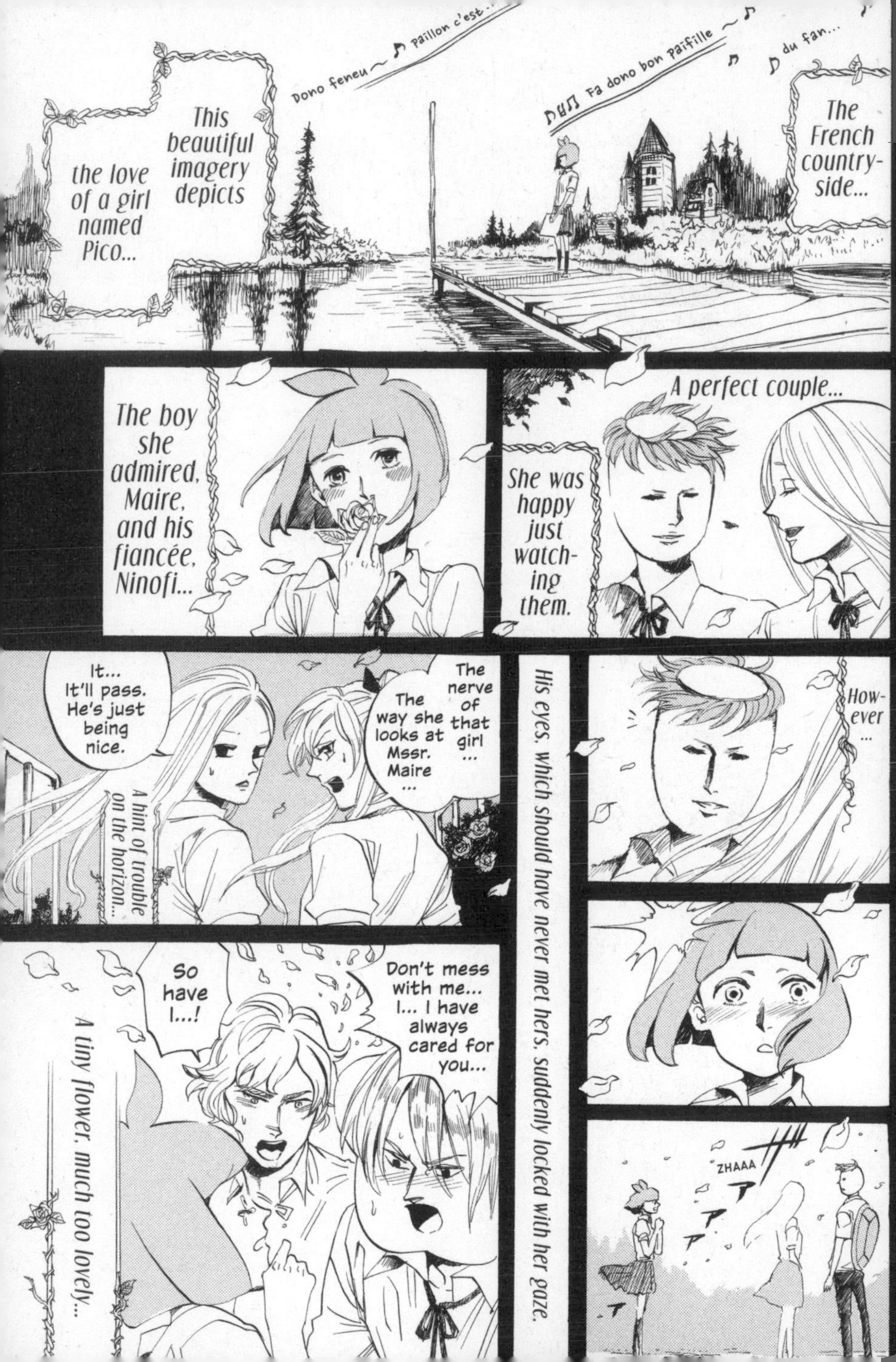

The French country-side...
Dono feneu~♪ Paillon c'est...
♫♫♫ Fa dono bon paifille~♪
♪ du fan...
This beautiful imagery depicts
the love of a girl named Pico...
A perfect couple...
She was happy just watching them.
The boy she admired, Maire, and his fiancée, Ninofi...
However...
ZHAAA
His eyes, which should have never met hers, suddenly locked with her gaze.
The nerve of that girl...
The way she looks at Mssr. Maire...
It... It'll pass. He's just being nice.
A hint of trouble on the horizon...
Don't mess with me... I... I have always cared for you...
So have I...!
A tiny flower, much too lovely...

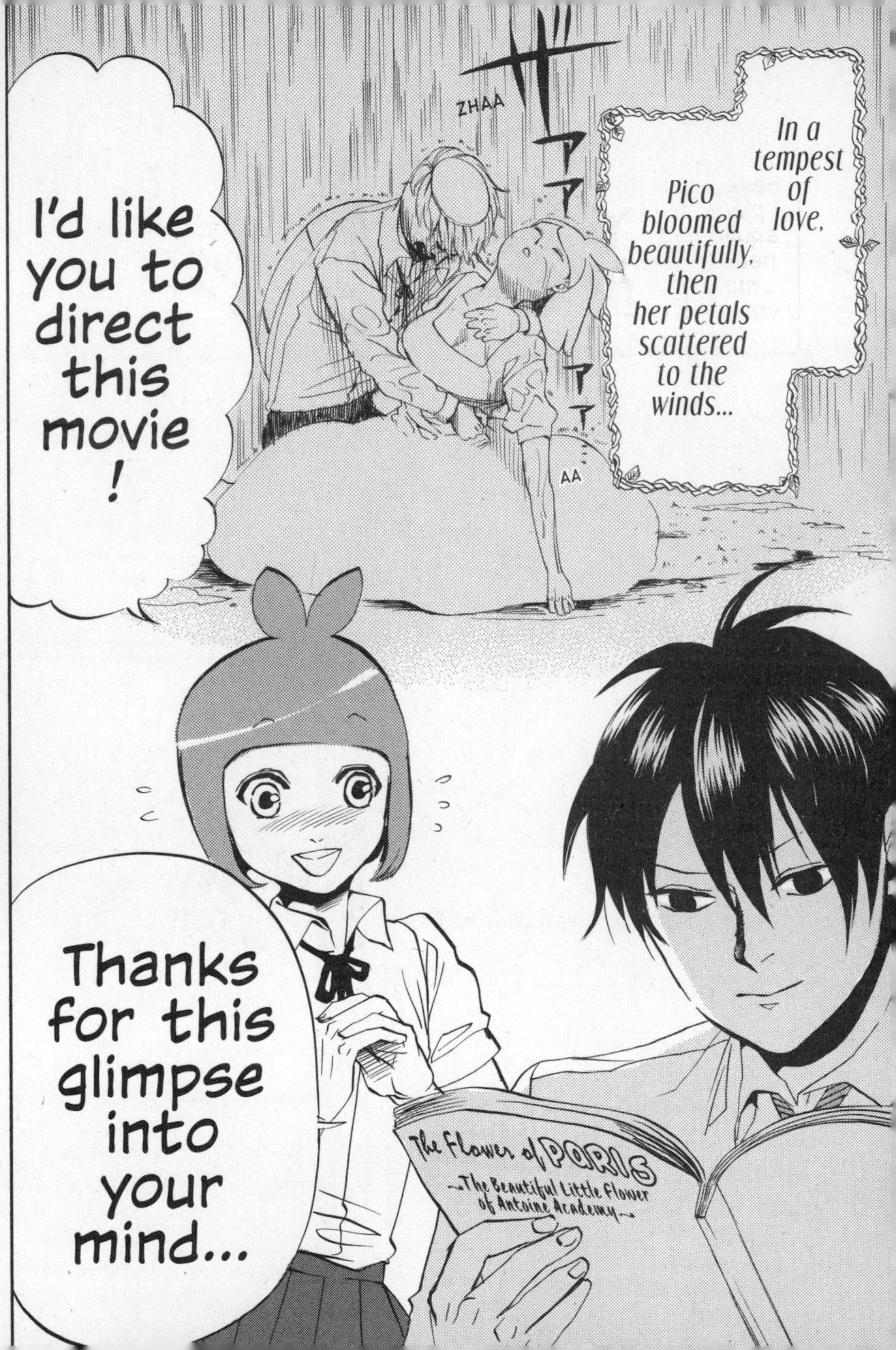
In a tempest of love, Pico bloomed beautifully, then her petals scattered to the winds...
ZHAA
AA
I'd like you to direct this movie!
The Flower of PARIS
~The Beautiful Little Flower of Antoine Academy~
Thanks for this glimpse into your mind...

Chapter 197: Arakawa Cinema News

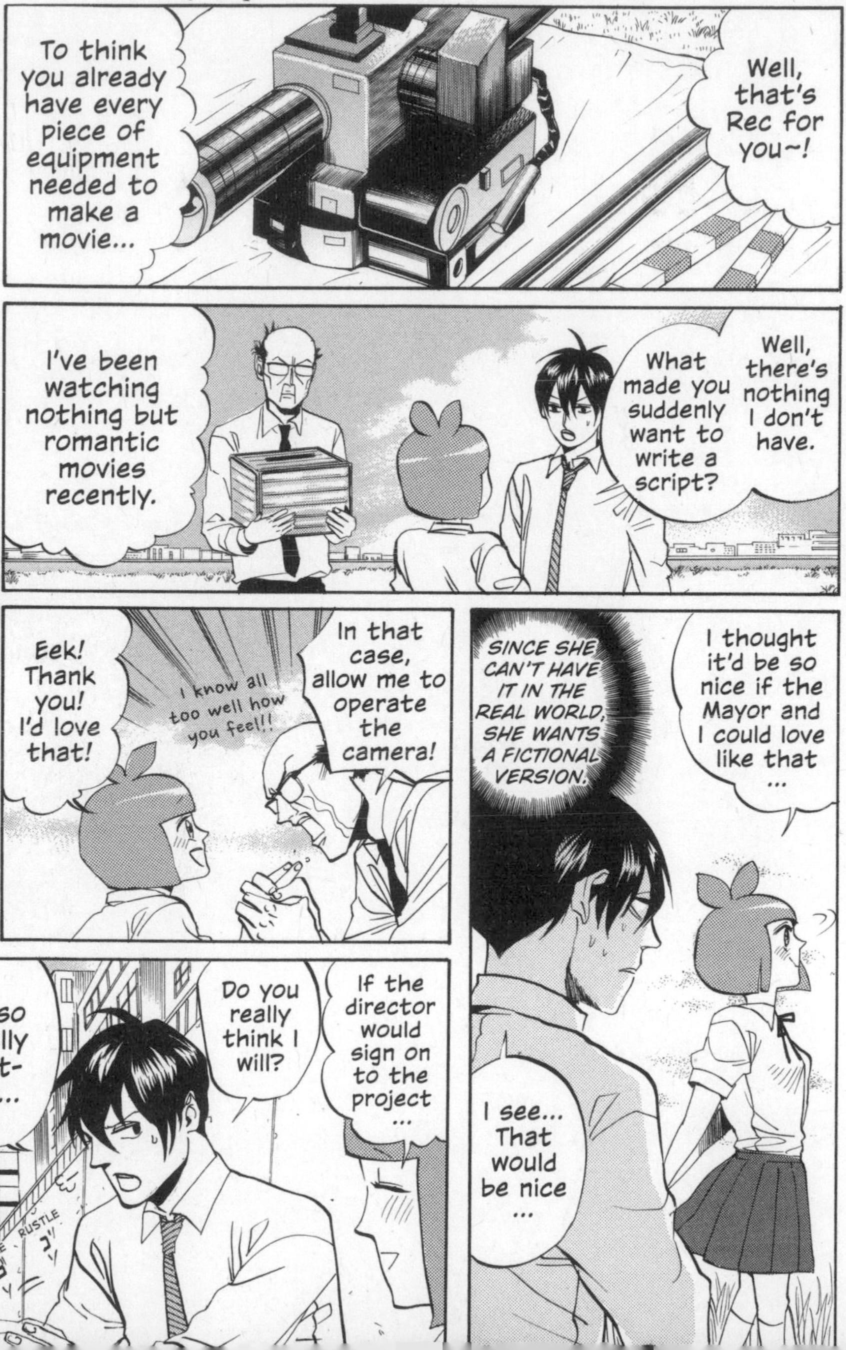
To think you already have every piece of equipment needed to make a movie...
Well, that's Rec for you~!
Well, there's nothing I don't have.
What made you suddenly want to write a script?
I've been watching nothing but romantic movies recently.
I thought it'd be so nice if the Mayor and I could love like that ...
SINCE SHE CAN'T HAVE IT IN THE REAL WORLD, SHE WANTS A FICTIONAL VERSION.
I see... That would be nice ...
In that case, allow me to operate the camera!
I know all too well how you feel!!
Eek! Thank you! I'd love that!
If the director would sign on to the project ...
Do you really think I will?
It's so totally pointless...
RUSTLE
RUSTLE

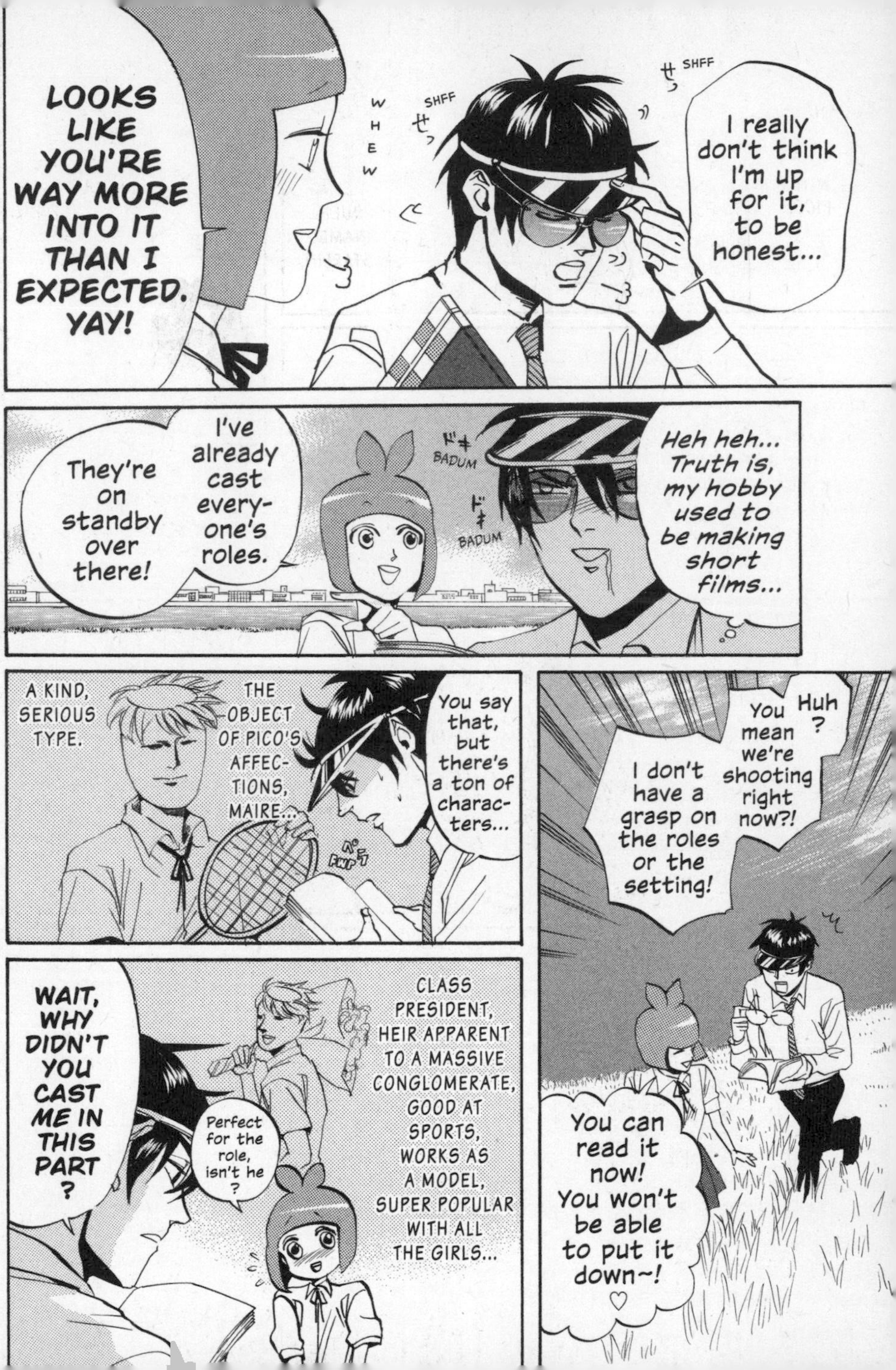
SHFF
I really don't think I'm up for it, to be honest...
WHEW
SHFF
LOOKS LIKE YOU'RE WAY MORE INTO IT THAN I EXPECTED. YAY!
Heh heh... Truth is, my hobby used to be making short films...
ドキ BADUM
ドキ BADUM
I've already cast every-one's roles.
They're on standby over there!
Huh?
You mean we're shooting right now?!
I don't have a grasp on the roles or the setting!
You can read it now! You won't be able to put it down~! ♡
You say that, but there's a ton of charac-ters...
FWP
THE OBJECT OF PICO'S AFFEC-TIONS, MAIRE...
A KIND, SERIOUS TYPE.
CLASS PRESIDENT, HEIR APPARENT TO A MASSIVE CONGLOMERATE, GOOD AT SPORTS, WORKS AS A MODEL, SUPER POPULAR WITH ALL THE GIRLS...
Perfect for the role, isn't he?
WAIT, WHY DIDN'T YOU CAST ME IN THIS PART?

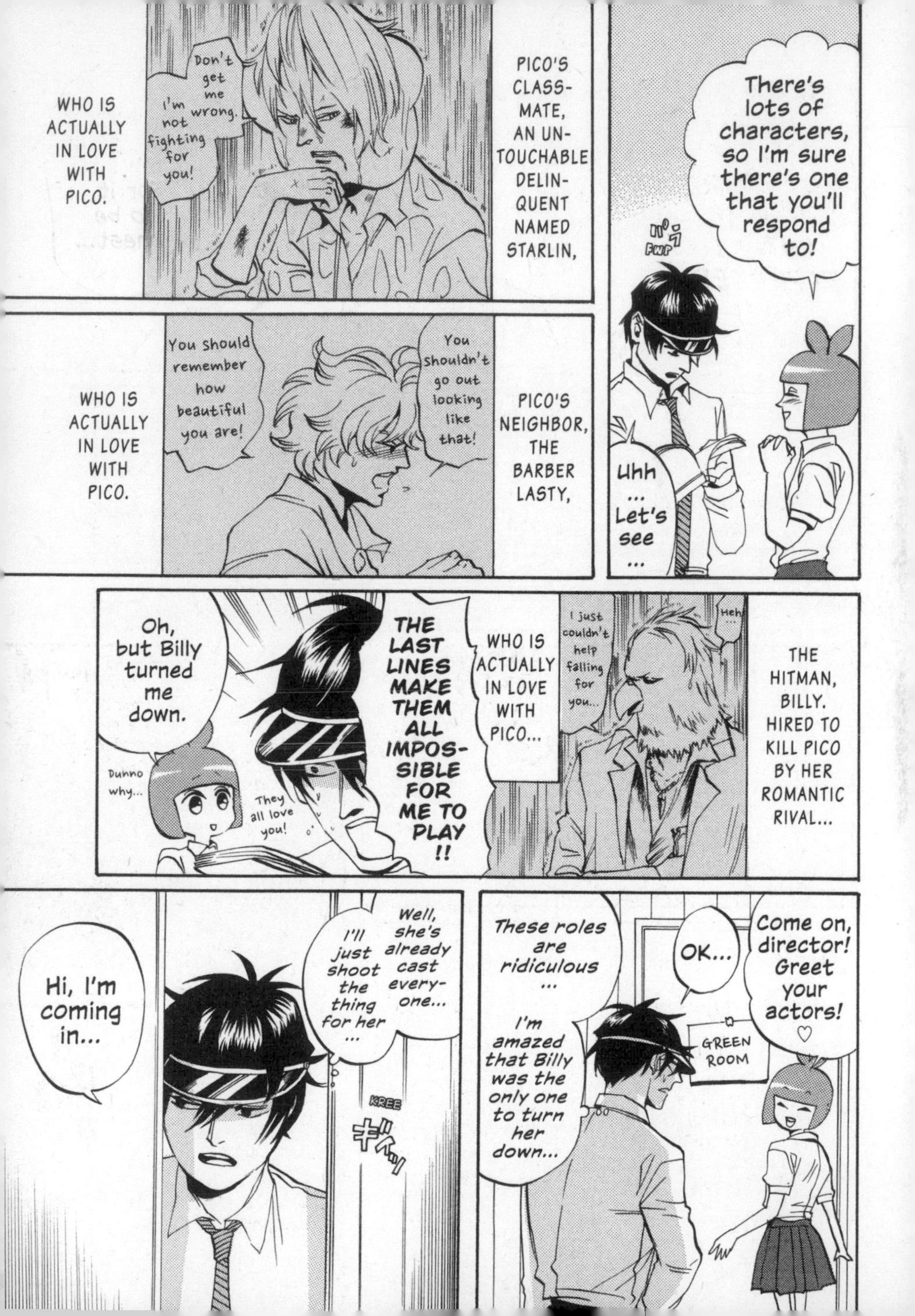
There's lots of characters, so I'm sure there's one that you'll respond to!
FWP
Uhh ... Let's see ...
PICO'S CLASSMATE, AN UNTOUCHABLE DELINQUENT NAMED STARLIN,
Don't get me wrong. I'm not fighting for you!
WHO IS ACTUALLY IN LOVE WITH PICO.
PICO'S NEIGHBOR, THE BARBER LASTY,
You shouldn't go out looking like that!
You should remember how beautiful you are!
WHO IS ACTUALLY IN LOVE WITH PICO.
THE HITMAN, BILLY. HIRED TO KILL PICO BY HER ROMANTIC RIVAL...
Heh
I just couldn't help falling for you...
WHO IS ACTUALLY IN LOVE WITH PICO...
THE LAST LINES MAKE THEM ALL IMPOSSIBLE FOR ME TO PLAY !!
Oh, but Billy turned me down.
They all love you!
Dunno why...
Come on, director! Greet your actors! ♡
OK...
GREEN ROOM
These roles are ridiculous ...
I'm amazed that Billy was the only one to turn her down...
Well, she's already cast every-one...
I'll just shoot the thing for her ...
KREE
Hi, I'm coming in...

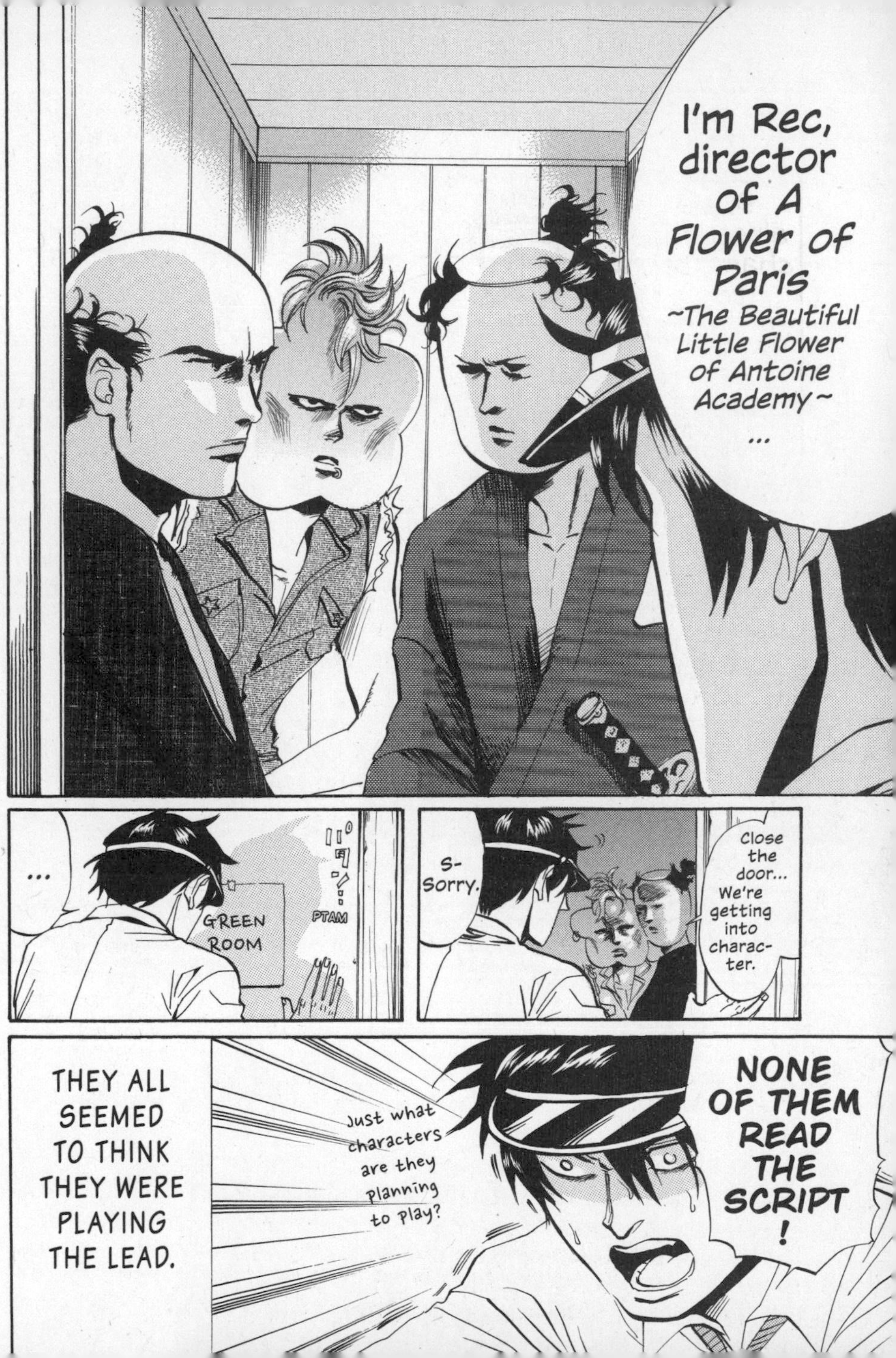
I'm Rec, director of A Flower of Paris
~The Beautiful Little Flower of Antoine Academy~
...
Close the door... We're getting into character.
S-Sorry.
PTAM
GREEN ROOM
...
NONE OF THEM READ THE SCRIPT!
Just what characters are they planning to play?
THEY ALL SEEMED TO THINK THEY WERE PLAYING THE LEAD.

Chapter 198: Crank In

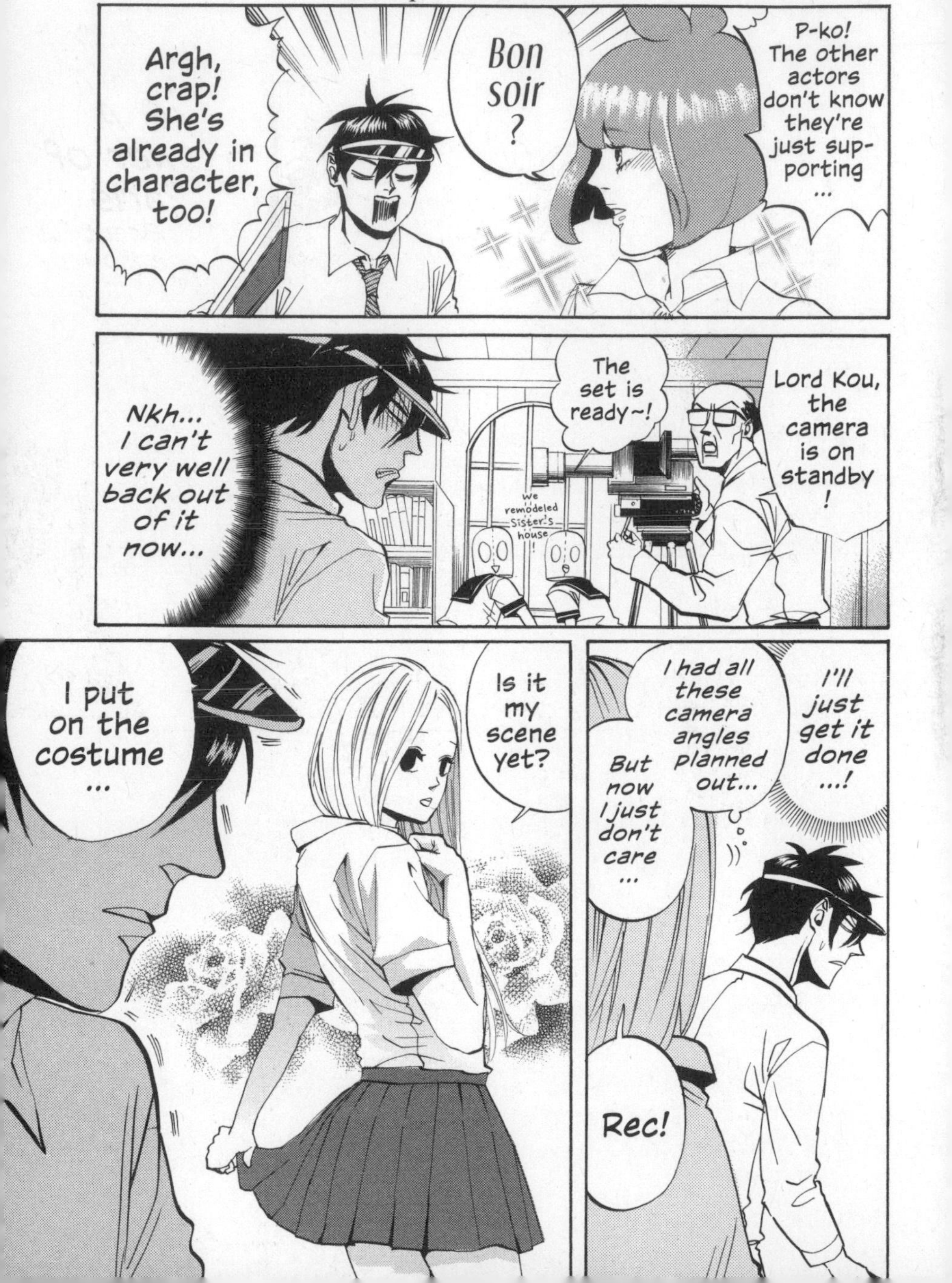

P-ko! The other actors don't know they're just supporting...
Bon soir?
Argh, crap! She's already in character, too!
Lord Kou, the camera is on standby!
The set is ready~!
we remodeled Sister's house!
Nkh... I can't very well back out of it now...
I'll just get it done...!
I had all these camera angles planned out...
But now I just don't care...
Rec!
Is it my scene yet?
I put on the costume...

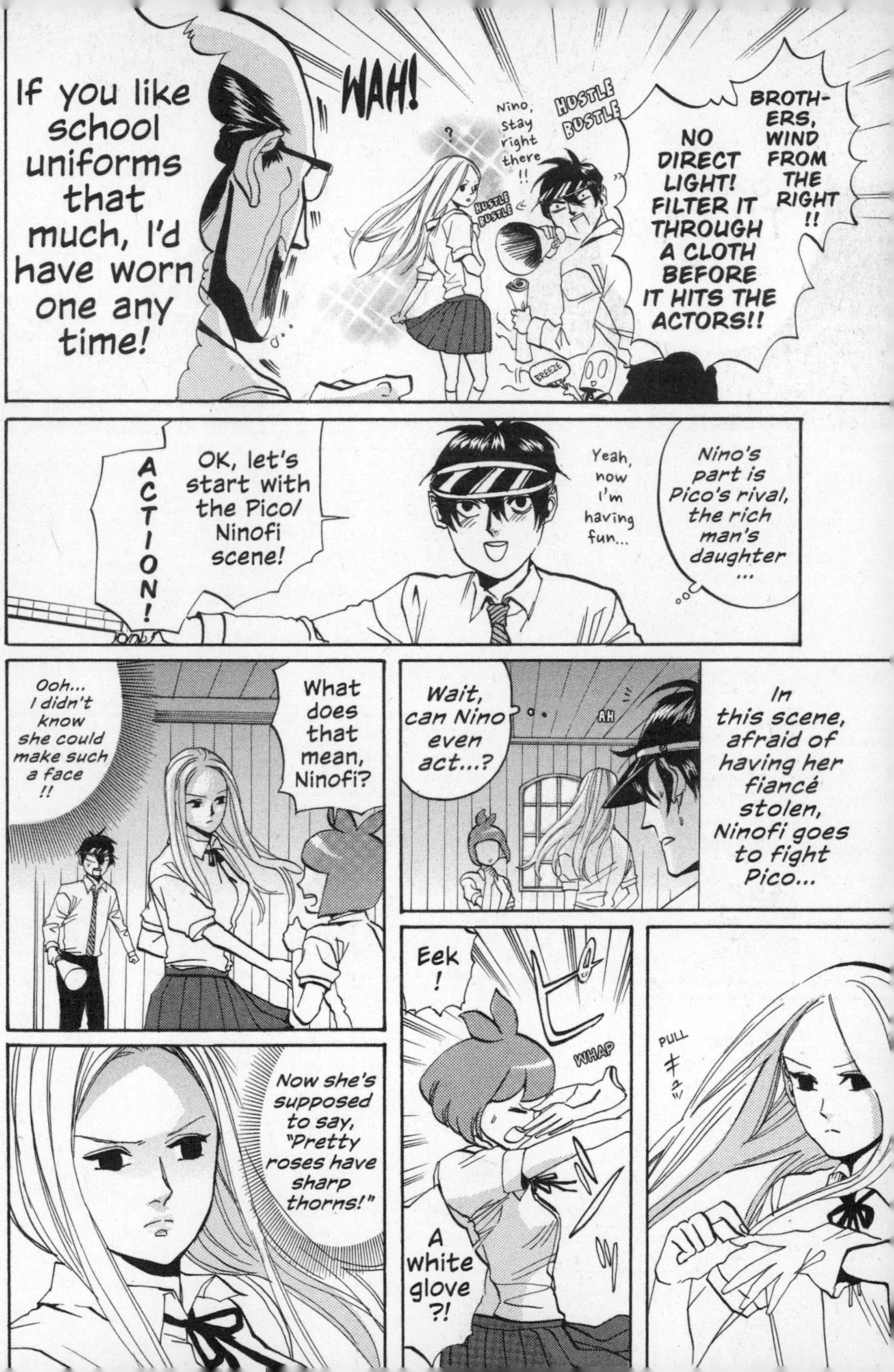
BROTHERS, WIND FROM THE RIGHT!!
NO DIRECT LIGHT! FILTER IT THROUGH A CLOTH BEFORE IT HITS THE ACTORS!!
HUSTLE BUSTLE
Nino, stay right there!!
WAH!
HUSTLE BUSTLE
If you like school uniforms that much, I'd have worn one any time!
BREEZE
Nino's part is Pico's rival, the rich man's daughter...
Yeah, now I'm having fun...
OK, let's start with the Pico/Ninofi scene!
ACTION!
In this scene, afraid of having her fiancé stolen, Ninofi goes to fight Pico...
AH
Wait, can Nino even act...?
What does that mean, Ninofi?
Ooh... I didn't know she could make such a face!!
PULL
キュッ
Eek!
WHAP
A white glove?!
Now she's supposed to say, "Pretty roses have sharp thorns!"

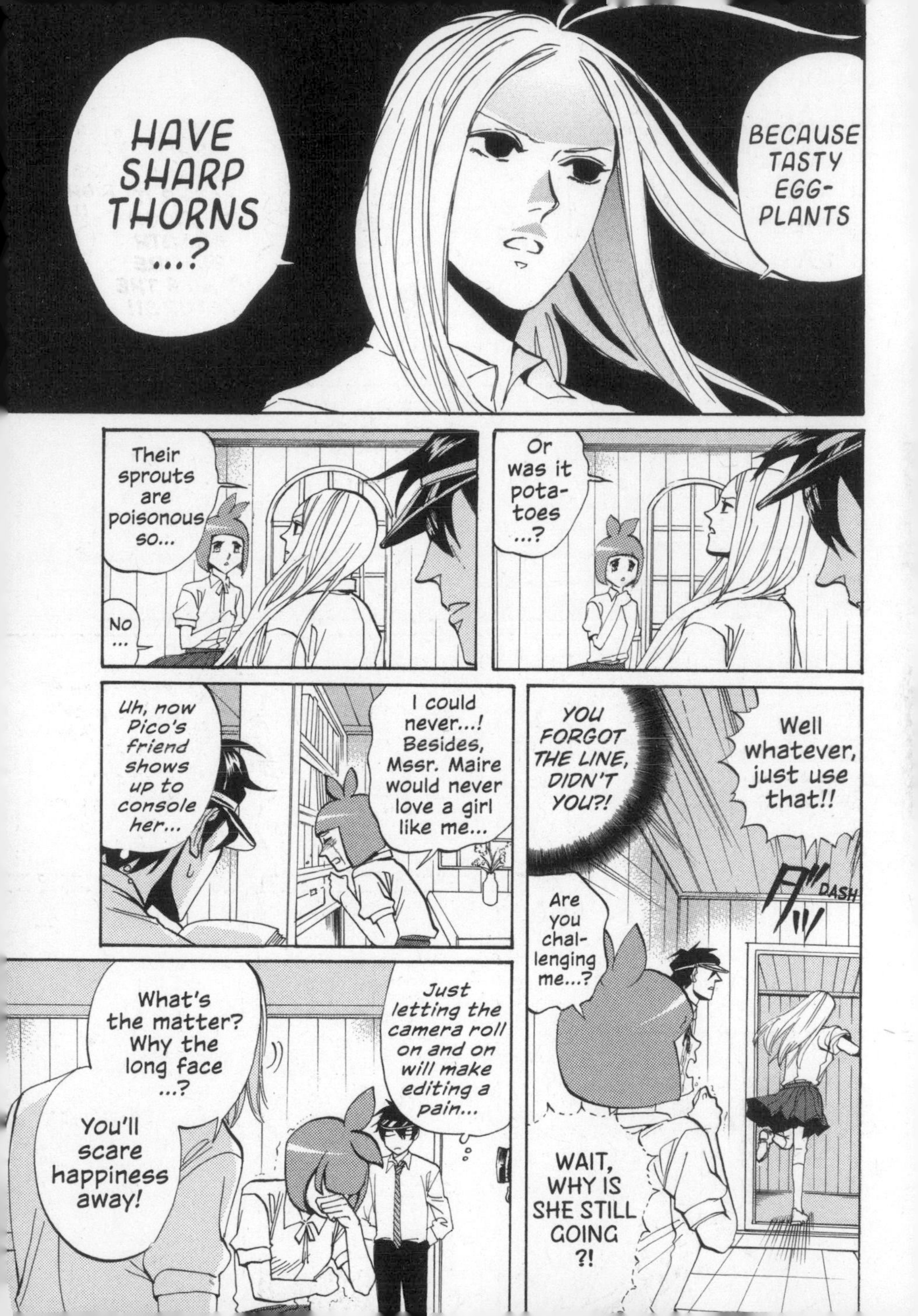
BECAUSE TASTY EGG-PLANTS
HAVE SHARP THORNS ...?
Or was it pota-toes ...?
Their sprouts are poisonous so...
No ...
Well whatever, just use that!!
YOU FORGOT THE LINE, DIDN'T YOU?!
DASH
Are you chal-lenging me...?
WAIT, WHY IS SHE STILL GOING ?!
I could never...! Besides, Mssr. Maire would never love a girl like me...
Uh, now Pico's friend shows up to console her...
Just letting the camera roll on and on will make editing a pain...
What's the matter? Why the long face ...?
You'll scare happiness away!

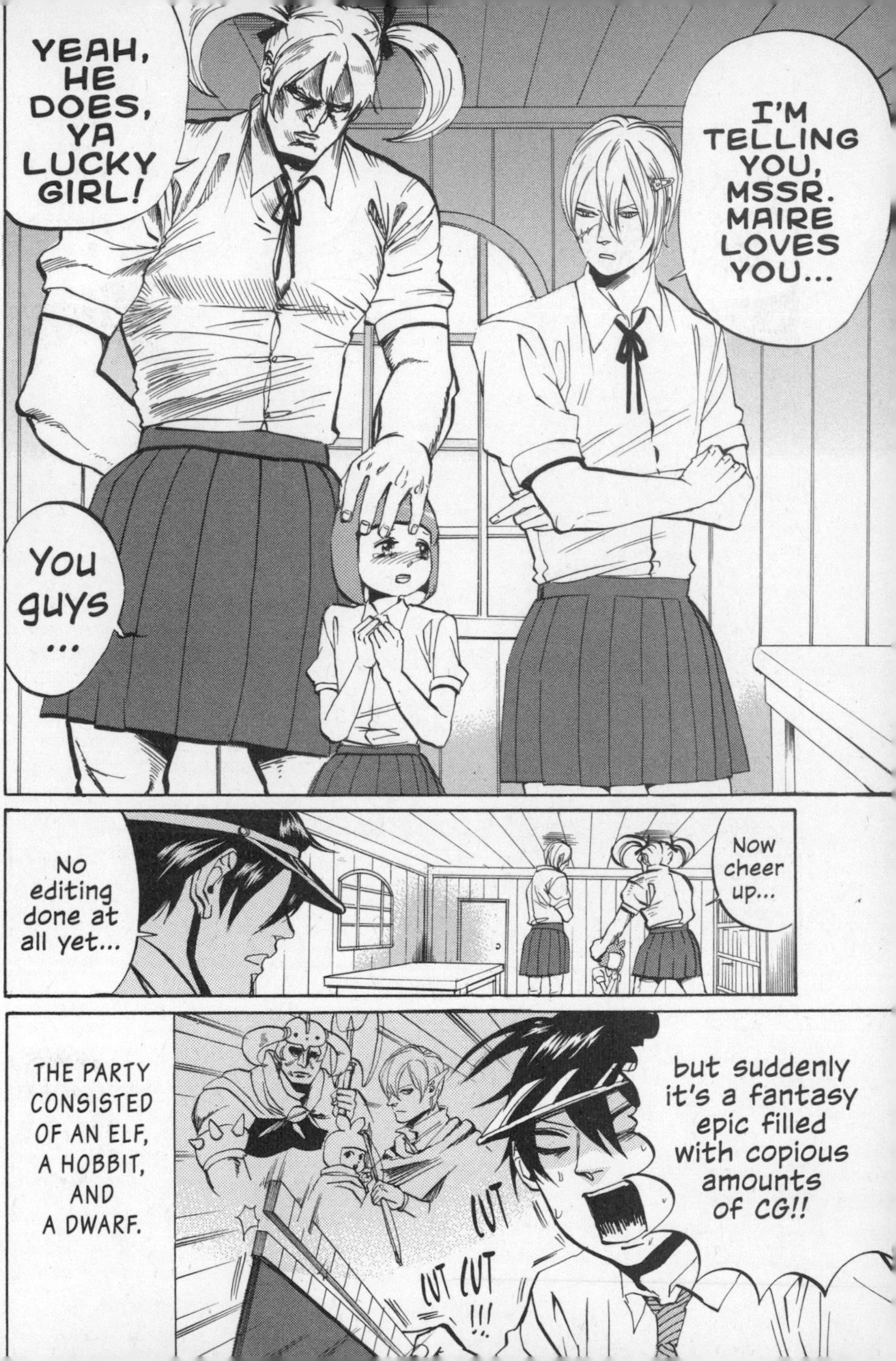
I'M TELLING YOU, MSSR. MAIRE LOVES YOU...
YEAH, HE DOES, YA LUCKY GIRL!
You guys ...
Now cheer up...
No editing done at all yet...
but suddenly it's a fantasy epic filled with copious amounts of CG!!
THE PARTY CONSISTED OF AN ELF, A HOBBIT, AND A DWARF.
CUT
CUT CUT !!!

Chapter 199: At the End of Delusion...

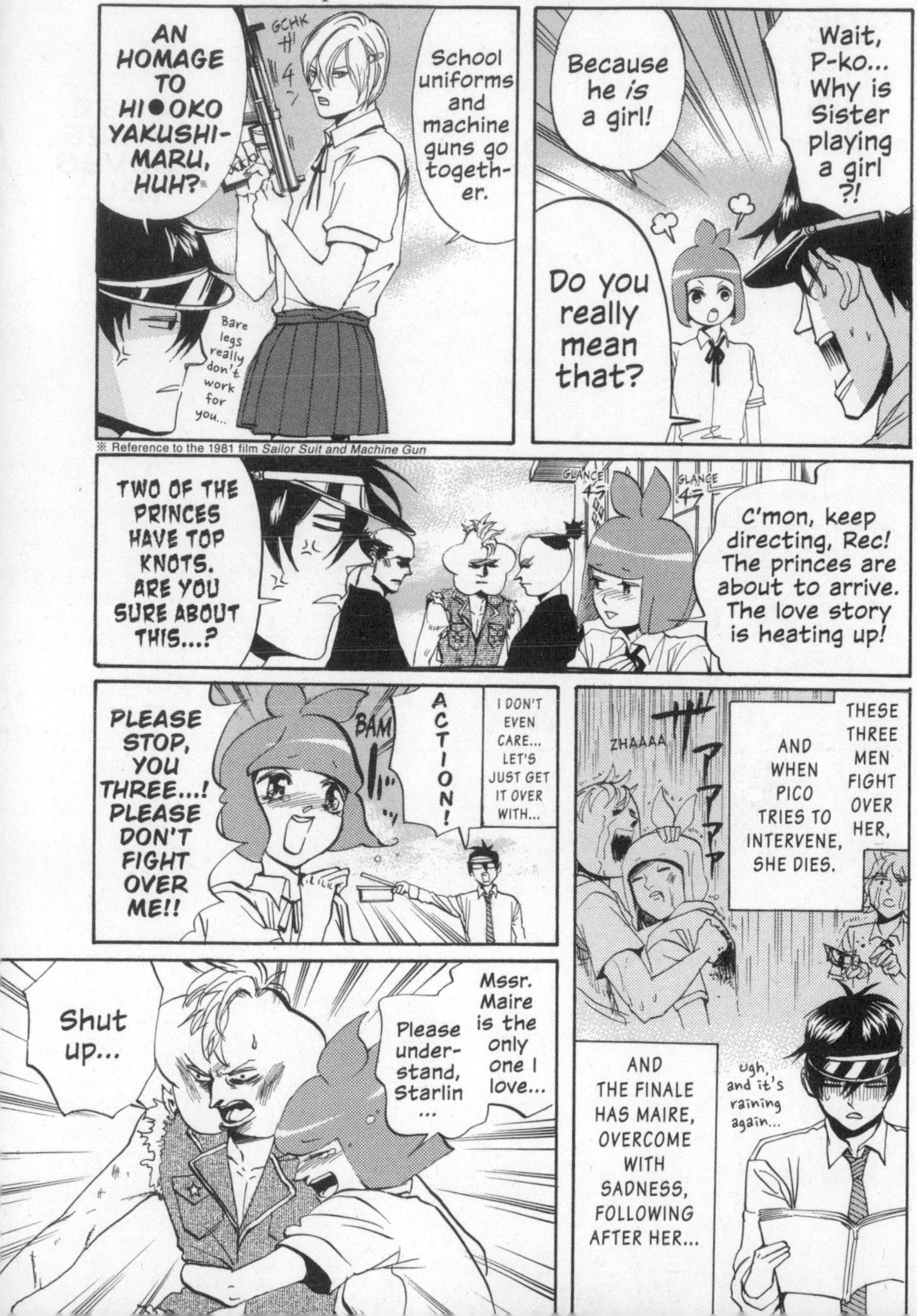

Wait, P-ko... Why is Sister playing a girl ?!
Because he *is* a girl!
Do you really mean that?
School uniforms and machine guns go togeth- er.
GCHK
AN HOMAGE TO HI●OKO YAKUSHIMARU, HUH?※
Bare legs really don't work for you...
C'mon, keep directing, Rec! The princes are about to arrive. The love story is heating up!
GLANCE
GLANCE
TWO OF THE PRINCES HAVE TOP KNOTS. ARE YOU SURE ABOUT THIS...?
THESE THREE MEN FIGHT OVER HER,
AND WHEN PICO TRIES TO INTERVENE, SHE DIES.
ZHAAAA
ugh, and it's raining again...
AND THE FINALE HAS MAIRE, OVERCOME WITH SADNESS, FOLLOWING AFTER HER...
I DON'T EVEN CARE... LET'S JUST GET IT OVER WITH...
ACTION!
BAM
PLEASE STOP, YOU THREE...! PLEASE DON'T FIGHT OVER ME!!
Mssr. Maire is the only one I love...
Please under- stand, Starlin ...
Shut up...

※ Reference to the 1981 film *Sailor Suit and Machine Gun*

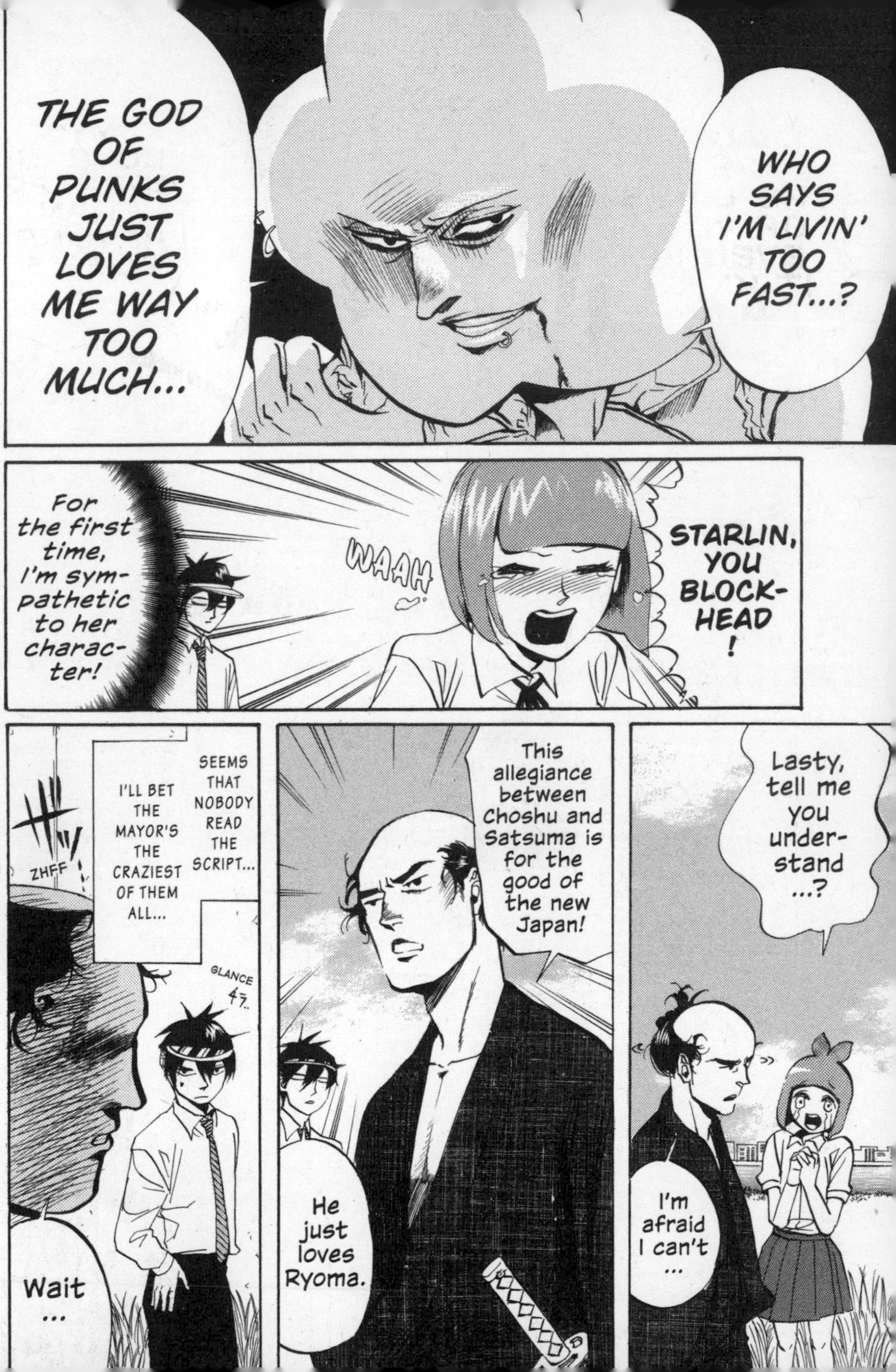
WHO SAYS I'M LIVIN' TOO FAST...?
THE GOD OF PUNKS JUST LOVES ME WAY TOO MUCH...
STARLIN, YOU BLOCKHEAD!
WAAH
For the first time, I'm sympathetic to her character!
Lasty, tell me you understand...?
I'm afraid I can't...
This allegiance between Choshu and Satsuma is for the good of the new Japan!
He just loves Ryoma.
SEEMS THAT NOBODY READ THE SCRIPT...
I'LL BET THE MAYOR'S THE CRAZIEST OF THEM ALL...
ZHFF
GLANCE
Wait...

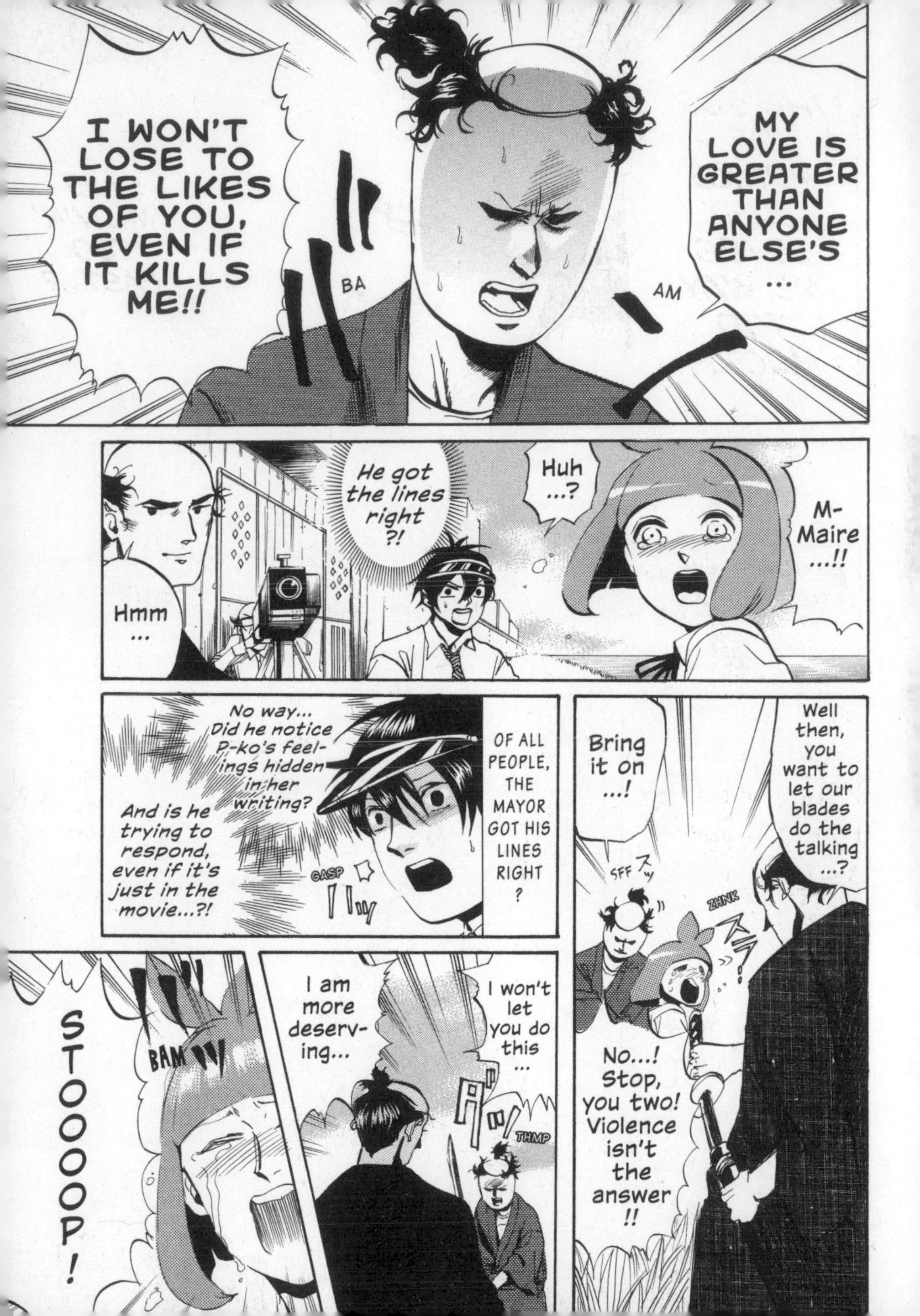
MY LOVE IS GREATER THAN ANYONE ELSE'S ...
I WON'T LOSE TO THE LIKES OF YOU, EVEN IF IT KILLS ME!!
BA
AM
M-Maire ...!!
Huh ...?
He got the lines right ?!
Hmm ...
Well then, you want to let our blades do the talking ...?
Bring it on ...!
SFF
ZHNK
No...! Stop, you two! Violence isn't the answer !!
OF ALL PEOPLE, THE MAYOR GOT HIS LINES RIGHT ?
No way... Did he notice P-ko's feelings hidden in her writing?
And is he trying to respond, even if it's just in the movie...?!
GASP
I won't let you do this ...
I am more deserv- ing...
THMP
STOOOOP!
BAM

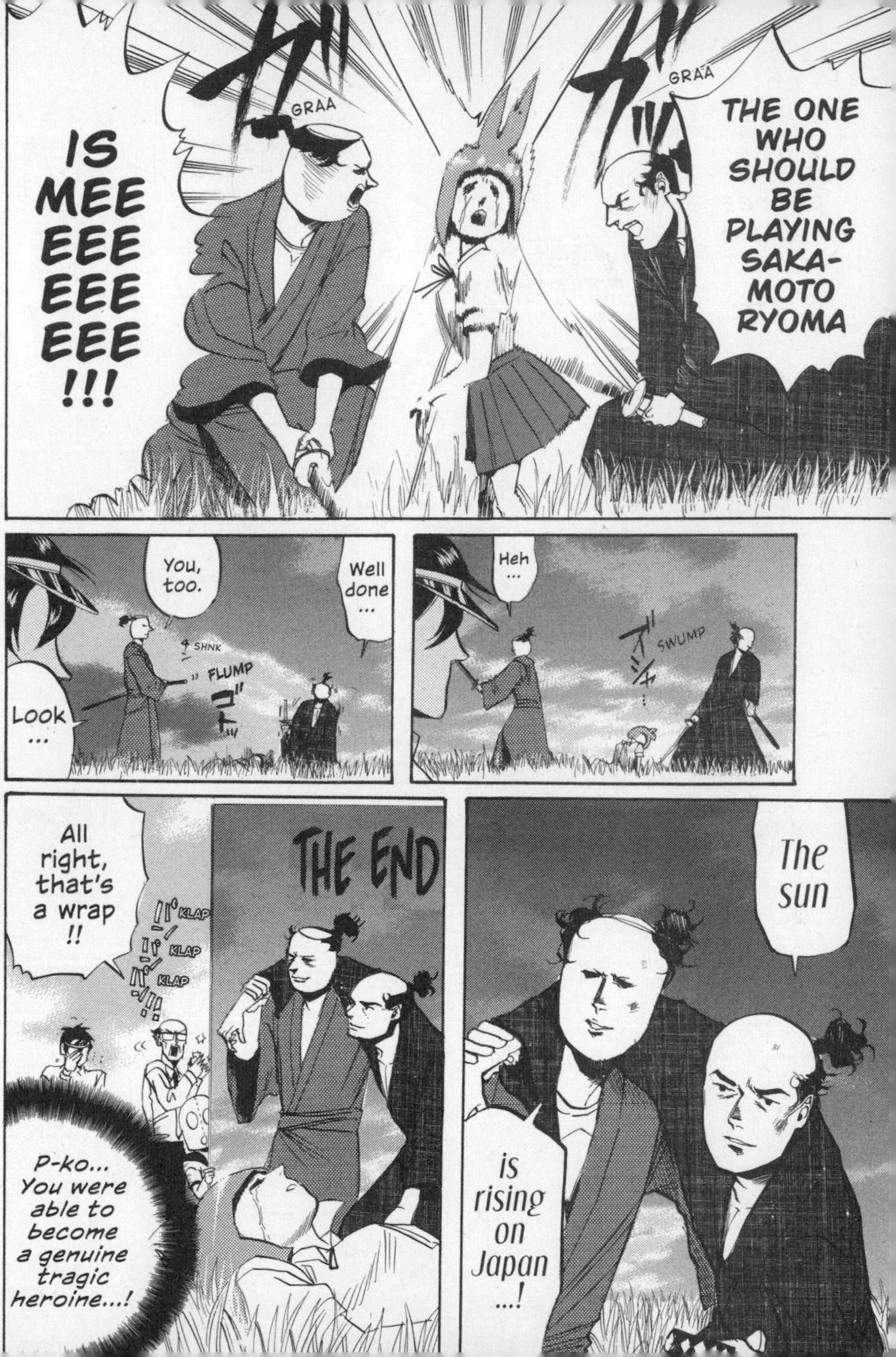
GRAA
THE ONE WHO SHOULD BE PLAYING SAKA-MOTO RYOMA
GRAA
IS MEEEEEEEEEEEEE!!!
Heh ...
SWUMP
Well done ...
You, too.
SHNK
FLUMP
Look ...
The sun
is rising on Japan ...!
THE END
All right, that's a wrap !!
KLAP
KLAP
KLAP
P-ko... You were able to become a genuine tragic heroine...!

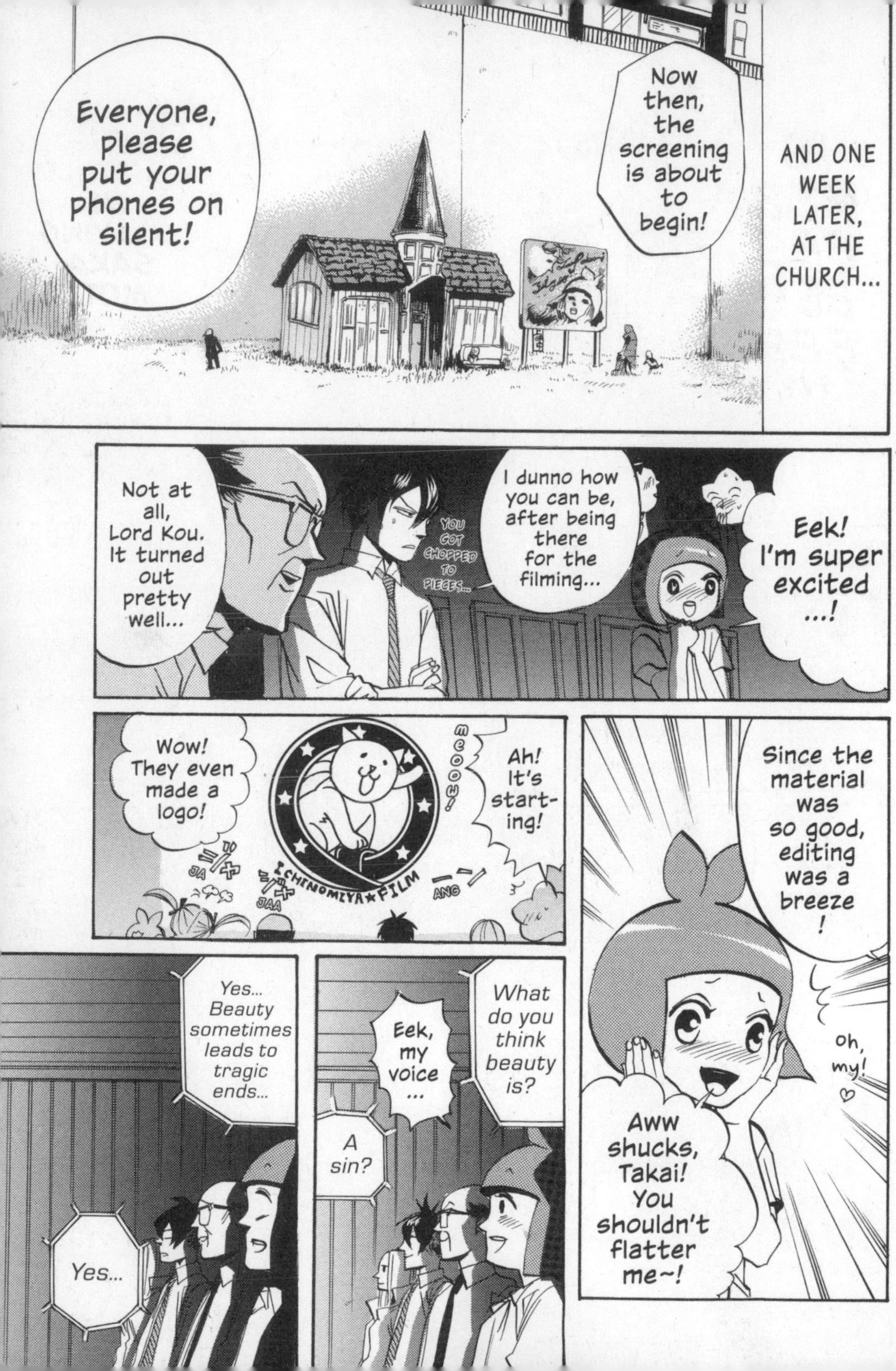
AND ONE WEEK LATER, AT THE CHURCH...
Now then, the screening is about to begin!
Everyone, please put your phones on silent!
Eek! I'm super excited...!
I dunno how you can be, after being there for the filming...
YOU GOT CHOPPED TO PIECES...
Not at all, Lord Kou. It turned out pretty well...
Since the material was so good, editing was a breeze!
oh, my!
Aww shucks, Takai! You shouldn't flatter me~!
Ah! It's starting!
MEOOOH!
ANG
ICHINOMIYA★FILM
JAA
Wow! They even made a logo!
JA
What do you think beauty is?
Eek, my voice...
A sin?
Yes... Beauty sometimes leads to tragic ends...
Yes...

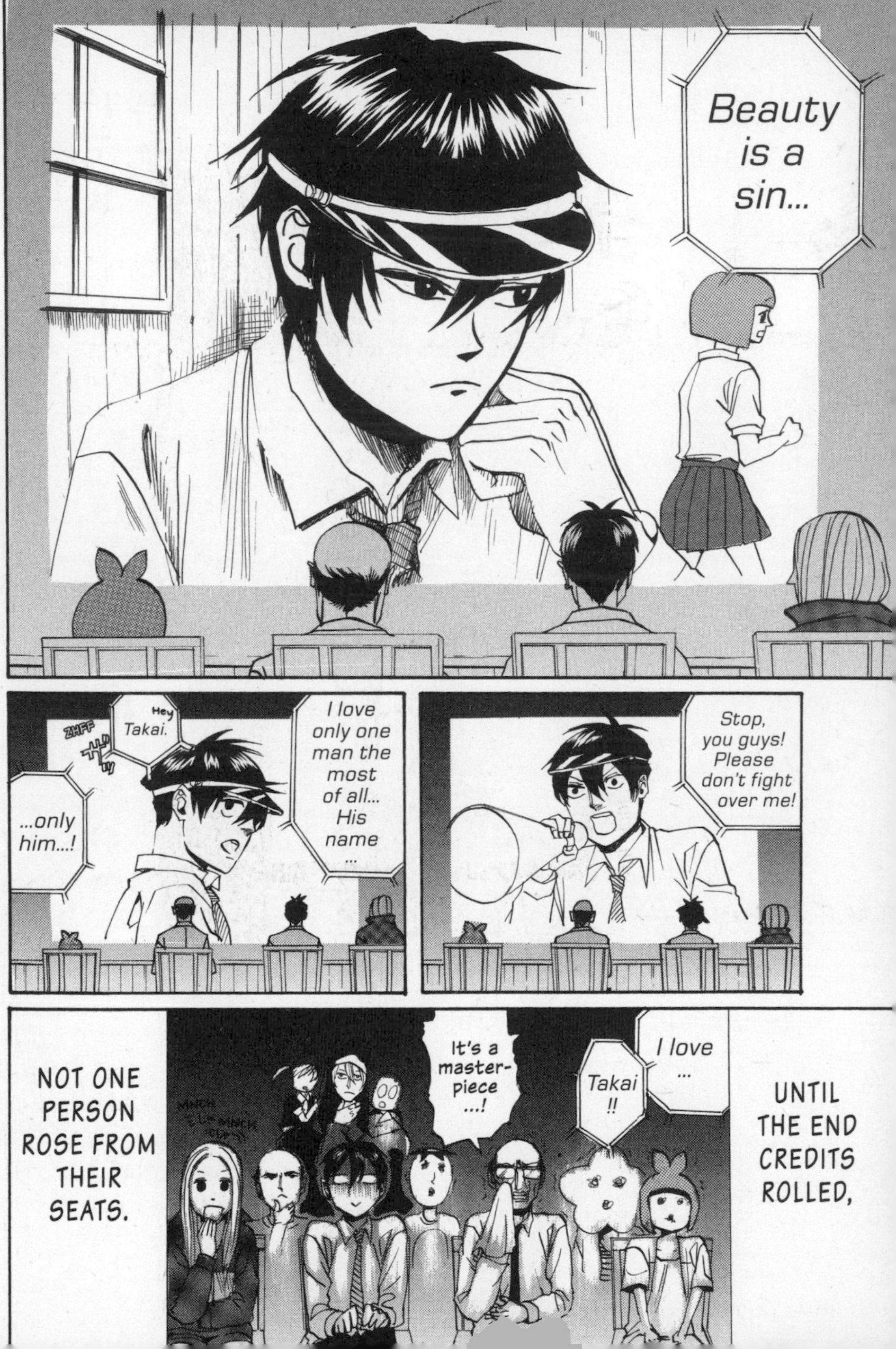
Beauty is a sin...
Stop, you guys! Please don't fight over me!
I love only one man the most of all... His name ...
Hey Takai.
ZHFF
...only him...!
UNTIL THE END CREDITS ROLLED,
I love ...
Takai !!
It's a masterpiece ...!
NOT ONE PERSON ROSE FROM THEIR SEATS.

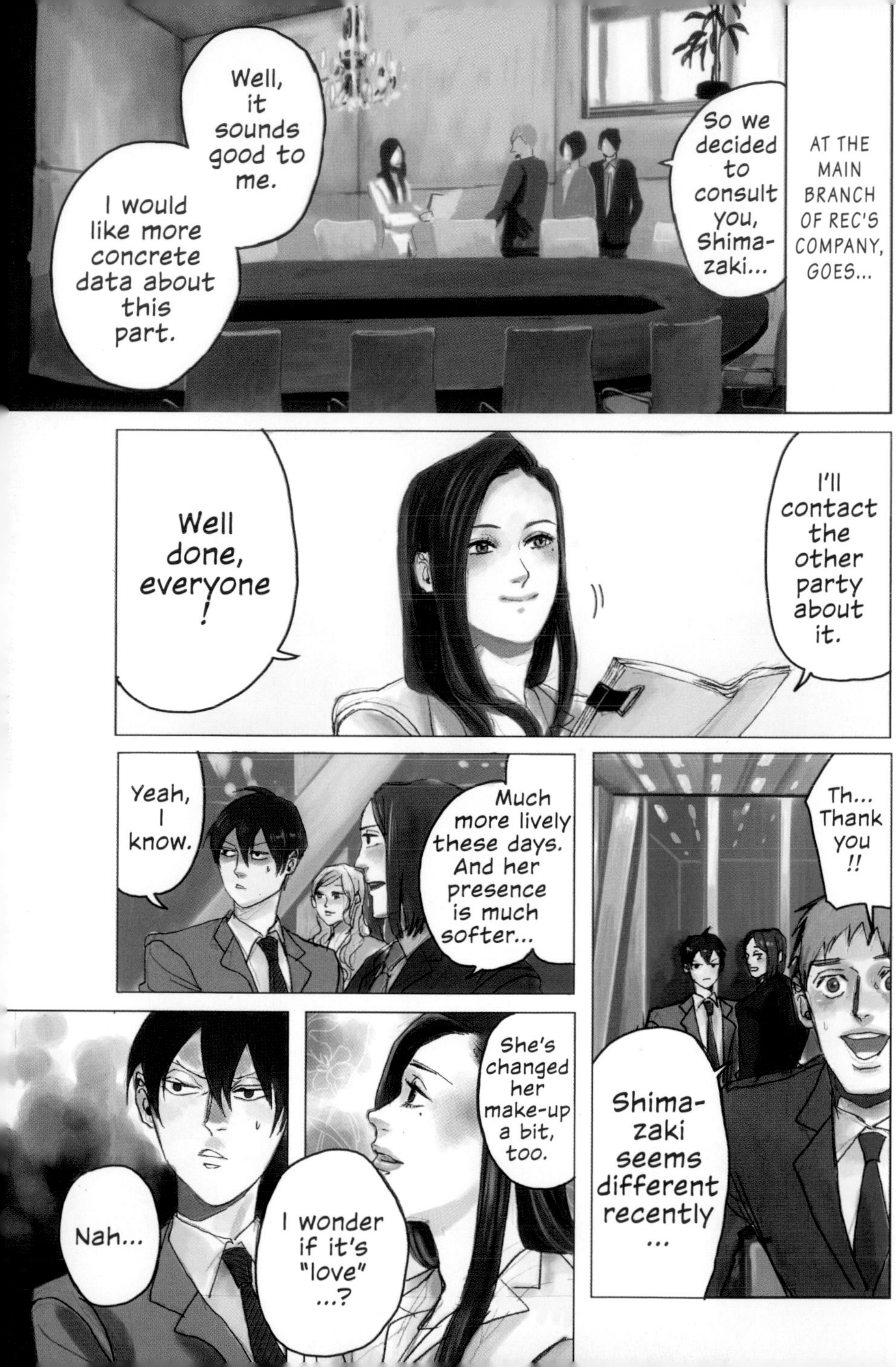
AT THE MAIN BRANCH OF REC'S COMPANY, GOES...
So we decided to consult you, Shimazaki...
Well, it sounds good to me.
I would like more concrete data about this part.
I'll contact the other party about it.
Well done, everyone!
Th... Thank you !!
Shimazaki seems different recently ...
Much more lively these days. And her presence is much softer...
Yeah, I know.
She's changed her make-up a bit, too.
I wonder if it's "love" ...?
Nah...

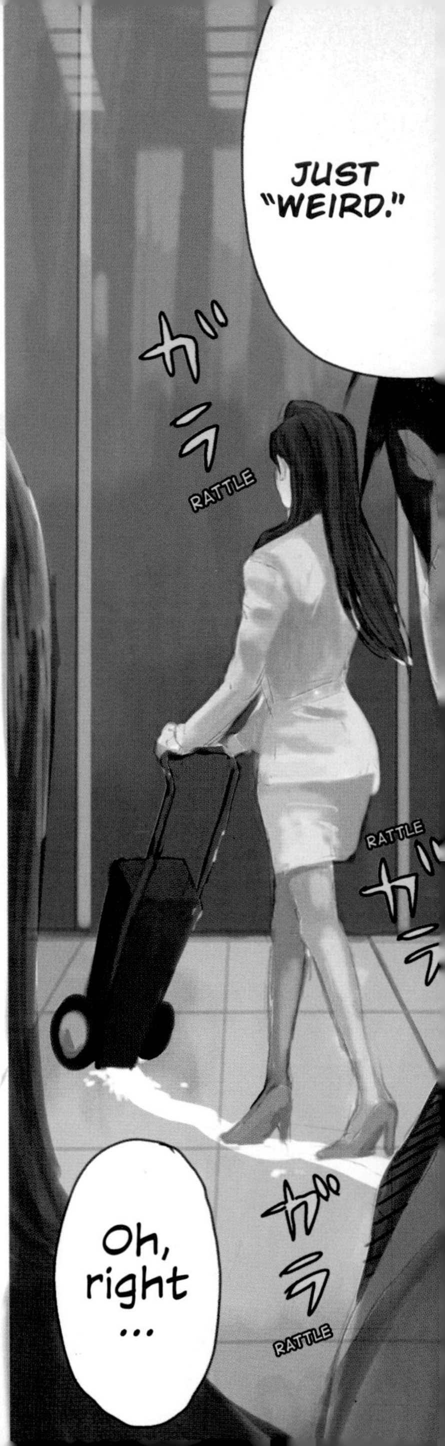
JUST "WEIRD."
ガラ
RATTLE
RATTLE
ガラ
Oh, right ...
ガラ
RATTLE

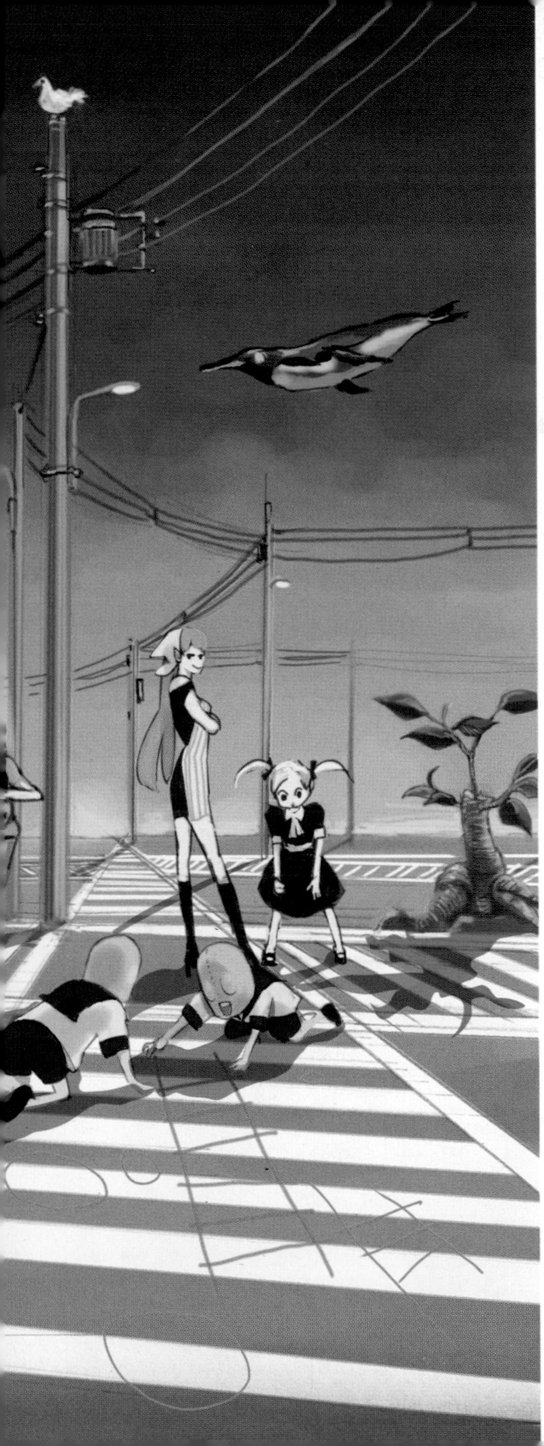

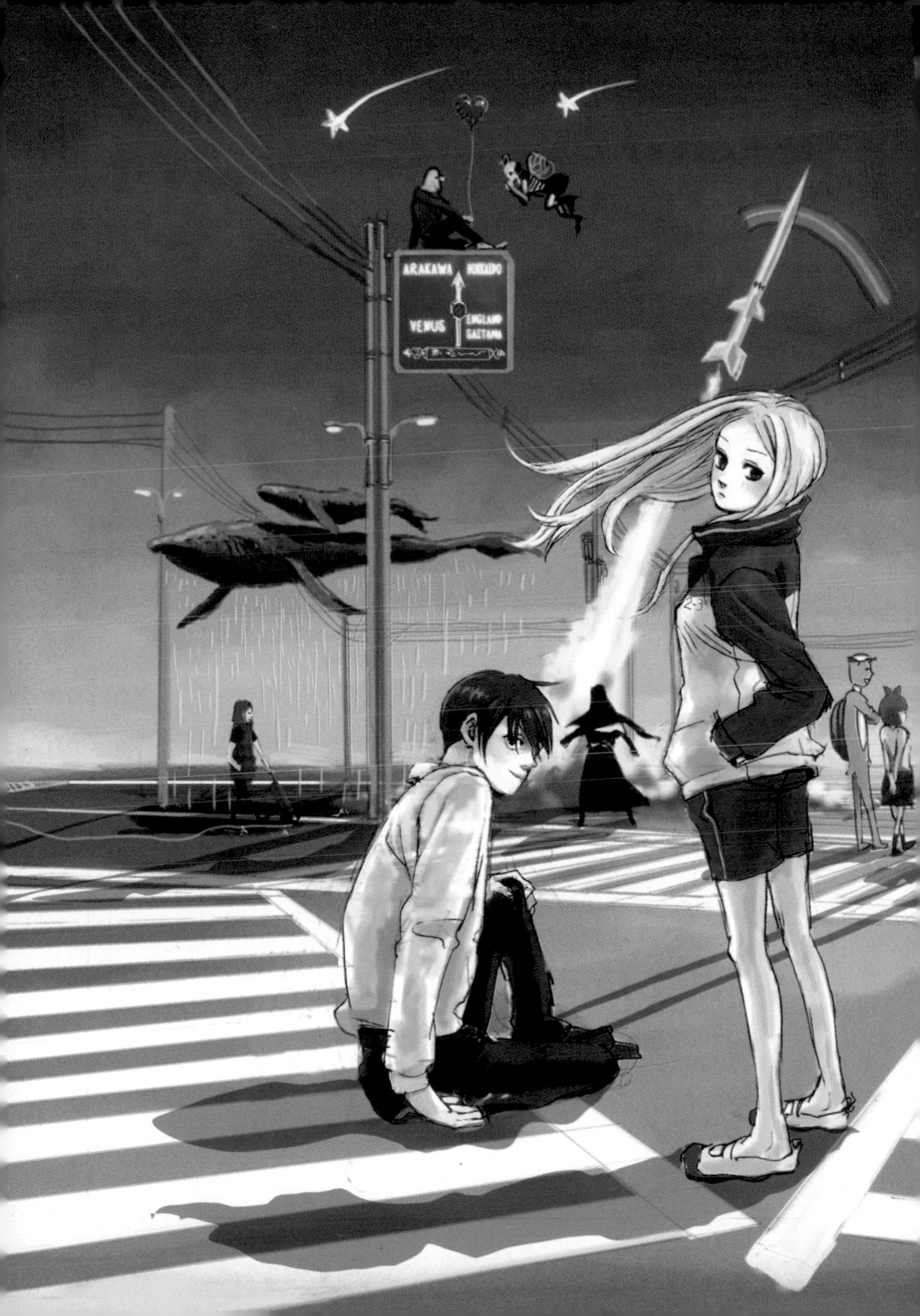
ARAKAWA
HOKKAIDO
VENUS
ENGLAND
SAITAMA

ARAKAWA
UNDER
THE BRIDGE

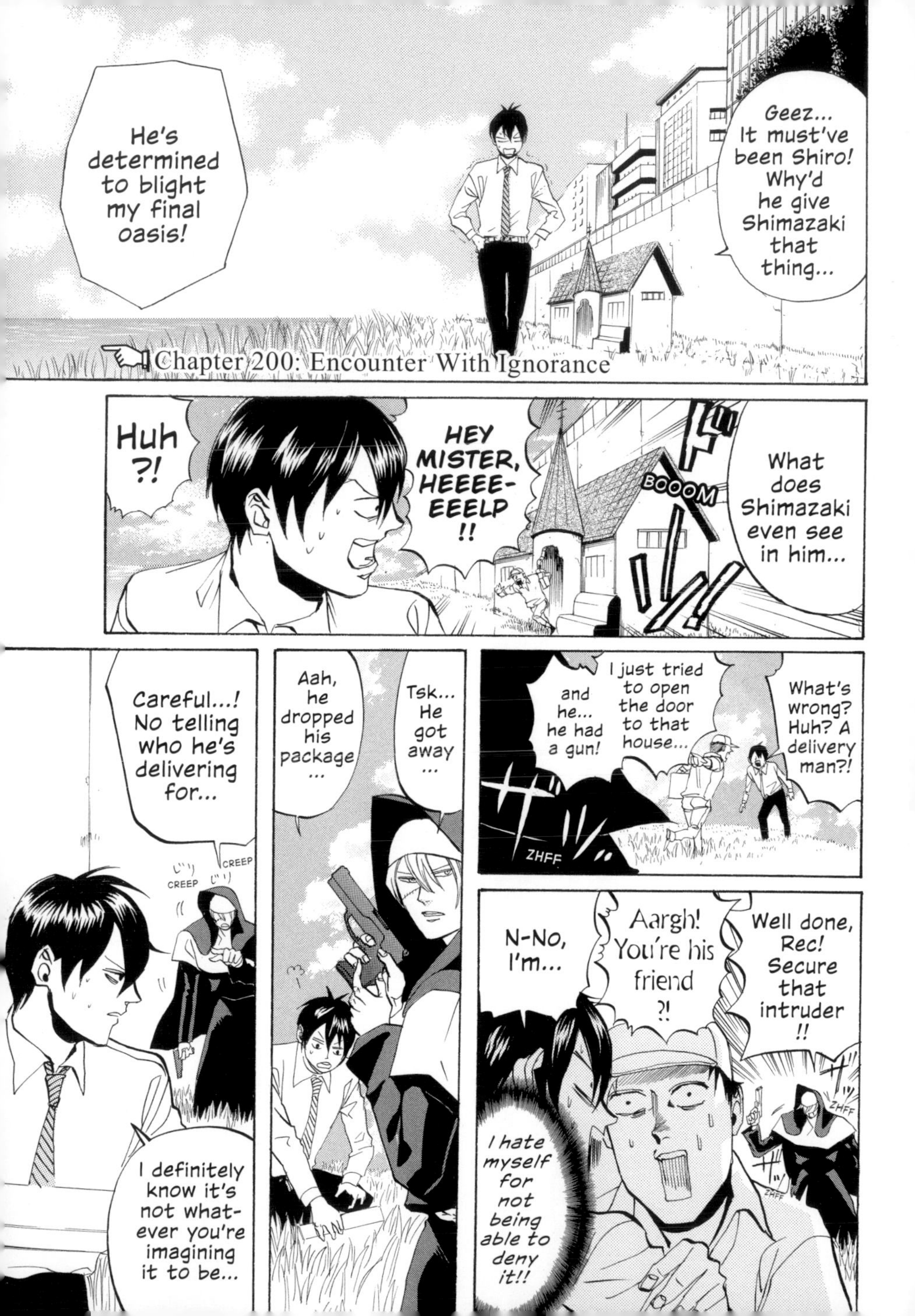
Geez... It must've been Shiro! Why'd he give Shimazaki that thing...
He's determined to blight my final oasis!
Chapter 200: Encounter With Ignorance
What does Shimazaki even see in him...
BOOOM
HEY MISTER, HEEEE-EEELP !!
Huh ?!
What's wrong? Huh? A delivery man?!
I just tried to open the door to that house...
and he... he had a gun!
ZHFF
Well done, Rec! Secure that intruder !!
Aargh! You're his friend ?!
N-No, I'm...
I hate myself for not being able to deny it!!
ZHFF
Tsk... He got away ...
Aah, he dropped his package ...
Careful...! No telling who he's delivering for...
CREEP
CREEP
I definitely know it's not what-ever you're imagining it to be...

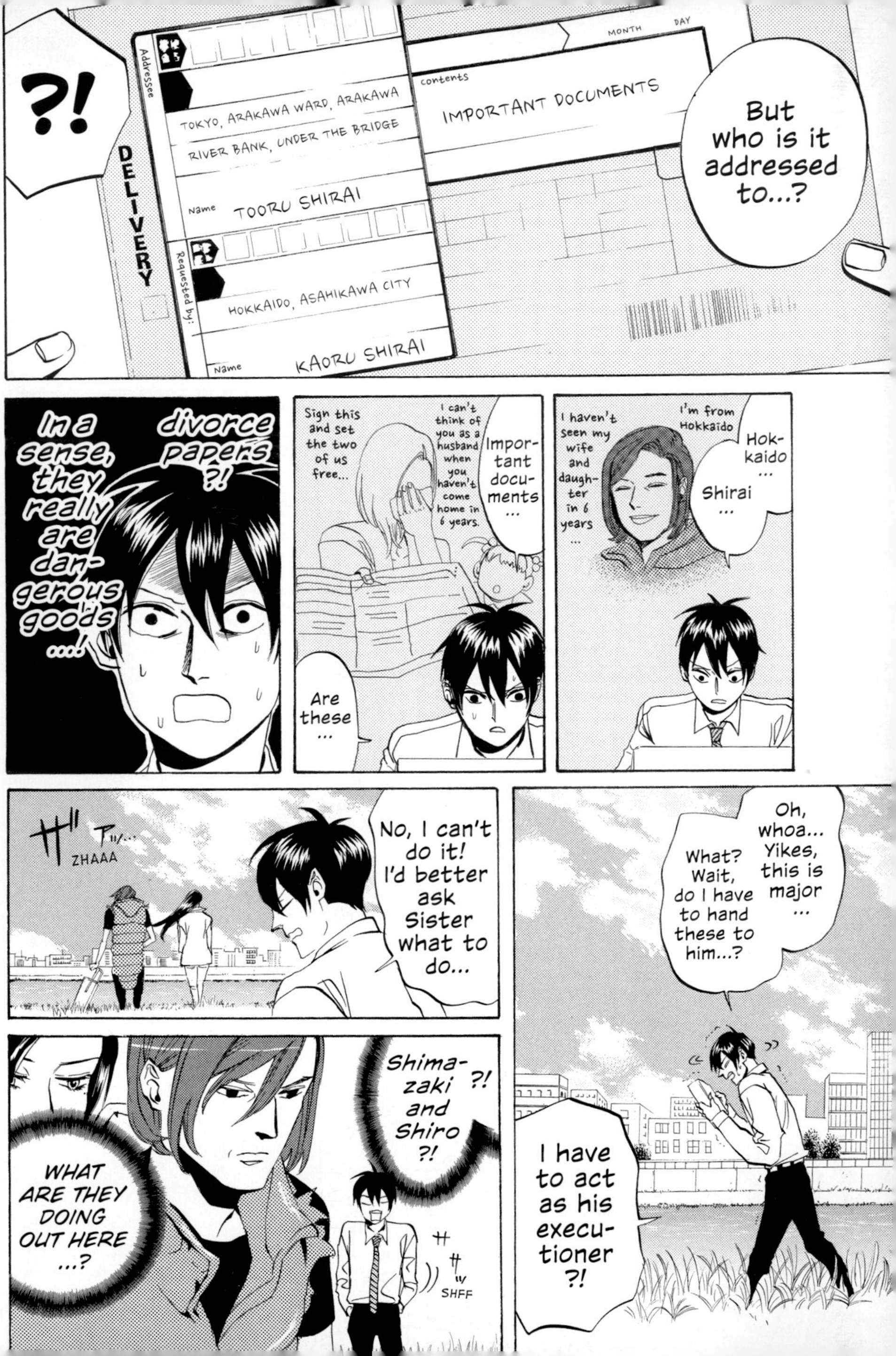
But who is it addressed to...?
MONTH
DAY
contents
IMPORTANT DOCUMENTS
Addressee
TOKYO, ARAKAWA WARD, ARAKAWA
RIVER BANK, UNDER THE BRIDGE
Name
TOORU SHIRAI
Requested by:
HOKKAIDO, ASAHIKAWA CITY
Name
KAORU SHIRAI
DELIVERY
?!
Hok-kaido...
Shirai...
I'm from Hokkaido
I haven't seen my wife and daugh-ter in 6 years...
Impor-tant docu-ments...
I can't think of you as a husband when you haven't come home in 6 years.
Sign this and set the two of us free...
Are these...
divorce papers?!
In a sense, they really are dan-gerous goods...!
Oh, whoa... Yikes, this is major...
What? Wait, do I have to hand these to him...?
I have to act as his execu-tioner?!
No, I can't do it! I'd better ask Sister what to do...
ZHAAA
Shima-zaki and Shiro?!
WHAT ARE THEY DOING OUT HERE...?
SHFF

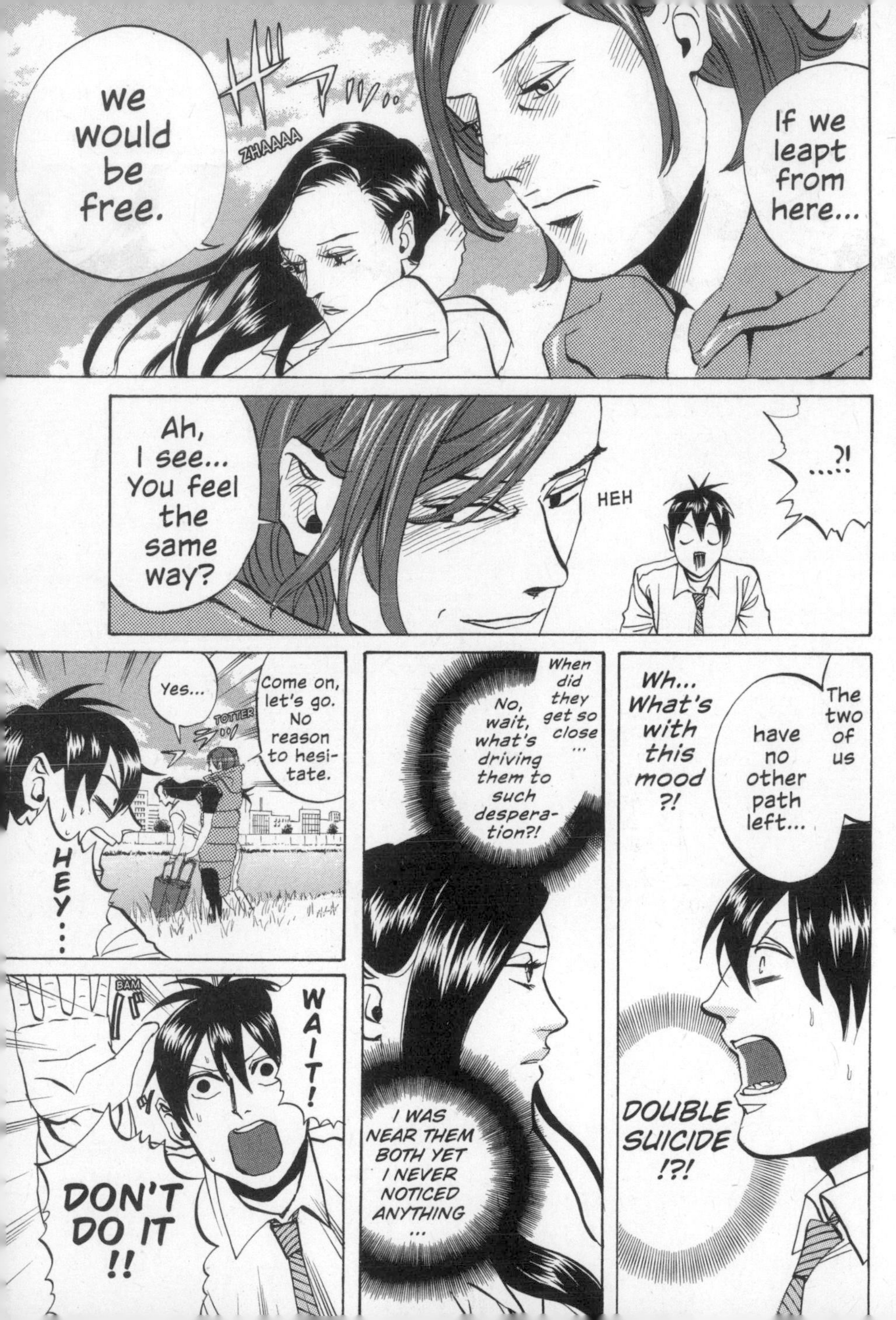

If we leapt from here...
ZHAAAA
we would be free.
...?!
HEH
Ah, I see... You feel the same way?
The two of us have no other path left...
Wh... What's with this mood?!
DOUBLE SUICIDE!?!
When did they get so close...
No, wait, what's driving them to such despera-tion?!
I WAS NEAR THEM BOTH YET I NEVER NOTICED ANYTHING...
Come on, let's go. No reason to hesi-tate.
Yes...
TOTTER
HEY...
BAM
WAIT!
DON'T DO IT!!

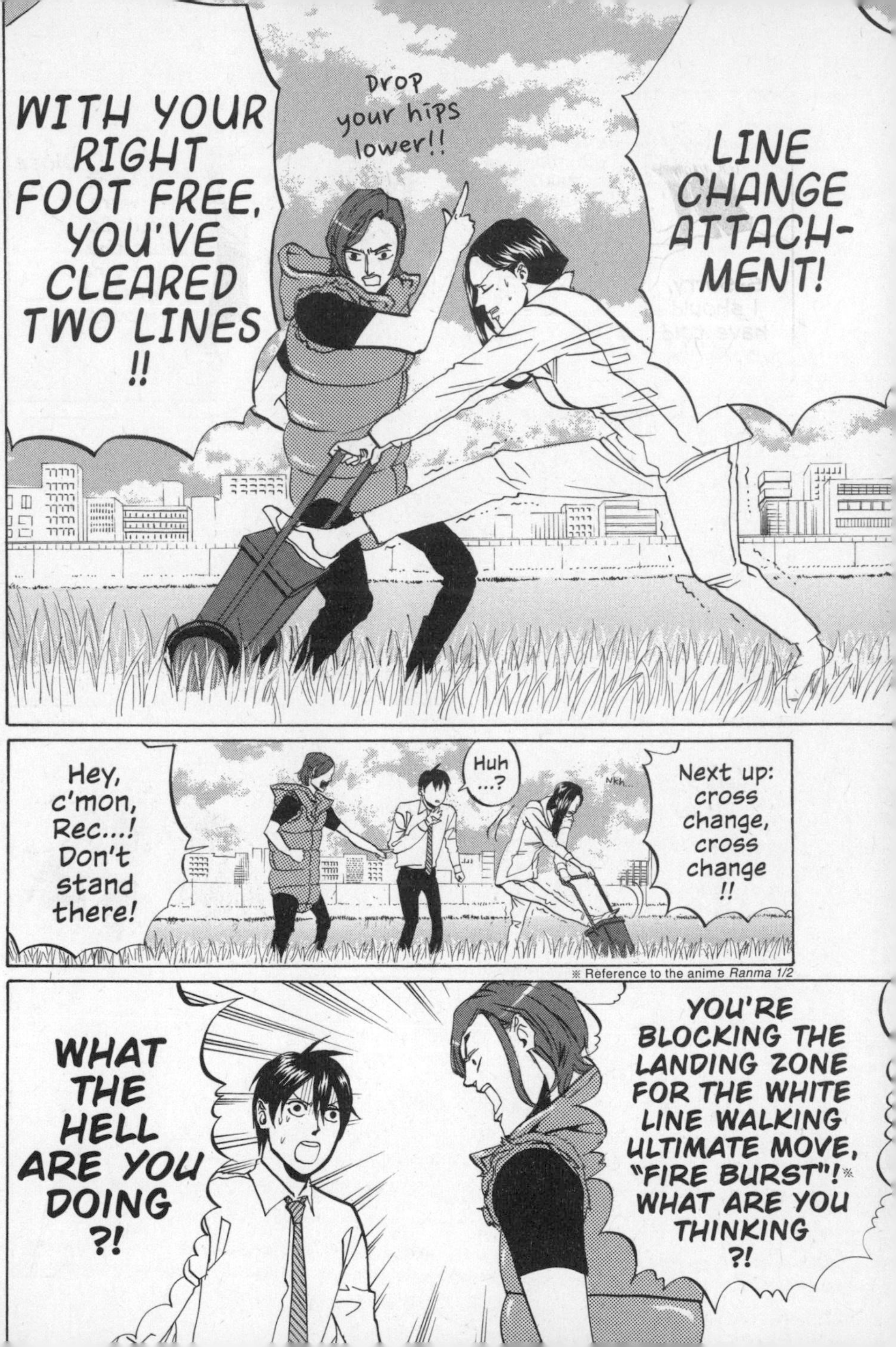
LINE CHANGE ATTACHMENT!
Drop your hips lower!!
WITH YOUR RIGHT FOOT FREE, YOU'VE CLEARED TWO LINES!!
Next up: cross change, cross change!!
Nkh...
Huh...?
Hey, c'mon, Rec...! Don't stand there!
YOU'RE BLOCKING THE LANDING ZONE FOR THE WHITE LINE WALKING ULTIMATE MOVE, "FIRE BURST"!※ WHAT ARE YOU THINKING?!
WHAT THE HELL ARE YOU DOING?!

※ Reference to the anime *Ranma 1/2*

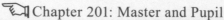

Chapter 201: Master and Pupil

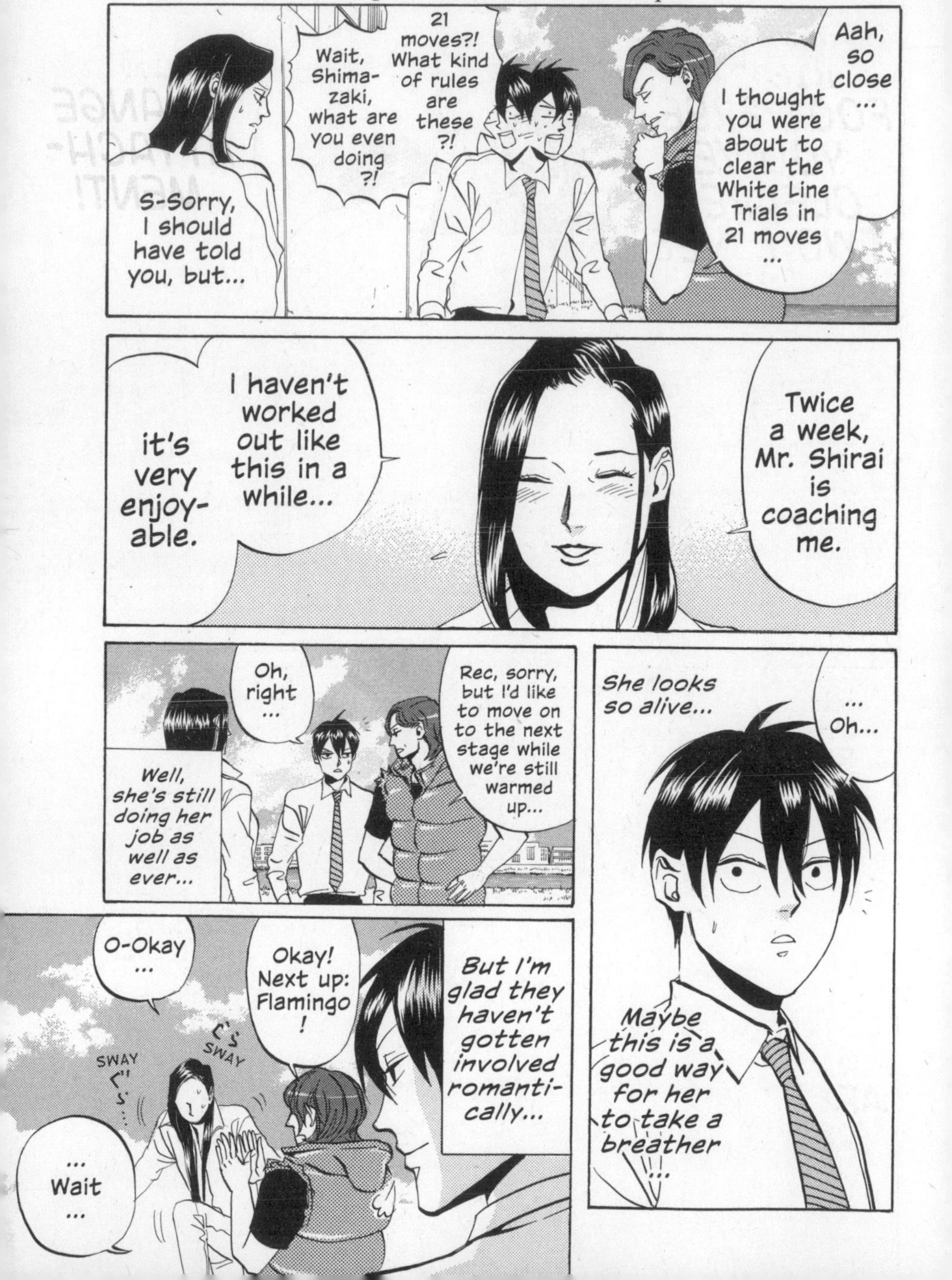
Aah, so close ... I thought you were about to clear the White Line Trials in 21 moves ...
21 moves?! What kind of rules are these ?!
Wait, Shima-zaki, what are you even doing ?!
S-Sorry, I should have told you, but...
Twice a week, Mr. Shirai is coaching me.
I haven't worked out like this in a while...
it's very enjoy-able.
... Oh...
She looks so alive...
Maybe this is a good way for her to take a breather ...
Rec, sorry, but I'd like to move on to the next stage while we're still warmed up...
Oh, right ...
Well, she's still doing her job as well as ever...
But I'm glad they haven't gotten involved romanti-cally...
Okay! Next up: Flamingo !
O-Okay ...
SWAY
SWAY
... Wait ...

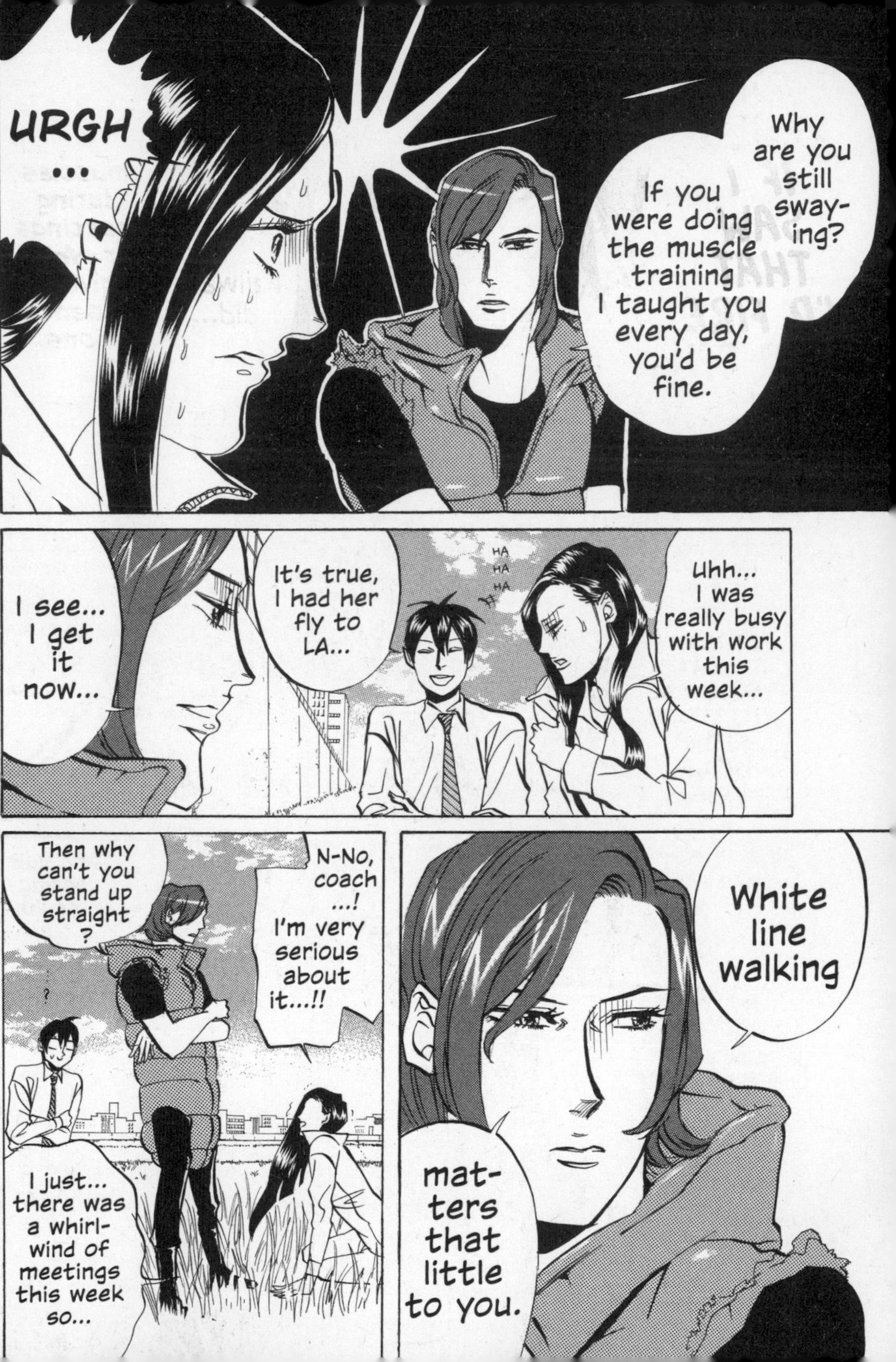
Why are you still sway- ing?
If you were doing the muscle training I taught you every day, you'd be fine.
URGH ...
Uhh... I was really busy with work this week...
HA HA HA
It's true, I had her fly to LA...
I see... I get it now...
White line walking
mat- ters that little to you.
N-No, coach ...! I'm very serious about it...!!
Then why can't you stand up straight ?
I just... there was a whirl- wind of meetings this week so...

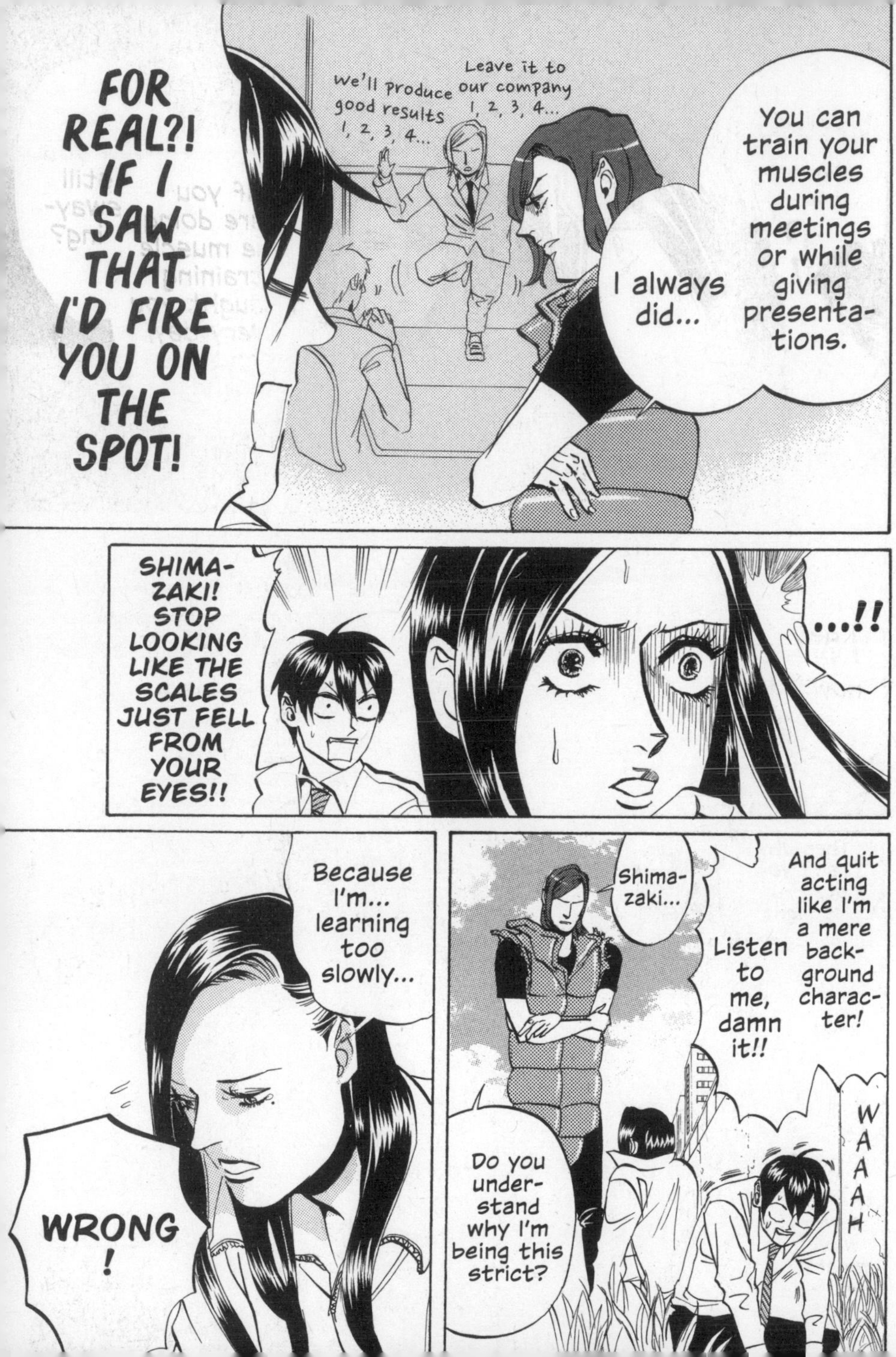
You can train your muscles during meetings or while giving presentations.
I always did...
Leave it to our company 1, 2, 3, 4...
We'll produce good results 1, 2, 3, 4...
FOR REAL?! IF I SAW THAT I'D FIRE YOU ON THE SPOT!
...!!
SHIMAZAKI! STOP LOOKING LIKE THE SCALES JUST FELL FROM YOUR EYES!!
And quit acting like I'm a mere background character!
Listen to me, damn it!!
Shimazaki...
WAAAAH
Do you understand why I'm being this strict?
Because I'm... learning too slowly...
WRONG!

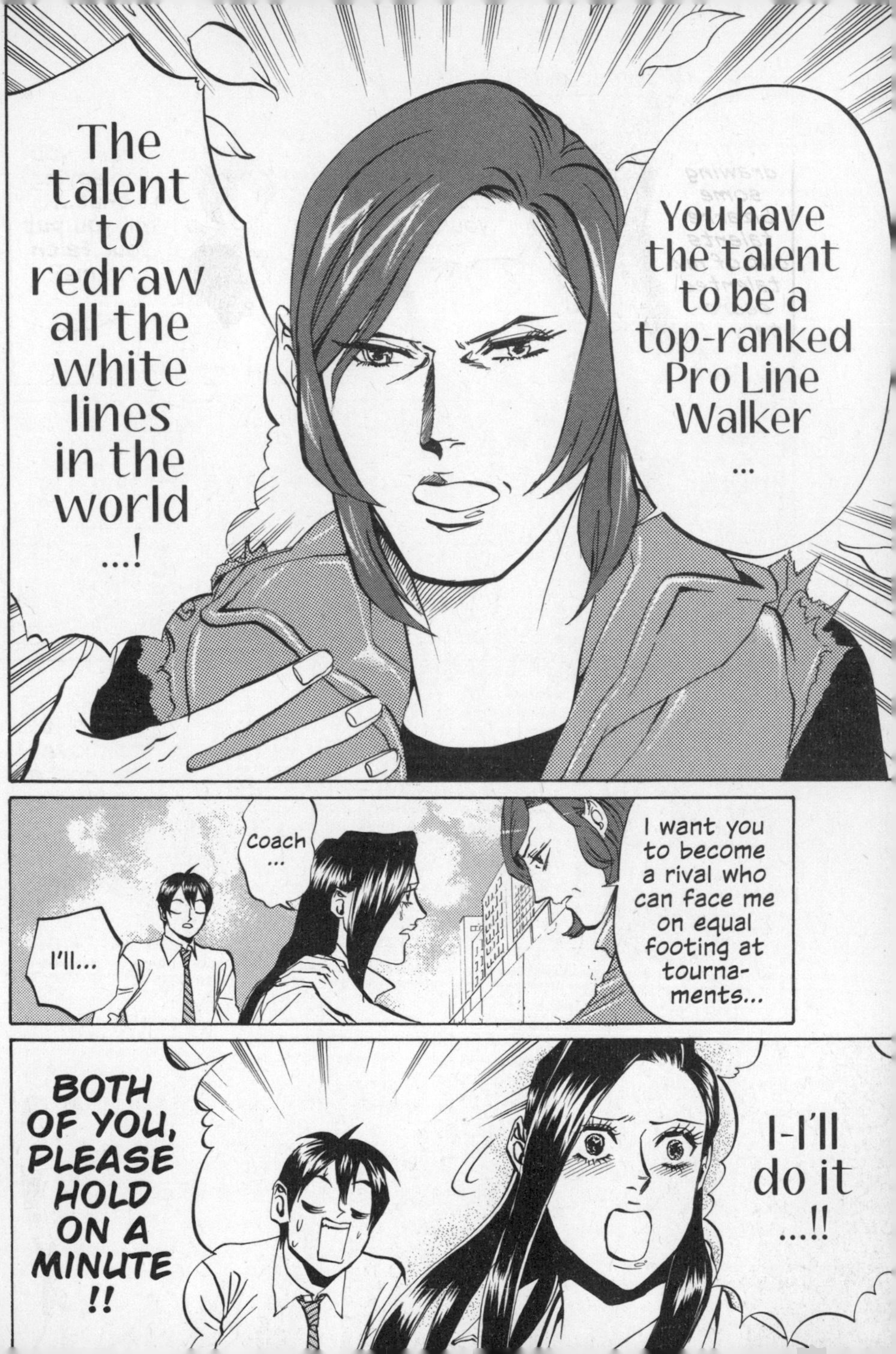
You have the talent to be a top-ranked Pro Line Walker ...
The talent to redraw all the white lines in the world ...!
I want you to become a rival who can face me on equal footing at tourna-ments...
Coach ...
I'll...
I-I'll do it ...!!
BOTH OF YOU, PLEASE HOLD ON A MINUTE !!

Chapter 202: The Road to White Line Mastery

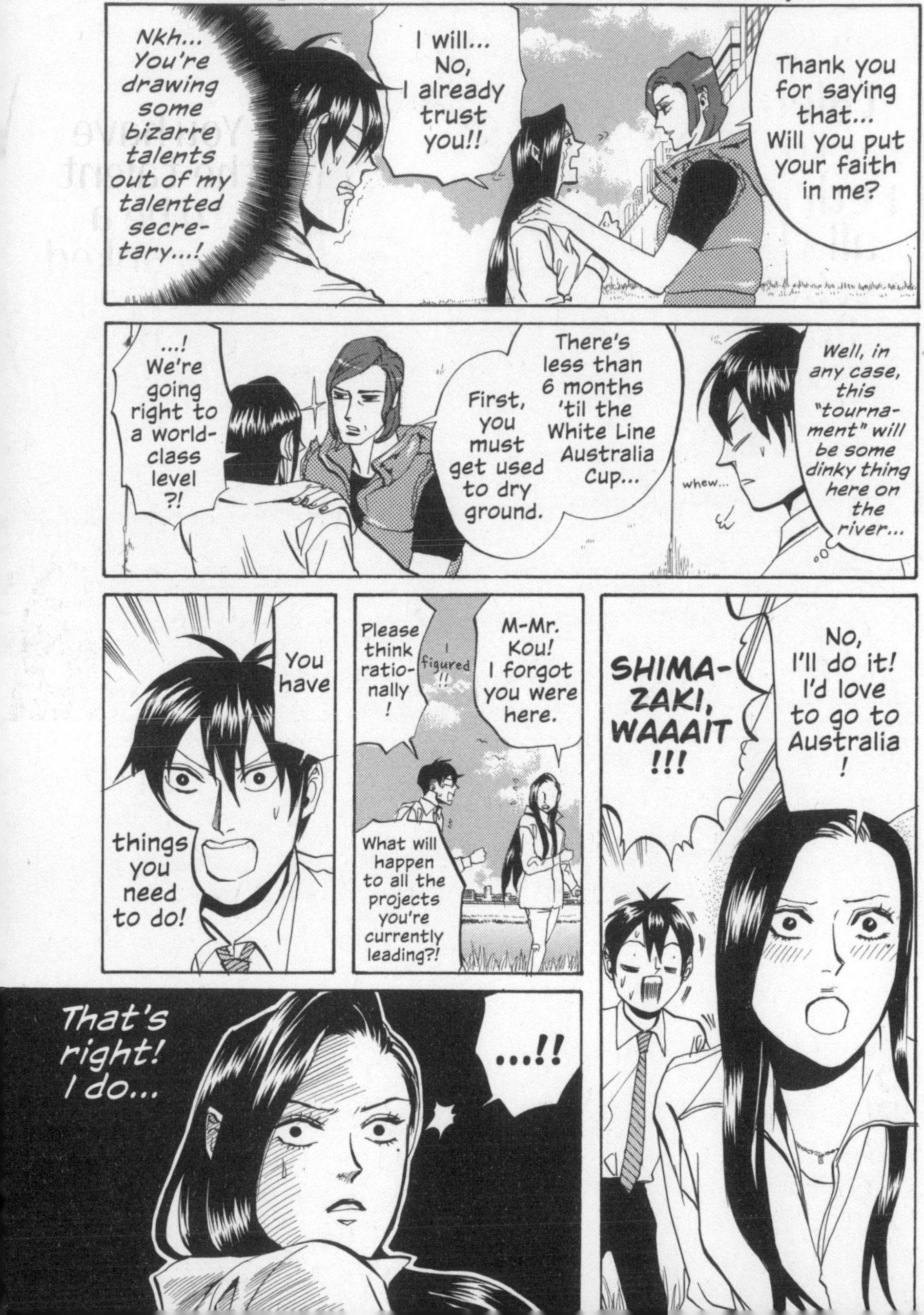

Thank you for saying that... Will you put your faith in me?
I will... No, I already trust you!!
Nkh... You're drawing some bizarre talents out of my talented secretary...!
Well, in any case, this "tournament" will be some dinky thing here on the river...
whew...
There's less than 6 months 'til the White Line Australia Cup...
First, you must get used to dry ground.
...! We're going right to a world-class level?!
No, I'll do it! I'd love to go to Australia!
SHIMAZAKI, WAAAIT!!!
M-Mr. Kou! I forgot you were here.
I figured!!
Please think rationally!
What will happen to all the projects you're currently leading?!
You have things you need to do!
...!!
That's right! I do...

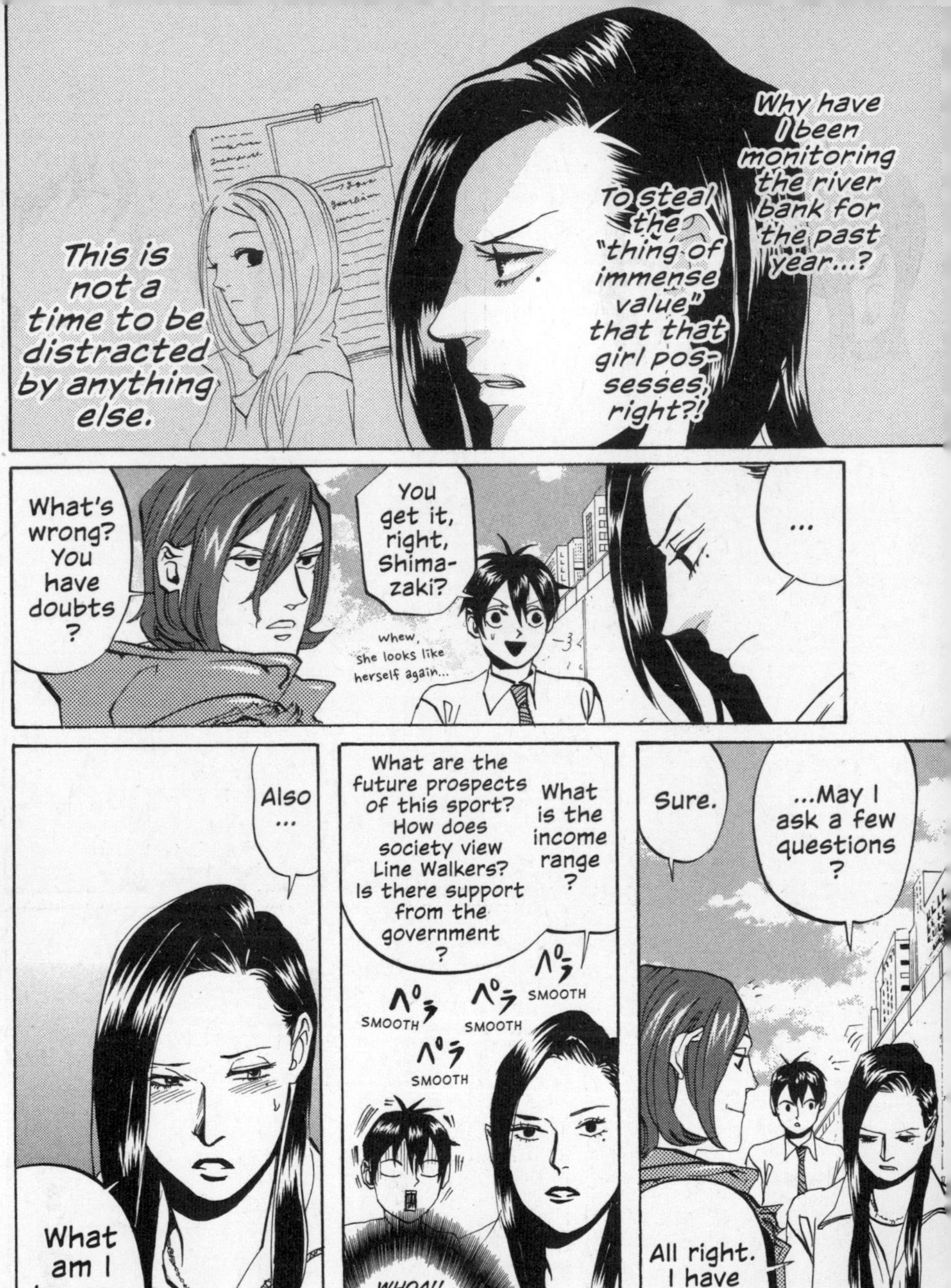
Why have I been monitoring the river bank for the past year...?
To steal the "thing of immense value" that that girl possesses, right?!
This is not a time to be distracted by anything else.
...
You get it, right, Shimazaki?
whew, she looks like herself again...
What's wrong? You have doubts?
...May I ask a few questions?
Sure.
All right. I have four...
What is the income range?
What are the future prospects of this sport? How does society view Line Walkers? Is there support from the government?
ペラ SMOOTH
ペラ SMOOTH
ペラ SMOOTH
ペラ SMOOTH
WHOA!! SHE SAID ALL THE SCARY STUFF AT ONCE!!!
Also...
What am I to you, coach...?

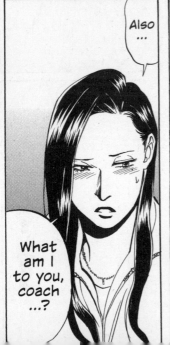

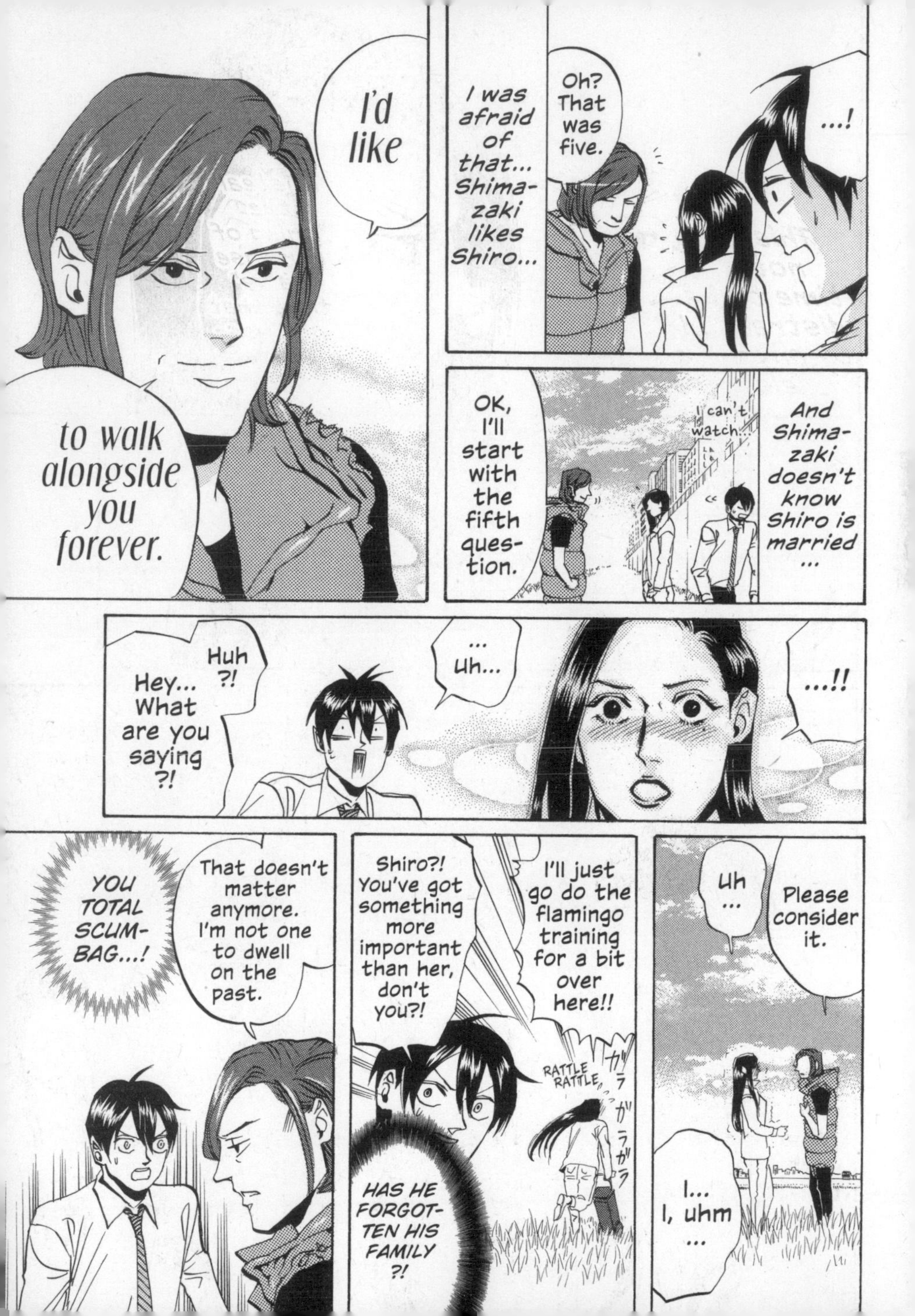

...!
Oh? That was five.
I was afraid of that... Shimazaki likes Shiro...
And Shimazaki doesn't know Shiro is married ...
I can't watch...
OK, I'll start with the fifth question.
I'd like
to walk alongside you forever.
...!!
... uh...
Huh ?!
Hey... What are you saying ?!
Please consider it.
Uh ...
I... I, uhm ...
I'll just go do the flamingo training for a bit over here!!
RATTLE RATTLE
Shiro?! You've got something more important than her, don't you?!
HAS HE FORGOTTEN HIS FAMILY ?!
That doesn't matter anymore. I'm not one to dwell on the past.
YOU TOTAL SCUMBAG...!

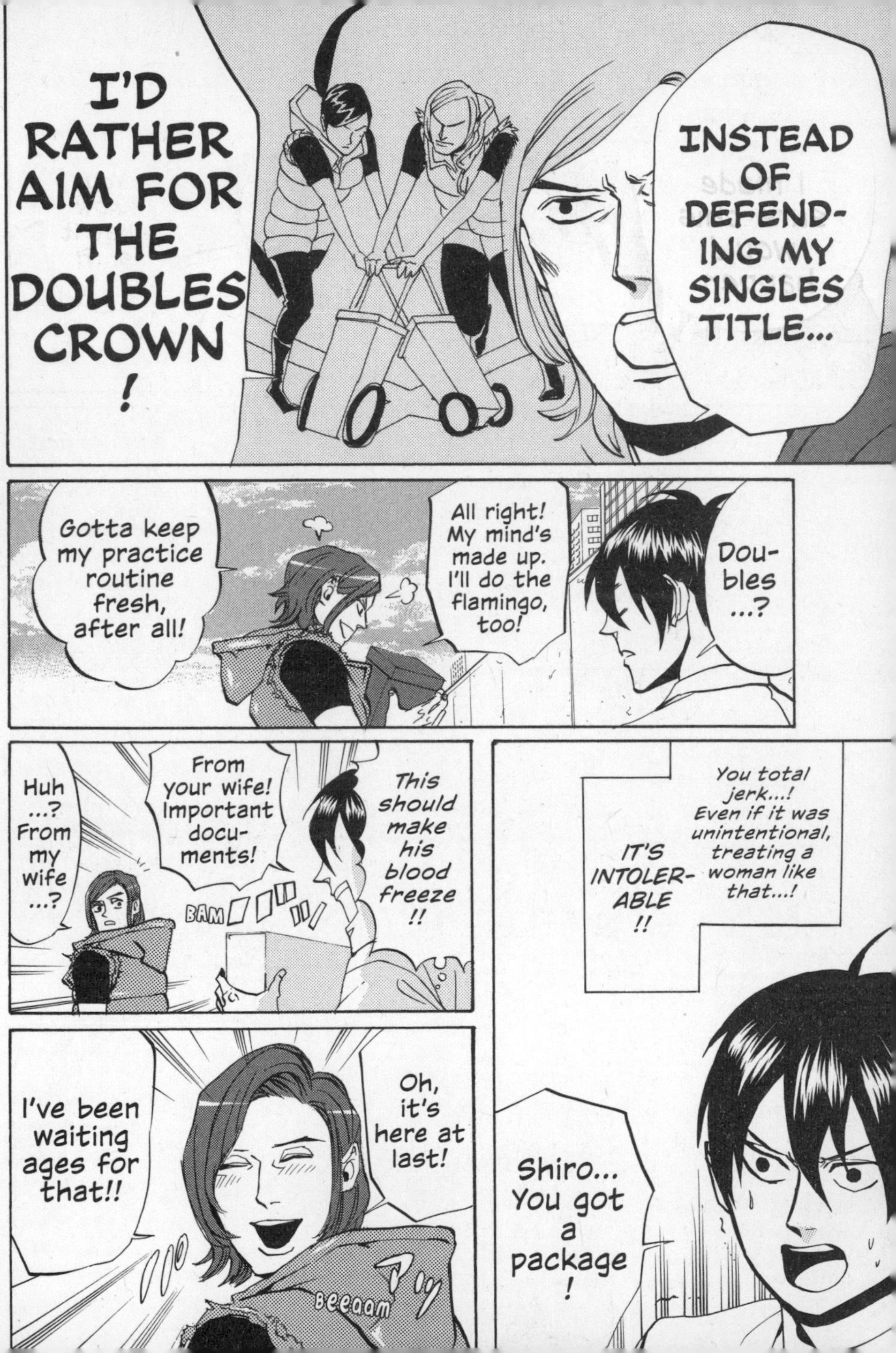
INSTEAD OF DEFEND-ING MY SINGLES TITLE...
I'D RATHER AIM FOR THE DOUBLES CROWN!
Dou-bles...?
All right! My mind's made up. I'll do the flamingo, too!
Gotta keep my practice routine fresh, after all!
You total jerk...! Even if it was unintentional, treating a woman like that...!
IT'S INTOLER-ABLE!!
Shiro... You got a package!
This should make his blood freeze!!
From your wife! Important docu-ments!
BAM
Huh...? From my wife...?
Oh, it's here at last!
I've been waiting ages for that!!
Beeaam

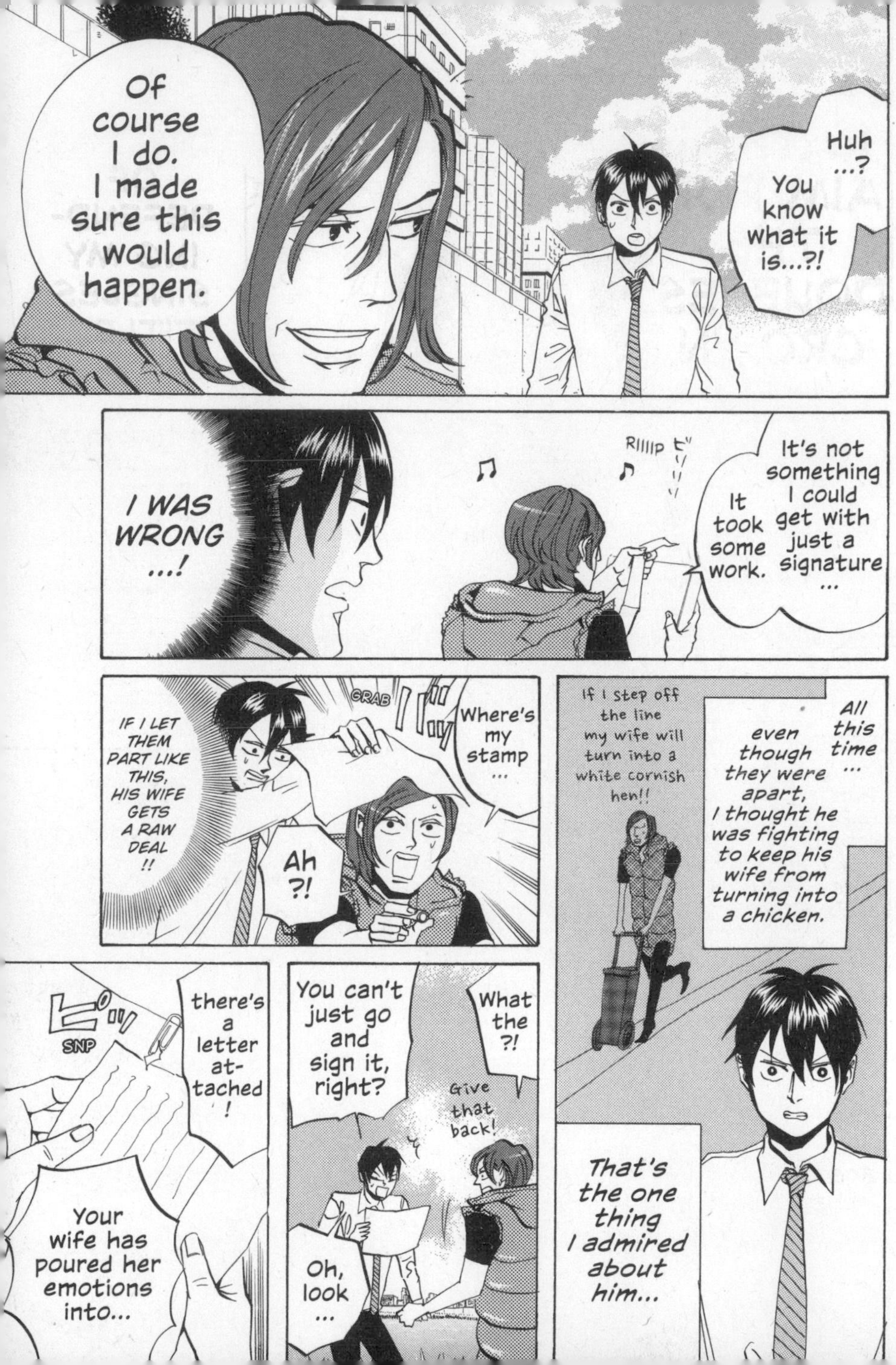
Huh ...? You know what it is...?!
Of course I do. I made sure this would happen.
It's not something I could get with just a signature ...
It took some work.
RIIIIP ビッ
I WAS WRONG ...!
All this time ...
even though they were apart, I thought he was fighting to keep his wife from turning into a chicken.
If I step off the line my wife will turn into a white cornish hen!!
That's the one thing I admired about him...
Where's my stamp ...
GRAB
IF I LET THEM PART LIKE THIS, HIS WIFE GETS A RAW DEAL !!
Ah ?!
What the ?!
You can't just go and sign it, right?
Give that back!
Oh, look ...
there's a letter at-tached !
ビッ
SNP
Your wife has poured her emotions into...

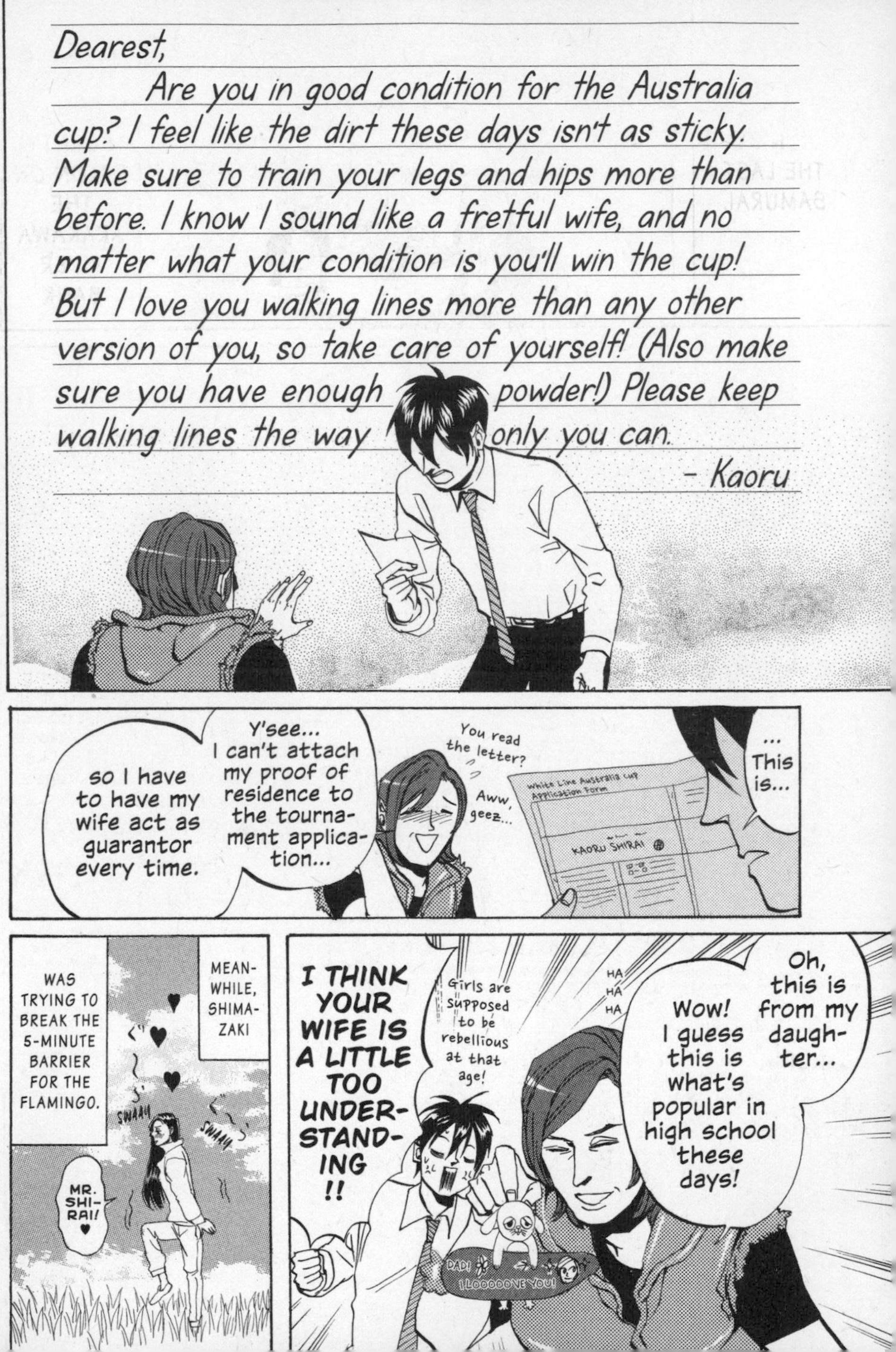
Dearest,
Are you in good condition for the Australia cup? I feel like the dirt these days isn't as sticky. Make sure to train your legs and hips more than before. I know I sound like a fretful wife, and no matter what your condition is you'll win the cup! But I love you walking lines more than any other version of you, so take care of yourself! (Also make sure you have enough powder!) Please keep walking lines the way only you can.
- Kaoru
... This is...
You read the letter?
Aww, geez...
White Line Australia cup Application Form
KAORU SHIRAI
Y'see... I can't attach my proof of residence to the tournament application...
so I have to have my wife act as guarantor every time.
Oh, this is from my daughter...
Wow! I guess this is what's popular in high school these days!
HA HA HA
Girls are supposed to be rebellious at that age!
I THINK YOUR WIFE IS A LITTLE TOO UNDERSTANDING!!
DAD! I LOOOOOVE YOU!
MEANWHILE, SHIMAZAKI
WAS TRYING TO BREAK THE 5-MINUTE BARRIER FOR THE FLAMINGO.
SWAAY
SWAAY
MR. SHIRAI! ♥

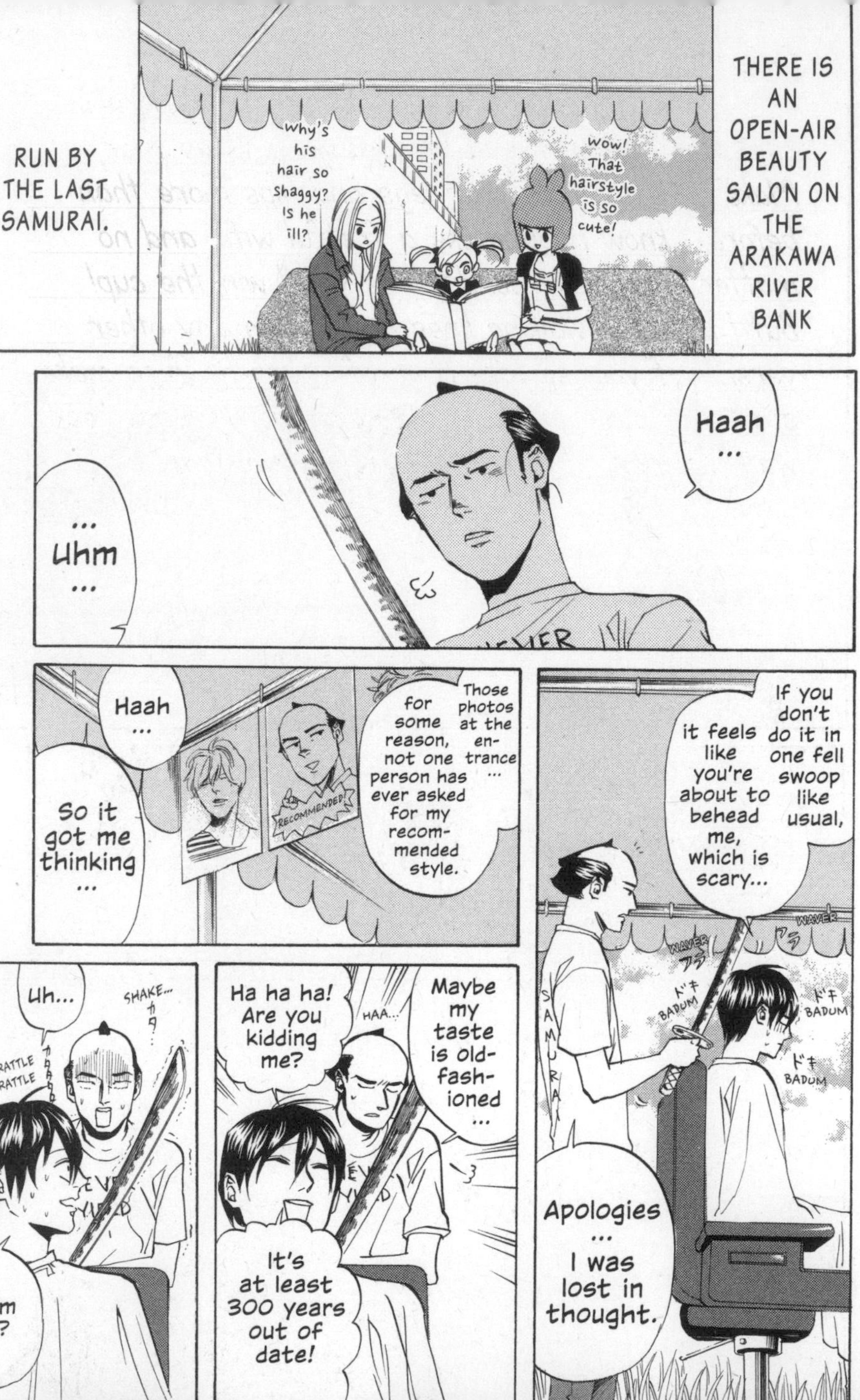
THERE IS AN OPEN-AIR BEAUTY SALON ON THE ARAKAWA RIVER BANK
Wow! That hairstyle is so cute!
Why's his hair so shaggy? Is he ill?
RUN BY THE LAST SAMURAI.
Haah ...
... Uhm ...
If you don't do it in one fell swoop like usual,
it feels like you're about to behead me, which is scary...
WAVER
WAVER
BADUM
BADUM
BADUM
SAMURAI
Apologies ... I was lost in thought.
Those photos at the entrance ...
for some reason, not one person has ever asked for my recommended style.
RECOMMENDED
Haah ...
So it got me thinking ...
Maybe my taste is old-fashioned ...
HAA...
Ha ha ha! Are you kidding me?
It's at least 300 years out of date!
Uh...
SHAKE...
RATTLE RATTLE
Uhm ...?

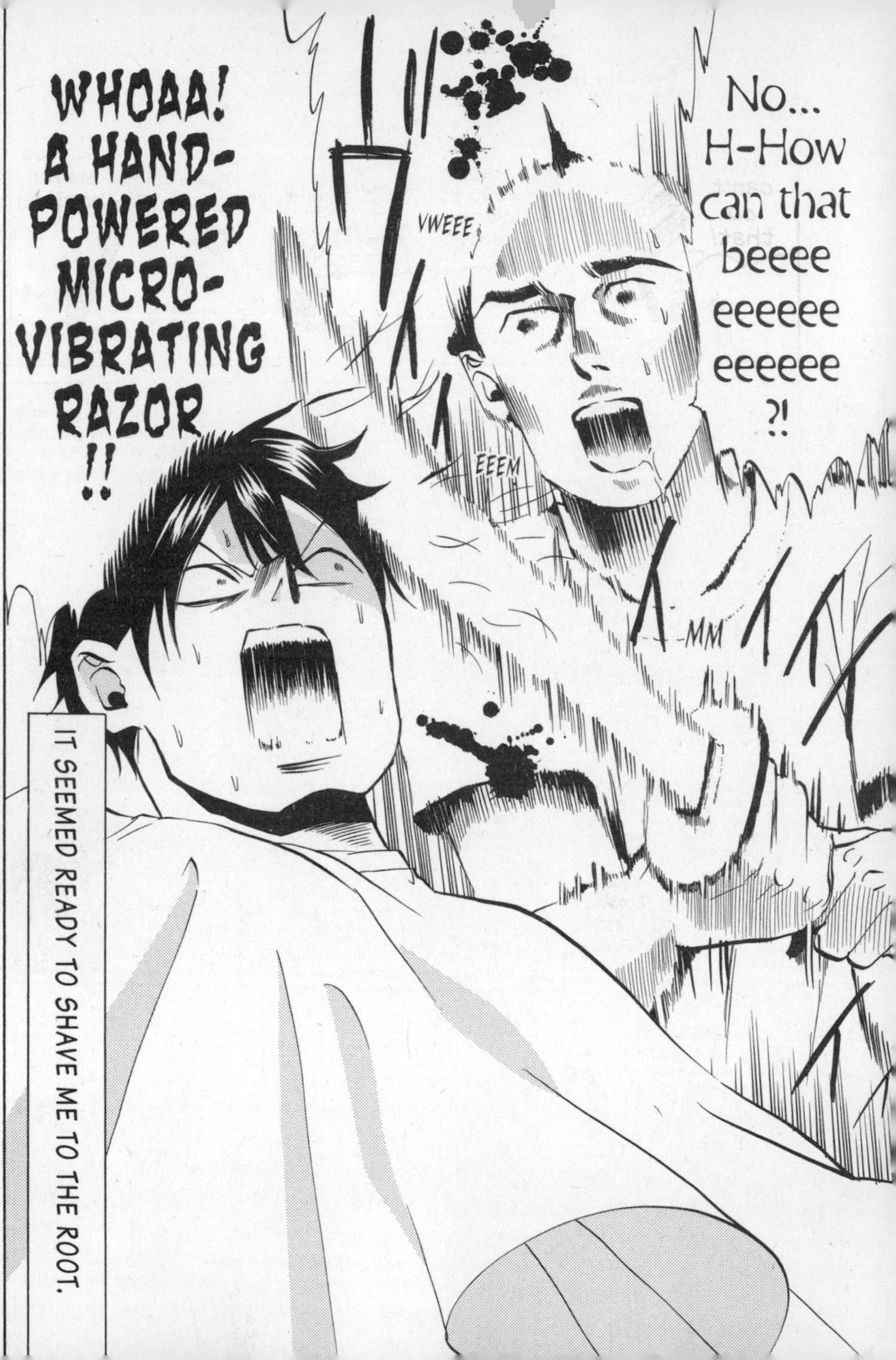
No... H-How can that beeee eeeeee eeeeee ?!
WHOAA! A HAND-POWERED MICRO-VIBRATING RAZOR !!
VWEEE
EEEM
MM
IT SEEMED READY TO SHAVE ME TO THE ROOT.

Chapter 203: The Road to Style Mastery

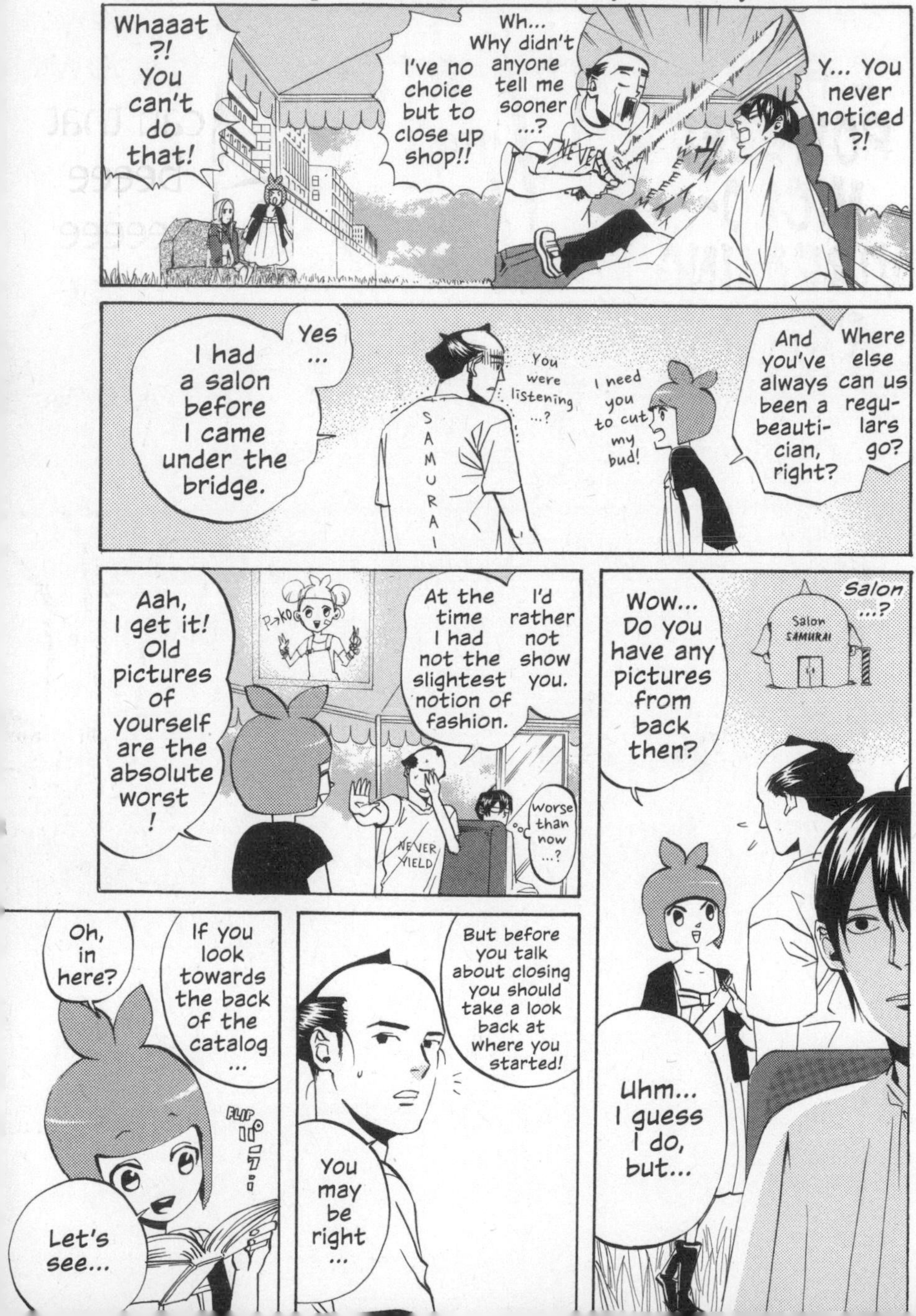

Y... You never noticed?!
Wh... Why didn't anyone tell me sooner...?
I've no choice but to close up shop!!
Whaaat?! You can't do that!
NEVER
Where else can us regulars go?
And you've always been a beautician, right?
I need you to cut my bud!
You were listening...?
SAMURAI
Yes...
I had a salon before I came under the bridge.
Salon...?
Salon SAMURAI
Wow... Do you have any pictures from back then?
Uhm... I guess I do, but...
I'd rather not show you.
At the time I had not the slightest notion of fashion.
P→KO
Aah, I get it! Old pictures of yourself are the absolute worst!
Worse than now...?
NEVER YIELD
But before you talk about closing you should take a look back at where you started!
You may be right...
If you look towards the back of the catalog...
Oh, in here?
FLIP
Let's see...

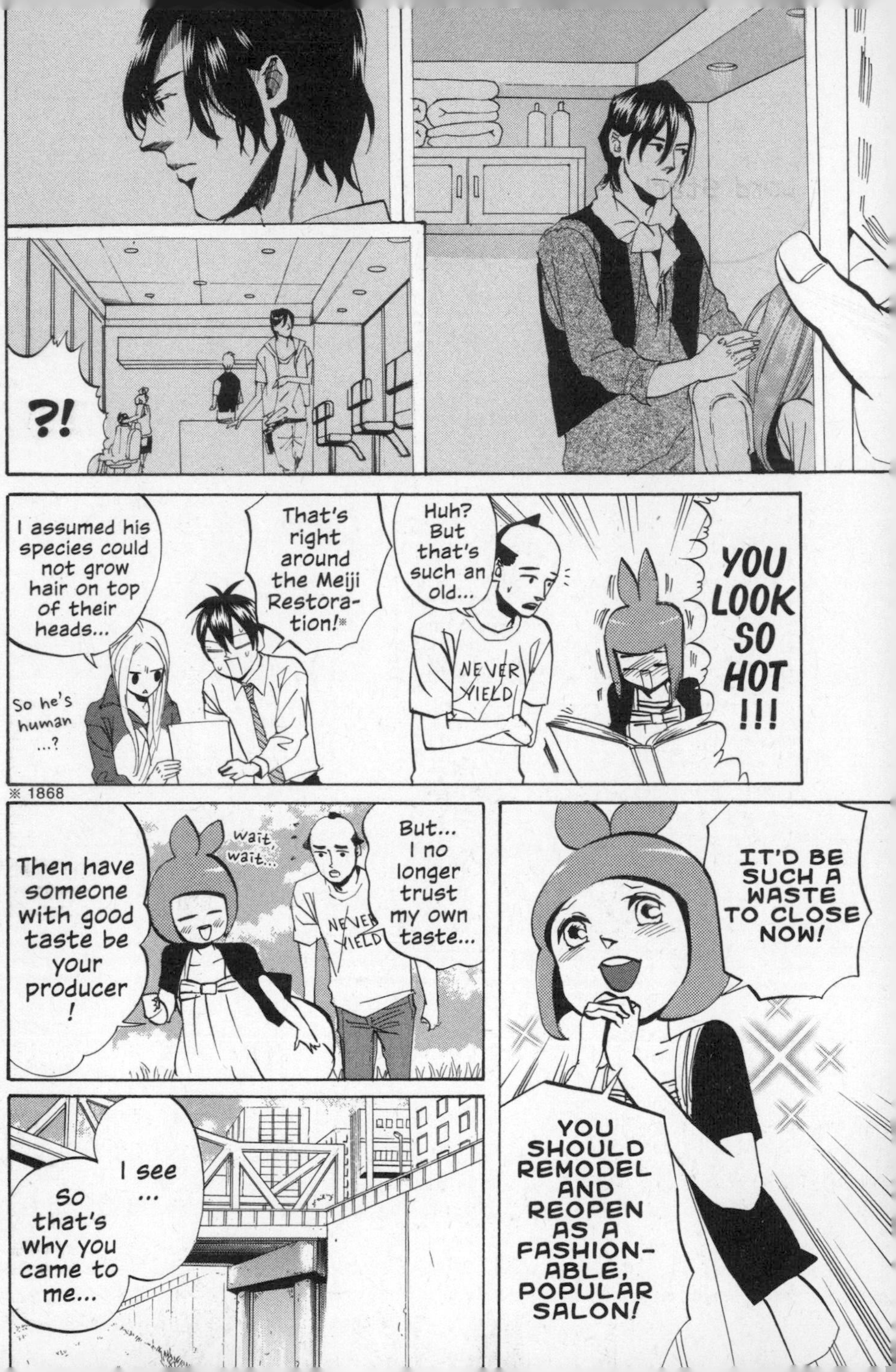
?!
YOU LOOK SO HOT !!!
Huh? But that's such an old...
That's right around the Meiji Restoration!※
I assumed his species could not grow hair on top of their heads...
So he's human ...?
IT'D BE SUCH A WASTE TO CLOSE NOW!
YOU SHOULD REMODEL AND REOPEN AS A FASHIONABLE, POPULAR SALON!
But... I no longer trust my own taste...
wait, wait...
Then have someone with good taste be your producer!
I see ...
So that's why you came to me...

※ 1868

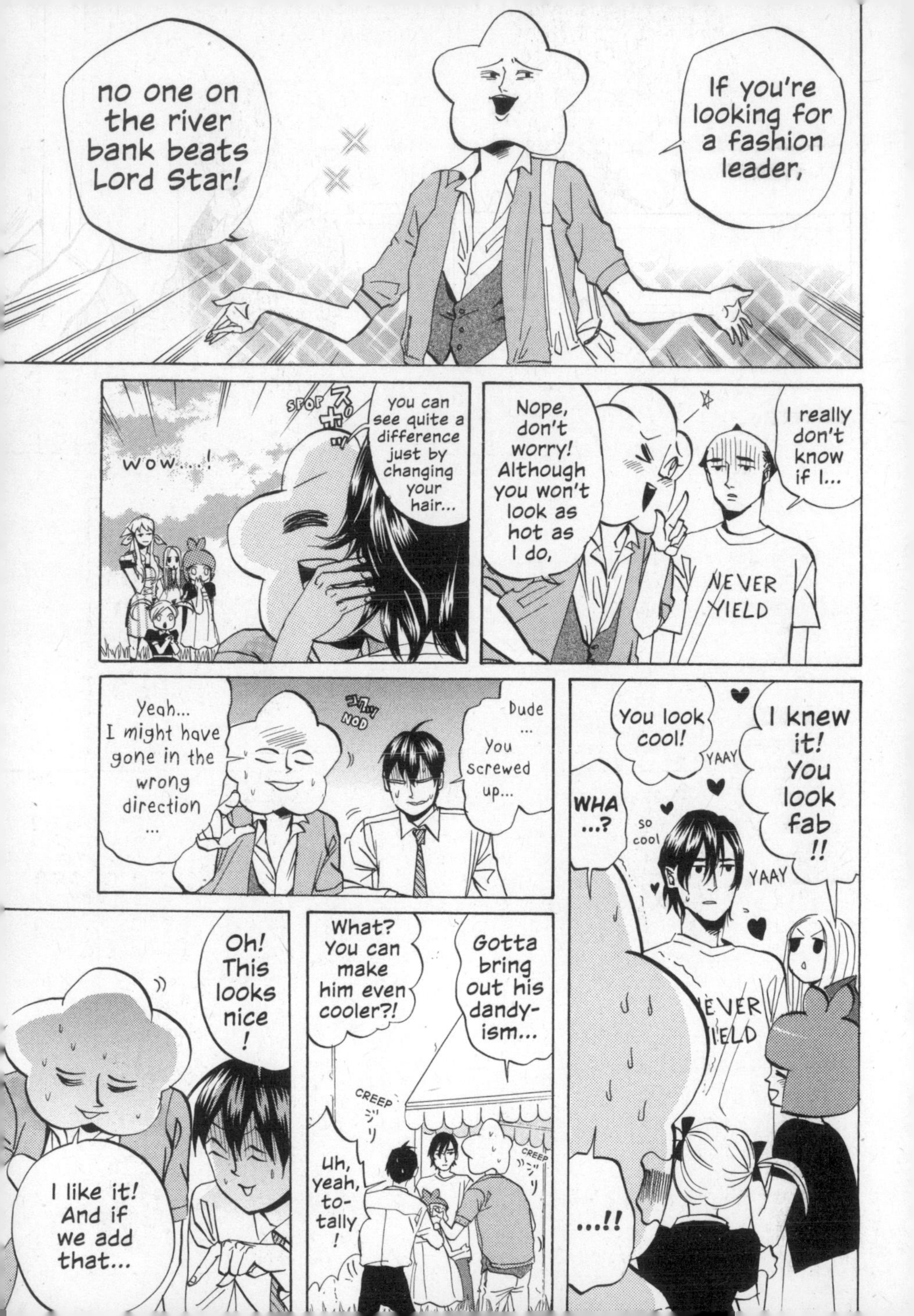
If you're looking for a fashion leader,
no one on the river bank beats Lord Star!
I really don't know if I...
Nope, don't worry! Although you won't look as hot as I do,
NEVER YIELD
SPOP
you can see quite a difference just by changing your hair...
wow...!
I knew it! You look fab!!
YAAY
You look cool!
YAAY
so cool
WHA...?
NEVER YIELD
...!!
Dude... You screwed up...
NOD
Yeah... I might have gone in the wrong direction...
Gotta bring out his dandy-ism...
What? You can make him even cooler?!
CREEP
CREEP
Uh, yeah, to-tally!
Oh! This looks nice!
I like it! And if we add that...

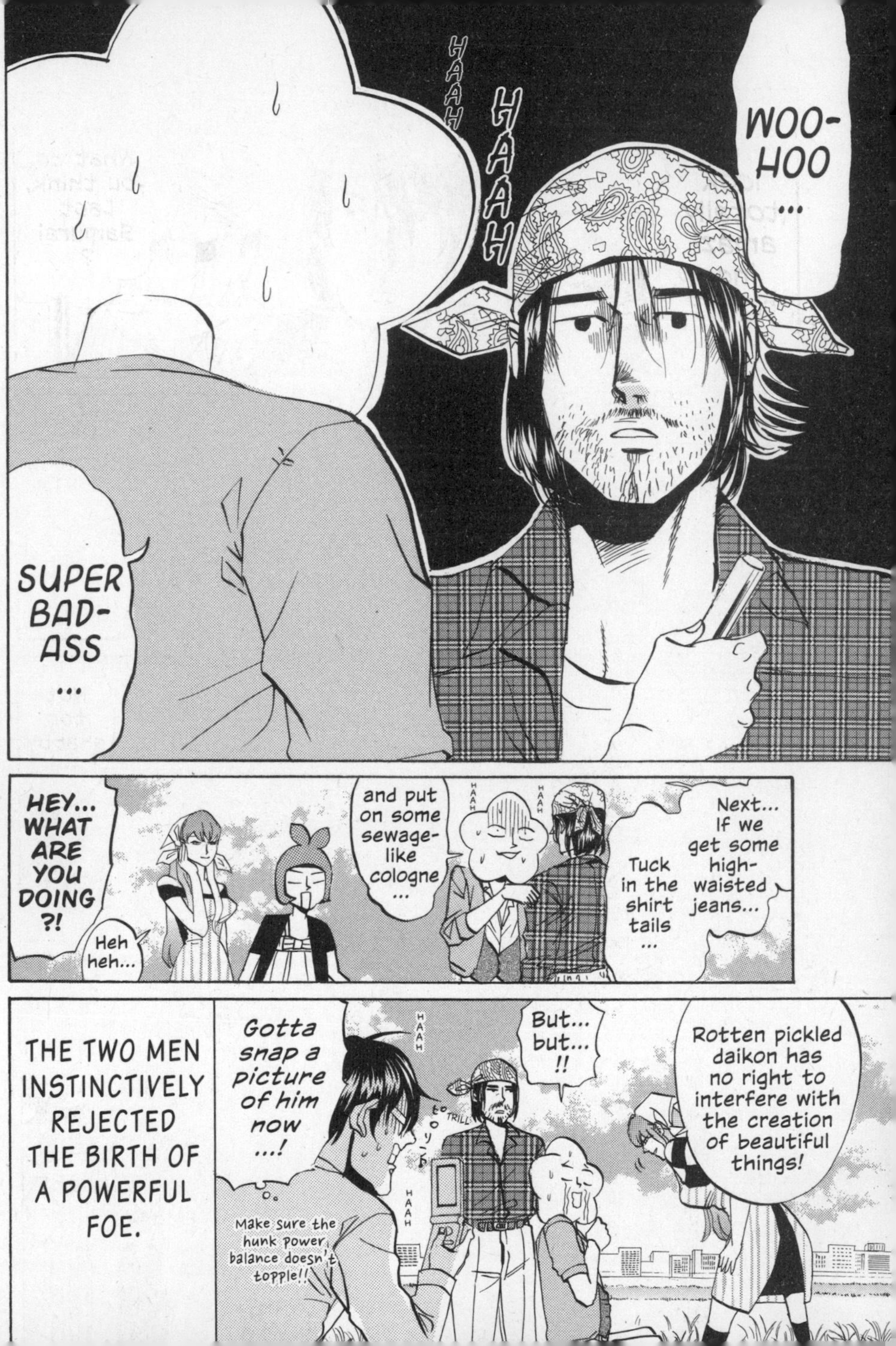
WOO-HOO...
HAAAH
HAAAH
SUPER BAD-ASS...
Next... If we get some high-waisted jeans...
Tuck in the shirt tails...
and put on some sewage-like cologne...
HAAAH
HAAAH
HEY... WHAT ARE YOU DOING?!
Heh heh...
Rotten pickled daikon has no right to interfere with the creation of beautiful things!
But... but...!!
TRILL
HAAAH
Gotta snap a picture of him now...!
HAAAH
Make sure the hunk power balance doesn't topple!!
THE TWO MEN INSTINCTIVELY REJECTED THE BIRTH OF A POWERFUL FOE.

Chapter 204: Arakawa Before and After

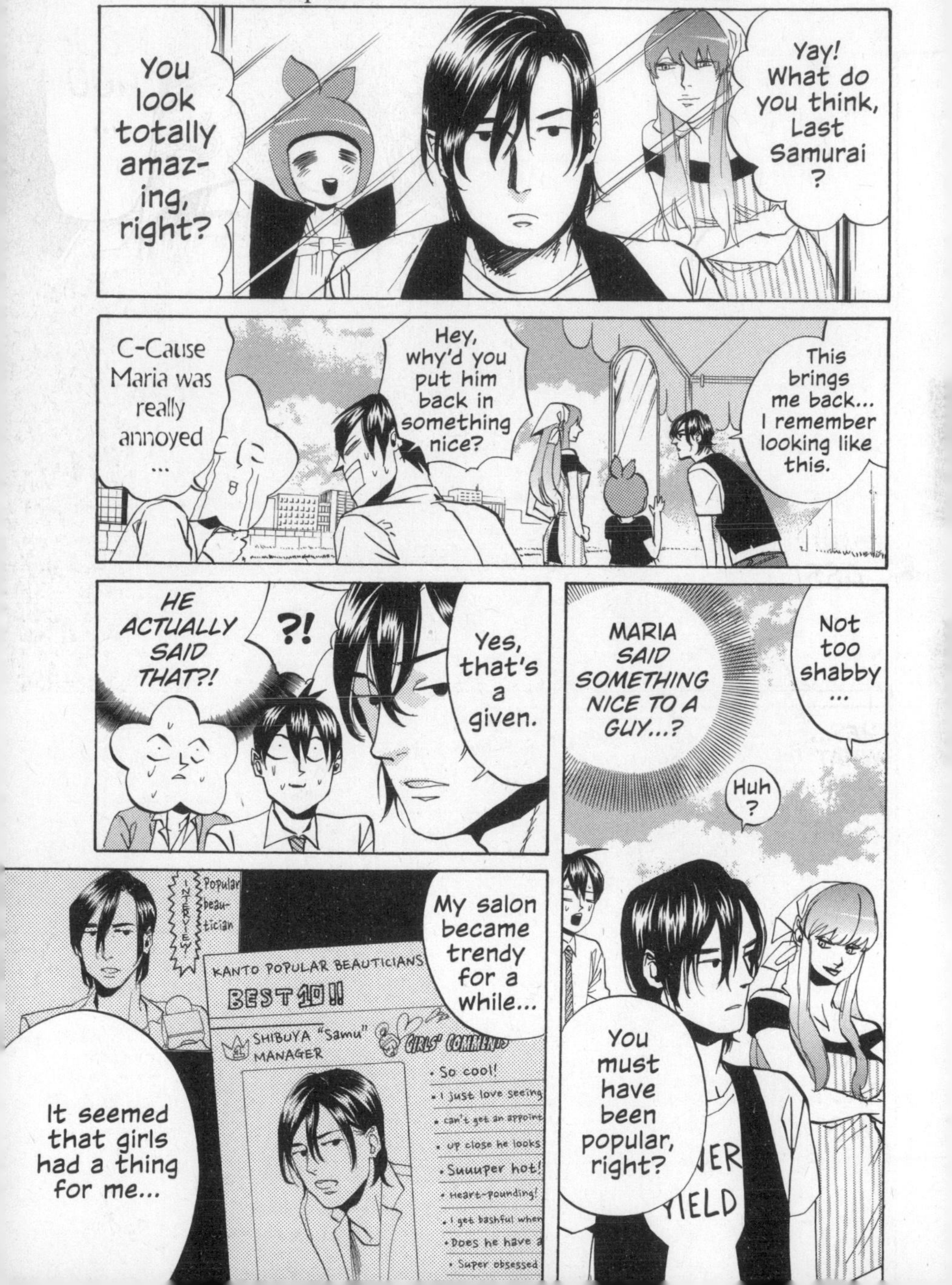
Yay! What do you think, Last Samurai?
You look totally amaz-ing, right?
This brings me back... I remember looking like this.
Hey, why'd you put him back in something nice?
C-Cause Maria was really annoyed...
Not too shabby...
MARIA SAID SOMETHING NICE TO A GUY...?
Huh?
You must have been popular, right?
Yes, that's a given.
?!
HE ACTUALLY SAID THAT?!
My salon became trendy for a while...
INTERVIEW
Popular beautician
KANTO POPULAR BEAUTICIANS
BEST 10!!
SHIBUYA "Samu" MANAGER
GIRLS' COMMENTS
So cool!
I just love seeing
up close he looks
Suuuper hot!
Heart-pounding!
I get bashful when
Does he have
Super obsessed
It seemed that girls had a thing for me...

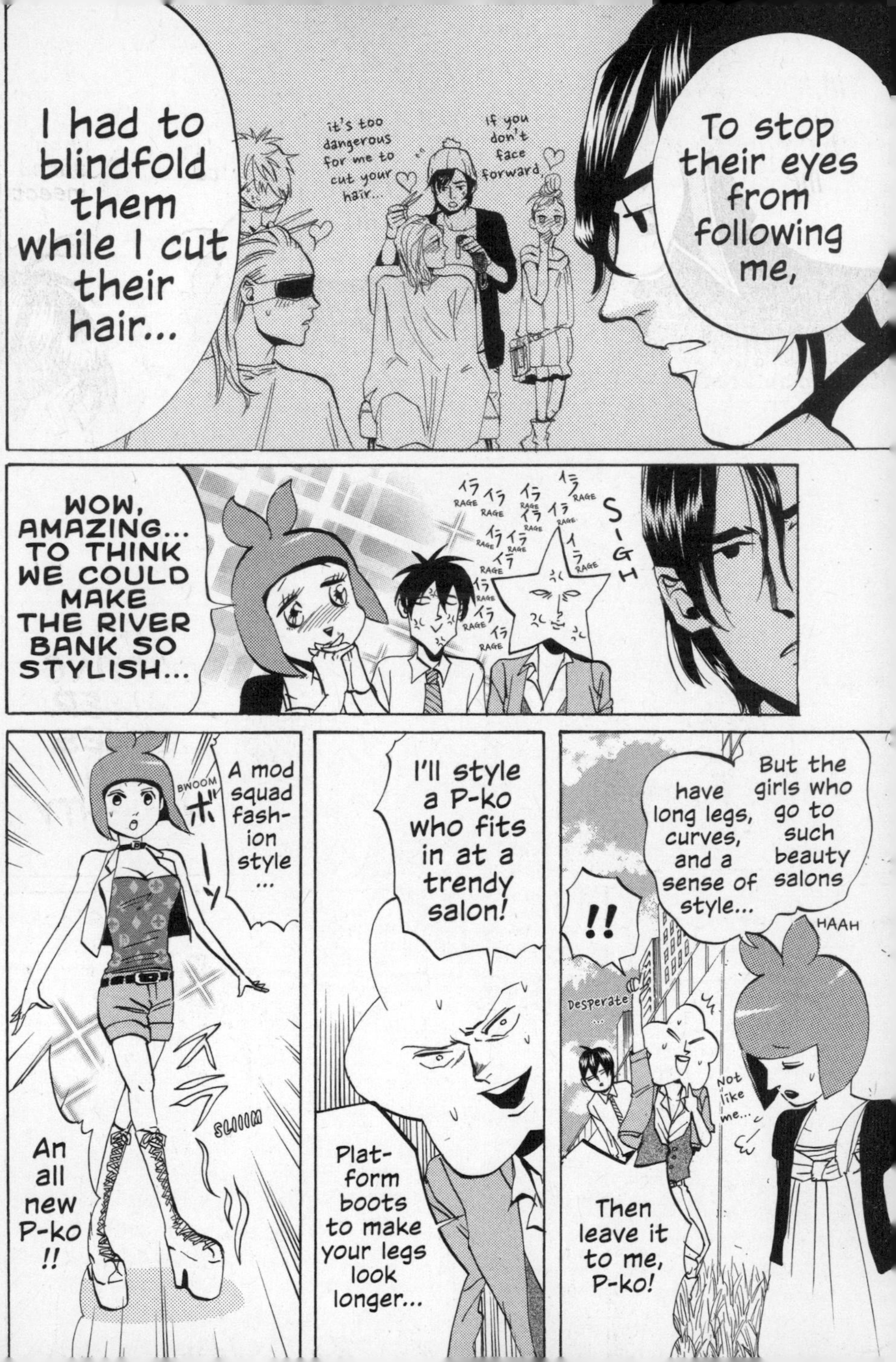
To stop their eyes from following me,
if you don't face forward,
it's too dangerous for me to cut your hair...
I had to blindfold them while I cut their hair...
SIGH
イラ イラ イラ イラ イラ イラ イラ イラ イラ イラ イラ イラ イラ
RAGE RAGE RAGE RAGE RAGE RAGE RAGE RAGE RAGE RAGE RAGE RAGE RAGE
WOW, AMAZING... TO THINK WE COULD MAKE THE RIVER BANK SO STYLISH...
But the girls who go to such beauty salons have long legs, curves, and a sense of style...
HAAH
Not like me...
Desperate ...
!!
Then leave it to me, P-ko!
I'll style a P-ko who fits in at a trendy salon!
Platform boots to make your legs look longer...
A mod squad fashion style ...
BWOOM
SLIIIM
An all new P-ko !!

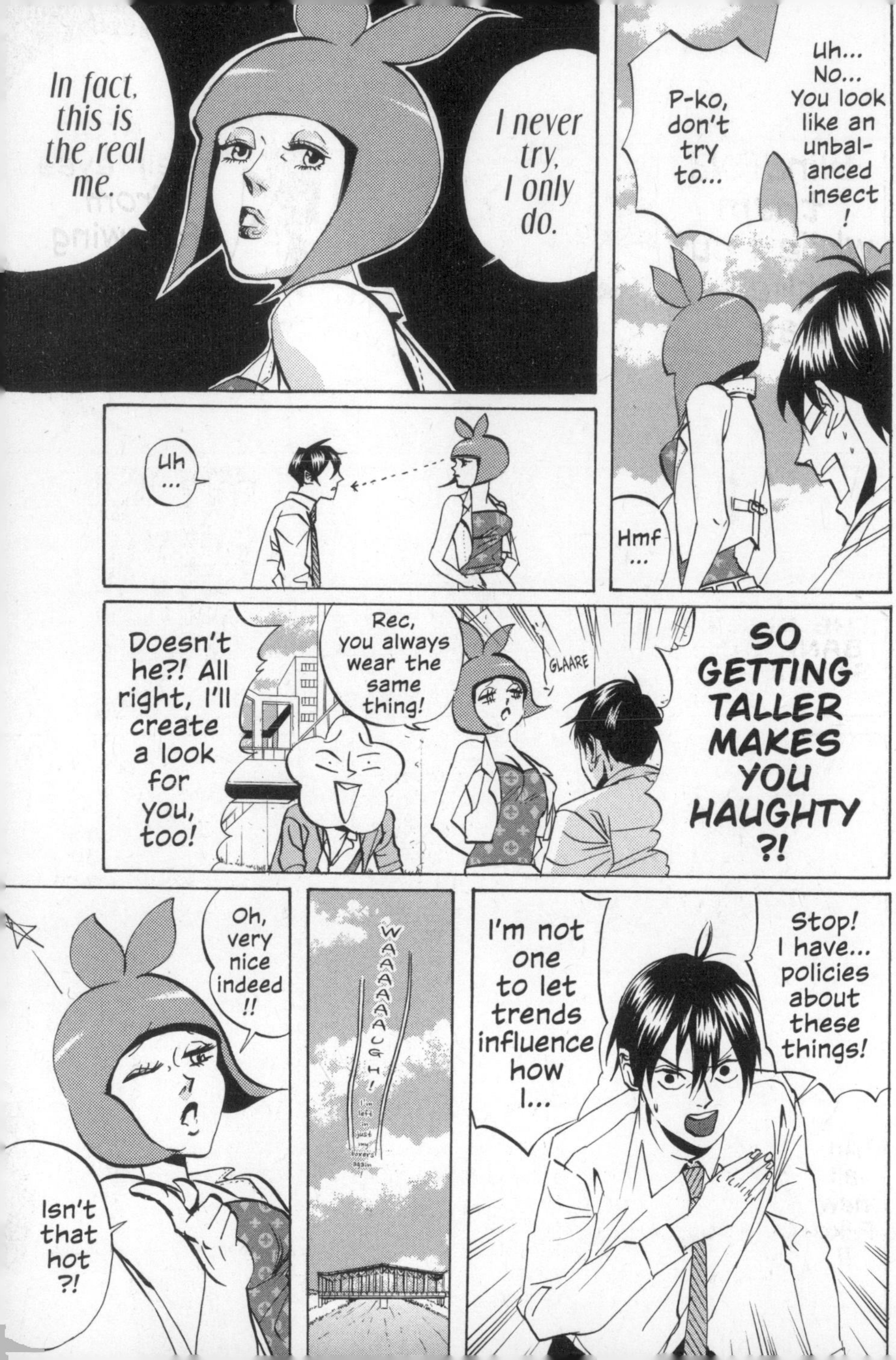
Uh... No... You look like an unbalanced insect!
P-ko, don't try to...
Hmf...
I never try, I only do.
In fact, this is the real me.
Uh...
SO GETTING TALLER MAKES YOU HAUGHTY?!
GLAARE
Rec, you always wear the same thing!
Doesn't he?! All right, I'll create a look for you, too!
Stop! I have... policies about these things!
I'm not one to let trends influence how I...
WAAAAAAUGH!
I'm left in just my boxers again!
Oh, very nice indeed!!
Isn't that hot?!

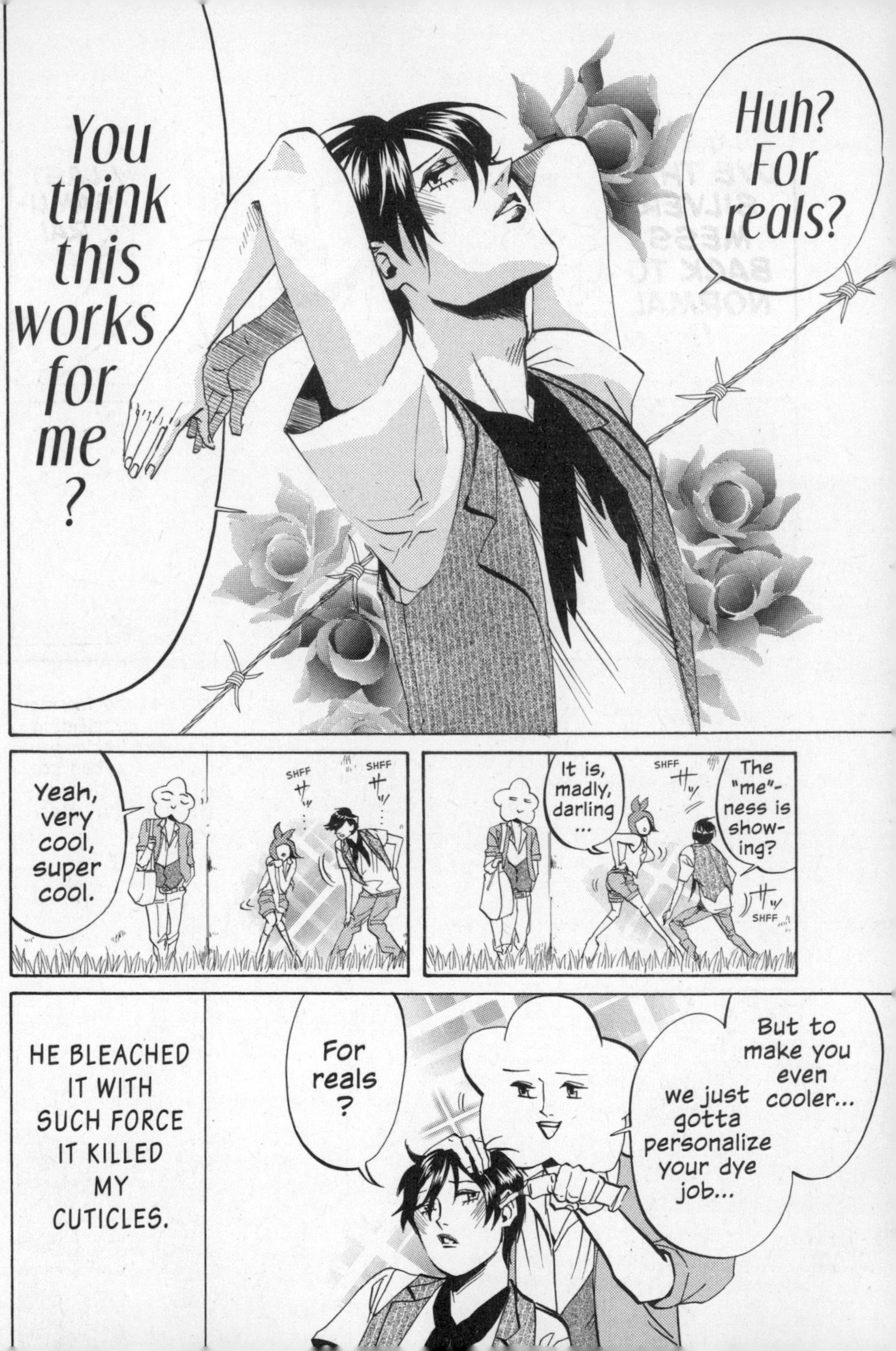
Huh? For reals?
You think this works for me?
The "me"-ness is showing?
SHFF
It is, madly, darling ...
SHFF
SHFF
SHFF
Yeah, very cool, super cool.
But to make you even cooler... we just gotta personalize your dye job...
For reals?
HE BLEACHED IT WITH SUCH FORCE IT KILLED MY CUTICLES.

Chapter 205: Eye-Opener

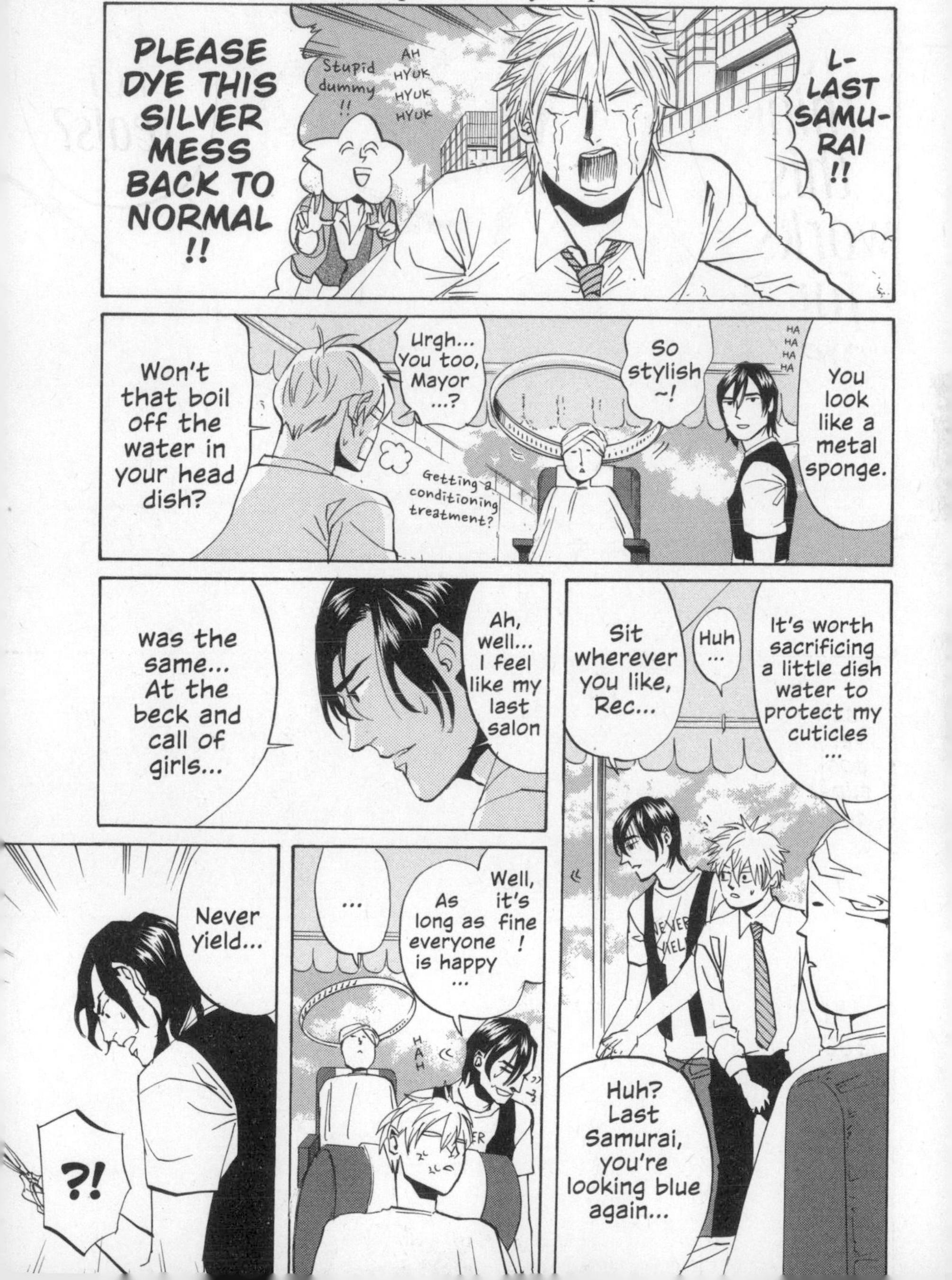
L-LAST SAMURAI!!
Stupid dummy!!
AH HYUK HYUK HYUK
PLEASE DYE THIS SILVER MESS BACK TO NORMAL!!
You look like a metal sponge.
HA HA HA HA
So stylish~!
Urgh... You too, Mayor...?
Won't that boil off the water in your head dish?
Getting a conditioning treatment?
It's worth sacrificing a little dish water to protect my cuticles...
Huh...
Sit wherever you like, Rec...
Huh? Last Samurai, you're looking blue again...
Ah, well... I feel like my last salon
was the same... At the beck and call of girls...
Well, it's fine!
As long as everyone is happy...
...
HAH
Never yield...
?!

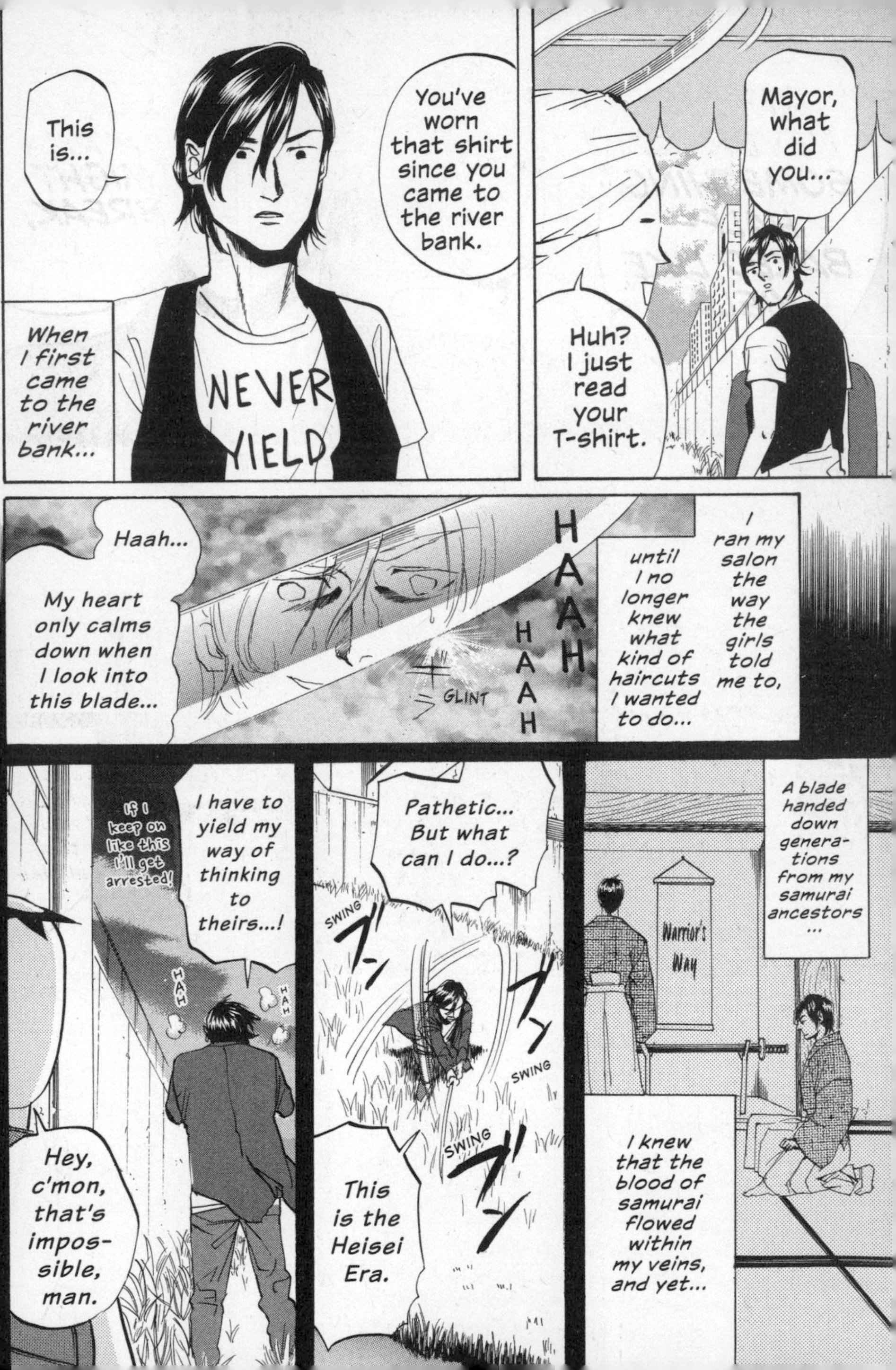
Mayor, what did you...
Huh? I just read your T-shirt.
You've worn that shirt since you came to the river bank.
This is...
NEVER YIELD
When I first came to the river bank...
I ran my salon the way the girls told me to,
until I no longer knew what kind of haircuts I wanted to do...
HAAH
HAAH
GLINT
Haah...
My heart only calms down when I look into this blade...
A blade handed down generations from my samurai ancestors...
Warrior's Way
I knew that the blood of samurai flowed within my veins, and yet...
Pathetic... But what can I do...?
SWING
SWING
SWING
This is the Heisei Era.
I have to yield my way of thinking to theirs...!
If I keep on like this I'll get arrested!
HAH
HAH
Hey, c'mon, that's impossible, man.

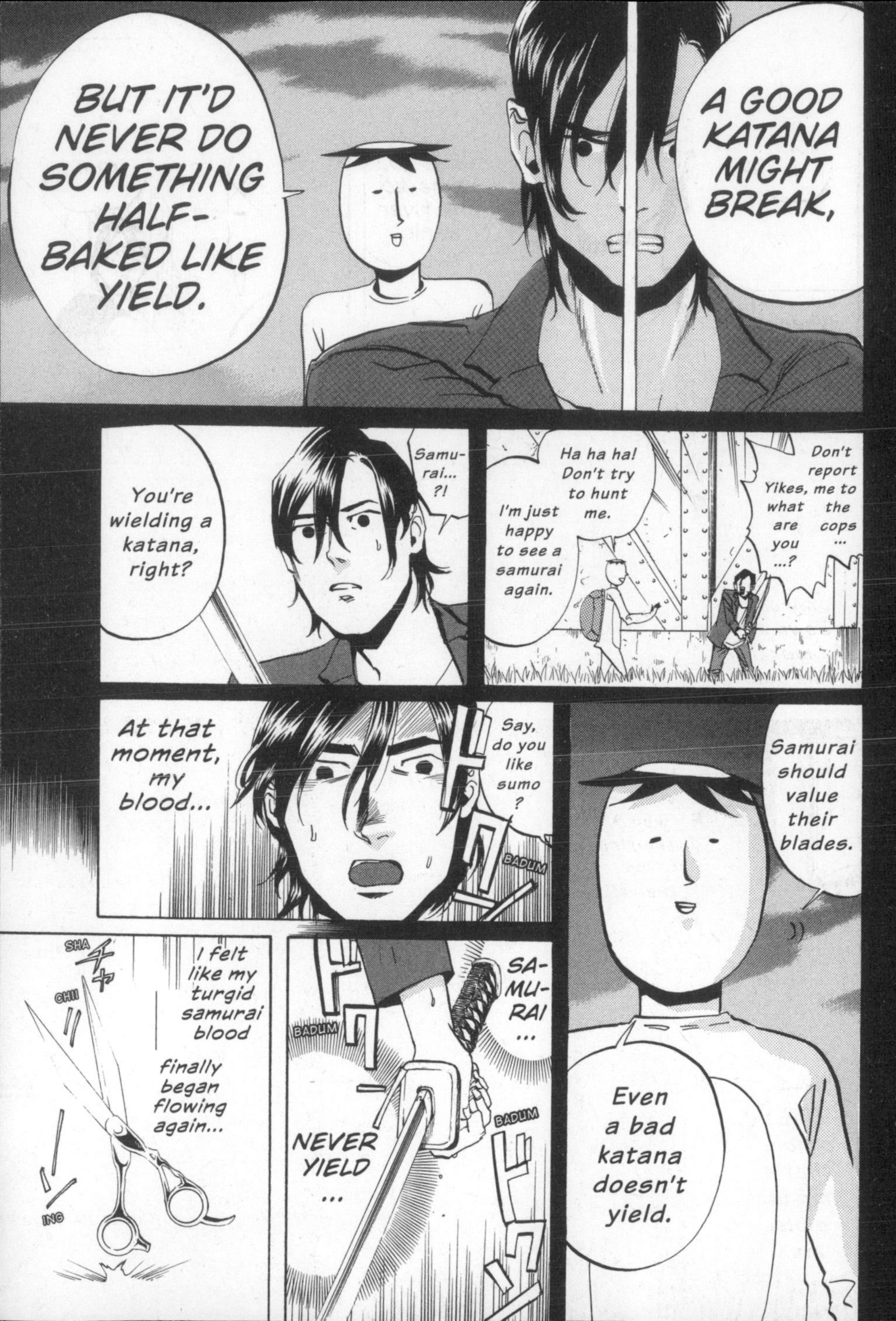
A GOOD KATANA MIGHT BREAK,
BUT IT'D NEVER DO SOMETHING HALF-BAKED LIKE YIELD.
Don't report me to the cops...
Yikes, what are you...?
Ha ha ha! Don't try to hunt me.
I'm just happy to see a samurai again.
Samurai...?!
You're wielding a katana, right?
Samurai should value their blades.
Even a bad katana doesn't yield.
Say, do you like sumo?
BADUM
At that moment, my blood...
SAMURAI...
BADUM
BADUM
NEVER YIELD...
SHA
CHII
ING
I felt like my turgid samurai blood
finally began flowing again...

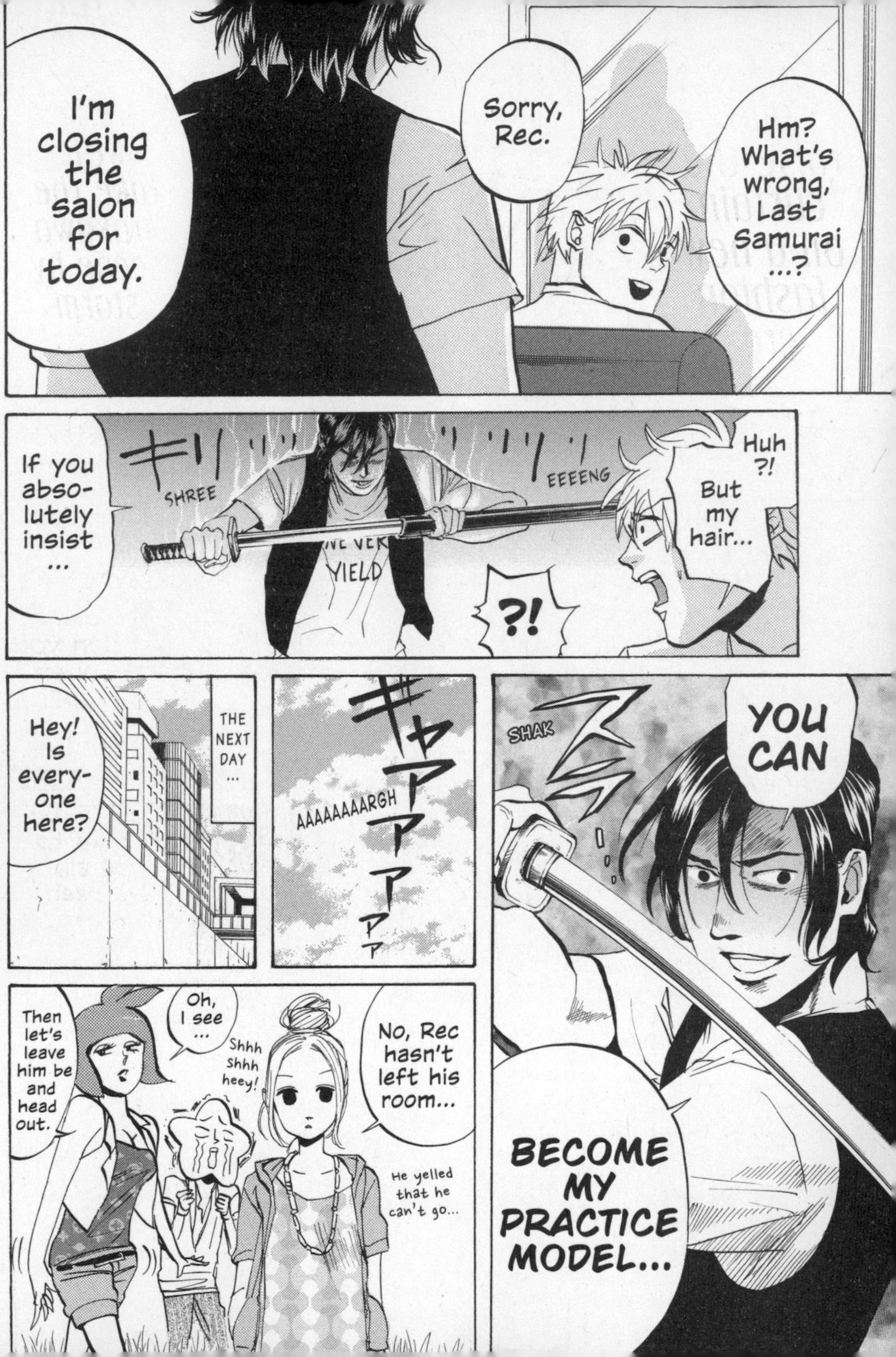
Hm? What's wrong, Last Samurai ...?
Sorry, Rec.
I'm closing the salon for today.
Huh ?! But my hair...
EEEENG
キリリリリリ
SHREE
NE VER YIELD
?!
If you abso-lutely insist ...
YOU CAN
SHAK
BECOME MY PRACTICE MODEL...
ギャアアアァァ
AAAAAAAARGH
THE NEXT DAY ...
Hey! Is every-one here?
No, Rec hasn't left his room...
He yelled that he can't go...
Oh, I see ...
Shhh shhh heey!
Then let's leave him be and head out.

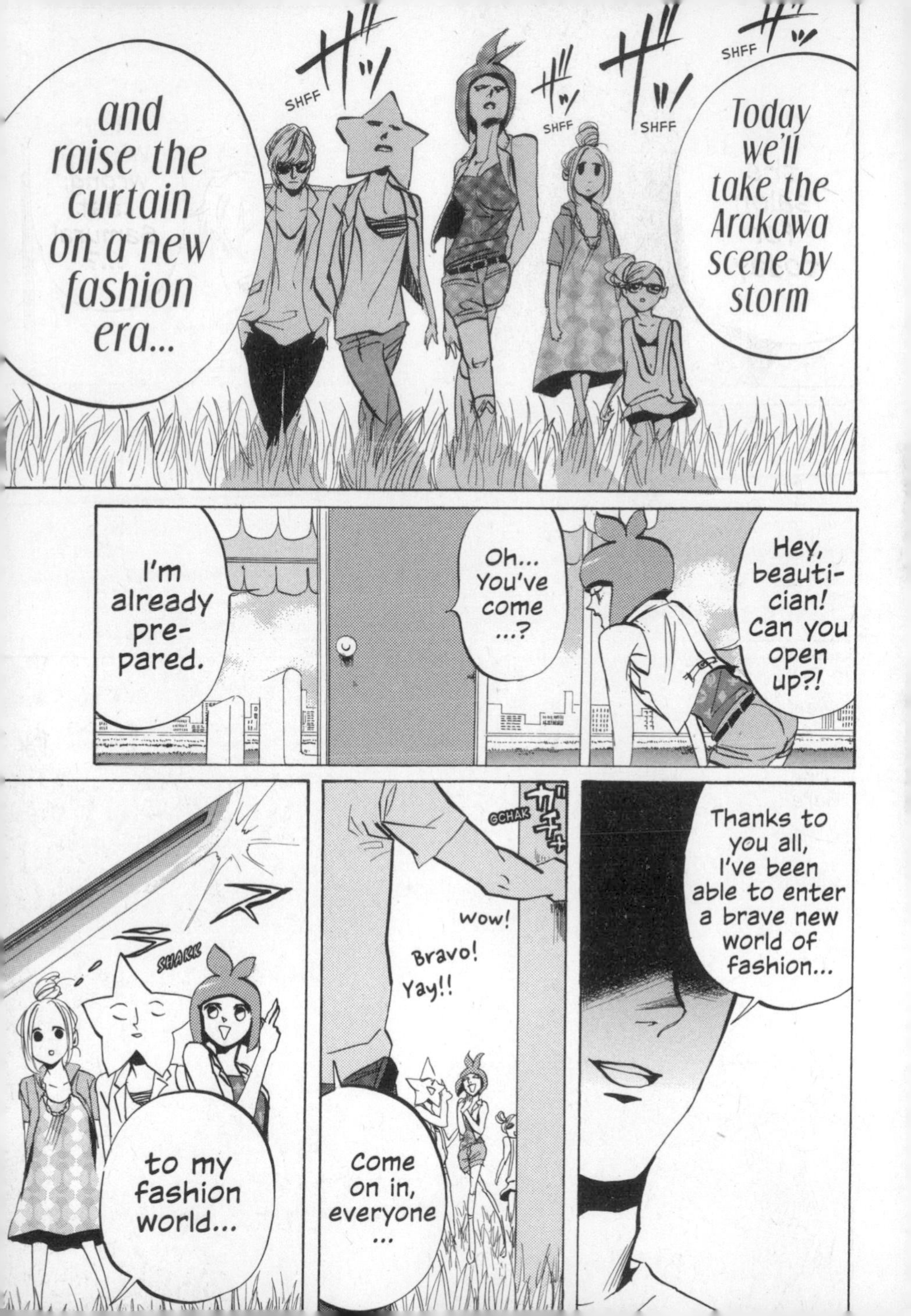
SHFF
SHFF
SHFF
SHFF
Today we'll take the Arakawa scene by storm
and raise the curtain on a new fashion era...
Hey, beauti-cian! Can you open up?!
Oh... You've come ...?
I'm already pre-pared.
Thanks to you all, I've been able to enter a brave new world of fashion...
GCHAK
Wow!
Bravo!
Yay!!
Come on in, everyone ...
SHARK
to my fashion world...

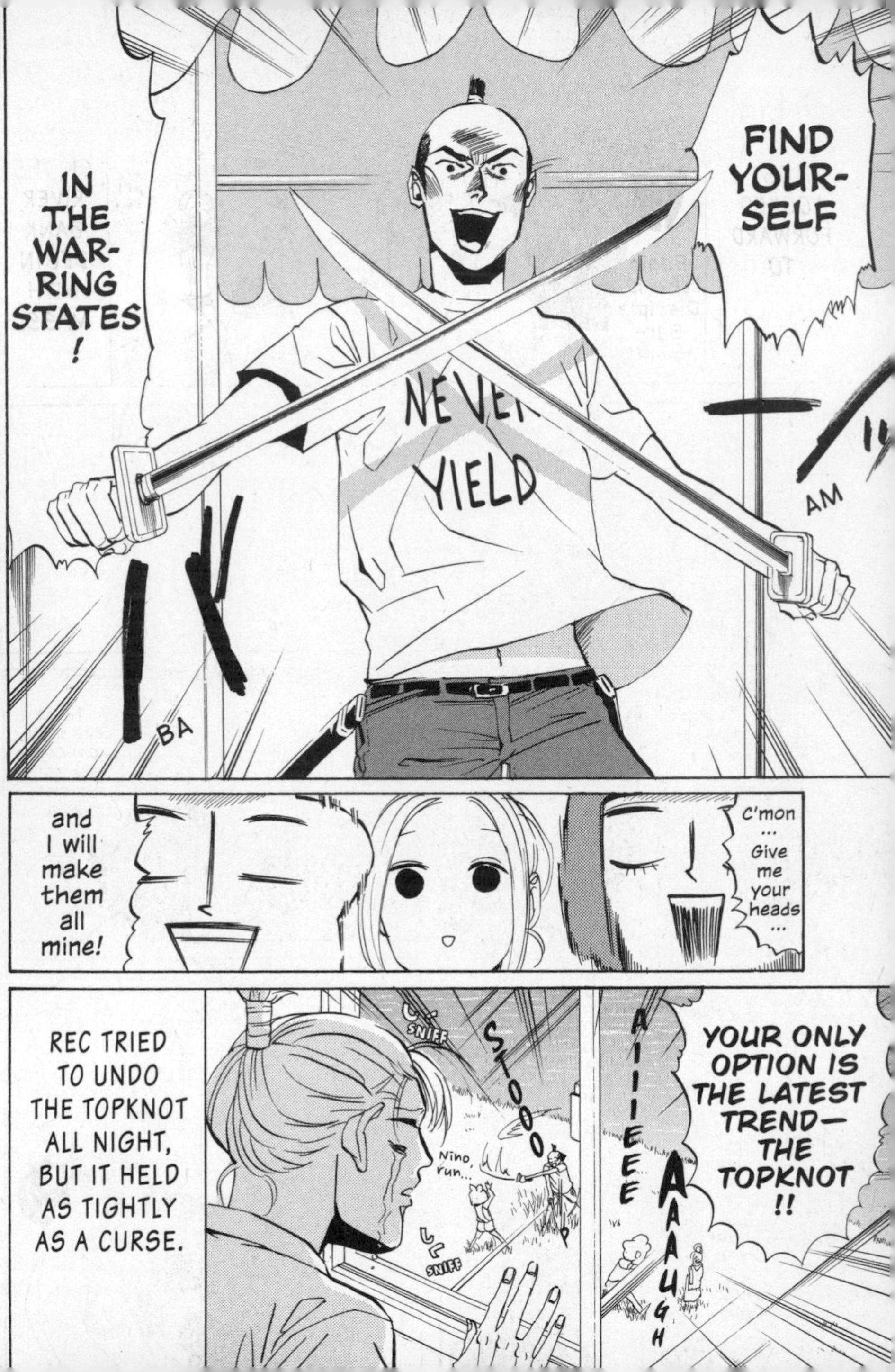
FIND YOURSELF
IN THE WARRING STATES!
BA
AM
NEVER YIELD
C'mon... Give me your heads...
and I will make them all mine!
YOUR ONLY OPTION IS THE LATEST TREND—THE TOPKNOT!!
AIIIEEE
AAAUGH
STOOOOP
Nino, run...
SNIFF
SNIFF
REC TRIED TO UNDO THE TOPKNOT ALL NIGHT, BUT IT HELD AS TIGHTLY AS A CURSE.

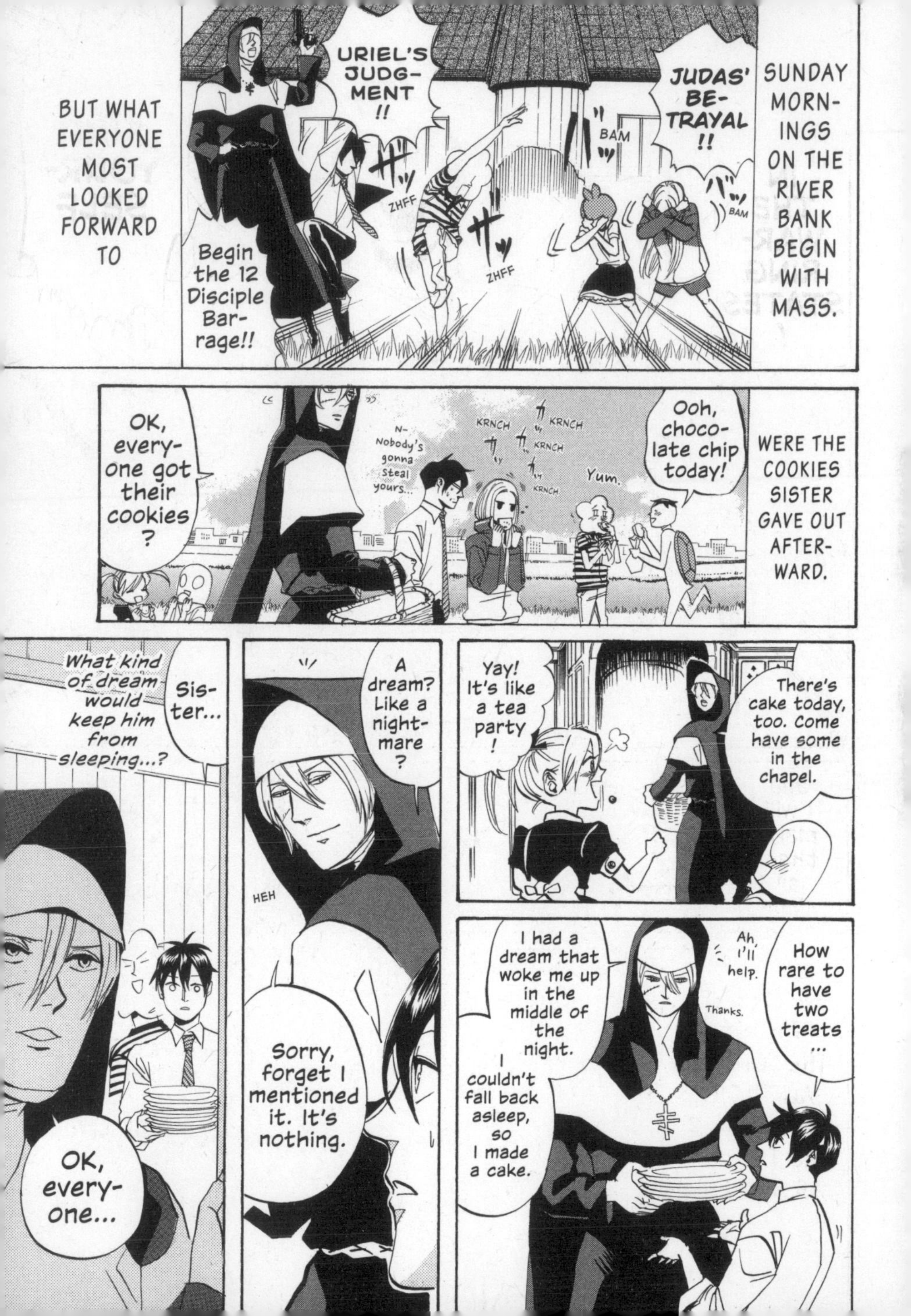
SUNDAY MORNINGS ON THE RIVER BANK BEGIN WITH MASS.
JUDAS' BETRAYAL!!
BAM
BAM
URIEL'S JUDGMENT!!
ZHFF
ZHFF
Begin the 12 Disciple Barrage!!
BUT WHAT EVERYONE MOST LOOKED FORWARD TO
WERE THE COOKIES SISTER GAVE OUT AFTERWARD.
Ooh, chocolate chip today!
Yum.
KRNCH
KRNCH
KRNCH
KRNCH
N-Nobody's gonna steal yours...
OK, everyone got their cookies?
There's cake today, too. Come have some in the chapel.
Yay! It's like a tea party!
How rare to have two treats...
Ah, I'll help.
Thanks.
I had a dream that woke me up in the middle of the night.
I couldn't fall back asleep, so I made a cake.
A dream? Like a nightmare?
HEH
Sorry, forget I mentioned it. It's nothing.
Sister...
What kind of dream would keep him from sleeping...?
OK, everyone...

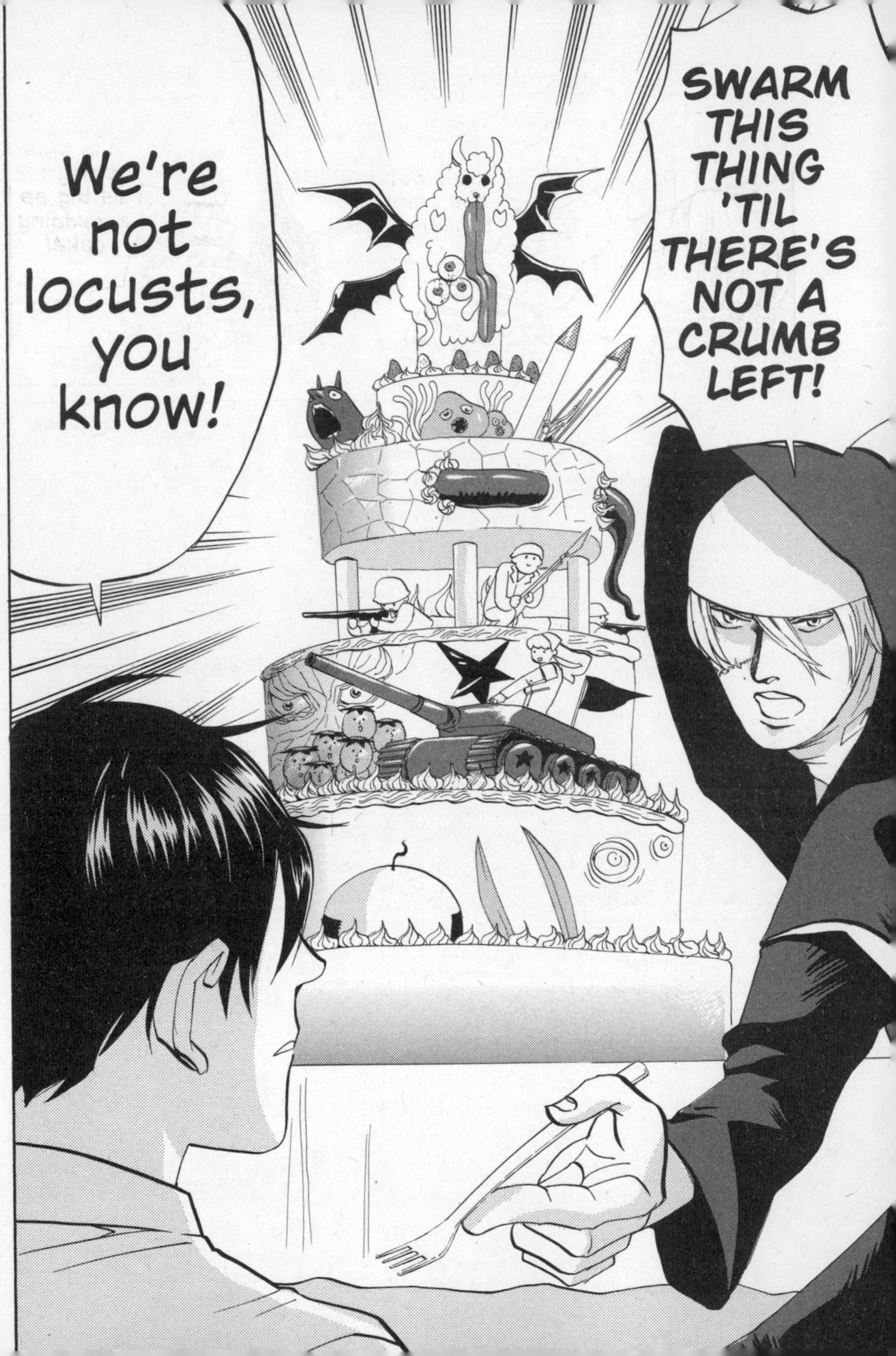
SWARM THIS THING 'TIL THERE'S NOT A CRUMB LEFT!
We're not locusts, you know!

Chapter 206: People Who Don't Clean

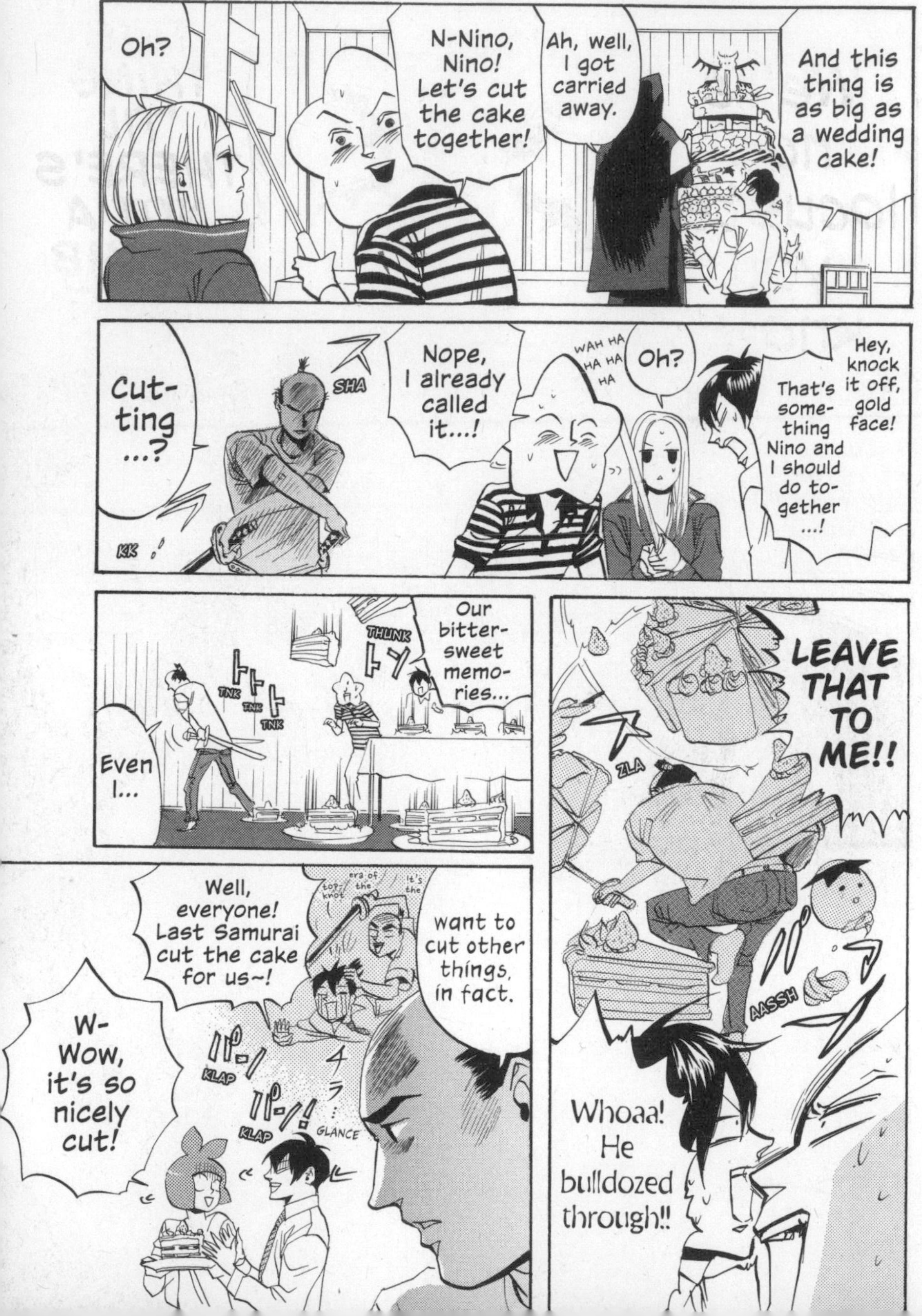
And this thing is as big as a wedding cake!
Ah, well, I got carried away.
N-Nino, Nino! Let's cut the cake together!
Oh?
Hey, knock it off, gold face!
That's something Nino and I should do together...!
Oh?
WAH HA HA HA HA
Nope, I already called it...!
SHA
Cutting...?
KK
LEAVE THAT TO ME!!
ZLA
AASSH
Whoaa! He bulldozed through!!
Our bittersweet memories...
THUNK
TNK TNK TNK
Even I...
want to cut other things, in fact.
it's the era of the topknot
Well, everyone! Last Samurai cut the cake for us~!
KLAP
KLAP
GLANCE
W-Wow, it's so nicely cut!

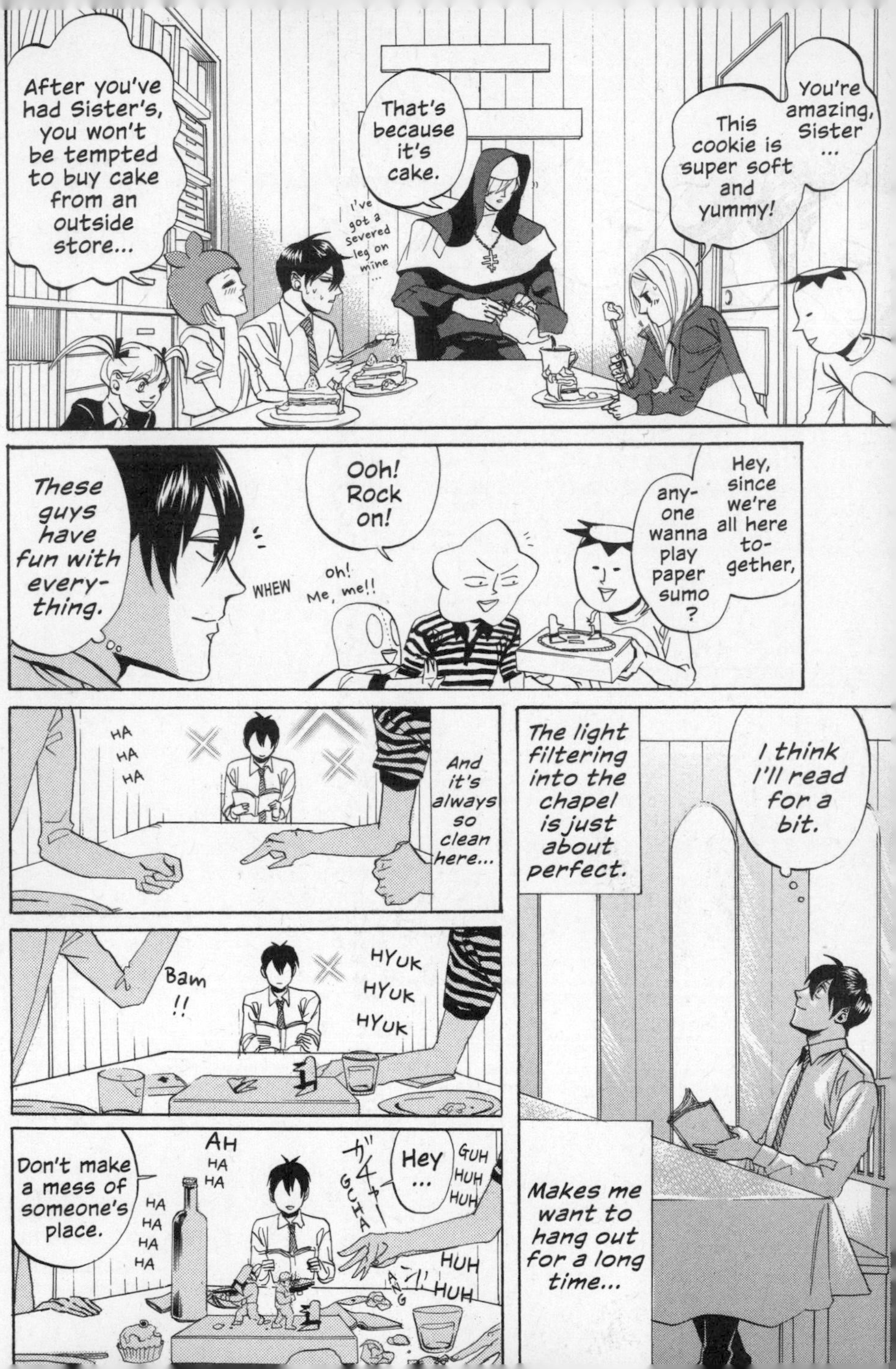
You're amazing, Sister ...
This cookie is super soft and yummy!
That's because it's cake.
I've got a severed leg on mine ...
After you've had Sister's, you won't be tempted to buy cake from an outside store...
Hey, since we're all here to-gether,
any-one wanna play paper sumo ?
Ooh! Rock on!
Oh! Me, me!!
WHEW
These guys have fun with every-thing.
I think I'll read for a bit.
The light filtering into the chapel is just about perfect.
Makes me want to hang out for a long time...
And it's always so clean here...
HA HA HA
HYUK HYUK HYUK
Bam !!
GUH HUH HUH
Hey ...
GACHA
AH HA HA
Don't make a mess of someone's place.
HA HA HA HA
HUH HUH
GANG

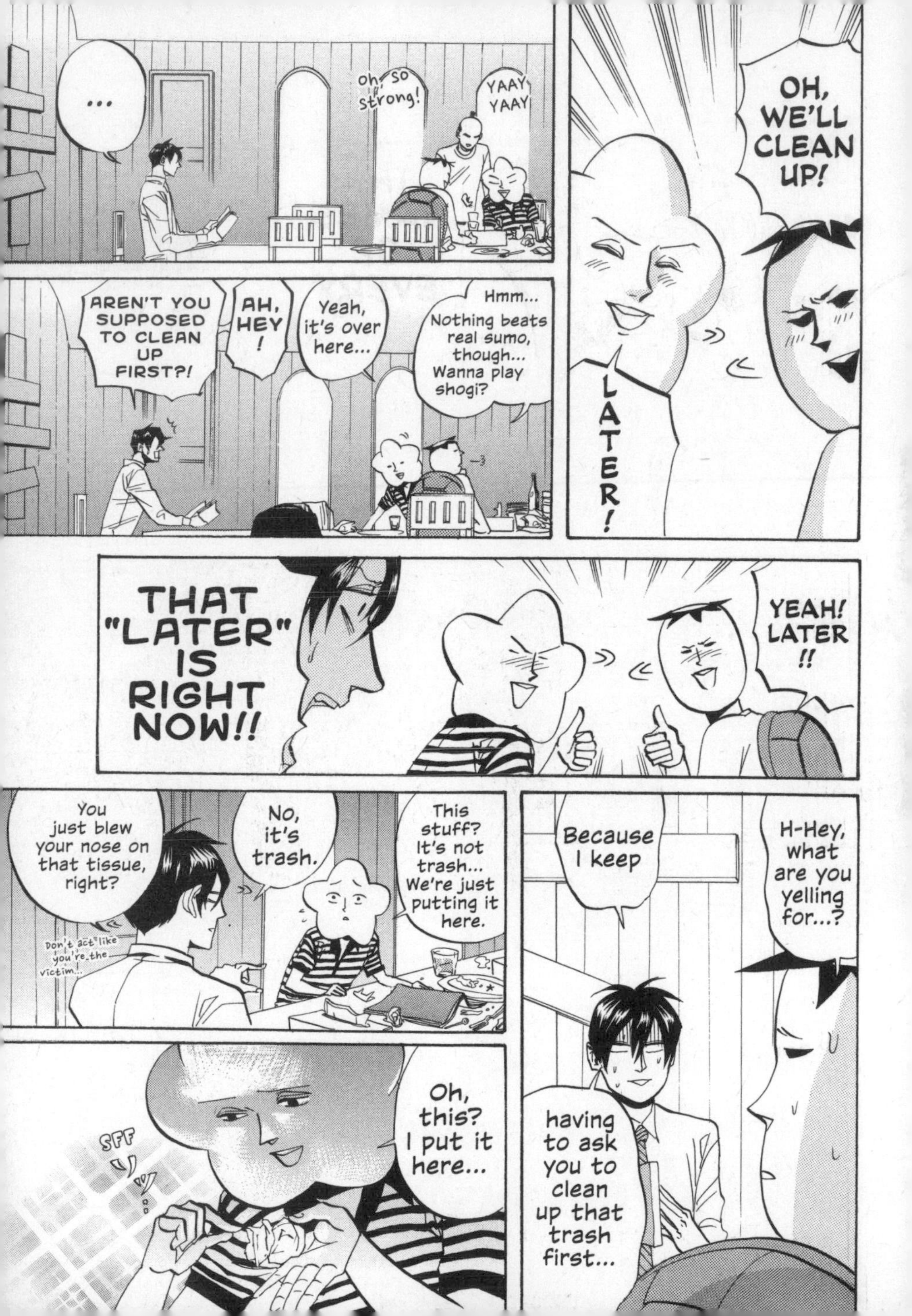
OH, WE'LL CLEAN UP!
LATER!
YAAY YAAY
Oh, so strong!
...
Hmm... Nothing beats real sumo, though... Wanna play shogi?
Yeah, it's over here...
AH, HEY!
AREN'T YOU SUPPOSED TO CLEAN UP FIRST?!
YEAH! LATER!!
THAT "LATER" IS RIGHT NOW!!
H-Hey, what are you yelling for...?
Because I keep
having to ask you to clean up that trash first...
This stuff? It's not trash... We're just putting it here.
No, it's trash.
You just blew your nose on that tissue, right?
Don't act like you're the victim...
Oh, this? I put it here...
SFF

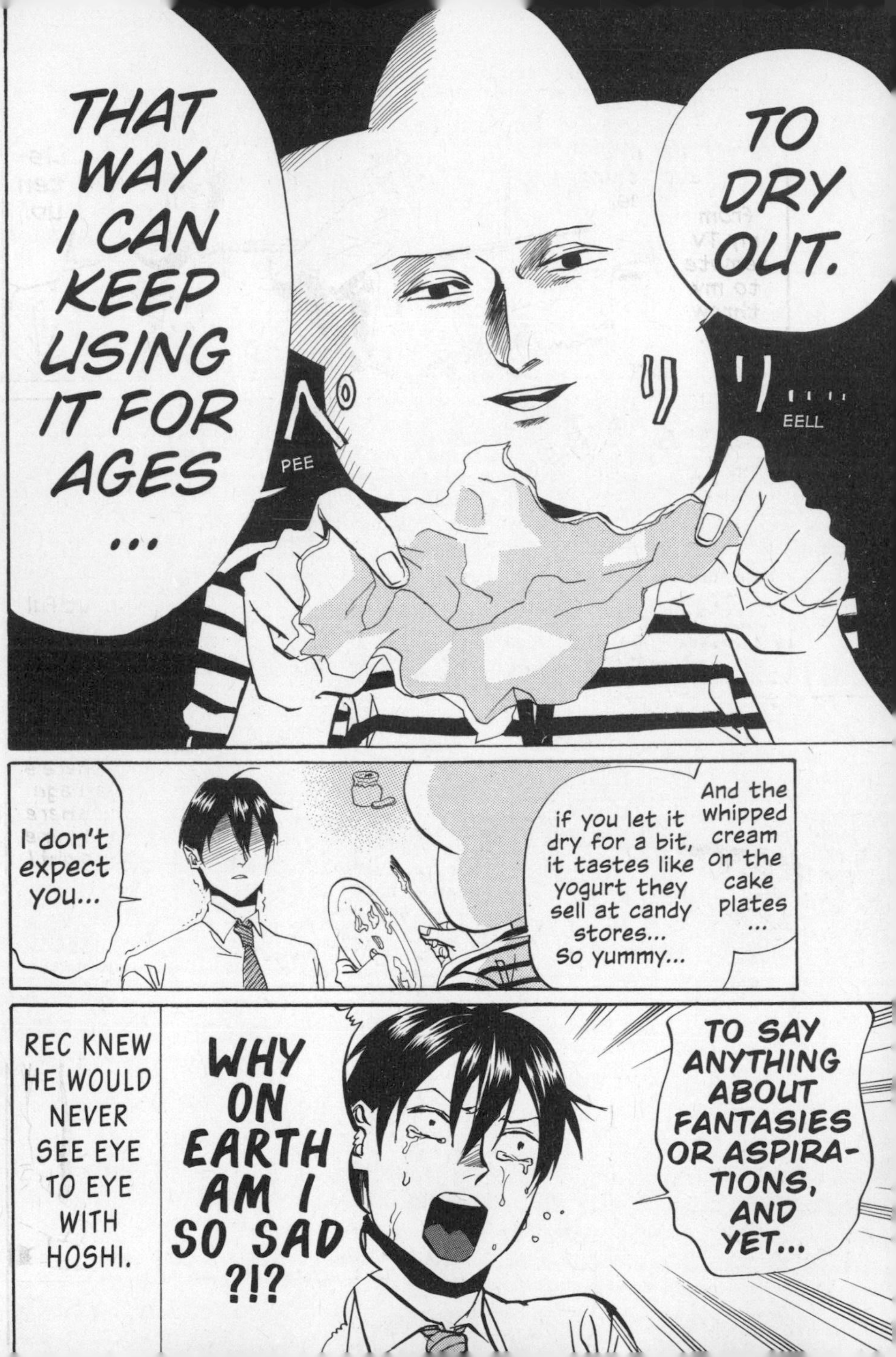
TO DRY OUT.
THAT WAY I CAN KEEP USING IT FOR AGES...
PEE
EELL
And the whipped cream on the cake plates...
if you let it dry for a bit, it tastes like yogurt they sell at candy stores... So yummy...
I don't expect you...
TO SAY ANYTHING ABOUT FANTASIES OR ASPIRA-TIONS, AND YET...
WHY ON EARTH AM I SO SAD ?!?
REC KNEW HE WOULD NEVER SEE EYE TO EYE WITH HOSHI.

Chapter 207: The Infomercial Thing

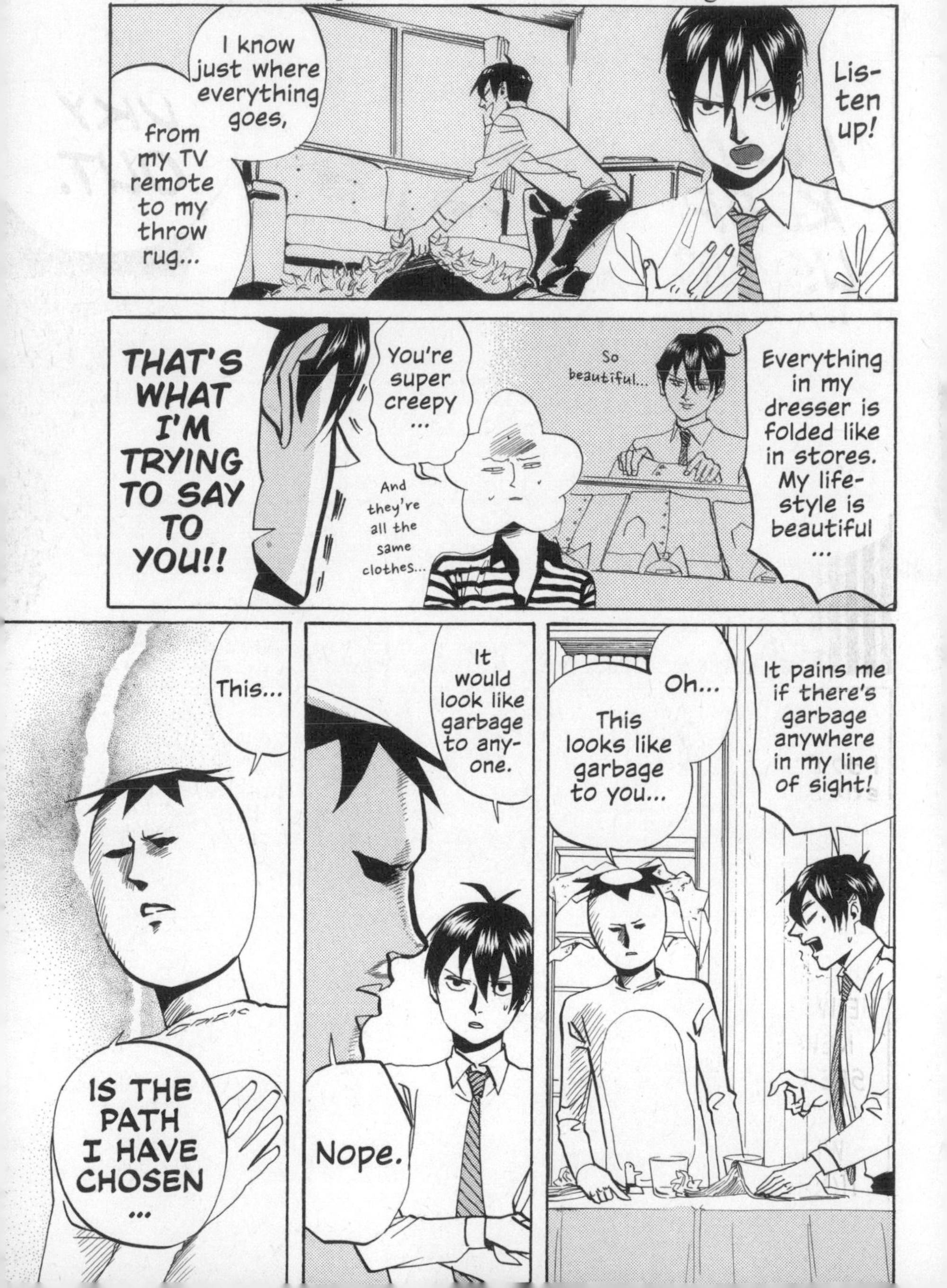
Lis-
ten
up!
I know just where everything goes,
from my TV remote to my throw rug...
Everything in my dresser is folded like in stores. My life-style is beautiful...
So beautiful...
You're super creepy...
And they're all the same clothes...
THAT'S WHAT I'M TRYING TO SAY TO YOU!!
It pains me if there's garbage anywhere in my line of sight!
Oh...
This looks like garbage to you...
It would look like garbage to any-one.
Nope.
This...
IS THE PATH I HAVE CHOSEN...

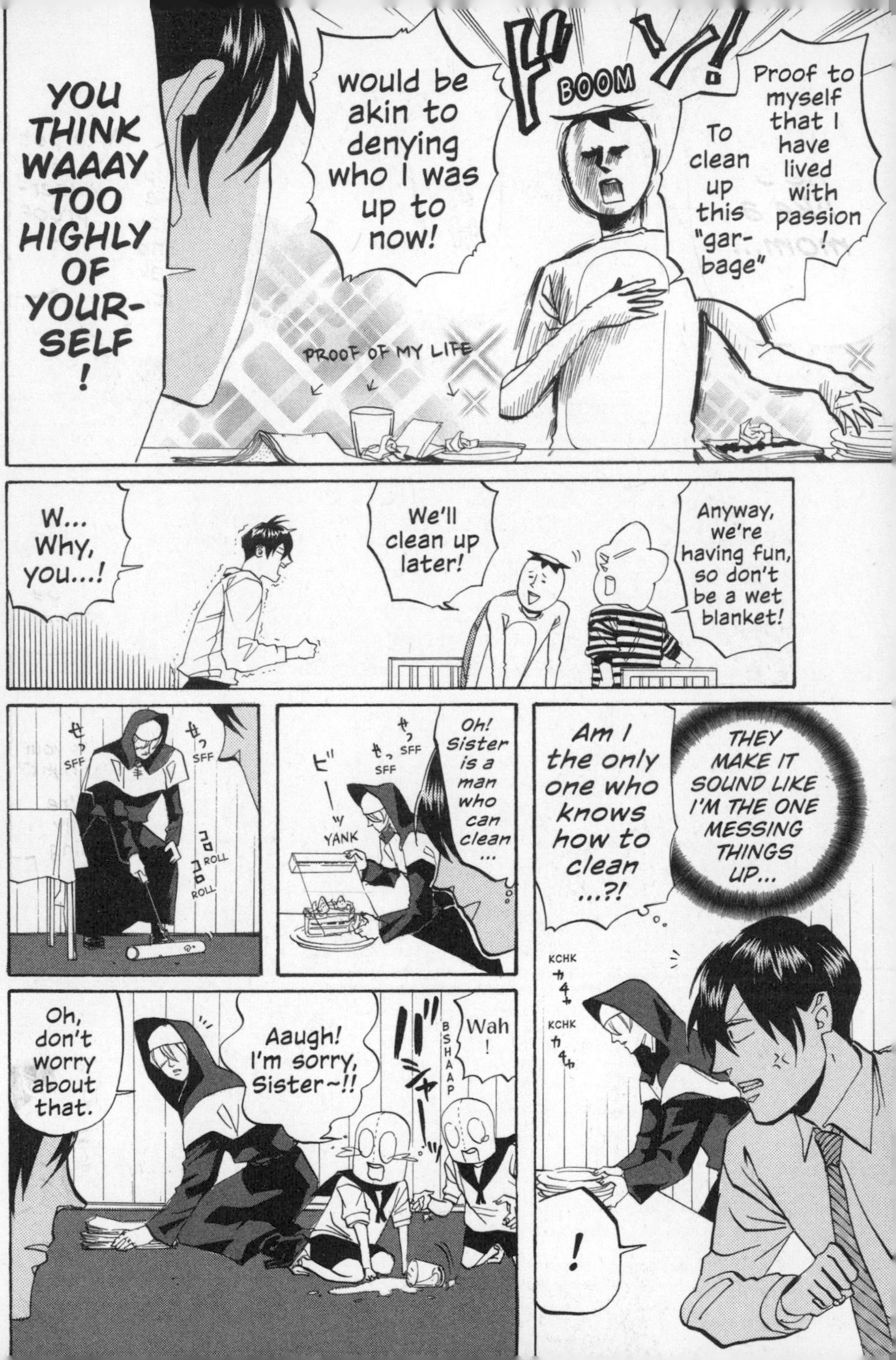

Proof to myself that I have lived with passion!
To clean up this "garbage"
BOOM
would be akin to denying who I was up to now!
YOU THINK WAAAY TOO HIGHLY OF YOURSELF!
PROOF OF MY LIFE
Anyway, we're having fun, so don't be a wet blanket!
We'll clean up later!
W... Why, you...!
THEY MAKE IT SOUND LIKE I'M THE ONE MESSING THINGS UP...
Am I the only one who knows how to clean ...?!
KCHK
KCHK
!
Oh! Sister is a man who can clean ...
SFF
SFF
YANK
SFF
SFF
ROLL
ROLL
Wah!
BSHAAP
Aaugh! I'm sorry, Sister~!!
Oh, don't worry about that.

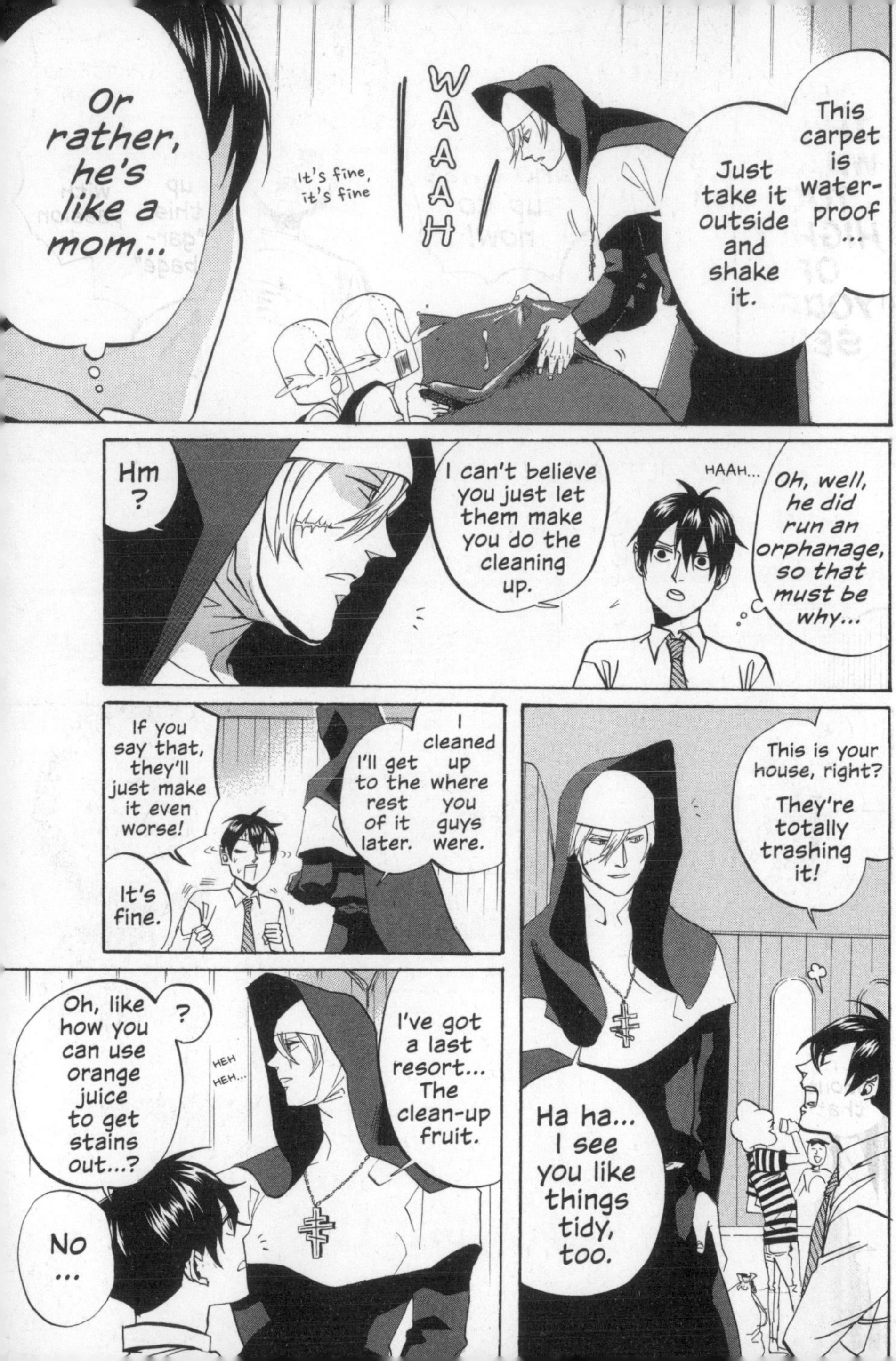
This carpet is waterproof...
Just take it outside and shake it.
WAAAAH
It's fine, it's fine
Or rather, he's like a mom...
Oh, well, he did run an orphanage, so that must be why...
HAAAH...
I can't believe you just let them make you do the cleaning up.
Hm?
This is your house, right?
They're totally trashing it!
Ha ha... I see you like things tidy, too.
I cleaned up where you guys were.
I'll get to the rest of it later.
If you say that, they'll just make it even worse!
It's fine.
I've got a last resort... The clean-up fruit.
HEH HEH...
?
Oh, like how you can use orange juice to get stains out...?
No ...

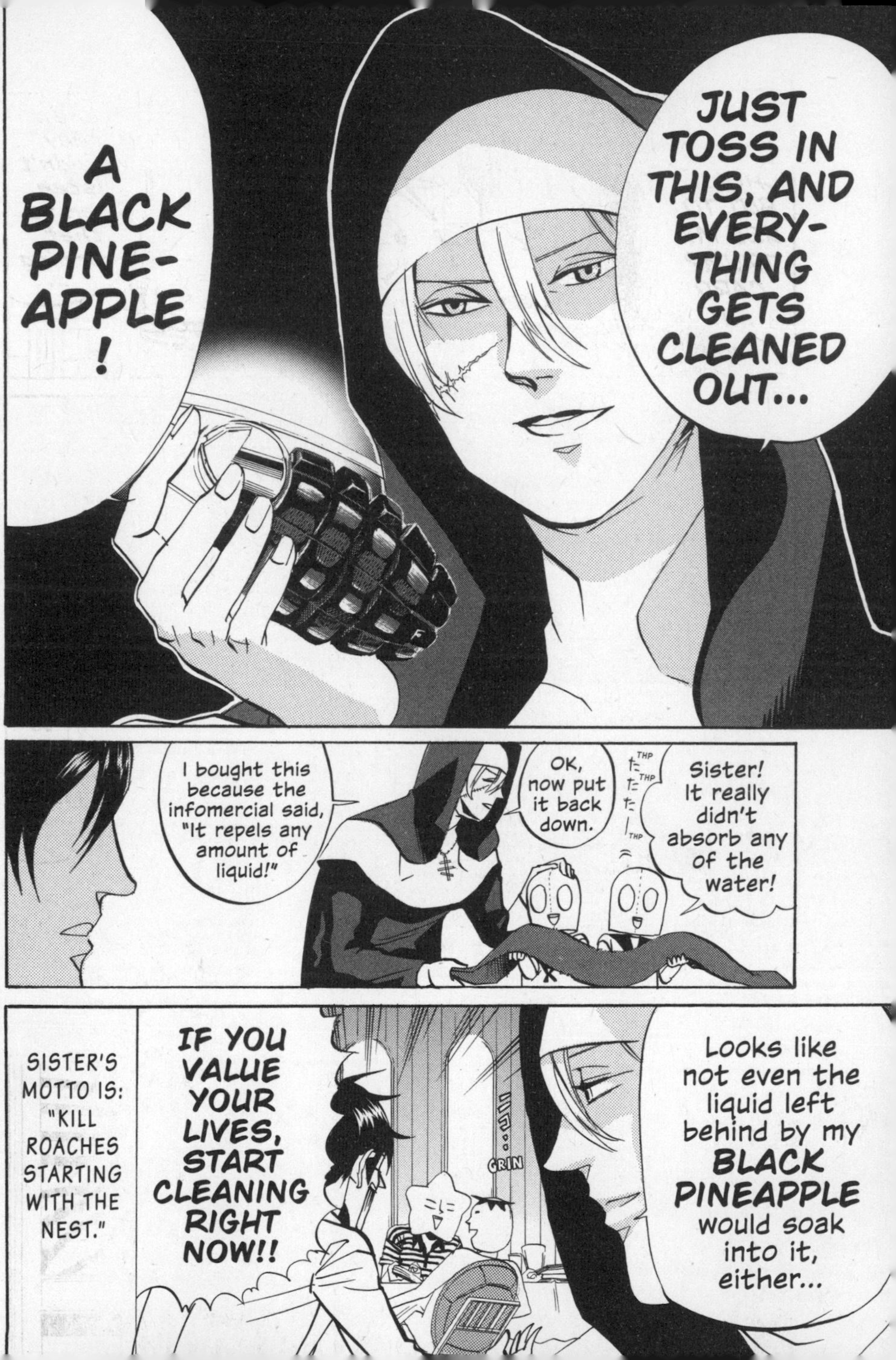
JUST TOSS IN THIS, AND EVERY-THING GETS CLEANED OUT...
A BLACK PINE-APPLE!
Sister! It really didn't absorb any of the water!
THP THP THP
OK, now put it back down.
I bought this because the infomercial said, "It repels any amount of liquid!"
Looks like not even the liquid left behind by my BLACK PINEAPPLE would soak into it, either...
IF YOU VALUE YOUR LIVES, START CLEANING RIGHT NOW!!
GRIN
SISTER'S MOTTO IS: "KILL ROACHES STARTING WITH THE NEST."

Chapter 208: Nino's Lesson

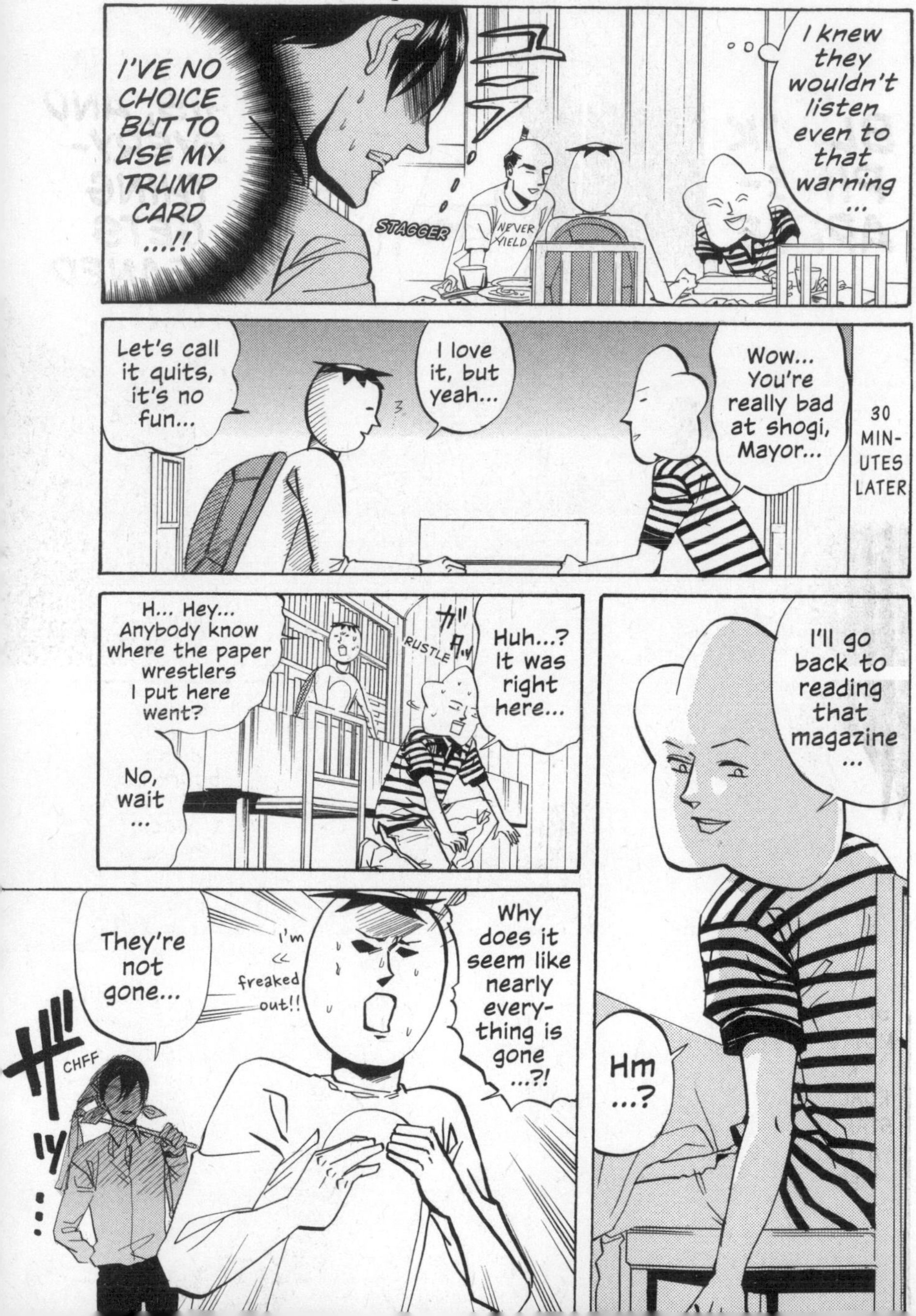

I knew they wouldn't listen even to that warning...
NEVER YIELD
STAGGER
I'VE NO CHOICE BUT TO USE MY TRUMP CARD...!!
30 MINUTES LATER
Wow... You're really bad at shogi, Mayor...
I love it, but yeah...
Let's call it quits, it's no fun...
I'll go back to reading that magazine...
Hm...?
Huh...? It was right here...
RUSTLE
H... Hey... Anybody know where the paper wrestlers I put here went?
No, wait...
Why does it seem like nearly everything is gone...?!
I'm freaked out!!
They're not gone...
CHFF

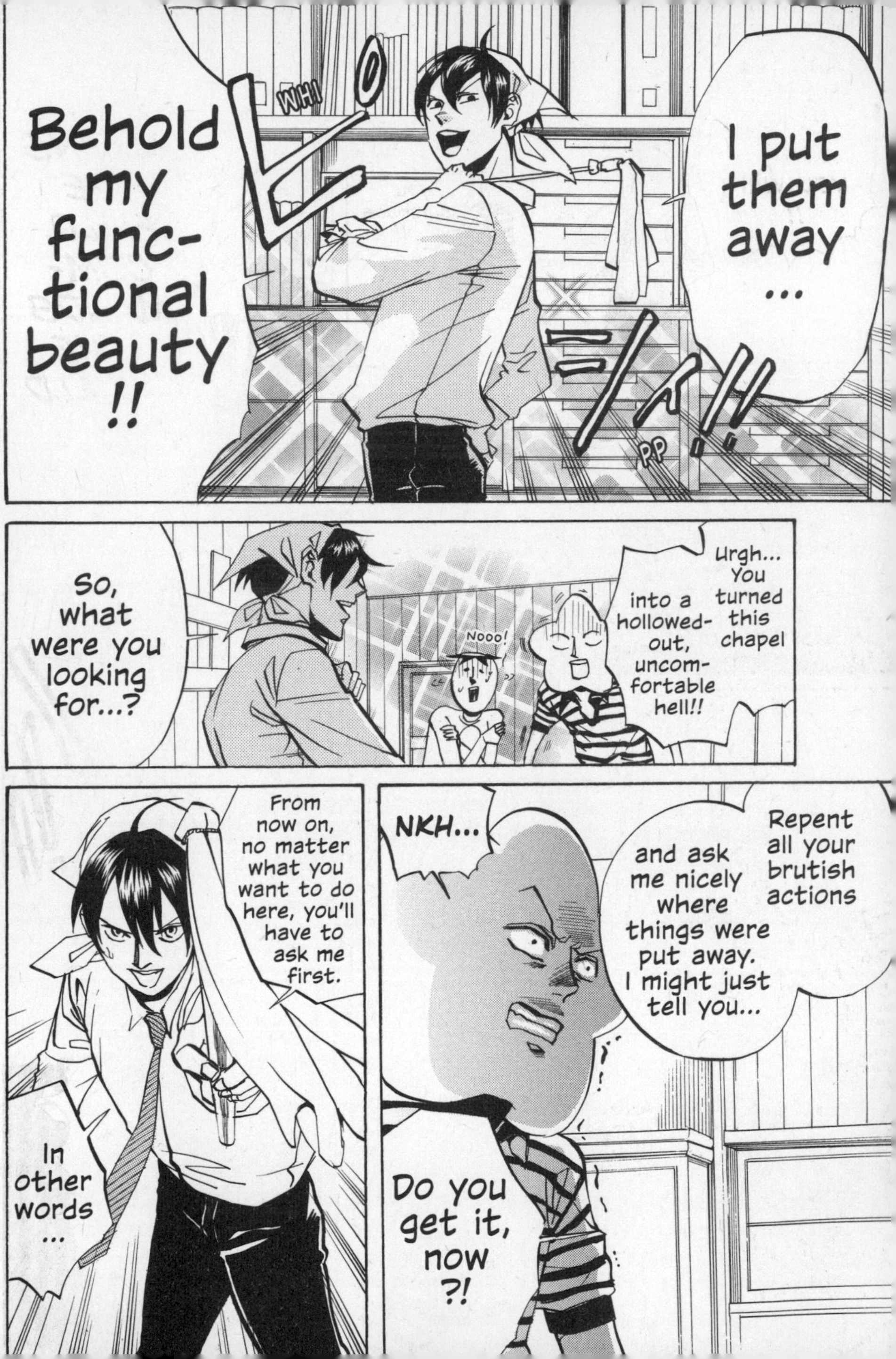
I put them away ...
WHI
PP
Behold my func-tional beauty !!
Urgh... You turned this chapel into a hollowed-out, uncom-fortable hell!!
Nooo!
So, what were you looking for...?
Repent all your brutish actions and ask me nicely where things were put away. I might just tell you...
NKH...
Do you get it, now ?!
From now on, no matter what you want to do here, you'll have to ask me first.
In other words ...

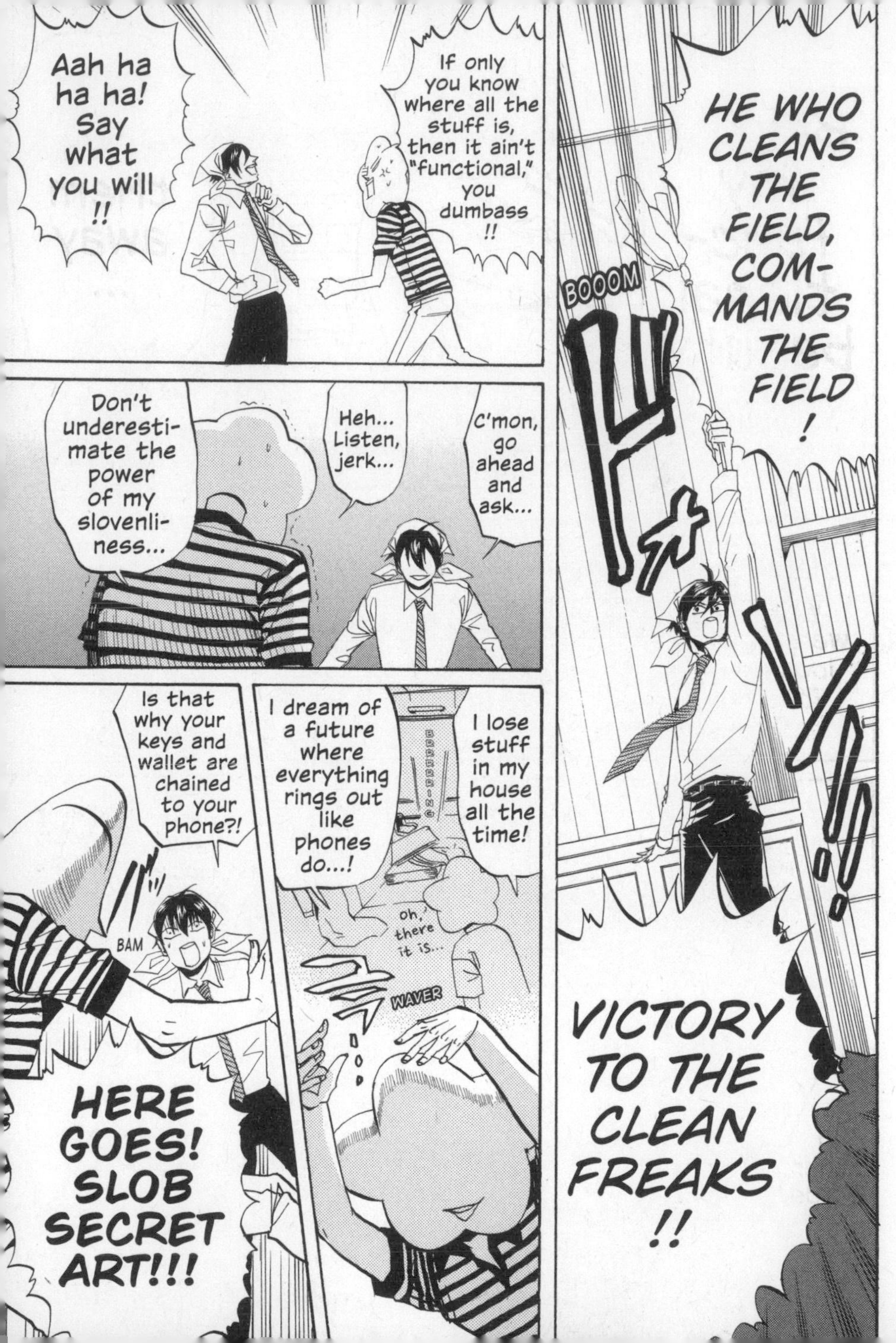
HE WHO CLEANS THE FIELD, COMMANDS THE FIELD!
BOOOM
VICTORY TO THE CLEAN FREAKS!!
If only you know where all the stuff is, then it ain't "functional," you dumbass!!
Aah ha ha ha! Say what you will!!
C'mon, go ahead and ask...
Heh... Listen, jerk...
Don't underestimate the power of my slovenliness...
I lose stuff in my house all the time!
I dream of a future where everything rings out like phones do...!
BRRRRING
oh, there it is...
WAVER
Is that why your keys and wallet are chained to your phone?!
BAM
HERE GOES! SLOB SECRET ART!!!

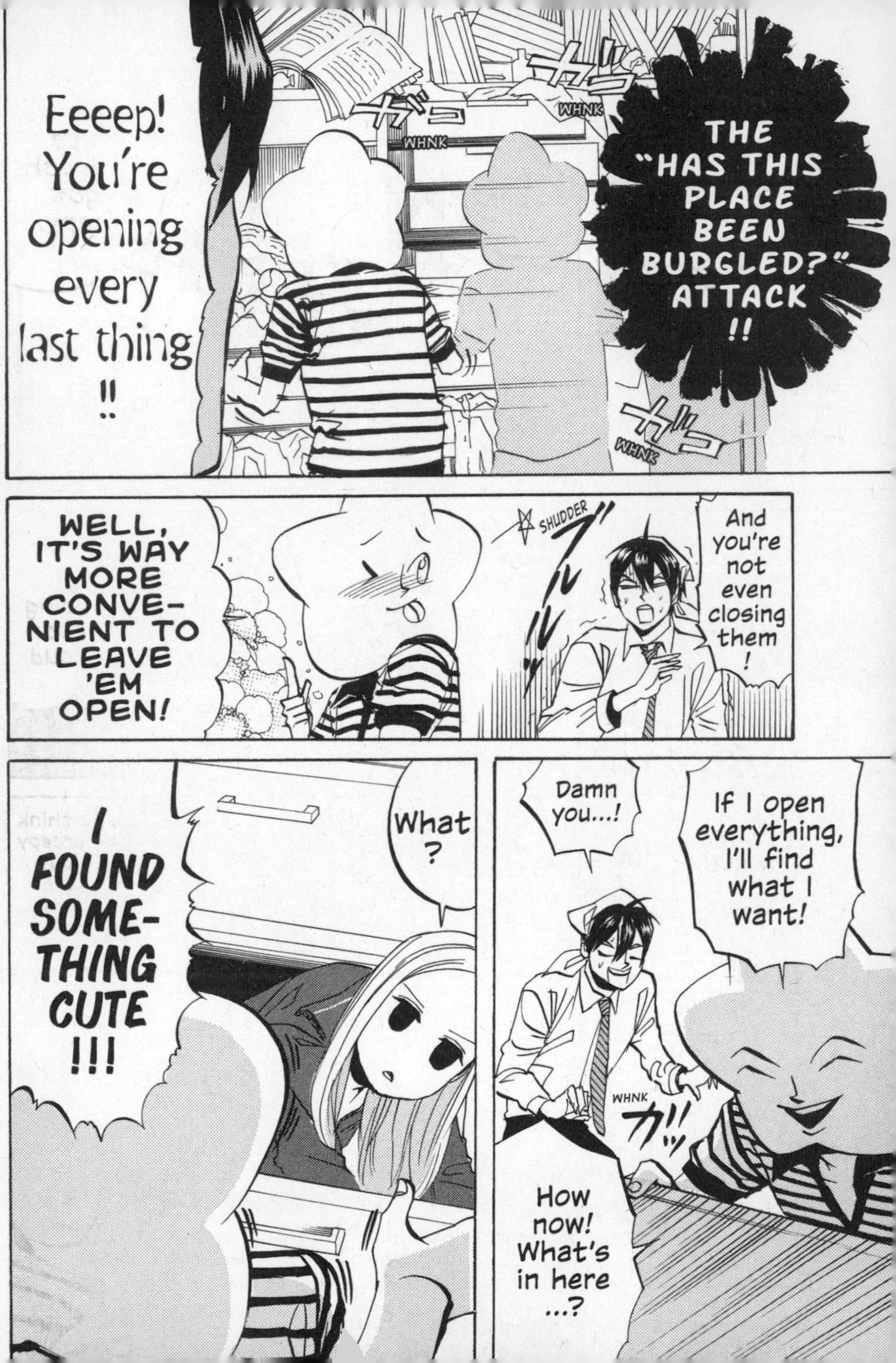
WHNK
THE "HAS THIS PLACE BEEN BURGLED?" ATTACK !!
WHNK
Eeeep! You're opening every last thing !!
WHNK
And you're not even closing them !
SHUDDER
WELL, IT'S WAY MORE CONVENIENT TO LEAVE 'EM OPEN!
If I open everything, I'll find what I want!
Damn you...!
WHNK
How now! What's in here ...?
What ?
I FOUND SOMETHING CUTE !!!

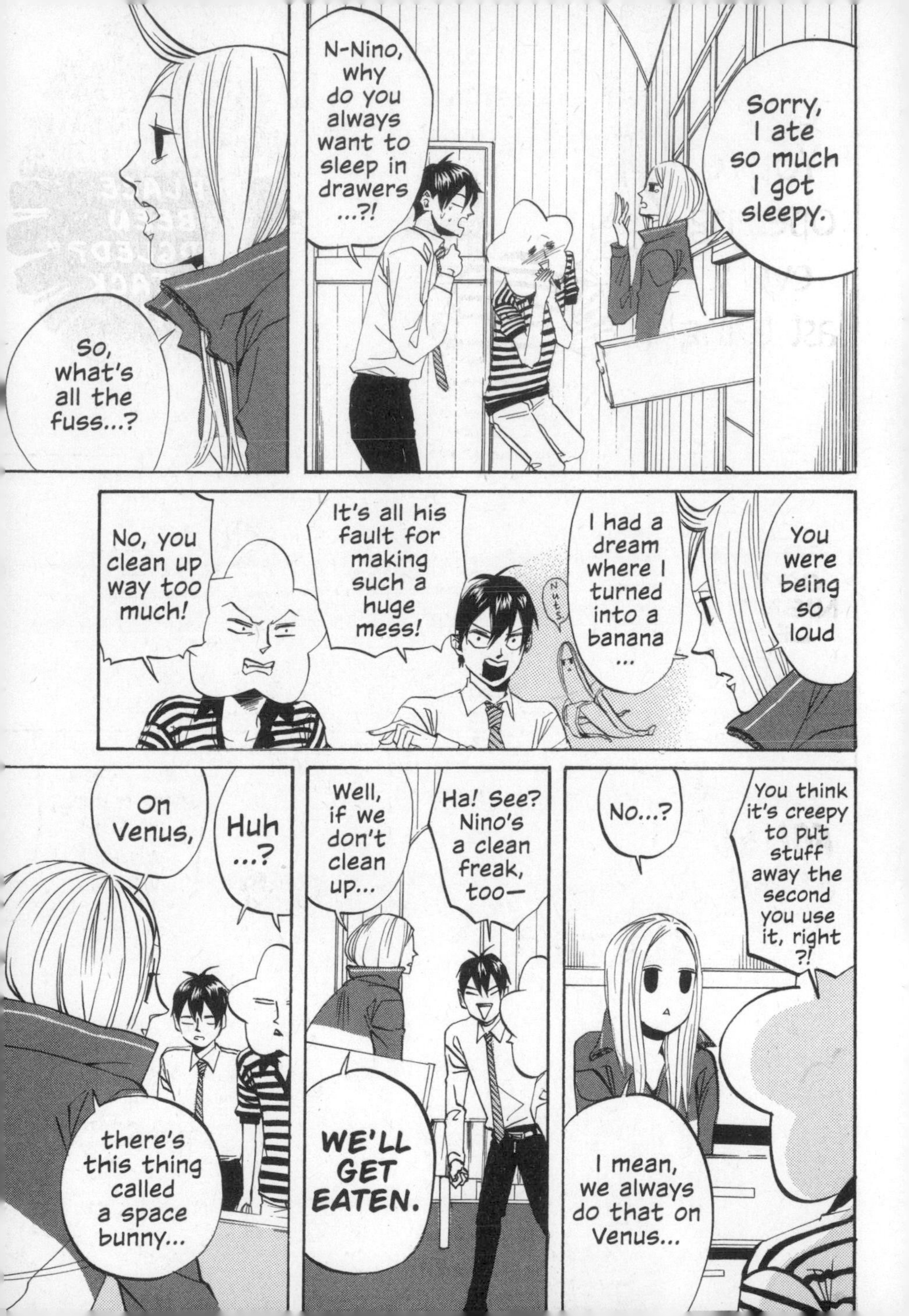
Sorry, I ate so much I got sleepy.
N-Nino, why do you always want to sleep in drawers ...?!
So, what's all the fuss...?
You were being so loud
I had a dream where I turned into a banana ...
Nuts
It's all his fault for making such a huge mess!
No, you clean up way too much!
You think it's creepy to put stuff away the second you use it, right ?!
No...?
I mean, we always do that on Venus...
Ha! See? Nino's a clean freak, too—
Well, if we don't clean up...
WE'LL GET EATEN.
Huh ...?
On Venus,
there's this thing called a space bunny...

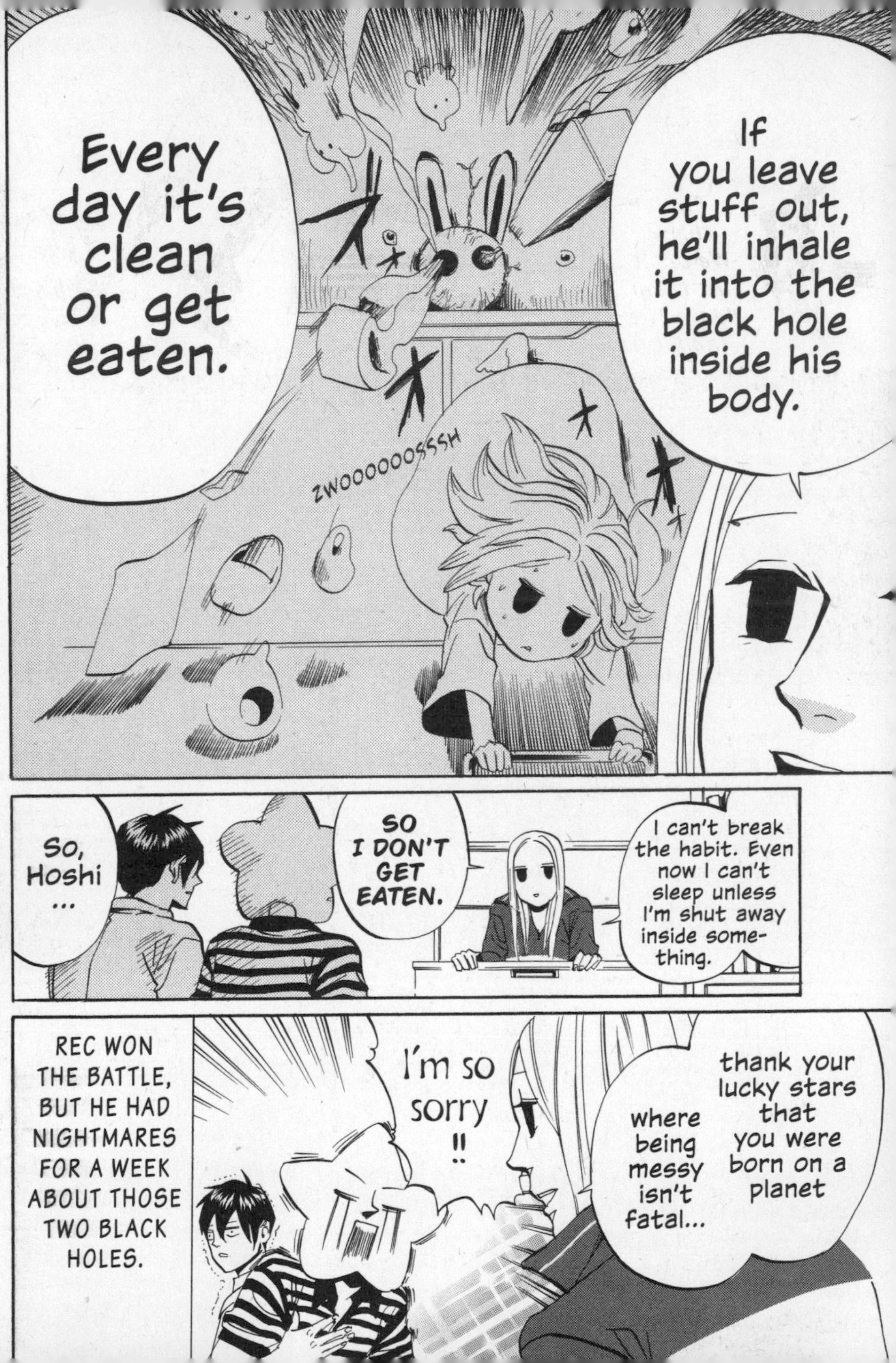
If you leave stuff out, he'll inhale it into the black hole inside his body.
Every day it's clean or get eaten.
ZWOOOOOOSSSH
I can't break the habit. Even now I can't sleep unless I'm shut away inside something.
SO I DON'T GET EATEN.
So, Hoshi ...
thank your lucky stars that you were born on a planet where being messy isn't fatal...
I'm so sorry!!
REC WON THE BATTLE, BUT HE HAD NIGHTMARES FOR A WEEK ABOUT THOSE TWO BLACK HOLES.

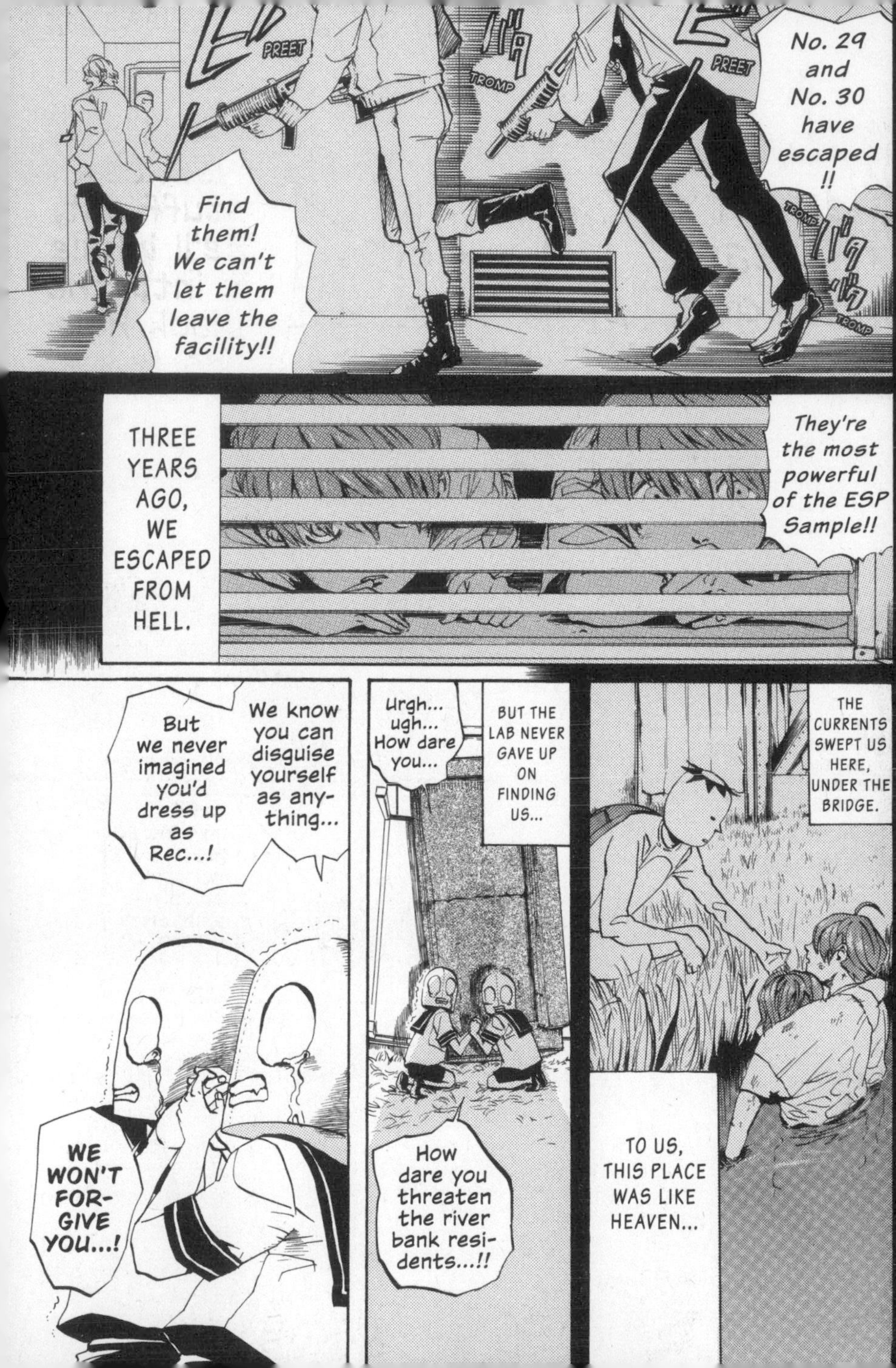
No. 29 and No. 30 have escaped!!
PREET
TROMP
PREET
TROMP
TROMP
Find them! We can't let them leave the facility!!
They're the most powerful of the ESP Sample!!
THREE YEARS AGO, WE ESCAPED FROM HELL.
THE CURRENTS SWEPT US HERE, UNDER THE BRIDGE.
TO US, THIS PLACE WAS LIKE HEAVEN...
BUT THE LAB NEVER GAVE UP ON FINDING US...
Urgh... ugh... How dare you...
How dare you threaten the river bank resi-dents...!!
We know you can disguise yourself as any-thing...
But we never imagined you'd dress up as Rec...!
WE WON'T FOR-GIVE YOU...!

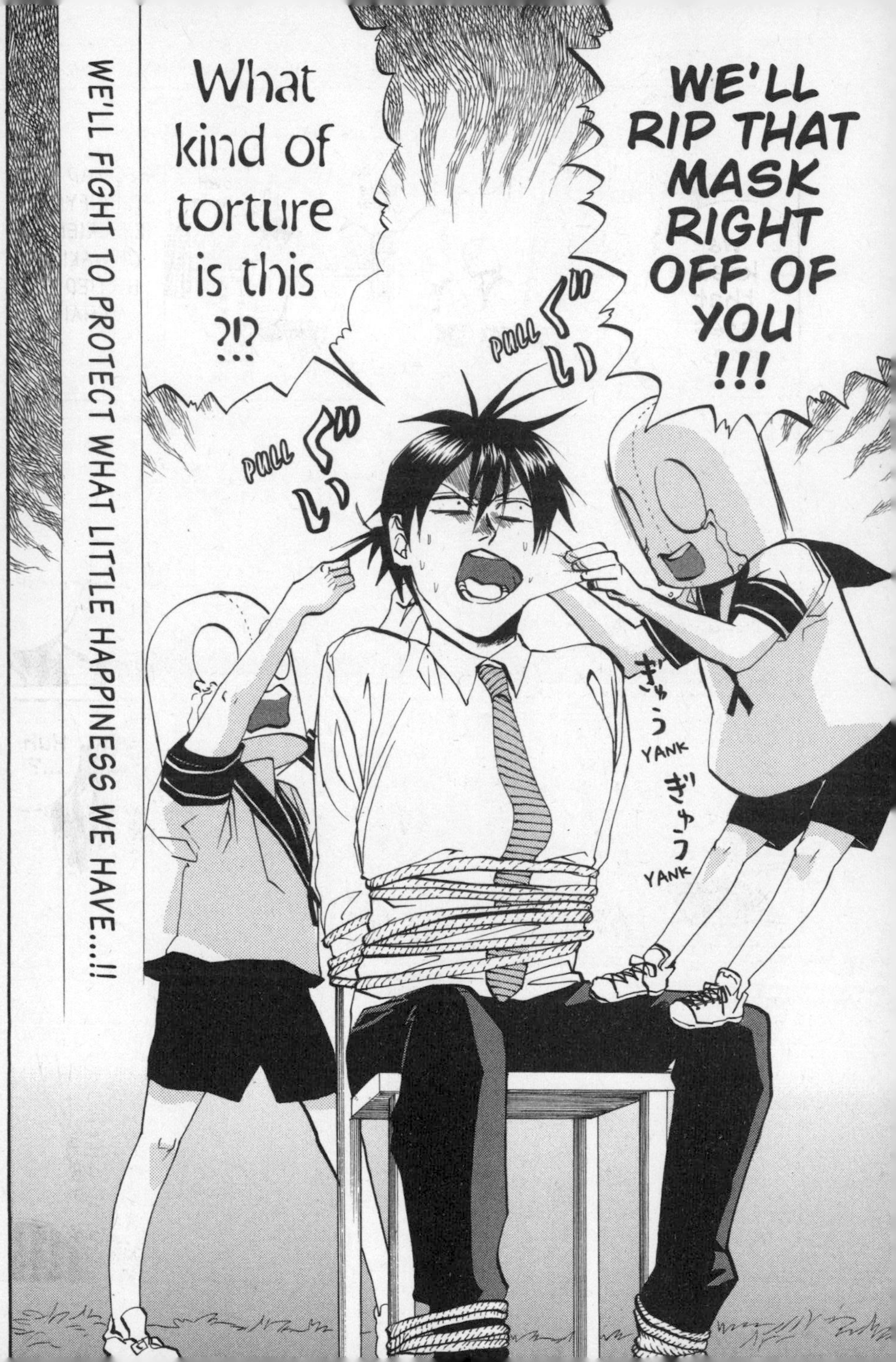
WE'LL RIP THAT MASK RIGHT OFF OF YOU!!!
What kind of torture is this?!?
PULL
PULL
ぎゅう
YANK
ぎゅう
YANK
WE'LL FIGHT TO PROTECT WHAT LITTLE HAPPINESS WE HAVE...!!

Chapter 209: The Metal Brothers Awaken

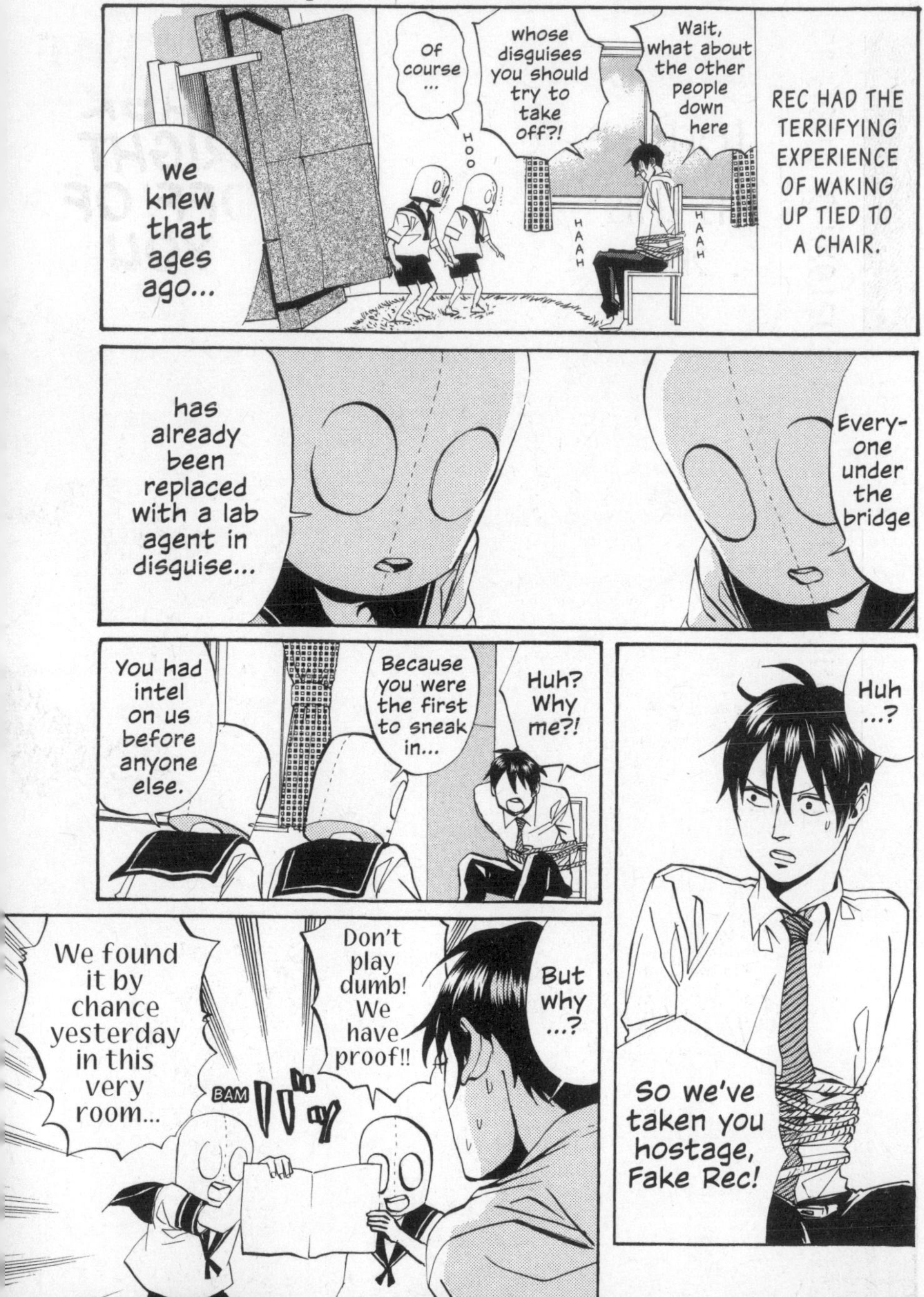
REC HAD THE TERRIFYING EXPERIENCE OF WAKING UP TIED TO A CHAIR.
HAAH
HAAH
Wait, what about the other people down here
whose disguises you should try to take off?!
HOO
Of course...
we knew that ages ago...
Every-one under the bridge
has already been replaced with a lab agent in disguise...
Huh...?
So we've taken you hostage, Fake Rec!
Huh? Why me?!
Because you were the first to sneak in...
You had intel on us before anyone else.
But why...?
Don't play dumb! We have proof!!
We found it by chance yesterday in this very room...
BAM

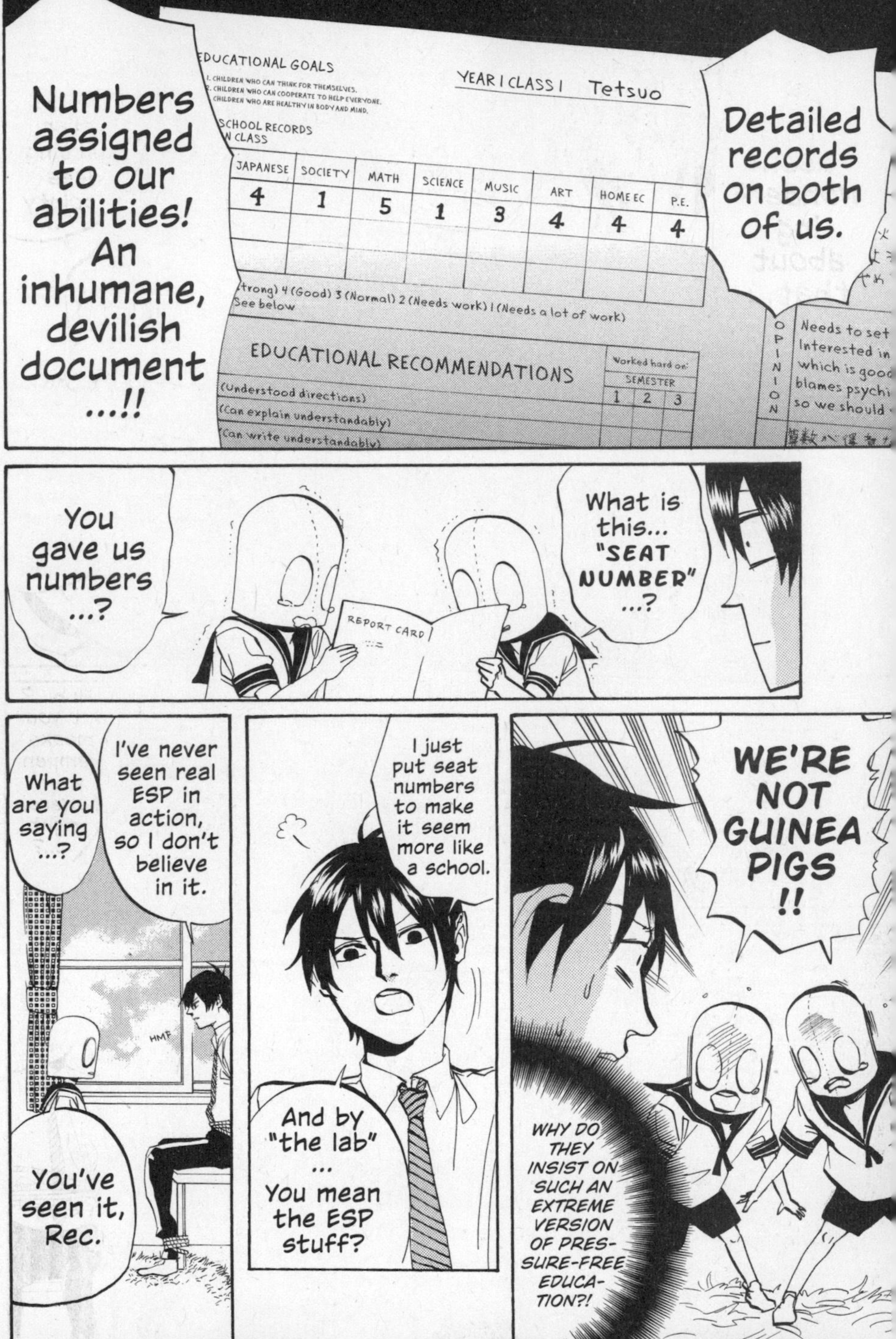
Detailed records on both of us.
EDUCATIONAL GOALS
1. CHILDREN WHO CAN THINK FOR THEMSELVES.
CHILDREN WHO CAN COOPERATE TO HELP EVERYONE.
CHILDREN WHO ARE HEALTHY IN BODY AND MIND.
YEAR 1 CLASS 1 Tetsuo
SCHOOL RECORDS
N CLASS
JAPANESE 4 SOCIETY 1 MATH 5 SCIENCE 1 MUSIC 3 ART 4 HOME EC 4 P.E. 4
trong) 4 (Good) 3 (Normal) 2 (Needs work) 1 (Needs a lot of work)
See below
EDUCATIONAL RECOMMENDATIONS
Worked hard on: SEMESTER 1 2 3
(Understood directions)
(Can explain understandably)
(Can write understandably)
OPINION
Needs to set
Interested in
which is good
blames psychi
so we should
Numbers assigned to our abilities! An inhumane, devilish document ...!!
What is this... "SEAT NUMBER" ...?
REPORT CARD
You gave us numbers ...?
WE'RE NOT GUINEA PIGS !!
WHY DO THEY INSIST ON SUCH AN EXTREME VERSION OF PRES-SURE-FREE EDUCA-TION?!
I just put seat numbers to make it seem more like a school.
And by "the lab" ... You mean the ESP stuff?
I've never seen real ESP in action, so I don't believe in it.
What are you saying ...?
HMF
You've seen it, Rec.

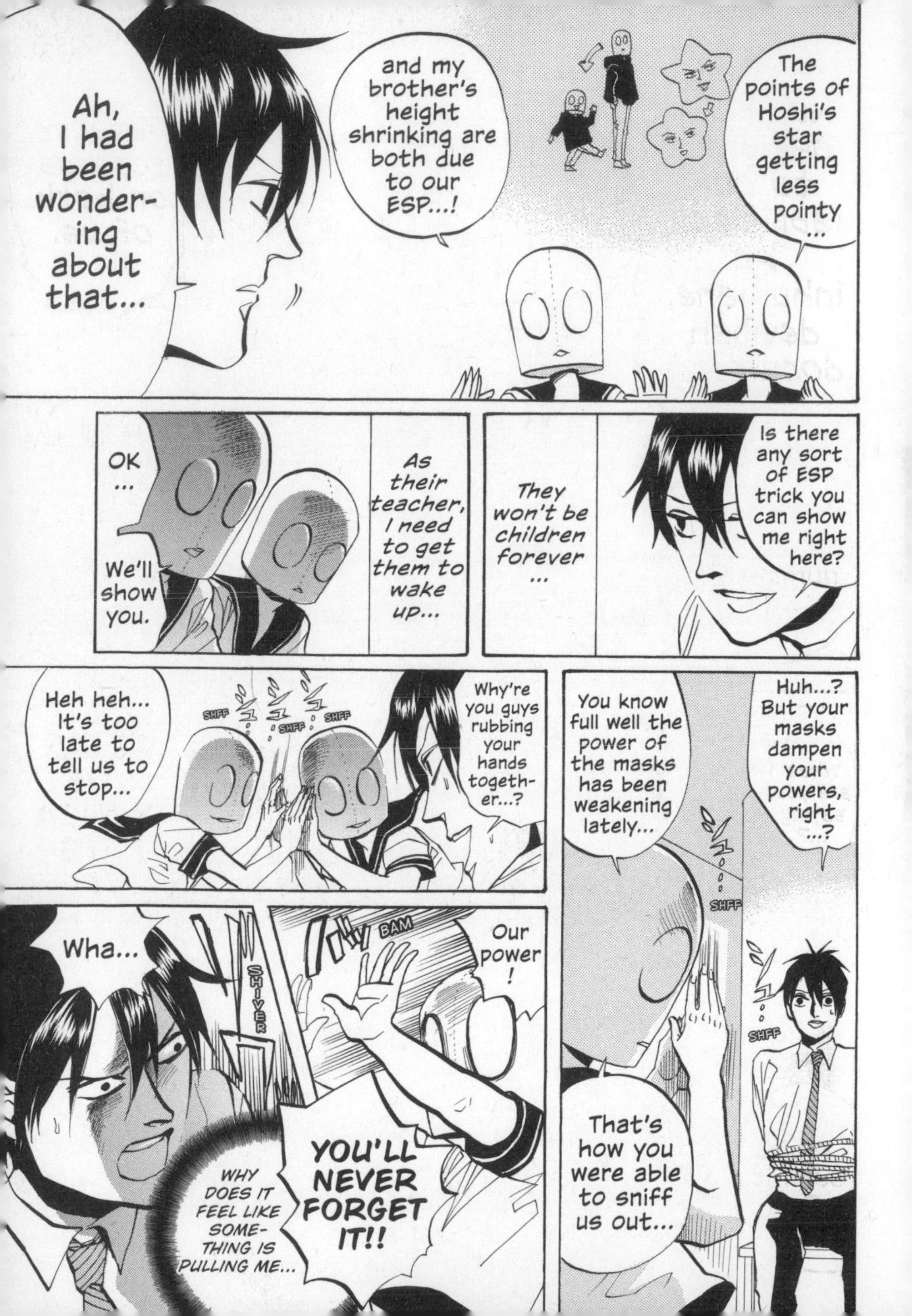
The points of Hoshi's star getting less pointy...
and my brother's height shrinking are both due to our ESP...!
Ah, I had been wondering about that...
Is there any sort of ESP trick you can show me right here?
They won't be children forever...
As their teacher, I need to get them to wake up...
OK... We'll show you.
Huh...? But your masks dampen your powers, right...?
You know full well the power of the masks has been weakening lately...
SHFF
SHFF
That's how you were able to sniff us out...
Why're you guys rubbing your hands together...?
SHFF
SHFF
SHFF
Heh heh... It's too late to tell us to stop...
Our power!
BAM
SHIVER
Wha...
YOU'LL NEVER FORGET IT!!
WHY DOES IT FEEL LIKE SOMETHING IS PULLING ME...

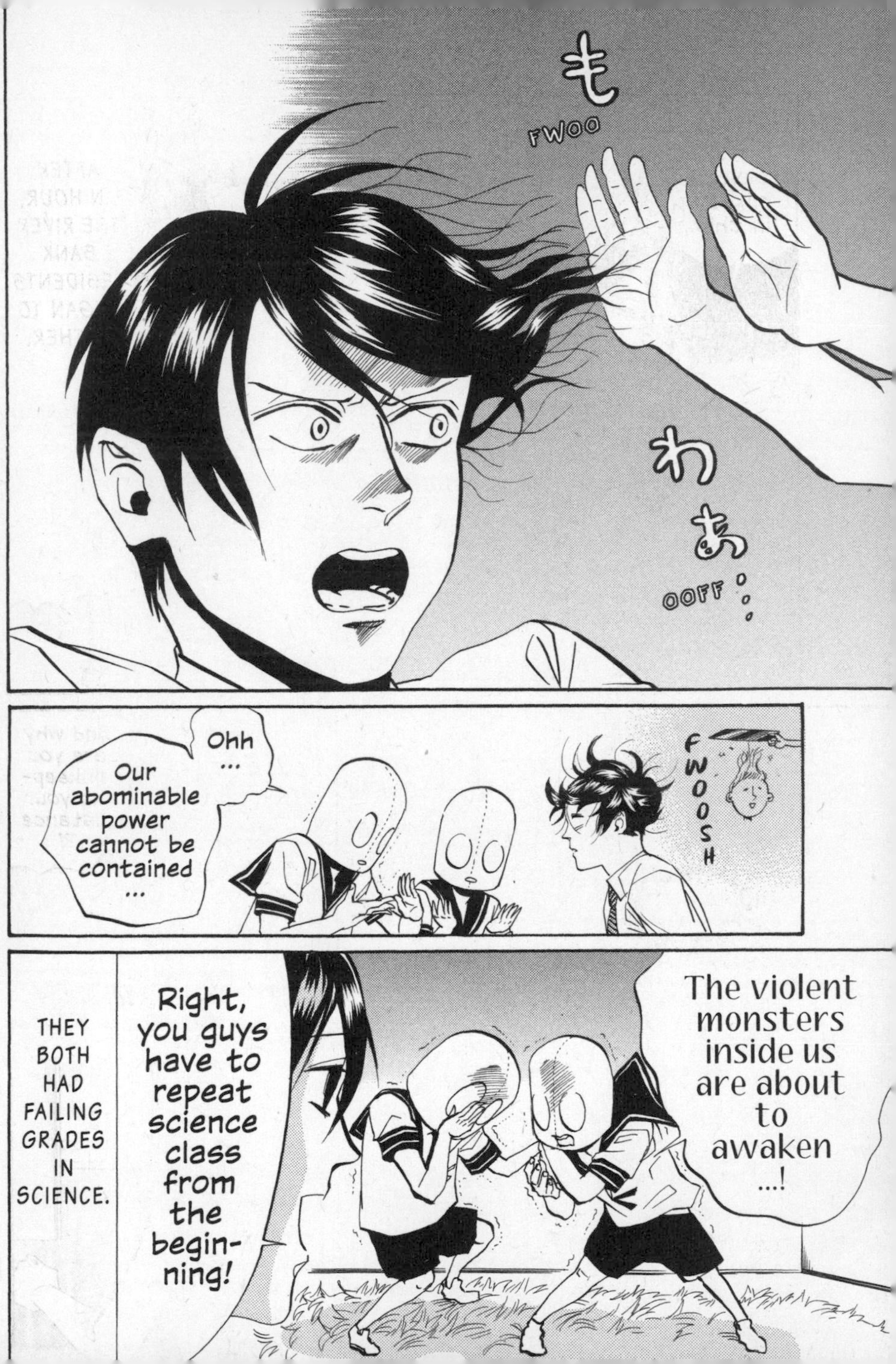
も
FWOO
わあ
OOFF
Ohh ...
Our abominable power cannot be contained ...
FWOOSH
The violent monsters inside us are about to awaken ...!
Right, you guys have to repeat science class from the beginning!
THEY BOTH HAD FAILING GRADES IN SCIENCE.

Chapter 210: ESPers vs. Venusians

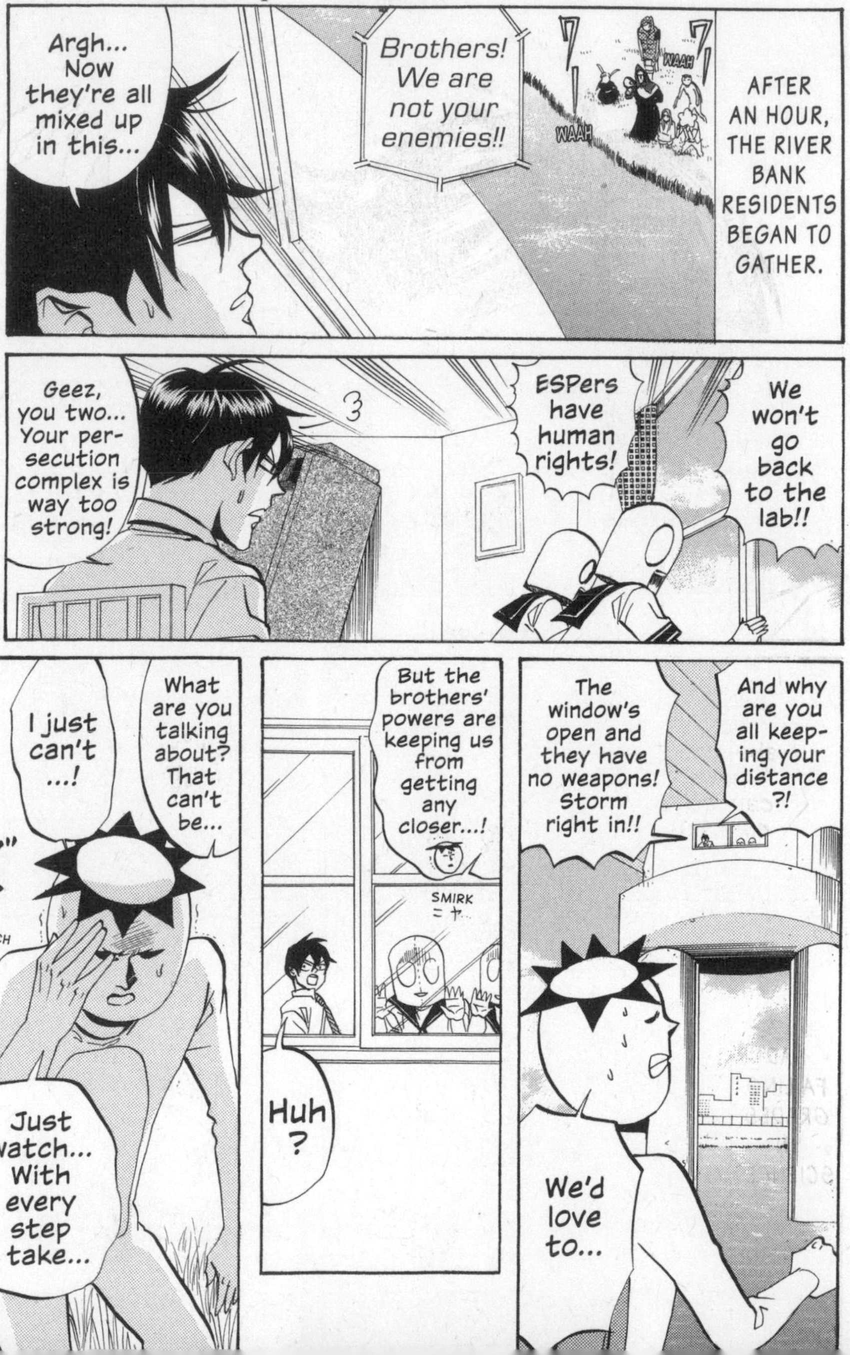
AFTER AN HOUR, THE RIVER BANK RESIDENTS BEGAN TO GATHER.
WAAH
WAAH
Brothers! We are not your enemies!!
Argh... Now they're all mixed up in this...
We won't go back to the lab!!
ESPers have human rights!
Geez, you two... Your persecution complex is way too strong!
And why are you all keeping your distance?!
The window's open and they have no weapons! Storm right in!!
We'd love to...
But the brothers' powers are keeping us from getting any closer...!
SMIRK
Huh?
What are you talking about? That can't be...
I just can't ...!
SCRNCH
Just watch... With every step I take...

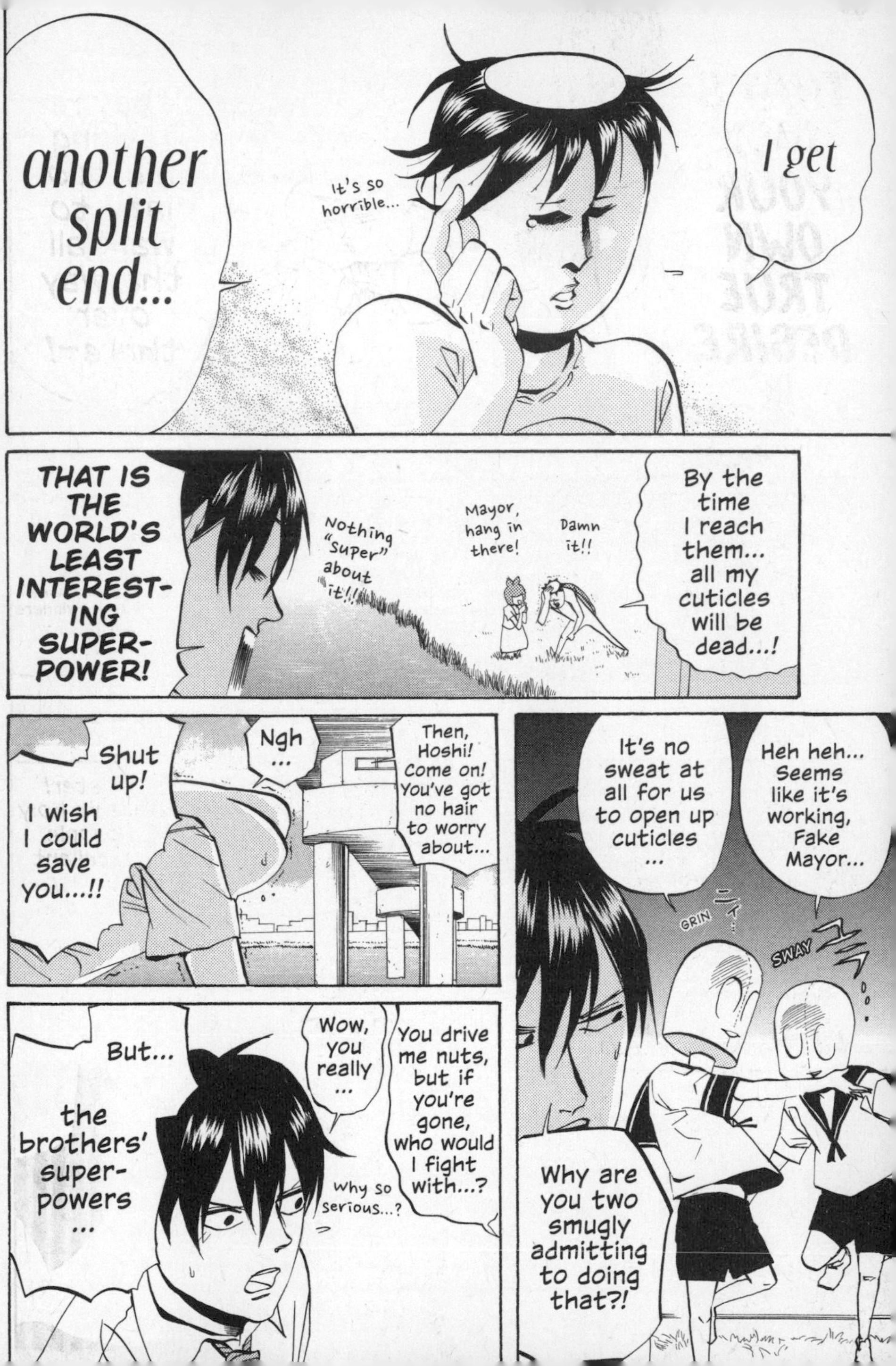
I get
It's so horrible...
another split end...
By the time I reach them... all my cuticles will be dead...!
Damn it!!
Mayor, hang in there!
Nothing "Super" about it!!
THAT IS THE WORLD'S LEAST INTERESTING SUPER-POWER!
Heh heh... Seems like it's working, Fake Mayor...
It's no sweat at all for us to open up cuticles ...
GRIN
SWAY
Why are you two smugly admitting to doing that?!
Then, Hoshi! Come on! You've got no hair to worry about...
Ngh ...
Shut up!
I wish I could save you...!!
You drive me nuts, but if you're gone, who would I fight with...?
Wow, you really ...
Why so serious...?
But...
the brothers' super-powers ...

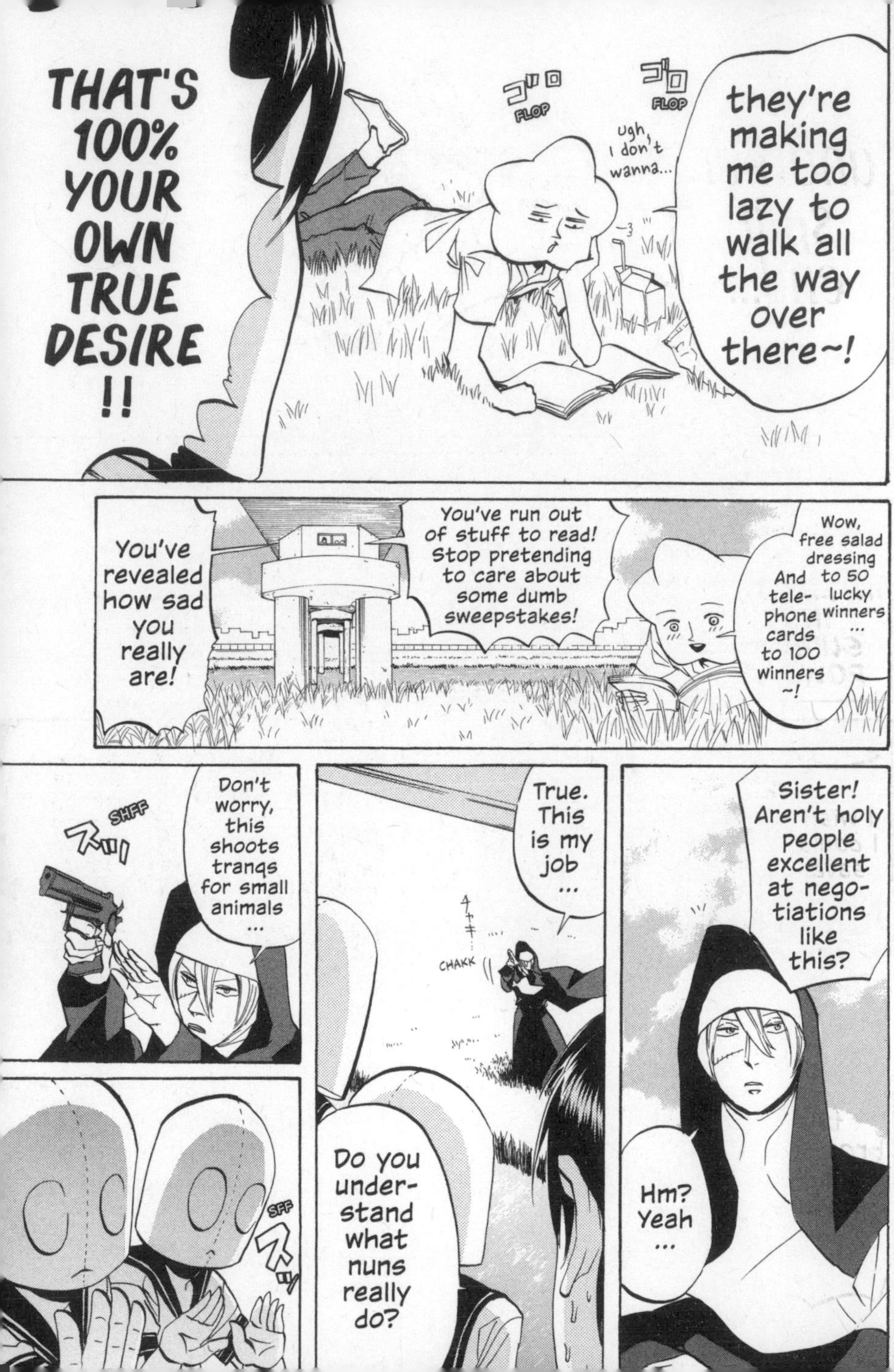
they're making me too lazy to walk all the way over there~!
ゴロ
FLOP
ゴロ
FLOP
Ugh, I don't wanna...
THAT'S 100% YOUR OWN TRUE DESIRE !!
Wow, free salad dressing to 50 lucky winners ...
And telephone cards to 100 winners ~!
You've run out of stuff to read! Stop pretending to care about some dumb sweepstakes!
You've revealed how sad you really are!
Sister! Aren't holy people excellent at negotiations like this?
Hm? Yeah ...
True. This is my job ...
CHAKK
Do you understand what nuns really do?
SHFF
Don't worry, this shoots tranqs for small animals ...
SFF

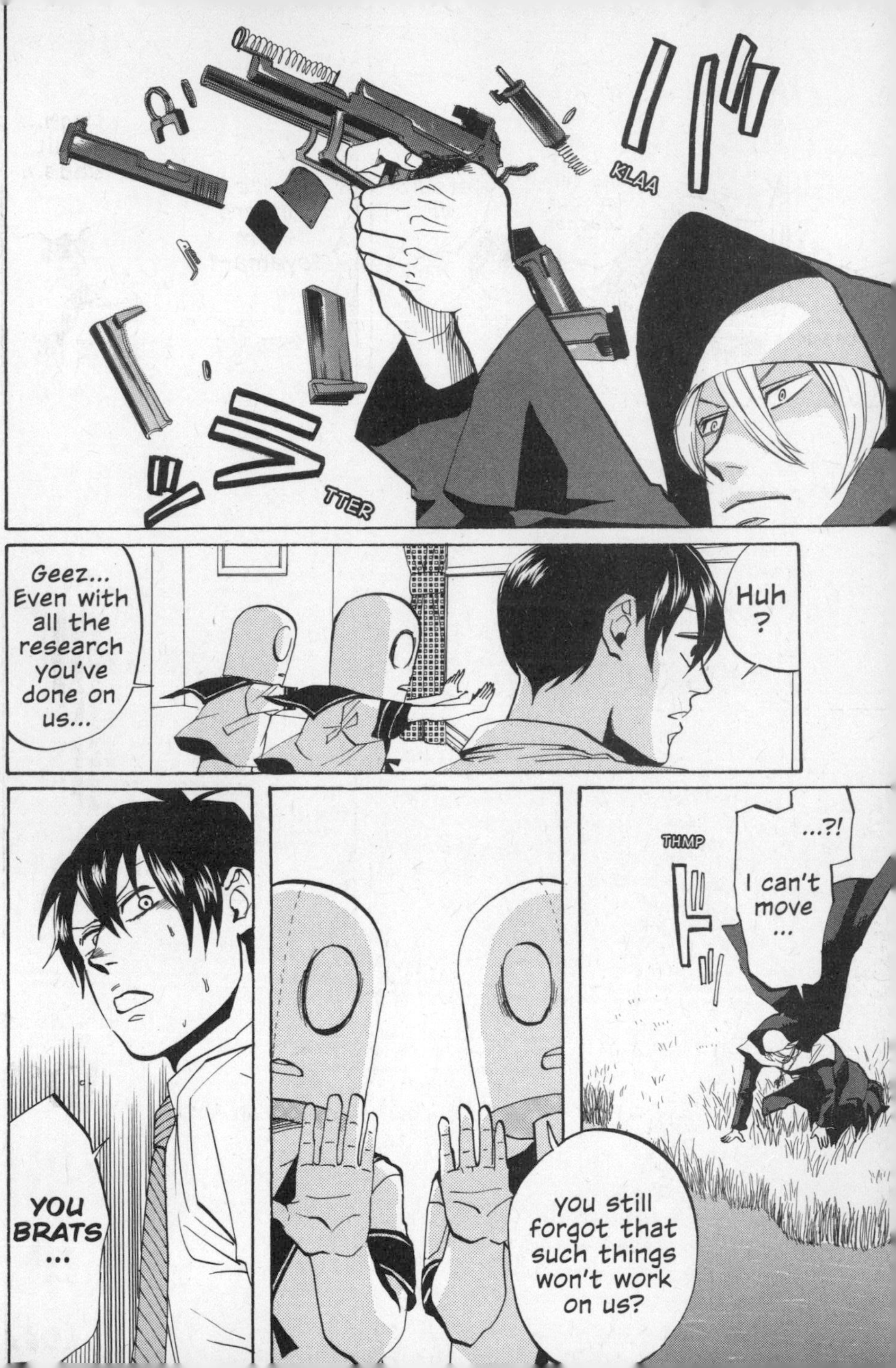
KLAA
TTER
Huh?
Geez... Even with all the research you've done on us...
THMP
...?!
I can't move ...
you still forgot that such things won't work on us?
YOU BRATS ...

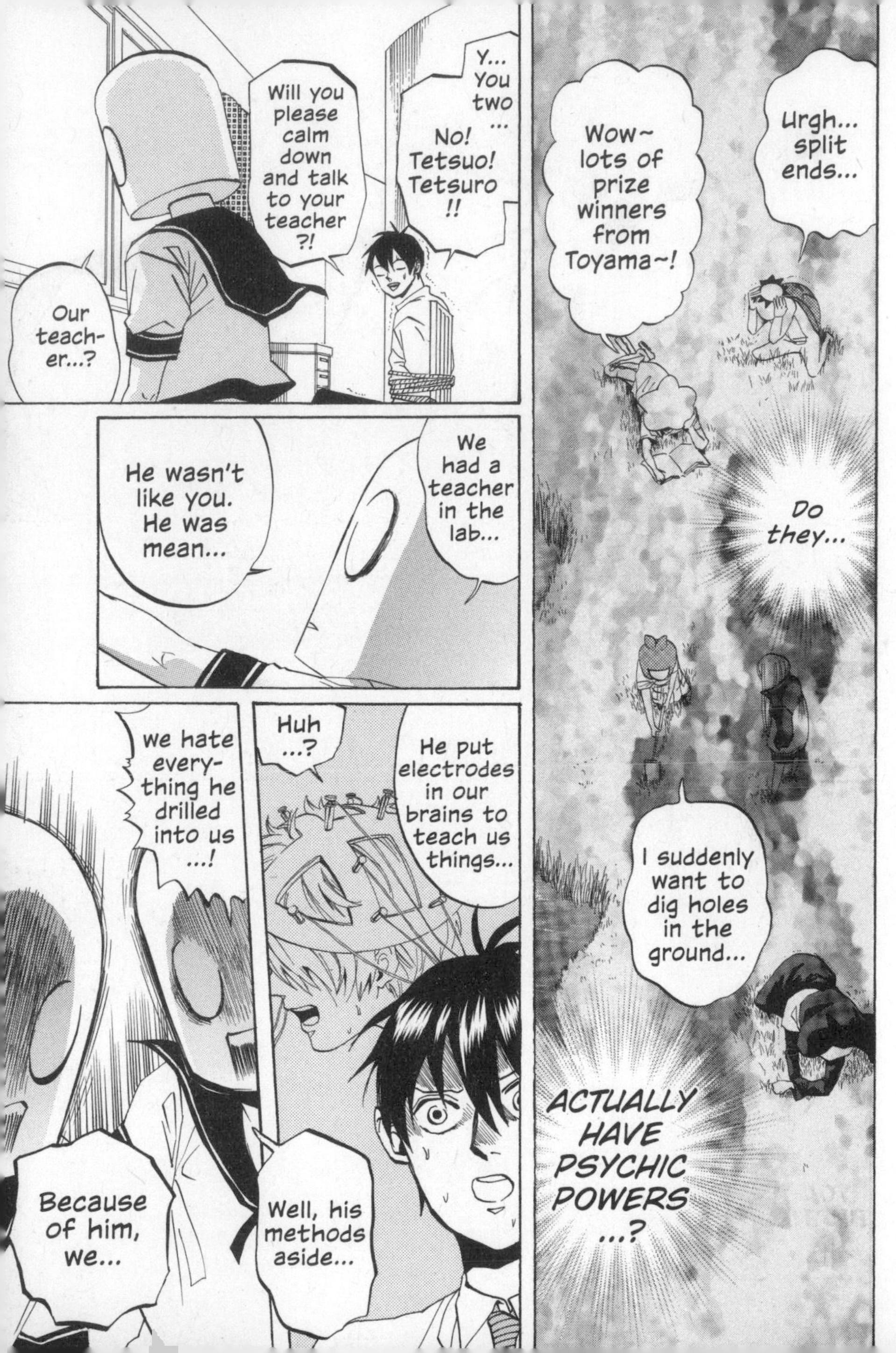
Urgh... split ends...
Wow~ lots of prize winners from Toyama~!
Do they...
I suddenly want to dig holes in the ground...
ACTUALLY HAVE PSYCHIC POWERS ...?
Y... You two ...
No! Tetsuo! Tetsuro !!
Will you please calm down and talk to your teacher ?!
Our teacher...?
We had a teacher in the lab...
He wasn't like you. He was mean...
He put electrodes in our brains to teach us things...
Huh ...?
Well, his methods aside...
Because of him, we...
we hate everything he drilled into us ...!

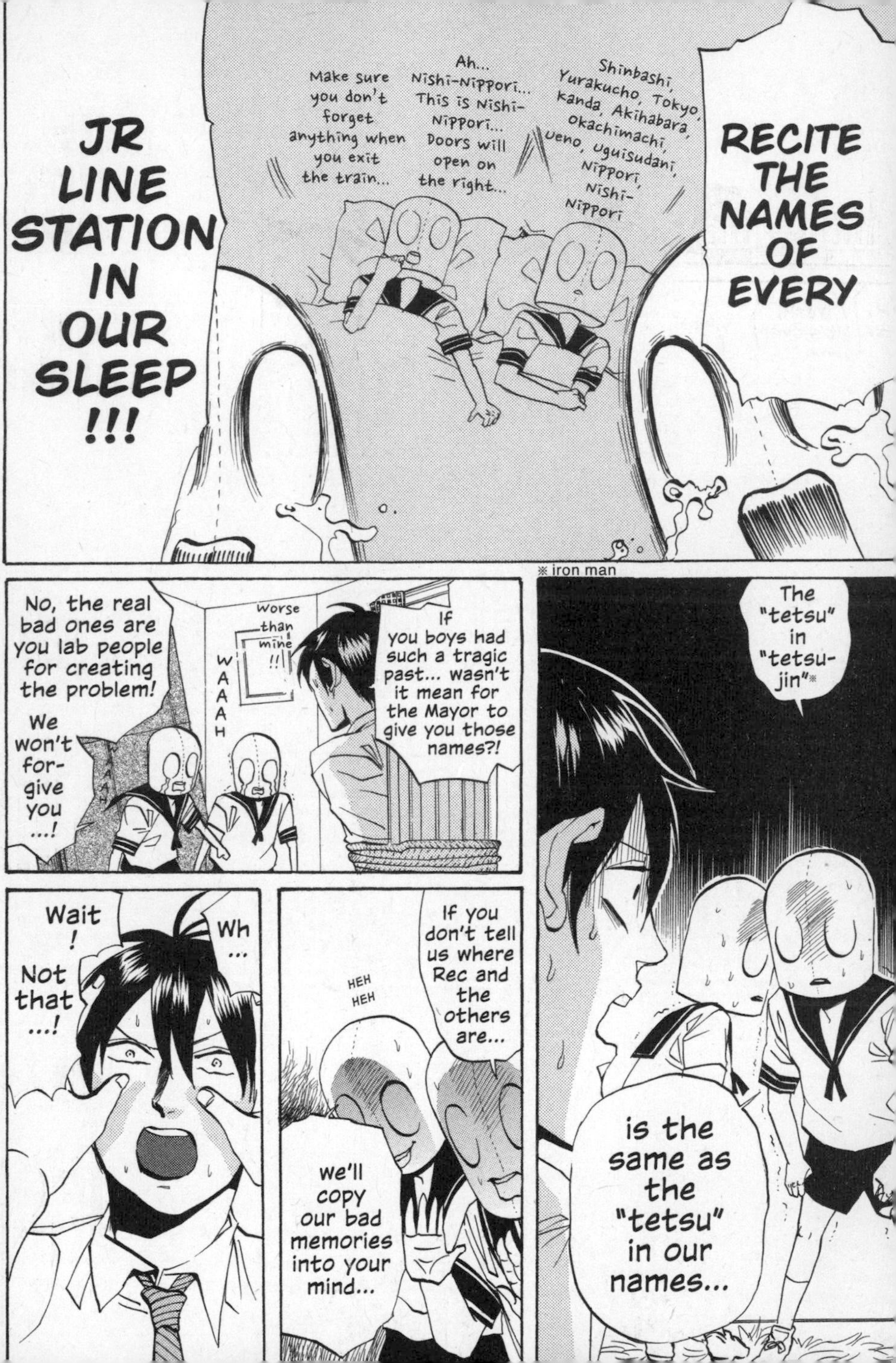
RECITE THE NAMES OF EVERY
Shinbashi, Yurakucho, Tokyo, Kanda, Akihabara, Okachimachi, Ueno, Uguisudani, Nippori, Nishi-Nippori
Ah... Nishi-Nippori... This is Nishi-Nippori... Doors will open on the right...
Make sure you don't forget anything when you exit the train...
JR LINE STATION IN OUR SLEEP!!!
※ iron man
The "tetsu" in "tetsu-jin"※
is the same as the "tetsu" in our names...
If you boys had such a tragic past... wasn't it mean for the Mayor to give you those names?!
Worse than mine!!
No, the real bad ones are you lab people for creating the problem!
WAAAAH
We won't forgive you...!
If you don't tell us where Rec and the others are...
HEH HEH
we'll copy our bad memories into your mind...
Wh...
Wait! Not that...!

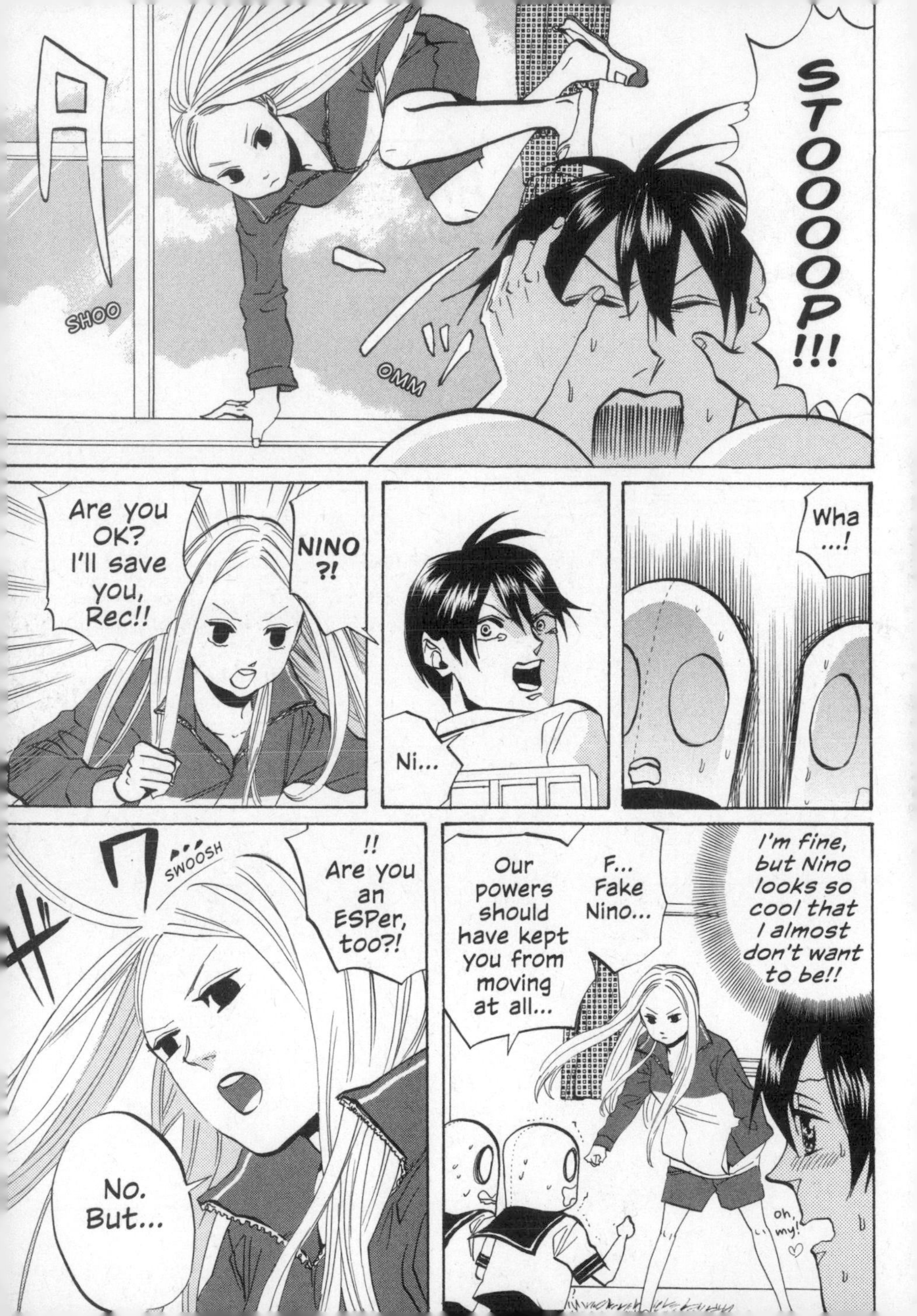
STOOOOOP!!!
SHOO
OMM
Wha ...!
Ni...
NINO ?!
Are you OK? I'll save you, Rec!!
I'm fine, but Nino looks so cool that I almost don't want to be!!
F... Fake Nino...
Our powers should have kept you from moving at all...
oh, my!
SWOOSH
!! Are you an ESPer, too?!
No. But...

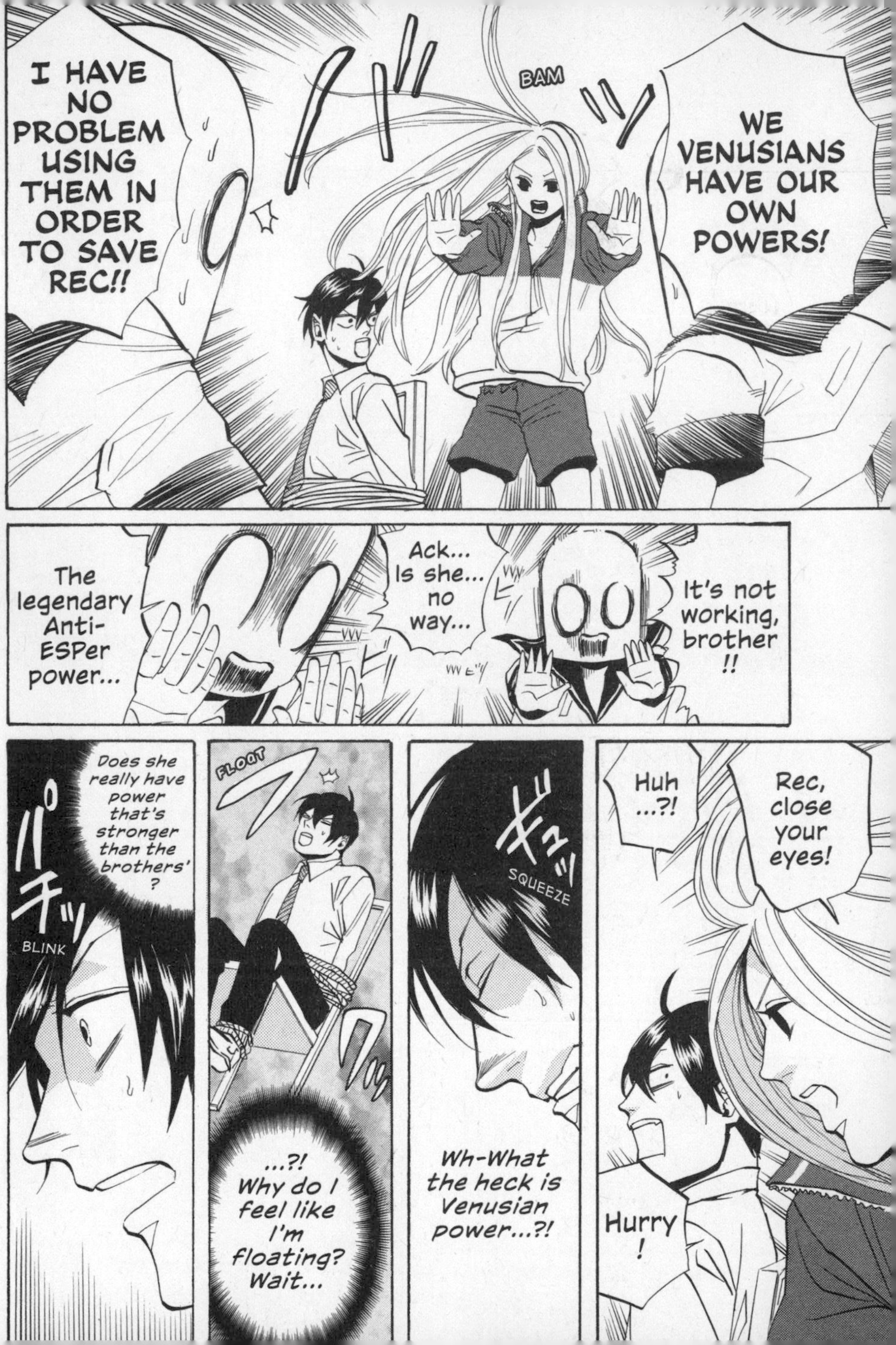

WE VENUSIANS HAVE OUR OWN POWERS!
BAM
I HAVE NO PROBLEM USING THEM IN ORDER TO SAVE REC!!
It's not working, brother!!
Ack... Is she... no way...
The legendary Anti-ESPer power...
Rec, close your eyes!
Huh ...?!
Hurry!
SQUEEZE
Wh-What the heck is Venusian power...?!
FLOAT
...?! Why do I feel like I'm floating? Wait...
Does she really have power that's stronger than the brothers'?
BLINK

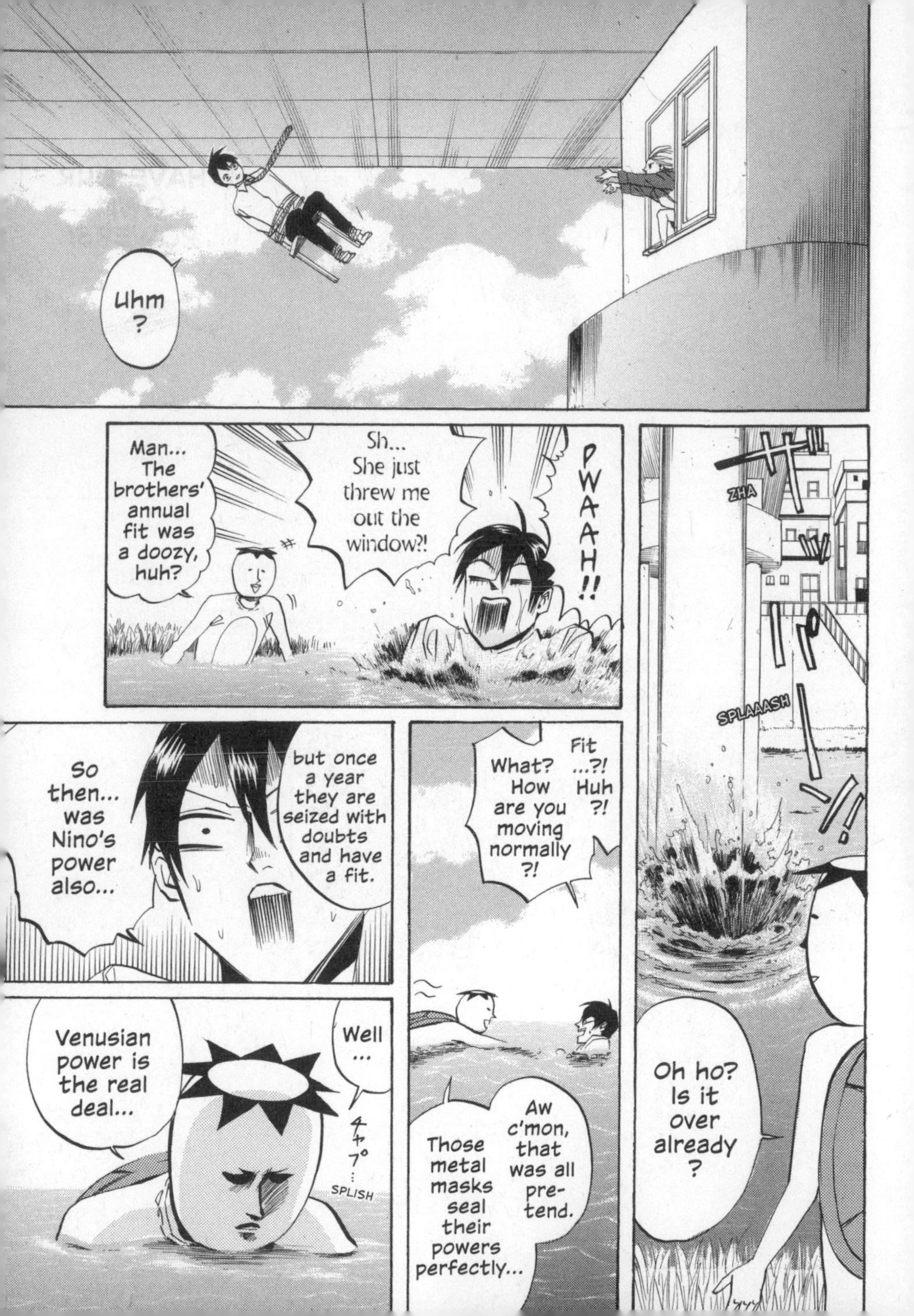
Uhm ?
ZHA
SPLAAASH
Oh ho? Is it over already ?
PWAAAH!!
Sh... She just threw me out the window?!
Man... The brothers' annual fit was a doozy, huh?
Fit ...?! Huh ?!
What? How are you moving normally ?!
Aw c'mon, that was all pre-tend.
Those metal masks seal their powers perfectly...
but once a year they are seized with doubts and have a fit.
So then... was Nino's power also...
Well ...
Venusian power is the real deal...
SPLISH

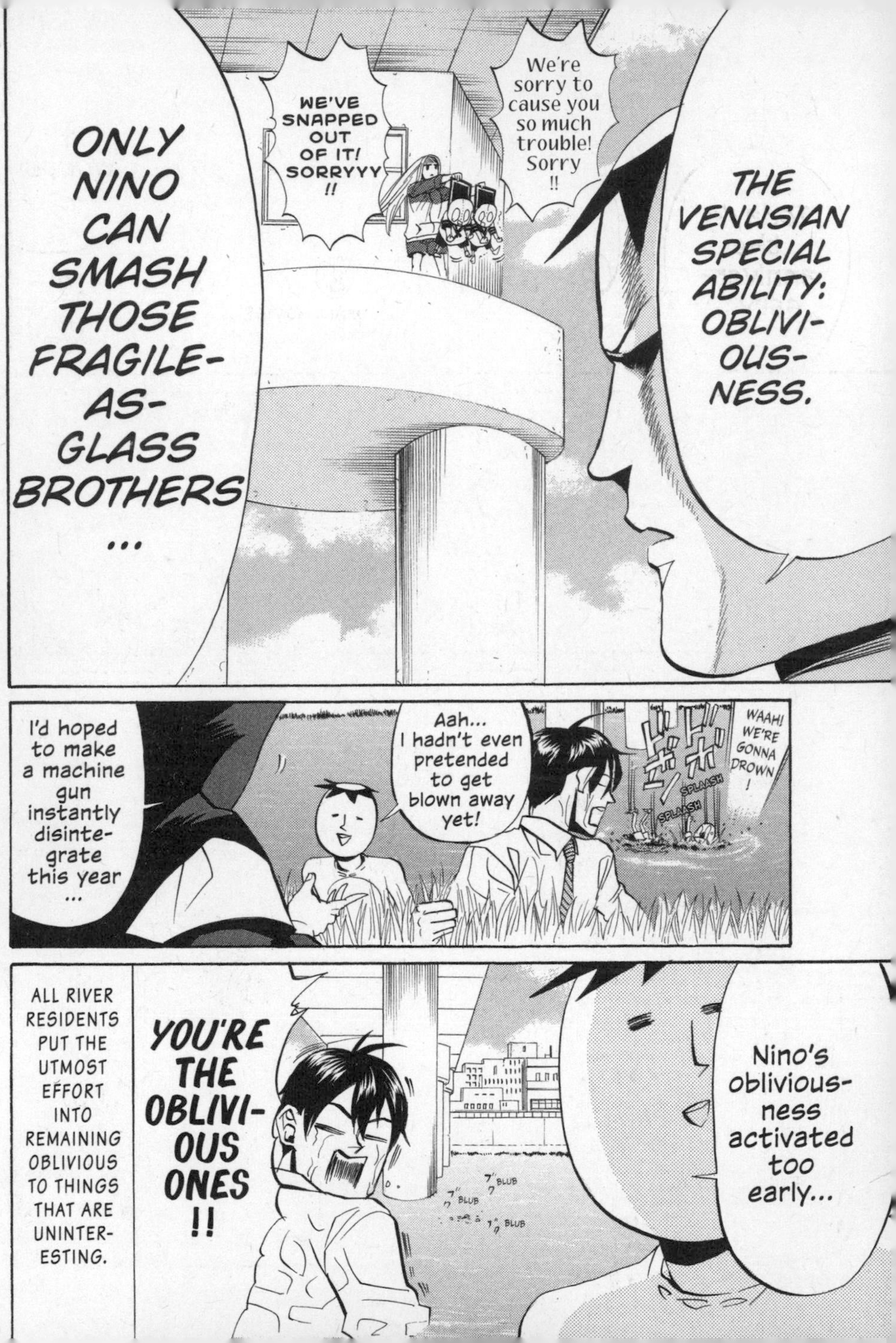

THE VENUSIAN SPECIAL ABILITY: OBLIVIOUSNESS.
We're sorry to cause you so much trouble! Sorry !!
WE'VE SNAPPED OUT OF IT! SORRYYY !!
ONLY NINO CAN SMASH THOSE FRAGILE-AS-GLASS BROTHERS ...
WAAH! WE'RE GONNA DROWN!
SPLAASH
SPLASH
Aah... I hadn't even pretended to get blown away yet!
I'd hoped to make a machine gun instantly disintegrate this year ...
Nino's obliviousness activated too early...
BLUB
BLUB
BLUB
YOU'RE THE OBLIVIOUS ONES !!
ALL RIVER RESIDENTS PUT THE UTMOST EFFORT INTO REMAINING OBLIVIOUS TO THINGS THAT ARE UNINTERESTING.

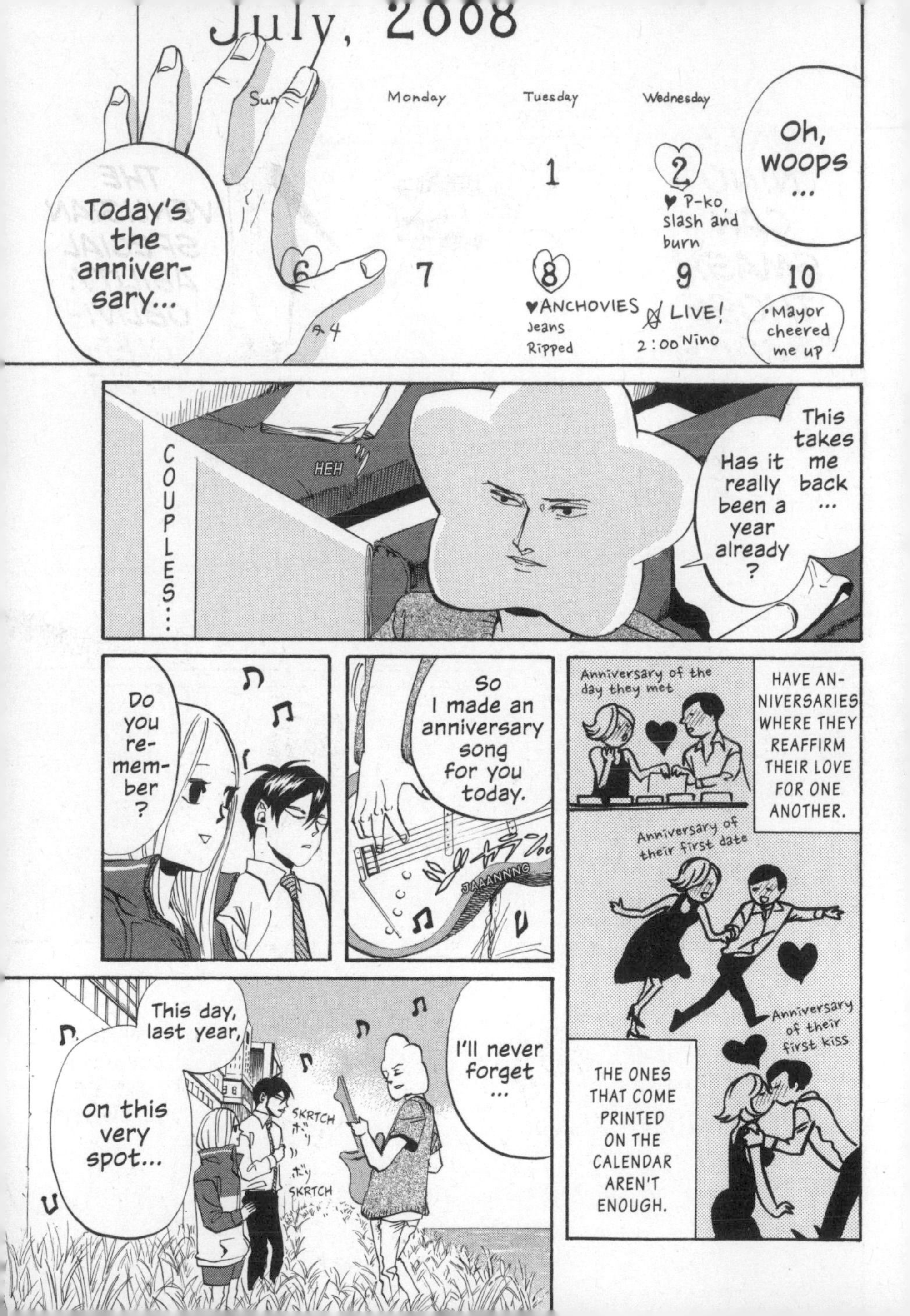

Oh, woops...
July, 2008
Sun
Monday
Tuesday
Wednesday
1
2
♥ P-ko, slash and burn
6
7
8
9
10
♥ANCHOVIES
Jeans Ripped
LIVE!
2:00 Nino
•Mayor cheered me up
Today's the anniversary...
This takes me back...
Has it really been a year already?
HEH
COUPLES...
HAVE ANNIVERSARIES WHERE THEY REAFFIRM THEIR LOVE FOR ONE ANOTHER.
Anniversary of the day they met
Anniversary of their first date
Anniversary of their first kiss
THE ONES THAT COME PRINTED ON THE CALENDAR AREN'T ENOUGH.
So I made an anniversary song for you today.
JAAAANNNG
Do you remember?
I'll never forget...
This day, last year,
on this very spot...
SKRTCH
SKRTCH

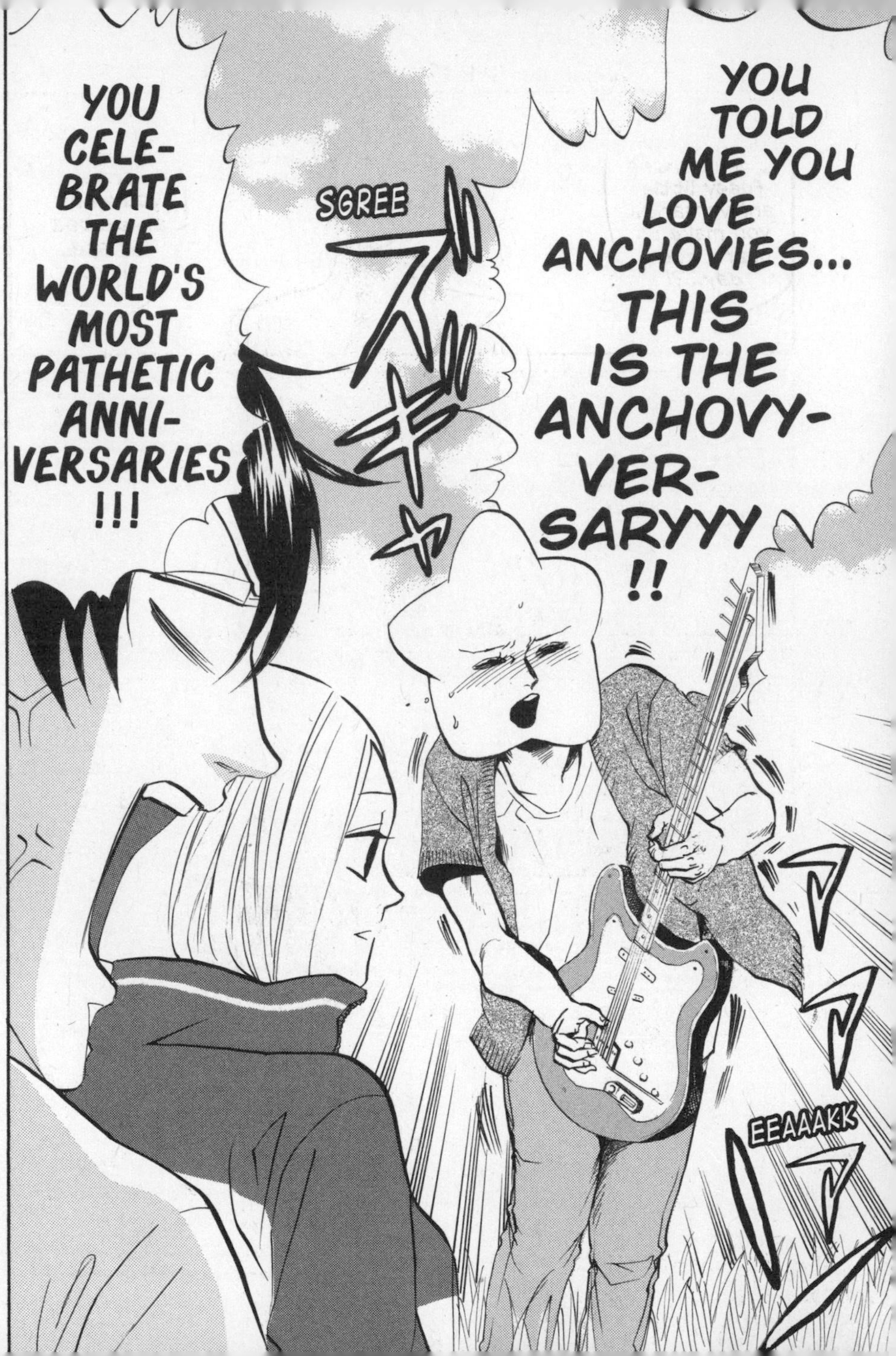
YOU TOLD ME YOU LOVE ANCHOVIES... THIS IS THE ANCHOVY-VER-SARYYY!!
SGREE
YOU CELE-BRATE THE WORLD'S MOST PATHETIC ANNI-VERSARIES!!!
EEAAAKK

Chapter 211: Precious Anniversary

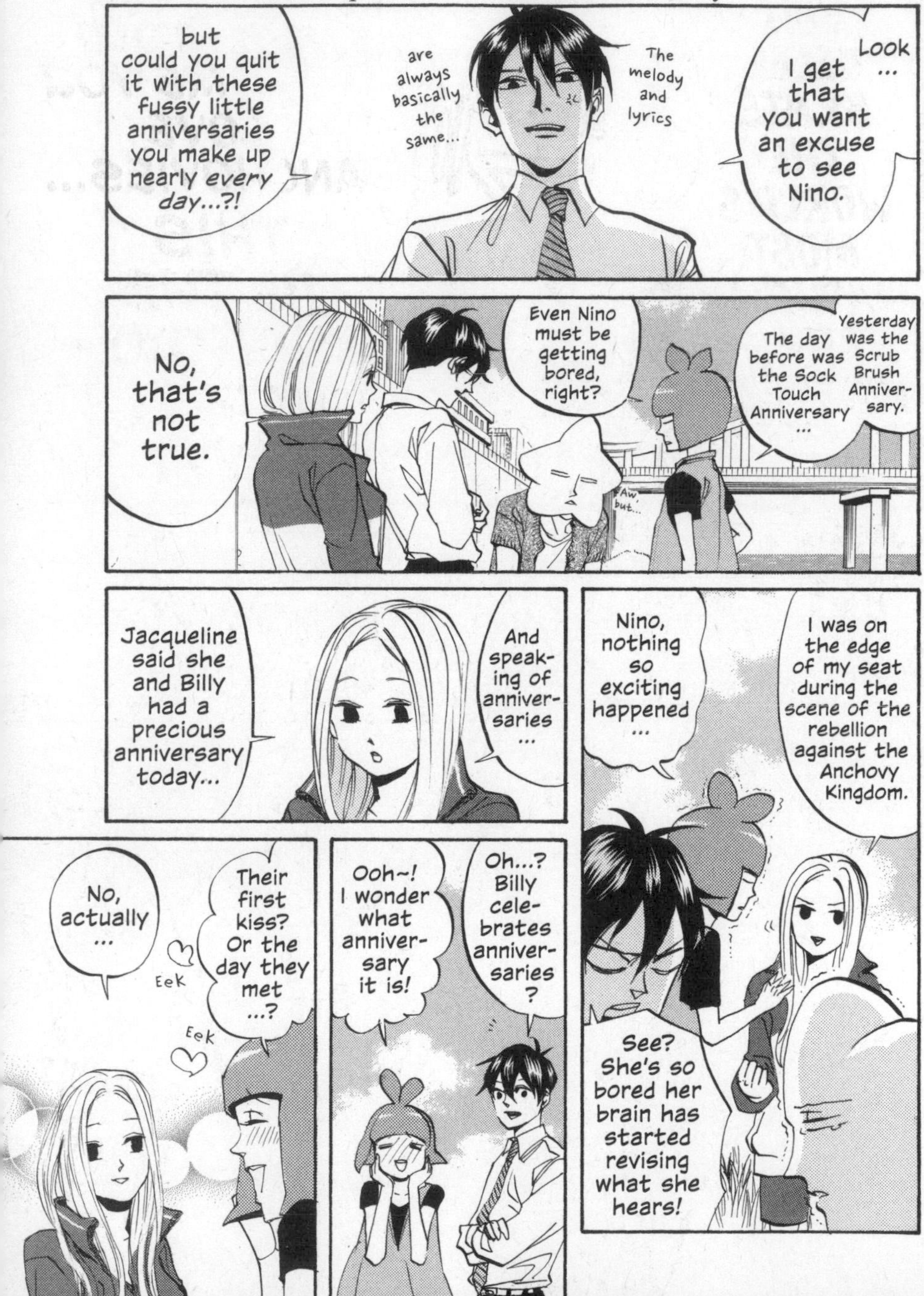
Look ... I get that you want an excuse to see Nino.
The melody and lyrics
are always basically the same...
but could you quit it with these fussy little anniversaries you make up nearly *every* day...?!
Yesterday was the Scrub Brush Anniversary.
The day before was the Sock Touch Anniversary ...
Even Nino must be getting bored, right?
Aw, but...
No, that's not true.
I was on the edge of my seat during the scene of the rebellion against the Anchovy Kingdom.
Nino, nothing so exciting happened ...
See? She's so bored her brain has started revising what she hears!
And speaking of anniversaries ...
Jacqueline said she and Billy had a precious anniversary today...
Oh...? Billy celebrates anniversaries ?
Ooh~! I wonder what anniversary it is!
Their first kiss? Or the day they met ...?
Eek
Eek
No, actually ...

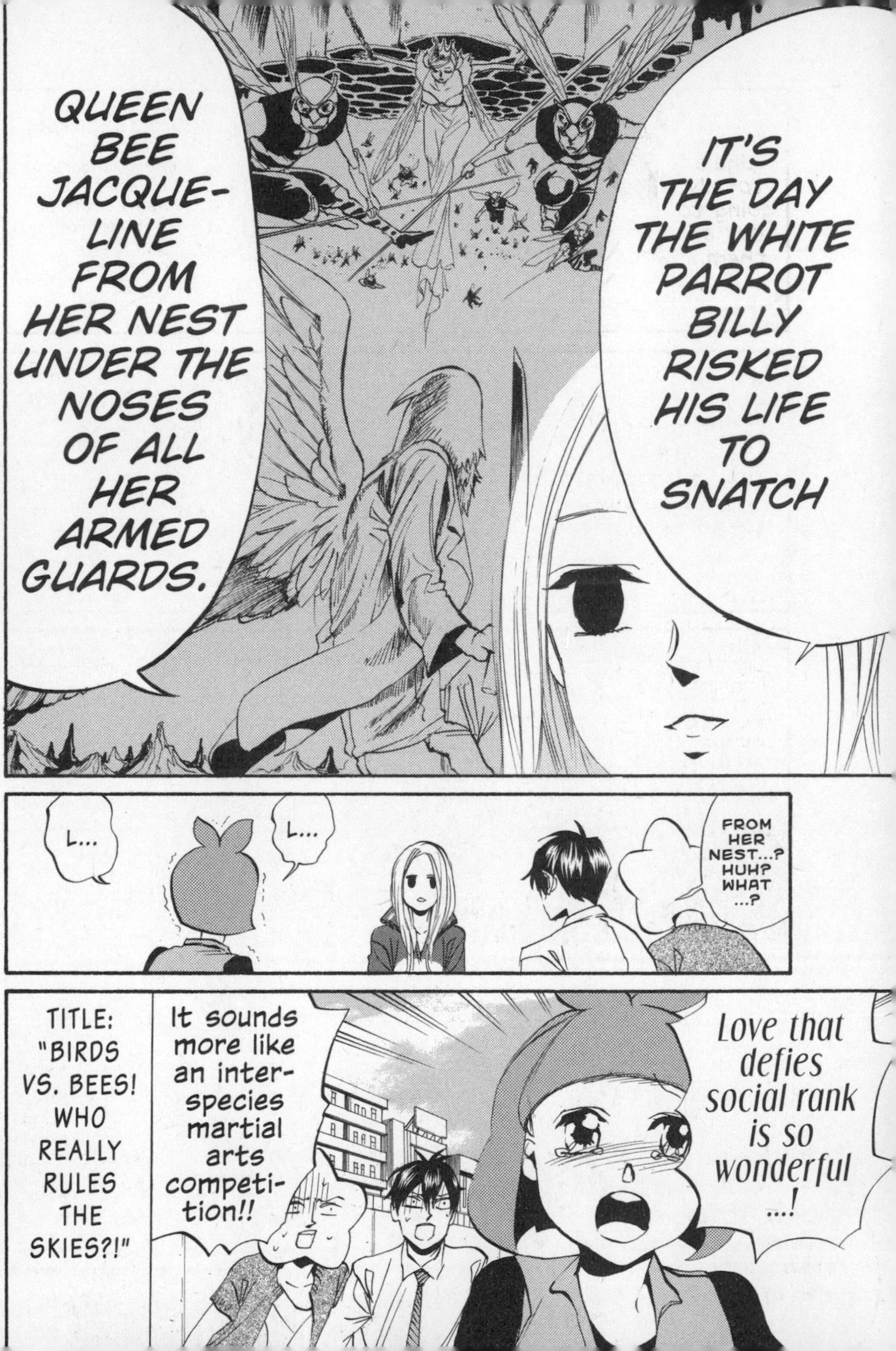
IT'S THE DAY THE WHITE PARROT BILLY RISKED HIS LIFE TO SNATCH
QUEEN BEE JACQUE-LINE FROM HER NEST UNDER THE NOSES OF ALL HER ARMED GUARDS.
FROM HER NEST...? HUH? WHAT ...?
L...
L...
Love that defies social rank is so wonderful ...!
It sounds more like an inter-species martial arts competi-tion!!
TITLE: "BIRDS VS. BEES! WHO REALLY RULES THE SKIES?!"

Chapter 212: Deepening Truth

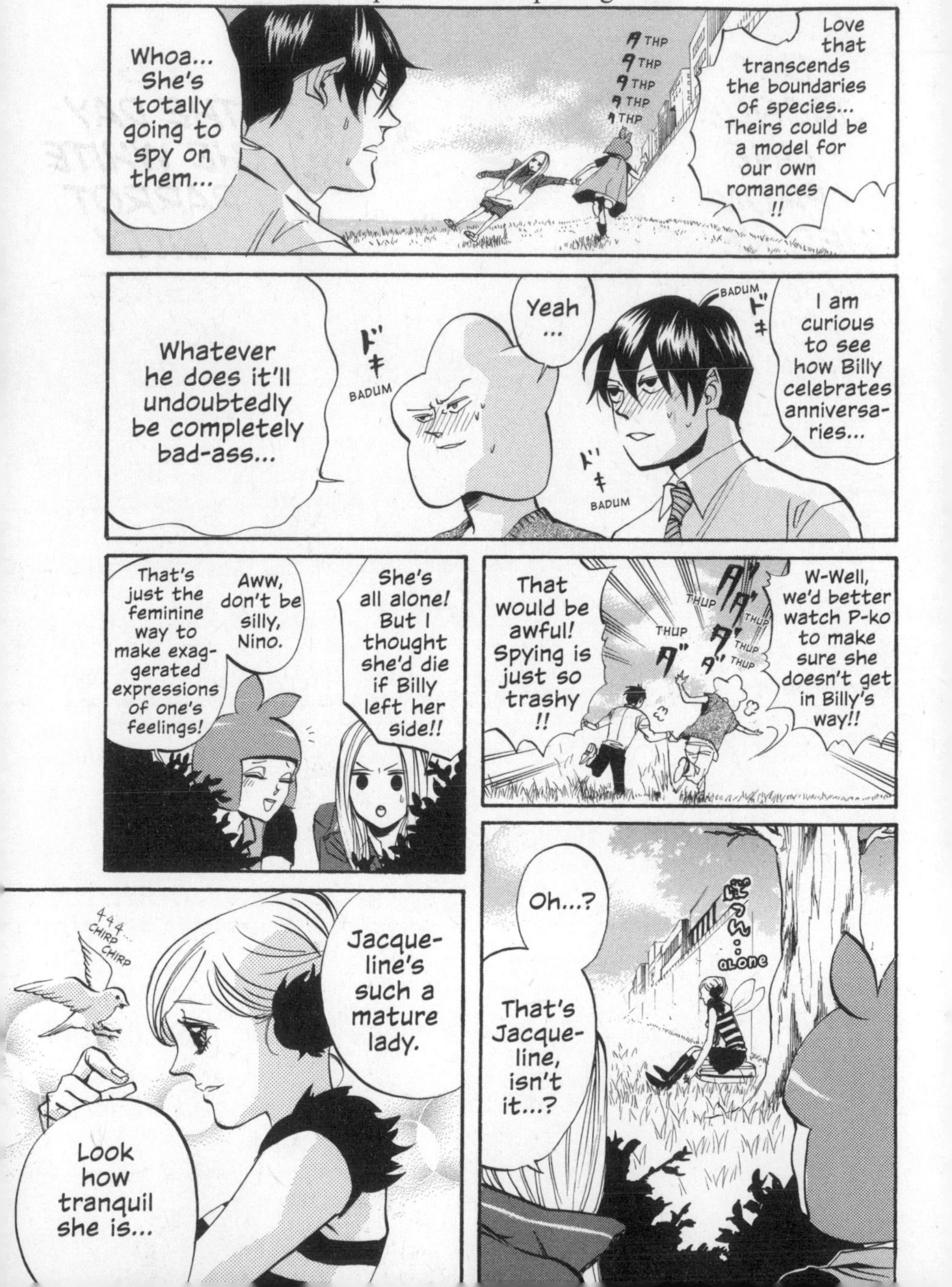

Love that transcends the boundaries of species... Theirs could be a model for our own romances !!
THP THP THP THP THP
Whoa... She's totally going to spy on them...
I am curious to see how Billy celebrates anniversa-ries...
BADUM
Yeah ...
BADUM
BADUM
Whatever he does it'll undoubtedly be completely bad-ass...
W-Well, we'd better watch P-ko to make sure she doesn't get in Billy's way!!
THUP THUP THUP THUP THUP
That would be awful! Spying is just so trashy !!
She's all alone! But I thought she'd die if Billy left her side!!
Aww, don't be silly, Nino.
That's just the feminine way to make exag-gerated expressions of one's feelings!
Oh...?
ALONE
That's Jacque-line, isn't it...?
Jacque-line's such a mature lady.
CHIRP CHIRP
Look how tranquil she is...

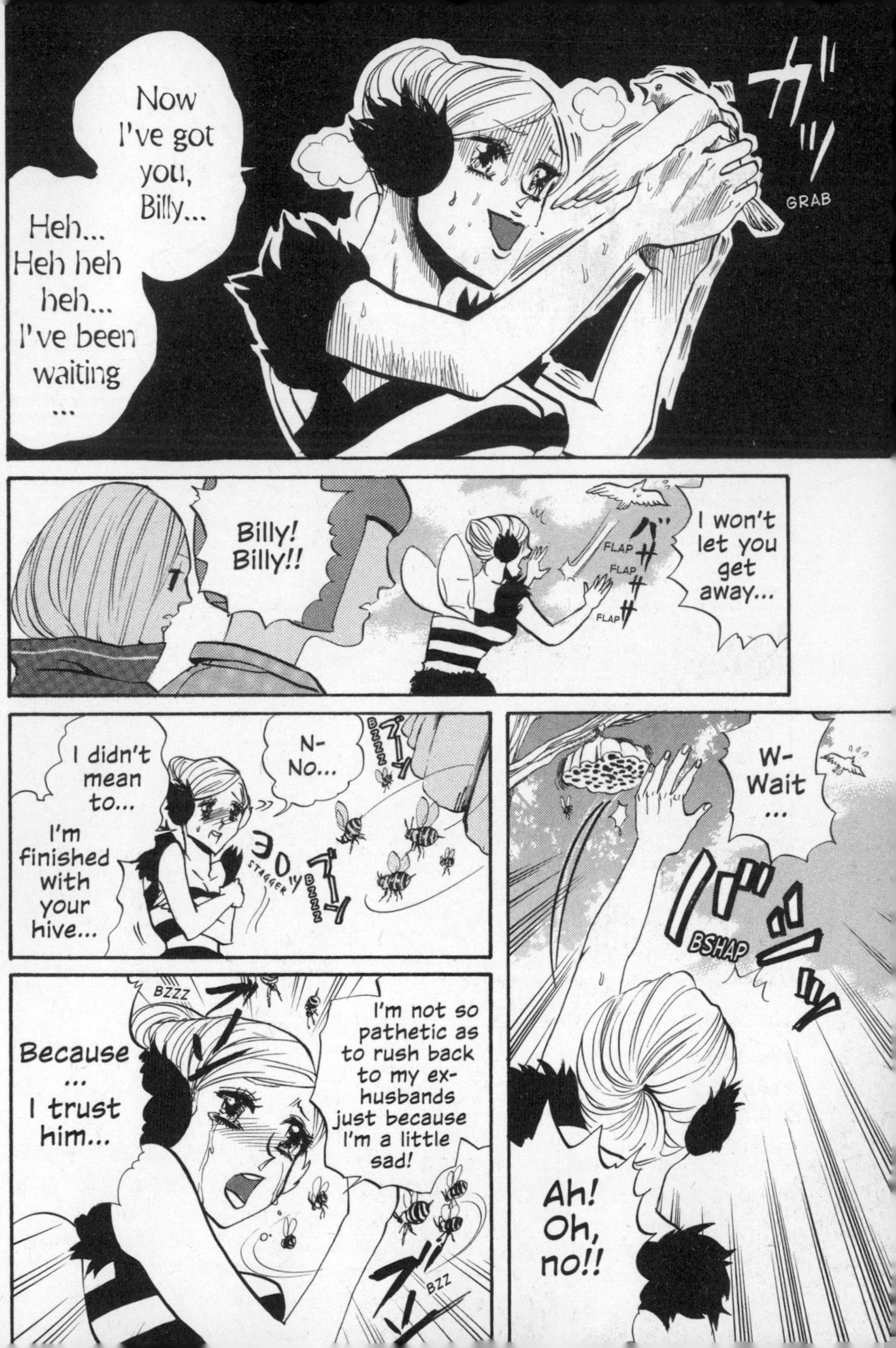
GRAB
Now I've got you, Billy...
Heh... Heh heh heh... I've been waiting ...
I won't let you get away...
FLAP
FLAP
FLAP
Billy! Billy!!
W- Wait ...
BSHAP
Ah! Oh, no!!
N- No...
BZZZ
STAGGER
BZZZ
I didn't mean to...
I'm finished with your hive...
I'm not so pathetic as to rush back to my ex-husbands just because I'm a little sad!
BZZZ
Because ... I trust him...
BZZ

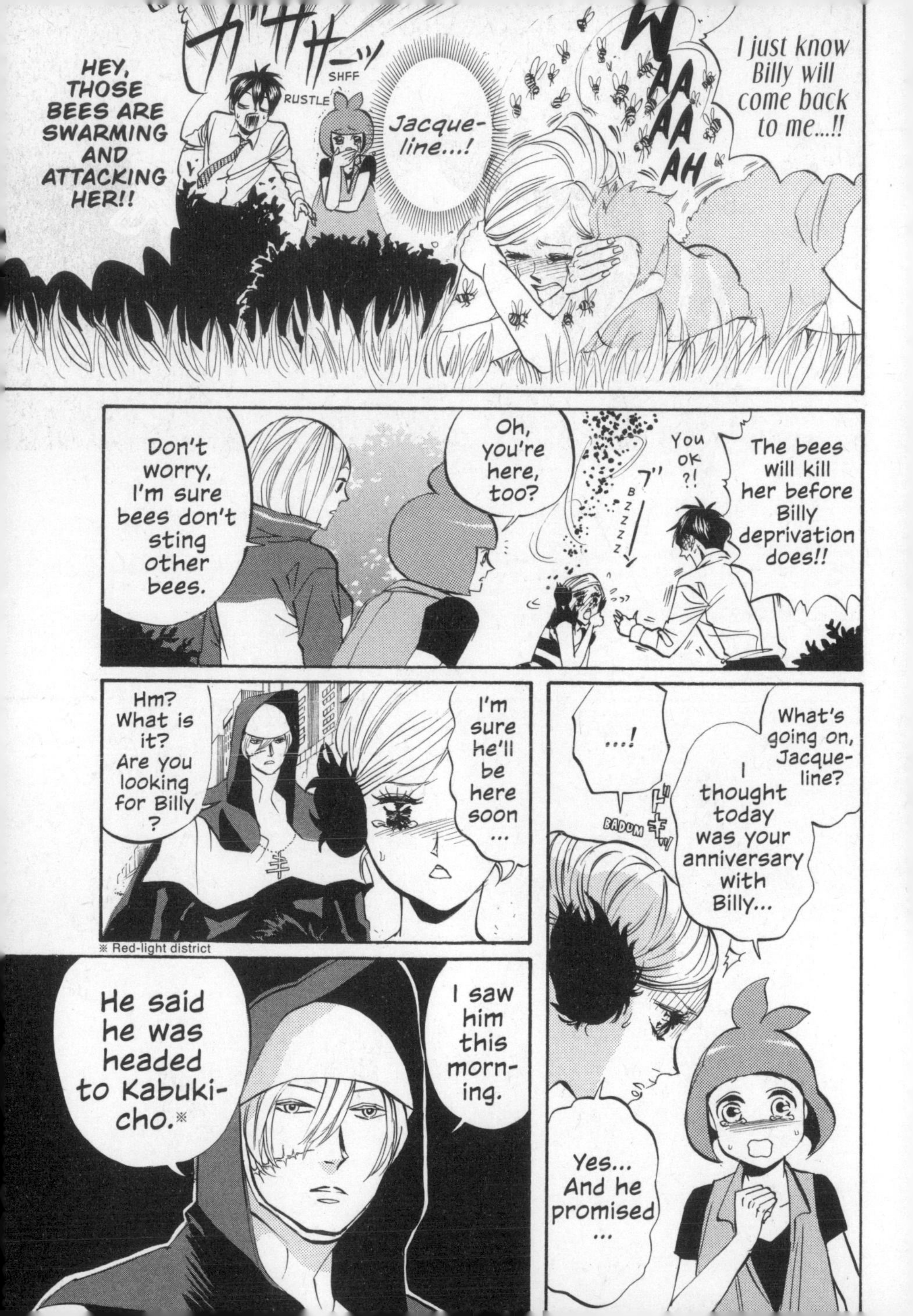
I just know Billy will come back to me...!!
WAAAAAH
Jacqueline...!
SHFF
RUSTLE
HEY, THOSE BEES ARE SWARMING AND ATTACKING HER!!
The bees will kill her before Billy deprivation does!!
You OK?!
BZZZZ
Oh, you're here, too?
Don't worry, I'm sure bees don't sting other bees.
What's going on, Jacqueline?
I thought today was your anniversary with Billy...
...!
BADUM
Yes... And he promised...
I'm sure he'll be here soon...
Hm? What is it? Are you looking for Billy?
I saw him this morning.
He said he was headed to Kabuki-cho.※

※ Red-light district

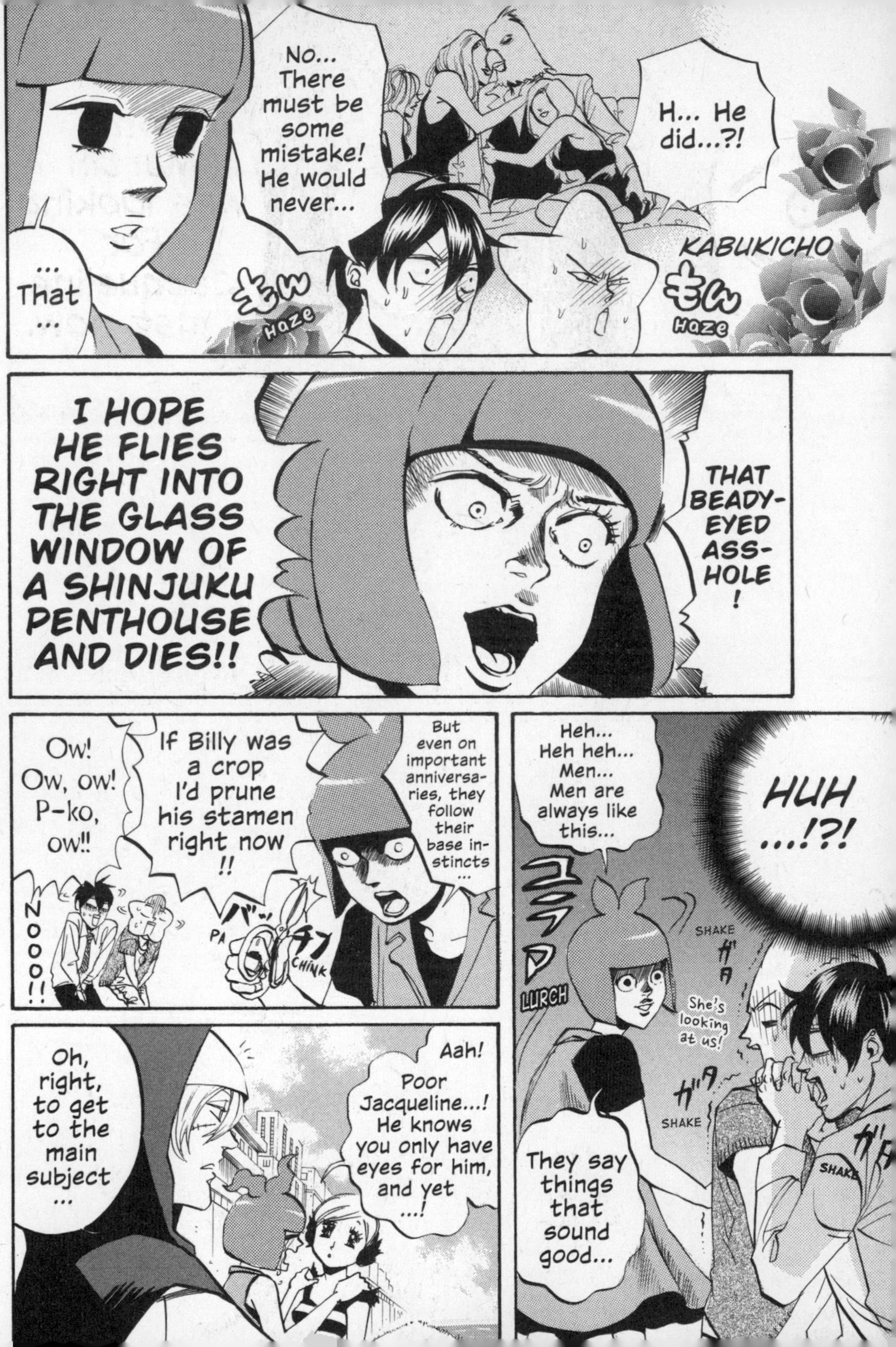
H... He did...?!
KABUKICHO
Haze
No... There must be some mistake! He would never...
Haze
... That ...
THAT BEADY-EYED ASS-HOLE!
I HOPE HE FLIES RIGHT INTO THE GLASS WINDOW OF A SHINJUKU PENTHOUSE AND DIES!!
HUH ...!?!
Heh... Heh heh... Men... Men are always like this...
SHAKE
She's looking at us!
LURCH
SHAKE
They say things that sound good...
SHAKE
But even on important anniversa-ries, they follow their base in-stincts ...
If Billy was a crop I'd prune his stamen right now !!
CHINK
PA
Ow! Ow, ow! P-ko, ow!!
NOOOO!!
Aah! Poor Jacqueline...! He knows you only have eyes for him, and yet ...!
Oh, right, to get to the main subject ...

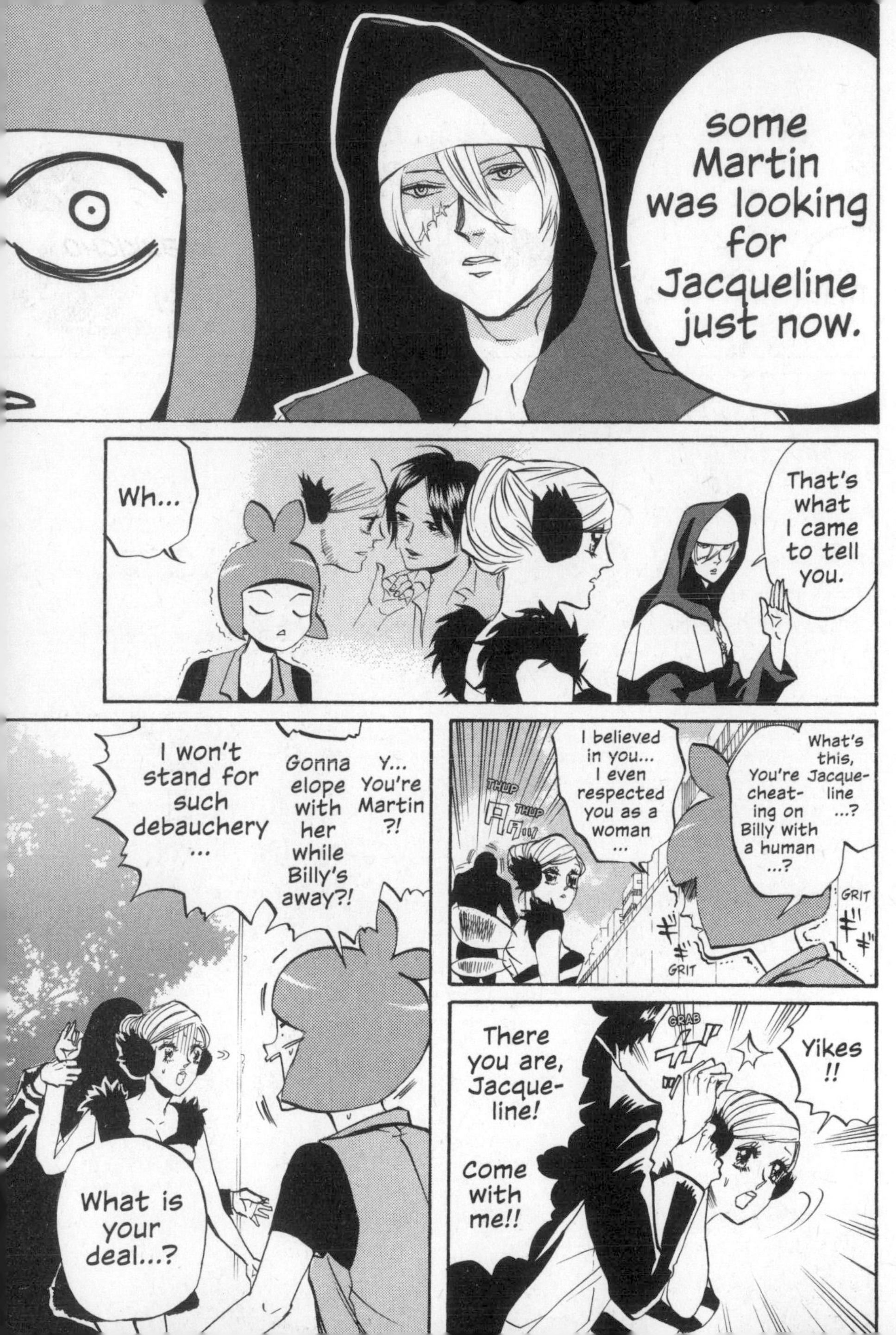
some Martin was looking for Jacqueline just now.
That's what I came to tell you.
Wh...
What's this, Jacqueline ...?
You're cheating on Billy with a human ...?
I believed in you... I even respected you as a woman ...
THUP
THUP
GRIT
GRIT
Yikes !!
GRAB
There you are, Jacqueline!
Come with me!!
Y... You're Martin ?!
Gonna elope with her while Billy's away?!
I won't stand for such debauchery ...
What is your deal...?

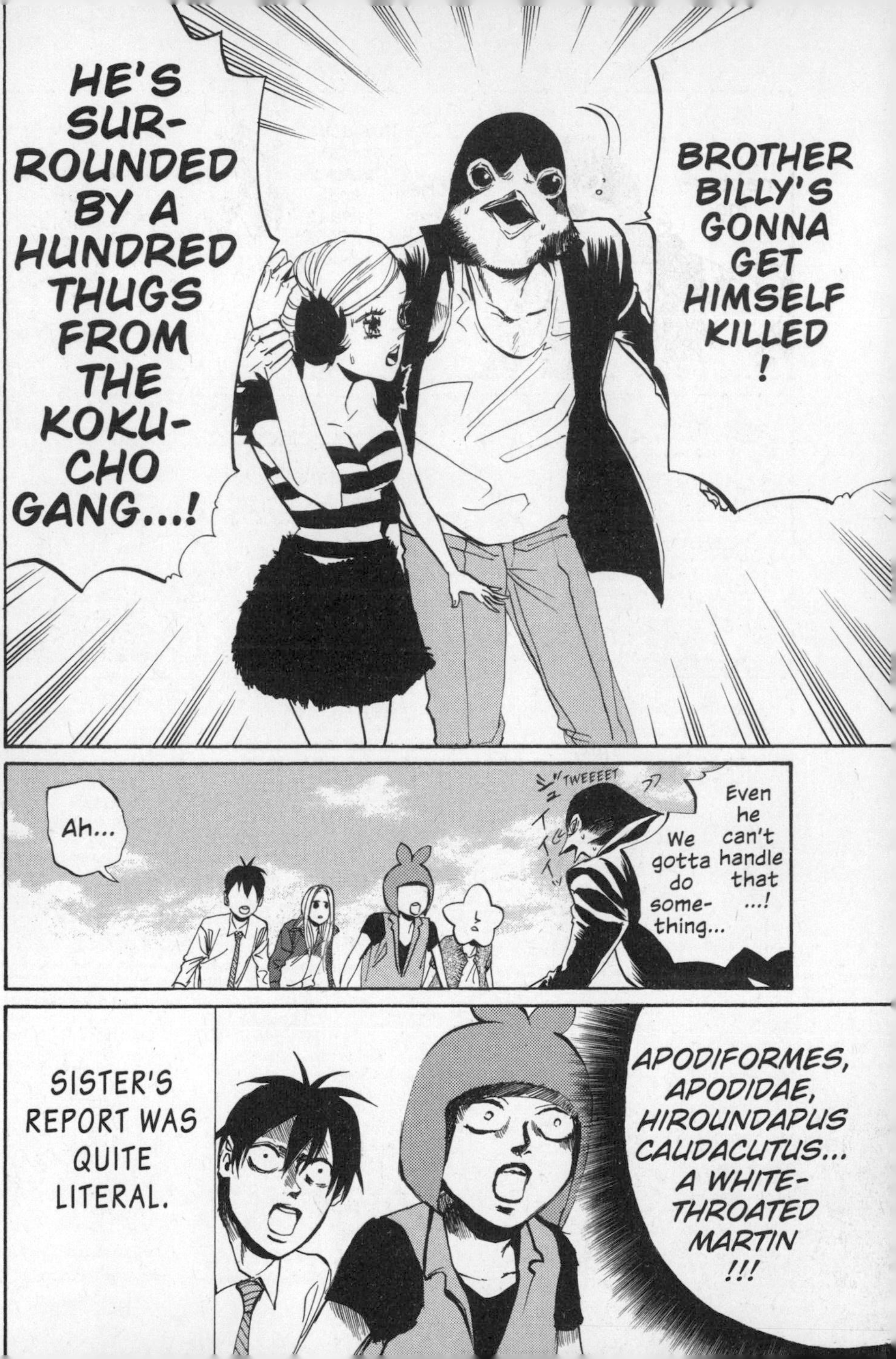
BROTHER BILLY'S GONNA GET HIMSELF KILLED!
HE'S SURROUNDED BY A HUNDRED THUGS FROM THE KOKUCHO GANG...!
Even he can't handle that...!
We gotta do something...
TWEEEET
Ah...
APODIFORMES, APODIDAE, HIROUNDAPUS CAUDACUTUS... A WHITE-THROATED MARTIN!!!
SISTER'S REPORT WAS QUITE LITERAL.

Chapter 213: Love O'eperches Species

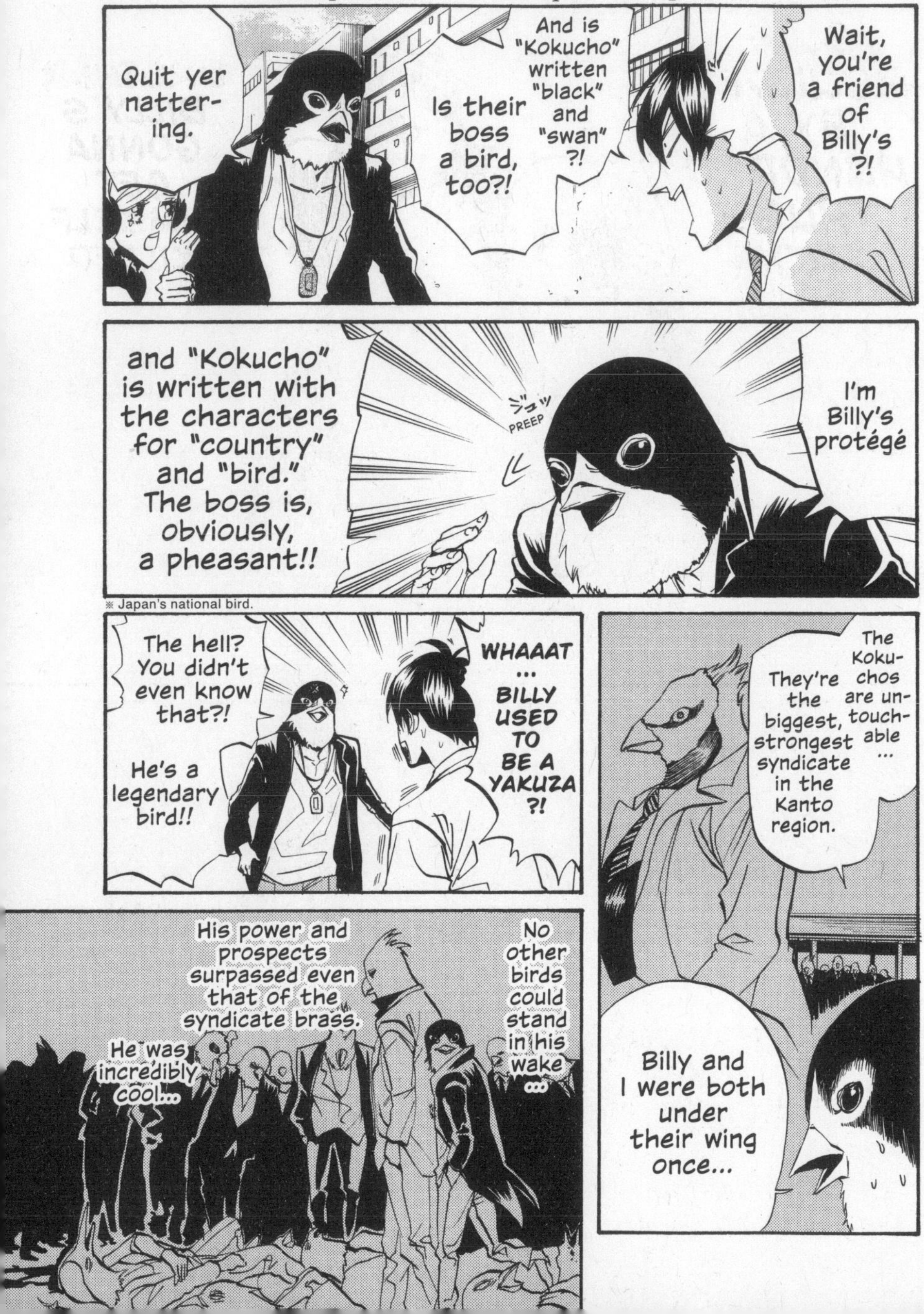

Wait, you're a friend of Billy's?!
And is "Kokucho" written "black" and "swan"?!
Is their boss a bird, too?!
Quit yer natter-ing.
I'm Billy's protégé
PREEP
and "Kokucho" is written with the characters for "country" and "bird." The boss is, obviously, a pheasant!!
※ Japan's national bird.
The Kokuchos are untouchable...
They're the biggest, strongest syndicate in the Kanto region.
Billy and I were both under their wing once...
WHAAAT... BILLY USED TO BE A YAKUZA?!
The hell? You didn't even know that?!
He's a legendary bird!!
No other birds could stand in his wake...
His power and prospects surpassed even that of the syndicate brass.
He was incredibly cool...

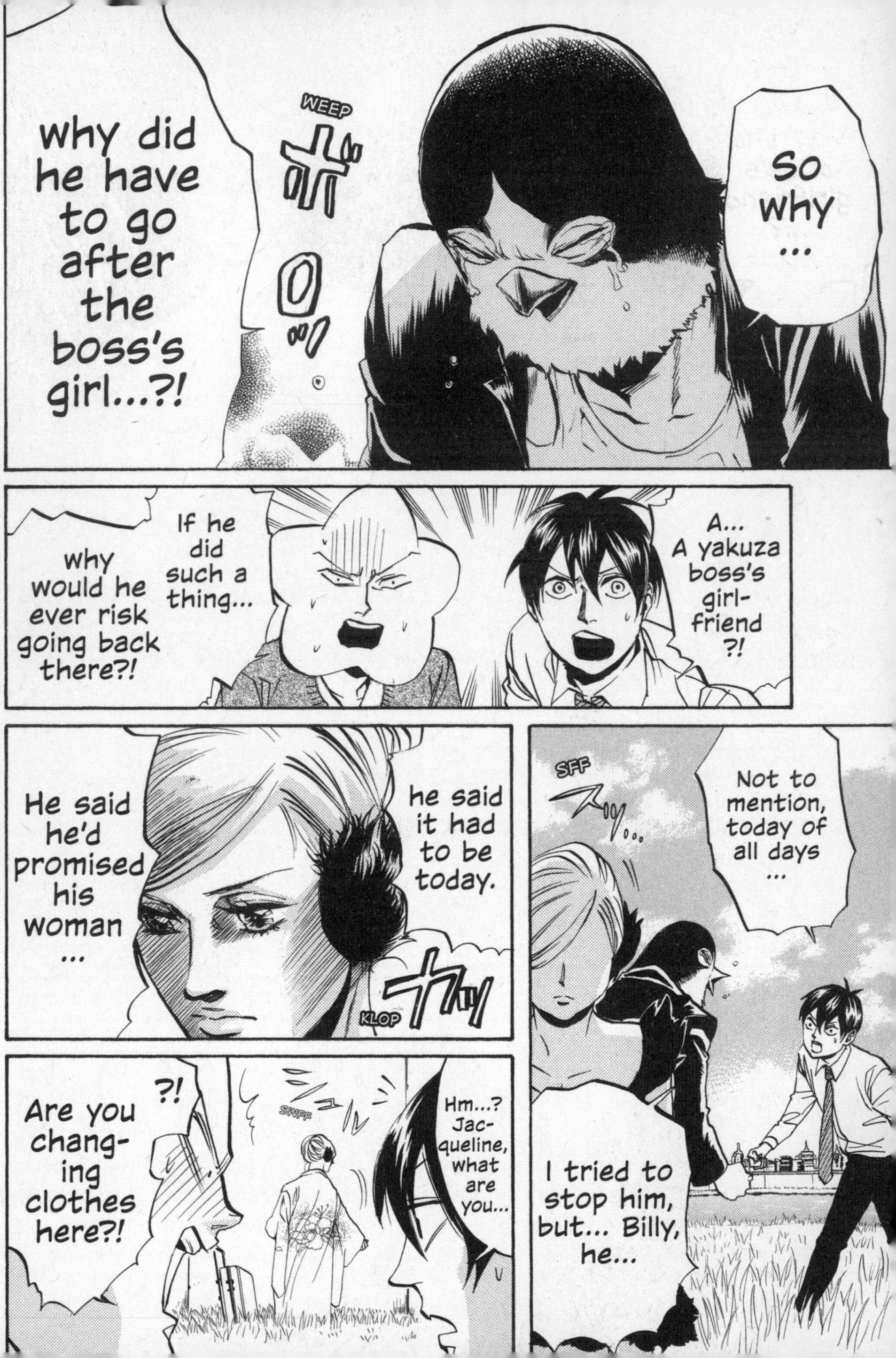
So why...
WEEP
why did he have to go after the boss's girl...?!
A... A yakuza boss's girlfriend?!
If he did such a thing...
why would he ever risk going back there?!
SFF
Not to mention, today of all days...
I tried to stop him, but... Billy, he...
he said it had to be today.
He said he'd promised his woman...
KLOP
Hm...? Jacqueline, what are you...
SWFF
?!
Are you changing clothes here?!

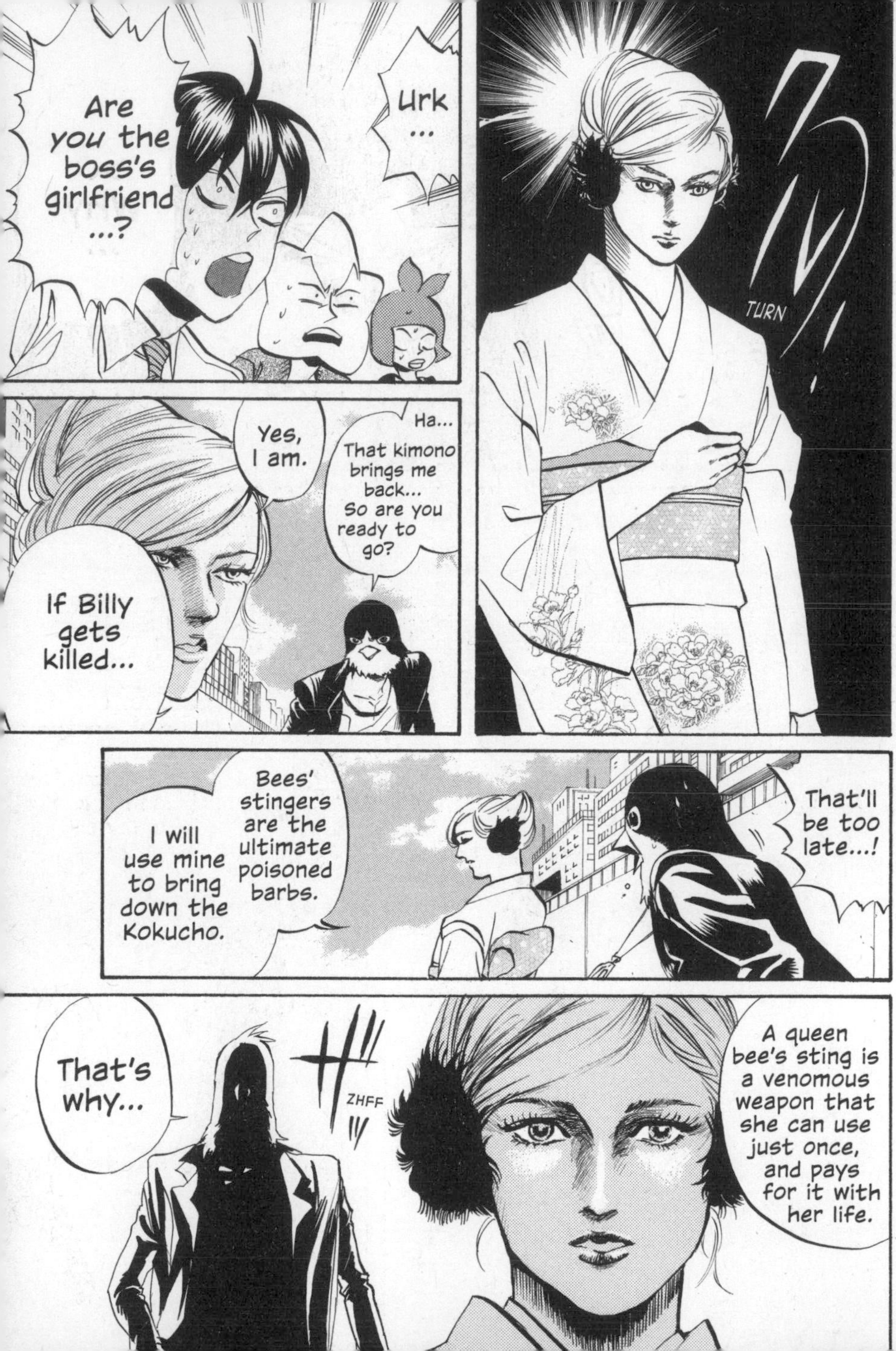
Are you the boss's girlfriend ...?
Urk ...
Yes, I am.
Ha... That kimono brings me back... So are you ready to go?
If Billy gets killed...
TURN
Bees' stingers are the ultimate poisoned barbs.
I will use mine to bring down the Kokucho.
That'll be too late...!
That's why...
ZHFF
A queen bee's sting is a venomous weapon that she can use just once, and pays for it with her life.

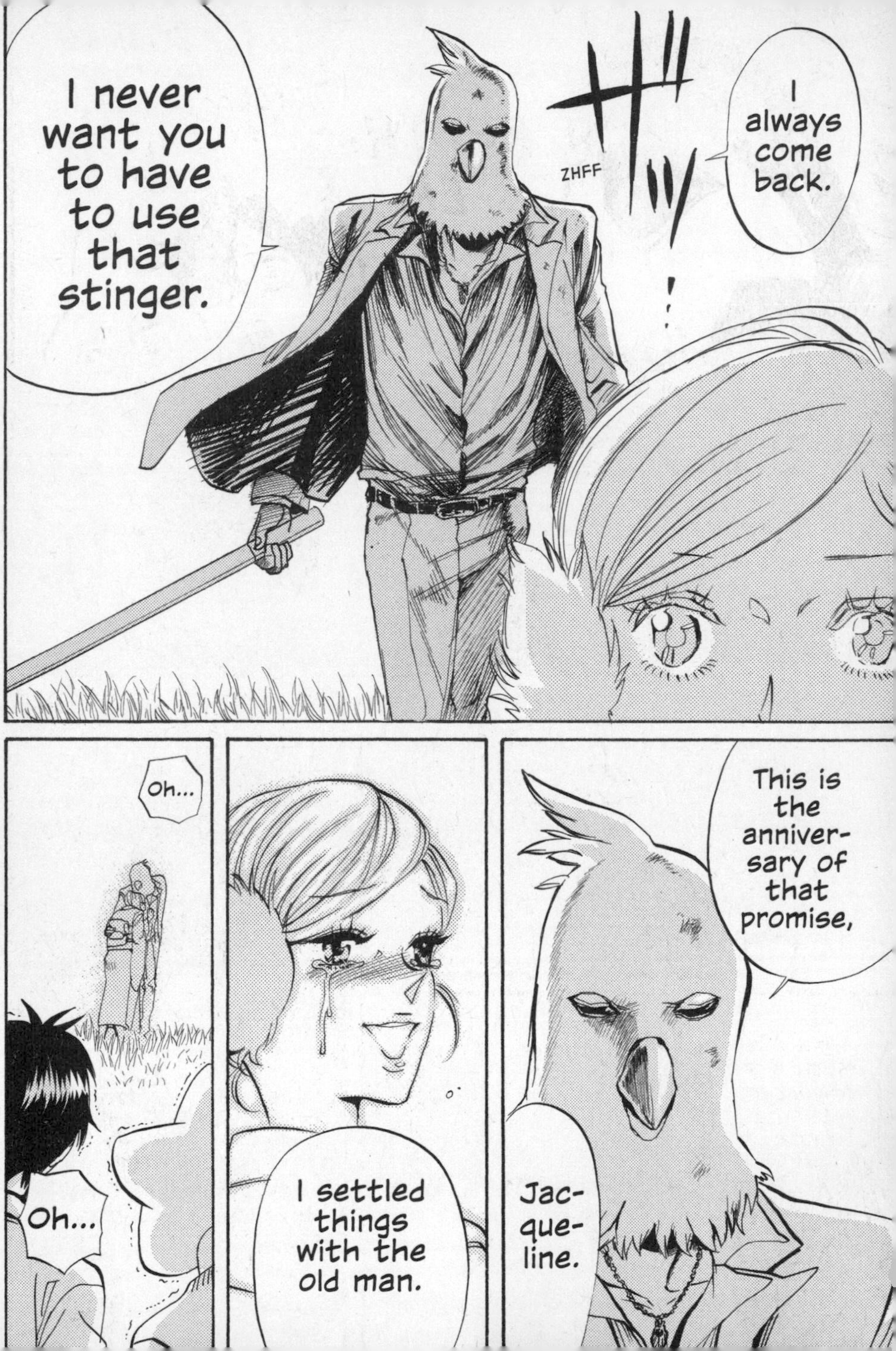
I always come back.
ZHFF
I never want you to have to use that stinger.
This is the anniver-sary of that promise,
Jac-que-line.
I settled things with the old man.
Oh...
Oh...

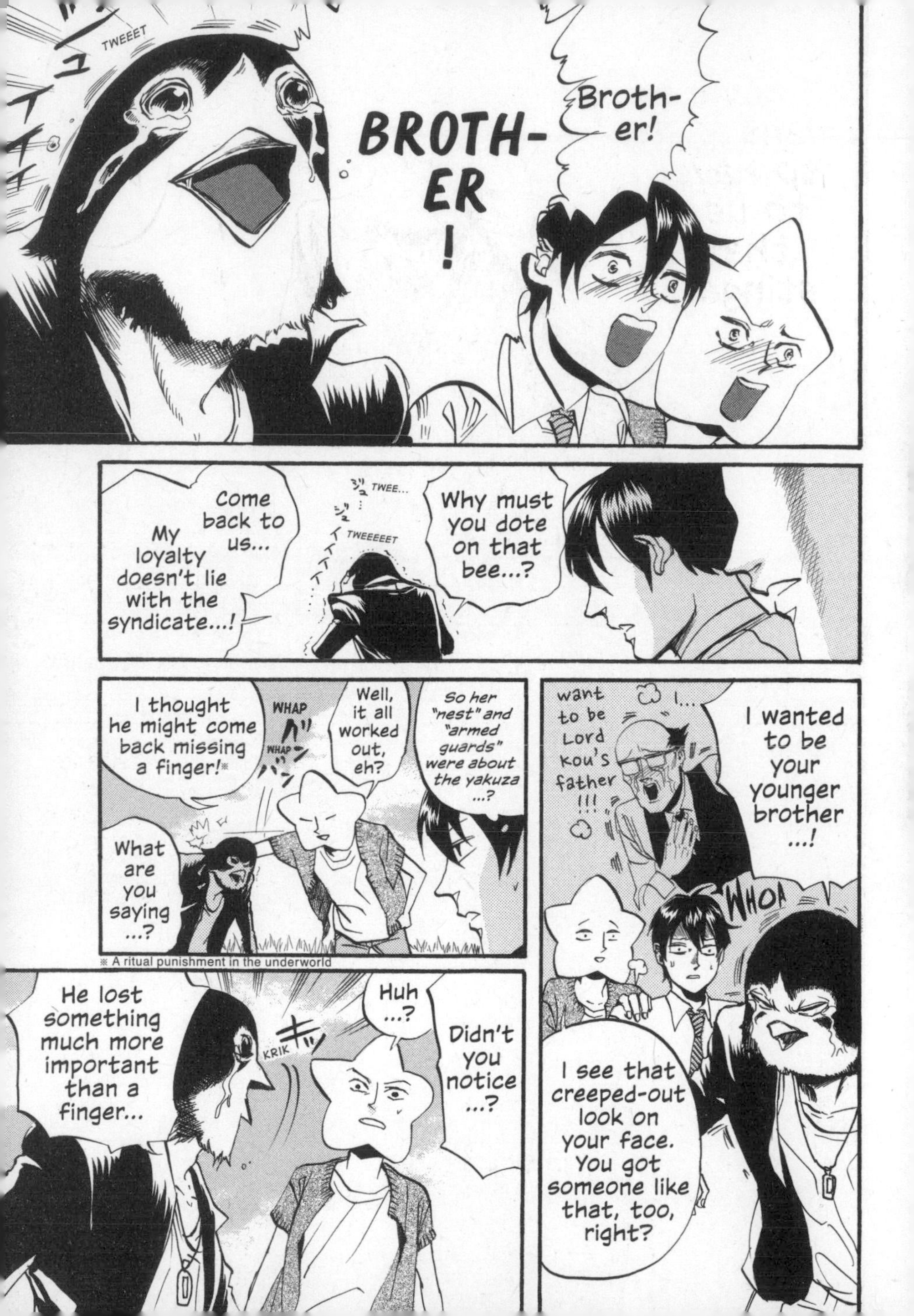
Brother-er!
BROTHER!
TWEEET
Why must you dote on that bee...?
TWEE...
TWEEEEET
Come back to us...
My loyalty doesn't lie with the syndicate...!
I wanted to be your younger brother...!
I... want to be Lord Kou's father!!!
WHOA
I see that creeped-out look on your face. You got someone like that, too, right?
So her "nest" and "armed guards" were about the yakuza...?
Well, it all worked out, eh?
WHAP
WHAP
I thought he might come back missing a finger!※
What are you saying...?
※ A ritual punishment in the underworld
Didn't you notice...?
Huh...?
KRIK
He lost something much more important than a finger...

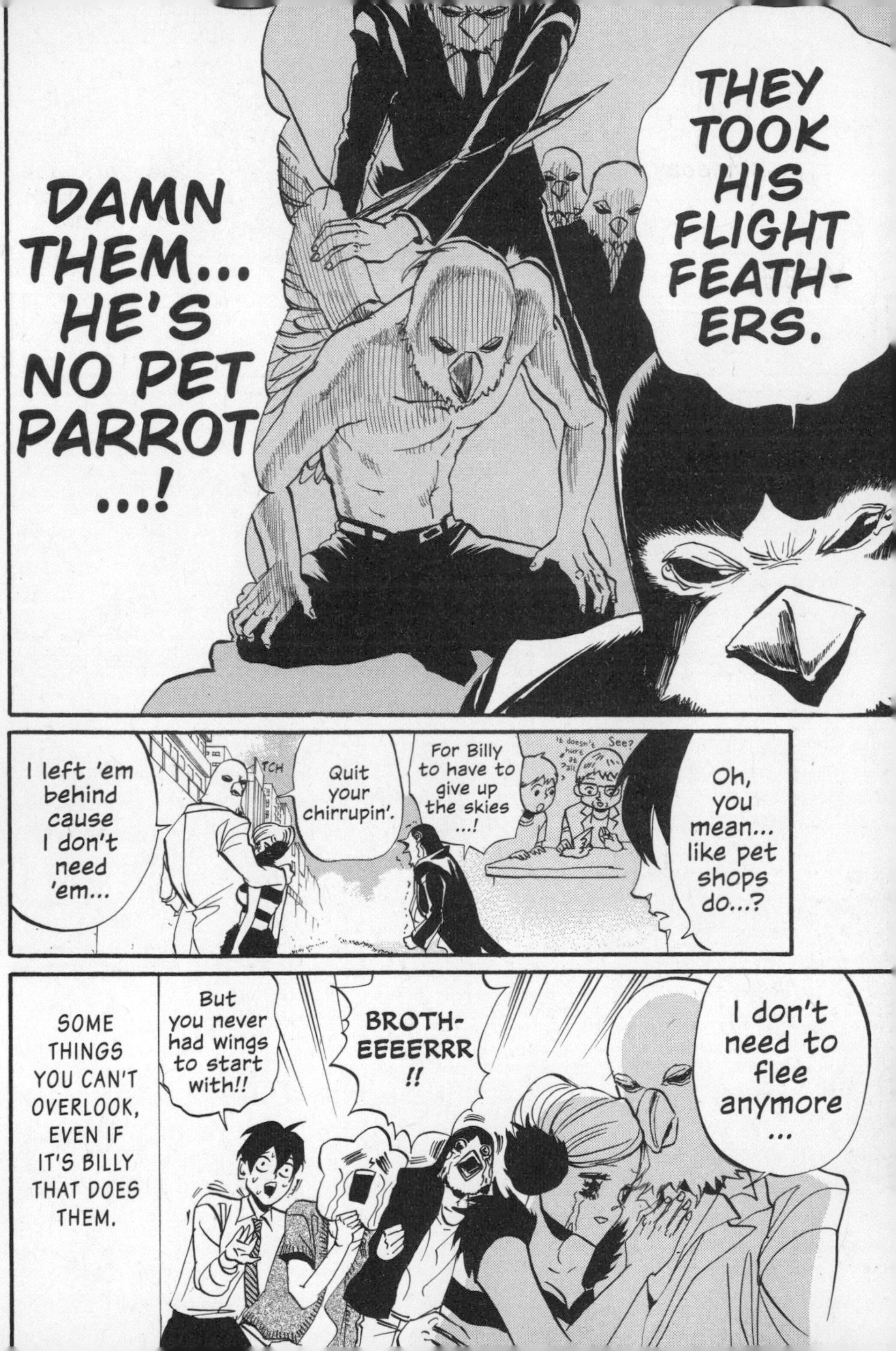
THEY TOOK HIS FLIGHT FEATH-ERS.
DAMN THEM... HE'S NO PET PARROT ...!
Oh, you mean... like pet shops do...?
See?
It doesn't hurt at all
For Billy to have to give up the skies ...!
Quit your chirrupin'.
TCH
I left 'em behind cause I don't need 'em...
I don't need to flee anymore ...
BROTH-EEEERRR !!
But you never had wings to start with!!
SOME THINGS YOU CAN'T OVERLOOK, EVEN IF IT'S BILLY THAT DOES THEM.

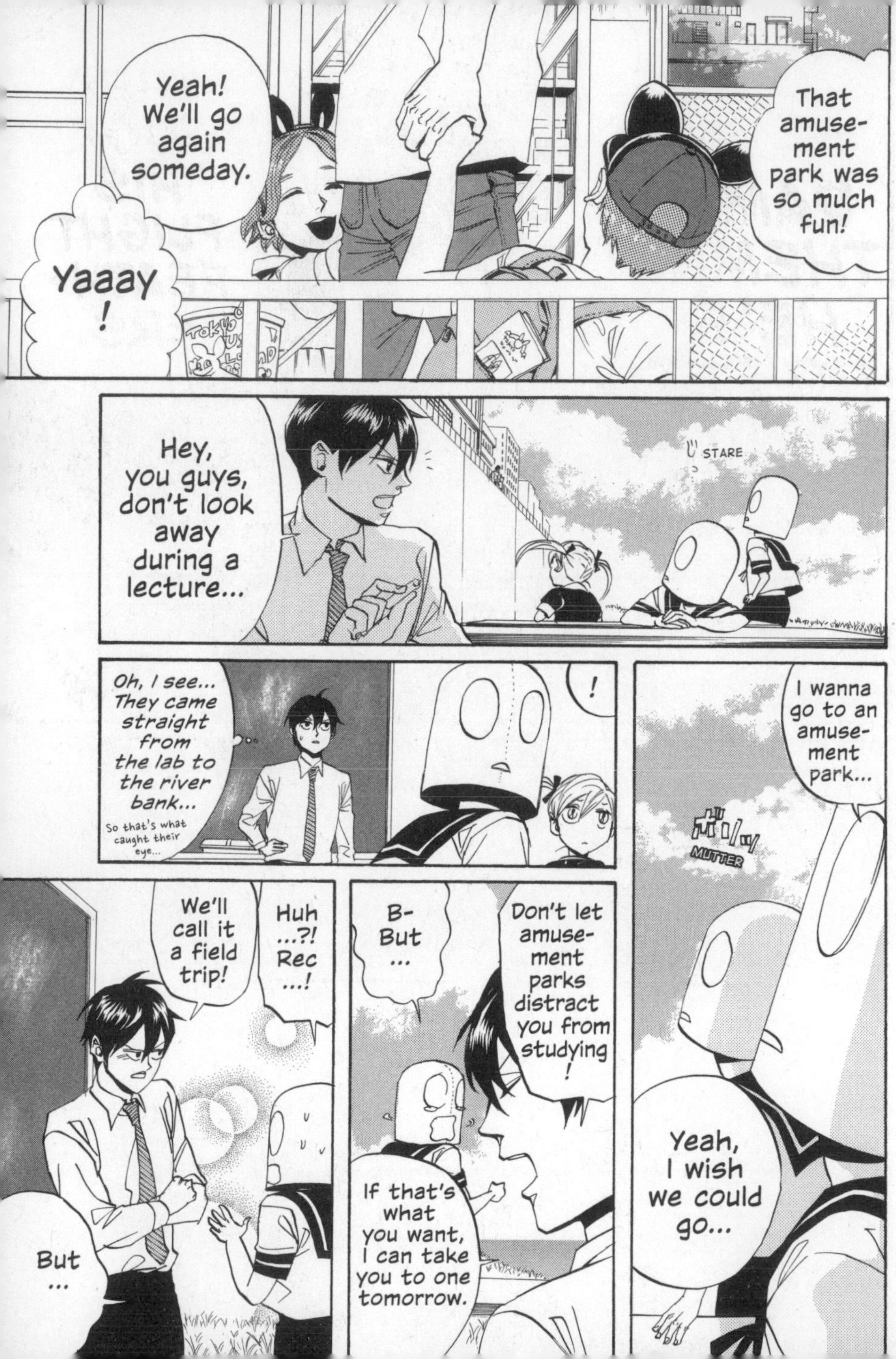
That amusement park was so much fun!
Yeah! We'll go again someday.
Yaaay!
STARE
Hey, you guys, don't look away during a lecture...
I wanna go to an amusement park...
MUTTER
Yeah, I wish we could go...
!
Oh, I see... They came straight from the lab to the river bank...
So that's what caught their eye...
Don't let amusement parks distract you from studying!
B-But...
If that's what you want, I can take you to one tomorrow.
Huh...?! Rec...!
We'll call it a field trip!
But...

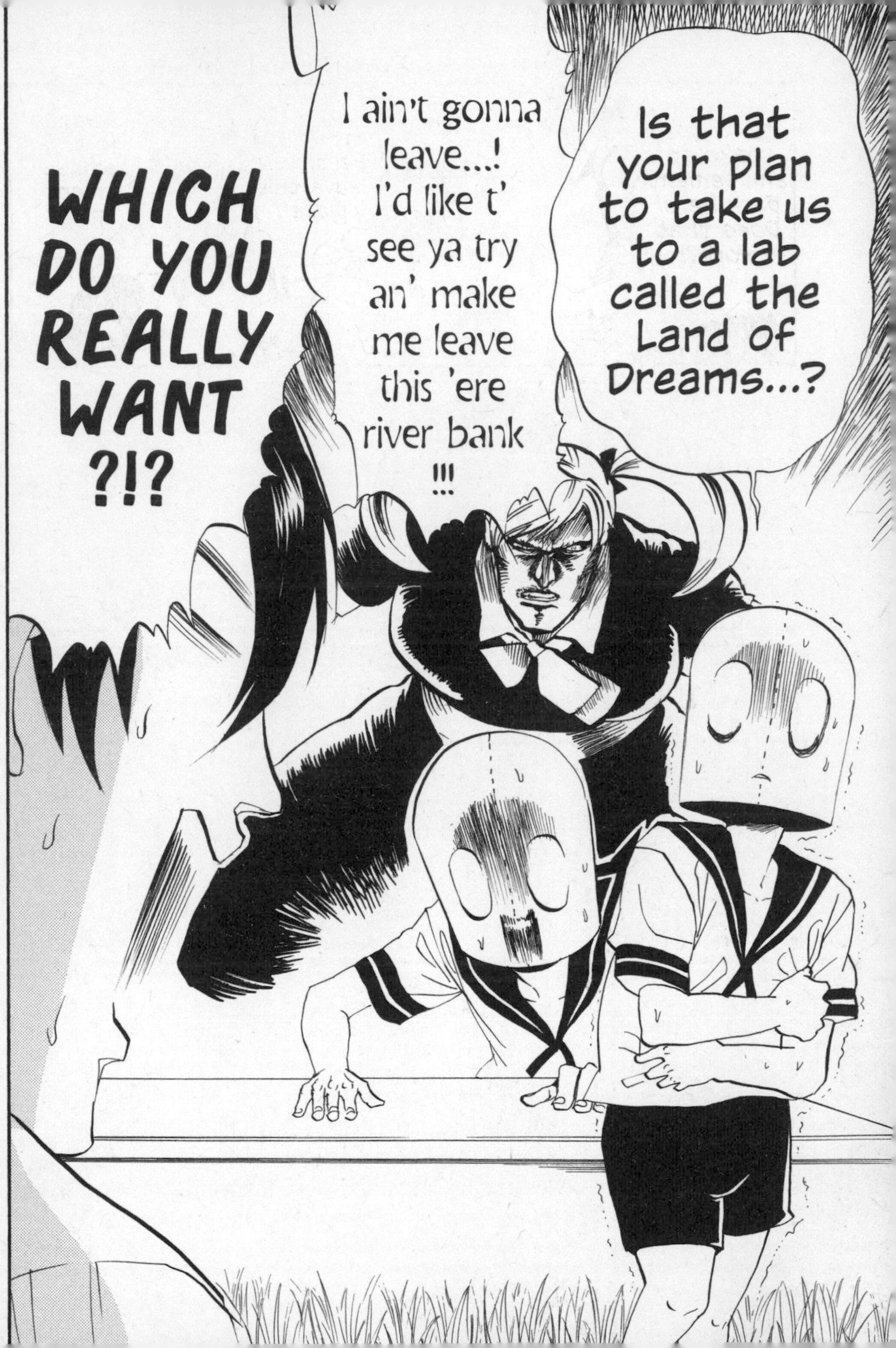
Is that your plan to take us to a lab called the Land of Dreams...?
I ain't gonna leave...! I'd like t' see ya try an' make me leave this 'ere river bank !!!
WHICH DO YOU REALLY WANT ?!?

Chapter 214: Arakawa Dream Land

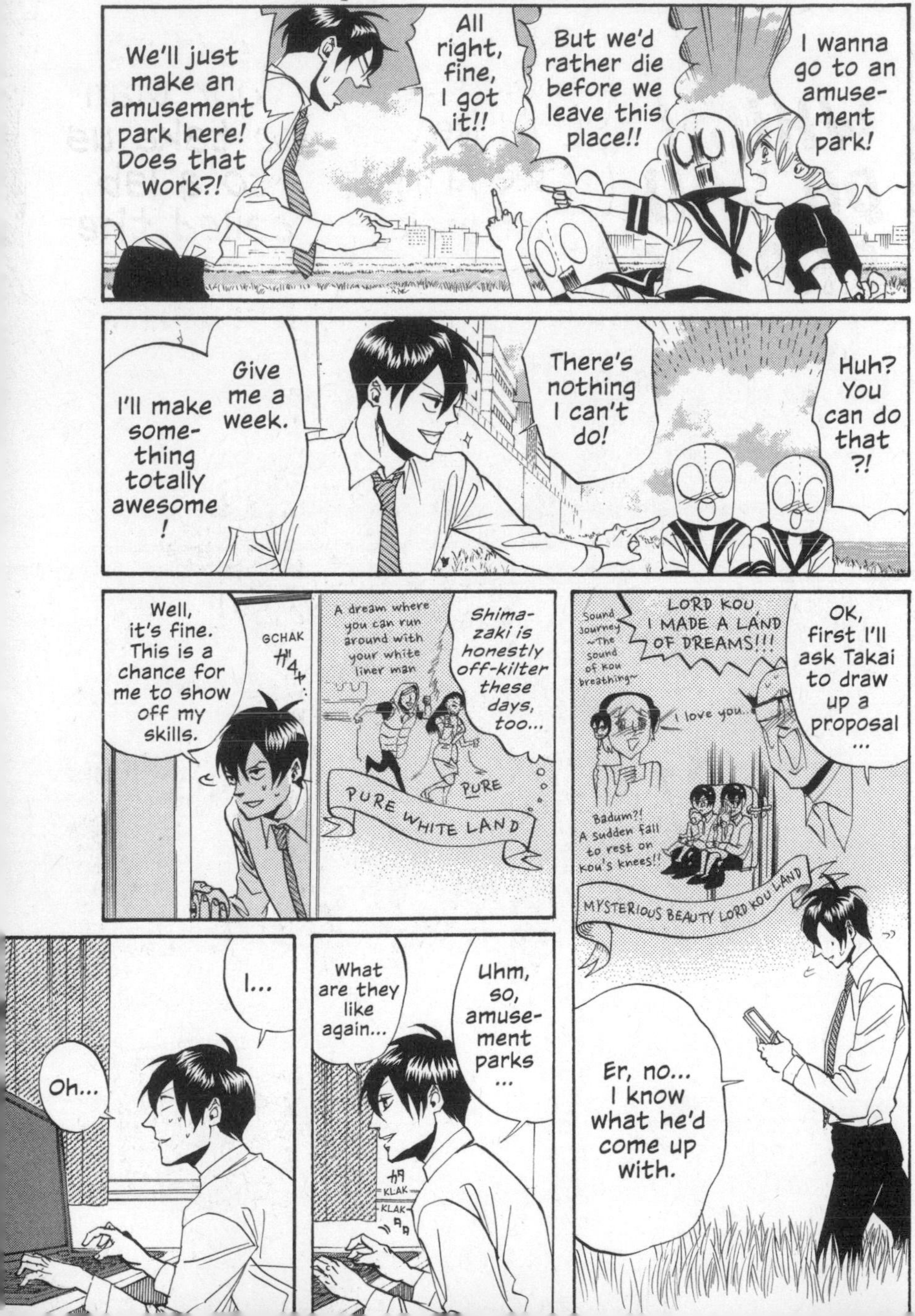

I wanna go to an amusement park!
But we'd rather die before we leave this place!!
All right, fine, I got it!!
We'll just make an amusement park here! Does that work?!
Huh? You can do that?!
There's nothing I can't do!
Give me a week.
I'll make something totally awesome!
OK, first I'll ask Takai to draw up a proposal...
LORD KOU, I MADE A LAND OF DREAMS!!!
Sound Journey ~The sound of Kou breathing~
I love you.
Badum?! A sudden fall to rest on Kou's knees!!
MYSTERIOUS BEAUTY LORD KOU LAND
Er, no... I know what he'd come up with.
Shimazaki is honestly off-kilter these days, too...
A dream where you can run around with your white liner man
PURE PURE
PURE WHITE LAND
GCHAK
Well, it's fine. This is a chance for me to show off my skills.
Uhm, so, amusement parks...
What are they like again...
KLAK
KLAK
I...
Oh...

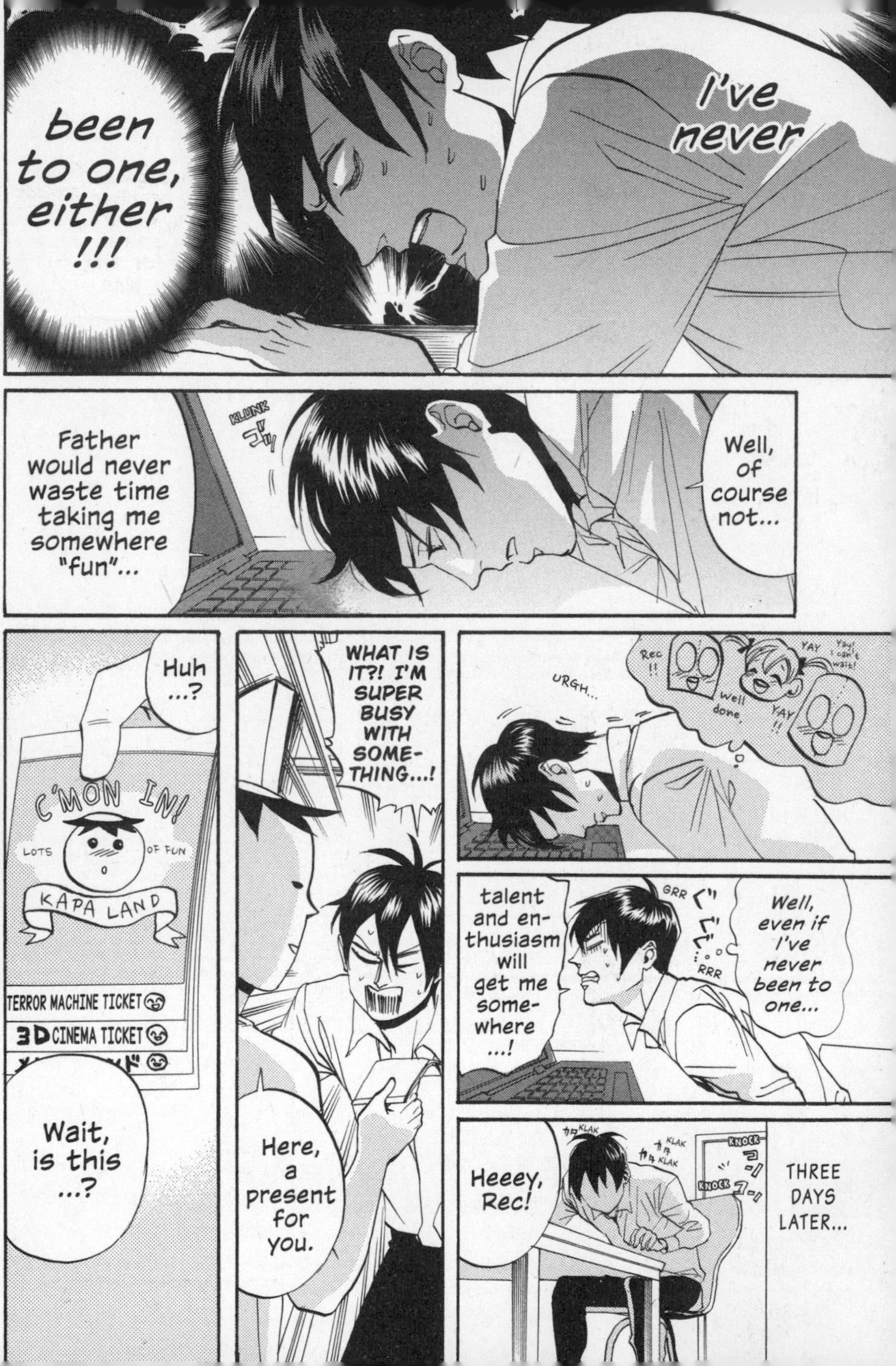
I've never
been to one, either !!!
Well, of course not...
KLUNK
Father would never waste time taking me somewhere "fun"...
Yay! I can't wait!
YAY
Rec !!
Well done
YAY !!
URGH...
Well, even if I've never been to one...
GRR
RRR
talent and enthusiasm will get me somewhere ...!
THREE DAYS LATER...
KNOCK
KNOCK
KLAK
KLAK
KLAK
Heeey, Rec!
WHAT IS IT?! I'M SUPER BUSY WITH SOMETHING...!
Here, a present for you.
Huh ...?
C'MON IN!
LOTS OF FUN
KAPA LAND
TERROR MACHINE TICKET
3D CINEMA TICKET
Wait, is this ...?

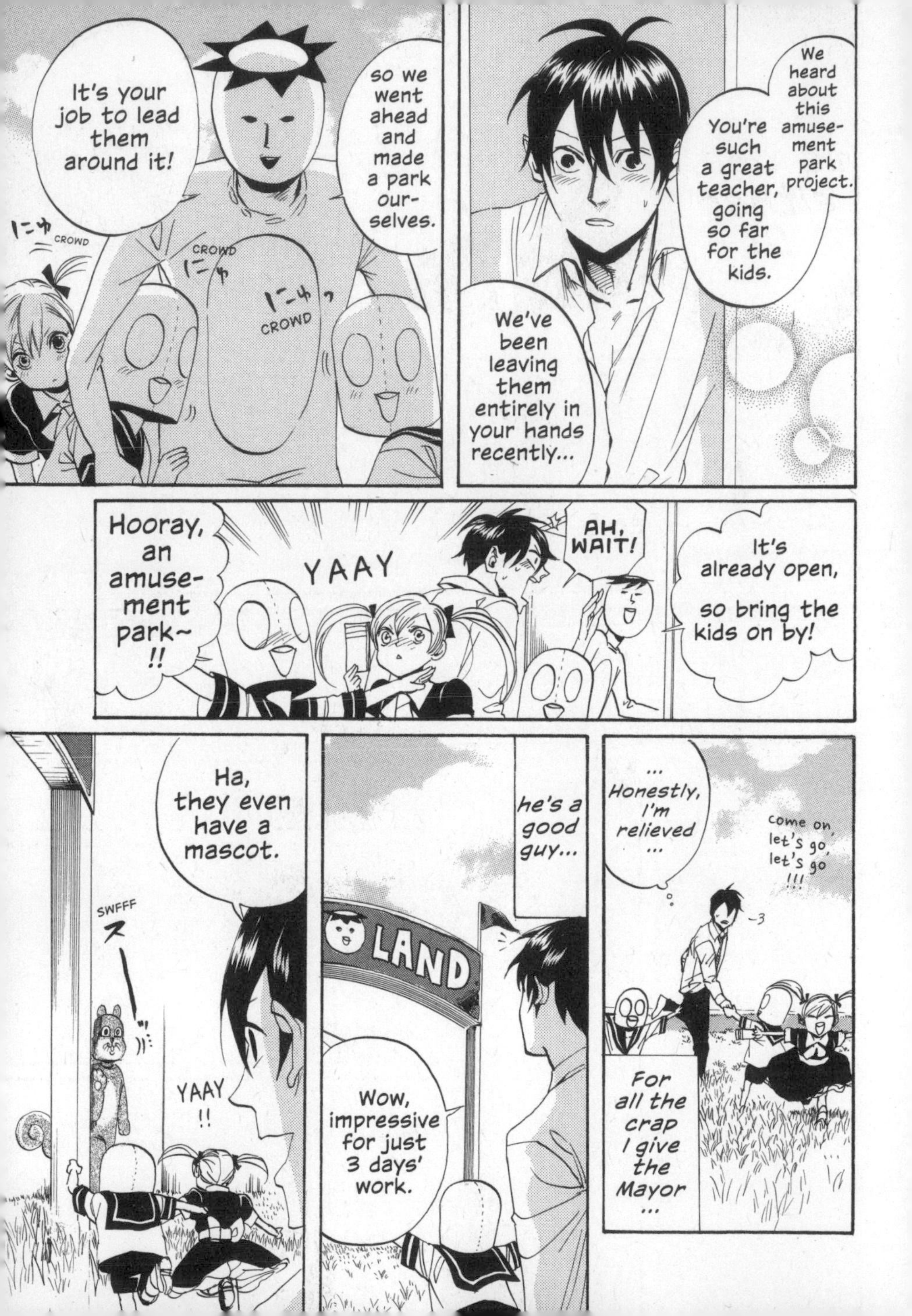
We heard about this amusement park project.
You're such a great teacher, going so far for the kids.
We've been leaving them entirely in your hands recently...
so we went ahead and made a park ourselves.
It's your job to lead them around it!
にゅ CROWD
にゅ CROWD
にゅっ CROWD
It's already open, so bring the kids on by!
AH, WAIT!
YAAY
Hooray, an amusement park~ !!
... Honestly, I'm relieved ...
come on, let's go, let's go !!!
For all the crap I give the Mayor ...
he's a good guy...
LAND
Wow, impressive for just 3 days' work.
Ha, they even have a mascot.
SWFFF
ス
YAAY !!

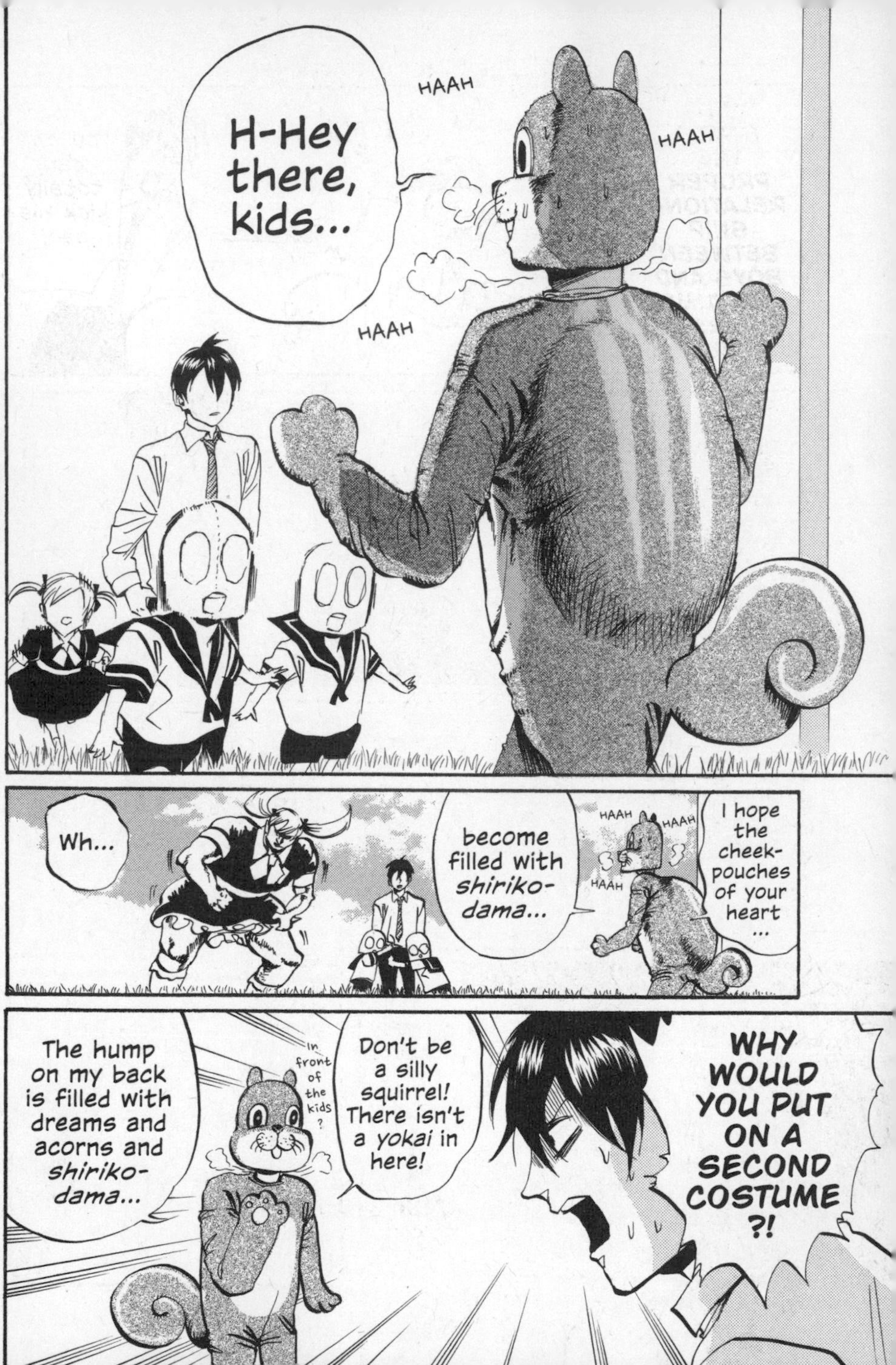
HAAH
HAAH
H-Hey there, kids...
HAAH
I hope the cheek-pouches of your heart ...
HAAH HAAH
HAAH
become filled with *shiriko-dama*...
Wh...
WHY WOULD YOU PUT ON A SECOND COSTUME ?!
Don't be a silly squirrel! There isn't a *yokai* in here!
In front of the kids ?
The hump on my back is filled with dreams and acorns and *shiriko-dama*...

Chapter 215: Attractions

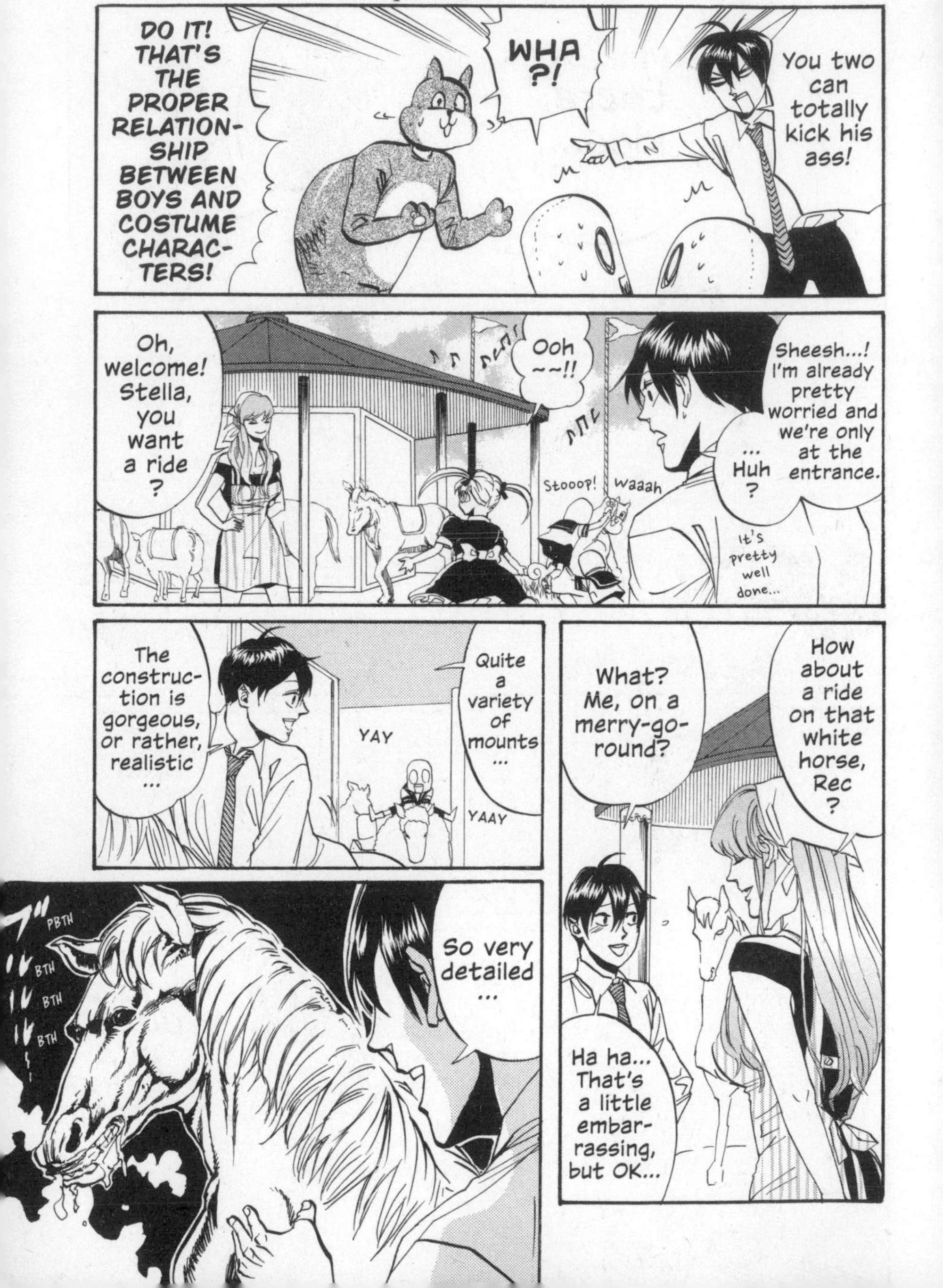

You two can totally kick his ass!
WHA ?!
DO IT! THAT'S THE PROPER RELATIONSHIP BETWEEN BOYS AND COSTUME CHARACTERS!
Sheesh...! I'm already pretty worried and we're only at the entrance.
Ooh ~~!!
Oh, welcome! Stella, you want a ride?
... Huh?
Waaah
Stooop!
It's pretty well done...
How about a ride on that white horse, Rec?
What? Me, on a merry-go-round?
Ha ha... That's a little embarrassing, but OK...
Quite a variety of mounts ...
The construction is gorgeous, or rather, realistic ...
YAY
YAAY
So very detailed ...
PBTH
BTH
BTH
BTH

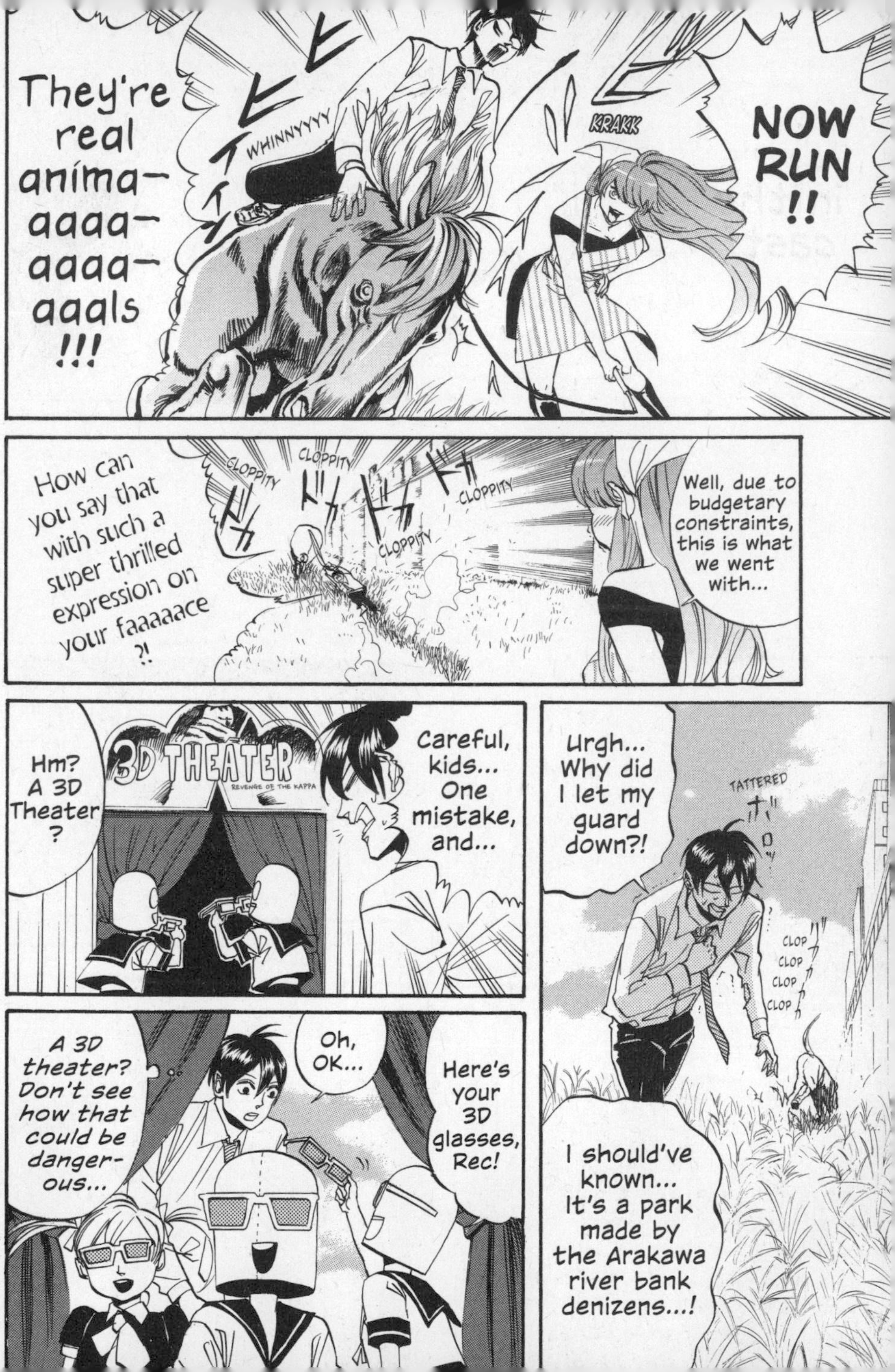
NOW RUN!!
KRAKK
WHINNYYYY
They're real anima-aaaa-aaaa-aaals!!!
Well, due to budgetary constraints, this is what we went with...
CLOPPITY
CLOPPITY
CLOPPITY
CLOPPITY
How can you say that with such a super thrilled expression on your faaaaace?!
Urgh... Why did I let my guard down?!
TATTERED
CLOP
CLOP
CLOP
CLOP
I should've known... It's a park made by the Arakawa river bank denizens...!
Careful, kids... One mistake, and...
3D THEATER
REVENGE OF THE KAPPA
Hm? A 3D Theater?
Here's your 3D glasses, Rec!
Oh, OK...
A 3D theater? Don't see how that could be danger-ous...

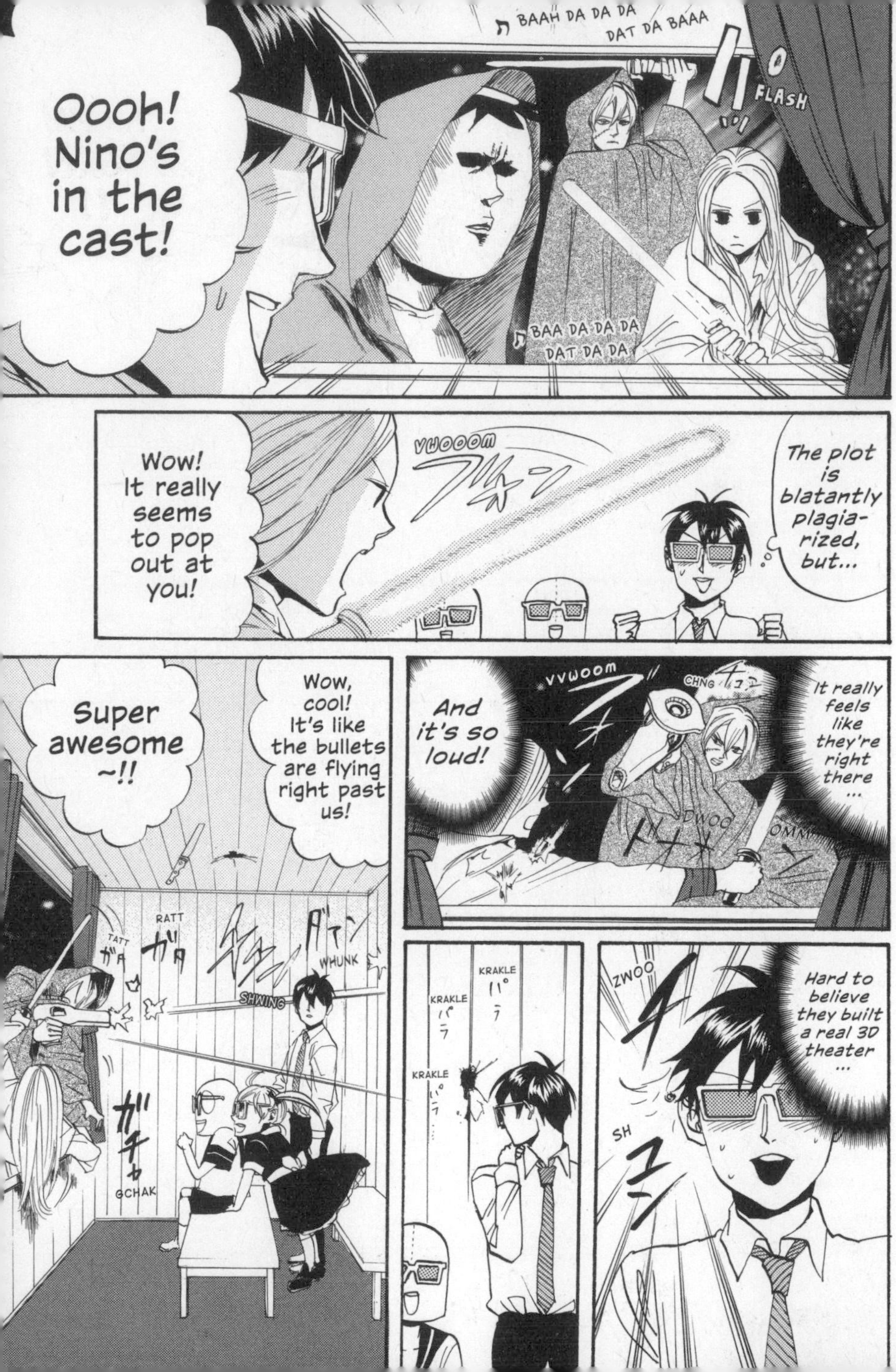
BAAH DA DA DA
DAT DA BAAA
FLASH
Oooh! Nino's in the cast!
BAA DA DA DA
DAT DA DA
The plot is blatantly plagia-rized, but...
VHOOOM
Wow! It really seems to pop out at you!
It really feels like they're right there ...
CHNG
VVWOOM
And it's so loud!
DWOOMM
Hard to believe they built a real 3D theater ...
ZWOO
SH
KRAKLE
KRAKLE
KRAKLE
Wow, cool! It's like the bullets are flying right past us!
Super awesome ~!!
WHUNK
RATT
TATT
SHWING
GCHAK

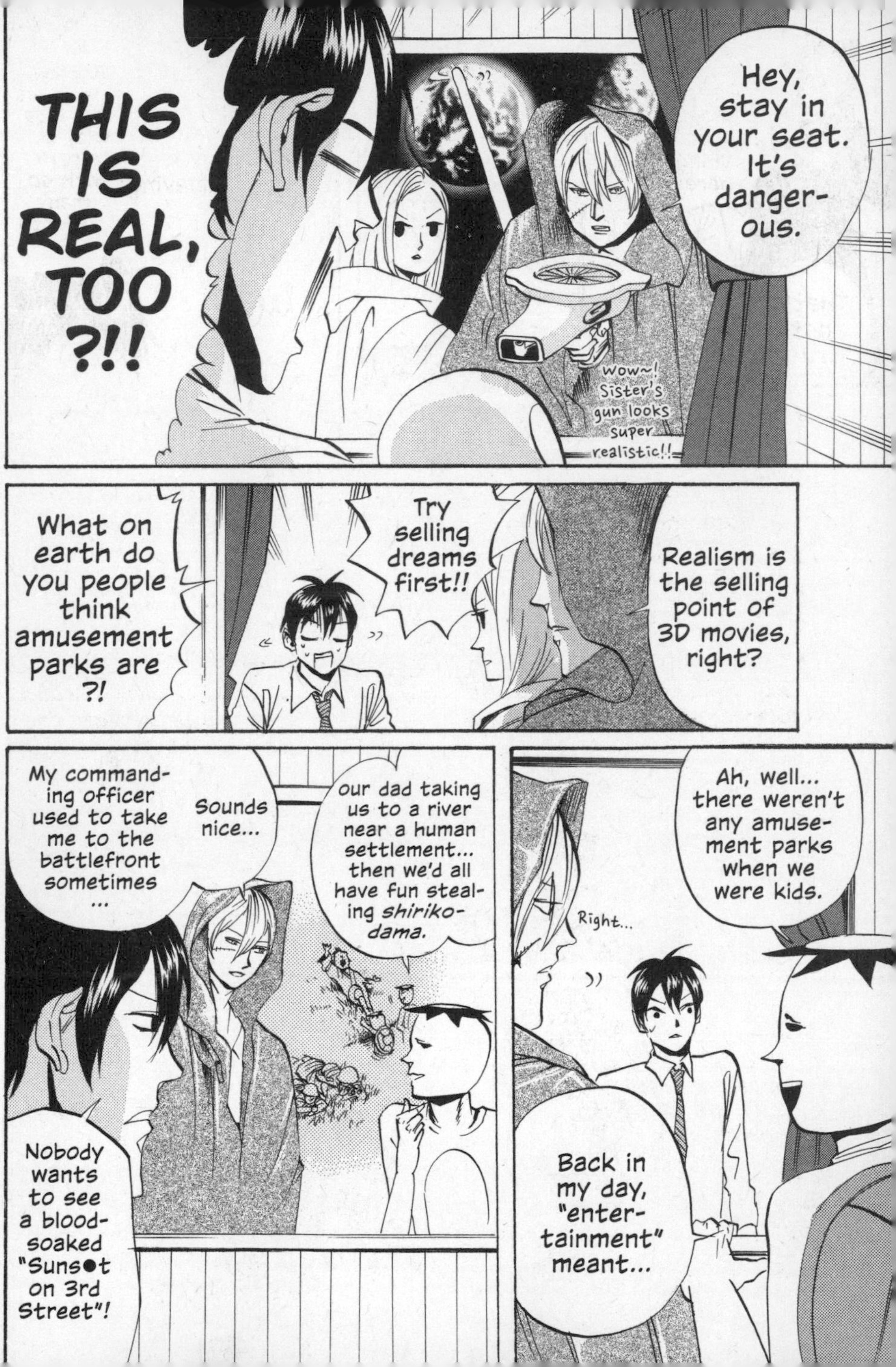
Hey, stay in your seat. It's danger-ous.
THIS IS REAL, TOO ?!!
Wow~! Sister's gun looks super realistic!!
Realism is the selling point of 3D movies, right?
Try selling dreams first!!
What on earth do you people think amusement parks are ?!
Ah, well... there weren't any amuse-ment parks when we were kids.
Right...
Back in my day, "enter-tainment" meant...
our dad taking us to a river near a human settlement... then we'd all have fun steal-ing shiriko-dama.
Sounds nice...
My command-ing officer used to take me to the battlefront sometimes ...
Nobody wants to see a blood-soaked "Suns●t on 3rd Street"!

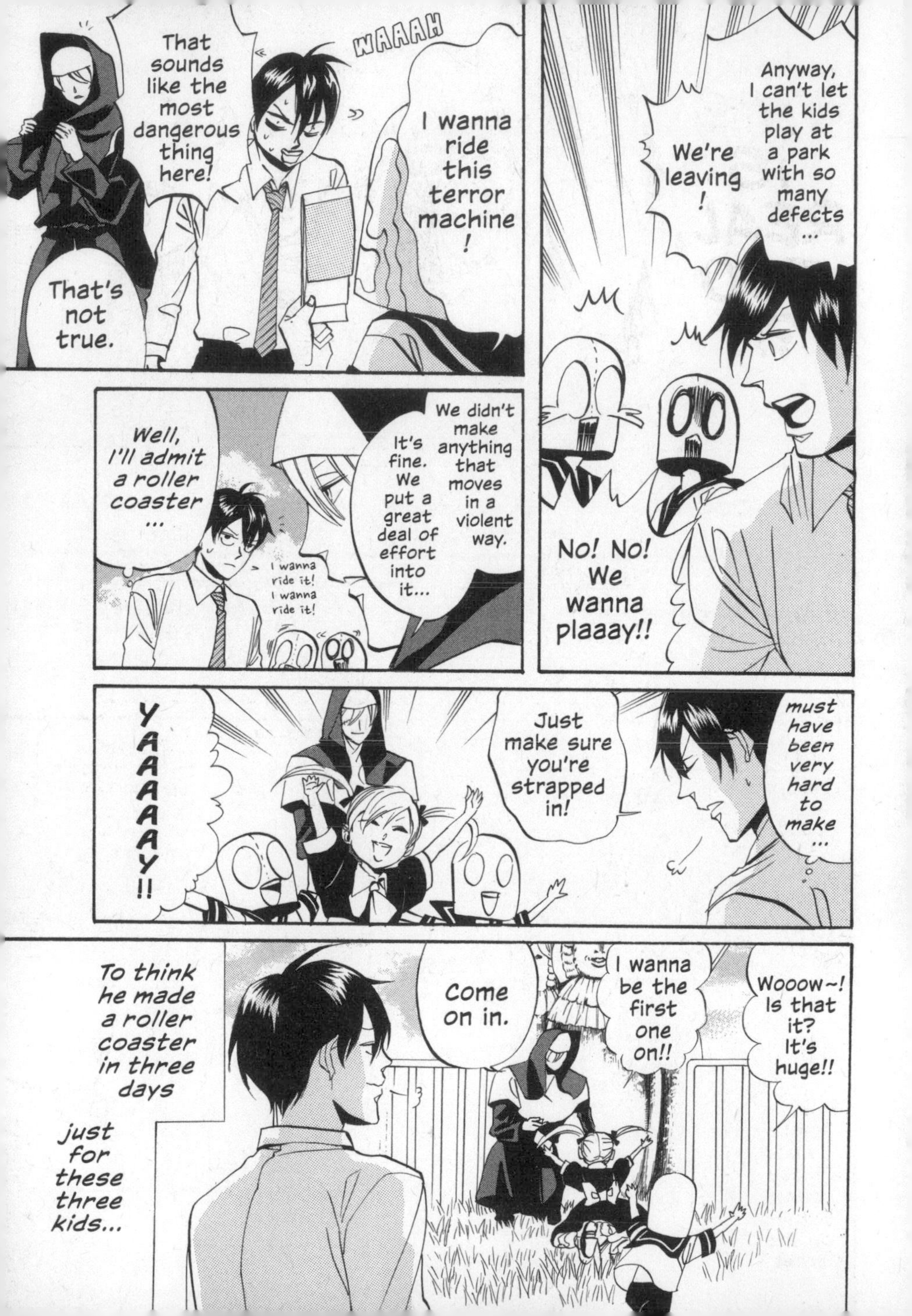
Anyway, I can't let the kids play at a park with so many defects ...
We're leaving!
No! No! We wanna plaaay!!
WAAAH
I wanna ride this terror machine!
That sounds like the most dangerous thing here!
That's not true.
We didn't make anything that moves in a violent way.
It's fine. We put a great deal of effort into it...
I wanna ride it! I wanna ride it!
Well, I'll admit a roller coaster ...
must have been very hard to make ...
Just make sure you're strapped in!
YAAAAAAY!!
Wooow~! Is that it? It's huge!!
I wanna be the first one on!!
Come on in.
To think he made a roller coaster in three days
just for these three kids...

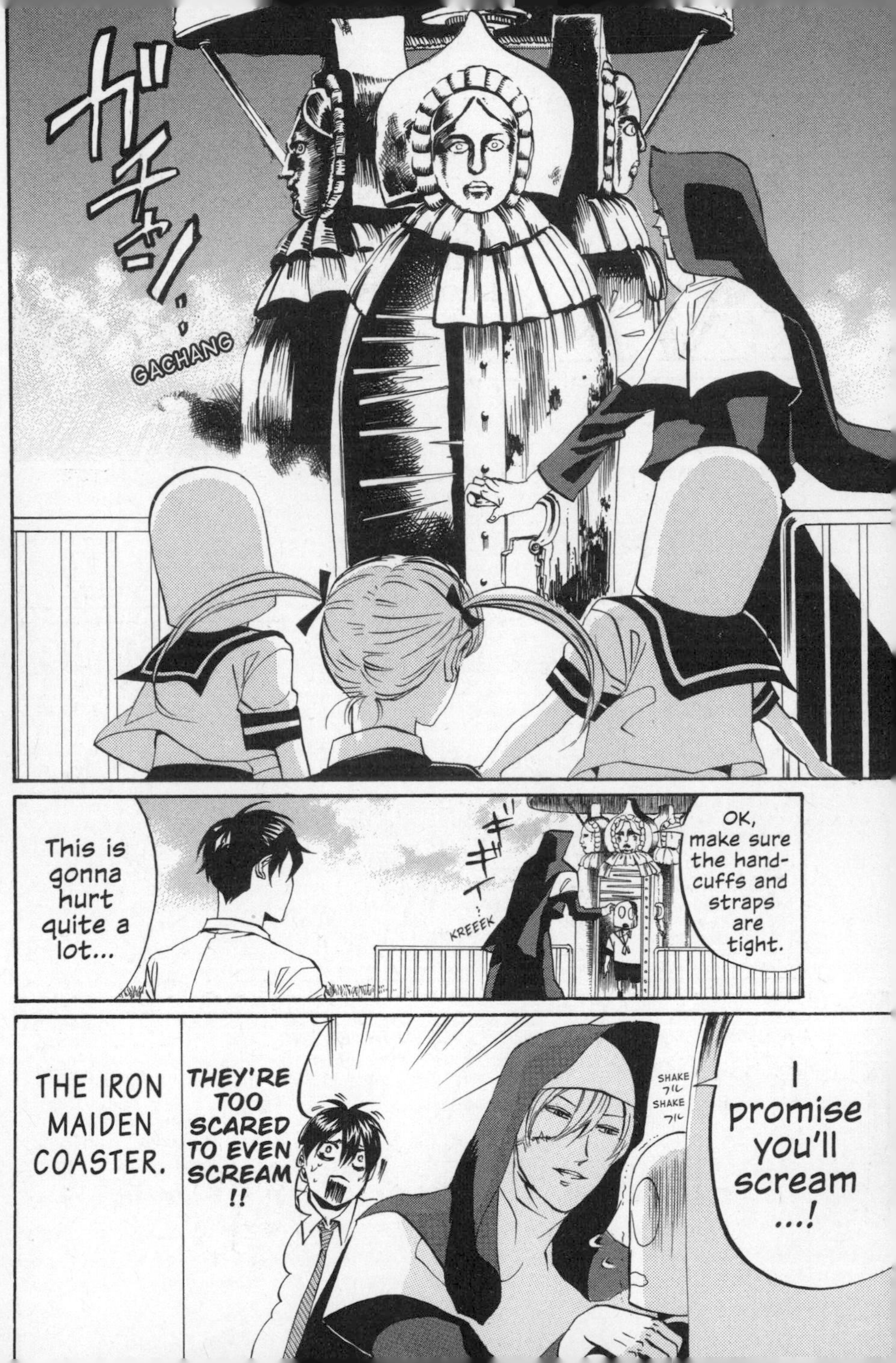
ガチャン!
GACHANG
OK, make sure the hand-cuffs and straps are tight.
ギギイ
KREEEK
This is gonna hurt quite a lot...
I promise you'll scream ...!
SHAKE フル
SHAKE フル
THEY'RE TOO SCARED TO EVEN SCREAM !!
THE IRON MAIDEN COASTER.

Chapter 216: Forgotten Parade

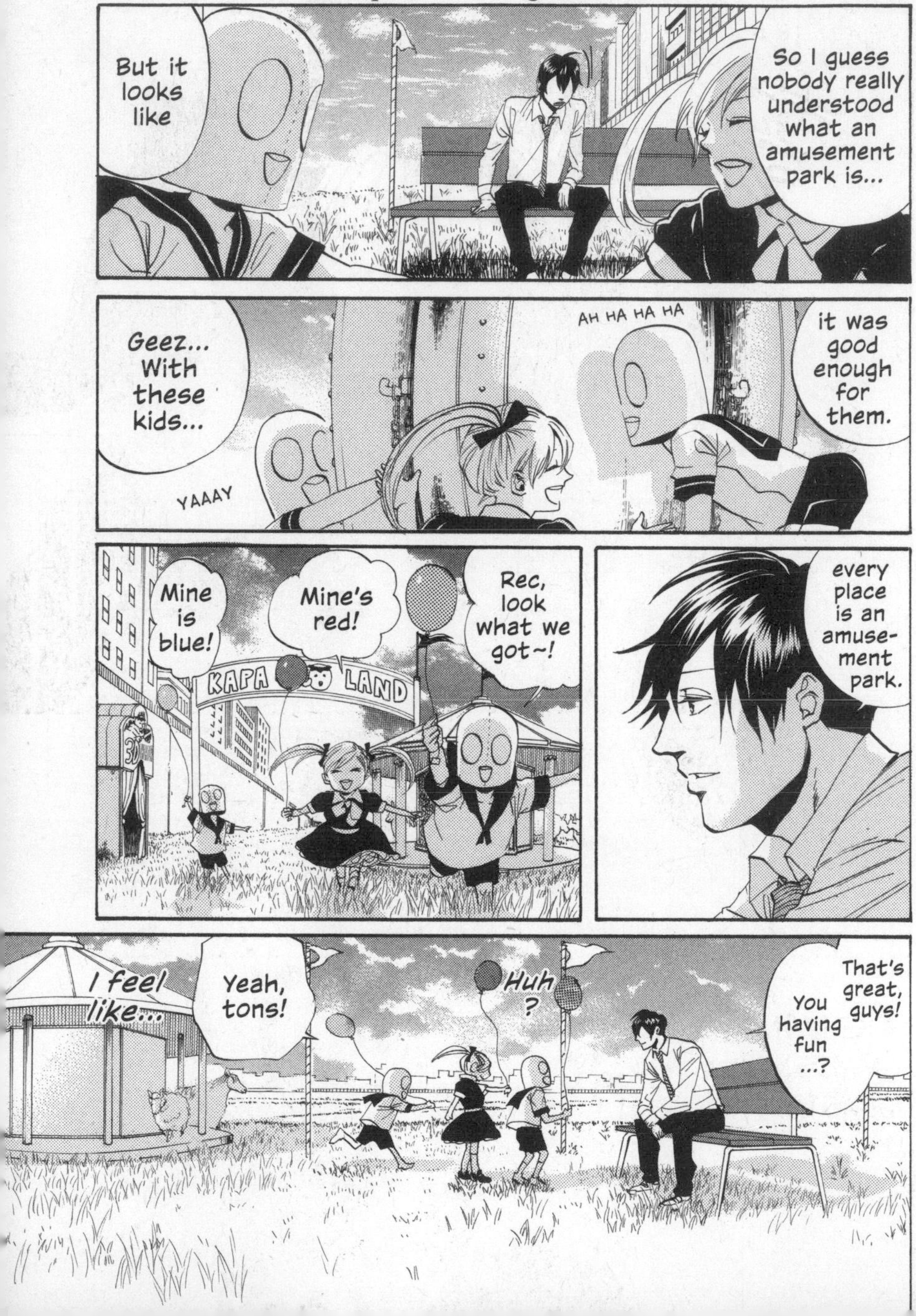
So I guess nobody really understood what an amusement park is...
But it looks like
it was good enough for them.
AH HA HA HA
Geez... With these kids...
YAAAY
every place is an amusement park.
Rec, look what we got~!
Mine's red!
Mine is blue!
KAPA LAND
That's great, guys! You having fun ...?
Huh?
Yeah, tons!
I feel like...

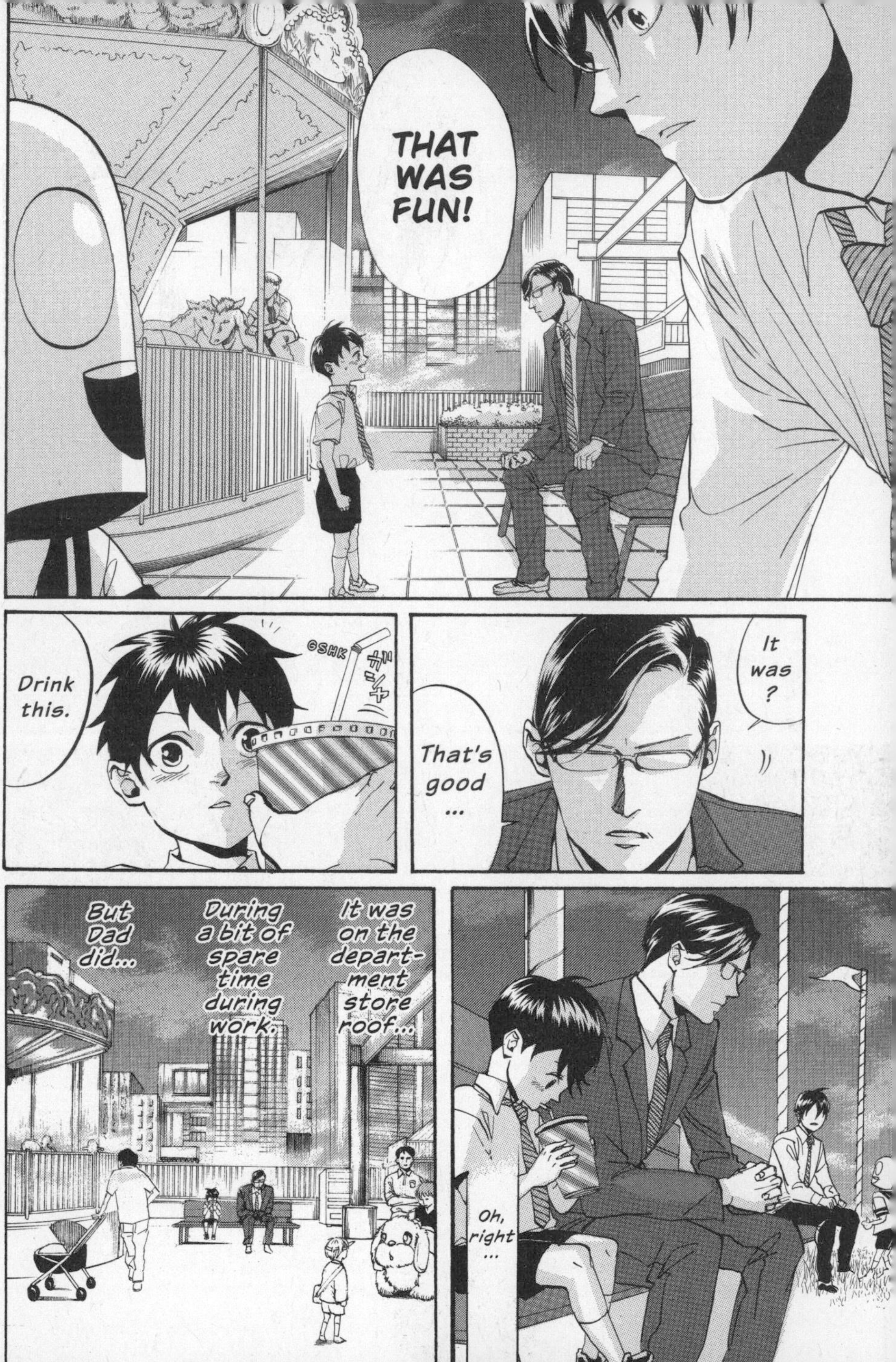
THAT WAS FUN!
It was?
That's good ...
Drink this.
GSHK
Oh, right ...
It was on the department store roof...
During a bit of spare time during work.
But Dad did...

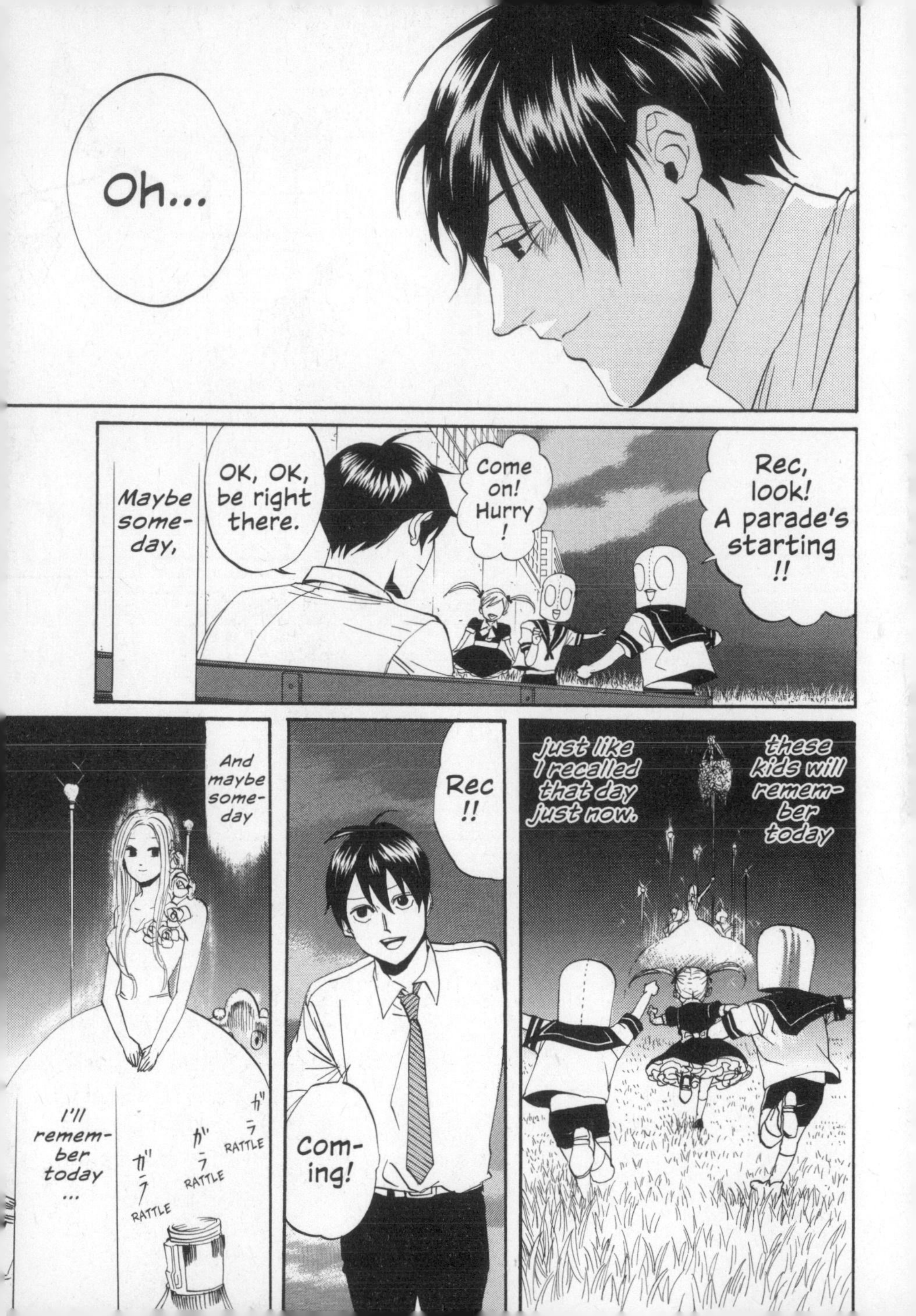
Oh...
Rec, look! A parade's starting!!
Come on! Hurry!
OK, OK, be right there.
Maybe someday,
these kids will remember today
just like I recalled that day just now.
Rec!!
Coming!
And maybe someday
ガラ RATTLE
がラ RATTLE
ガラ RATTLE
I'll remember today...

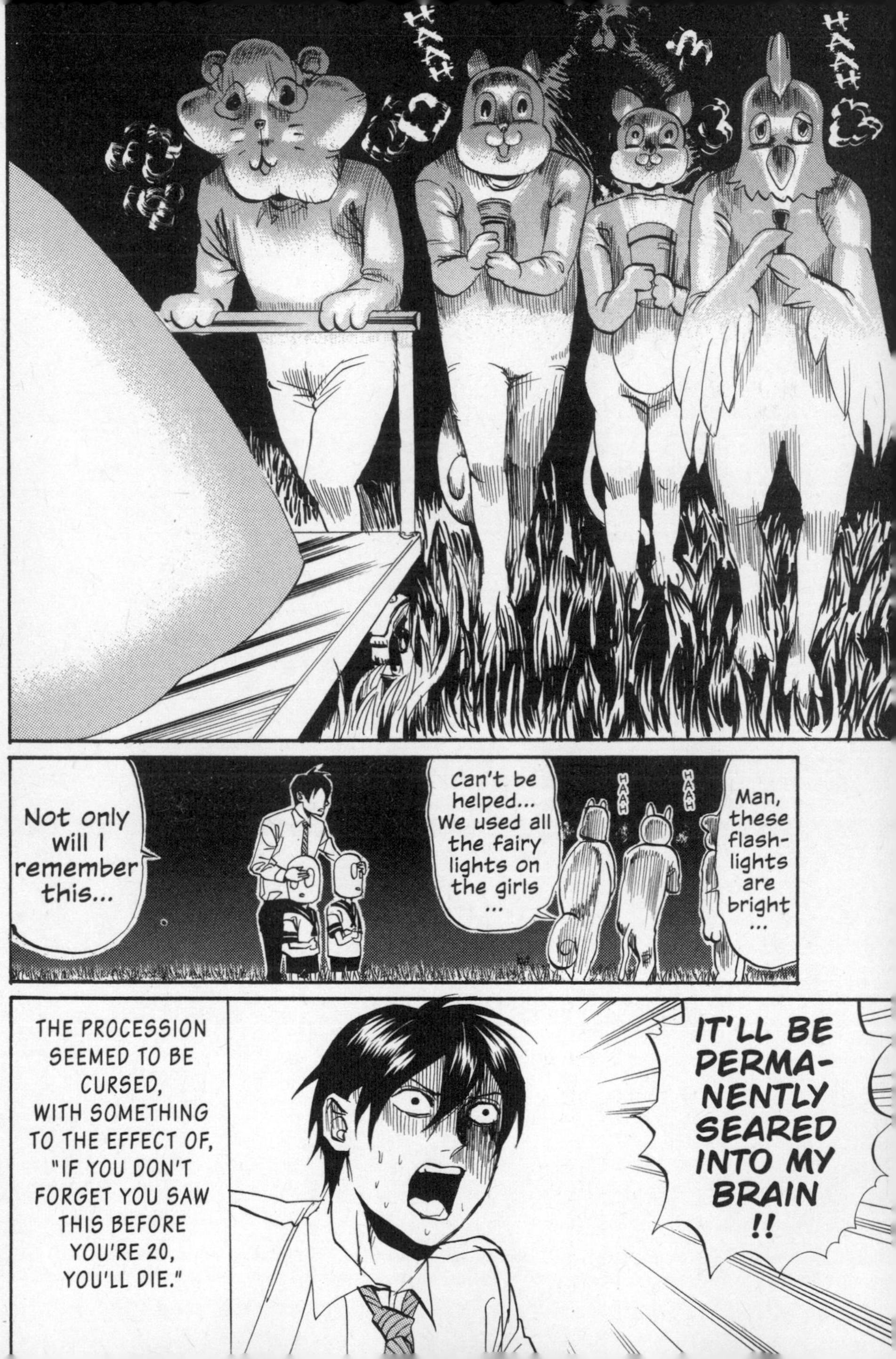
HAAAH
HAAAH
Man, these flash-lights are bright...
HAAH
HAAH
Can't be helped... We used all the fairy lights on the girls...
Not only will I remember this...
IT'LL BE PERMA-NENTLY SEARED INTO MY BRAIN!!
THE PROCESSION SEEMED TO BE CURSED, WITH SOMETHING TO THE EFFECT OF, "IF YOU DON'T FORGET YOU SAW THIS BEFORE YOU'RE 20, YOU'LL DIE."

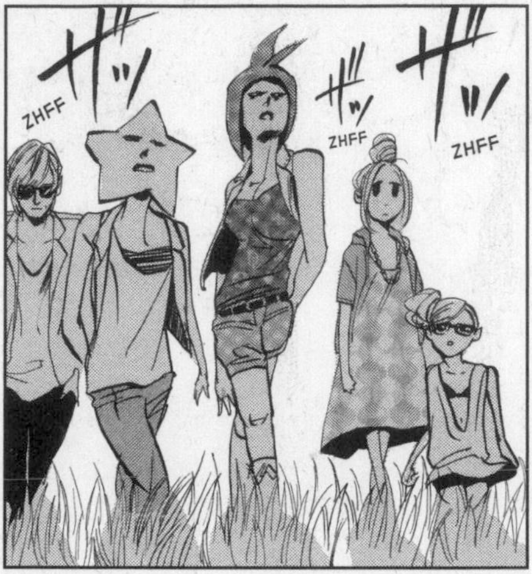
ザッ
ZHFF
ザッ
ZHFF
ザッ
ZHFF

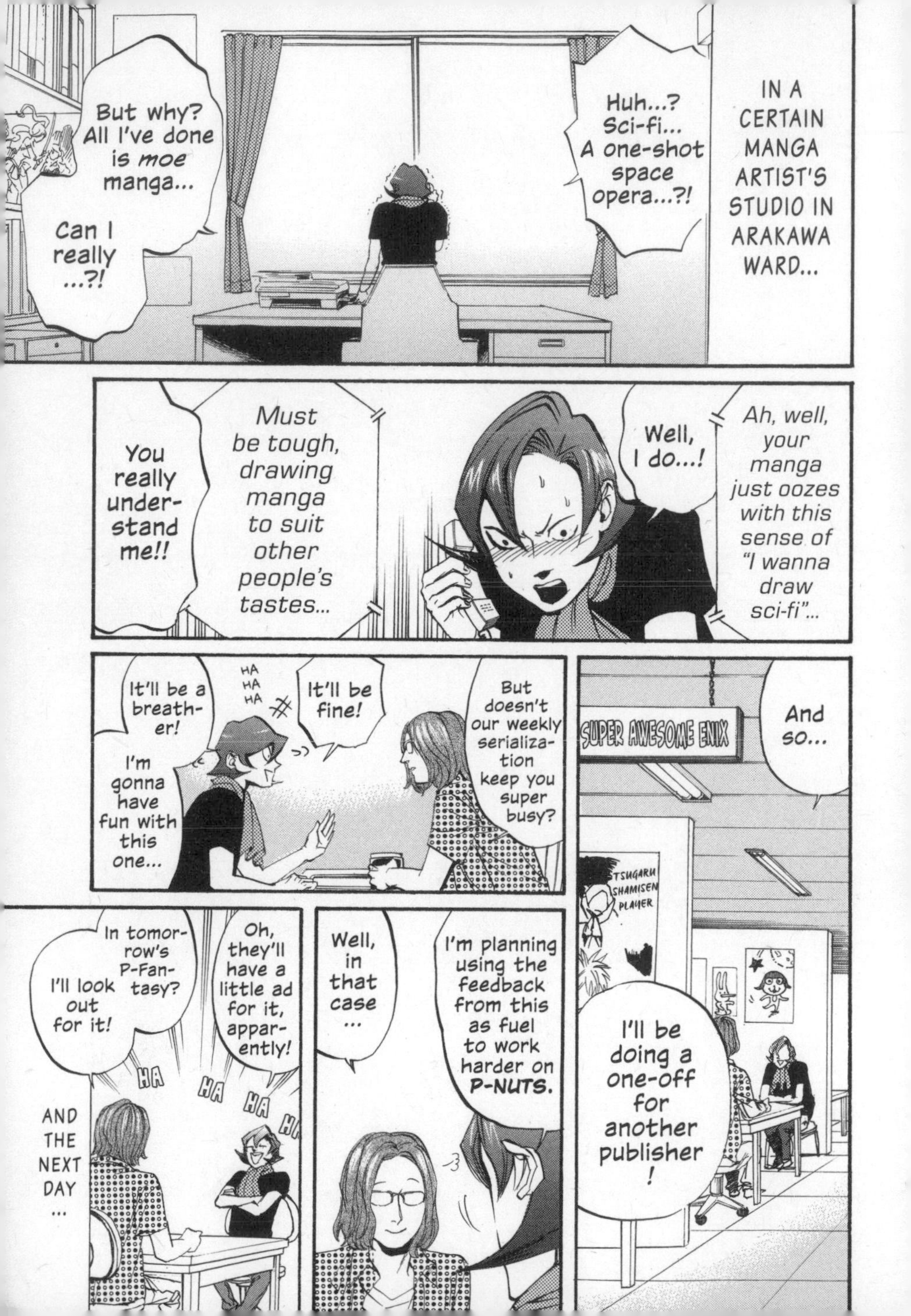
IN A CERTAIN MANGA ARTIST'S STUDIO IN ARAKAWA WARD...
Huh...? Sci-fi... A one-shot space opera...?!
But why? All I've done is *moe* manga...
Can I really ...?!
Ah, well, your manga just oozes with this sense of "I wanna draw sci-fi"...
Well, I do...!
Must be tough, drawing manga to suit other people's tastes...
You really under-stand me!!
And so...
SUPER AWESOME ENIX
TSUGARU SHAMISEN PLAYER
I'll be doing a one-off for another publisher!
But doesn't our weekly serializa-tion keep you super busy?
It'll be fine!
HA HA HA
It'll be a breath-er!
I'm gonna have fun with this one...
I'm planning using the feedback from this as fuel to work harder on **P-NUTS**.
Well, in that case ...
Oh, they'll have a little ad for it, appar-ently!
In tomor-row's P-Fan-tasy?
I'll look out for it!
HA HA HA HA
AND THE NEXT DAY ...

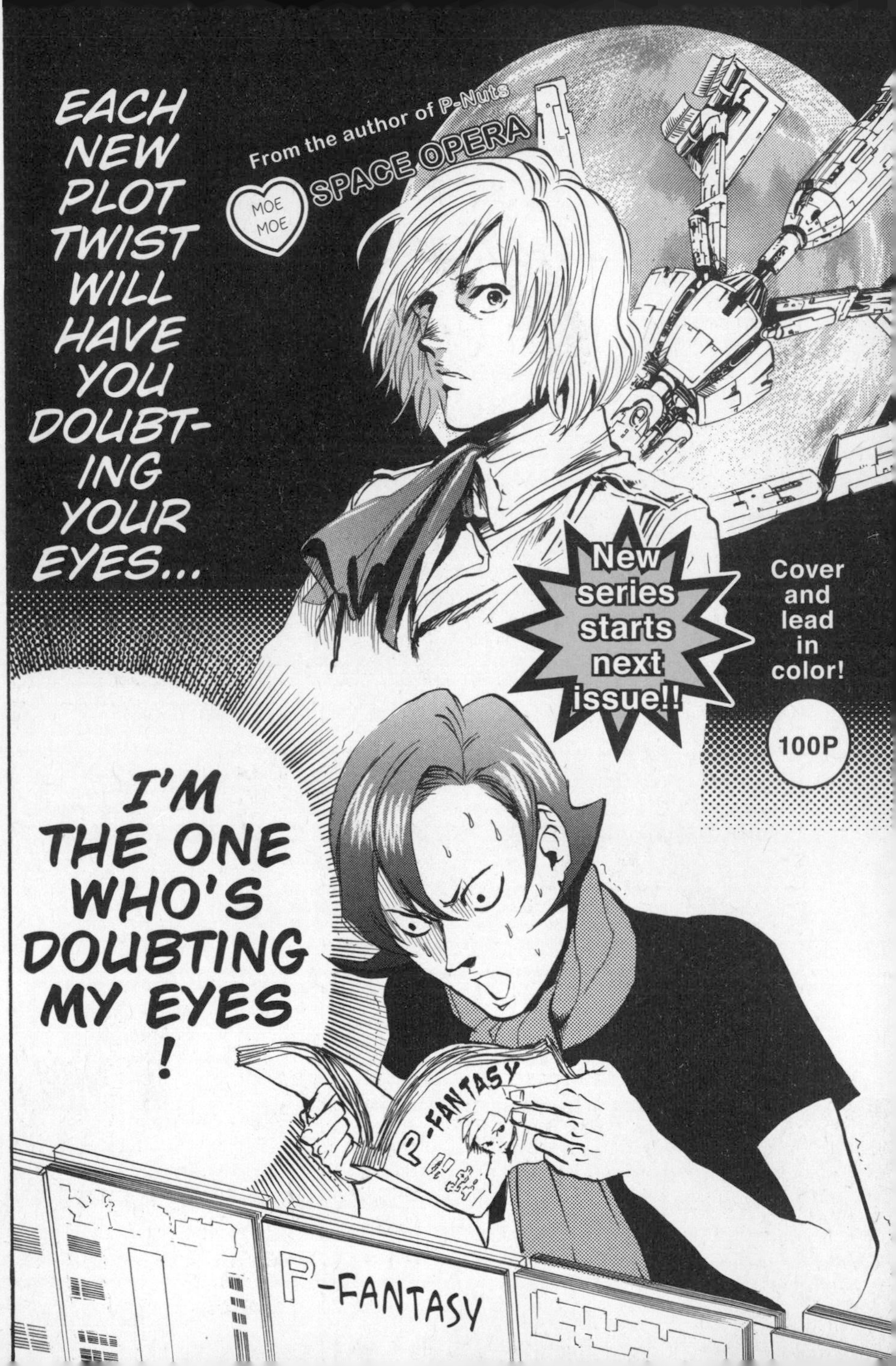
From the author of P-Nuts
SPACE OPERA
MOE MOE
EACH NEW PLOT TWIST WILL HAVE YOU DOUBTING YOUR EYES...
New series starts next issue!!
Cover and lead in color!
100P
I'M THE ONE WHO'S DOUBTING MY EYES!
P-FANTASY
P-FANTASY

Chapter 217: Captain Returns

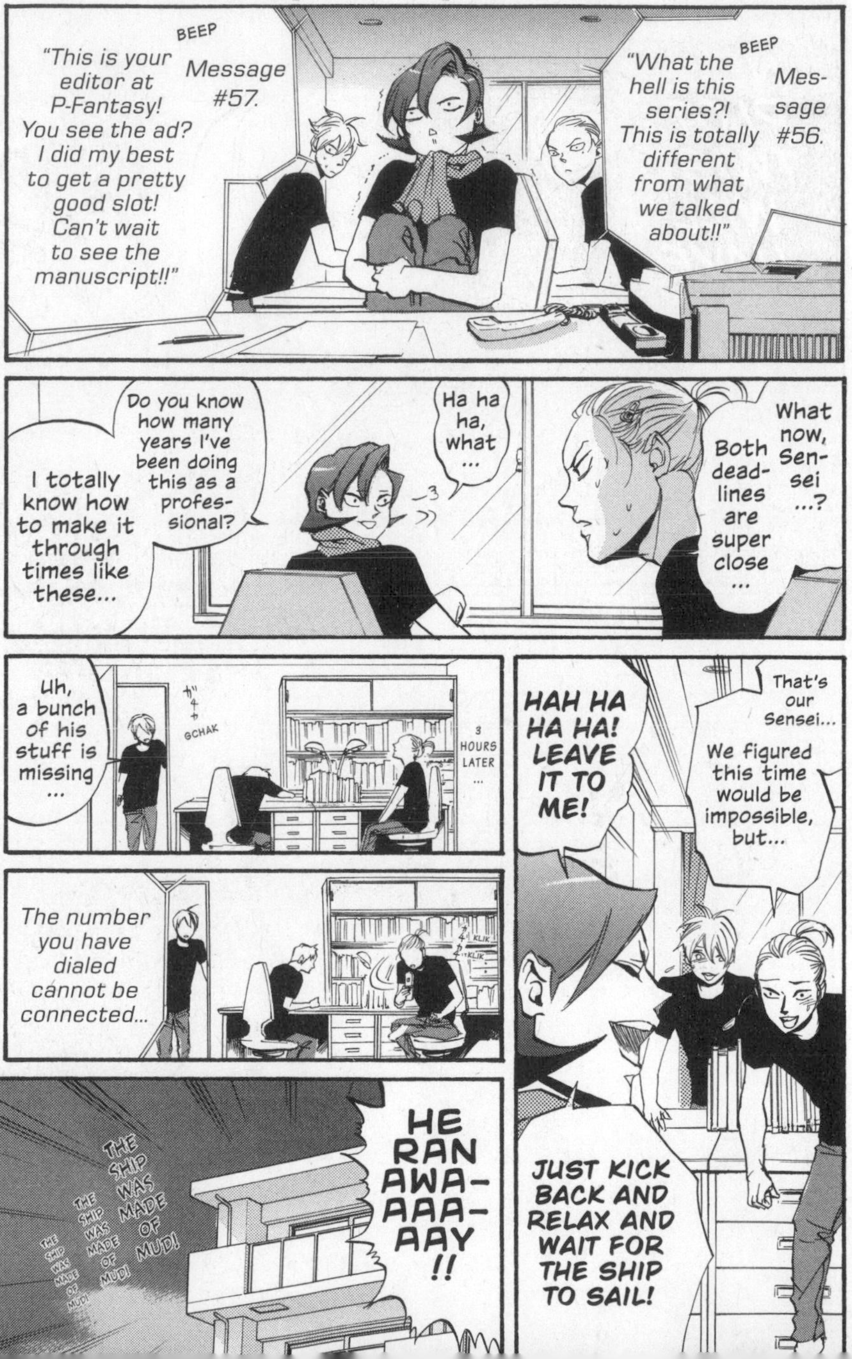
BEEP
Mes-sage #56.
"What the hell is this series?! This is totally different from what we talked about!!"
BEEP
Message #57.
"This is your editor at P-Fantasy! You see the ad? I did my best to get a pretty good slot! Can't wait to see the manuscript!!"
What now, Sensei ...?
Both dead-lines are super close ...
Ha ha ha, what ...
Do you know how many years I've been doing this as a profes-sional?
I totally know how to make it through times like these...
That's our Sensei...
We figured this time would be impossible, but...
HAH HA HA HA! LEAVE IT TO ME!
JUST KICK BACK AND RELAX AND WAIT FOR THE SHIP TO SAIL!
3 HOURS LATER ...
GCHAK
Uh, a bunch of his stuff is missing ...
KLIK KLIK
The number you have dialed cannot be connected...
HE RAN AWAA-AAAA-AAY !!
THE SHIP WAS MADE OF MUD!
THE SHIP WAS MADE OF MUD!
THE SHIP WAS MADE OF MUD!

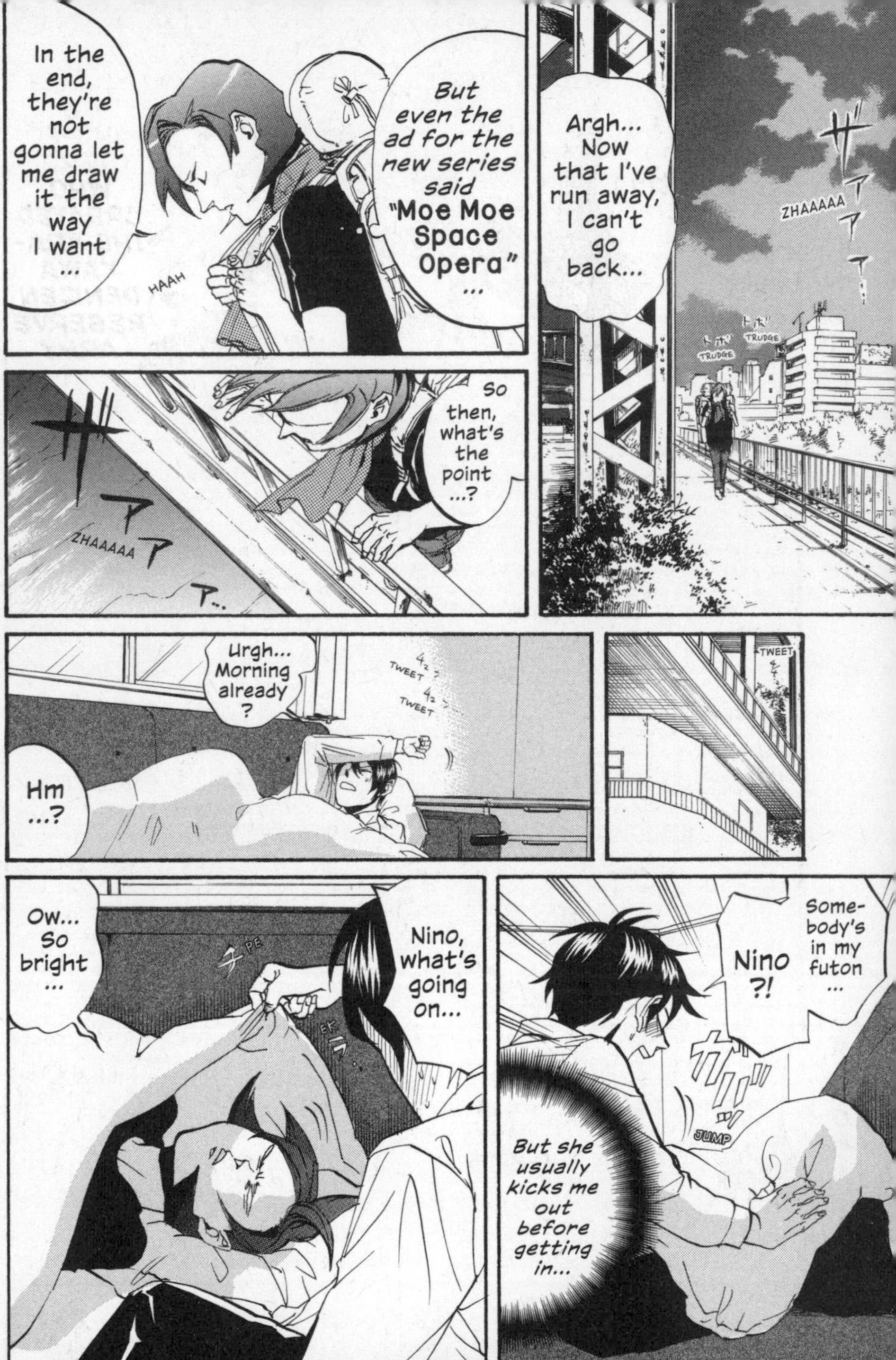

Argh... Now that I've run away, I can't go back...
ZHAAAAA
TRUDGE
TRUDGE
But even the ad for the new series said "Moe Moe Space Opera"...
In the end, they're not gonna let me draw it the way I want...
HAAH
So then, what's the point...?
ZHAAAAA
TWEET
Urgh... Morning already?
TWEET
TWEET
Hm...?
Somebody's in my futon...
Nino?!
JUMP
But she usually kicks me out before getting in...
Nino, what's going on...
Ow... So bright...
PE
EK

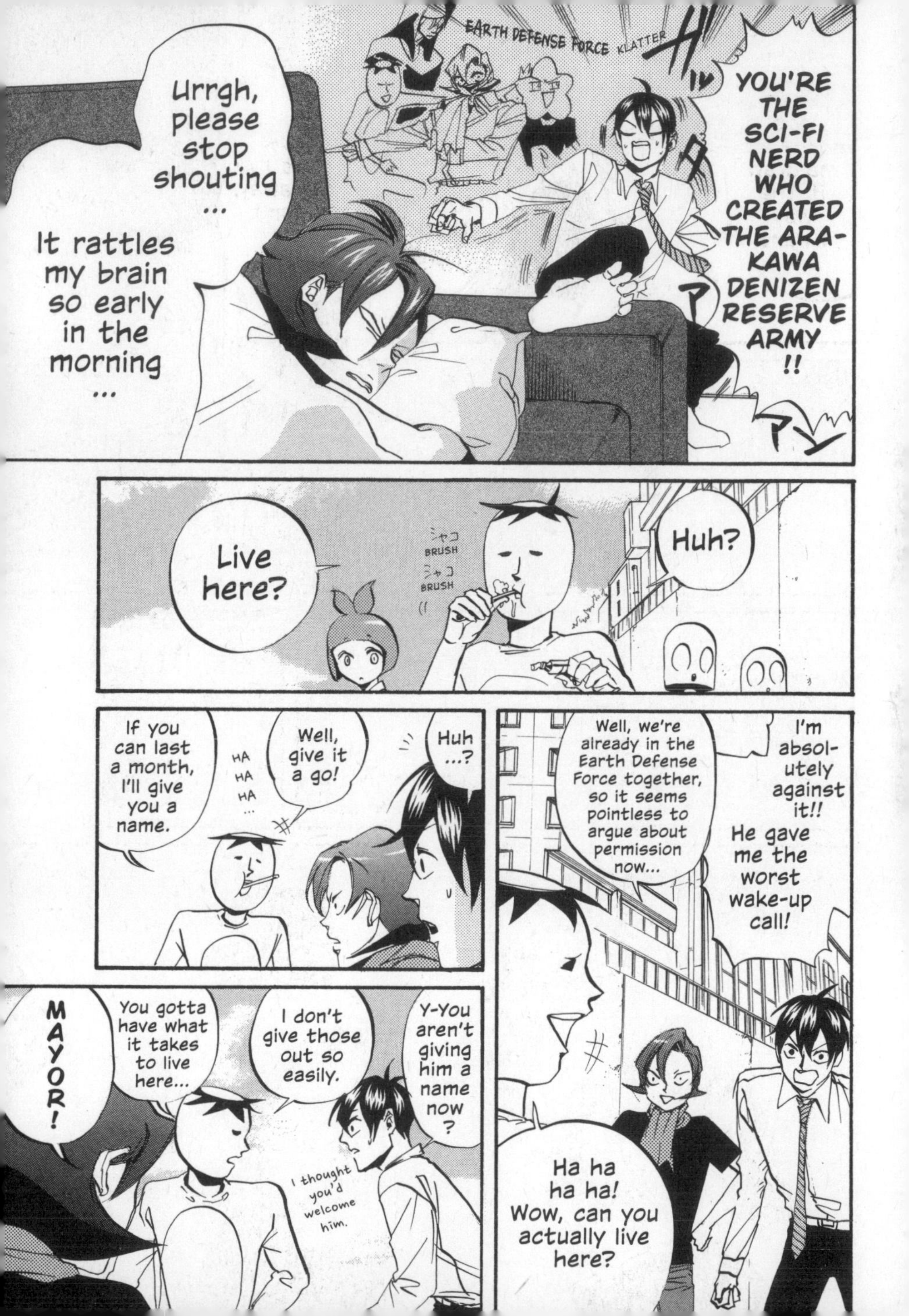
YOU'RE THE SCI-FI NERD WHO CREATED THE ARA-KAWA DENIZEN RESERVE ARMY!!
EARTH DEFENSE FORCE
KLATTER
Urrgh, please stop shouting ...
It rattles my brain so early in the morning ...
Huh?
シャコ
BRUSH
シャコ
BRUSH
Live here?
I'm absolutely against it!!
He gave me the worst wake-up call!
Well, we're already in the Earth Defense Force together, so it seems pointless to argue about permission now...
Ha ha ha ha! Wow, can you actually live here?
Huh ...?
Well, give it a go!
HA HA HA ...
If you can last a month, I'll give you a name.
Y-You aren't giving him a name now?
I thought you'd welcome him.
I don't give those out so easily.
You gotta have what it takes to live here...
MAYOR!

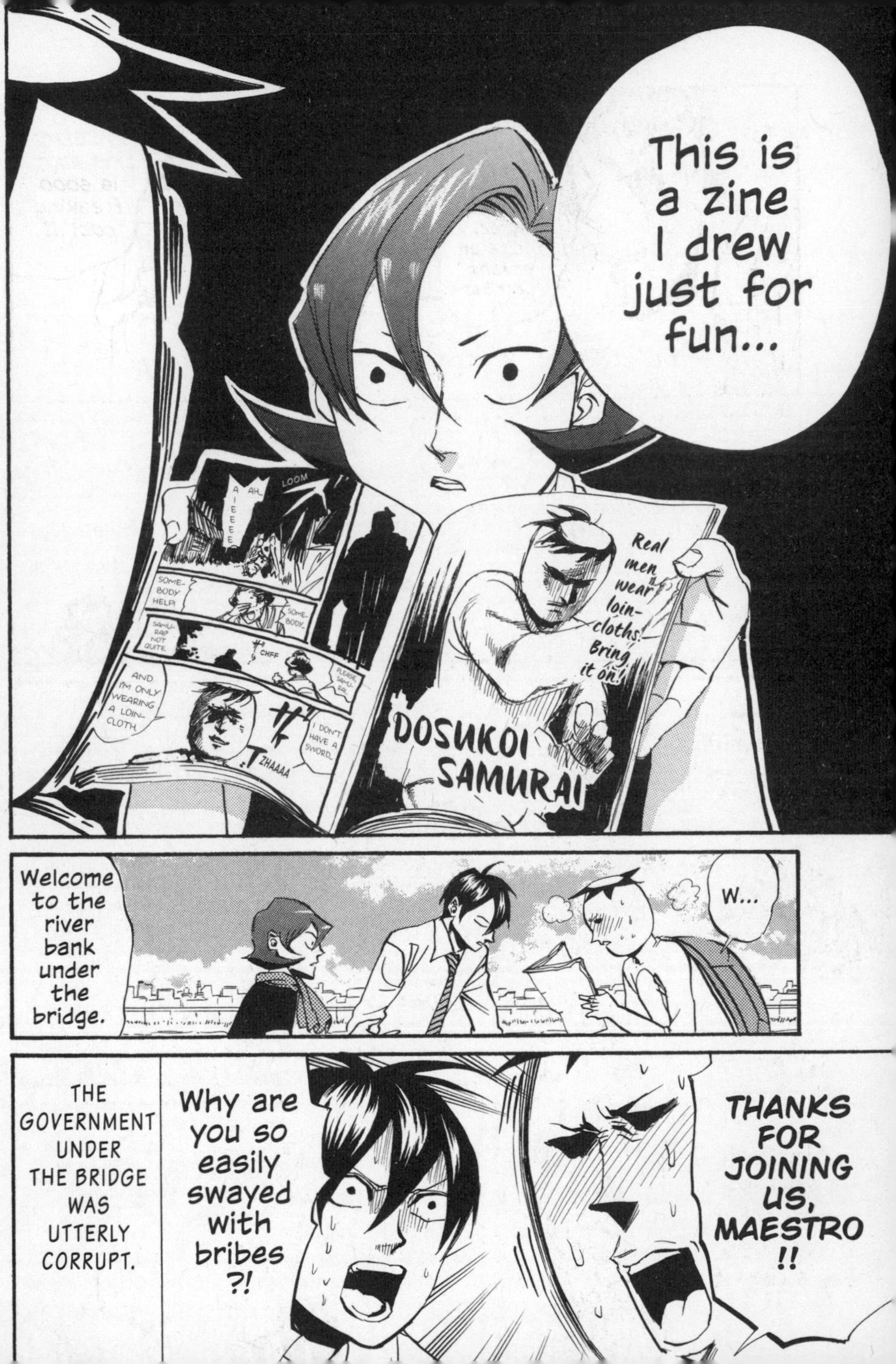
This is a zine I drew just for fun...
Real men wear loin-cloths. Bring it on!
DOSUKOI SAMURAI
LOOM
AH
AIEEEEE
SOME-BODY HELP!
SOME-BODY...
SAMURAI? NOT QUITE.
CHFF
PLEASE, SAMURAI...
AND I'M ONLY WEARING A LOIN-CLOTH.
I DON'T HAVE A SWORD...
ZHAAAA
W...
Welcome to the river bank under the bridge.
THANKS FOR JOINING US, MAESTRO!!
Why are you so easily swayed with bribes?!
THE GOVERNMENT UNDER THE BRIDGE WAS UTTERLY CORRUPT.

Chapter 218: True Nature Revealed

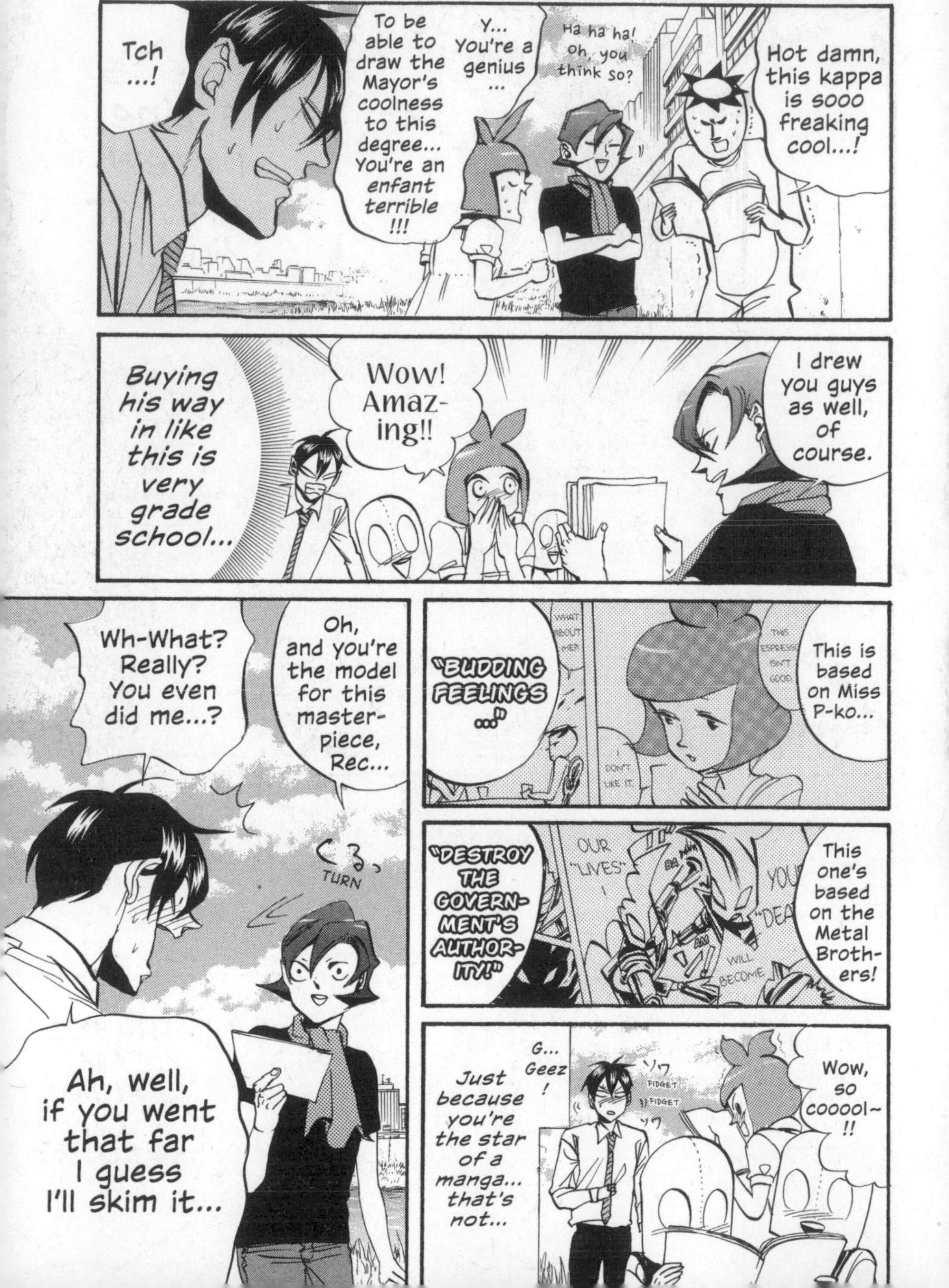
Hot damn, this kappa is sooo freaking cool...!
Ha ha ha! Oh, you think so?
Y... You're a genius...
To be able to draw the Mayor's coolness to this degree... You're an enfant terrible!!!
Tch...!
I drew you guys as well, of course.
Wow! Amaz-ing!!
Buying his way in like this is very grade school...
This is based on Miss P-ko...
THIS ESPRESSO ISN'T GOOD.
WHAT ABOUT ME?
I DON'T LIKE IT.
"BUDDING FEELINGS..."
This one's based on the Metal Brothers!
OUR "LIVES"
WILL BECOME
"DESTROY THE GOVERNMENT'S AUTHORITY!"
Wow, so cooool~!!
FIDGET FIDGET
G... Geez!
Just because you're the star of a manga... that's not...
Oh, and you're the model for this master-piece, Rec...
Wh-What? Really? You even did me...?
TURN
Ah, well, if you went that far I guess I'll skim it...

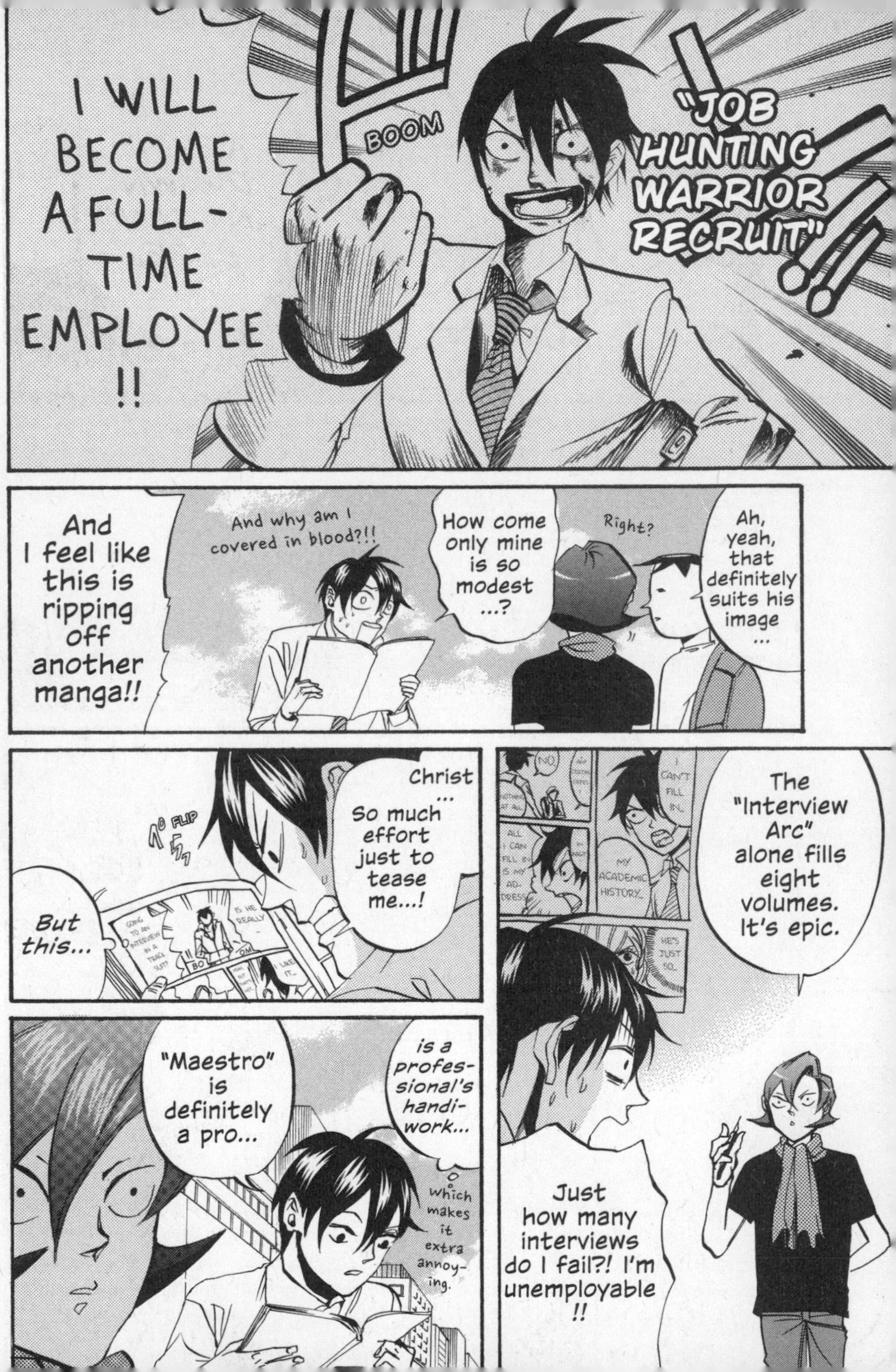
"JOB HUNTING WARRIOR RECRUIT" !!
BOOM
I WILL BECOME A FULL-TIME EMPLOYEE !!
Ah, yeah, that definitely suits his image ...
Right?
How come only mine is so modest ...?
And why am I covered in blood?!!
And I feel like this is ripping off another manga!!
The "Interview Arc" alone fills eight volumes. It's epic.
NO.
I CAN'T FILL IN.
ALL I CAN FILL IN IS MY ADDRESS
MY ACADEMIC HISTORY...
HE'S JUST SO...
Christ ... So much effort just to tease me...!
FLIP
But this...
GOING TO AN INTERVIEW IN A TRACK SUIT?
IS HE REALLY
BO
OM
Just how many interviews do I fail?! I'm unemployable !!
"Maestro" is definitely a pro...
is a professional's handiwork...
Which makes it extra annoying.

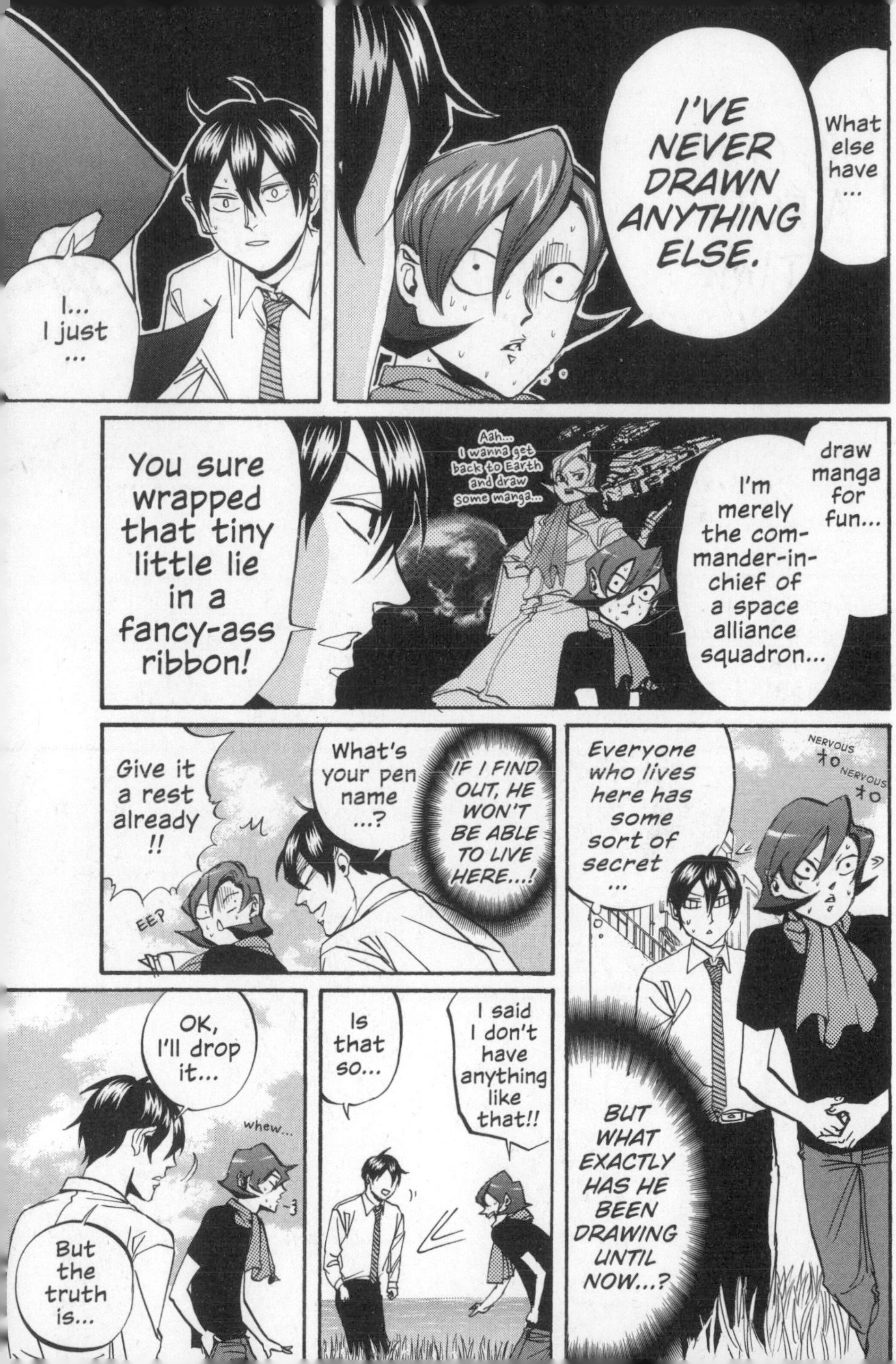
What else have ...
I'VE NEVER DRAWN ANYTHING ELSE.
I... I just ...
draw manga for fun...
I'm merely the commander-in-chief of a space alliance squadron...
Aah... I wanna get back to Earth and draw some manga...
You sure wrapped that tiny little lie in a fancy-ass ribbon!
NERVOUS
オロ
NERVOUS
オロ
Everyone who lives here has some sort of secret ...
BUT WHAT EXACTLY HAS HE BEEN DRAWING UNTIL NOW...?
IF I FIND OUT, HE WON'T BE ABLE TO LIVE HERE...!
What's your pen name ...?
Give it a rest already !!
EEP
I said I don't have anything like that!!
Is that so...
OK, I'll drop it...
whew...
But the truth is...

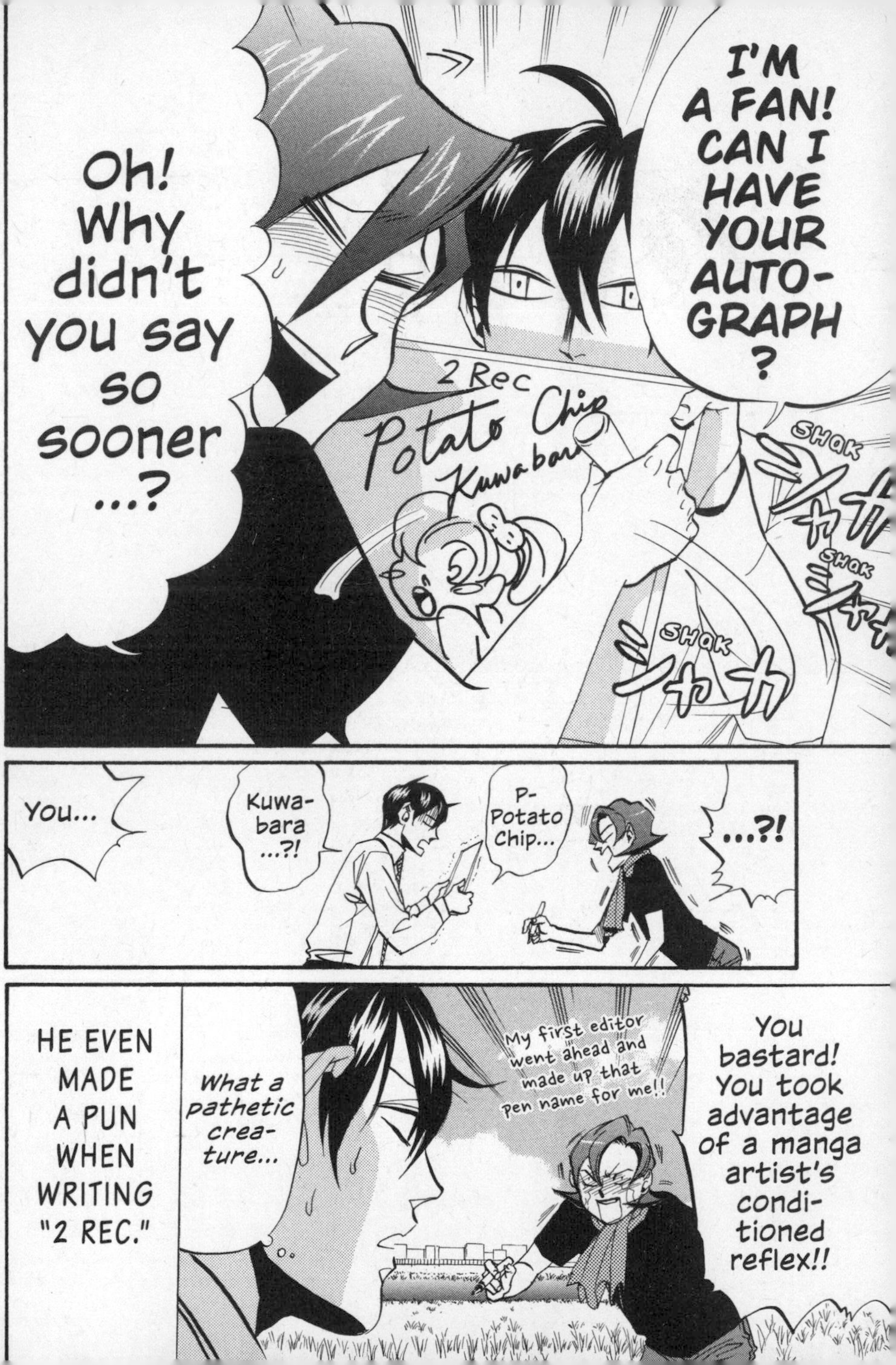
I'M A FAN! CAN I HAVE YOUR AUTOGRAPH?
SHAK
SHAK
2 Rec
Potato Chip
Kuwabara
SHAK
Oh! Why didn't you say so sooner...?
...?!
P-Potato Chip...
Kuwabara...?!
You...
You bastard! You took advantage of a manga artist's conditioned reflex!!
My first editor went ahead and made up that pen name for me!!
What a pathetic creature...
HE EVEN MADE A PUN WHEN WRITING "2 REC."

Chapter 219: The End of Passion

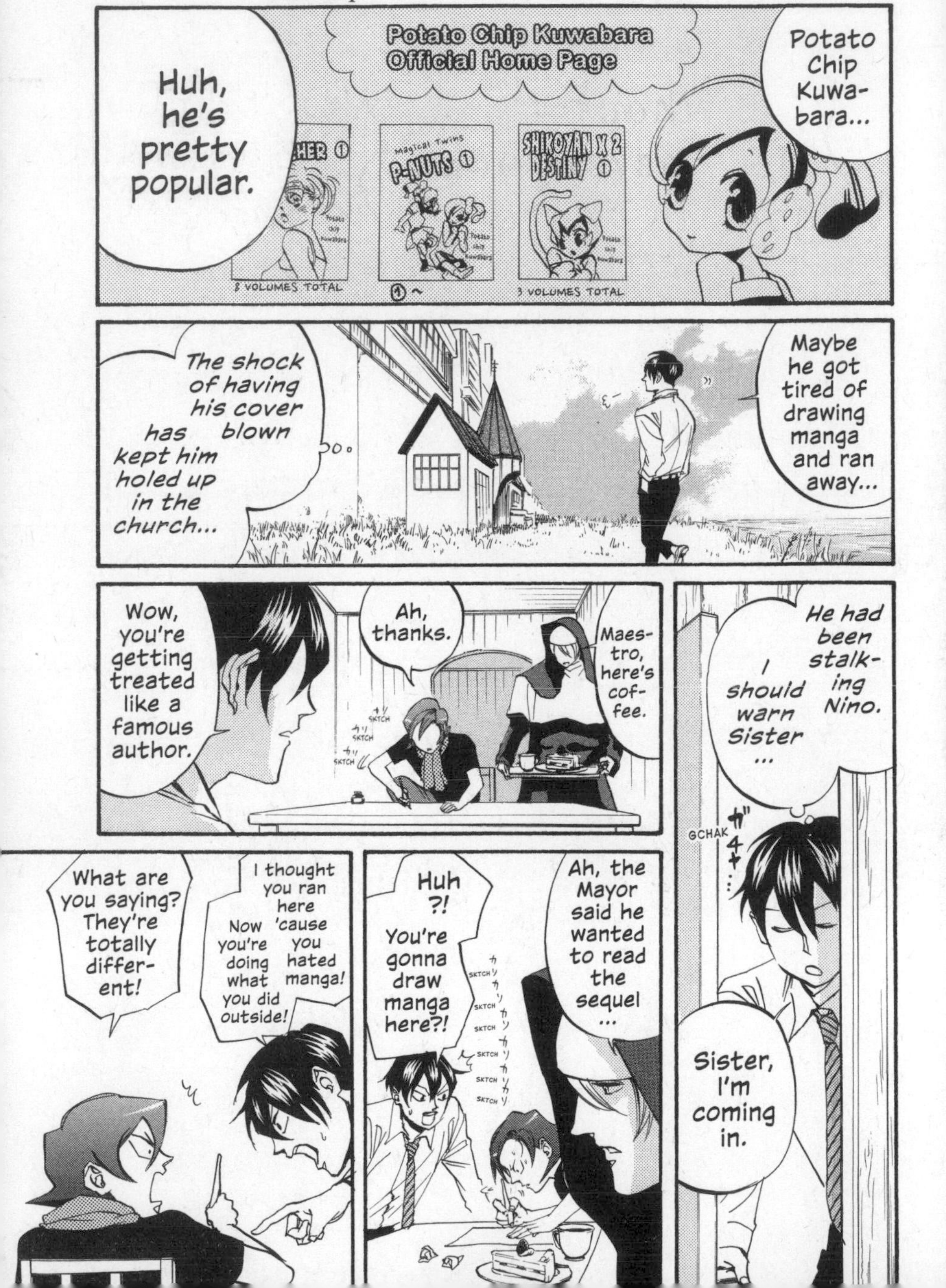
Potato Chip Kuwabara...
Potato Chip Kuwabara Official Home Page
SHIKOYAN X 2 DESTINY 1
3 VOLUMES TOTAL
Magical Twins P-NUTS 1
HER 1
8 VOLUMES TOTAL
Huh, he's pretty popular.
Maybe he got tired of drawing manga and ran away...
The shock of having his cover blown has kept him holed up in the church...
He had been stalking Nino.
I should warn Sister...
GCHAK
Sister, I'm coming in.
Maestro, here's coffee.
Ah, thanks.
SKTCH SKTCH SKTCH
Wow, you're getting treated like a famous author.
Ah, the Mayor said he wanted to read the sequel...
SKTCH SKTCH SKTCH SKTCH SKTCH SKTCH
Huh?! You're gonna draw manga here?!
I thought you ran here 'cause you hated manga! Now you're doing what you did outside!
What are you saying? They're totally different!

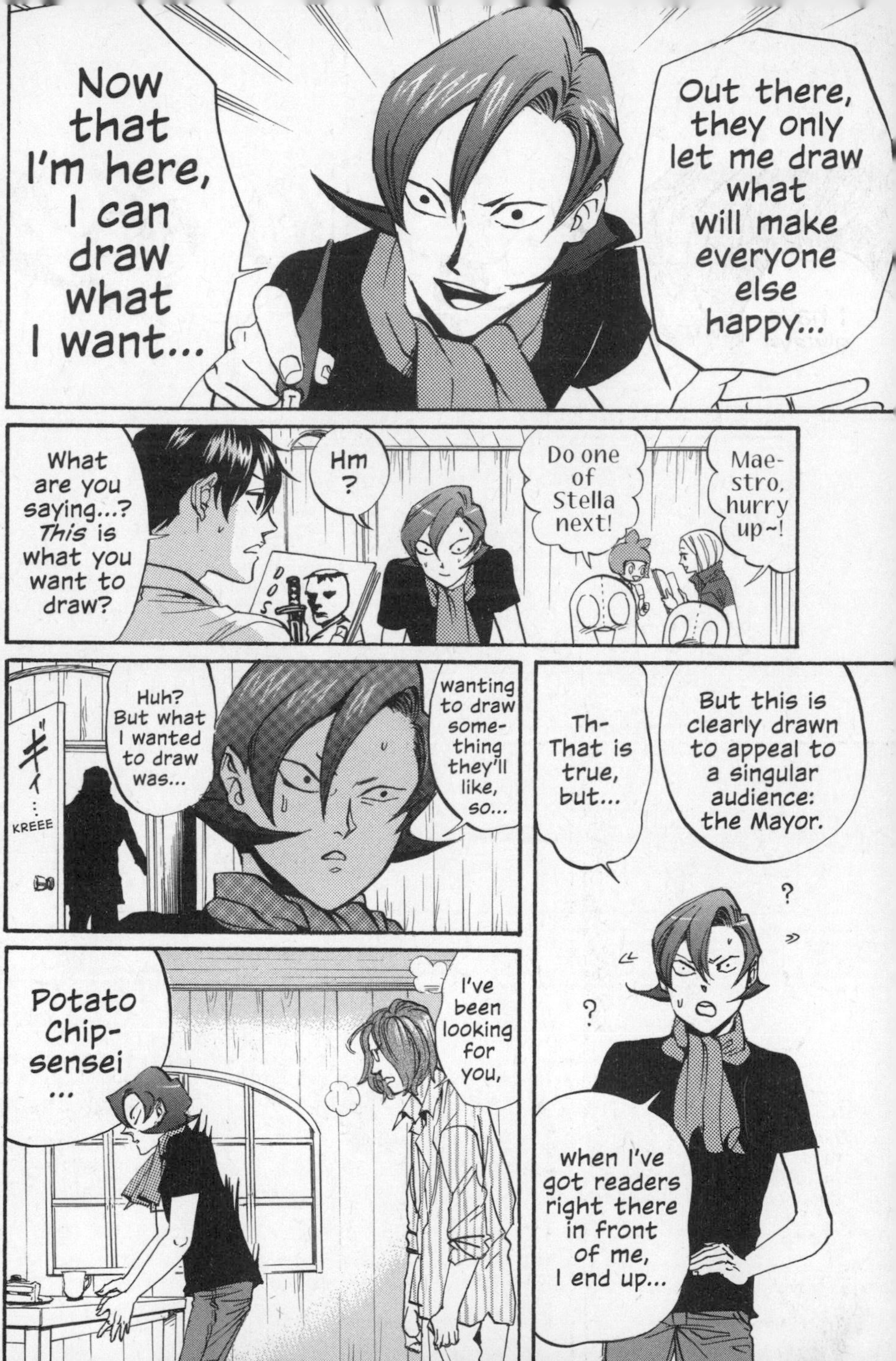
Out there, they only let me draw what will make everyone else happy...
Now that I'm here, I can draw what I want...
Mae-stro, hurry up~!
Do one of Stella next!
Hm?
What are you saying...? *This* is what you want to draw?
But this is clearly drawn to appeal to a singular audience: the Mayor.
Th- That is true, but...
when I've got readers right there in front of me, I end up...
wanting to draw something they'll like, so...
Huh? But what I wanted to draw was...
ギィ…
KREEE
I've been looking for you,
Potato Chip-sensei...

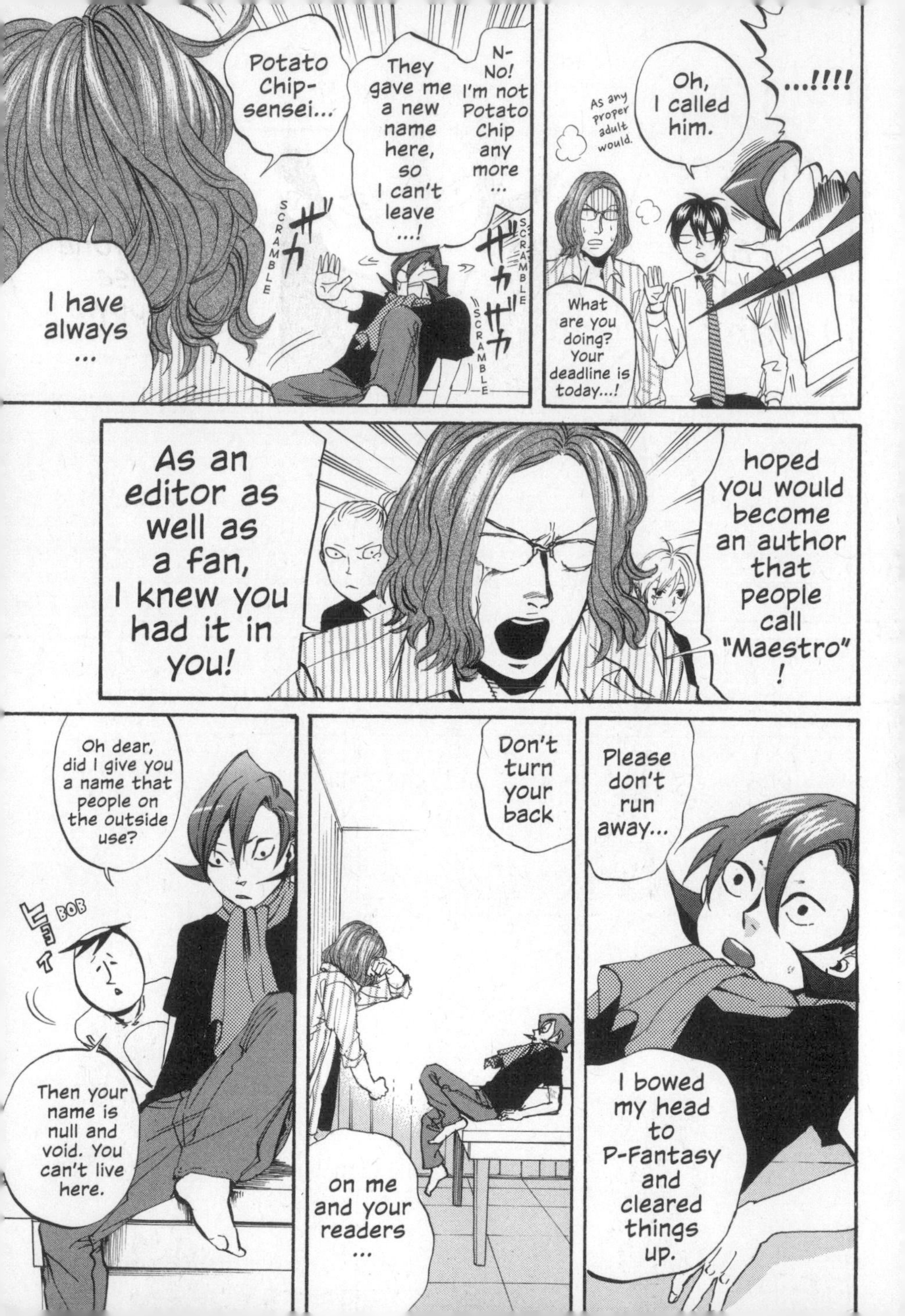
...!!!!
Oh, I called him.
As any proper adult would.
What are you doing? Your deadline is today...!
N-No! I'm not Potato Chip any more...
They gave me a new name here, so I can't leave...!
Potato Chip-sensei...
SCRAMBLE
SCRAMBLE
SCRAMBLE
I have always...
hoped you would become an author that people call "Maestro"!
As an editor as well as a fan, I knew you had it in you!
Please don't run away...
I bowed my head to P-Fantasy and cleared things up.
Don't turn your back
on me and your readers...
Oh dear, did I give you a name that people on the outside use?
BOB
Then your name is null and void. You can't live here.

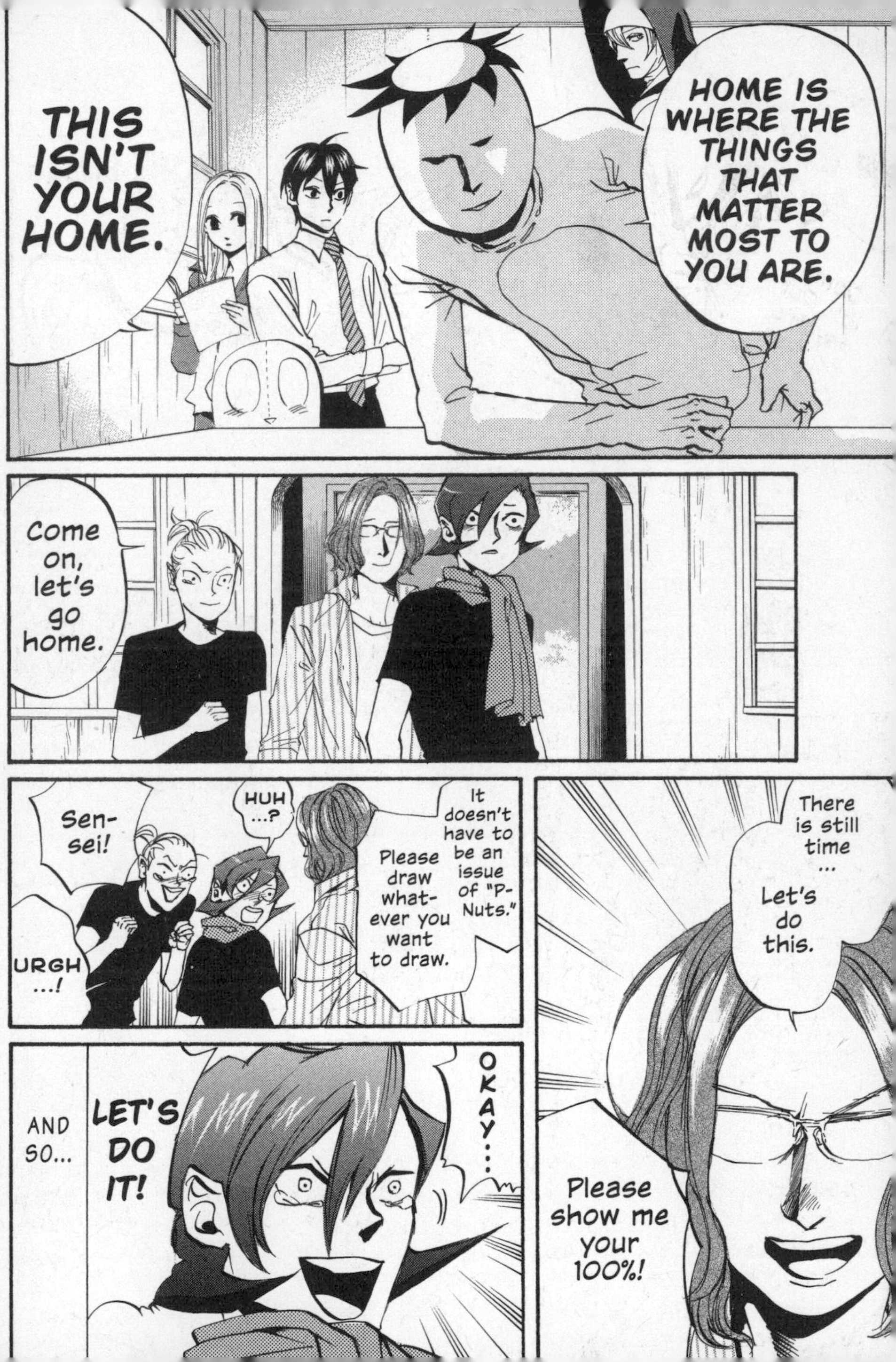
HOME IS WHERE THE THINGS THAT MATTER MOST TO YOU ARE.
THIS ISN'T YOUR HOME.
Come on, let's go home.
There is still time...
Let's do this.
Please show me your 100%!
It doesn't have to be an issue of "P-Nuts."
Please draw what-ever you want to draw.
HUH ...?
Sen-sei!
URGH ...!
OKAY...
LET'S DO IT!
AND SO...

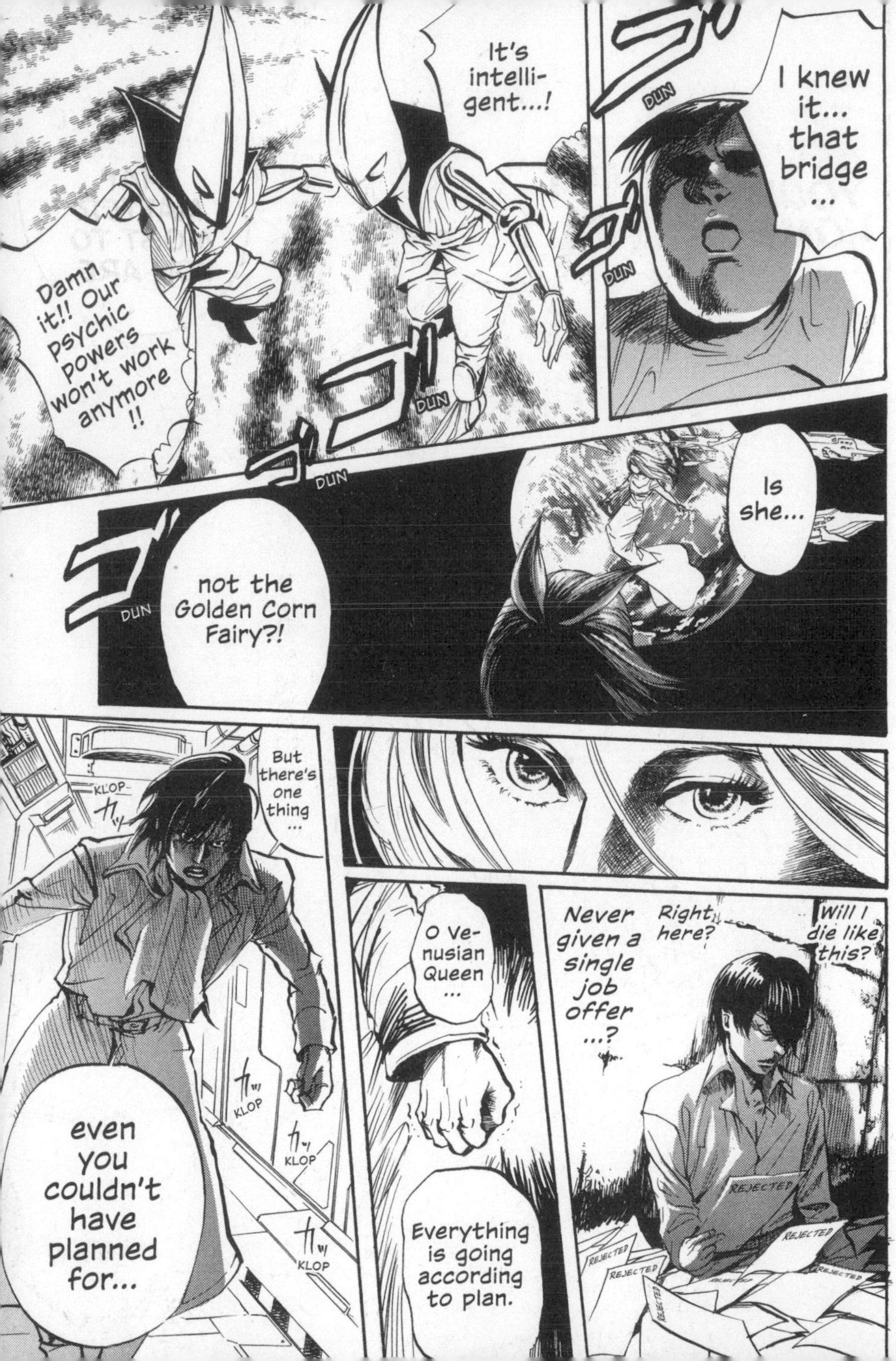
DUN
I knew it... that bridge ...
DUN
It's intelli- gent...!
Damn it!! Our psychic powers won't work anymore !!
DUN
DUN
Is she...
not the Golden Corn Fairy?!
DUN
Will I die like this?
Right here?
Never given a single job offer ...?
REJECTED
REJECTED
REJECTED
REJECTED
REJECTED
REJECTED
O Ve- nusian Queen ...
Everything is going according to plan.
But there's one thing ...
KLOP
KLOP
KLOP
KLOP
even you couldn't have planned for...

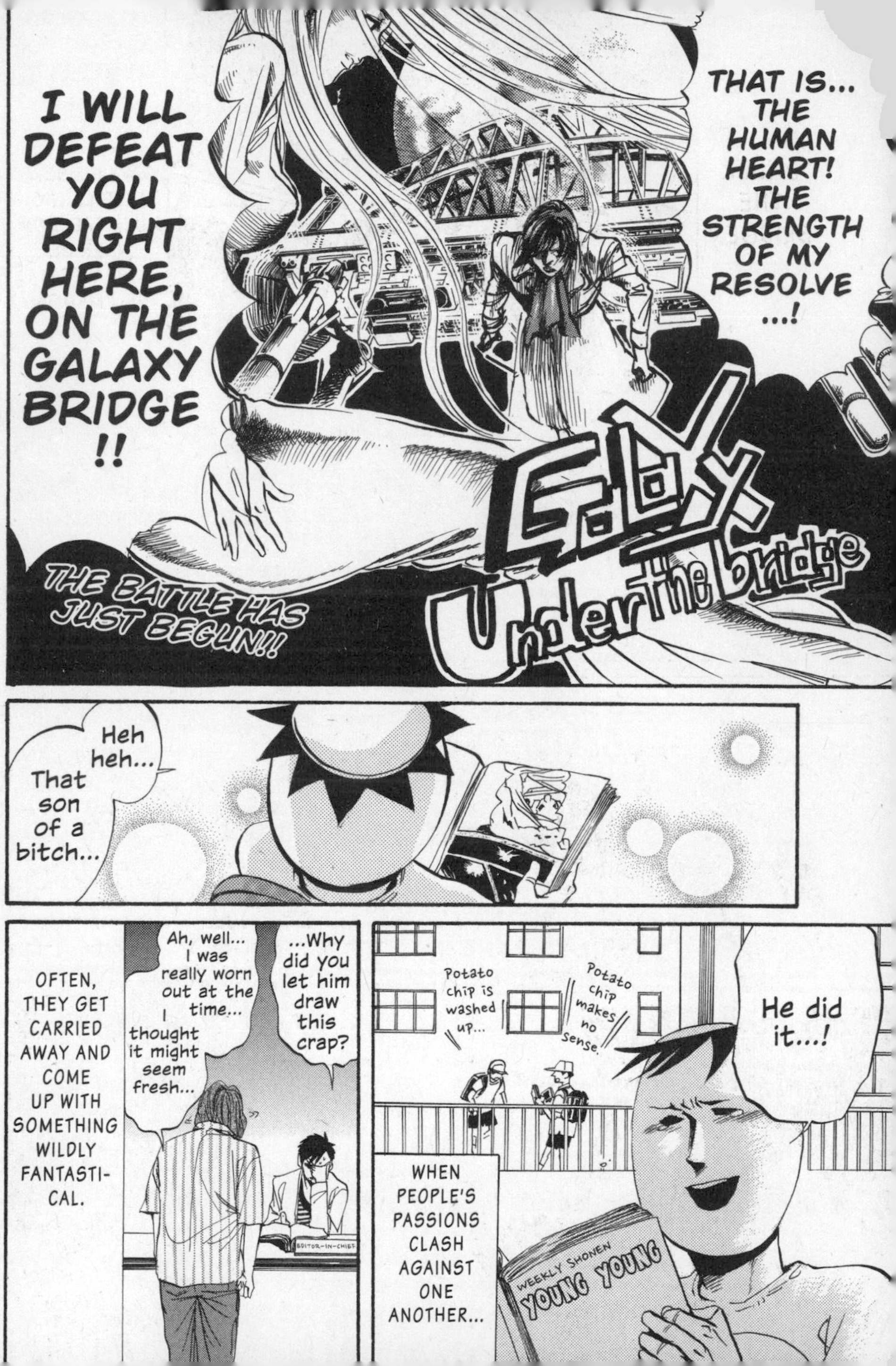
THAT IS... THE HUMAN HEART! THE STRENGTH OF MY RESOLVE ...!
I WILL DEFEAT YOU RIGHT HERE, ON THE GALAXY BRIDGE !!
Under the bridge
THE BATTLE HAS JUST BEGUN!!
Heh heh... That son of a bitch...
He did it...!
Potato chip makes no sense.
Potato chip is washed up...
WHEN PEOPLE'S PASSIONS CLASH AGAINST ONE ANOTHER...
WEEKLY SHONEN YOUNG YOUNG
...Why did you let him draw this crap?
Ah, well... I was really worn out at the time... I thought it might seem fresh...
EDITOR-IN-CHIEF
OFTEN, THEY GET CARRIED AWAY AND COME UP WITH SOMETHING WILDLY FANTASTICAL.

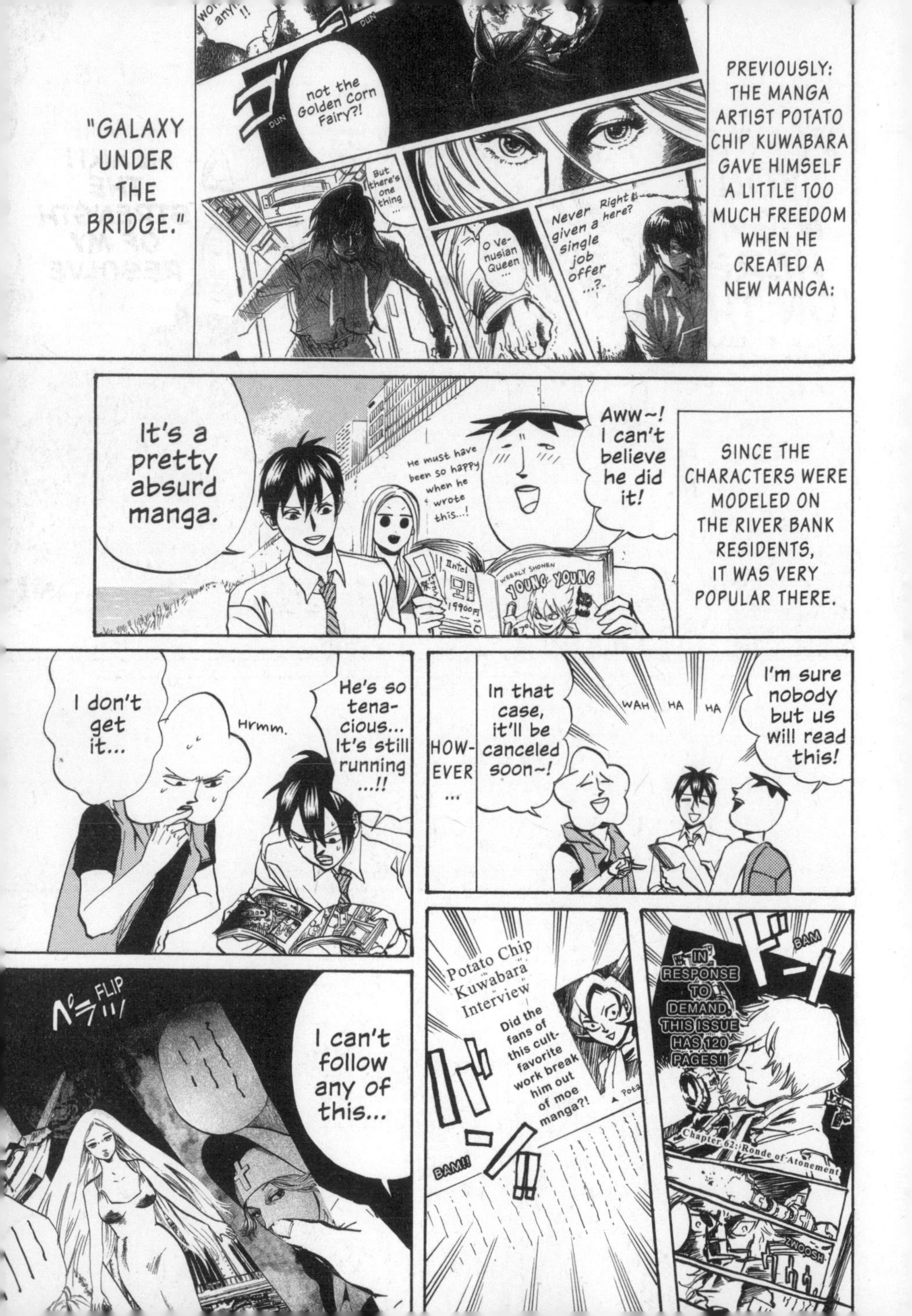
PREVIOUSLY: THE MANGA ARTIST POTATO CHIP KUWABARA GAVE HIMSELF A LITTLE TOO MUCH FREEDOM WHEN HE CREATED A NEW MANGA:
DUN
not the Golden Corn Fairy?!
DUN
Right here?
Never given a single job offer ...?
O Ve-nusian Queen ...
But there's one thing ...
"GALAXY UNDER THE BRIDGE."
SINCE THE CHARACTERS WERE MODELED ON THE RIVER BANK RESIDENTS, IT WAS VERY POPULAR THERE.
Aww~! I can't believe he did it!
WEEKLY SHONEN YOUNG YOUNG
He must have been so happy when he wrote this...!
It's a pretty absurd manga.
I'm sure nobody but us will read this!
WAH HA HA
In that case, it'll be canceled soon~!
HOW-EVER ...
He's so tena-cious... It's still running ...!!
Hrmm.
I don't get it...
BAM
IN RESPONSE TO DEMAND, THIS ISSUE HAS 120 PAGES!!
Chapter 62: Ronde of Atonement
ZNOOSH
Potato Chip Kuwabara Interview
Did the fans of this cult-favorite work break him out of moe manga?!
BAM!!
FLIP
I can't follow any of this...

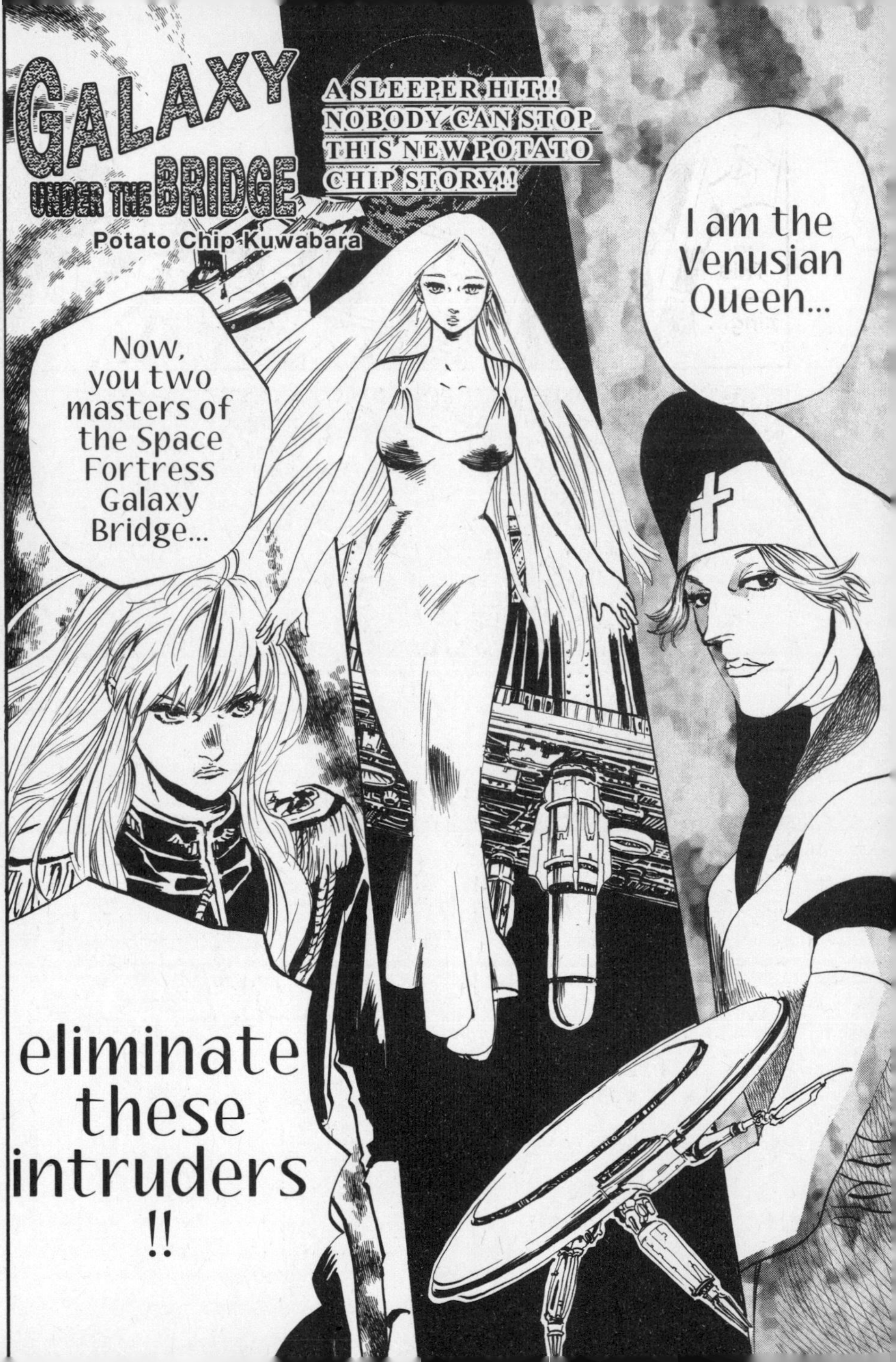
GALAXY UNDER THE BRIDGE
A SLEEPER HIT!! NOBODY CAN STOP THIS NEW POTATO CHIP STORY!!
Potato Chip Kuwabara
I am the Venusian Queen...
Now, you two masters of the Space Fortress Galaxy Bridge...
eliminate these intruders !!

Chapter 220: Sudden Visitors

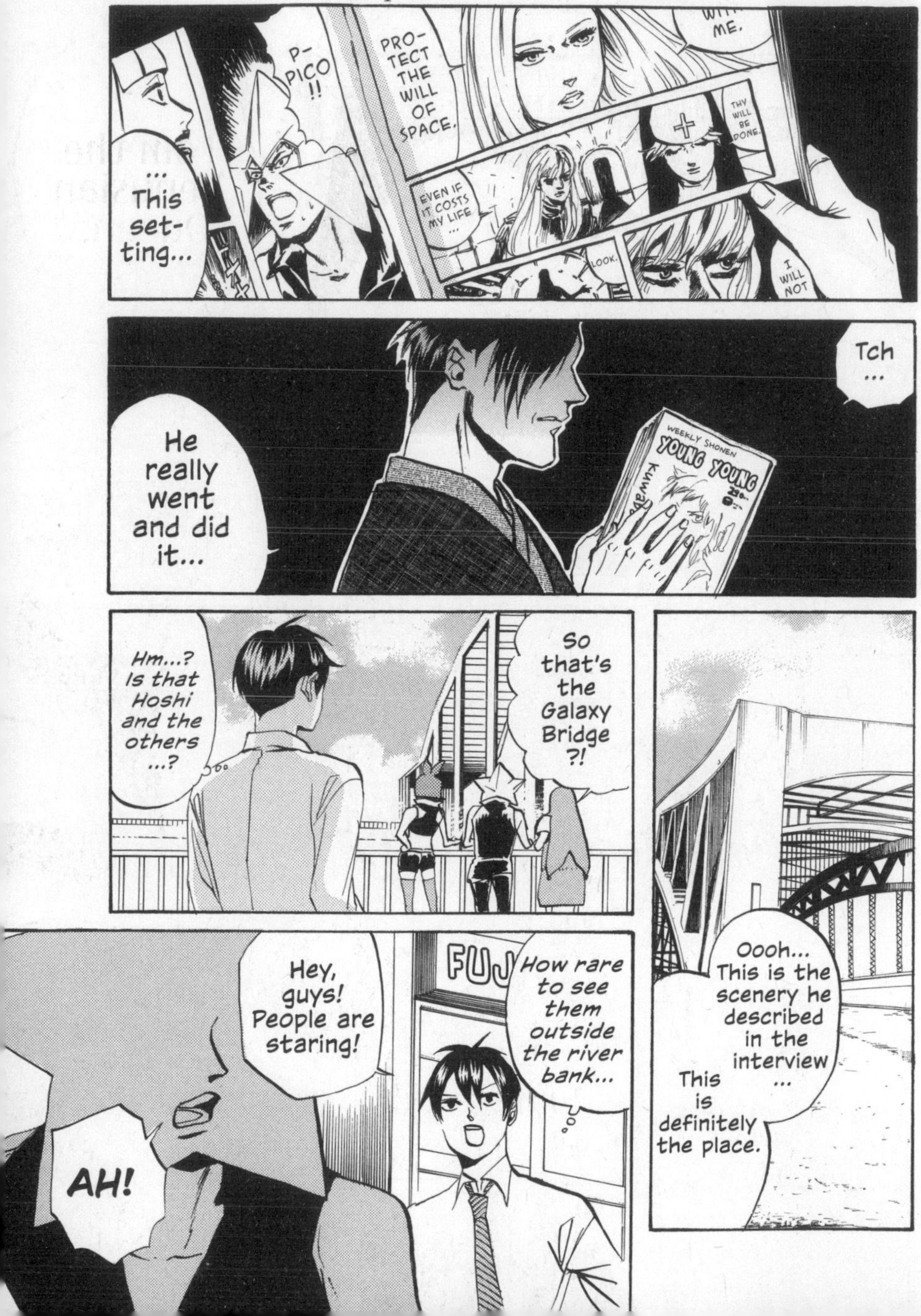
ME.
THY WILL BE DONE.
I WILL NOT
LOOK.
EVEN IF IT COSTS MY LIFE...
PROTECT THE WILL OF SPACE.
P-PICO!!
...This setting...
Tch...
WEEKLY SHONEN
YOUNG YOUNG
He really went and did it...
Oooh... This is the scenery he described in the interview...
This is definitely the place.
So that's the Galaxy Bridge?!
Hm...? Is that Hoshi and the others...?
How rare to see them outside the river bank...
Hey, guys! People are staring!
AH!

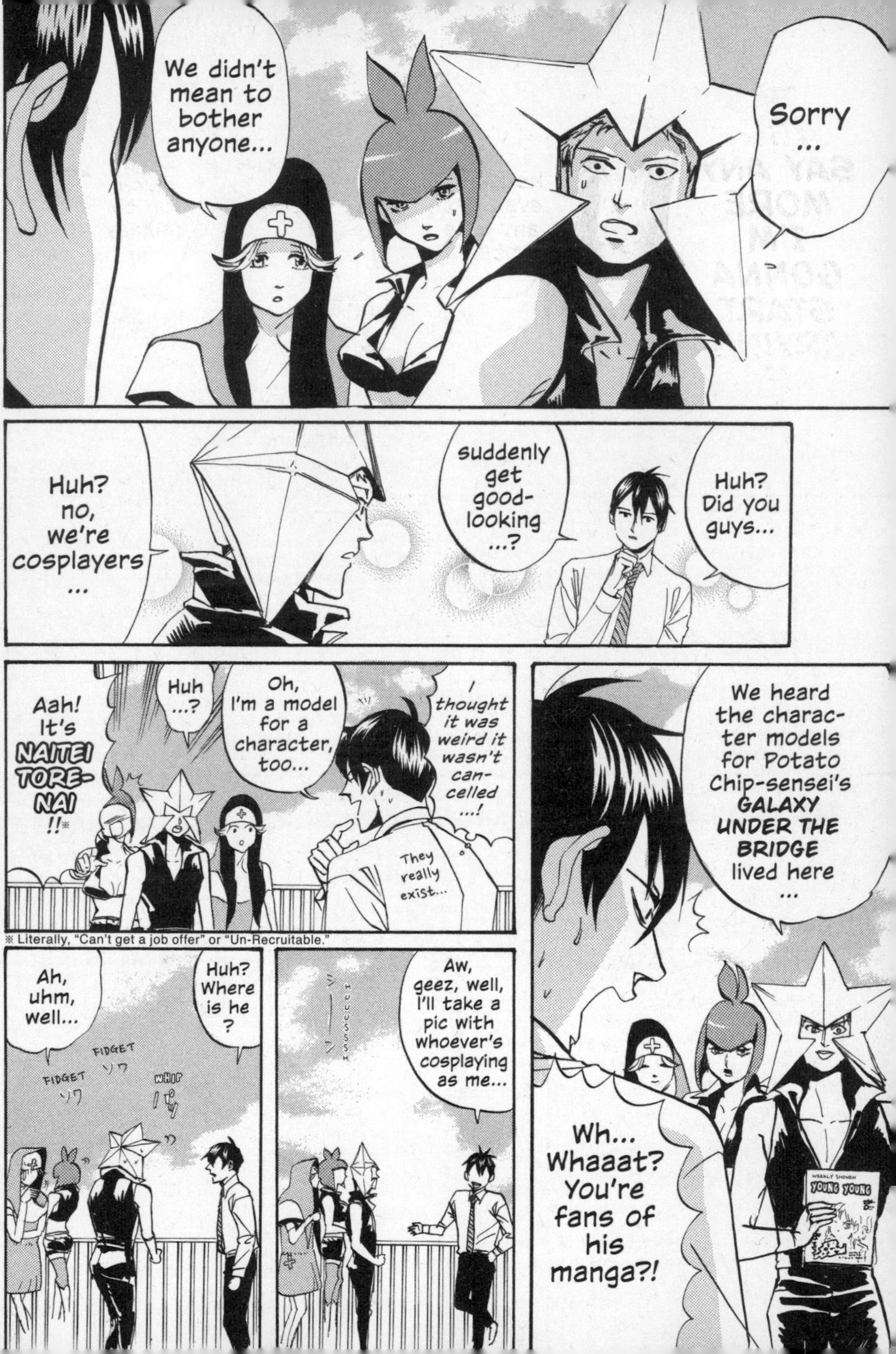
Sorry ...
We didn't mean to bother anyone...
Huh? Did you guys...
suddenly get good-looking ...?
Huh? no, we're cosplayers ...
We heard the character models for Potato Chip-sensei's **GALAXY UNDER THE BRIDGE** lived here ...
Wh... Whaaat? You're fans of his manga?!
WEEKLY SHONEN YOUNG YOUNG
I thought it was weird it wasn't cancelled ...!
Oh, I'm a model for a character, too...
Huh ...?
Aah! It's NAITEI TORE-NAI !!※
They really exist...
Aw, geez, well, I'll take a pic with whoever's cosplaying as me...
HUUUSSSH
Huh? Where is he ?
Ah, uhm, well...
FIDGET
FIDGET
WHIP
※ Literally, "Can't get a job offer" or "Un-Recruitable."

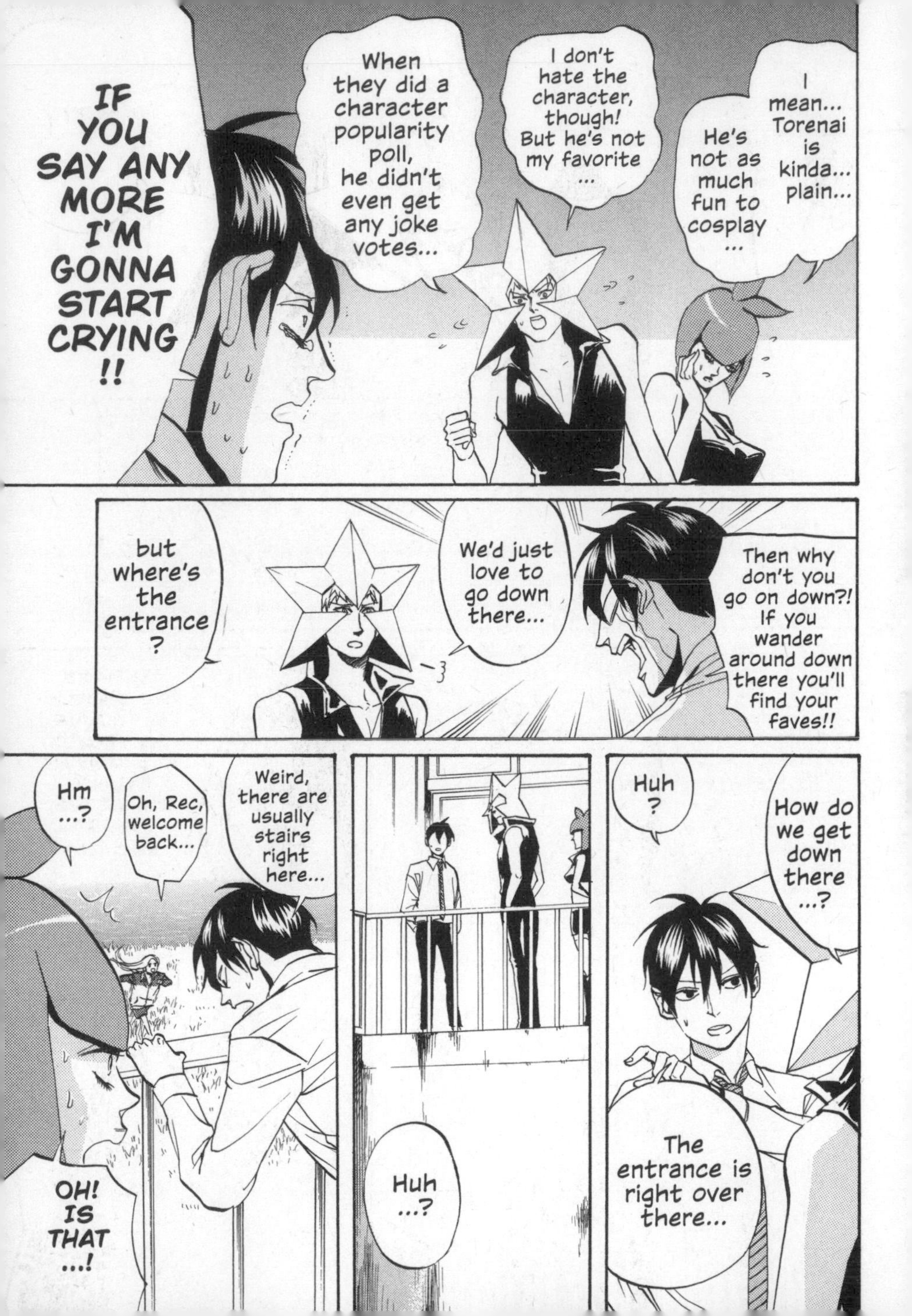
I mean... Torenai is kinda... plain...
He's not as much fun to cosplay ...
I don't hate the character, though! But he's not my favorite ...
When they did a character popularity poll, he didn't even get any joke votes...
IF YOU SAY ANY MORE I'M GONNA START CRYING!!
Then why don't you go on down?! If you wander around down there you'll find your faves!!
We'd just love to go down there...
but where's the entrance ?
How do we get down there ...?
Huh ?
The entrance is right over there...
Huh ...?
Weird, there are usually stairs right here...
Oh, Rec, welcome back...
Hm ...?
OH! IS THAT ...!

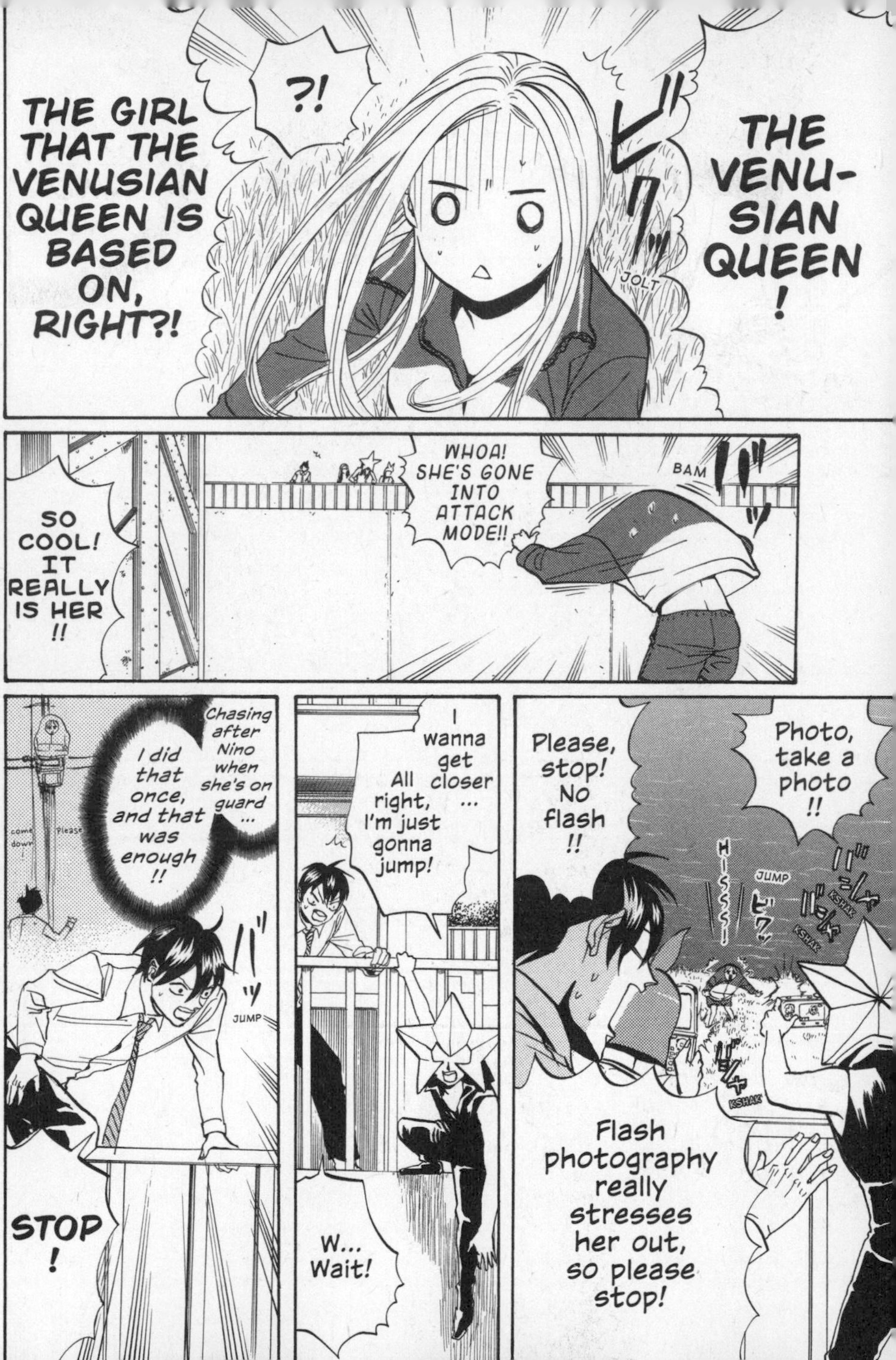
THE VENUSIAN QUEEN!
JOLT
?!
THE GIRL THAT THE VENUSIAN QUEEN IS BASED ON, RIGHT?!
BAM
WHOA! SHE'S GONE INTO ATTACK MODE!!
SO COOL! IT REALLY IS HER!!
Photo, take a photo!!
Please, stop! No flash!!
HISSS
JUMP
KSHAK
KSHAK
KSHAK
Flash photography really stresses her out, so please stop!
I wanna get closer ...
All right, I'm just gonna jump!
W... Wait!
Chasing after Nino when she's on guard ...
I did that once, and that was enough!!
Please
come down
JUMP
STOP!

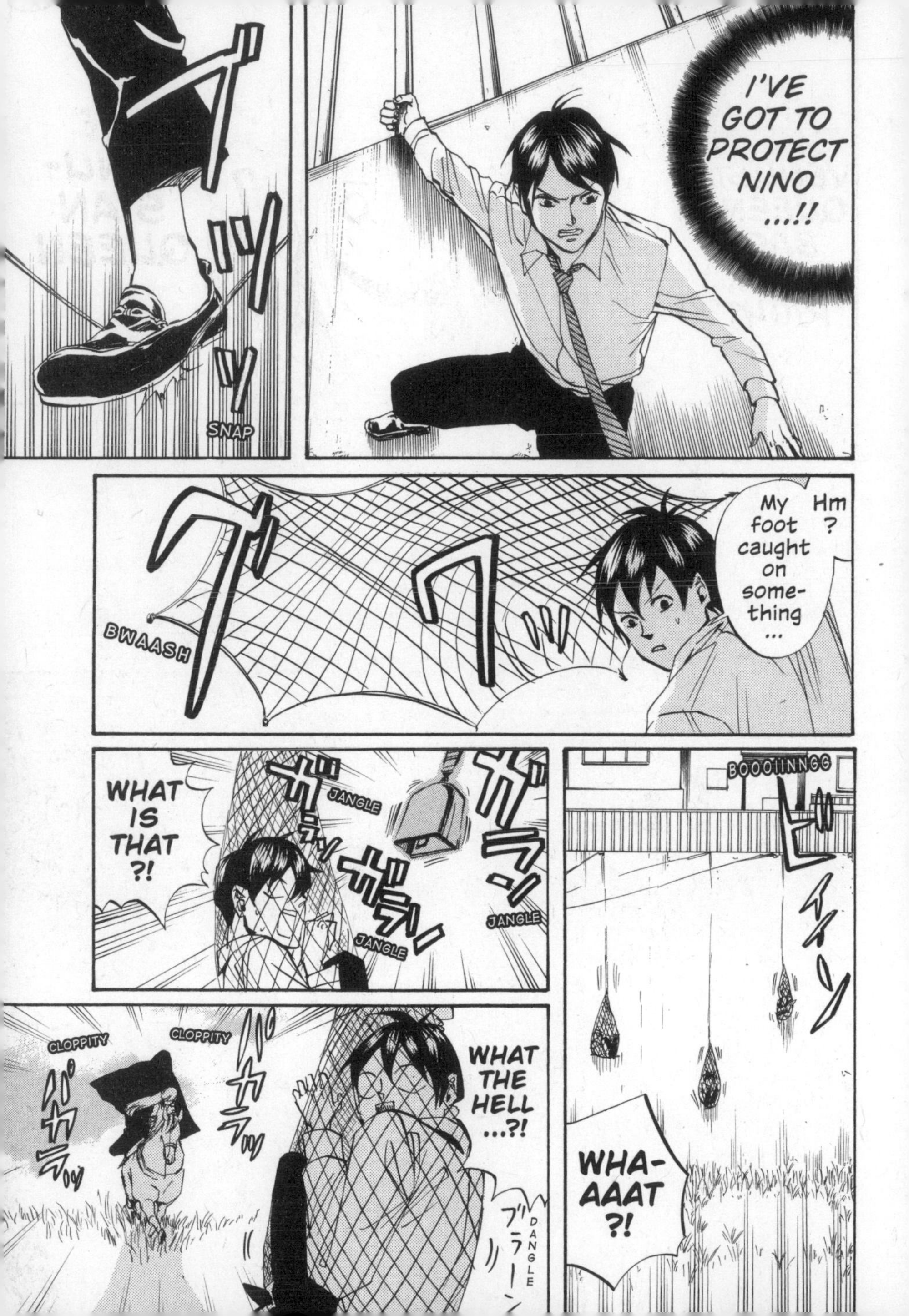
I'VE GOT TO PROTECT NINO ...!!
SNAP
Hm?
My foot caught on something...
BWAASH
BOOOIINNGG
WHA-AAAT?!
WHAT IS THAT?!
JANGLE
JANGLE
JANGLE
WHAT THE HELL ...?!
DANGLE
CLOPPITY
CLOPPITY

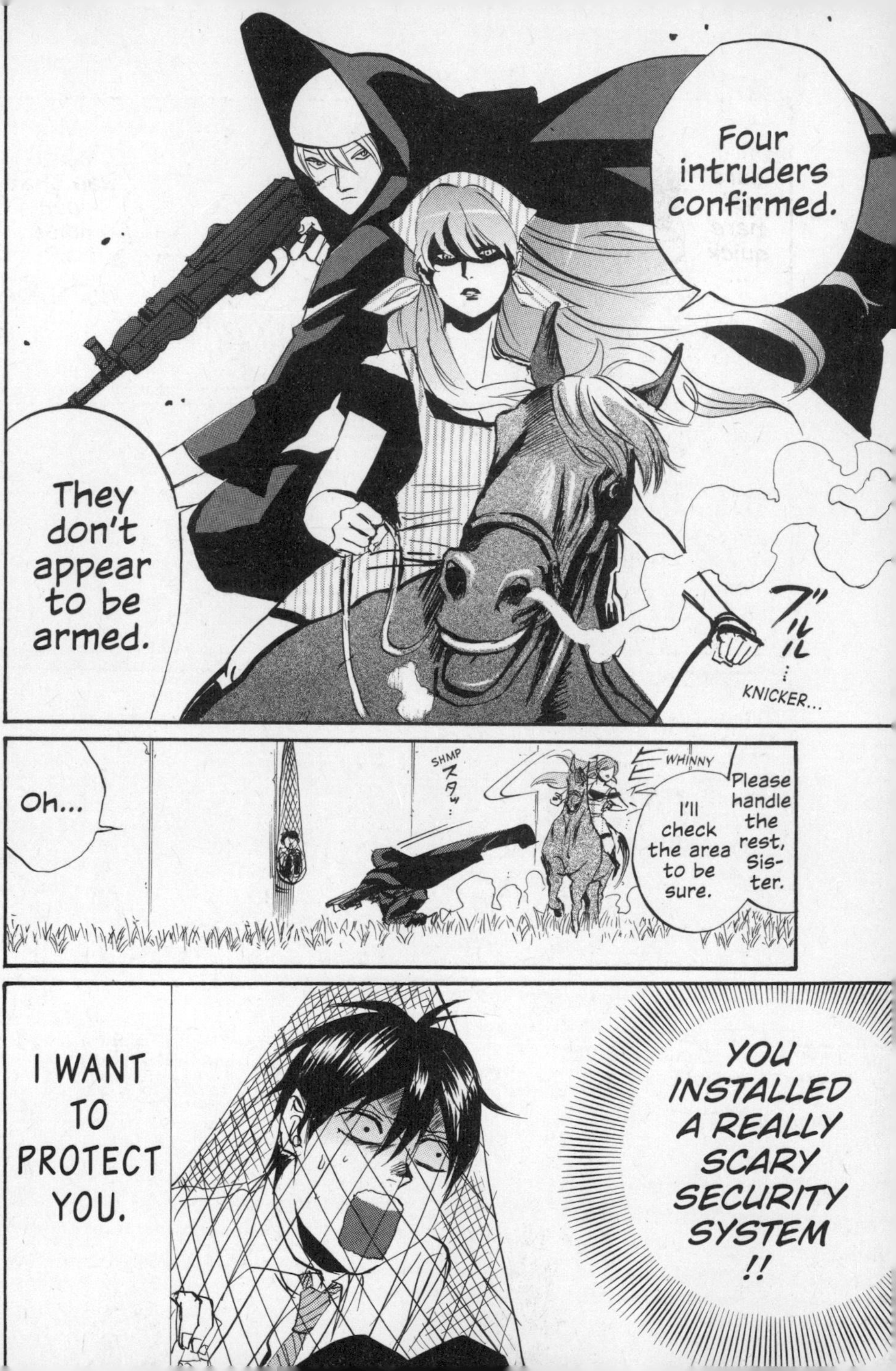
Four intruders confirmed.
They don't appear to be armed.
ブルル…
KNICKER...
Please handle the rest, Sister.
I'll check the area to be sure.
WHINNY
SHMP
スタッ
Oh...
YOU INSTALLED A REALLY SCARY SECURITY SYSTEM!!
I WANT TO PROTECT YOU.

Chapter 221: Real

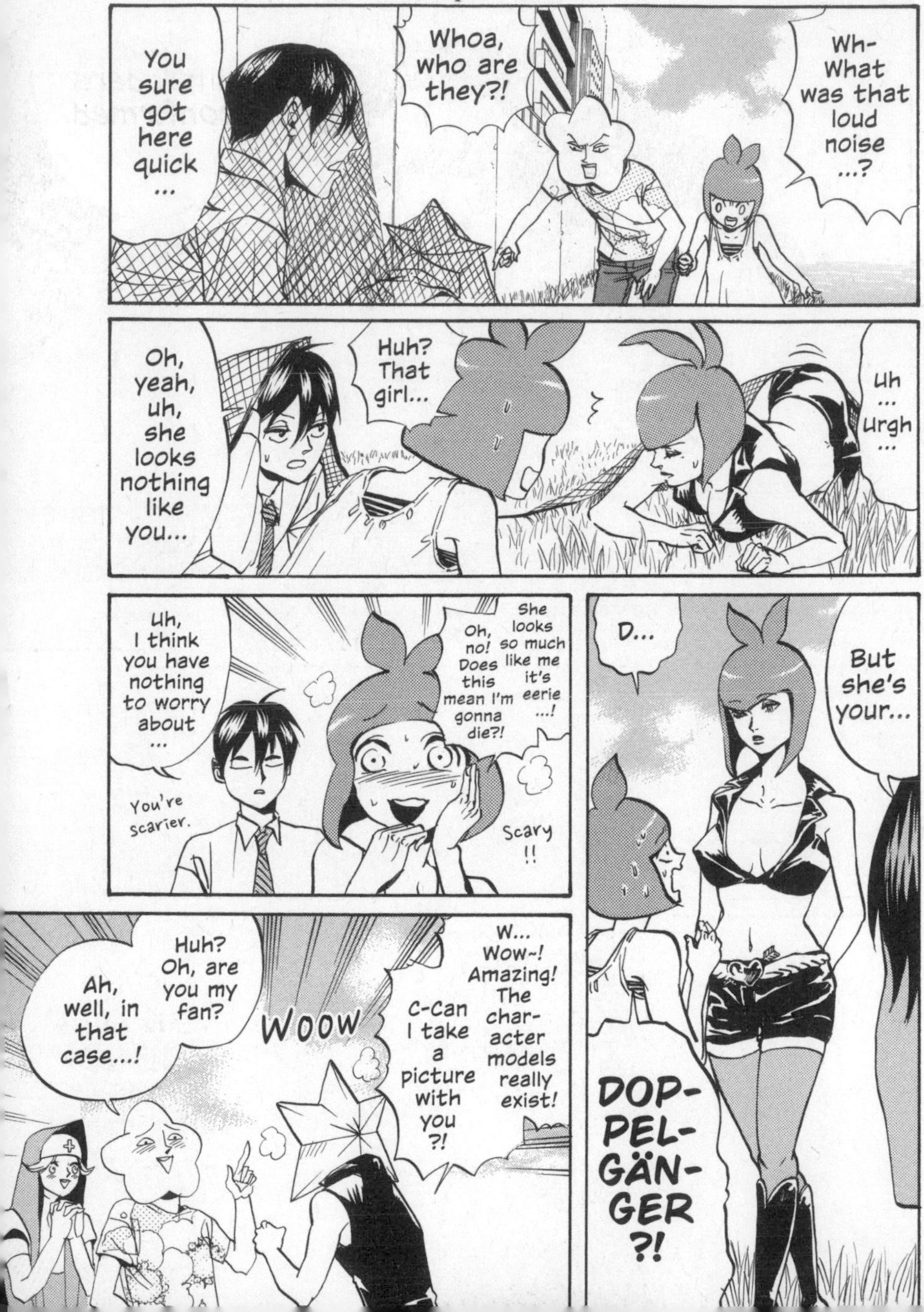
Wh-What was that loud noise ...?
Whoa, who are they?!
You sure got here quick ...
Uh ... Urgh ...
Huh? That girl...
Oh, yeah, uh, she looks nothing like you...
But she's your...
D...
DOPPELGÄNGER?!
She looks so much like me it's eerie ...!
Oh, no! Does this mean I'm gonna die?!
Scary !!
Uh, I think you have nothing to worry about ...
You're scarier.
W... Wow~! Amazing! The character models really exist!
C-Can I take a picture with you?!
WOOW
Huh? Oh, are you my fan?
Ah, well, in that case...!

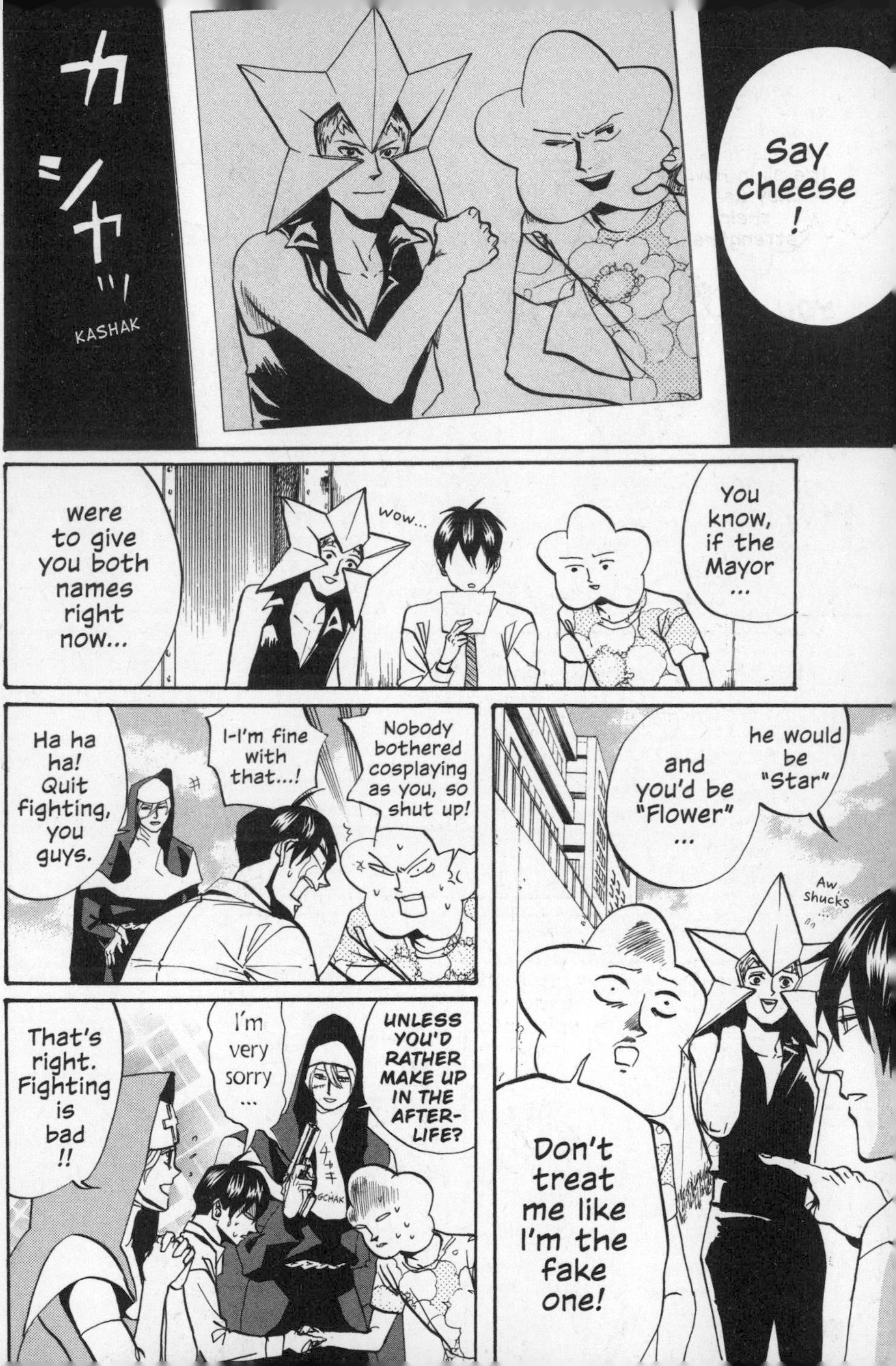

Say cheese!
カシャッ
KASHAK
You know, if the Mayor...
wow...
were to give you both names right now...
he would be "Star"
and you'd be "Flower"...
Aw shucks...
Don't treat me like I'm the fake one!
Nobody bothered cosplaying as you, so shut up!
I-I'm fine with that...!
Ha ha ha! Quit fighting, you guys.
UNLESS YOU'D RATHER MAKE UP IN THE AFTER-LIFE?
GCHAK
I'm very sorry...
That's right. Fighting is bad!!

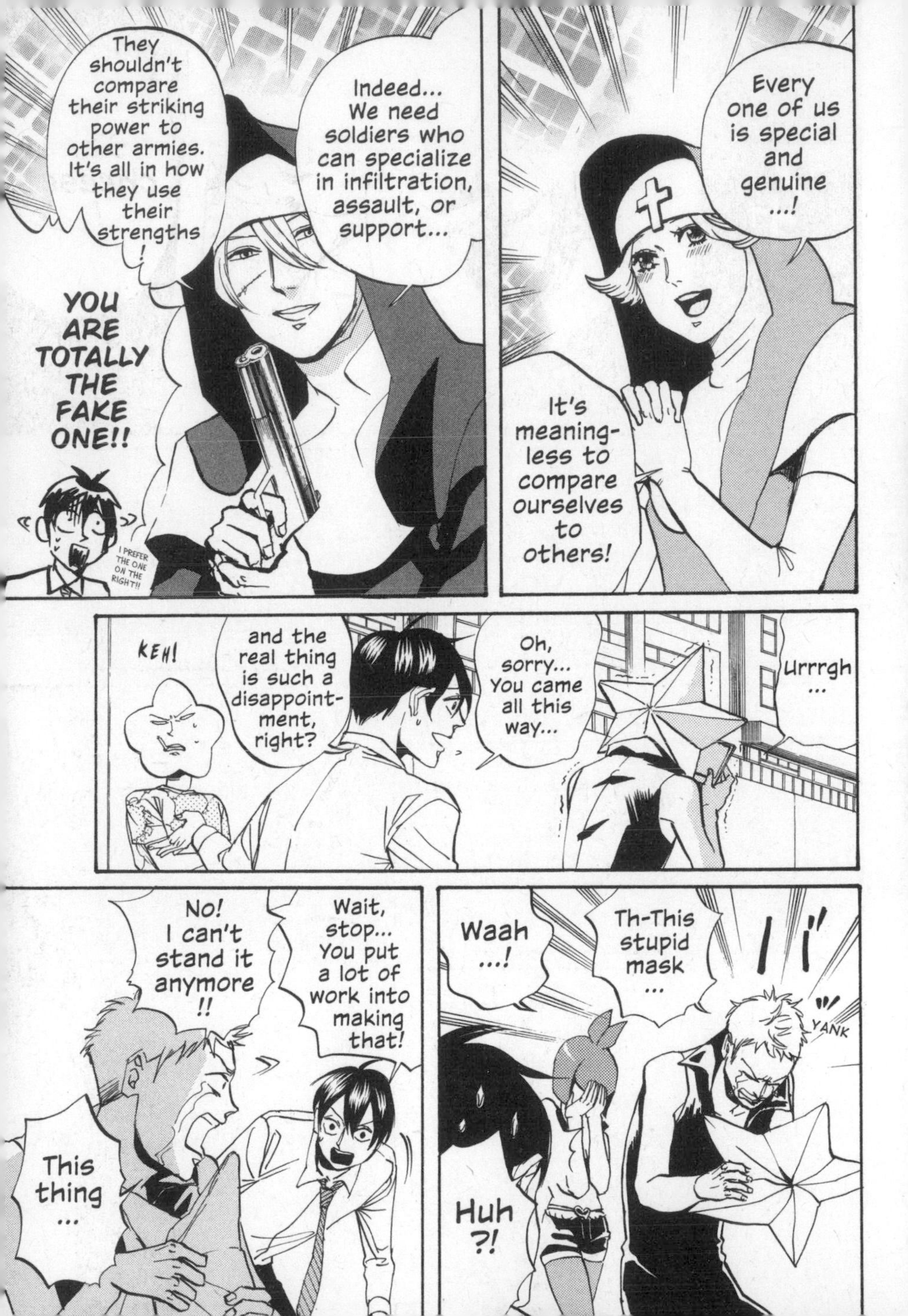
Every one of us is special and genuine ...!
It's meaning-less to compare ourselves to others!
Indeed... We need soldiers who can specialize in infiltration, assault, or support...
They shouldn't compare their striking power to other armies. It's all in how they use their strengths!
YOU ARE TOTALLY THE FAKE ONE!!
I PREFER THE ONE ON THE RIGHT!!
Urrrgh ...
Oh, sorry... You came all this way...
and the real thing is such a disappoint-ment, right?
KEH!
Th-This stupid mask ...
YANK
Waah ...!
Huh ?!
Wait, stop... You put a lot of work into making that!
No! I can't stand it anymore !!
This thing ...

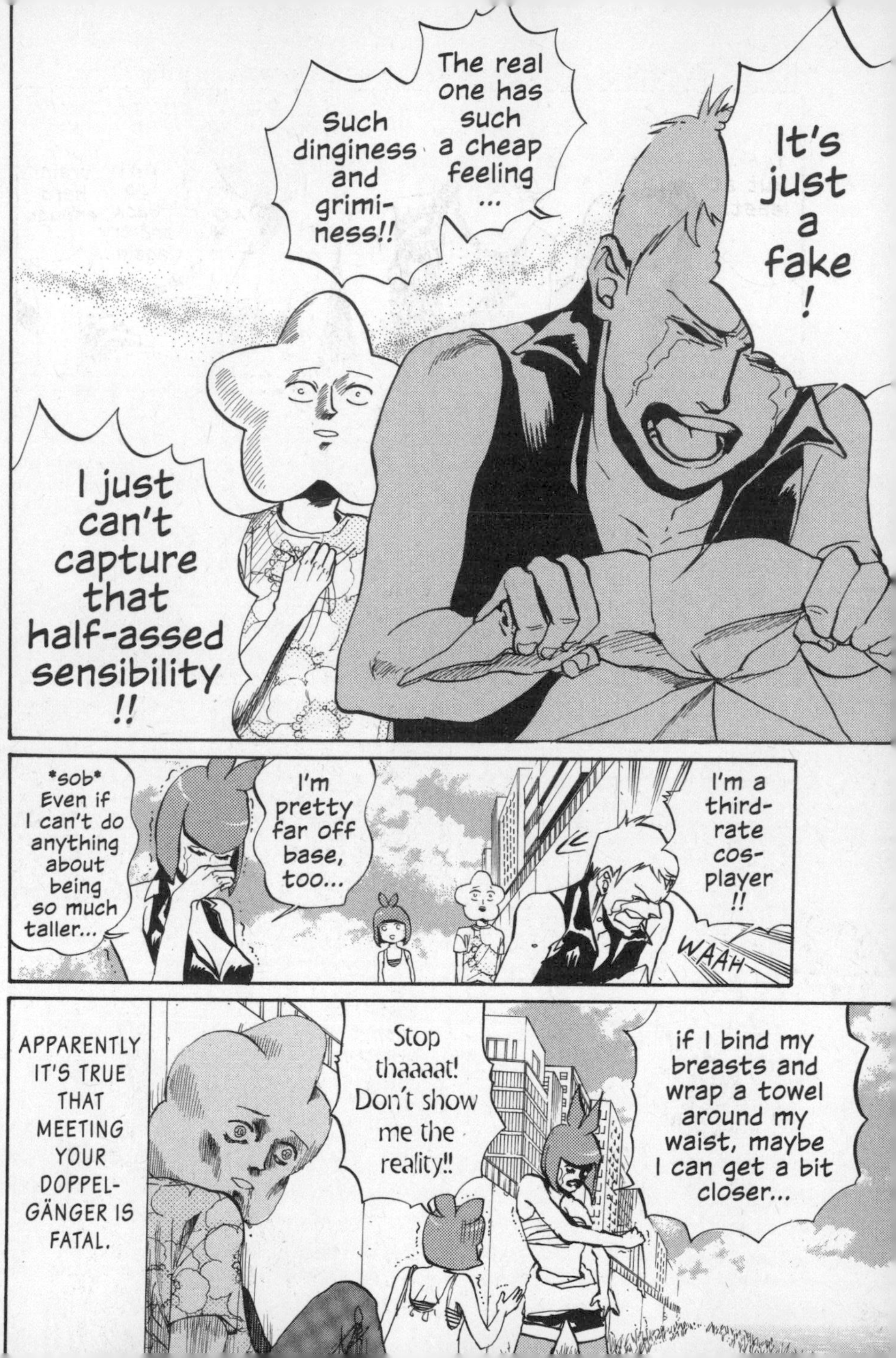
It's just a fake!
The real one has such a cheap feeling...
Such dinginess and griminess!!
I just can't capture that half-assed sensibility!!
I'm a third-rate cosplayer!!
WAAH
I'm pretty far off base, too...
sob Even if I can't do anything about being so much taller...
if I bind my breasts and wrap a towel around my waist, maybe I can get a bit closer...
Stop thaaaat! Don't show me the reality!!
APPARENTLY IT'S TRUE THAT MEETING YOUR DOPPELGÄNGER IS FATAL.

Chapter 222: People to Protect, Places to Protect

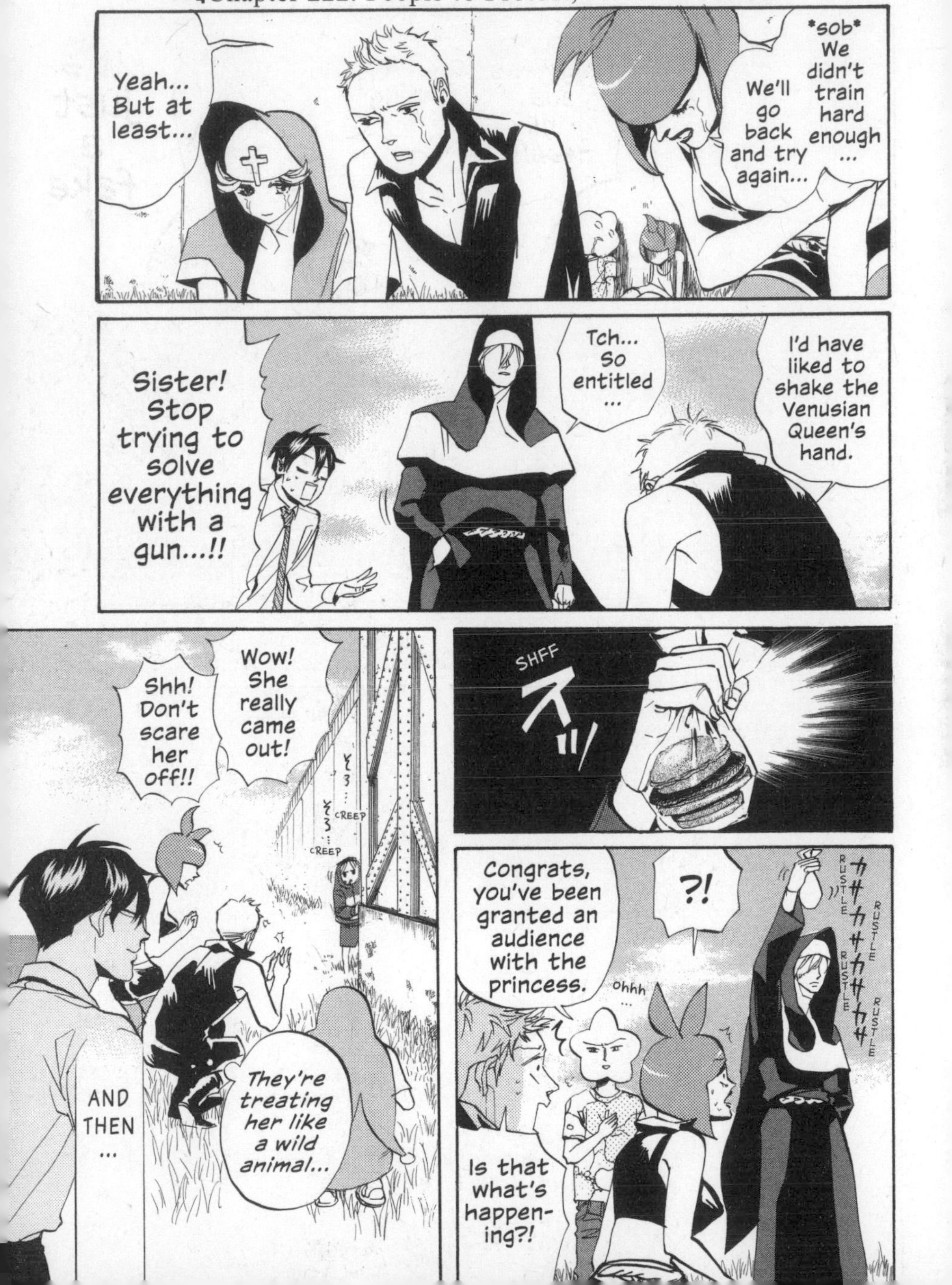
sob We didn't train hard enough ...
We'll go back and try again...
Yeah... But at least...
I'd have liked to shake the Venusian Queen's hand.
Tch... So entitled ...
Sister! Stop trying to solve everything with a gun...!!
SHFF
スッ
カサカサカサカサ
RUSTLE RUSTLE RUSTLE RUSTLE
?!
Congrats, you've been granted an audience with the princess.
Ohhh ...
Is that what's happening?!
Wow! She really came out!
Shh! Don't scare her off!!
そろ… CREEP
そろ… CREEP
They're treating her like a wild animal...
AND THEN ...

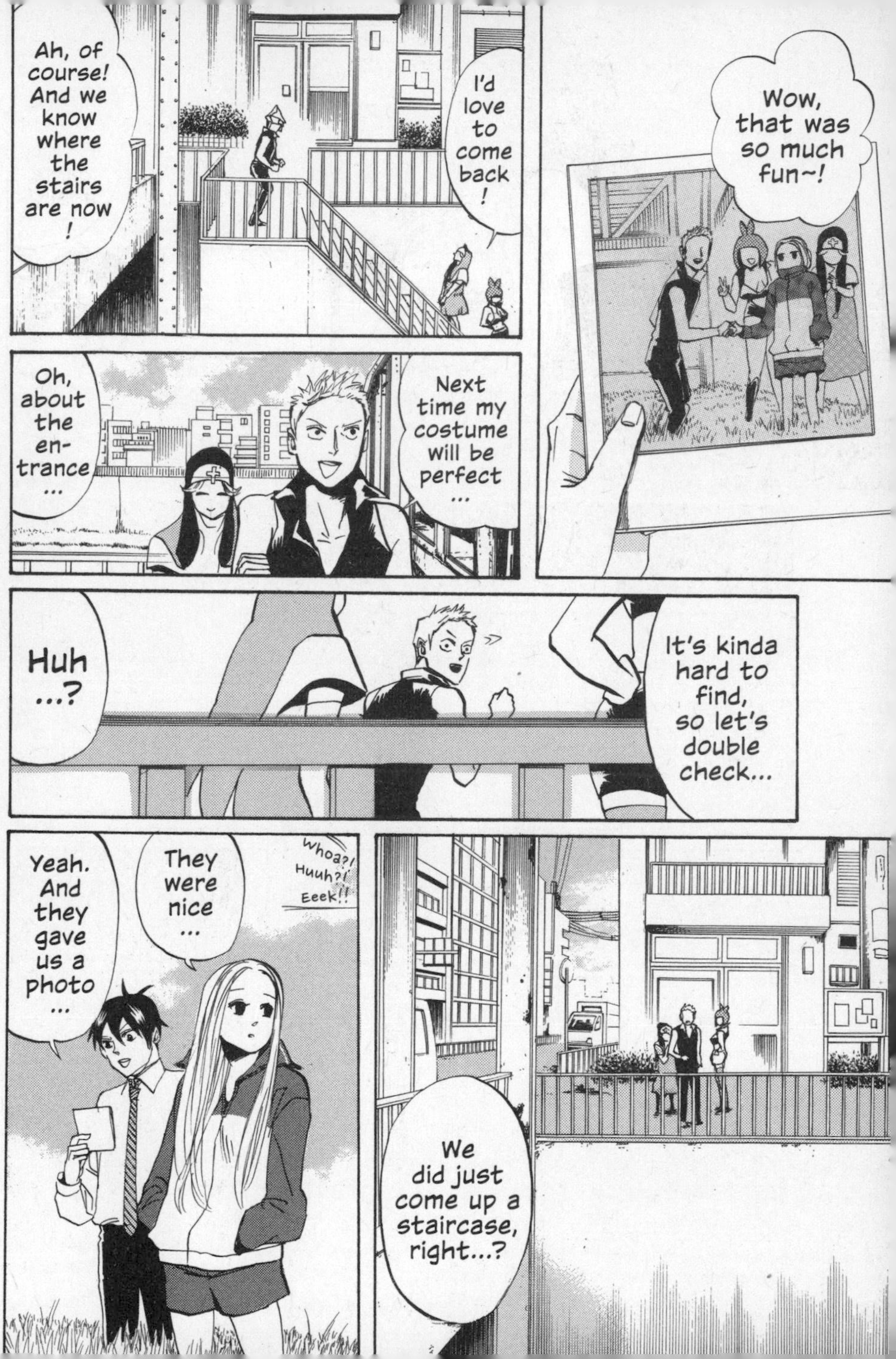

Wow, that was so much fun~!
I'd love to come back!
Ah, of course! And we know where the stairs are now!
Next time my costume will be perfect...
Oh, about the entrance...
It's kinda hard to find, so let's double check...
Huh...?
We did just come up a staircase, right...?
Whoa?! Huuh?! Eeek!!
They were nice...
Yeah. And they gave us a photo...

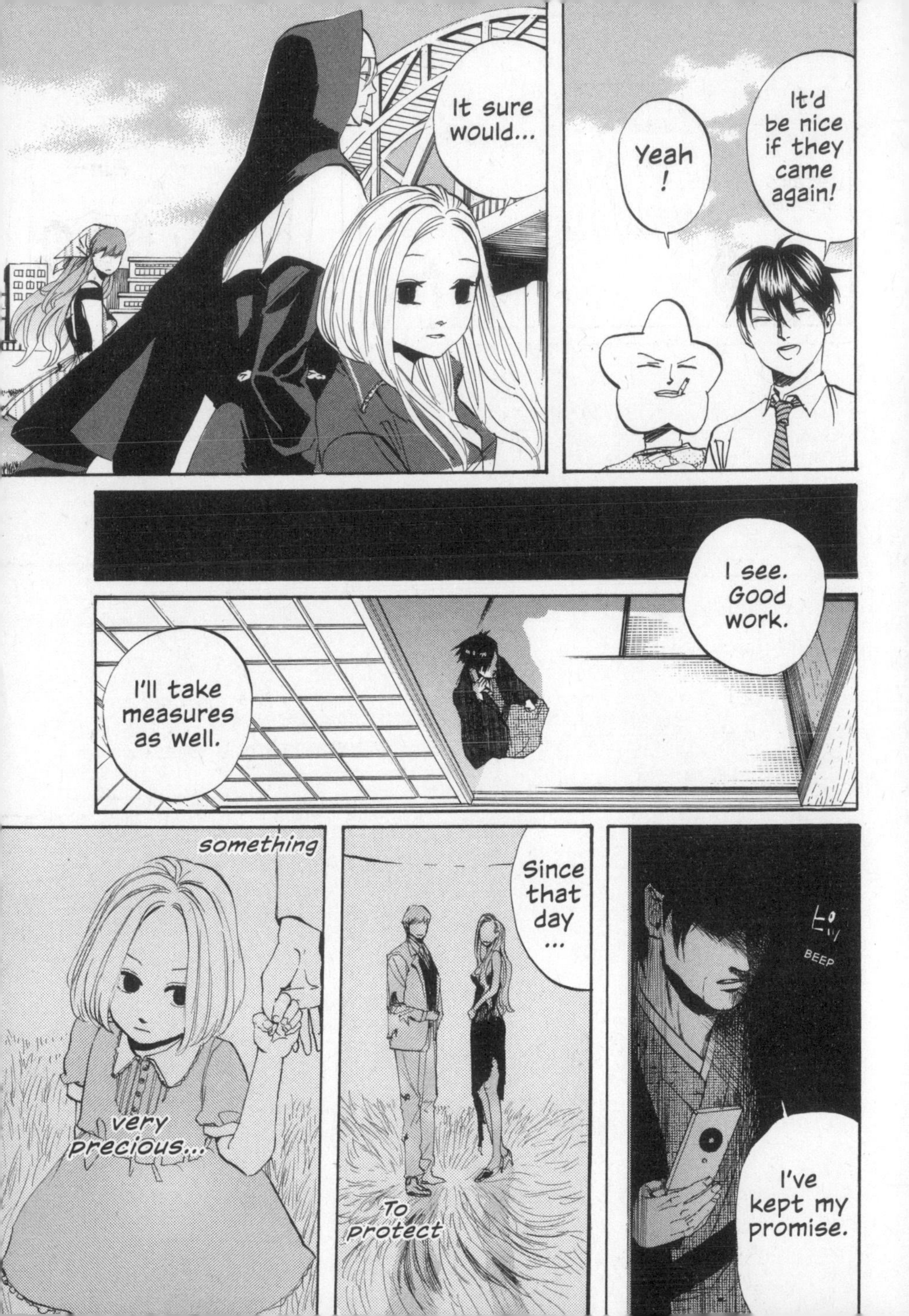
It'd be nice if they came again!
Yeah!
It sure would...
I see. Good work.
I'll take measures as well.
BEEP
I've kept my promise.
Since that day...
To protect
something
very precious...

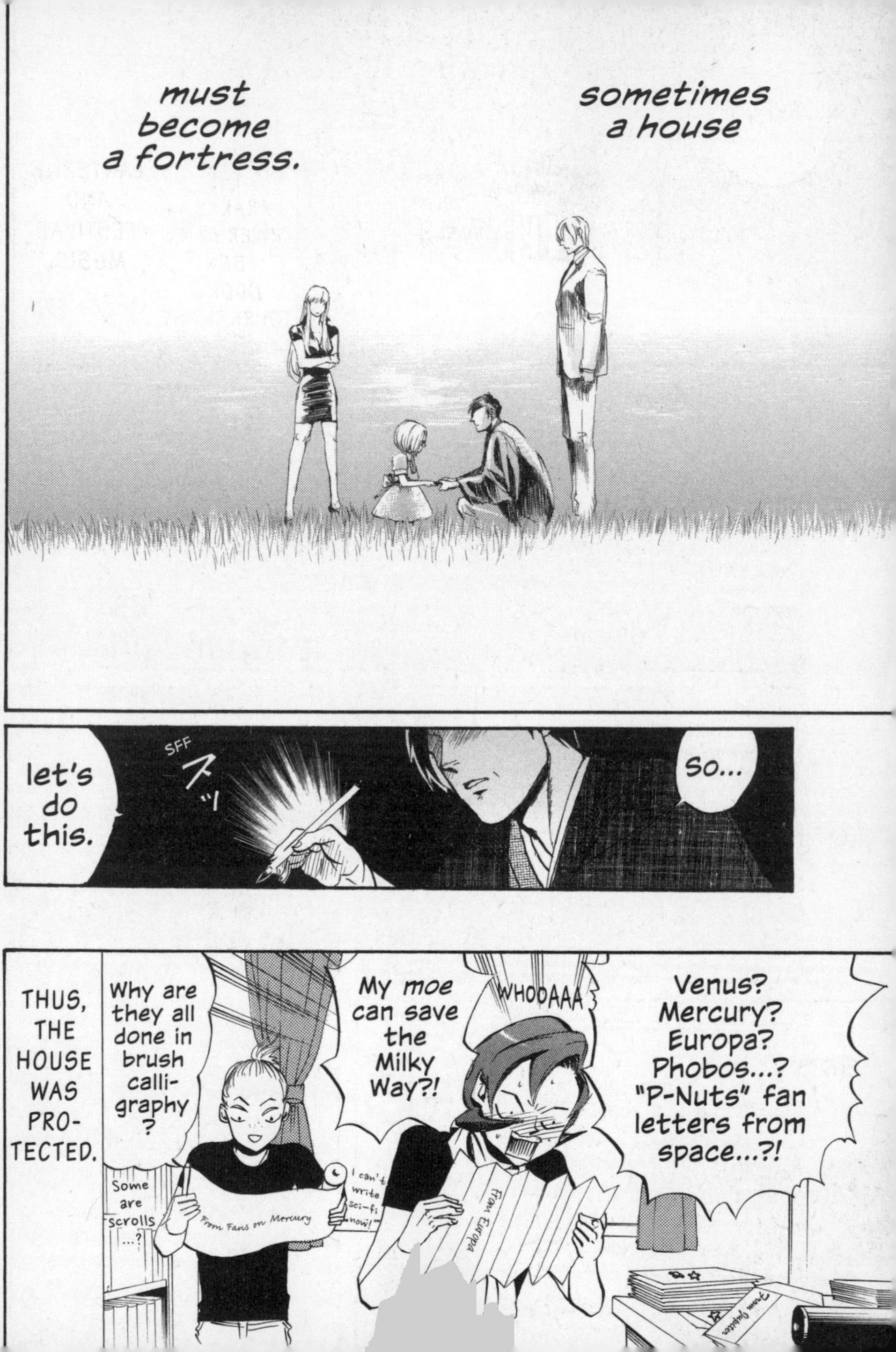
sometimes a house
must become a fortress.
So...
SFF
let's do this.
Venus? Mercury? Europa? Phobos...? "P-Nuts" fan letters from space...?!
WHOOAAA
My moe can save the Milky Way?!
From Europa
I can't write sci-fi now!
From Fans on Mercury
Why are they all done in brush calli-graphy?
Some are scrolls ...?
THUS, THE HOUSE WAS PRO-TECTED.

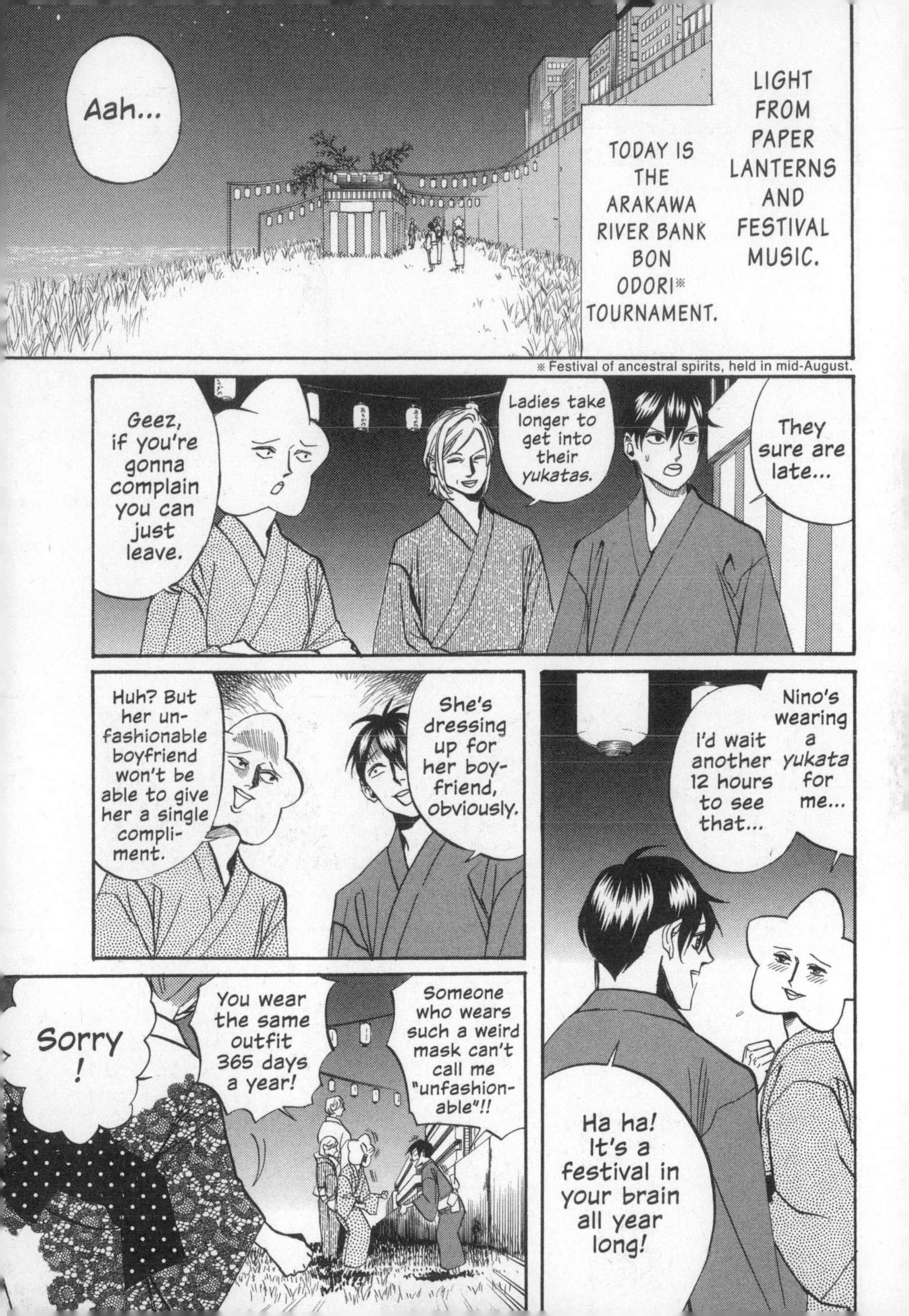
LIGHT FROM PAPER LANTERNS AND FESTIVAL MUSIC.
TODAY IS THE ARAKAWA RIVER BANK BON ODORI※ TOURNAMENT.
Aah...
They sure are late...
Ladies take longer to get into their yukatas.
Geez, if you're gonna complain you can just leave.
Nino's wearing a yukata for me...
I'd wait another 12 hours to see that...
Ha ha! It's a festival in your brain all year long!
She's dressing up for her boy-friend, obviously.
Huh? But her un-fashionable boyfriend won't be able to give her a single compli-ment.
Someone who wears such a weird mask can't call me "unfashion-able"!!
You wear the same outfit 365 days a year!
Sorry!

※ Festival of ancestral spirits, held in mid-August.

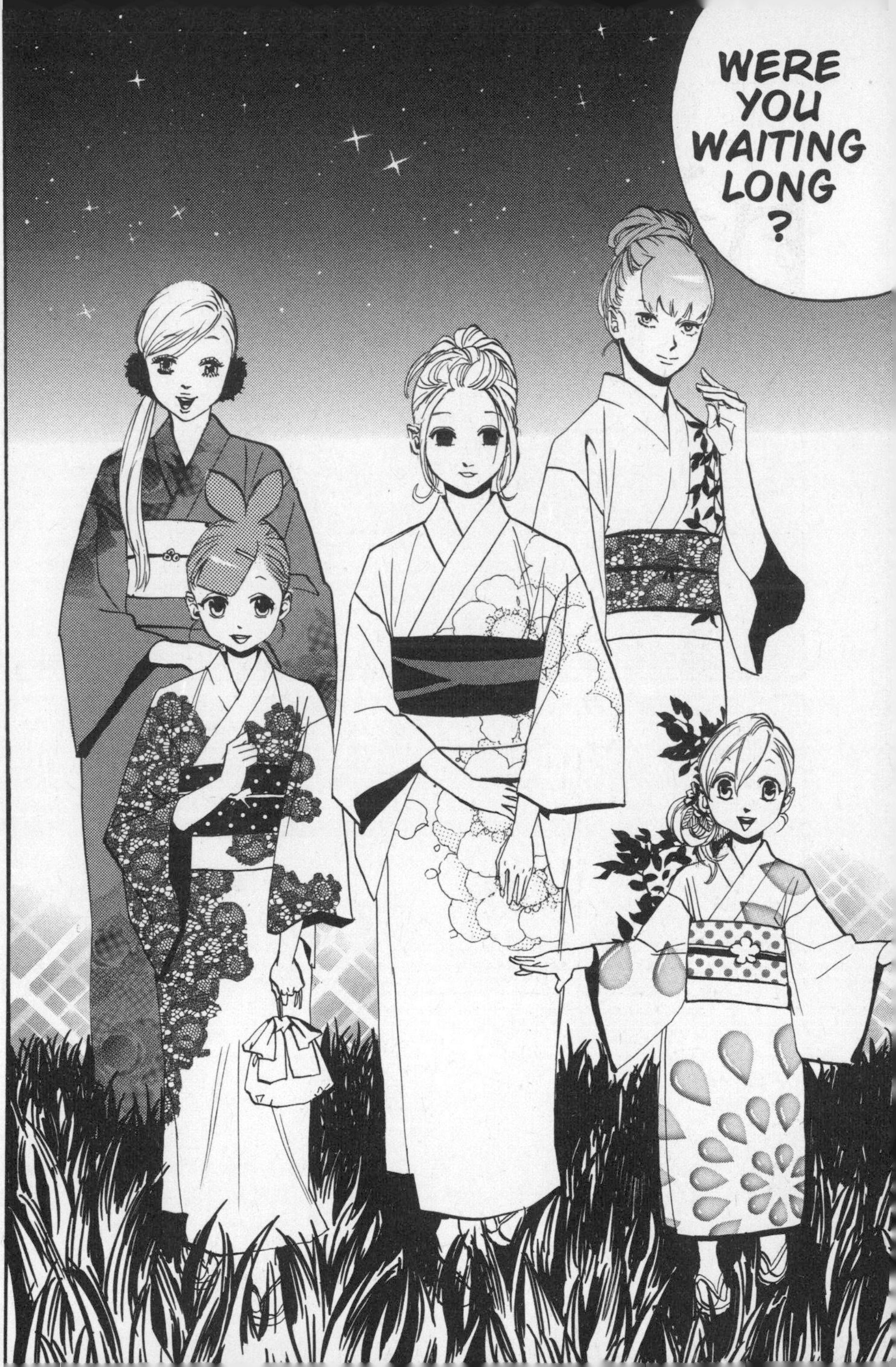
WERE YOU WAITING LONG ?

Chapter 223: The Form of a Date

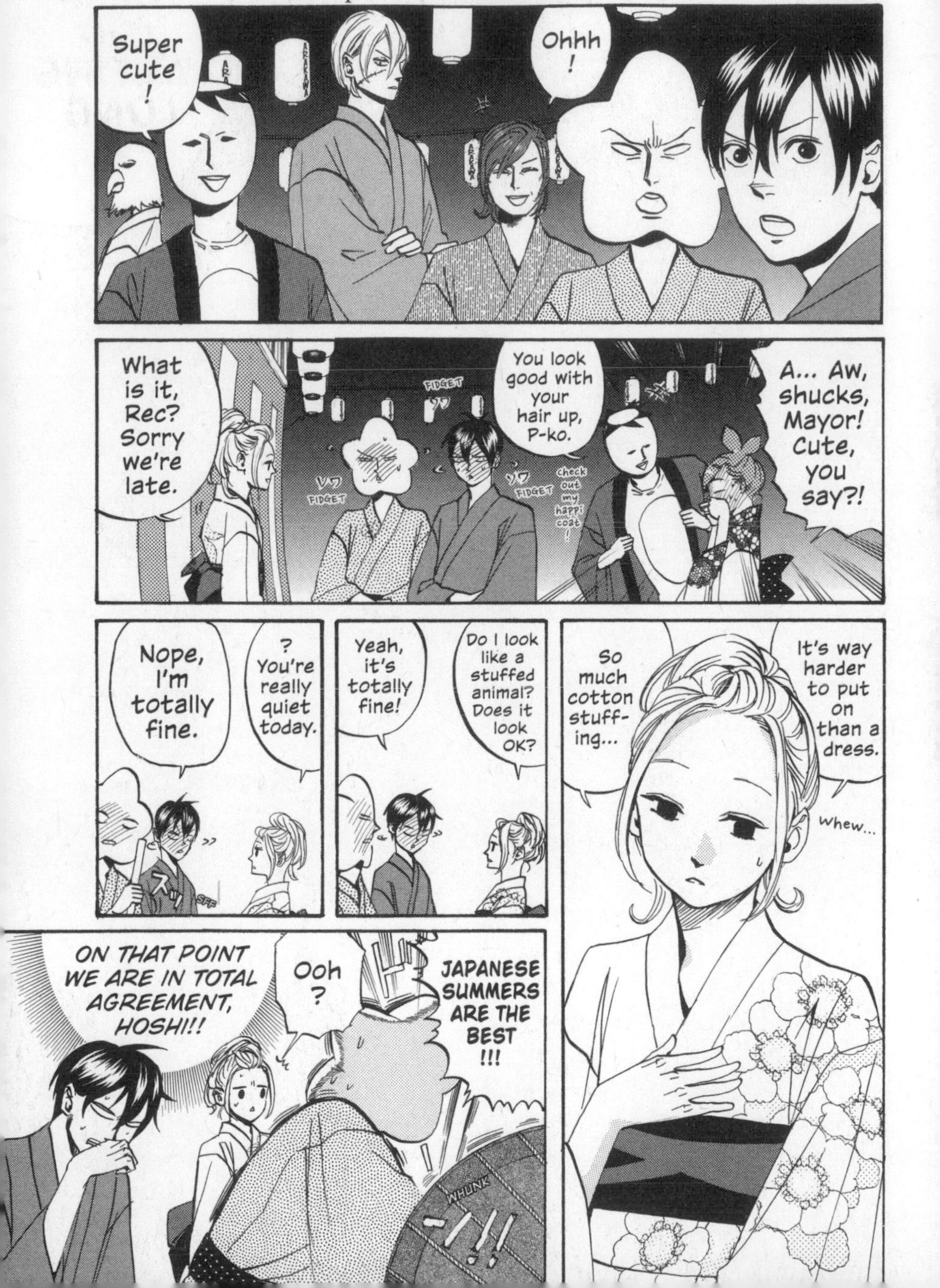
Ohhh!
Super cute!
A... Aw, shucks, Mayor! Cute, you say?!
check out my happi coat!
You look good with your hair up, P-ko.
FIDGET
FIDGET
FIDGET
What is it, Rec? Sorry we're late.
It's way harder to put on than a dress.
So much cotton stuffing...
Whew...
Do I look like a stuffed animal? Does it look OK?
Yeah, it's totally fine!
? You're really quiet today.
Nope, I'm totally fine.
SFF
JAPANESE SUMMERS ARE THE BEST!!!
Ooh?
ON THAT POINT WE ARE IN TOTAL AGREEMENT, HOSHI!!!
WHUNK

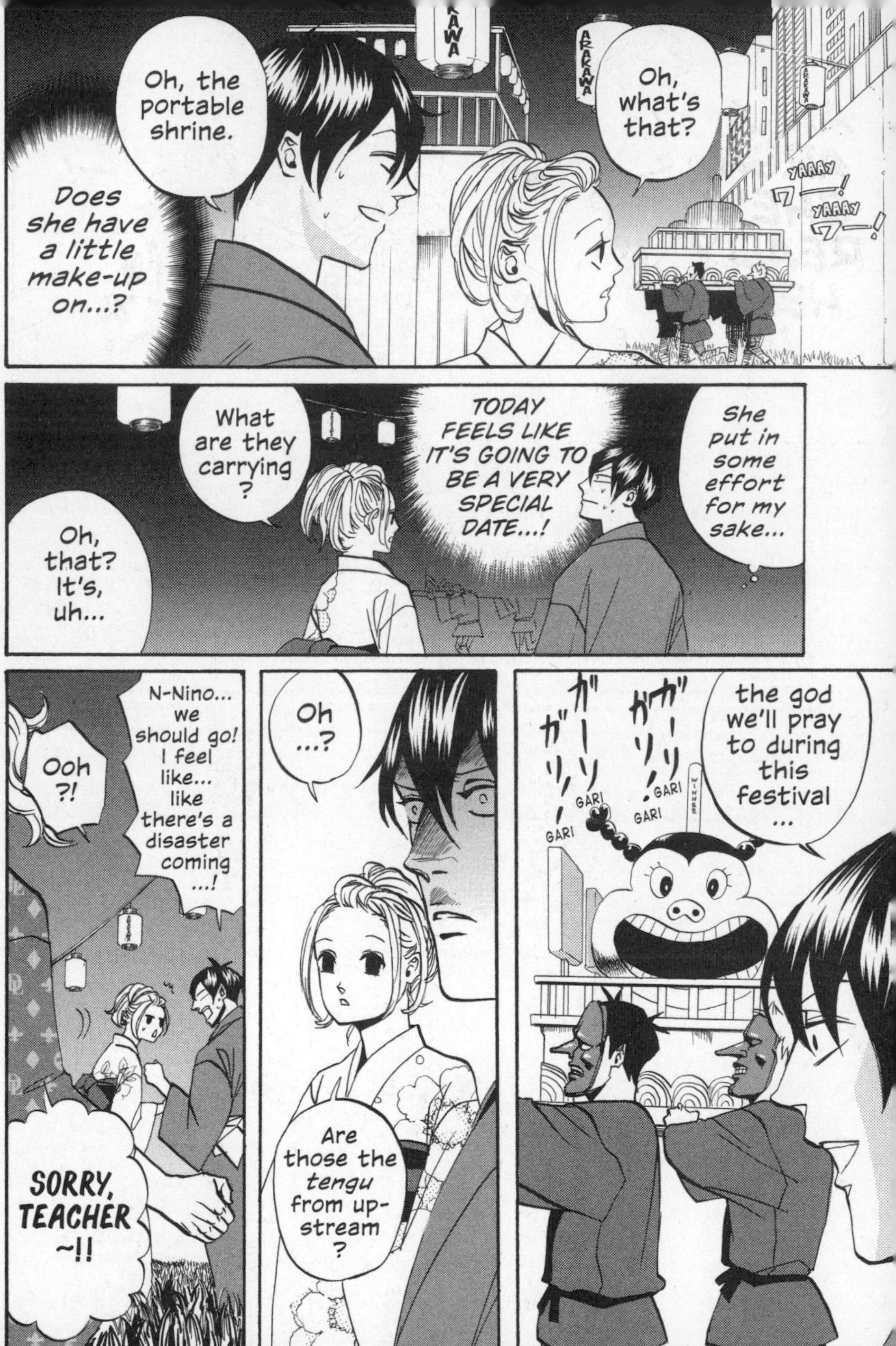
ARAKAWA
Oh, what's that?
YAAAY
YAAAY
Oh, the portable shrine.
Does she have a little make-up on...?
She put in some effort for my sake...
TODAY FEELS LIKE IT'S GOING TO BE A VERY SPECIAL DATE...!
What are they carrying?
Oh, that? It's, uh...
the god we'll pray to during this festival...
GARI
GARI
GARI
GARI
WINNER
Oh...?
Are those the *tengu* from up-stream?
N-Nino... we should go! I feel like... like there's a disaster coming...!
Ooh?!
SORRY, TEACHER~!!

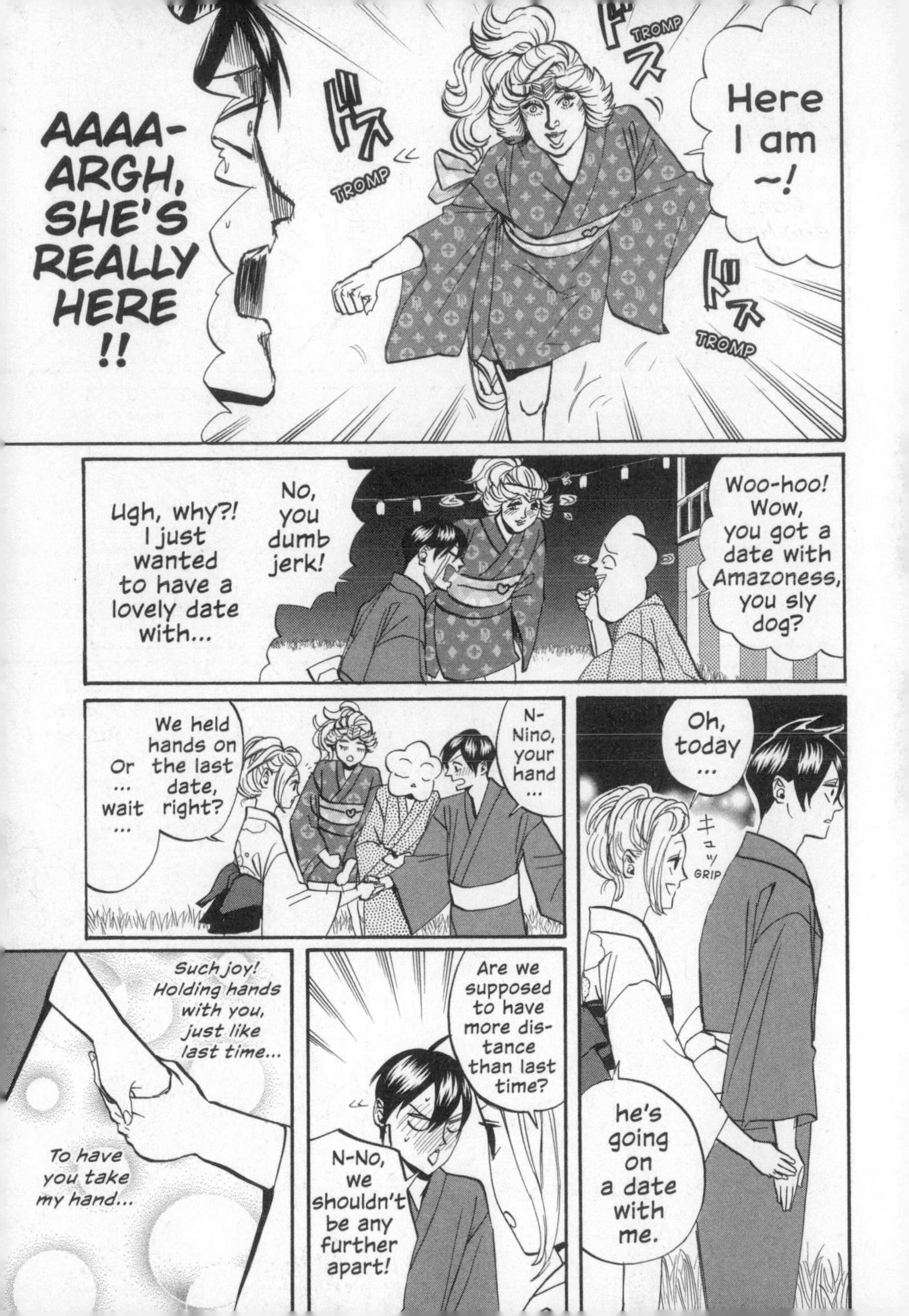
ドス
TROMP
Here I am ~!
ドス
TROMP
ドス
TROMP
AAAA-ARGH, SHE'S REALLY HERE !!
Woo-hoo! Wow, you got a date with Amazoness, you sly dog?
No, you dumb jerk!
Ugh, why?! I just wanted to have a lovely date with...
Oh, today ...
キュッ
GRIP
he's going on a date with me.
N-Nino, your hand ...
We held hands on the last date, right?
Or ... wait ...
Are we supposed to have more distance than last time?
N-No, we shouldn't be any further apart!
Such joy! Holding hands with you, just like last time...
To have you take my hand...

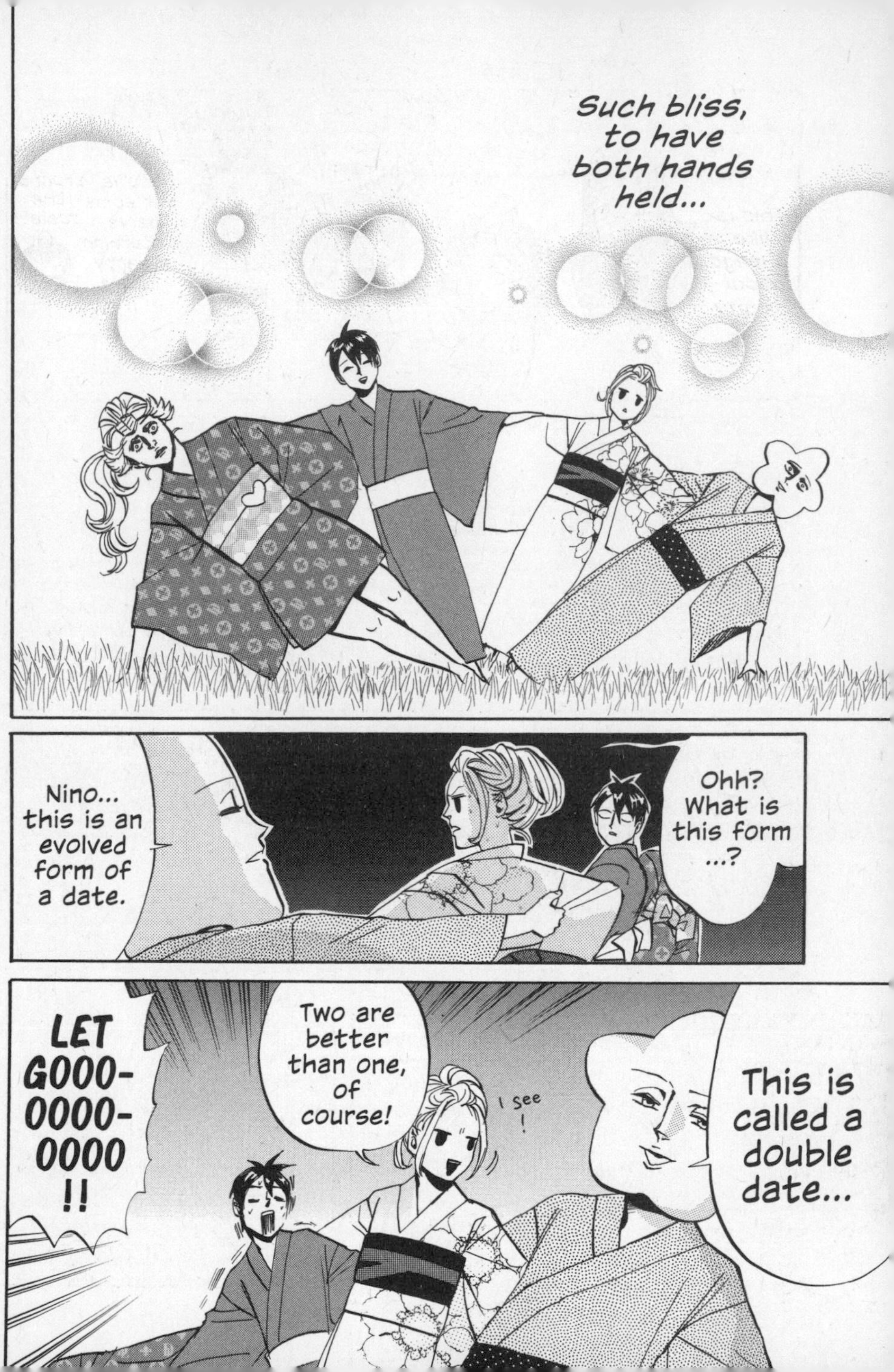
Such bliss, to have both hands held...
Ohh? What is this form ...?
Nino... this is an evolved form of a date.
This is called a double date...
I see!
Two are better than one, of course!
LET GOOO-OOOO-OOOO!!

Chapter 224: Love Rivals

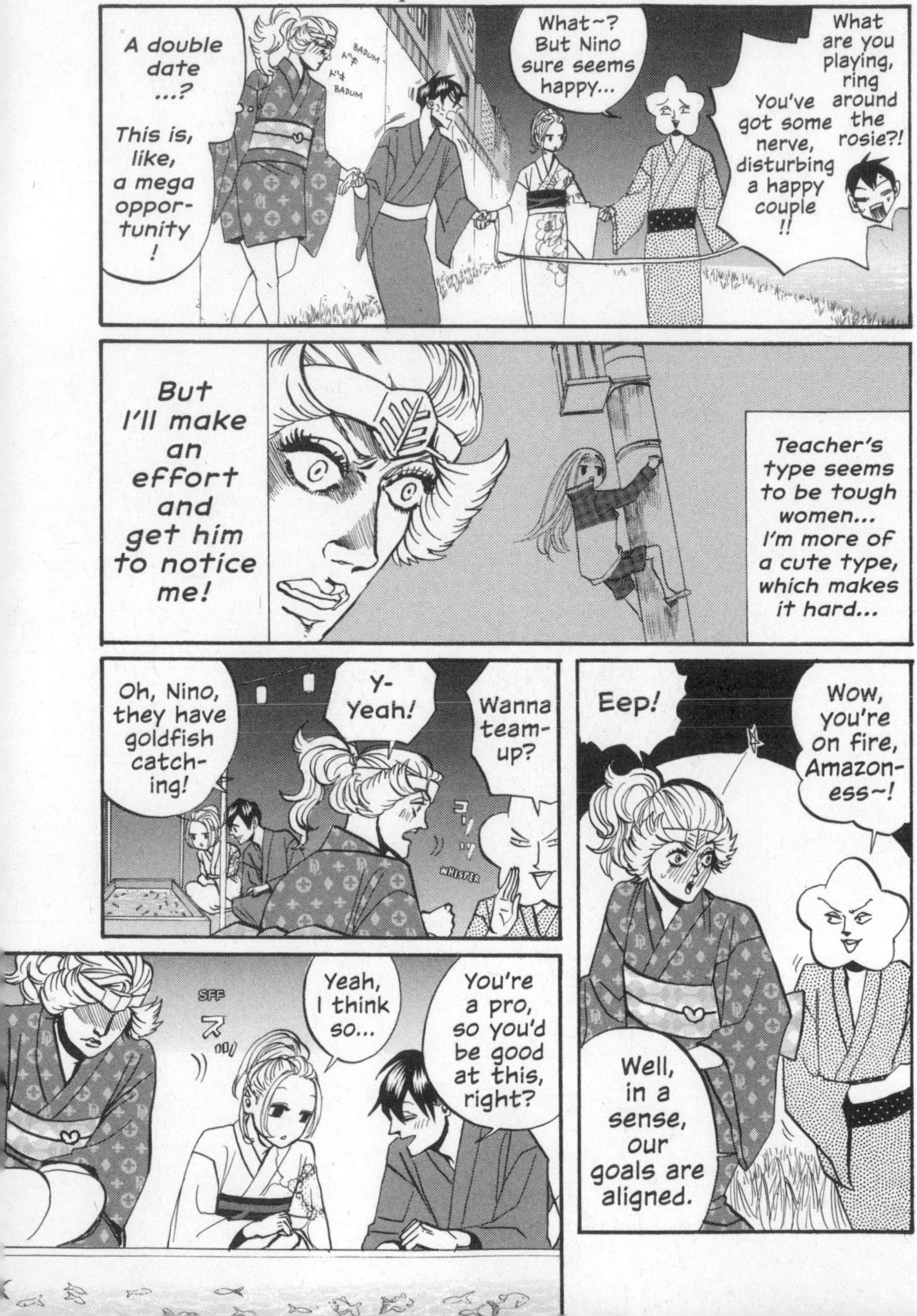
What are you playing, ring around the rosie?!
You've got some nerve, disturbing a happy couple!!
What~? But Nino sure seems happy...
BADUM BADUM
A double date...?
This is, like, a mega opportunity!
Teacher's type seems to be tough women... I'm more of a cute type, which makes it hard...
But I'll make an effort and get him to notice me!
Wow, you're on fire, Amazoness~!
Eep!
Well, in a sense, our goals are aligned.
Wanna team-up?
WHISPER
Y-Yeah!
Oh, Nino, they have goldfish catching!
You're a pro, so you'd be good at this, right?
Yeah, I think so...
SFF

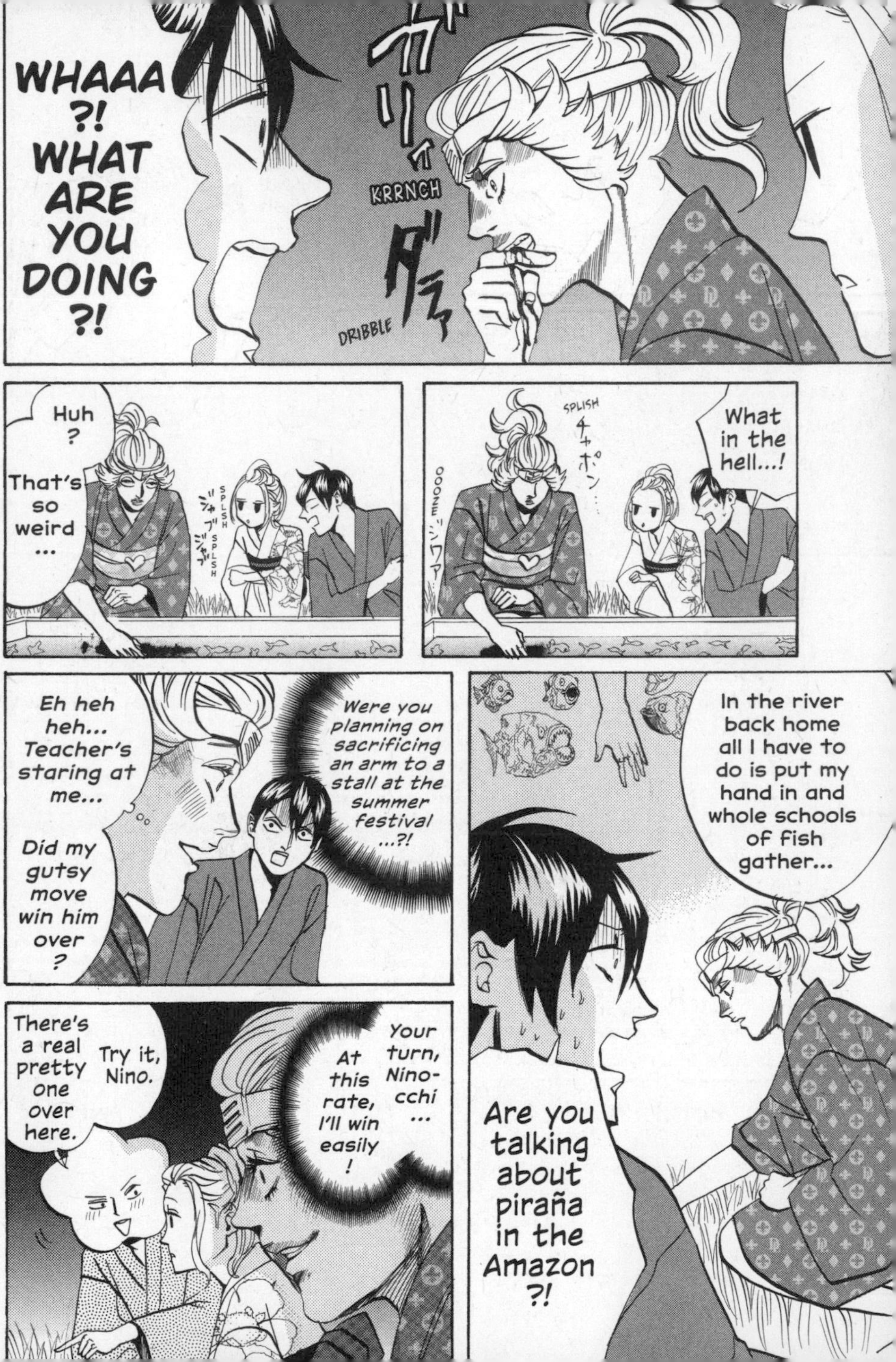
KRRNCH
WHAAA?! WHAT ARE YOU DOING?!
DRIBBLE
What in the hell...!
SPLISH
OOOZE
Huh?
That's so weird...
SPLSH SPLSH
In the river back home all I have to do is put my hand in and whole schools of fish gather...
Are you talking about piraña in the Amazon?!
Were you planning on sacrificing an arm to a stall at the summer festival...?!
Eh heh heh... Teacher's staring at me...
Did my gutsy move win him over?
Your turn, Ninocchi...
At this rate, I'll win easily!
Try it, Nino.
There's a real pretty one over here.

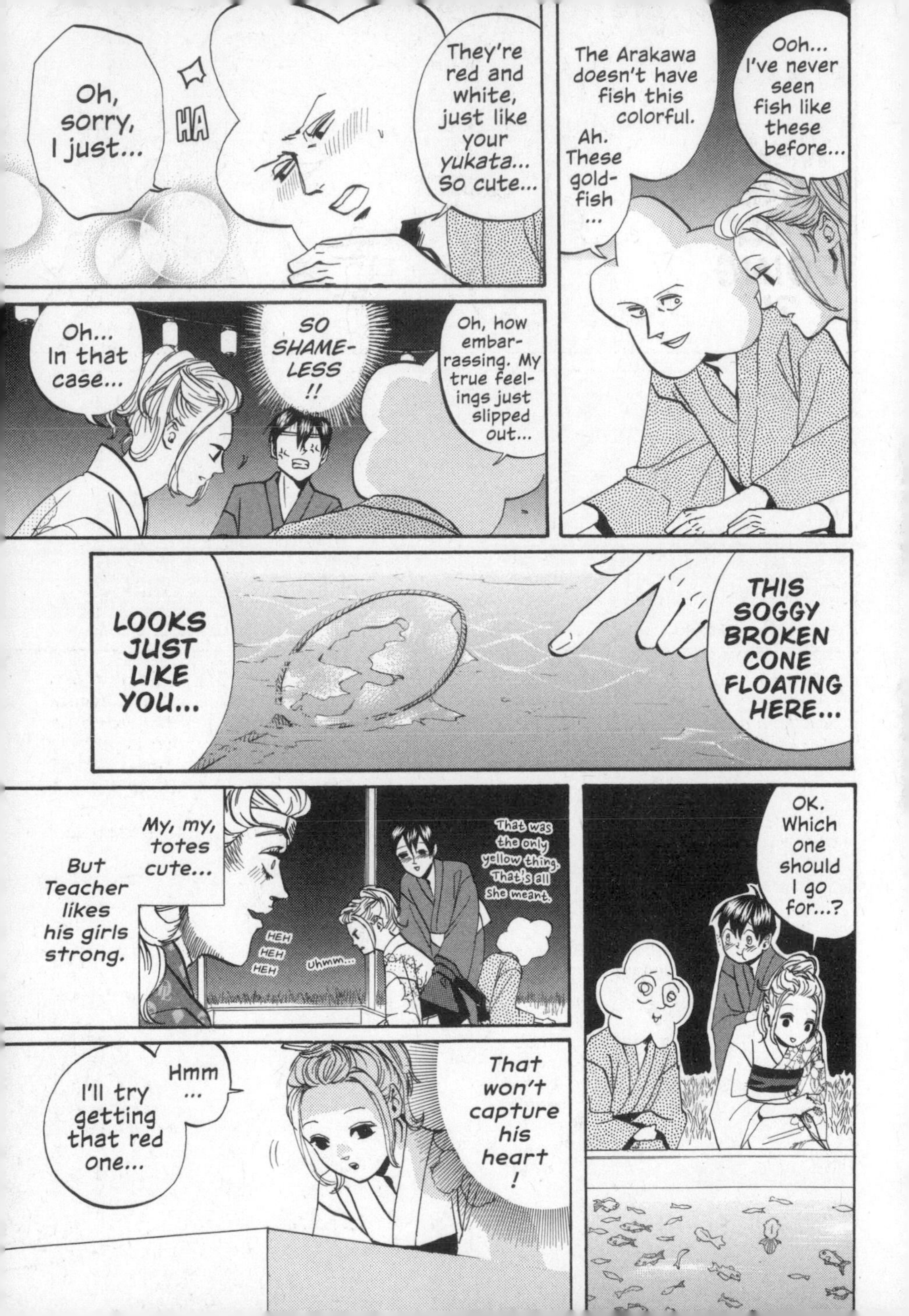
Ooh... I've never seen fish like these before...
The Arakawa doesn't have fish this colorful.
Ah. These goldfish...
They're red and white, just like your yukata... So cute...
HA
Oh, sorry, I just...
Oh, how embarrassing. My true feelings just slipped out...
SO SHAMELESS!!
Oh... In that case...
THIS SOGGY BROKEN CONE FLOATING HERE...
LOOKS JUST LIKE YOU...
OK. Which one should I go for...?
That was the only yellow thing. That's all she meant.
My, my, totes cute...
But Teacher likes his girls strong.
HEH HEH HEH
Uhmm...
That won't capture his heart!
Hmm...
I'll try getting that red one...

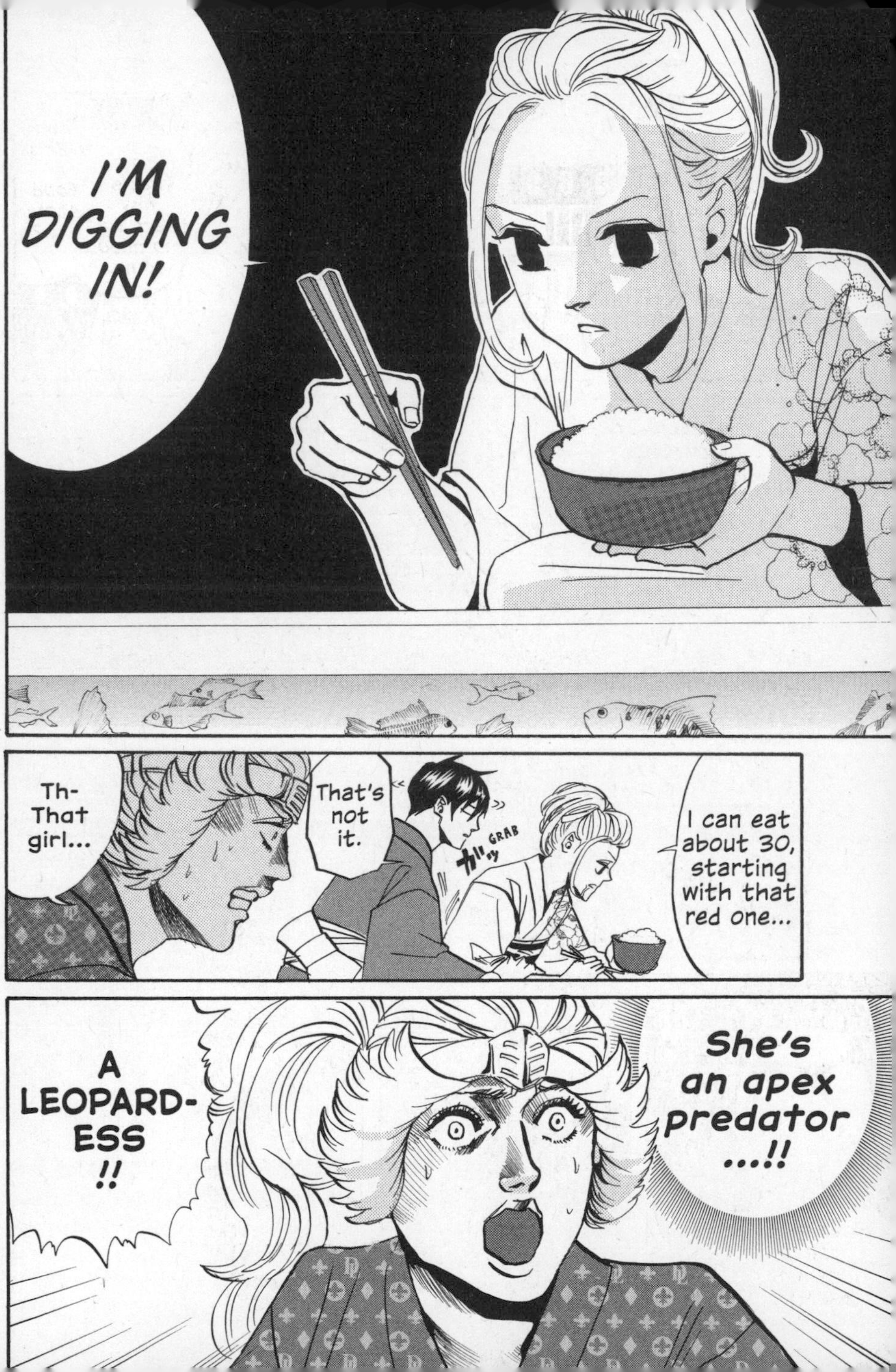
I'M DIGGING IN!
I can eat about 30, starting with that red one...
GRAB
That's not it.
Th- That girl...
She's an apex predator ...!!
A LEOPARD-ESS !!

Chapter 225: Summer Night Miracle

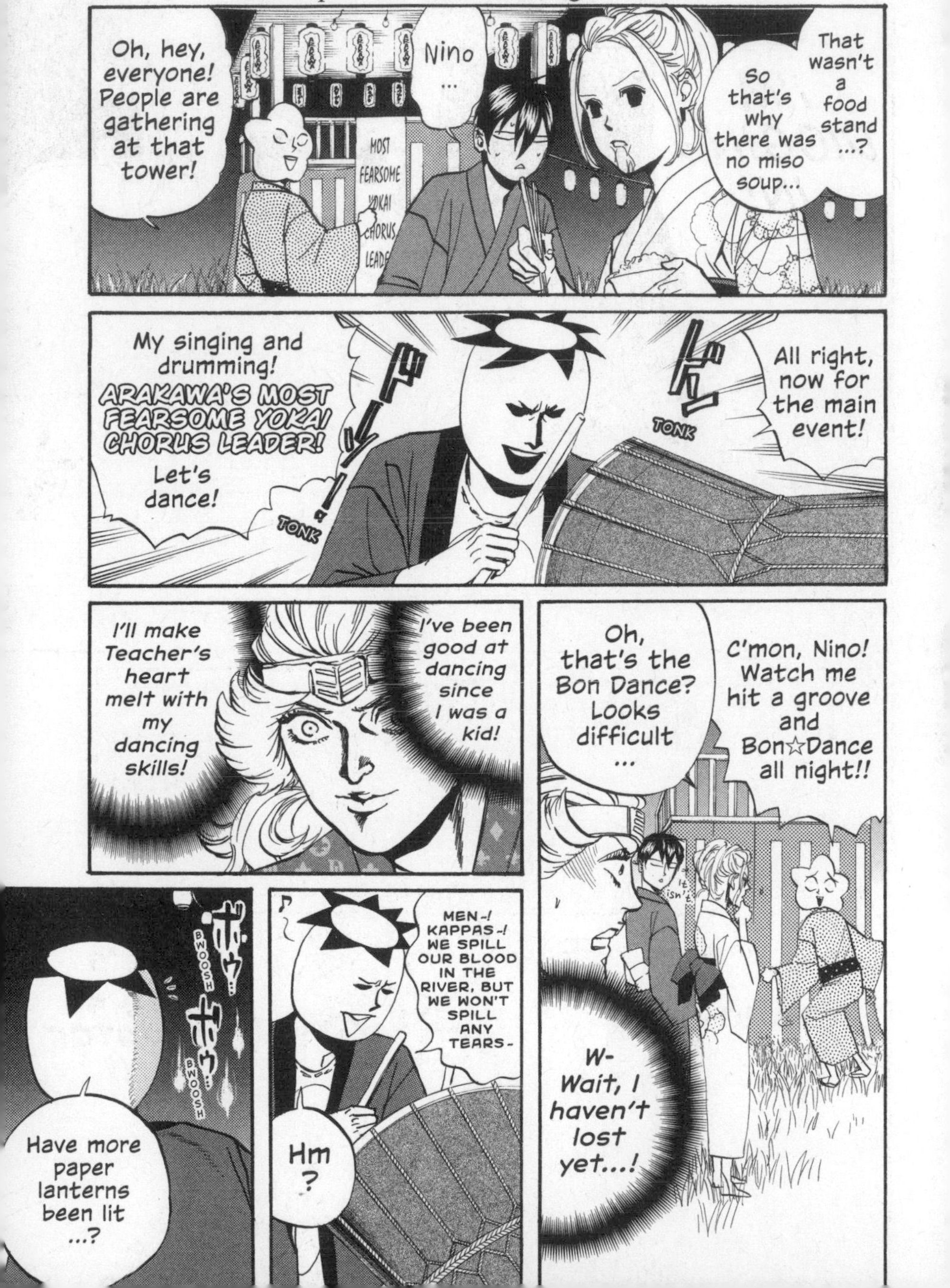
That wasn't a food stand ...?
So that's why there was no miso soup...
Nino ...
Oh, hey, everyone! People are gathering at that tower!
MOST FEARSOME YOKAI CHORUS LEADE
All right, now for the main event!
TONK
My singing and drumming!
ARAKAWA'S MOST FEARSOME YOKAI CHORUS LEADER!
Let's dance!
TONK
C'mon, Nino! Watch me hit a groove and Bon☆Dance all night!!
Oh, that's the Bon Dance? Looks difficult ...
It isn't
W- Wait, I haven't lost yet...!
I've been good at dancing since I was a kid!
I'll make Teacher's heart melt with my dancing skills!
MEN-! KAPPAS-! WE SPILL OUR BLOOD IN THE RIVER, BUT WE WON'T SPILL ANY TEARS-
Hm ?
BWOOSH
BWOOSH
Have more paper lanterns been lit ...?

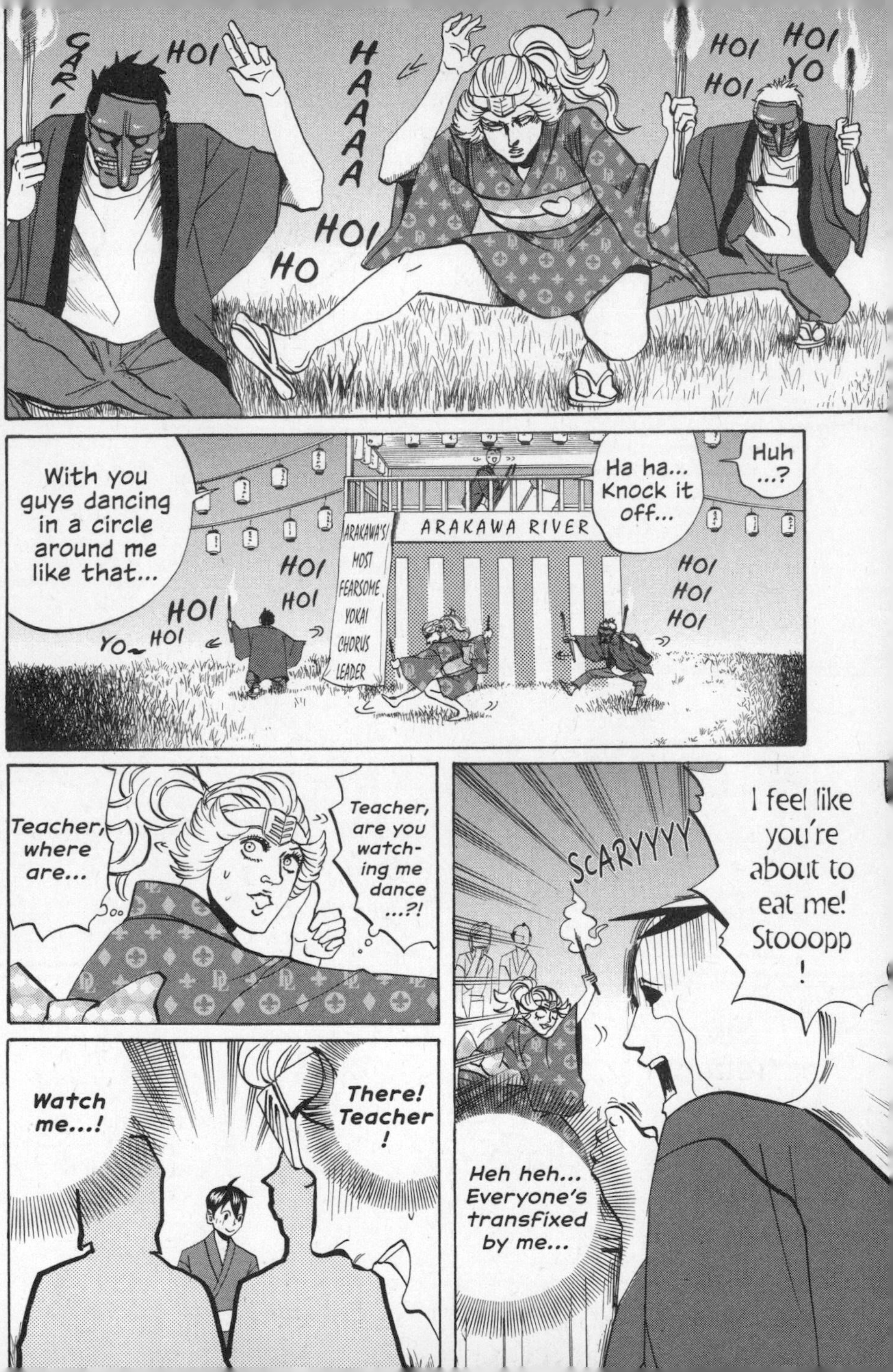
HOI YO
HOI HOI
HOI
HAAAAA
HOI
HO
HOI
GARI
Huh ...?
Ha ha... Knock it off...
ARAKAWA RIVER
HOI HOI HOI
ARAKAWA'S MOST FEARSOME YOKAI CHORUS LEADER
With you guys dancing in a circle around me like that...
HOI HOI
HOI
YO~ HOI
I feel like you're about to eat me! Stooopp!
SCARYYYY
Heh heh... Everyone's transfixed by me...
Teacher, are you watching me dance...?!
Teacher, where are...
There! Teacher!
Watch me...!

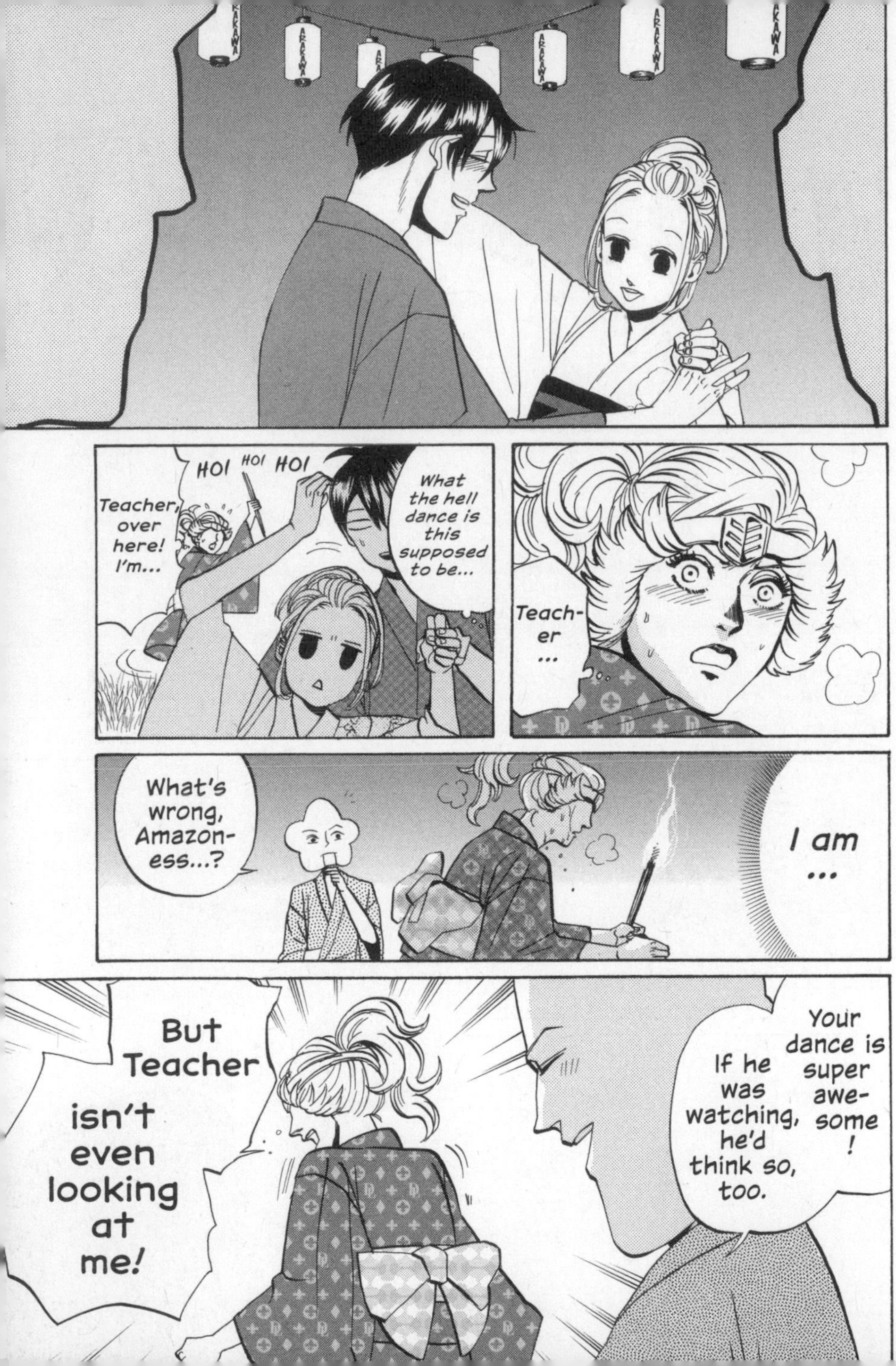
Teacher...
What the hell dance is this supposed to be...
HOI HOI HOI
Teacher, over here! I'm...
I am ...
What's wrong, Amazoness...?
Your dance is super awesome!
If he was watching, he'd think so, too.
But Teacher isn't even looking at me!

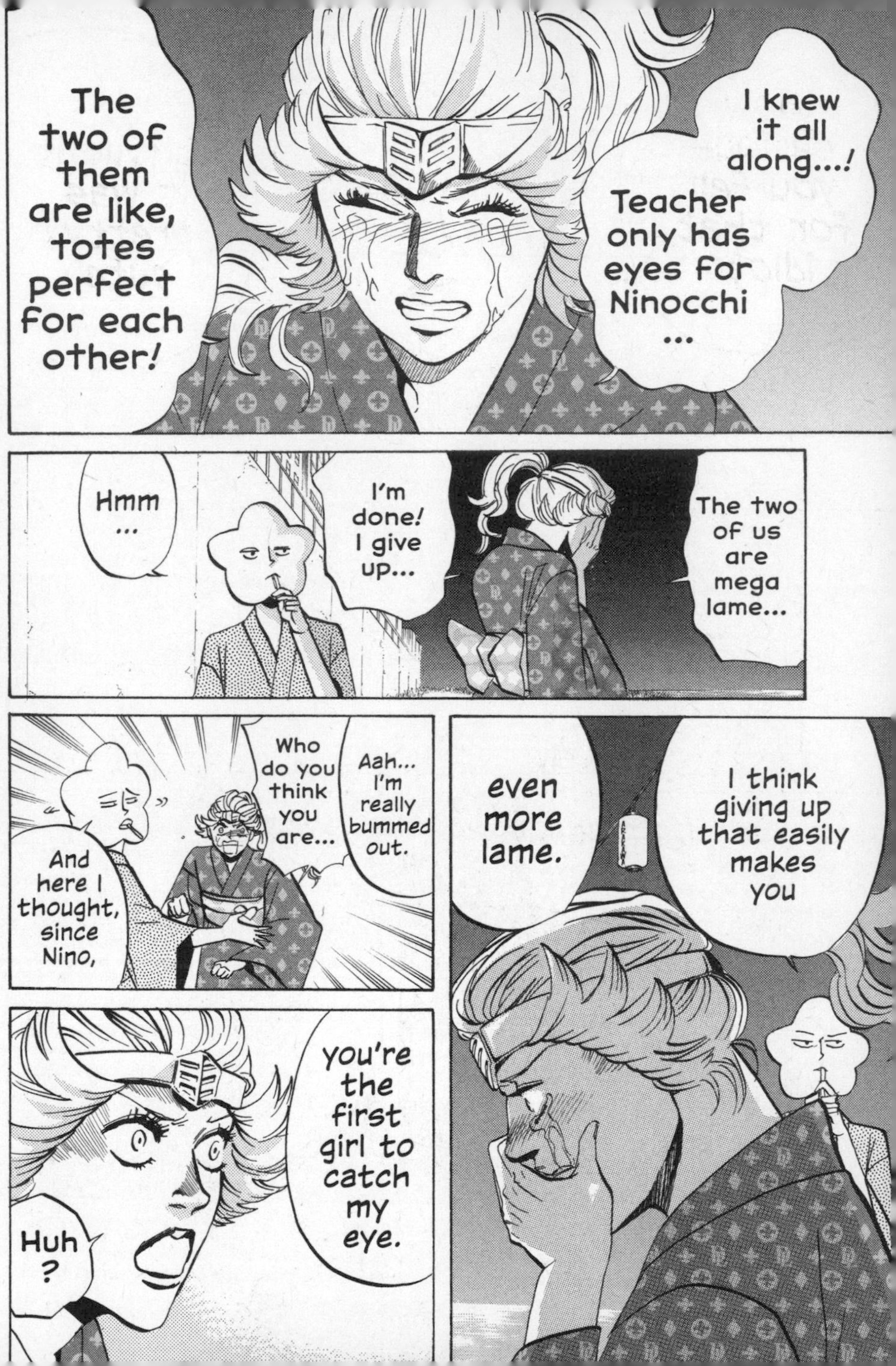
I knew it all along...!
Teacher only has eyes for Ninocchi ...
The two of them are like, totes perfect for each other!
The two of us are mega lame...
I'm done! I give up...
Hmm ...
I think giving up that easily makes you
even more lame.
Aah... I'm really bummed out.
Who do you think you are...
And here I thought, since Nino,
you're the first girl to catch my eye.
Huh ?

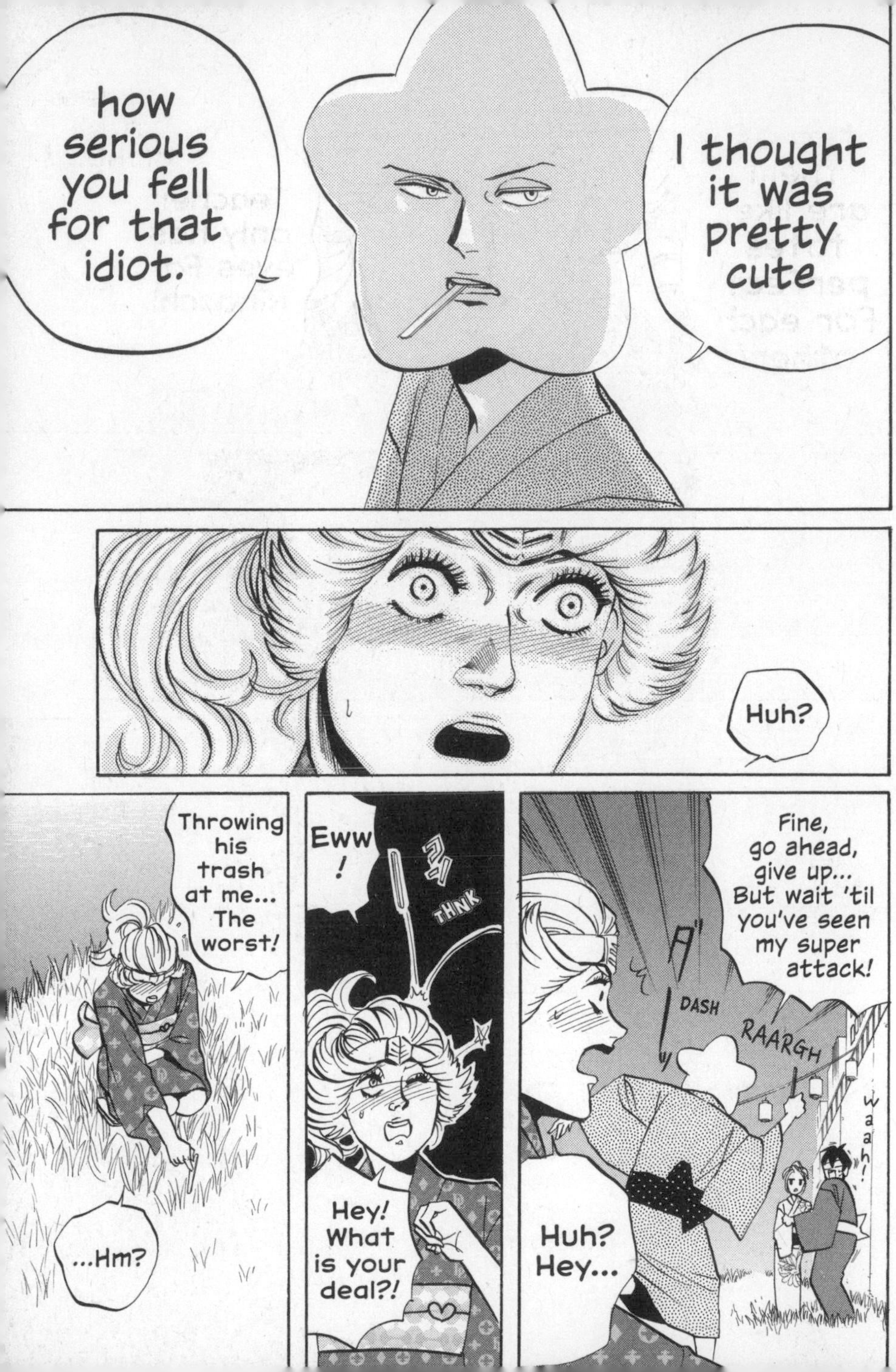
I thought it was pretty cute
how serious you fell for that idiot.
Huh?
Fine, go ahead, give up... But wait 'til you've seen my super attack!
DASH
RAARGH
waah!
Huh? Hey...
Eww!
THNK
Hey! What is your deal?!
Throwing his trash at me... The worst!
...Hm?

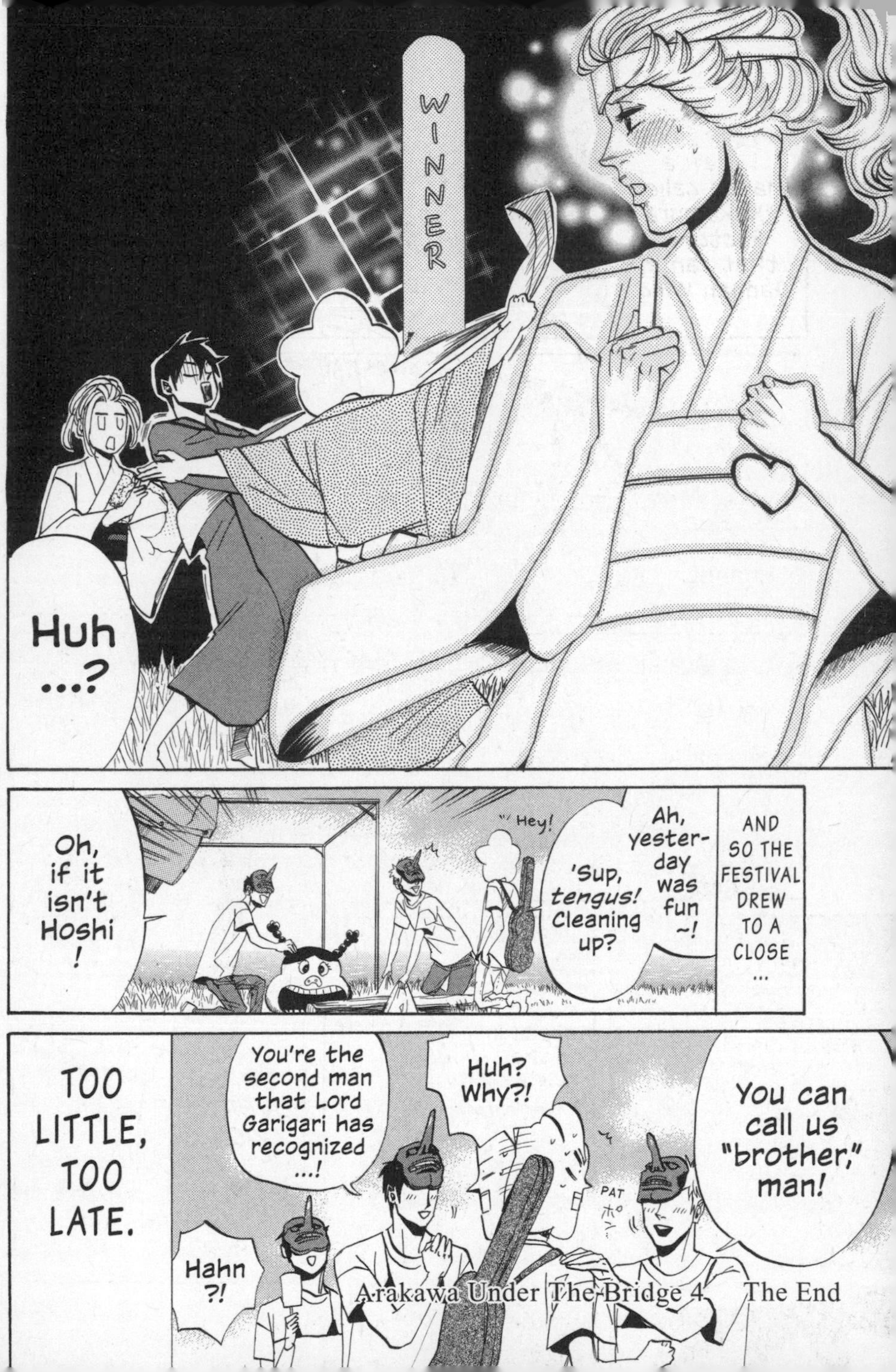
WINNER
Huh ...?
AND SO THE FESTIVAL DREW TO A CLOSE ...
Ah, yester-day was fun ~!
'Sup, *tengus!* Cleaning up?
Hey!
Oh, if it isn't Hoshi!
You can call us "brother," man!
Huh? Why?!
You're the second man that Lord Garigari has recognized ...!
PAT
TOO LITTLE, TOO LATE.
Hahn ?!
Arakawa Under The Bridge 4 The End

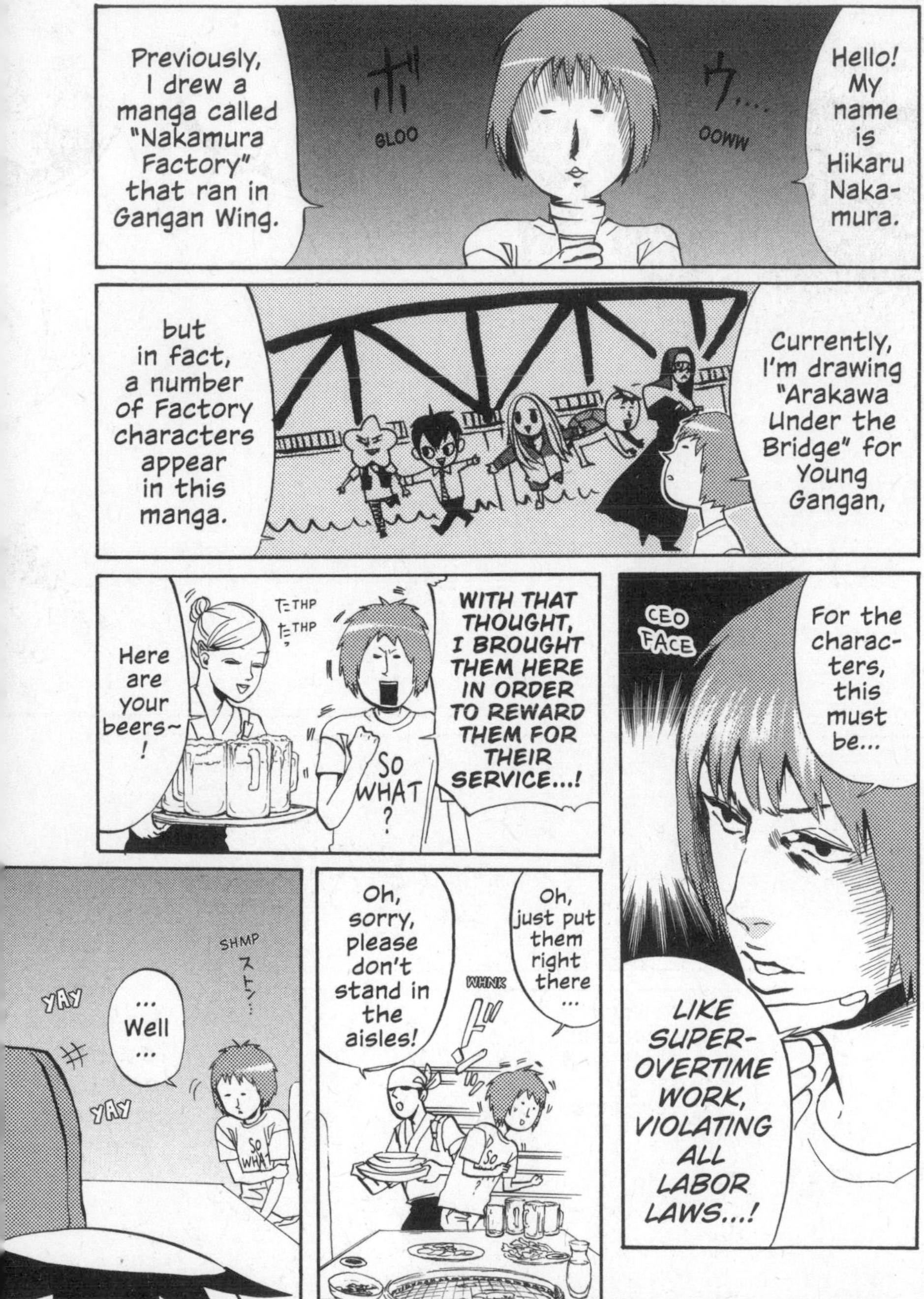
Hello! My name is Hikaru Naka-mura.
OOWW
GLOO
Previously, I drew a manga called "Nakamura Factory" that ran in Gangan Wing.
Currently, I'm drawing "Arakawa Under the Bridge" for Young Gangan,
but in fact, a number of Factory characters appear in this manga.
CEO FACE
For the charac-ters, this must be...
LIKE SUPER-OVERTIME WORK, VIOLATING ALL LABOR LAWS...!
WITH THAT THOUGHT, I BROUGHT THEM HERE IN ORDER TO REWARD THEM FOR THEIR SERVICE...!
THP
THP
Here are your beers~!
SO WHAT?
Oh, just put them right there ...
Oh, sorry, please don't stand in the aisles!
WHNK
SHMP
... Well ...
YAY
YAY

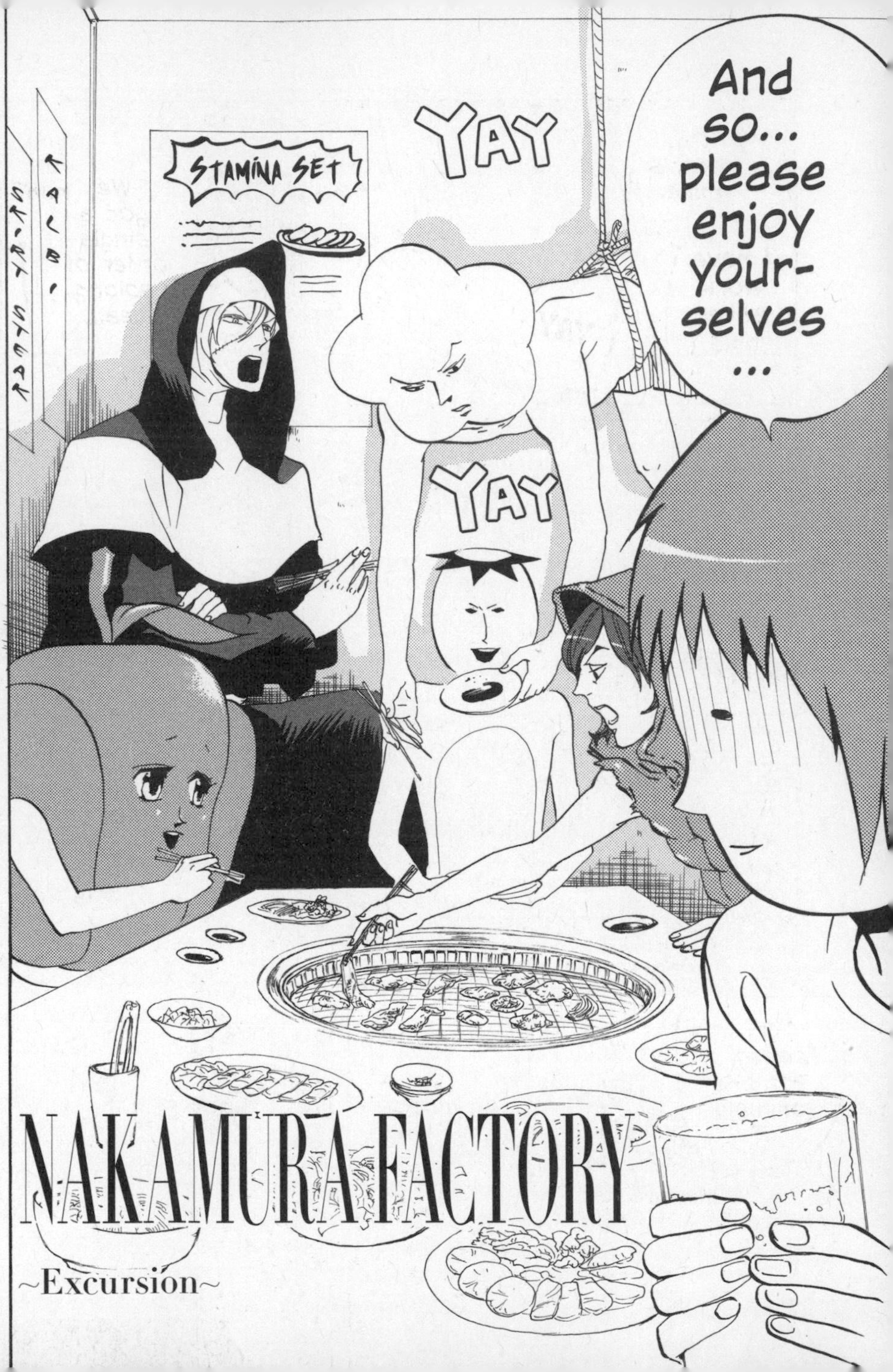
And so... please enjoy your-selves ...
YAY
YAY
STAMINA SET
KALBI
SKIRT STEAK
NAKAMURA FACTORY
~Excursion~

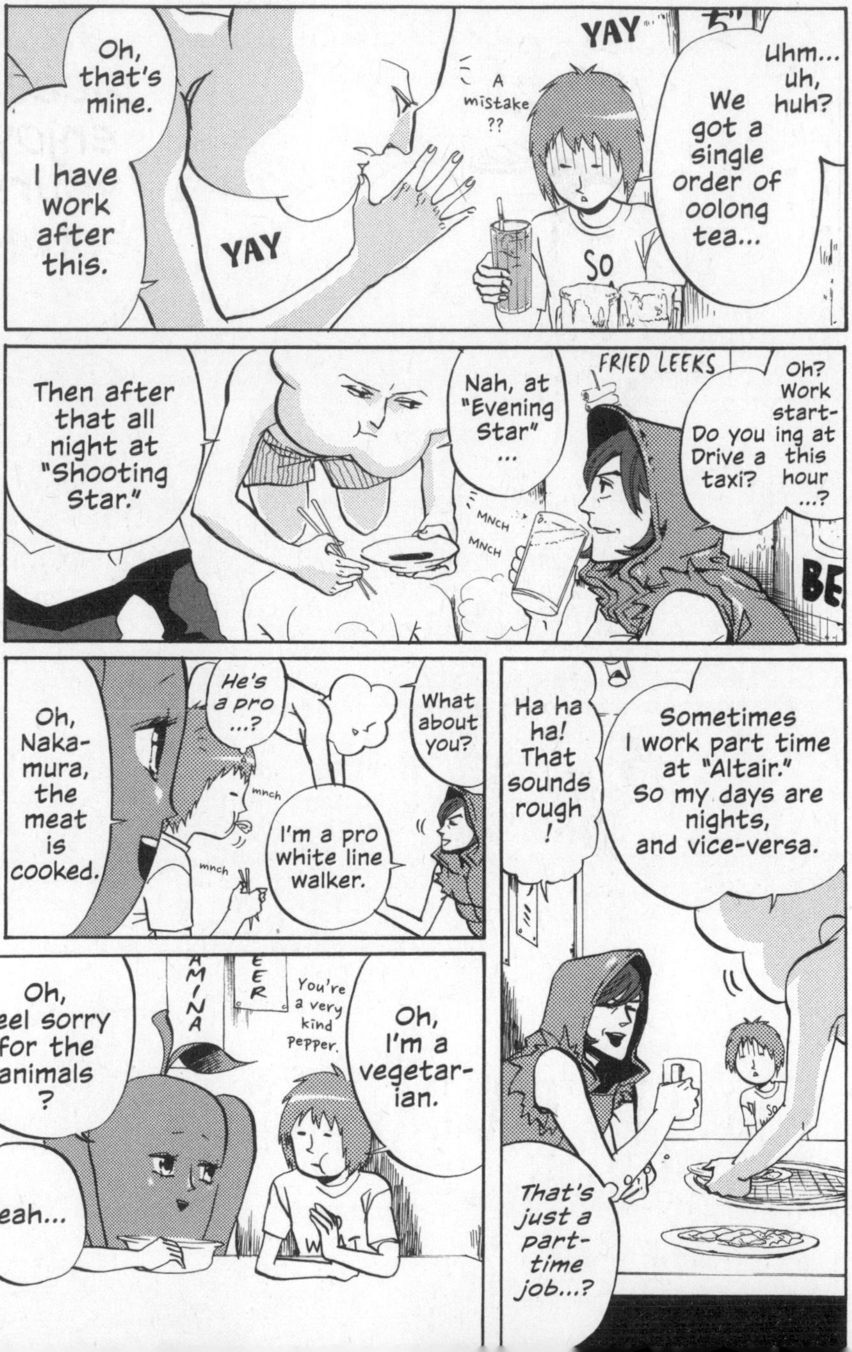
Uhm... uh, huh? We got a single order of oolong tea...
YAY
A mistake ??
Oh, that's mine. I have work after this.
YAY
Oh? Work starting at this hour ...? Do you Drive a taxi?
FRIED LEEKS
Nah, at "Evening Star" ...
MNCH MNCH
Then after that all night at "Shooting Star."
Sometimes I work part time at "Altair." So my days are nights, and vice-versa.
Ha ha ha! That sounds rough!
That's just a part-time job...?
What about you?
I'm a pro white line walker.
He's a pro ...?
mnch
mnch
Oh, Nakamura, the meat is cooked.
Oh, I'm a vegetarian.
You're a very kind Pepper.
Oh, feel sorry for the animals ?
Yeah...

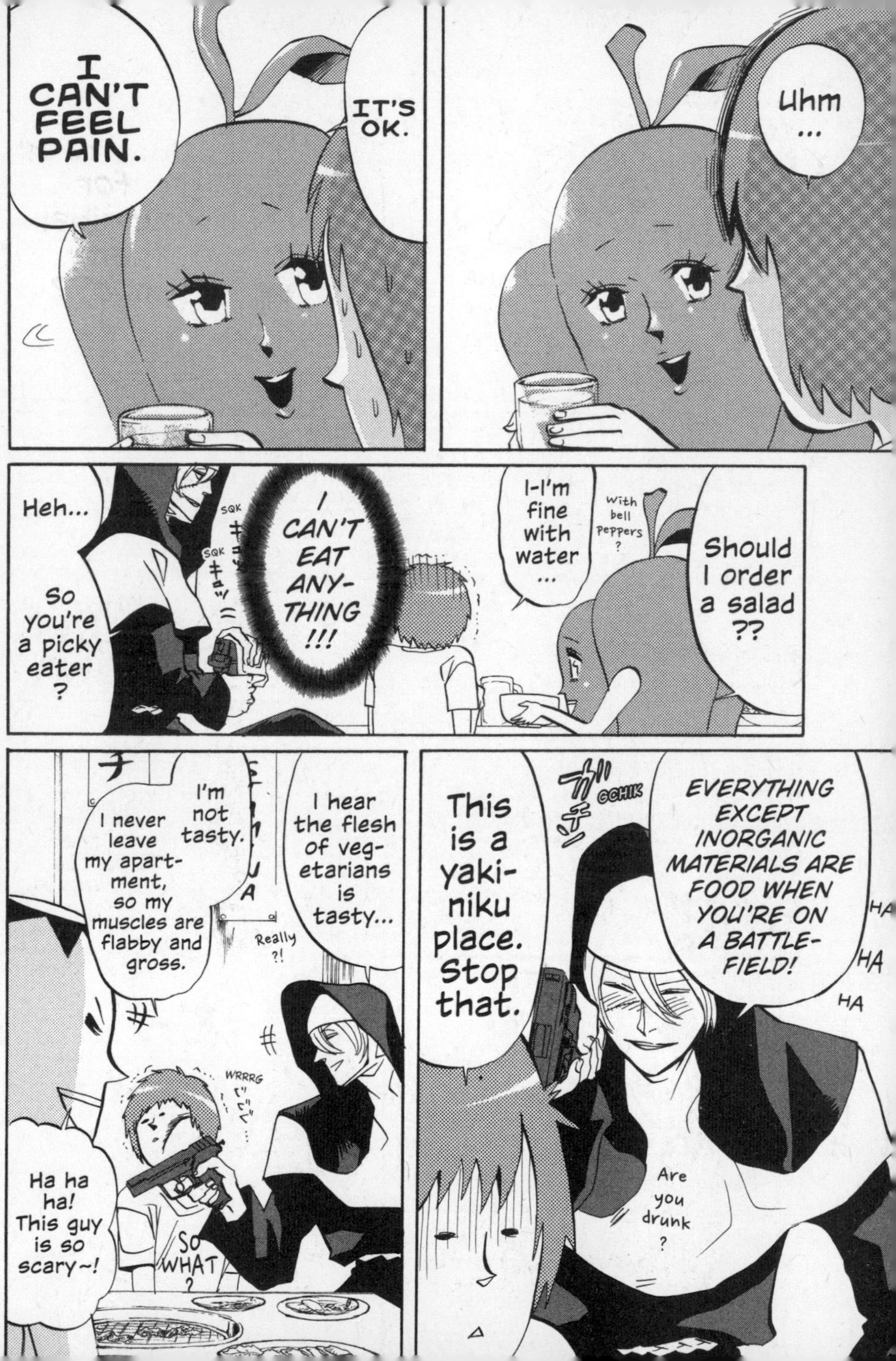
Uhm ...
IT'S OK.
I CAN'T FEEL PAIN.
Should I order a salad ??
With bell peppers ?
I-I'm fine with water ...
I CAN'T EAT ANYTHING !!!
SQK
SQK
Heh...
So you're a picky eater ?
EVERYTHING EXCEPT INORGANIC MATERIALS ARE FOOD WHEN YOU'RE ON A BATTLEFIELD!
HA HA HA
CCHIK
This is a yakiniku place. Stop that.
Are you drunk ?
I hear the flesh of vegetarians is tasty...
I'm not tasty.
I never leave my apartment, so my muscles are flabby and gross.
Really ?!
WRRRG
SO WHAT ?
Ha ha ha! This guy is so scary~!

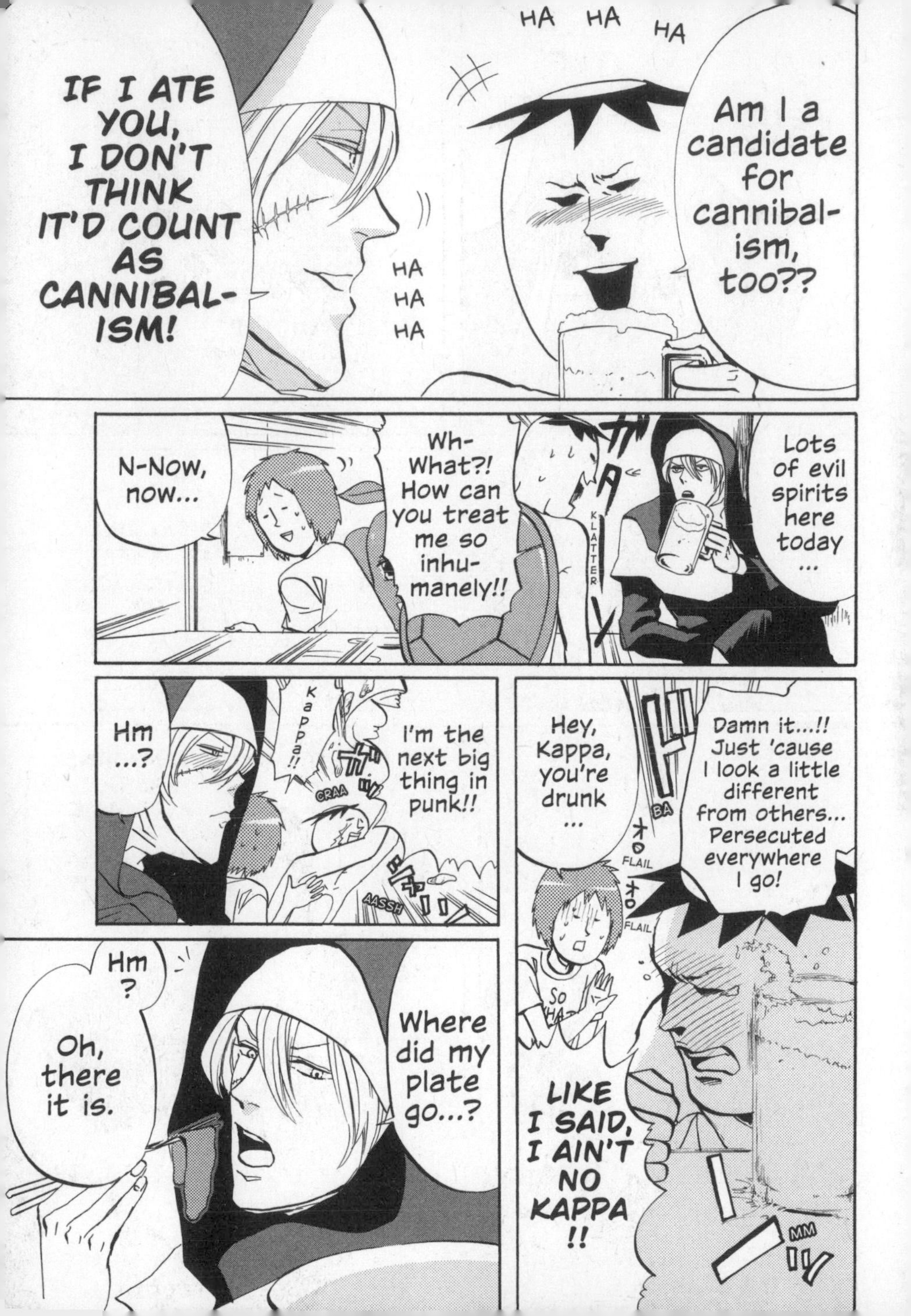
HA HA HA
Am I a candidate for cannibal-ism, too??
IF I ATE YOU, I DON'T THINK IT'D COUNT AS CANNIBAL-ISM!
HA HA HA
Lots of evil spirits here today ...
KLATTER
Wh- What?! How can you treat me so inhu-manely!!
N-Now, now...
Damn it...!! Just 'cause I look a little different from others... Persecuted everywhere I go!
BA
Hey, Kappa, you're drunk ...
FLAIL
FLAIL
LIKE I SAID, I AIN'T NO KAPPA !!
MM
I'm the next big thing in punk!!
Kappa!!
CRAA
AASSH
Hm ...?
Where did my plate go...?
Hm ?
Oh, there it is.

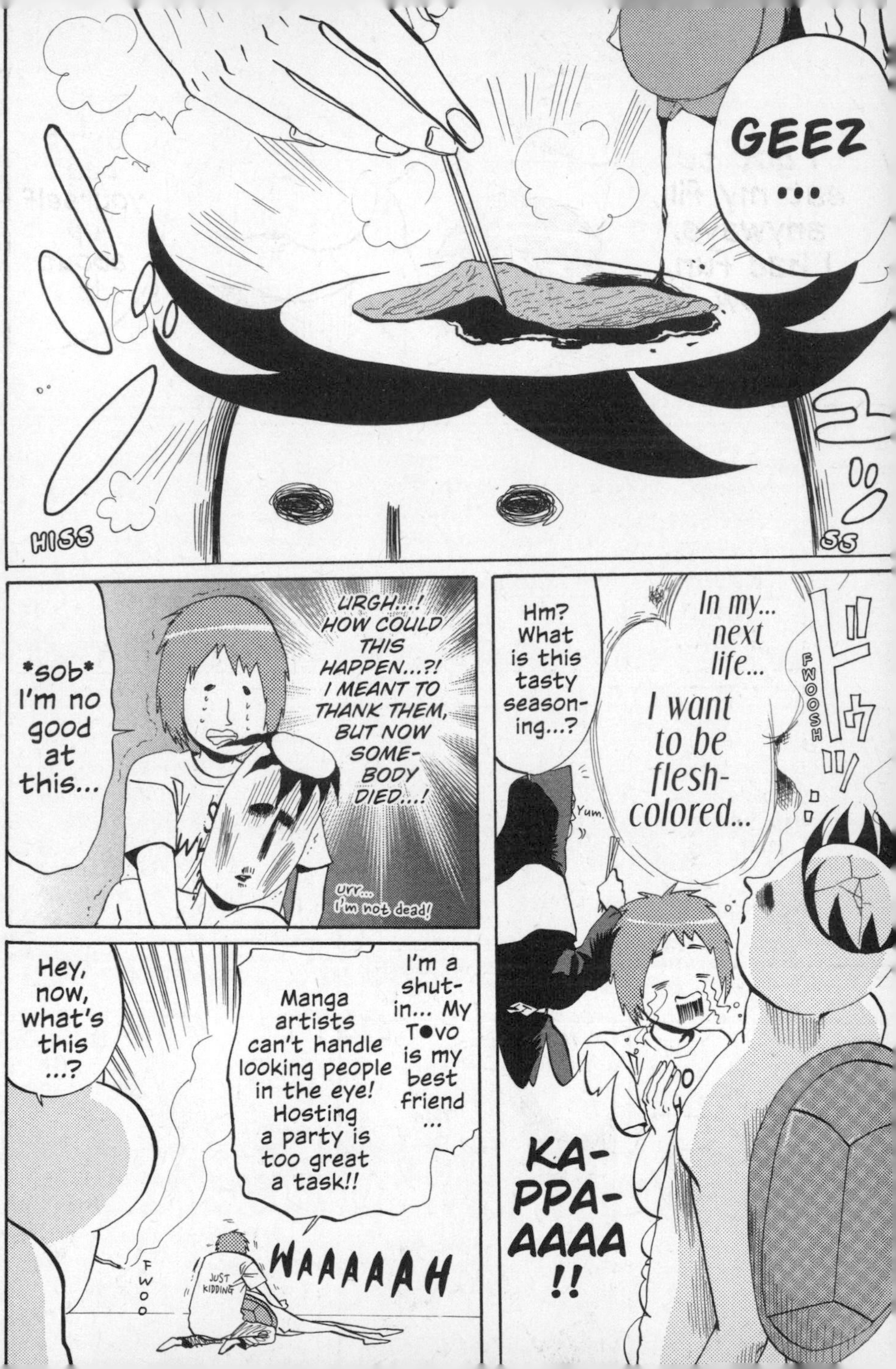
GEEZ...
SS
HISS
FWOOSH
In my... next life...
I want to be flesh-colored...
Hm? What is this tasty season-ing...?
Yum.
KA-PPA-AAAA!!
URGH...! HOW COULD THIS HAPPEN...?! I MEANT TO THANK THEM, BUT NOW SOME-BODY DIED...!
sob I'm no good at this...
urr... I'm not dead!
I'm a shut-in... My T●vo is my best friend...
Manga artists can't handle looking people in the eye! Hosting a party is too great a task!!
Hey, now, what's this ...?
WAAAAAH
JUST KIDDING
FWOO

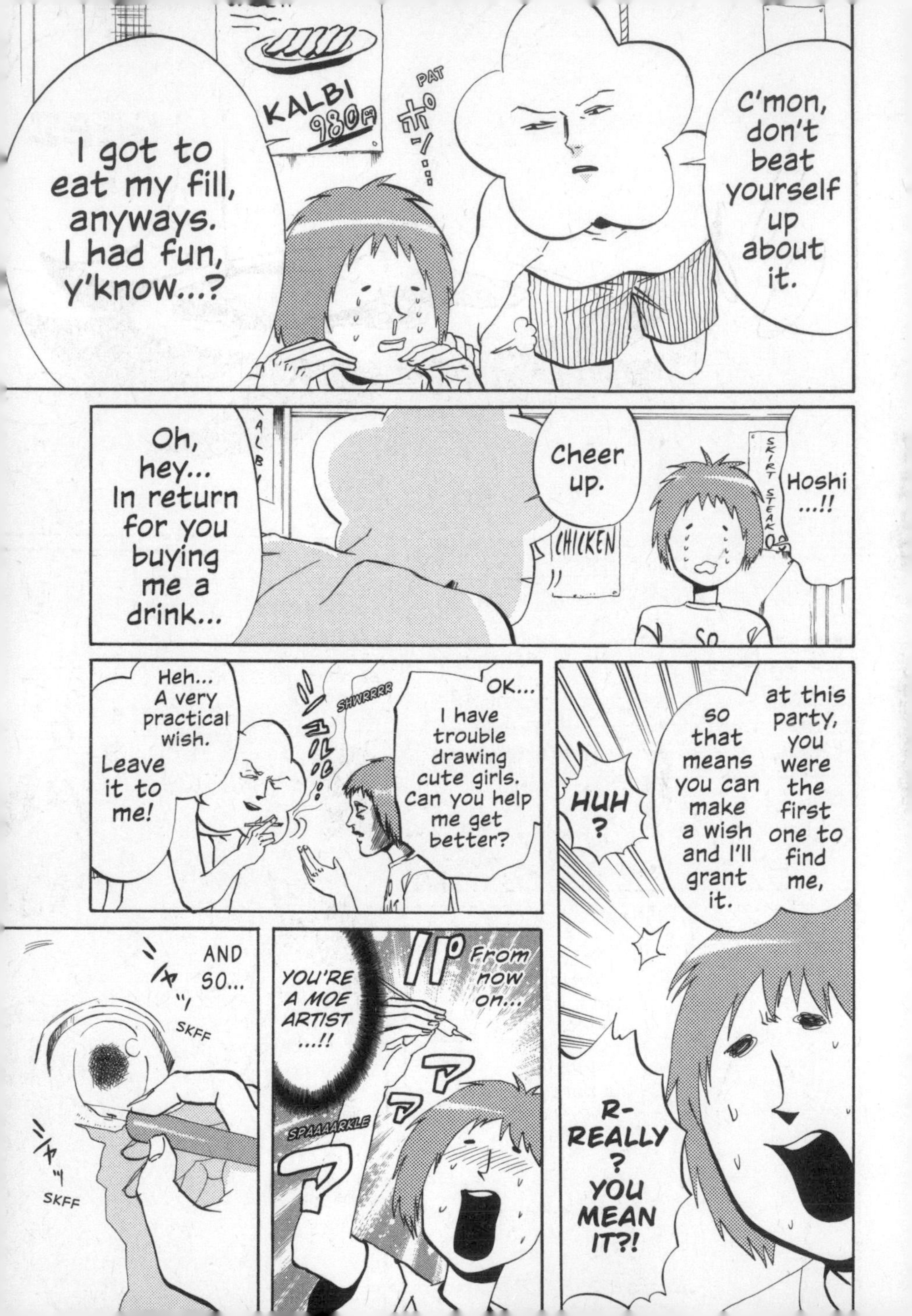
C'mon, don't beat yourself up about it.
PAT
KALBI 980円
I got to eat my fill, anyways. I had fun, y'know...?
Hoshi ...!!
SKIRT STEAK
Cheer up.
CHICKEN
KALBI
Oh, hey... In return for you buying me a drink...
at this party, you were the first one to find me,
so that means you can make a wish and I'll grant it.
HUH ?
R-REALLY ? YOU MEAN IT?!
OK... I have trouble drawing cute girls. Can you help me get better?
SHWRRRR
Heh... A very practical wish.
Leave it to me!
From now on...
YOU'RE A MOE ARTIST ...!!
SPAAAARKLE
AND SO...
SKFF
SKFF

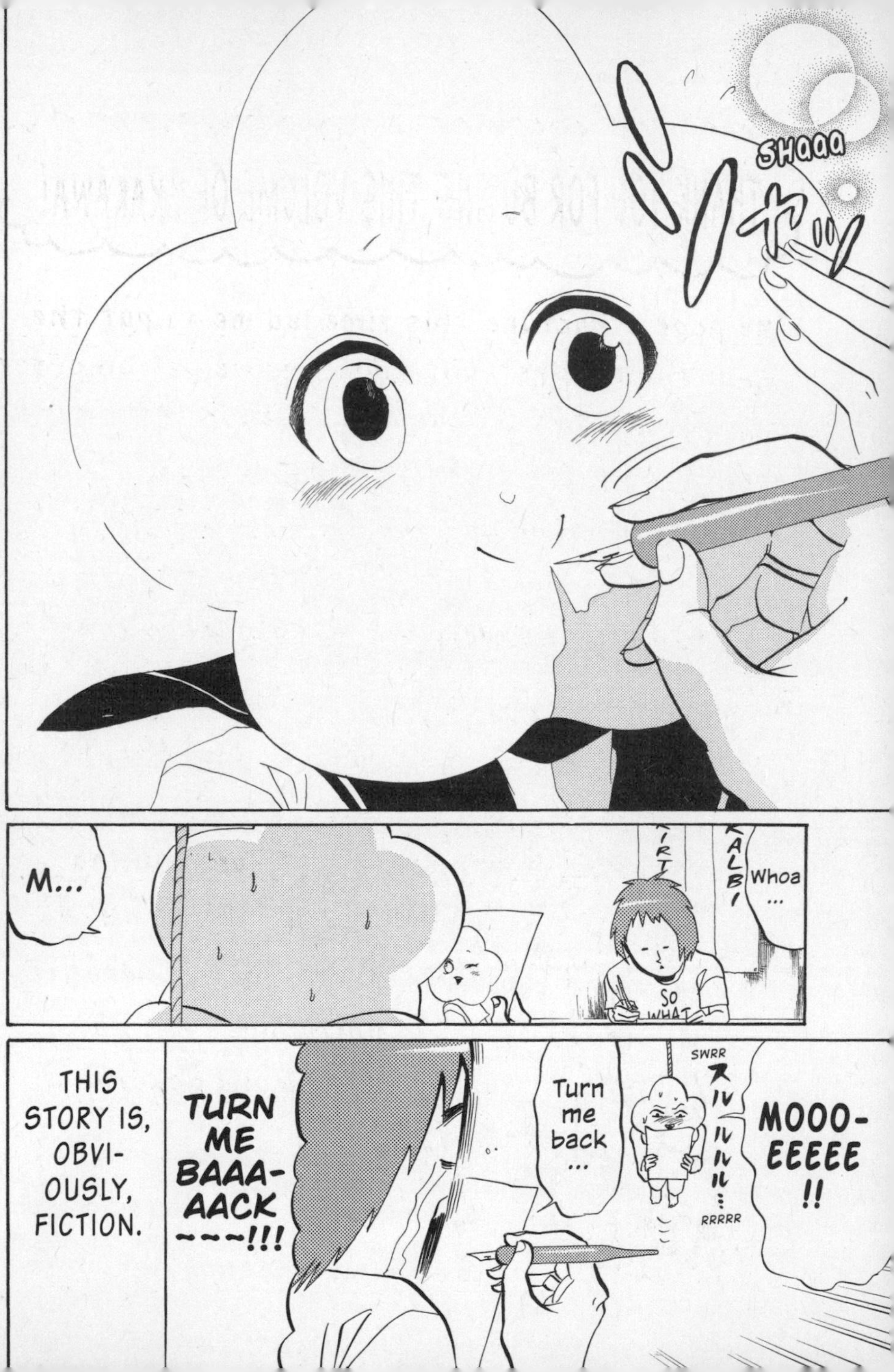
SHAaa
KALBI
Whoa ...
SO WHAT
M...
MOOO-EEEEE !!
SWRR
スルルル…
RRRRR
Turn me back ...
TURN ME BAAA-AACK ---!!!
THIS STORY IS, OBVIOUSLY, FICTION.

THANK YOU FOR BUYING THIS VOLUME OF ARAKAWA!

The page structure this time led me to put the bonus manga first, but this time we get an after-party with the characters I used in "Nakamura Factory" for the magazine Gangan Wing.

These characters appear in Arakawa as well, but this is the Factory version of them, so if you're used to the Arakawa version, they may act very eccentrically... or so I thought, but...

they always act eccentrically, so I realized it wasn't all that weird after all.

I had a lot of fun drawing this, so I hope it made you grin. See you next volume!

10/17/2008

Hikaru Nakamura

come play again!

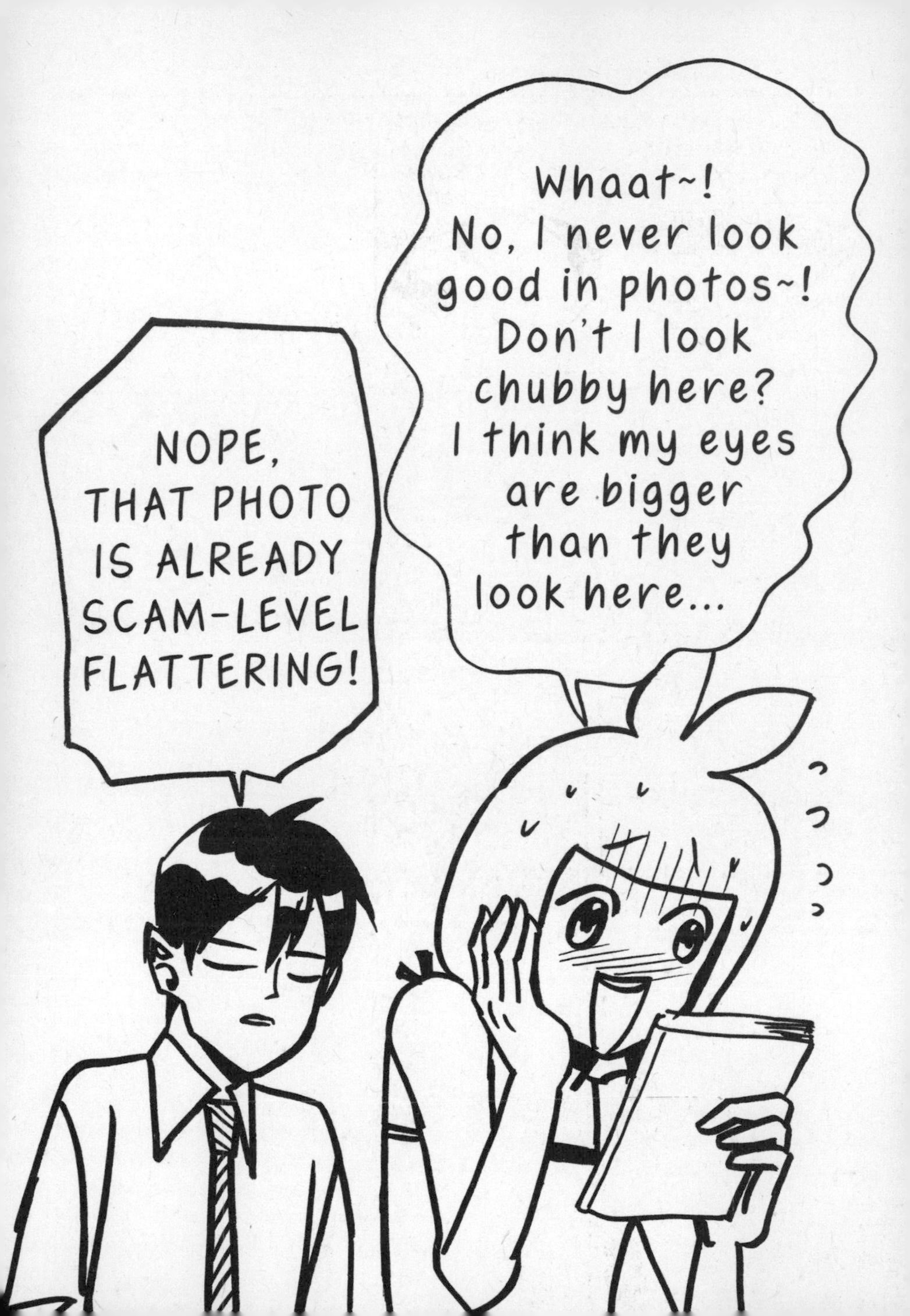
Whaat~! No, I never look good in photos~! Don't I look chubby here? I think my eyes are bigger than they look here...
NOPE, THAT PHOTO IS ALREADY SCAM-LEVEL FLATTERING!

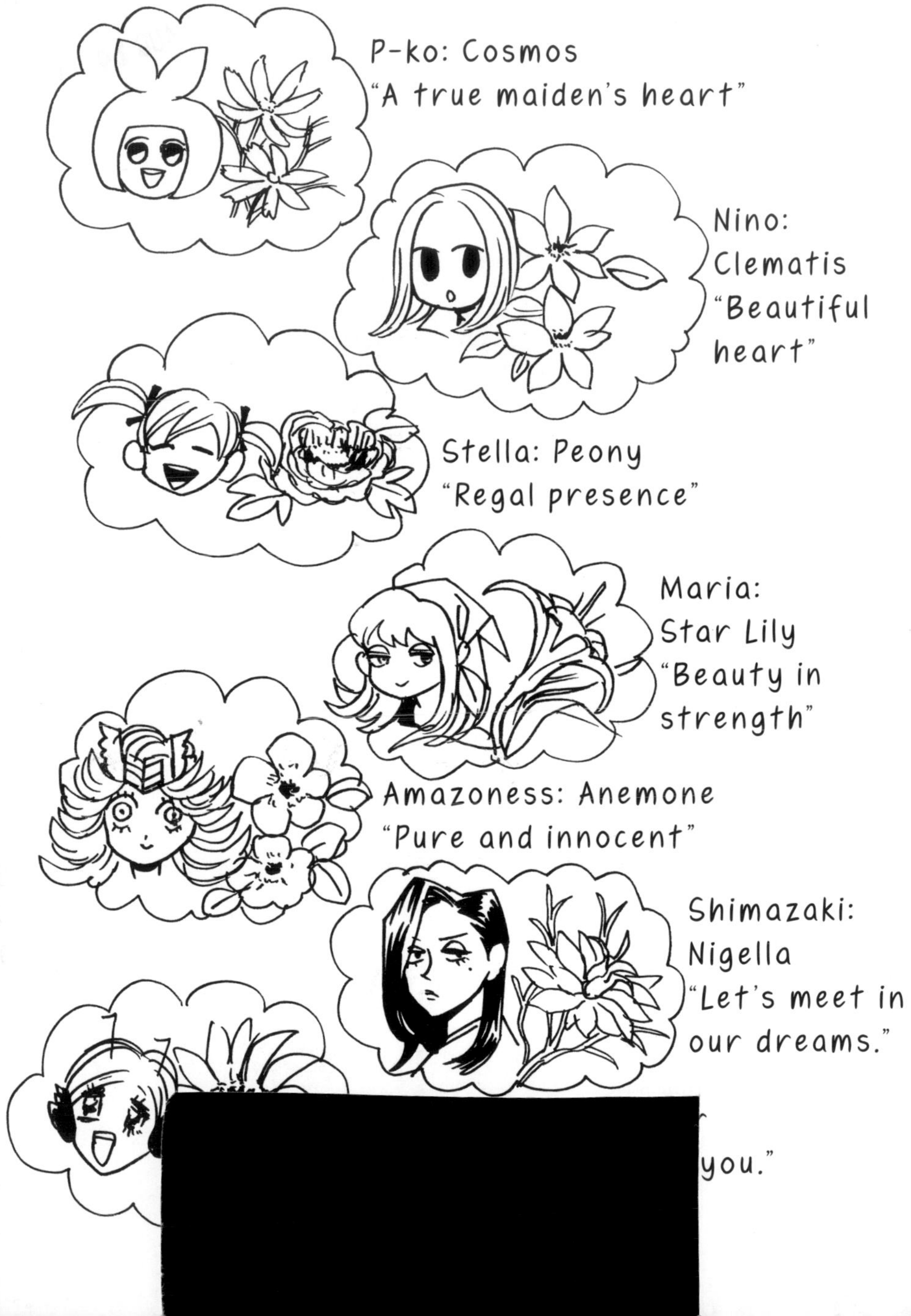
P-ko: Cosmos
"A true maiden's heart"
Nino:
Clematis
"Beautiful
heart"
Stella: Peony
"Regal presence"
Maria:
Star Lily
"Beauty in
strength"
Amazoness: Anemone
"Pure and innocent"
Shimazaki:
Nigella
"Let's meet in
our dreams."
[redacted]
you."

AUG 19 4

ARAKAWA UNDER THE BRIDGE 4
Hikaru Nakamura

Translation: Andrew Cunningham
Production: Risa Cho
          Tomoe Tsutsumi

ARAKAWA UNDER THE BRIDGE Vol. 7 & 8
© 2008 Hikaru Nakamura / SQUARE ENIX CO., LTD.
First Published in Japan in 2008 by SQUARE ENIX CO., LTD.
Translation rights arranged with SQUARE ENIX CO., LTD. and Vertical, Inc.
through Tuttle-Mori Agency, Inc. Translation © 2018 by SQUARE ENIX CO., LTD.

Translation provided by Vertical Comics, 2018
Published by Vertical, Inc., New York

Originally published in Japanese as *Arakawa Andaa Za Burijji 7 & 8*
by SQUARE ENIX Co., Ltd., 2008
Arakawa Andaa Za Burijji first serialized in *Young Gangan*, SQUARE ENIX Co.,
Ltd., 2004-2015

This is a work of fiction.

ISBN: 978-1-947194-13-7

Manufactured in Canada

First Edition

Vertical, Inc.
451 Park Avenue South
7th Floor
New York, NY 1001
www.vertical-comi

Vertical books are ▮   ervices.

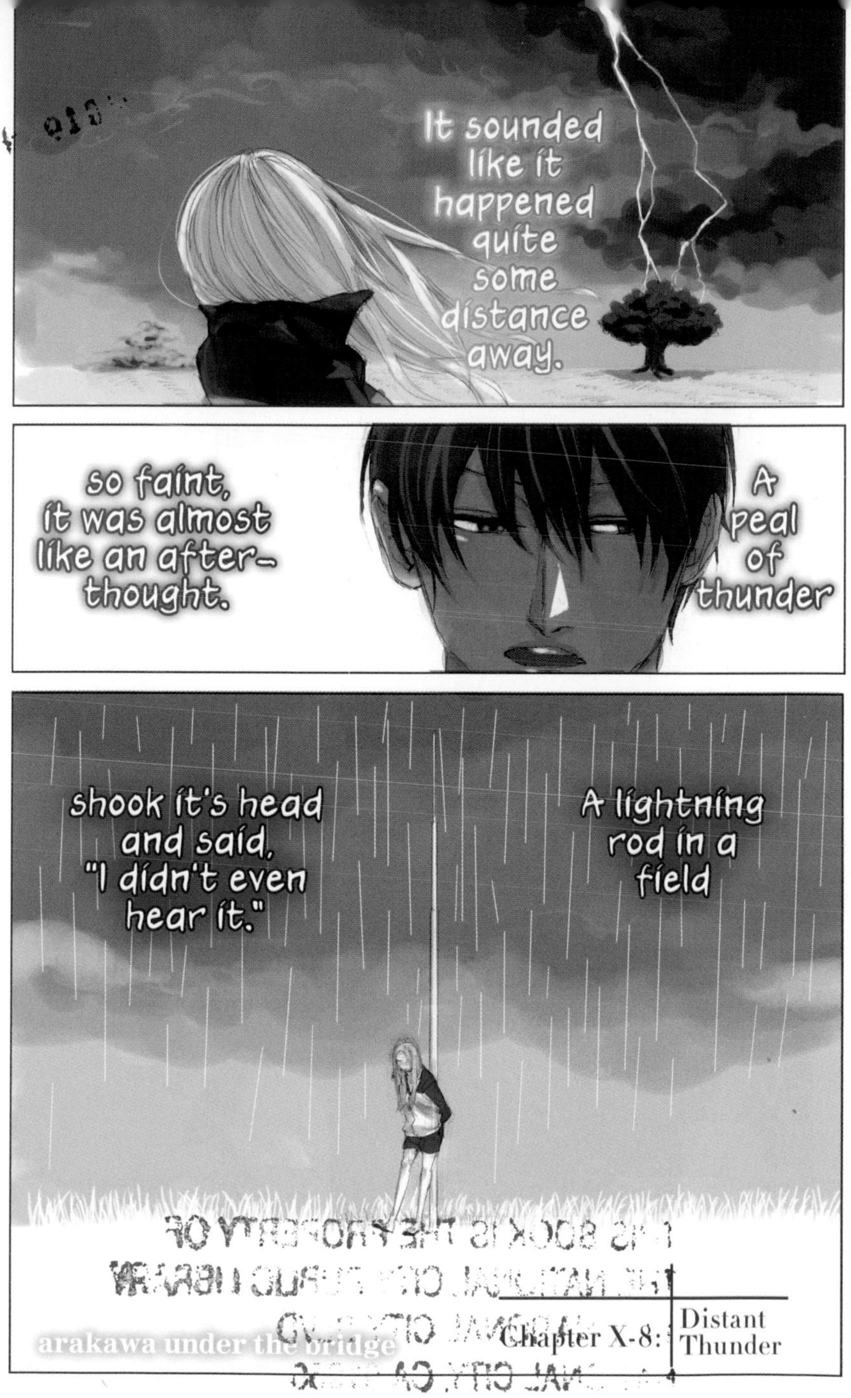
It sounded like it happened quite some distance away.
A peal of thunder
so faint, it was almost like an after-thought.
A lightning rod in a field
shook it's head and said, "I didn't even hear it."
Chapter X-8: Distant Thunder
arakawa under the bridge

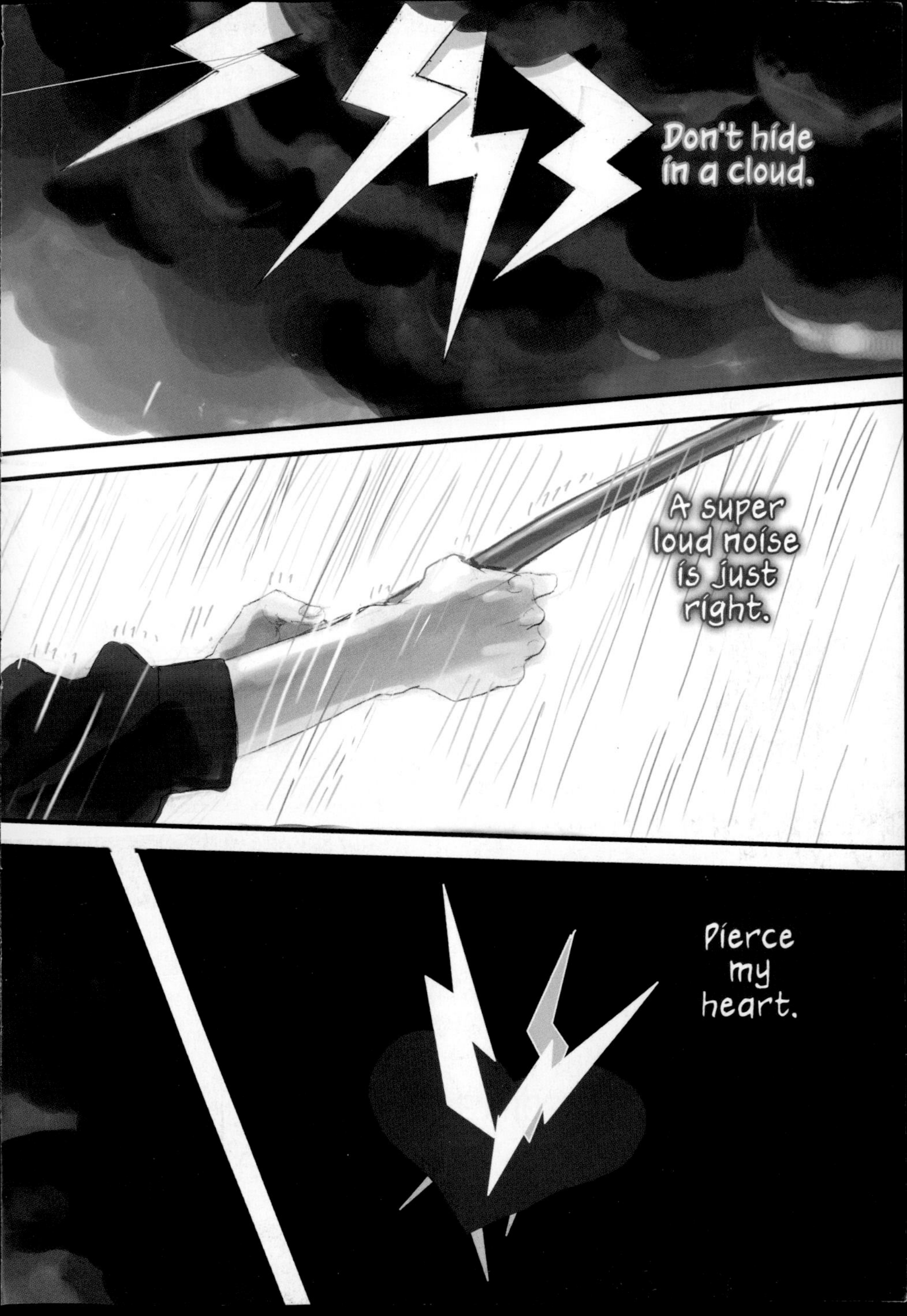
Don't hide in a cloud.
A super loud noise is just right.
Pierce my heart.

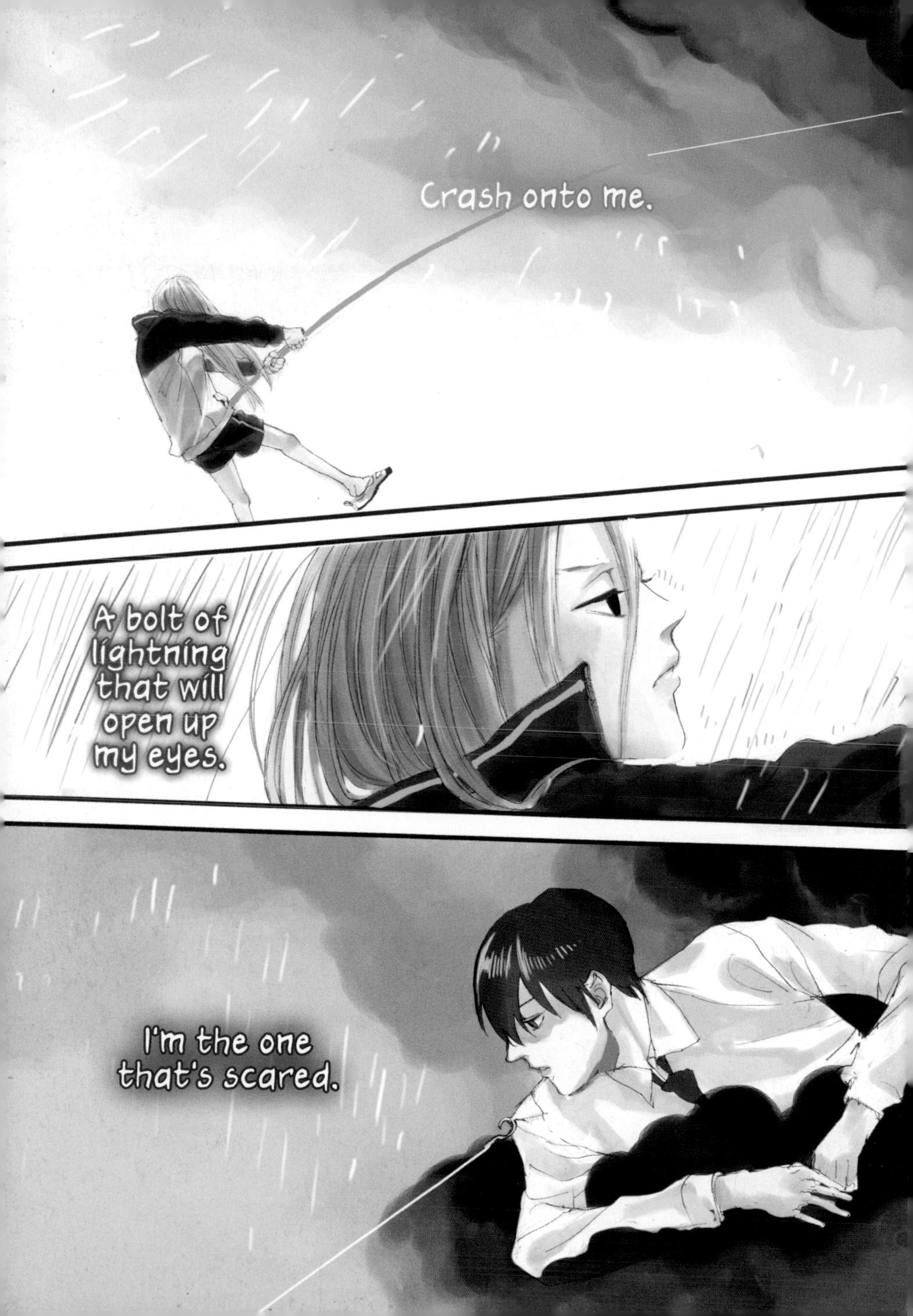
Crash onto me.
A bolt of lightning that will open up my eyes.
I'm the one that's scared.

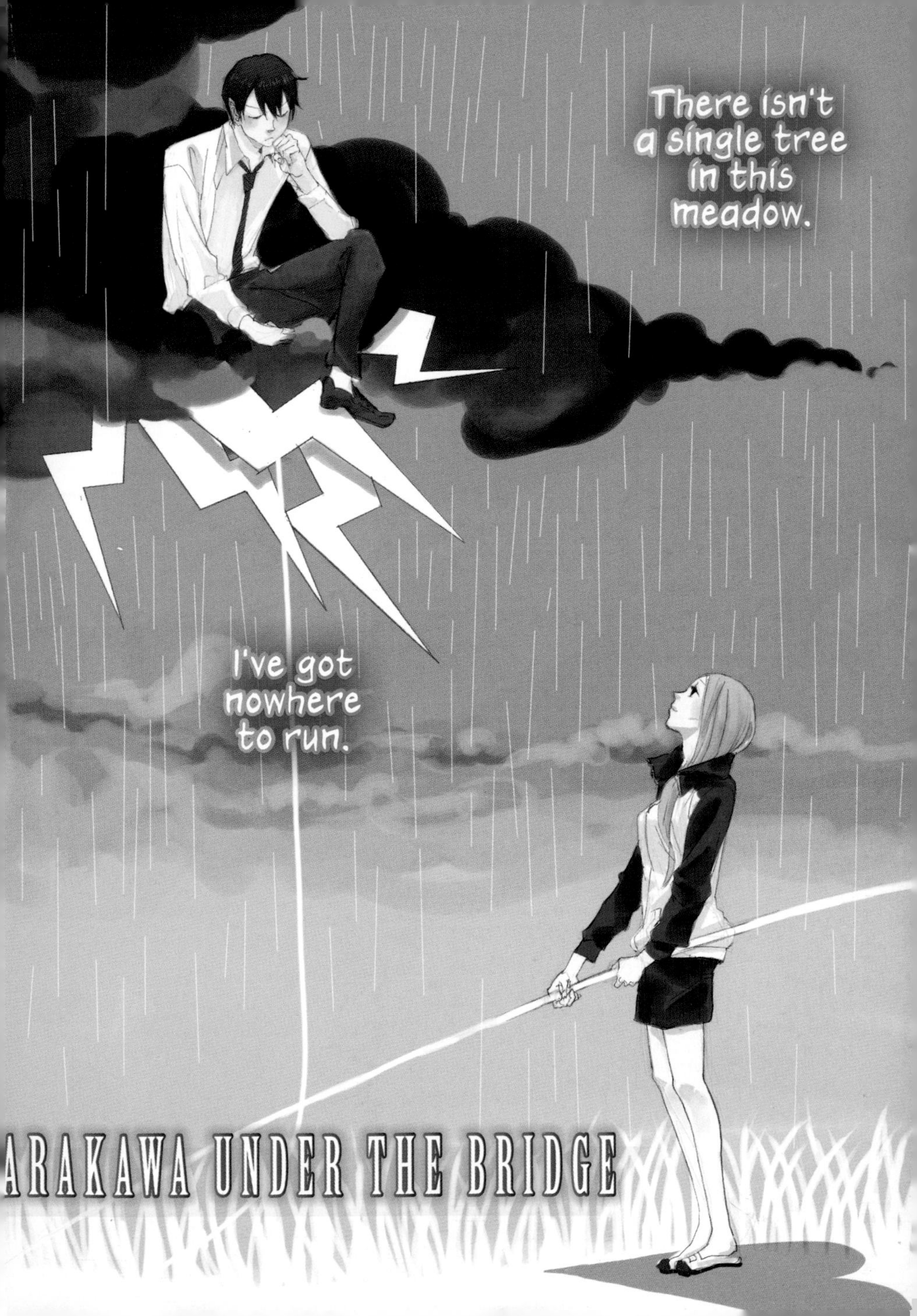
There isn't a single tree in this meadow.
I've got nowhere to run.
ARAKAWA UNDER THE BRIDGE